EGYPTIAN AND SEMITO-HAMITIC (AFRO-ASIATIC) STUDIES IN MEMORIAM W. VYCICHL

EDITED BY

GÁBOR TAKÁCS

BRILL
LEIDEN · BOSTON
2004

This book is printed on acid-free paper.

Library of Congress Cataloging-in-Publication Data

Egyptian and Semito-Hamitic (Afro-Asiatic) studies : in memoriam W. Vycichl / edited by Gábor Takács.
p. cm. — (Studies in Semitic languages and linguistics, ISSN 0081-8461 ; v. 39)
Consists of articles in English, French, and German.
Includes bibliographical references and index.
ISBN 90-04-13245-7 (hard back)
1. Afroasiatic languages. 2. Egyptian philology. I. Vycichl, Werner. II. Takács, Gábor. III. Studies in Semitic languages and linguistics ; 39

PJ992.E33 2003
492—dc21 2003052101

ISSN 0081-8461
ISBN 90 04 13245 7

PRINTED IN THE NETHERLANDS

EGYPTIAN AND SEMITO-HAMITIC (AFRO-ASIATIC) STUDIES IN MEMORIAM W. VYCICHL

STUDIES IN SEMITIC LANGUAGES AND LINGUISTICS

EDITED BY

T. MURAOKA AND C.H.M. VERSTEEGH

VOLUME XXXIX

EGYPTIAN AND SEMITO-HAMITIC (AFRO-ASIATIC) STUDIES IN MEMORIAM W. VYCICHL

Werner Vycichl (1934)

Werner Vycichl (1909–1999)

CONTENTS

SECTION ONE
EGYPTOLOGY AND COPTOLOGY

SECTION TWO
SEMITIC LINGUISTICS

SECTION THREE
BEJA LINGUISTICS

SECTION FOUR
CHADIC LINGUISTICS

SECTION FIVE
COMPARATIVE SEMITO-HAMITIC (AFRO-ASIATIC) LINGUISTICS

Werner Vycichl in 1987 with the oldest member of the Siwa Berbers

WERNER VYCICHL (1909–1999)

The last great representative of the old generation of Egypto-Semitic and Afro-Asiatic (Semito-Hamitic)[1] comparative linguistics is gone. Together with W.A. Ward and C.T. Hodge, both of whom passed away recently (in 1996 and in 1998, respectively), he belonged to what can be described as the "old school" of Egypto-Semitic (and Egypto-Afro-Asiatic) studies, a rather neglected field of research, which was "kept alive" on the behalf of Egyptology up to the 1990s practically only by these three long surviving scholars.

The range of W. Vycichl's scholarly activities was enormously wide, going far beyond the limits of Afro-Asiatic: Egyptian language history, vocalisation of Old Egyptian, Coptic language and culture, Arabic (esp. its Egyptian and Sudanese dialects), Amharic, Berberology, Beja (Bed'awye), and Hausa (Chadic) linguistics, Armenian, and even Finno-Ugric languages (including Hungarian).

In remembrance of W. Vycichl, already two memorial volumes have recently appeared in two different areas of his activities: Egyptian philology[2] and Berberology.[3] The present volume is paying homage to his memory and scholarly heritage with a collection of articles contributing to the huge domain to which W. Vycichl devoted his research most intensively and extensively: Afro-Asiatic languages (excepting Berber)[4] and comparative Afro-Asiatic linguistics.

---

[1] W. Vycichl used the traditional term "Semito-Hamitic" (kept in the title of this volume and in certain further cases out of respect for him), which, however, has been recently replaced by J.H. Greenberg's scientifically more correct and commonly accepted "Afro-Asiatic" (and I.M. Diakonoff's "Afrasian" used in the Russian works).

[2] *Bulletin de la Société d'Égyptologie, Genève* 23 (1999).

[3] Naït-Zerrad, K. (ed.): *Articles de linguistique berbère. Mémorial Werner Vycichl.* Paris, 2002, L'Harmattan.

[4] Originally, still in late 1999 and early 2000, when I put forward the idea of an Afro-Asiatic *Gedenkschrift* for W. Vycichl, K. Naït-Zerrad and I were thinking of one common volume for all Afro-Asiatic contributions, but—due to the quantity of the incoming papers—we soon realized the need for two separate and fully independent volumes: one purely Berberological (undertaken by K. Naït-Zerrad) and a further one comprising all the rest of the Afro-Asiatic language family (initiated by G. Takács).

Since a detailed biography and bibliography of W. Vycichl has been most recently published,[5] this remembrance will be restricted to mentioning only the most important facts of his life.

He graduated from the famous *Institut für Ägyptologie und Afrikanistik der Universität Wien* (founded by Leo Reinisch, directed later by Wilhelm Czermak) in 1932 with a Ph.D. dissertation entitled *Untersuchungen über das Hausa-Dialekt von Kano* (which was partly published in his fundamental study on the comparison of Hausa and Egyptian).[6] He spent 5 years (1934–38) in Luxor, thanks to which he possessed an excellent knowledge of Arabic and its Egyptian dialect. His joint research with William H. Worrell (University of Michigan), a highly esteemed specialist of the subject, on the survival of Coptic traditions in Upper Egypt started in 1936 in Luxor, which resulted in their joint work on the *Popular Traditions of the Coptic Language*.[7] The Second World War interrupted his career for a while. In 1947, he married Armène Vycichl (stemming from the Armenian Barsamian family),[8] a loving wife for his entire life.[9] The period between 1948 and 1960 he spent in Paris. In 1960, he moved to Genève. His academic career restarted in fact only in 1968, when he was appointed *privat-docent* of the University of Fribourg (he became a *professeur titulaire* in 1973). He took part in the foundation of the *Société d'Égyptologie Genève* in 1978 accepting the position of the vice president. He retired from the university of Fribourg in 1980, and devoted all his time to completing his long awaited *magnum opus*, *Dictionnaire étymologique de la langue copte* (Louvain, 1983, Peeters), which was fol-

---

[5] A. Vycichl: "Werner Vycichl: éléments biographiques." = Naït-Zerrad, K. (ed.): *Op. cit.*, pp. 15–17. G. Takács: Publications de Werner Vycichl. = *Ibidem*, pp. 19–41. A further version of the biography and the bibliography was published by Mme Armène Vycichl in the 54/2002 issue of the journal "*Discussions in Egyptology*" (Oxford), pp. 5–33. A bibliography listing the works published by W. Vycichl in 1933–1980 appeared in *Bulletin de la Société d'Égyptologie, Genéve* 4 (1980), 9–18. A third biography appeared in the journal *Wiener Zeitschrift für die Kunde des Morgenlandes* 91 (2001), 9–14.

[6] "Hausa und Ägyptisch. Ein Beitrag zur historischen Hamitistik." = *Mitteilungen des Seminars für Orientalische Sprachen an der Friedrich-Wilhelms-Universität zu Berlin* 37 (1934), 36–116.

[7] In: *Coptic Texts of the University of Michigan Collection*. Ann Arbor, 1942. The University of Michigan. Pp. 294–354.

[8] The painful history of this family has been painted by Meguerditch Barsamian in his poetic "*Histoire du village qui meurt*" (Paris, 1990, V. et A. Barsamian).

[9] I wish to express my best thanks to Mme Armène Vycichl (Genève) for her vivid attention, enthusiasm, and all the information with which she helped the preparation of this volume.

lowed by his fundamental *La vocalisation de la langue égyptienne. Tome 1er: La phonétique* (Le Caire, 1990, IFAO). He carried out field research several times on the Berber dialects of Djerba and Siwa (the last one was made in 1987), which greatly contributed to his gigantic monograph *Die Berbersprachen*, which, unfortunately, is up to now unpublished.[10]

The importance of the heritage left behind by Werner Vycichl for comparative Afro-Asiatic linguistics can be compared only to that of Igor M. Diakonoff (1915–1999),[11] while his extraordinary contribution (continuing the best traditions of the once flourishing "old school") to the prehistory of Egyptian phonology and lexicon has made him an outstanding authority of this field.

It is my pleasure to express my best thanks to Miss Ingrid Heijckers and Mrs. Trudy Kamperveen for their careful work on this volume as well as to Brill Academic Publishers for publishing it in its Semitic series.

G.T.
Székesfehérvár, April 2003

[10] Mme A. Vycichl submitted the manuscript (counting some 2,500 pp.) to the *Institut für Afrikanistik* in Bayreuth. Most of the manuscripts, field research records (also those concerning Siwa Berber) of Werner Vycichl were deposited in the "Fonds Werner Vycichl" of the "Oswin-Köhler-Archiv" of the Institut für Afrikanische Sprachwissenschaften (Frankfurt a/M). Werner Vycichl's monumental monograph "Die Berbersprachen" is now in preparation (edited by Maarten Kossmann and Dymitr Ibriszimow), and will be published probably in Germany.

[11] There have appeared already two distinct memorial volumes paying homage to Prof. Diakonoff in different areas of his activity. One in the field of Oriental studies in general, cf. Livšic, V.A. & Medvedskaja, I.N. & Jakobson, V.A. (eds.): *Istorija i jazyki Drevnego Vostoka: Pamjati I.M. D'jakonova* (Sankt-Peterburg, 2002., Sankt-Peterburgskij Filial IV RAN). Contributions from comparative Afro-Asiatic have been collected by Bender, M.L. (chief ed.) & Appleyard, D. & Takács, G. (eds.) in: *Selected Comparative-Historical Afrasian Linguistic Studies in Memory of Igor M. Diakonoff* (München & Newcastle, 2003, Lincom Europa).

SECTION ONE

EGYPTOLOGY AND COPTOLOGY

THE LEXICAL ITEM NFT OF AN OLD EGYPTIAN INSCRIPTION

Francesco Aspesi
(University of Milano)

The Seasons Chamber in the Sun Temple of the Fifth Dynasty of Ny-User-Rēˁ at Abu Ghorab (about 2500/2400 BC) gives us the most ancient depicted representation in Egypt of the treatment of honey and the only example to come down from the Old Kingdom period.[1]

In it, seven men are busy, either alone or in pairs, with a series of operations that finish with the sealing of the jars of honey with a rope loop and their storage on a shelf. An inscription, in the top part of the register, completes the carrying out of the scene in its different stages.[2] Despite initial and central fractures that compromise the perfect understanding of the operations represented and described, the inscription is composed of three singular lexical items in succession, respectively *nft/mḥj/]ˁf[*,[3] followed by the syntagma *ḫtm bjt*.

The correspondence between the scene that constitutes the extreme right of the relief where a man on his knees is carefully fixing a top onto a jar, and the significance of the standing over inscription *ḫtm bjt* "sealing the honey",[4] appears obvious. In the same way, we have to think that the three separate lexical items that precede it, specify with their positioning and their meaning three other sections indentifiable in the overall representation.

[1] Except for a small fragment of a similar relief coming from the excavations of the entrance passage of the Unas pyramid at the end of the same dynasty (Leclant 1968, 52, note 4, Leclant 1975, 786, Chouliara-Raïos 1989, 26).

[2] A good reproduction of this scene is found in Bissing 1955, pl. XIII. On the subject, see Borchard, Schäfer 1900 and Kees 1928, in addition to the later studies quoted in Chouliara-Raïos 1989, 25, note 23.

[3] Divided by vertical strokes.

[4] *Bjt* is the noun for "honey" of general use in Egyptian. Only in Late Egyptian the noun *ḥḏt* "white" is also use for "honey" to underline its characteristics of luminosity and purity. The same consonant sequence *bjt* as a rule seems specifies also the noun for "bee", which sometimes assumes the denomination *ˁfj bjt* "honey fly" (or, for ellipsis, simply *ˁfj*: see following note 6).

Of these sections, only the second from left results integral; it shows three servants intent on pouring the contents of two jars into two containers on the ground and in fact it appears perfectly in correlation with the verb *mḥj* "fill", written above. The third term *]ˁf[* is unfortunately inscribed above the central fracture which leaves identifiable only the outline of a man bending forwards. Either by adopting the reading *[j]ˁf* "mixing" of Kuény (1950, 92) or by privileging the interpretation of Faulkner *ˁf[j]* "press",[5] it appears certain that also this stem is the infinitive of a verb expressing the action represented in the corresponding mutilated scene.[6]

However, different seems to me the status of the first lexical element, *nft*, on the interpretation of which the present study is centred.

The scene referred to, precisely the first one, is also damaged by a fracture which, even if smaller than the central one, is such as to compromise a true understanding of the operation illustrated. In fact a man appears kneeling on only one knee in front of a row of heaped objects, evidently horizontal jars and is holding in his hands the bottom of a jar, the mouth of which, in the same way as the front part of the individual, have been destroyed by the breakage of the support. The proportions of the figure and of the bottom of the vase have led the scholars to believe that the man is bringing the mouth of the jar to his mouth. In the heap of horizontal jars, it would seem possible to notice a type of bee hive apparently documented in the other two bee-keeping scenes of Pharaonic Egypt, more recent, those of the Theban tombs of Rekh-mi-Rēˁ of the fifteenth century and of Pa-bu-Sa of the seventh,[7] and which would find confirmation in the cylinder-shape beehives still used in modern Egypt.[8] All this led to a reconstruction of the scene which induces to interpret *nft* as the infinitive of a verb *nfj* "to blow", thought elsewhere witnessed only in Late Egyptian.

Originally the operation of blowing into a jar, element of a bee-

[5] Quoted and shared by Neufeld (1978, 233), althought a careful examination of the inscription shows evident traces of a sign *j* placed before the group *ˁf*.

[6] The hypothesis of an interpretation of *ˁfj* as a noun for "fly" and, with *bjt* implied, "honey fly", that is "bee", also hinted at in Neufeld 1978, 233, contrasts with the epigraphic and figurative context. On this noun are to be seen the relevant etymological-comparative considerations by Prof. Vycichl (1983, 21).

[7] Neufeld 1978, 233–38, here included also the bibliographical indications to integrate with the later ones of Chouliara-Raïos 1989, 25–8, notes 23–29.

[8] Kuény 1950, 88–9.

keeping, was understood as a means to get rid of the bees,[9] but appropriately Kuény (1950, 90) underlines the foolishness of blowing directly with one's mouth into a bee hive "étant donné la nature agressive des abeilles".[10]

Therefore Kuény puts forward the supposition that *nft* means the emission of a sound by which the kneeling person calls the bees out of the hive;[11] the scholar reveals correctly that the yar half seen between the hands of this man has the same characteristics of the jar that the first man of the second scene (the one specified by *mḥj* "fill"), is using to fill the container on the ground. Therefore it would not be an element of the presumed bee hive, but a jar containing honey or one of its ingredients,[12] to which once again in the second scene, other two men are adding something else, perhaps water,[13] poured from a smaller roundish jar.

Despite the persuasive observations of Kuény, an interpretation of *nft* as "emit a noise with the mouth" leaves one puzzled not only for the lack of other evidence of the verb *nfj* in the whole Old and Middle Kingdom, but for the obvious incongruity of carrying out such an action with one's mouth near the mouth of a jar of honey, probably the same from which the honey is being pured in the following scene. More recently Neufeld (1978, 233), quoting the two interpretations of *nft* understood as an infinitive, and that is "blowing" or "breathing", concludes in fact that "the actual meaning is uncertain".

In the whole inscription correlated to the honey treatment scene of the Seasons Chamber, as we have seen *nft mḥj]ʿf [ḫtm bjt*, the final substance sealed in the jar to be stored is identified as *bjt*, that is with the generic Egyptian term for "honey".[14] It appears evident that, at least in this context, the honey *bjt* is the result of the pouring

---

[9] Ransome 1937, 26: "blowing or smoking", perhaps therefore also "blowing smoke", according to the known technique of distancing the bees from the hive in order to extract honey. Such an opinion was originnaly proposed by Wreszinski (1923–36, I, pl. 378).

[10] Opinion given also by Leclant himself (1968, 52).

[11] Kuény 1950, 90 and note 15.

[12] "Elle contenait donc du miel ou tout au moins un produit servant à traiter le miel": *ibidem*.

[13] According to Kuény (cit. 92). Neufeld (1978, 233) thinks instead about the "additional ingredients, possibly fruit juices, to produce honey syrup or honey beer". However, since at the end they store honey (*bjt*), it would be better to think about the addition of more honey, perhaps of a different quality.

[14] See above, note 4.

and of the mixing of different ingredients, starting from the substance contained in the jar handled both by the man on one knee in the first scene and by the first "pourer" in the second.

This fundamental ingredient, in some way a basic substance as regards the final honey *bjt*, cannot but be in its turn other honey, subject however to further treatment and probably named in a different way.

Nft therefore, instead of being an infinitive of difficult interpretation, could be more adequately understood as the isolated evidence in Egyptian of the noun for this type of honey or honey substance.

From a textual point of view, such a succession of terms to illustrate a scene of temple or domestic economy[15] finds precise correspondences in reliefs more or less contemporary with tombs of officials of high rank.

At Meir, for example, in the tomb of Pepy-Ankh the Black,[16] Vizier of the Pharaoh of the Sixth Dynasty Pepy II, a part of the east wall relief of the entrance room shows three kneeling men intent on picking grapes, followed by another three who are pressing it in a low jar: the succession of terms of the relative inscription *j3rrt 3mʿ jrp* "Vine. To press the wine" presents a syntax "noun plus infinitive with noun" just the same as that deriving from an interpretation of *nft mḥj]ʿf[ḫtm bjt* as "Basic honey. Fill up. Mix (or press). Seal the finished honey". Such a syntax is based on the absolute topicalisation of a noun, in the specific case *j3rrt*, that assumes the function of theme, downright title of that who is represented and described. The semantics of these two texts of the end of the Old Kingdom, which define two strictly similar scenes of food production, seems so to develop along a perfectly parallel course, starting off from the noun of an initial product, the vine grape and the honey to process, in order to arrive at the final product, by way of the infinitives that specify the phases of the working.

Even if a hypothetical name *nft* "honey of some kind" constitutes today a *hapax* for Egyptian, the ambit of Egypto-Semitic comparison would seem to give us elements on the matter.[17]

---

[15] In particular, honey, at least its best qualities, seems to be in Pharaonic Egypt a royal prerogative (Kuény 1950, 85, Forbes 1957, 81) and thus also divine. On the possible existence of priest-bee keepers, refer to Montet 1950. The scenes in the tomb of the Viziers are in addition often connected directly to Court economy.

[16] Blackman 1914–35.

[17] Ambit of research carried out in a masterly way by Prof. Vycichl, as in his

Among the different Semitic nouns for "honey", referred both to the produce of the bees and the vegetable honey derived from dates,[18] Ugaritic and Hebrew, North-West Semitic languages, testify respectively also *nbt* and *nōpet̲* which, in spite of the imperfect phonetic correspondence of the central labial, are certainly assimilable.[19]

The noun for honey which is found much more often in the Hebrew Bible and with a wider correspondence in other Semitic languages is *dᵉb̲aš*.[20] *Nōpet̲* finds certain evidence in the Biblical text, in addition to the metaphoric uses of *Cant.* 4.11 and of *Prov.* 5.3 plus 2.13, only in *Ps.* 19.11 where it figures as specification of *dᵉb̲aš* to indicate more exactly the honey "dripping from honeycombs" and in *Pr.* 27.7, even here with reference to the honey contained in the honeycomb.[21]

The sporadic evidence of the noun for "honey" *nōpet̲* in the Biblical text in general and its concentration in wisdom and poetic texts can make it suspected as being a Canaanite contribution,[22] especially in consideration of the fact that such a noun does not exist elsewhere in Semitic, if not just in Ugaritic, a Canaanite language with Amorite influences of the second half of the second millennium. The strict relationship of Hebrew *nōpet̲* with Ugaritic *nbt* seems to find confirmation also in the association, of probable formulary nature, with a name for "oil" common to both languages.[23] The same difficulty to bring back the two terms to a common Semitic heredity due to the afore-mentioned phonetic incongruity[24] brings us to consider the

fundamental *Dictionnaire étymologique de la langue copte*, mentioned above. In the wider domain of Hamito-Semitic (Afrasiatic), I am particularly pleased to remember here the presence of Professor Vycichl during four of the *Giornate di Studi Camito-Semitici e Indeuropei* organised in Italy (the third, the fourth, the sixth and the seventh), in the course of which I had the privilege to know him better.

[18] Halévy 1910, 499–501.

[19] The Ugaritic noun, in particular, refers to a root **NWB* which is at the base of Semitic nouns for "bee" common, in a complementary way, only in the East and South Semitic languages (Akkadian *nūbtu(m)* "bee", Arabic *nūb* "bee", South Arabian Mehri *nōbēt*, Ethiopic Geʿez and Tigre *nehb* "bee").

[20] Cohen 1993, 215–6, *sub voce DB/Pš.*

[21] A further recurrence *nōpet̲* subtended to the Masoretic text of the *Psalms* 119,129 is testified by the documentation of Qumran (11Q Ps[a]).

[22] For the importance of Canaanite in the formation in particular of the wisdom books of the Bible, refer to Albright 1955, Dahood 1852 e 1963, Fisher 1972 and 1975, Rummel 1981.

[23] Hebrew *šemen* and Ugaritic *šmn.*: Fisher 1972, II, 376. For the Hebrew, refer, for example, to the quoted *Pr.* 5.3.

[24] Moreover not completely isolated. On the analogue anomaly in the corrispondence of the labials between Ugaritic *bʿl* and Hebrew *pāʿal*, placed in the widest phenomena of the possibility of inter-exchange of the labials in the phonetics of the

unusual Hebrew term as the continuation of a specific noun for "honey" characteristic in the Bronze Age of the Semitic component of the urbanised peoples of the Syrian-Palestine coast.[25]

At this point a connection between an Egyptian noun *nft* "honey of a certain type" and the Canaanite Semitic *nbt/npt* "honey", suggested by the same form of the significants,[26] can be proposed both on the basis of the fundamental congruity between Egyptian and Semitic languages on account of the belonging of such languages to the common Hamito-Semitic linguistic family (Afrasiatic), and in consideration of the very close contacts between Egypt and the peoples along the Syrian-Palestine coast over the millenniums.

In connection with this basic food itself,[27] the annals of Thutmosi III (about 1490–1436) refer to the considerable tributes of honey to the Pharaoh from part of the regions of Syria-Palestine: 264 jars from *rtn*[28] and 470 from *dh*;[29] similar honey tributes came "from every port town" along the Phoenician coast and were sent just to Rekh-mi-Rēᶜ, Vizier of the same King and owner of the Theban tomb with the representation of the second of the three honey scenes left to us by Old Egypt.[30]

Even if Egypt has always been known as a honey-producing country, "il miele appare tra i prodotti basilari del commercio estero delle città siriane dell'età del bronzo";[31] in fact we have reference to this in an administrative document from the records of the harbour city

Semitic languages, can be seen, amongst others, Grabbe 1979. The phonetics of labials is in Hebrew furthermore complicated by the specific phenomena of the change of inter-vocal occlusives into fricatives.

[25] Also the root **NWB* at the base of this particular North-West Semitic noun for "honey" (besides the nouns for "bee" in other Semitic languages listed in note 19), appears residual in so far more or less unproductive as verbal root and attributable "allo strato più antico del semitico occidentale" (Aspesi 1999 and 2001).

[26] To the phoneme */f/* of Old Egyptian corresponds in Semitic both */p/* and */b/* (Dolgopolsky 1999, 38, according to O. Rössler).

[27] The bee honey is, together with vegetable one, the only sweetening substance of ancient times, besides being a basic medicinal essence.

[28] *Retenu*, region to be found along the Syrian coast.

[29] *Diahi*, locality to be found on the coast south of *rtn*.

[30] Neufeld 1978, 225 with bibliographical references quoted in the notes. Because of an excess of synthesis, Neufeld seems to hint at an unlikely temple of Rekh-mi-Rēᶜ, whereas the inscription reported by Breasted (1906, 290, no. 748) refers to the office of "master of secret things" held by this Vizier in the temple of Amon at Thebes.

[31] Aravantinos 1985, 19. Again in Ptolemaic age, there is documentation of honey sent to Egypt from Syria and Palestine via Gaza (Chouliara-Raïos 1989, 111).

of Ugarit in a period shortly after that of Thutmosi III. Here we can read of a deposit of *'alp kd nbt* "a thousand jars of honey".[32]

It is true that, if the palaces of high Egyptian officials and, even more so, of the king[33] seem to be well provided with Syrian-Palestine honey at the beginning of the Late Bronze Age, the relief of Abu Ghorab takes us back a good millennium in time. However, there are no particular reasons to exclude that the victualling to the Egyptian court of the high quality Syrian-Palestine honey to integrate the local product was already active right at the end of the Old Kingdom, probably not as a tribute of a subjected city, a situation more in keeping with the later expansionistic political policy of Egypt, but rather as a result of the very close trade network long set up by Egypt with the Levantine regions.

It would therefore seem correct to attribute to this exceptional attestation of a noun *nft* for honey to Abu Ghorab, contextual to the Egyptian generic term for honey *bjt*,[34] the nature of a loan, also in consideration of the ownership of such lexical item to the semantic field of food, one of the lexical sectors particularly exposed to linguistic interference. Following on the honey that designates, the loan would come from Syrian-Palestinian Semitic dialects of the third millennium, or from another linguistic substratum to the semitic Canaanite proved starting from the successive Ugaritic archives.

Returning to the honey scene in which *nft* appears, the supposition of the linguistic loan would get us to interpret the heap of jars on the extreme left not so much as a beehive, but simply as a deposit of collected honey jars, in this case honey *nft* of Levantine origin: the figure kneeling before[35] would be taking one of these jars, the contents of which will later in the picture be mixed with other ingredients[36] to obtain the final honey *bjt*.

---

[32] Gordon 1965, 163 (*UT* 12+97, 2 and 8).

[33] Kuény (1950, 85) claims that the production of honey represented in the tomb of Rekh-mi-Rēʿ was not destined for the table of the Vizier, but that also in the New Kingdom, at least in its first stages, "le miel est encore en premier lieu réservé aux dieux et aux rois". See also note 15 above.

[34] See again note 4.

[35] With just one knee on the ground and thence in a dynamic position, suitable for extracting a jar before standing up again immediately: such posture was in contra-position to the static one of the third and last person, on both knees, intent as they were on continuative work.

[36] See above, note 13. In the hypothesis that the added ingredients are actually of other types of honey, since the final product is explicitly denominated as *bjt*, the

If this were the case, then the sole attestation which would date the acquisition of the techniques of bee keeping back to the third millennium would be nullified, and Egypt would thus be in line with the other Mediterranean countries which limit themselves to harvest wild honey presumably until the end of the Bronze Age.

The alternative interpretation of the heap of jars as a very old bee hive, favoured by most people,[37] would be connected instead to the necessity to consider the *nft* of Abu Ghorab as the sole testimony of another archaic Egyptian noun for "honey" inherited, together with the North-West Semitic,[38] from a common Hamito- or Egypto-Semitic lexical patrimony. The description of honey as "somewhat unrefined" and in any case to submit to further procedures of processing such as mixing and remixing, which comes from the context of the epigraph-relief of Abu Ghorab, would in this way find a distant and postponed answer to the value of "unrefined honeycomb honey" preserved by the occasional biblical reference of the Hebrew *nōp̱eṯ* considered above.

Bibliography

Albright (W.F.): 1955 "Canaanite and Phoenician Sources of Hebrew Wisdom", *Vetus Testamentum—Supplementum* 3, pp. 1–15.

Aravantinos (V.L.): 1985 "L'apicultura nel mondo minoico-miceneo", *Minos* N.S. 1 & 2, pp. 11–27.

Aspesi (F.): 1999 "Considerazioni etimologiche su ebraico *nāḇî*'", Lamberti (M.), Tonelli (L.), Eds., *Papers from the 9th Italian Meeting of Afro-Asiatic (Hamito-Semitic) Linguistics, Trieste, April 23–24, 1998*, Trieste, pp. 47–62.

——: 2001 "Nympha Orientalis", Finazzi (R.B.), Tornaghi (P.), Eds., *Cinquant'anni di ricerche linguistiche: problemi, risultati e prospettive per il terzo millennio. Atti del IX Convegno Internazionale di Linguisti tenuto a Milano nei giorni 8–10 ottobre 1998*, Alessandria, pp. 135–49.

Bissing (W.F. Von): 1955 "La chambre des trois saison du Sanctuaires Solaire du Roi Rathourès (Ve Dynastie) à Abousir", *Annales du Service des Antiquités de l'Égypte* 53, 319–38 and pl. XIII.

Blackman (A.M.): 1914–35 *The Rock Tombs of Meir*, I–VI, London.

honey added to the Levantine substance, of a particular high-class quality, could be of Egyptian production: "le miel égyptien était en géneral moins estimé—claims Chouliara-Raïos (1989, 109)—sauf le miel blanc du Delta".

[37] According to the interpretations referred to above (page 2 and relative notes). Also Crane (1983, 36–9, Crane, Graham, 2–5) considers that the heap of pots of the relief of Abu Ghorab constitutes the most ancient representation of a beehive.

[38] Where also it is a residual noun outside Ugaritic (see above, page 8 and note 25).

Borchard (L.), Schäfer (H.): 1900 "Das Re Heiligtum des König Ne-user rē, *Zeitschrift für ägyptische Sprache und Altertumskunde* 38.
Breasted (J.H.), 1906, *Ancient Records of Egypt*, II, Chicago.
Chauvin (R., Ed.): 1968 *Traité de biologie de l'abeille*. V, *Histoire, ethnographie et folklore*, Paris.
Chouliara-Raïos (H.): 1989 *L'abeille et le miel en Égypte d'après les papyrus grecs*, Joannina
Cohen (D.): 1993 *Dictionnaire des racines sémitiques ou attestées dans les langues sémitiques*, fasc. 3: GLD—DHML/R, Leuven.
Crane (E.): 1983 *The Archaeology of Beekeeping*, London.
Crane (E.), Graham (A.J.): 1985 "Bee Hives of the Ancient World", *Bee World* 66, 25–41, 148–70.
Dahood (M.J.): 1952 "Canaanite-Phoenician Influence on Qohelet", *Biblica* 23, 191–221.
——: 1963 *Proverbs and North-West Semitic Philology*, Roma.
Dolgopolski (A.): 1999 *From Proto-Semitic to Hebrew. Phonology. Etymological Approach in a Hamito-Semitic Perspective*, Milano.
Fisher (L.R., Ed.): 1972 *Ras Sharma Parallel. The Texts from Ugarit and the Hebrew Bible, I*, Roma.
——: 1975 *Ras Sharma Parallel. The Texts from Ugarit and the Hebrew Bible, II*, Roma.
Forbes (R.J.): 1957 *Studies in Ancient Technology*, I–V, Leiden.
Gordon (C.H.): 1965 *Ugaritic Textbook*, Roma.
Grabbe (L.L.): 1979 "Hebrew *pāʿal* / Ugaritic *bʿl* and the Supposed *B/P* Interchange in Semitic", *Ugarit-Forschungen* 11, 307–14.
Halévy (J.): 1910 "Le nom de l'abeille et du miel dans les langues sémitiques", *Revue Sémitique* 18, 497–506.
Kees (H.): 1928 *Die grosse Festdarstellung*, III vol. of BISSING (F.W., Ed.): 1905–28—*Das Re-Heiligtum des Königs Ne-Woser-Re (Rathures)*, I–III, Leipzig.
Kuény (G.): 1950 "Scènes apicoles dans l'ancienne Égypte", *Journal of Near Eastern Srudies* 9, 84–93.
Leclant (J.): 1968 "L'abeille et le miel dans l'Égypte pharanoique", Chauvin 1968, V, 51–60.
——: 1975 "Biene", Helck (W.), Otto (E.), Eds., *Lexikon der Ägyptologie*, Wiesbaden, I, 786–9.
Montet (P.): 1950 "Études sur quelques prètres et fonctionnaires du dieu Min", *Journal of Near Eastern Studies* 9, 18–27.
Neufeld (E.): 1978 "Apiculture in Ancient Palestine (Early and Middle Iron Age) within the Framework of the Ancient Near East", *Ugarit-Forschungen* 10, 219–47.
Ransome (H.M.): 1937 *The Sacred Bee in Ancient Times and Folklore*, Boston.
Rummel (St., Ed.): 1981 *Ras Sharma Parallel. The Texts from Ugarit and the Hebrew Bible*, III, Roma.
Vycichl (W.): 1983 *Dictionnaire étymologique de la langue copte*, Leuven.
Wreszinski (W.): 1923–36 *Atlas zur altaegyptischen Kulturgeschichte*, I–III, Leipzig.

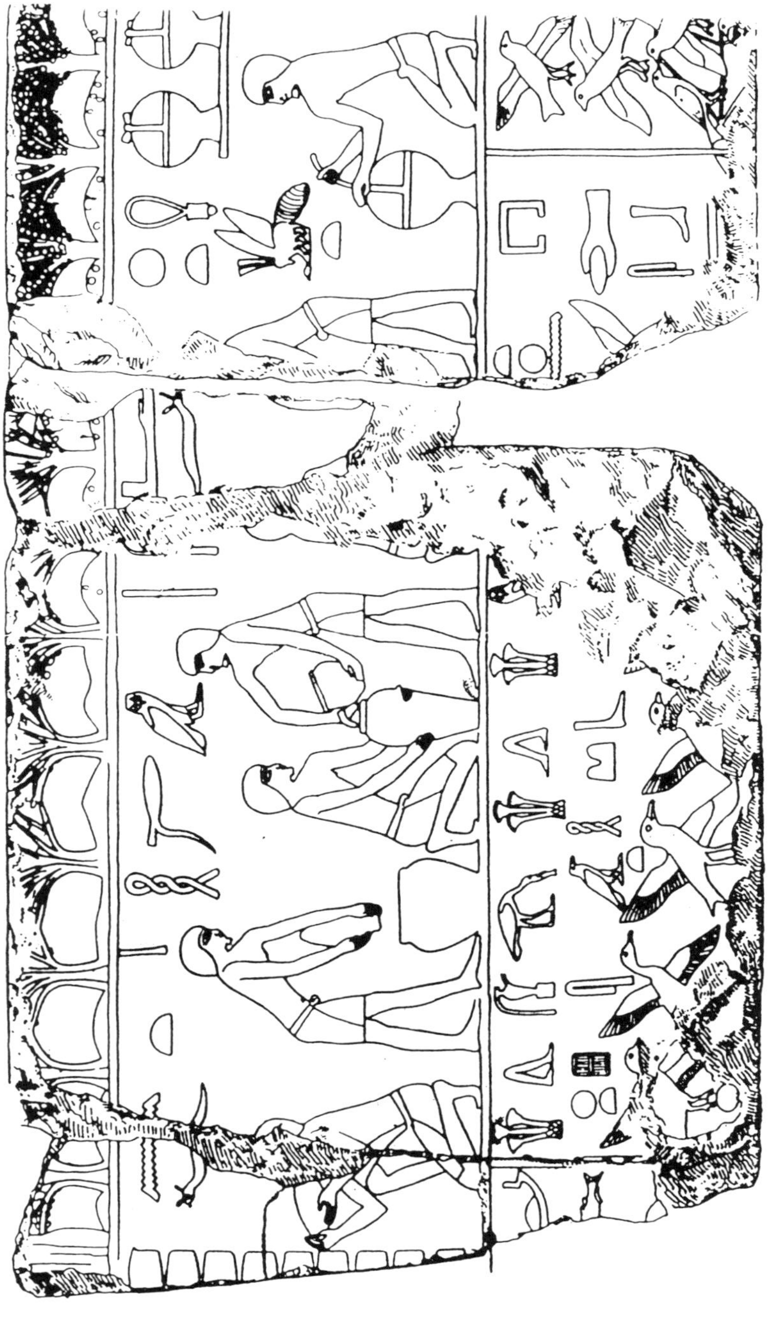

Fig. 1. Drawn from Borchard, Schafer 1990

EIN ARAMÄISCHES LEHNWORT FÜR „KATARAKT" IN DER BESCHREIBUNG ELEPHANTINES AUF DER HUNGERSNOTSTELE UND ÜBERLEGUNGEN ZUR DATIERUNG DERSELBEN ANHAND DER NENNUNG EINES MEROITISCHEN FUNKTIONÄRS

Francis Amadeus Karl Breyer
(University of Tübingen)

Die sogenannte Hungersnotstele[1] hat Generationen von Ägyptologen und besonders auch Theologen aus drei Gründen interessiert. Zum einen ist dieses Pseudoepigraph neben einer Statue aus der 26. Dynastie[2] der wichtigste Beleg für die Identität des Τοσορθρος oder Σεσορθος (d.h. *Č̦sr* = *Djoser*) der späteren Überlieferung[3] mit dem auf zeitgenössischen Steindenkmälern allein bezeugten *Ḥr(.w) Nčr.ỉ-ẖ.t.* bzw. *Nčr.ỉ-ẖ.t-Nb.tỉ*. Für die Theologen ist zum anderen die Erwähnung einer siebenjährigen Hungersnot von gewisser Bedeutung. Der Historiker dagegen wird bei der Nennung eines Landstücks mit den Ausmaßen von *12 ỉtr.w*[4] hellhörig, da ihm die Bezeichnung *Dodekaschoinos* vor Augen schwebt. Trotzdem hat die Inschrift als Text verhältnismäßig wenig Beachtung erfahren, was wahrscheinlich darauf zurückzuführen ist, daß man sich auf der Bearbeitung P. Barguets ausruhen zu können glaubte. H. Goedicke hat sich in jüngster Zeit wieder an einer Bearbeitung versucht, die allerdings in vielen Punkten recht abstruse Lösungen anbietet und eher einen Rückschritt darstellt. So ist denn auch der Text entgegen der Meinung Goedickes in ziemlich verwildertem Ägyptisch geschrieben, wird doch allenorten deutlich, daß der Schreiber nur noch rudimentäre Vorstellungen von der klassisch-ägyptischen Sprache hat.

---

[1] P. Barguet, La Stèle de la Famine à Séhel, BdE 24, 1953 und H. Goedicke, Comments on the „Famine Stela", San Antonio 1994.

[2] Statue Berlin 14765, siehe A. Erman, Geschichtliche Inschriften aus dem Berliner Museum, in: ZÄS 38, 1900, 114–121.

[3] J.v. Beckerath, in: LÄ I, 1111–1112, s.v. Djoser und DERS., Handbuch der ägyptischen Königsnamen, MÄS 49, ²1999, 48f.

[4] Diskussion referiert bei H. Goedicke, Comments on the „Famine Stela", San Antonio 1994, 100–101 und besonders auch bei M. Lichtheim, The Famine Stela, in: W. Hallo, K. Lawson Younger, Jr., Hrsg., The Context of Scripture I, Canonical Compositions from the Biblical World, Leiden 1997, 130–134.

Die in die Zeit des Djoser datierte Stele entlarvt sich nicht zuletzt durch den Gebrauch des ptolemäischen Schriftsystems als eine Art „Konstantinische Schenkung", d.h eine Fälschung wahrscheinlich der Chnum-Priester von Elephantine,[5] die den Zweck verfolgt, ihre Stellung gegen die mächtiger werdenden Isis-Priester von Philae zu behaupten. In Form eines Dekrets wird Djoser die Schilderung einer sieben Jahre währenden Hungersnot in den Mund gelegt. Um dieser zu begegnen, wird der in der Spätzeit als Gott verehrte Imhotep bemüht, der nach Studium der alten Schriften (*bꜣ.w-Rꜥ(.w)*) die Fragen Pharaos

śỉ ś.t-mśi̯ Ḥꜥpỉ . . . . pr-tr tw wn m ḥtp(.w) <ỉm>=f

Wo ist die Quelle des Nil?. . . . Wer ist denn (der Gott), der <in> ihm ruht?

ausführlich beantwortet und dabei eine sehr detaillierte Schilderung der Umgebung von Elephantine gibt. Sie kann inhaltlich in drei Abschnitte gegliedert werden.

Der erste Abschnitt ist eine Kurzbeschreibung der Lage von Elephantine und wird gefolgt von einer näheren und sehr drastischen Beschreibung der Nilflut mit gleichzeitiger Fokussierung auf die Rolle, die Chnum dabei spielt. Im letzten Teil wird genauer auf die Topographie, eingegangen, und dies mit der Nennung der dort verehrten Gottheiten und den in der Nähe anstehenden Gesteinsarten verbunden.

Innerhalb dieses Teiles wird näher auf den Katarakt eingegangen:

rç̣i̯ ẖr.(w)t=śn ꜥb.w r-ḫft ḥr n(.ỉ) H̱nm.w
m-pẖr=f
mỉ[t.t] rnp.w ꜥꜣ ḥrr.w nb(.w)

wn ḥꜣ.tỉ m ꜣbw
pḥ.w m Snm.t
wn ỉm ḥr ỉꜣb.tt ỉmn.tt
wn m-ḥr.ỉ-ỉb ỉ:trw
ḥbś-mw r tr=f n(.ỉ) rnp.t
ś.t ś:nç̣m n ś.ỉ-nb
ỉri̯ kꜣ.t n nn ỉnr(.w) ḥr śp.tỉ=ś
wn m-ỉ:trw m-śti̯ nꜣw.t tn n(.ỉ) ꜣbw ç̌ś<=ś>
wn ⌜ḫy⌝ ḥr.ỉ-[ỉb]
ḳsn.tỉ m ç̣.t=f
***grf ꜣbw** ḫr=tw r=f*

Gegeben ist ihr Bedarf, da sie versammelt sind vor dem Angesicht Chnums und um ihn herum,

[5] P. Barguet, La Stèle de la Famine à Séhel, BdE 24, 1953, 35 f. hält allerdings Ptolemaois V für den Auftraggeber der Fälschung, da er als Hintergrund dessen Expansion nach Nubien sieht.

ebenso viel Grünzeug und alle (Arten von) Blumen.
- Der Anfang ist Elephantine, das Ende ist Bigga -
die dort sind auf der Ost- und Westseite.
Es ist inmitten des Flusses, wenn er das Wasser flutet zu seiner Zeit des Jahres.
Es ist ein Ruheort für Jedermann. Es wird die Arbeit gemacht für diese
Steinbrüche an seinen beiden Rändern (lit. Lippen).
Es ist im Fluß bei der Stádt Elephantine.
Es ist die Flut darin,
der Engpass im Bergmassiv (lit.: in seinem Leib)
***„Katarakt von Elephantine"** ist sein Name.*

Die Stellen, die hier besonders interessieren, sind die beiden Aussagen

1. *„Der Anfang ist Elephantine, das Ende ist Bigga"*
2. *„Es ist die Flut darin,*
der Engpass im Bergmassiv (lit.: in seinem Leib)
***„Katarakt von Elephantine"** ist sein Name."*

Der erste Satz steckt den Rahmen ab, in dem sich die Beschreibung bewegt, die beiden äußeren Inseln des engeren Kataraktengebiets. Es wird kein Zufall sein, daß sich diese beiden Punkte auch zum Anbringungsort der Hungersnotstele in Beziehung setzen lassen, liegt doch die Insel Sehel exakt zwischen diesen beiden anderen Inseln.

Der zweite Satz sagt aus, daß das Stück zwischen den beiden Inseln Elephantine und Bigga ***grf ꜣbw*** genannt wird. Bei diesem Ausdruck handelt es sich um ein *hapax legomenon*, welches im Wörterbuch der Ägyptischen Sprache noch nicht aufgeführt ist. Barguet hat auf die Frage nach der Bedeutung eine wahrlich klassische Antwort gefunden: Herodot—genauer gesagt dessen Beschreibung der Nilquelle.[6]

Herodot gibt an, der Nil entspränge zwischen zwei Bergen mit Namen Κρῶφι und Μῶφι. Allein schon die Namensbildung[7] verleitet dazu, diese Aussage nicht ganz ernst zu nehmen—ganz abgesehen von den inhaltlichen Widersprüchen. Allerdings hat bereits Champollion einen Interpretationsvorschlag gemacht,[8] den Barguet wieder in die Diskussion einbringt.[9] Wie so oft betrachtet Champollion die Sache aus koptischer Sicht, indem er Μῶφι mit kopt. **ⲙⲟⲩϥⲓ** *„qui signifie le*

---

[6] Dies mit Literatur bei: A.B. Lloyd, Herodotus Book II, Commentary 1–98, EPRO 43, Leiden 1976, 111ff.

[7] Zur Bildung siehe J. Friedrich, AOF 20, 1963, 102.

[8] J.-F. Champollion le jeune, L'Égypte sous les Pharaons ou recherche sur la géographie, la religion, la langue, les écritures et l'histoire de l'Égypte avant l'invasion de Cambyse. Description géographique. Paris, De Bure, juillet 1814, I, 115.

[9] P. Barguet, La Stèle de la Famine à Séhel, BdE 24, 1953, 22f., Anm. 14 und Taf. IV.

bon" in Zusammenhang bringt, und Κρῶφι als Gegensatz dazu sieht *„qui, en langue égyptienne, a la valeur de mauvaise*". Champollions ⲙⲟⲩϥⲓ existiert zwar nicht, in dieser Form, doch sollte es keine Probleme bereiten, den im Koptischen häufigen Übergang von ⲛ> ⲙ hier geltend zu machen und an kopt.[10] ⲛⲟⲩϥⲓ (B., F.), ⲛⲟⲩϥⲉ (S., A.) <*nāfir* zu denken, was Champollion wohl auch getan hat. Champollion hat jedoch übersehen, daß ⲛⲟⲩϥⲉ ein Adjektiv ist, sogar eines der seltenen Primäradjektive ererbter afroasiatischer Bildungsweise (vgl. akkad. *pārisum*), und daß das Nomen nach Antritt einer Endung um eine Silbe länger sein muß, was auch dazu führt, daß der Vokal kurz ist und der dritte Radikal erhalten bleibt (ⲛⲟϥⲣⲉ < *nafrˇt.*).

Κρῶφι d.h. nach Champollion < kopt. ⲕⲣⲟϥ soll nun nach dem Vorschlag Barguets auch bei dem zur Diskussion stehenden ***grf ꜣbw*** vorliegen. Gegen diesen Ansatz hat sich Beinlich ausgesprochen.[11] Er geht auf ältere Vorschläge gar nicht ein, wartet aber doch mit einer sehr interessanten neuen Sicht der Dinge auf. Danach gehen sowohl Κρῶφι als auch Μῶφι jeweils auf einen zweigliedrigen Nominalsatz mit der Kopula *pw* zurück: dem. **ḳr pw*, kopt. > *ⲕⲣⲟ ⲡⲉ *„Das ist das Ufer*" und **mꜣw.t pw*, > kopt. ⲙⲟⲩⲉ ⲡⲉ *„Das ist die Insel*". Daß die Kopula ⲡⲉ /pʰe/[12] mit *phi* wiedergegeben wird, weil dieses zur Zeit Herodots noch aspiriert realisiert wurde, bedarf keiner weiteren Erklärung. Die restlichen lautlichen Erscheinungen werden hingegen von Beinlich relativ oberflächlich abgehandelt. Wenn schon die Κρῶφι zugrundeliegende Form mit *ⲕⲣⲟ ⲡⲉ angesetzt wird, muß man sich auch fragen, warum die griechische Wiedergabe dann *omega* schreibt und nicht *omikron.* Die „Meinung von Herrn Dr. Brunsch", nach der die Verwendung der Kopula auch erklären würde, warum sich der lange Vokal des *status absolutus* in der griechischen Wiedergabe erhalten hat,[13] ist sehr eigentümlich. Denn der *status absolutus* lautet ⲕⲟⲣ und nicht etwa *ⲕⲣⲱ! Da müßte man eher gleich an die Pluralform ⲕⲣⲱⲟⲩ /*kʰrōw*/[14] denken, bei welcher der Halbvokal verschliffen wurde. Der Plural ⲕⲡⲱⲟⲩ wird gerne *promiscue* gebraucht. Eine andere Frage ist die griechische Wiedergabe eines solchen /*kʰrōw*/. Analog zur Wiedergabe der Kopula würde man hier ein *chi* erwarten und in der Tat ist in den griechischen Handschriften nicht

[10] W. Westendorf, Koptisches Handwörterbuch, Heidelberg 1965–77, 133.
[11] H. Beinlich, Die Nilquellen nach Herodot, in: ZÄS 106, 1979, 11–14.
[12] Siehe bei C. Peust, Egyptian Phonology, Göttingen 1999, 133ff.
[13] H. Beinlich, Die Nilquellen nach Herodot, in: ZÄS 106, 1979, 13, Anm. 21.
[14] Zur Aspiration siehe C. Peust, Egyptian Phonology, Göttingen 1999, 107ff.

nur die Form Κρῶφι, sondern ebenso häufig auch die Schreibung Χρῶφι bezeugt![15]

Was die Gleichung Μῶφι—kopt. *ⲙⲟⲩⲉ ⲡⲉ <**m*ꜣ*w.t pw* betrifft, so sind auch hier Ungereimtheiten festzustellen. Beinlich erklärt nicht, wie er sich den Übergang von *ⲙⲟⲩⲉ ⲡⲉ /*mwe pe*/ zu Μῶφι genau vorstellt. Einleuchtender—und genauso ein Gegensatz zu ⲕⲣⲱⲟⲩ bildend—erscheint es mir, Μῶφι auf /*mōw pe*/ vgl. kopt. *ⲙⲱⲟⲩ ⲡⲉ *„Das ist das Wasser“* zurückzuführen.

Nach einer erneuten Betrachtung der von Beinlich aufgeführten Gleichung ist es wahrscheinlich, in den beiden Bergnamen Κρῶφι und Μῶφι die Nominalsätze *ⲕⲣⲱⲟⲩ ⲡⲉ und *ⲙⲱⲟⲩ ⲡⲉ zu sehen. Wieder einmal[16] haben wir es mit einem Beispiel zu tun, bei dem Herodot auf eine schlaue Frage eine sehr dumme Antwort erhalten hat. Man hat geradezu die „fachkundigen“ ägyptischen Fremdenführer vor Augen, die den gutgläubigen Touristen—und nichts anderes war Herodot ja—die Geschichte vom Pferd bzw. von Krophi und Mophi erzählen.

Die von Barguet stammende Gleichung von *grf* mit Κρῶφι lehnt Beinlich ab, weil dann aus seiner Sicht die gesamte Textstelle keinen Sinn ergäbe.[17] Seine eigene Lesung erscheint mir allerdings auch nicht viel überzeugender zu sein und er gibt selbst zu, die Stelle sei wohl etwas verderbt.

Ungeachtet der Frage, ob denn nun *grf* mit Κρῶφι verbunden werden kann, möchte ich den Blick in eine ganz andere Richtung lenken.

Grundvoraussetzung für die folgenden Überlegungen ist die Datierung der Hungersnotstele in die Ptolemäerzeit und die Tatsache, daß seit der Perserherrschaft auf Elephantine ein aramäisch sprechender Bevölkerungsteil nachzuweisen ist.[18] Was liegt da näher, als bei einem unverständlichen Wort mit Elephantine im Kontext an das Aramäische zu denken. Die Inschrift gibt uns geradezu die Lösung vor, heißt es doch über ***grf* ꜣ*bw*:** *ḫr=tw r=f „sagt man dazu“* und mit *„man“* werden sicherlich die Bewohner der Insel, d.h jene aramäisch sprechenden Juden gemeint sein.

---

15 P. Barguet, La Stèle de la Famine à Séhel, BdE 24, 1953, 22f., Anm. 14.

16 W. Schenkel hat in seiner Miszelle „Wie das ägyptische Labyrinth zu seinem Namen kam“ in: GM 159, 1997, 87–90 eine sehr passende Anekdote zum Besten gegeben, die demonstriert, daß man auf die Frage „was ist das“ harmlose Antworten erhalten kann, die geradezu beleidigend sind.

17 H. Beinlich, Die Nilquellen nach Herodot, in: ZÄS 106, 1979, 13.

18 Siehe H. Shirun, in: LÄ I, 362–670 s.v. Aramäische Texte aus Ägypten, und L. Kákosy, in: LÄ I, 1221, s.v. Elephantine.

Leider finden wir im *Dictionary of the North-West Semitic Inscriptions*[19] keinen alt- oder reichsaramäischen Beleg für die Wurzel √*grp*, doch ist die Wurzel sonst im Semitischen gut bekannt. Es finden sich folgende Belege:[20]

Nordwest-Semitisch			
	jüdisch-aramäisch:	*g^{e}raf*	*wegfegen, weg-, fortschaufeln*
	syrisch	*graf*	*abspühlen, wegfegen*
	bibelhebräisch	*gāraf*	*mit sich fortreißen, wegspülen*
		ʾ^{æ}g^{e}rōf	*Faust, Gewalt*
		**m^{æ}g^{e}rāfāh*	unsicher, *Erdscholle ?*
	mittelhebräisch	√*grp*	*wegfegen, -spülen*
Zentral-Semitisch			
	arabisch	*ǧarafa*	*wegspülen, -waschen, wegschaufeln, entfernen, mitnehmen*
		ǧurf, ǧuruf	*Ufer, Bank, Hang*
		maǧraf	*Sturzbach*
		ǧārif	*reißend, ungestüm*
Süd-Semitisch			
	geʿez	*garafa*	*Fallen stellen, Netz auswerfen*
		g^{w}arif	*Flut (Lw aus dem Amharischen)*
	amharisch	*g^{w}ärif*	*Flut*
		g^{w}arrafa	*strömen (v. Gießbach)*

Auch die ägyptischen Ortsnamen, die mit dem Element *Ǧarf* gebildet werden, sind hierher zu stellen.[21]

Auf der lautlichen Ebene bereitet die Gleichung von *grf* mit der Wurzel √*grp* keinerlei Schwierigkeiten. In Wiedergaben nicht-ägyptischer Wörter in Hieroglyphen sind alle Entsprechungen belegt, z.B.:[22]

---

[19] J. Hoftijzer, K. Jongeling, Dictionary of the North-West Semitic Inscriptions, HdO I, 21, Leiden 1995.

[20] W. Gesenius, Hebräisches und Aramäisches Handwörterbuch über das Alte Testament, Berlin ^{18}1987, 230; L. Koehler und W. Baumgartner, Hebräisches und Aramäisches Lexikon zum Alten Testament, Leiden ^{3}1967, 196; H. Wehr, A Dictionary of Modern Written Arabic, Wiesbaden ^{3}1971, 120; W. Leslau, Comparative Dictionary of Geʿez, Wiesbaden 1987, 201.

[21] H. Halm, Ägypten nach den mamelukischen Lehensregistern, II. Das Delta, TAVO Beih. B 38/2, Wiesbaden 1982, 791.

[22] W. Schenkel, Einführung in die altägyptische Sprachwissenschaft, Darmstadt 1990, 35–38.

1. ägyptisches <*g*> entspricht semitischem (altkanaanäischem) /*g*/:
   [*m*]**g***ṭr* → *mi**g**dāl* “*Turm*”
2. ägyptisches <*r*> entspricht semitischem (altkanaanäischem) /*r*/:
   šʿr → *seʿīru* “*Wald*”
3. ägyptisches <*f*> entspricht semitischem (altkanaanäischem) <*p*>:
   Č̣ft → *Ṣapat* „*Ausguck*“, ein Toponym

Der Befund des letzten Konsonanten verdient unsere besondere Aufmerksamkeit. Ein Blick auf die oben gegebene Liste der verwandten Lexeme in anderen semitischen Sprachen zeigt, daß in allen Fällen die Spirantisierung dieses Radikals schon vollzogen war, der freilich im Nordwest-Semitischen noch in der Schrift in seiner ursprünglichen Form greifbar ist. Nun haben wir in der hieroglyphischen Schreibung ein <*f*> und kein <*p*>, wie man vielleicht erwarten könnte. Dies führt zu dem Schluß, daß bereits in dieser Zeit der *bgdkpt*-Konsonant *p* spirantisiert realisiert wurde. Segert bemerkt in seiner Altaramäischen Grammatik,[23] es sei nicht eindeutig festzustellen, ob bereits in der altaramäischen Periode (zu der er auch das Reichsaramäische zählt) die spirantischen Positionsvarianten berücksichtigt würden. Nach Beyer ist die spirantisierte Entsprechung des *gimel* vom 1. Jhd. v. Chr an belegt.[24] Auf jeden Fall kann die Spirantisierung nur nach der Aspirierung von *k*, *p* und *t* (um 200 v.Chr.) und dem Schwund der uraramäischen Laute *ġ*, *ḏ*, *ḫ* und *ṯ* (um 250 v.Chr.) erfolgt sein. Als *terminus post quem* besitzen wir den sog. Uruktext (um 150 v.Chr.), der keilschriftlich immer <*k*> und nicht <*ḫ*> schreibt, z.B. *za-ki-it* /*zakīt*/ „*ich siegte*“ zur Wurzel √*zky*.[25] Immerhin gibt es dagegen ältere Belege[26] in anderssprachigen Wiedergaben, z.B. keilschriftlich *Abdi-Milḫi* zur Wurzel √*mlk*. Hoch führt zwei sichere Belege in ägyptischen Texten auf:[27]

1. ägyptisch *ḥfč* für semitisch *ḥafaza*, √*ḥpz* „*eilen*“ und
2. ägyptisch *špt*/*šft* für semitisch *ṯapaṭa* „*richten*“.

Er spricht sich allerdings nicht für eine Spirantisierung des Frikativs aus, sondern deutet die Belege in Richtung eines „*affricated stop, namely* [pf]“[28]

---

[23] S. Segert, Altaramäische Grammatik, Leipzig 1975, 96.

[24] K. Beyer, Die aramäischen Texte vom Toten Meer, Göttingen 1984, 126–128 und 412.

[25] Siehe vorige Anm.

[26] Siehe Anm. 23.

[27] J. Hoch, Semitic Words in Egyptian Texts of the New Kingdom and Third Intermediate Period, Princeton, New Jersey 1994, 401, 430 und speziell 225, Nr. 310 und 278, Nr. 398.

[28] Siehe vorige Anm. 430.

und führt den altbekannten Wechsel der Graphien <*psi̯*>, <*fsi̯*> und <*pfsi̯*> „*kochen*" an. Bei diesen wird man besser mit Kammerzell von einem emphatischen Laut ausgehen, der im Alten Reich (wo der Graphiewechsel belegt ist) noch gesprochen worden wäre.[29]

Y. Muchiki hat sich nicht nur mit ägyptischen Lehnwörtern im Nordwest-Semitischen allgemein, sondern auch speziell mit Frage der Belege für die Spirantisierung beschäftigt,[30] mit dem Ergebnis, daß dieses Phänomen bei den ägyptischen Namen und Lehnwörtern im Phönizischen sehr schön nachgewiesen werden kann, hingegen im Aramäischen und Hebräischen keine Anzeichen dafür auszumachen seien. Die angeführten Belege decken den Zeitraum zwischen dem späten 6. Jhd. und dem Ende des 4. Jhd. v.Chr. ab:

1. PṬḤNM *pꜣ-č̣i̯-**H̱**nm(.w) Hermopolis, spätes 6. Jhd. v. Chr.*
2. NḤTḤWR *n**ḫ̮**t-Ḥr(.w) außerhalb Ägyptens, 5. Jhd. v. Chr.*
3. PḤWY *pꜣ-**ḫ̮**y Elephantine, Ende 4. Jhd.v. Chr.*

Der jüngste Beleg liegt noch jenseits des oben erwähnten *terminus post quem*. Die vorliegende Schreibung des aramäischen Lehnwortes *grf* in ägyptischen Hieroglyphen stellt somit einen weiteren Hinweis für eine recht früh beginnende Spirantisierung der *bgkpt* im Aramäischen dar und zwar zu einem Zeitpunkt, der auf jeden Fall früher anzusetzen ist, als bisher angenommen wurde.

Es sei noch erwähnt, daß über die Natur des ägyptischen <*f*>, gemessen an den Unsicherheiten bei der Interpretation anderer Konsonanten im Ägyptischen, erstaunlich wenig Schwierigkeiten bestehen.[31] Im Koptischen ist ϥ nicht umsonst eines der zum griechischen Alphabet hinzugefügten Sonderzeichen hieratischer Herkunft und bezeichnet konstant den labiodentalen stimmlosen Frikativ /*f*/. Als solcher wird er auch im Arabischen wiedergegeben.

Das hier angenommene Lexem „*Stromschnelle*" ist als Toponym auch aus anderem Kontext bekannt.[32] So taucht es in einer Aufstellung von Ortsnamen auf, die Darstellungen eines Syrienfeldzuges Ramses' II. im Jahre 8 beigeordnet sind, welche am Nordrand des Nordwestturmes des 1. Pylons im Ramesseum angebracht sind.[33] Dort lautet die

[29] F. Kammerzell, in: LingAeg. 2, 1992, 171f.

[30] Y. Muchiki, Spirantization in fifth-century BC north-west semitic, in: JNES 53, 1994, 125–130.

[31] C. Peust, Egyptian Phonology, Göttingen 1999, 133.

[32] W. Gesenius, Hebräisches und Aramäisches Handwörterbuch über das Alte Testament, Berlin [18]1987, 230.

[33] W. Helck, Die Beziehungen Ägyptens zu Vorderasien im 3. und 2. Jahrtausend v. Chr., ÄA 5, Wiesbaden 1962, 219.

Schreibung *k-ꜣ-r-p-w*, d.h. ohne die Spirantisierung. Lokalisiert wurde der Ort von Noth durch die Gleichung mit *Ğerabta* 8 km südöstlich von *el-Batrun* nördlich von Byblos auf dem Gebirge von Beth-Anat.[34]

Eine ganz andere Frage, die dieses Vorkommen aufwirft, ist die nach der fehlenden Verwendung der sogenannten syllabischen Schrift, ist es doch auffällig, daß im Falle der Hungersnotstele diese nicht zum Einsatz gekommen ist. M.E. liegt dies einfach in der Sprach- bzw. Schriftsituation begründet, die für Elephantine bestens belegt ist: das Nebeneinander der Verwendung von ägyptischen Hieroglyphen und der aramäischen Konsonantenschrift. Hinzu mag kommen, daß gerade bei einer an diesem Ort herrschenden Diglossiesituation das Wort gar nicht mehr als Lehnwort wahrgenommen wurde.

Damit wird auch schon ein weiterer Aspekt angeschnitten, der für die Beurteilung des Lehnwortes *grf* von Bedeutung ist: die Klassifikation des Entlehnungsvorgangs zum Zwecke der Beurteilung des herrschenden kulturellen Kontaktes zwischen den Sprechern der entlehnenden Matrix-Sprache und den Schreibern der Hungersnotstele. Unterscheidet man bei Entlehnungsvorgängen[35] nach dem Ort des Sprachkontakts *diatopisch* zwischen indirekter oder Fernentlehnung und direkter Entlehnung, so wird man mit Bestimmtheit das Vorkommen des Ortsnamens *k-ꜣ-r-p-w* auf ägyptischen Reliefs als einfache, aus kriegerischem Kontakt entsprungenen indirekte Fernentlehnung betrachten. Streng genommen handelt es sich eigentlich nur um die Nennung eines fremden Toponyms ohne Inkorporierung in den eigenen Wortschatz, d.h. nicht um ein Lehnwort im engeren Sinn. Im Gegensatz dazu ist der direkte Kontakt zwischen Ägyptern auf der einen und aramäischsprachigen Juden auf der anderen Seite durch vielfach festgestelltes Lehngut sehr gut dokumentiert.

Ein reicher Fundus für ägyptische Wörter ist die Arbeit von Kornfeld über die Onomastica Aramaica aus Ägypten,[36] zu denen Vittmann einige Ergänzungen beigesteuert hat.[37] Obschon nicht aus Elephantine, sondern aus Saqqara stammen weitere Aramaica, denen sich Zauzich gewidmet hat.[38] Abgesehen von diesen Personennamen

---

[34] M. Noth, Ramses II. in Syrien, ZDPV 64, 1941, 39–74, speziell 103f.

[35] Zur Klassifikation von Entlehnungsphänomenen, TESCH, Linguale Interferenz. Theoretische, terminologische und methodische Grundfragen zu ihrer Erforschung, Tübinger Beiträge zur Linguistik 105, Tübingen 19788, 61–74.

[36] W. Kornfeld, Onomastica Aramaica aus Ägypten, SÖAW 333, Wien 1978.

[37] G. Vittmann, Zu den ägyptischen Entsprechungen aramäisch überlieferter Personennamen, in: OrNS 58, 213–229.

[38] K.-Th. Zauzich, Ägyptologische Bemerkungen zu den neuen aramäischen Papyri aus Saqqara, in: Enchoria 13, 1985, 115–118.

sind einige ägyptische Wörter ins Aramäische entlehnt worden[39] und sogar Lehnübersetzungen lassen sich aufspüren.[40] Bei den aramäischen Entlehnungen im Ägyptischen sieht der Stand der Dinge ganz anders aus. Zwar hat Hoch ziemlich viele semitische Wörter gesammelt, die in ägyptischen Texten vorkommen und die größtenteils aus dem Nordwest-Semitischen stammen, doch bleibt eine exakte Zuordnung zu den beiden Zweigen Kanaanäisch und Aramäisch äußerst schwierig. Das vorliegende Lexem dürfte demnach das erste semitische Lehnwort im Ägyptischen sein, für das eine Herkunft aus dem Aramäischen sehr wahrscheinlich ist.

Die Forschungslage scheint zu suggerieren, daß der Kontakt, zumindest auf der Ebene sprachlicher Interferenz einseitig von der ägyptischen Seite ausging. Doch dieses Bild ist m.E. aus verschiedenen Gründen verzerrt. Zum einen ist da das ziemlich geschlossene Corpus der aramäischen Papyri aus Elephantine, dem keine vergleichbare Gruppe von ägyptischen Alltagstexten gegenübersteht. Mit anderen Worten—es liegt ein Ungleichgewicht bezüglich der Beleglage und der Textgattungen vor. Zum anderen ist es auch eine Frage der Erwartungshaltung. Der Aramaist, der sich mit den Elephantine-Papyri beschäftigt, erwartet von vorne herein schon das Vorkommen ägyptischen Lehnguts und ist solchermaßen geschärften Sinnes. Dagegen bedarf es erst einer solchen Ausnahmesituation, wie dem Auftreten eines *hapax legomenon*, um den Ägyptologen zu einem vorerst fruchtlos und abwegig erscheinenden Griff nach einem Wörterbuch des Aramäischen zu bewegen.

Daß es sich bei der Matrix-Sprache gerade um das Aramäische und nicht um irgend eine andere (nordwest)semitische Sprache handeln muß, ist durch den Kontext Elephantine sehr plausibel, auch wenn wir keine weiteren internen Kriterien dafür haben. Solche wären beispielsweise phonologischer Natur, etwa die Notation der Sibilanten, oder der kanaanäische Lautwandel ā́ > ō. Genausogut könnten morphologische Merkmale wie die unterschiedlichen Endungen des *m.pl. abs.* (aramä. *-n*, phöniz. *-m*) oder das Kausativmorphem zur Unterscheidung herangezogen werden.[41]

[39] B. Couroyer, Termes égyptien dans les papyri araméens du Musée de Brooklyn, in: RB 61, 1954, 555–559; J.F. Quack, Ein demotischer Ausdruck in aramäischer Transkription, in: WdO 23, 1992, 15–20; G. Vittmann, Ägyptisch-Aramäische Kleinigkeiten, in: WZKM 83, 1993, 233–246.

[40] J. Leibovitch, Quelques égyptianismes contenus dans les textes araméens d'Égypte, in: BIE 18, 1935f., 19–29.

[41] Siehe auch dazu J. Hoch, Semitic Words in Egyptian texts from the New Kingdom and Third Intermediate Period, Princeton New Jersey, 1994, 479–486.

Für die Untersuchung einer Motivation der Entlehnung des aramäischen Wortes für „Katarakt" muß noch ein weiterer Aspekt hinzugezogen werden. Ein Blick in Hochs Arbeit zeigt, daß noch eine weitere semitische Bezeichnung für „Strom" Eingang den ägyptischen Wortschatz genommen hat.[42] Es liegt in zwei verschiedenen Graphien vor und ist durch die Determinative ausreichend gesichert:

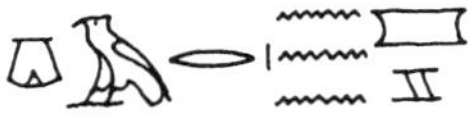

Auffälligerweise kommt bei diesem Lexem die syllabische Schreibung zum Einsatz und es liegt nicht in etwa ein Eintrag in einer Toponymliste vor, sondern das Wort scheint im Ägyptischen Sprachgebrauch verankert gewesen zu sein. Hoch stellt dieses *g-ꜣ-rʾ(-y)* zur Wurzel[43] √*gry*, wohingegen Helck die Wurzel √*grr* „ziehen, sich schlängeln" im Auge hatte.

Nordwest-Semitisch			
	mittelhebräisch	√*gry*	D, „reizen, sich erregen"
	bibelhebräisch	√*grh*	D, (Streit) erregen
	reichsaramäisch	√*gry*	reizen, verklagen, in Gang bringen
	syrisch	√*grʾ*	G, laufen, D, erregen
	jüdisch-aramäisch	√*grʾ*	D, reizen, abschießen (Pfeile)
Zentral-Seemitisch			
	arabisch	*ǧarā*	(v. Wasser) laufen, fließen, stattfinden
		ǧarayān	„Strom, Wasserlauf"
		maǧran	„Strom"
Ost-Semitisch			
	akkadisch	*garû, gerû*	„befehden, prozessieren"

Natürlich sind beides nichts anderes als Varianten derselben, ursprünglich zweiradikaligen Wurzel *√*gr*, die einmal durch Teilreduplikation

[42] J. Hoch, Semitic Words in Egyptian texts from the New Kingdom and Third Intermediate Period, Princeton New Jersey, 1994, 350, Nr. 515.

[43] W. Gesenius, Hebräisches und Aramäisches Handwörterbuch über das Alte Testament, Berlin [18]1987, 228.

(„Gemination“) zur Dreiradikalität gebracht wird, das andere mal durch die Wurzelerweiterung *y*.

Die drei Wurzeln √*grr*, √*gry* und √*grp* vor Augen—die doch immerhin fast bedeutungsgleich sind—ist man versucht, nach weiteren Wurzeln zu suchen, die in dieses Bild passen, d.h. die aus den beiden Radikalen *g* und *r* und einem zusätzlichen varriierenden Radikal bestehen, dabei gleichzeitig einer gemeinsamen Bedeutungsspäre angehören, die approximativ als „heftig niedergehen“ umschrieben werden kann. Ich verweise auf folgende Beispiele:[44]

Wurzel mit Variable an erster Stelle:

√*m***gr**	*„fallen, stürzen, hinwerfen“*
√*n***gr**	*„ausgegossen sein, fließen (v. Wasser), ausgießen“*
√*s***gr**	*sagᵉrîr „heftiger Regen“*
√*š***gr**	*„schicken, werfen, senden“*

Wurzel mit Variable an zweiter Stelle:

√**g***h***r**	*„sich zu Boden werfen“*

Wurzel mit Variable an dritter Stelle:

√**gr***h*	→ √*gry „fließen, laufen, stattfinden“*
√**gr***p*	*„wegfegen, -spülen, strömen*
√**gr**ʿ	*„tropfen, schlürfen, wegnehmen“*
√**gr***š*	*„sich scheiden, verstoßen, aufwühlen (die See)*

Das Phänomen primär zweikonsonantiger Wurzeln vom korrespondierenden Wortfeld mit einem variablen Radikal wurde schon von Gesenius-Kautzsch als Beleg für einen ehedem weiter verbreiteten Biradikalismus vorgebracht.[45] W.v. Soden hat es in seinem *Grundriss der Akkadischen Grammatik* sehr eindrücklich am Beispiel der zweiradikaligen Basis PR = "*trennen*" demonstriert,[46] das in jüngster Zeit von Kienast noch erweitert wurde.[47]

Nach diesem kurzen Ausflug in die Untiefen des Biradikalismus-Problems soll eine Motivationsanalyse sowie eine Klassifikation des Entlehnungsvorgangs vorgenommen werden.

Die Klassifikation nach Kontaktzonen in *direkte* vs. *indirekte* Entlehnung

[44] W. Gesenius, Hebräisches und Aramäisches Handwörterbuch über das Alte Testament, Berlin [18]1987, 204, 228, 230f. und W. Gesenius, Hebräisches und Aramäisches Handwörterbuch über das Alte Testament, Leipzig [14]1905, 359, 439, 487, 738, 134.

[45] E. Kautzsch, Gesenius‘ Hebräische Grammatik, Leipzig [28]1909, §30 f-o.

[46] W.v. Soden, Grundriss der Akkadischen Grammatik, AnOr 33, Rom [3]1995, §73 b.

[47] B. Kienast, Historische Semitische Sprachwissenschaft, Wisbaden 2001, 66f.

wurde bereits angesprochen. Ein Problem bei der weiteren Einteilung der indirekten Entlehnung in *adstratives*, *substratives* und *superstratives* Lehngut stellt das Unvermögen dar, bei letzterem zu entscheiden, wann eine Sprache als dominant und wann als rezessiv eingestuft werden sollte. In unserem konkreten Fall heißt das: ist das Ägyptische auf oder in der Nähe von Elephantine wirklich das vorherrschende Idiom? Die Masse der aramäischen Papyri geben die Antwort: nein! Bei solchermaßen gleichberechtigt nebeneinander bestehenden Sprachen gibt es mehrere daraus resultierende Schlüsse. Entweder war *grf* ein umgangssprachlicher Begriff, der sozusagen nur als "Ausrutscher" in einen offiziellen Text gekommen ist, was einem *vertikalen* Übernahmeprozess von unten nach oben gleichkommt, oder aber *grf* ist ein Wort aus der Fachsprache. Als *terminus technicus* könnte es durchaus von Schiffsleuten gebraucht worden sein—leider ist es ein *hapax legomenon.* Als horizontale Wanderbewegung von Fachsprache zu Fachsprache wäre *grf* in einem höheren Sprachniveau angesiedelt und ein gewisses Prestige kann ein entscheidender Faktor bei der Übernahme von fremden Wörtern sein. Es muß einen anderen Grund als einen sachbezogegen Zwang dafür geben, schließlich ist schwer vorstellbar, daß die Ägypter keine wirklich treffende Bezeichnung für den reißenden Katarakt gefunden hätten. Tatsächlich gibt es die Verbindung[48] *mw bỉn „schlechtes (Fahr)wasser“*, die sich auf die zerstörerischen Gegebenheiten des Flusses bezieht. Dagegen ist *ḳbḥ.w* zwar eine Bezeichnung des Kataraktengebiets, doch genauso ein allgemeines Wort für „Wassergebiet“[49] ohne die gefährliche Komponente—im Gegenteil. Hervorgehoben wird der wasser- und damit lebensspendende Aspekt. Trotzdem ist ***grf*** sprachökonomisch besser, weil prägnanter. Neben Sachzwang und Prestige kann schlichtweg Gewohnheit d.h. ein kommunikativer Aspekt für den Gebrauch des aramäischen Wortes das auslösende Moment gewesen sein. Das würde bedeuten, daß der Schreiber dem aramäischen Sprachmilieu sehr nahe stand.

Eine solche Annahme würde sich sehr gut ins Bild fügen angesichts des eingangs erwähnten *topos* von der sieben Jahre währenden Hungersnot. Selbst angesichts der Tatsache, daß die Hungersnot in Ägypten—besonders in der Ersten Zwischenzeit—ein weit verbreitetes *topos* ist,[50] wurde verschiedentlich eine Anlehnung der Hungersnotstele

[48] G. Dreyer, in: LÄ III, 356f. s.v. Katarakt(e).
[49] Wb. V, 29, 6–19.
[50] Dazu J.C. Garcia, Études sur l'administration, le pouvoir et l'idéologie en

an das Alte Testament erwogen.[51] Solche Stimmen erhalten durch eine eben vertretene Affinität zu den aramäisch sprechenden Juden Elephantines neues Gewicht, obschon man in Rechnung stellen muß, daß der Zeitraum von sieben Jahren im Orient gleichfalls ein Motiv ist, das sich großer Beliebtheit erfreute.[52]

Die Beschäftigung mit dem Umfeld des Schreibers muß unweigerlich zu der Problematik um den Auftraggeber und solchermaßen der Datierung der Hungersnotstele führen. Wie bereits erwähnt gibt die der Text vor, eine Inschrift aus der 3. Dynastie zu sein. Die Paläographie zeigt allerdings eindeutig, daß die Stele in die Ptolemäerzeit datiert werden muß. Barguet hat diesen Zeitraum weiter eingegrenzt und sich für eine Abfassung in der Zeit Ptolemaios V. ausgesprochen. Er begründet dies mit dem verstärkten Vorkommen des Imhotep in seiner Regierungszeit, in dessen 19. oder 20. Jahr dem vergöttlichten Wesir auf Philae ein Tempel errichtet wurde. Des weiteren führt er ins Feld, daß sich Ptolemaios V. als erster Herrscher der makedonischen Dynastie in Memphis krönen lies und damit eine gewisse Volksnähe bewiesen haben soll, die sich auf ähnliche Weise in der Rückbesinnung auf die Altvorderen Djoser und Imhotep spiegeln würde. Darüber hinaus habe die Schenkung eines Gebietes, das genau dem Dodekaschoinos entspricht, an den Chnum-Tempel den Sinn, das ptolemäische Einflußgebiet nach Süden hin abzustecken und nach der Revolte im Süden verlorenen Grund wiederzugewinnen. Zu allem Überfluss nimmt Barguet die Hungernot als reales Ereignis und setzt sie mit oben genannten Unruhen in Verbindung. Gegen diese Sicht der Dinge hat sich H. de Meulenaere gewandt,[53] der zu bedenken gibt, wie wenig eine solche Inschrift der ägyptischen Bräuchen gegenüber arroganten Art entspricht, die ptolemäische Herrscher sonst an den Tag legen. Wildung verweist darauf, wie außerordentlich es ist, daß ein König vollkommen hinter einem Vorgänger zurück-

Égypte de l'Ancien au Moyen Empire, Aegyptiaca Leodiensia 4, 1997, sowie L.D. Morenz, Versorgung mit Getreide: Historische Entwicklung und intertextuelle Bezüge zwischen ausgehendem Alten Reich und Erster Zwischenzeit in Achmim, in: SAK 26, 1998, 81–117.

[51] D.B. Redford, A Study of the Biblical Story of Joseph, VT Suppl. 20, 1970, 98, Anm.3 und 206f., vgl. auch K. Zibelius, in: LÄ III 84, s.v. Hungersnotstele.

[52] Für die Hungersnot im AAqhatu-Epos siehe W. Hallo et al. (Hg.) The Context of Scripture, Vol. I, Canonocal Compositions from the Biblical World, Leiden 1997, 351 und für das Auftreten des *topos* in Babylonien, siehe Tafel VI, 104 des Gilgamesch-Epos, vgl. S. Dalley, Myths from Mesopotamia. Creation, the flood, Gilgamesh and others, Oxford 1989, 80.

[53] H. de Meulenaere, in: BiOr 14, 1957, 33f.

tritt.[54] Gerade diesen Punkt halte ich ebenfalls für sehr problematisch, genauso wie den ganzen Datierungsansatz Barguet's. Vielmehr liegt es m.E nahe, das gesamte Szenario umzudrehen. Von einer Argumentation mit einer Hungersnot sollte man gerade wegen des *topos*-Charakters besser Abstand nehmen.

Die Krönung Ptolemaios' V. in Memphis diente selbstredend der Propaganda und steht vor dem Hintergrund von Zugeständnissen an die Priesterschaft, die aus der schwachen Position des Königs erwachsen sind. Ähnliches wird auf die Tempelbauten in Philae zutreffen. Die Rückbesinnung auf Djoser klingt eher wie ein nationalägyptischer Wiederbelebungsversuch, der die Selbständigkeit eines lokalen Fürsten untermauern soll. In Frage kommt da der in der Inschrift—im Gegensatz zu Ptolemaios V.—namentlich genannten

> *ḥꜣt.ỉ-<ʿ(.w)> ỉr.ỉ-pʿ.t ḥḳꜣ-ḥww.t-rsỉw.t ỉm.ỉ-rʾ ẖntỉ.w m ꜣbw M-s-(ỉ)r(ỉ)*
> *Fürst, Graf, Vorsteher der südlichen Domänen, Vorsteher der Nubier in Elephantine, Masar*

Die Lesung des Namens ist umstritten. Sethe hat ihn unter Vorbehalt als *Mʿdỉr* gelesen,[55] während Gardiner nach eigener Kollation *Mꜣỉ-ḥsꜣ*, d.h. Μιύσις liest[56] und somit immerhin einen Sinn herauslesen kann. Barguet[57] interpretiert explizit gegen Gardiner das unklare obere Zeichen im zweiten "Schriftquadrat" als *s* und liest *Msỉ-ỉr.t* *"Celui qui rapporte l'oeil"*.

Sethe: 

Gardiner: 

Barguet: 

H. de Meulenaere verwirft diese Lesung ihrerseits wieder mit dem Verweis auf inhaltliche Schwierigkeiten, macht allerdings keinen Gegenvorschlag. Er hat bestimmt Recht in der Annahme, der Name des „Vorstehers der Nubier in Elephantine“ müsse eher nubisch oder allenfalls griechisch sein, denn ägyptisch.

---

[54] D. Wildung, Die Rolle ägyptischer Könige im Bewußtsein ihrer Nachwelt I, MÄS 17, 1969, 88.

[55] K. Sethe, Dodekaschoinos. Das Zwölfmeilenland an der Grenze von Ägypten und Nubien, UGAÄ 2, 1901, 22.

[56] A.H. Gardiner, The House of Life, in: JEA 24, 1938, 157–179; 166 in Anm. 2.

[57] P. Barguet, La Stèle de la Famine à Séhel, BdE 24, 1953, 14, Anm. 3.

Eine andere Möglichkeit wäre die Interpretation als numidischen Namen. Bekanntlich ist das libysche Element MS *„Herr, Fürst“* in ägyptischen Texten bezeugt.[58] Es hat seine Entsprechung in Tuareg (Ahaggar)[59] *mess „maître“*, Tuareg (Niger)[60] *messi*. Bei Annahme einer Graphie <*m-s-r*> bietet sich eine Verbindung zur berberischen Wurzel √L *„in Besitz nehmen“* an, vgl. Tuareg (Ahagar)[61] *el „avoir“*. Numidisch ist dieser Namenstypus gut gezeugt,[62] vgl. MS-LT *„Herr, nimm ihn zu eigen“* (**Mas-elat*, RIL 895)[63] oder *Mas-ilan „Der Herr hat zu eigen“* (vgl. später latinisiert *Deushabet*). Der Name hätte dann wohl die Bedeutung *„Herr, nimm zu eigen“*. Zwar sind die berberischen Stämme in der gesamten Westwüste verbreitet und auch in Elephantine nicht undenkbar, doch erscheint es mir ratsamer an einem „nubischen“ Vorsteher der Nubier festzuhalten.

Unter dieser Prämisse lohnt es sich, eine meroitische Lösung in Erwägung zu ziehen. Im entsprechenden Onomastikon gibt es eine Reihe von Namen, die als erstes Element den Namen der Sonnengottheit *Mš* d.h. /*masa*/ aufweisen. Török hat sie gesammelt und den Standpunkt vertreten, *Mš* sei mit Amun-Re zu gleichen.[64]

Bereits von Griffith stammt die Hypothese, welche den Gottesnamen *Mš* /*masa*/ mit dem gemeinen nubischen Appellativum für „Sonne“ gleichsetzt:[65]

altnubisch:	ⲙⲁϣⲁⲗ
nobiin:	*màshà*
midob:	*pàssàr*

Die Verbindung des nubischen Lexems zum besagten meroitischen Gottesnamen wurde häufig in der Literatur angebracht, beispielsweise

---

[58] J. Yoyotte, Les principeautés du delta, in: Mélanges Maspero I: Orient Ancien Bd. 4, Paris/Kairo 121–179 speziell 123.

[59] Ch. de Foucauld, Dictionnaire touareg-français, Paris 1951–1952, III 1245.

[60] H. Barth, Reisen und Entdeckungen in Nord- und Central-Afrika, Gotha 1858, V 673.

[61] Ch. de Foucauld, Dictionnaire touareg-français, Paris 1951–1952, III 974.

[62] O. Rössler, Die Numider. Herkunft, Schrift, Sprache, in: T. Schneider, O. Rössler. Gesammelte Schriften zur Semitohamitistik, AOAT 287, Münster 2001, 658.

[63] J.-B. Chabot, Recueil des inscriptions libyques, Paris 1940.

[64] L. Török, Meroitic religion: Three contributions in a positivistic manner, in: Meroitica 7, 1984, 156–182.

[65] F.L. Griffith, Karanòg. The meroitic inscriptions of Shablûl ans Karanòg, Philadelphia 1911, 56 und 82f. und zu den nubischen Belegen: C. Peust, Das Napatanische, Göttingen 1999, 80.

von Trigger[66] oder Hofmann,[67] allerdings mit dem Prädikat „unsicher“.

Peust, der sich auf das äußerst unsichere Terrain herauswagt und ein Verwandschaftsverhältnis des Meroitischen mit dem Nubischen postuliert, stuft die Gleichung als wenig sicher ein, um gleichzeitig zu bemerken, daß das Nubische eine Liquida im Auslaut aufweist, die in der meroitischen Graphie unausgedrückt hätte bleiben müssen. Sollte sich der Zusammenhang zwischen meroitisch *Mš /masa/* und ⲙⲁϣⲁⲗ, *màshà*, *pàssàr* doch als richtig erweisen, besteht die Möglichkeit, in der Graphie  einen Beleg zu sehen, bei dem diese Liquida geschrieben wurde, weil es sich nicht um eine Schreibung in meroitischer Schrift handelt, sondern um eine ägyptisch-hieroglyphische. Nur ist doch sehr die Frage, ob es vorstellbar ist, daß jemand einen Gottesnamen allein trägt, ohne daß es sich um eine Kurzform wie *ꜣImn(.w).y* handelt.

Andererseits würde man bei einem Hypokoristikon eine entsprechende Endung erwarten, zumindest ein „Doppelschilfblatt“ *y*, man denke an den Namen *Ms-ye*.[68] Zur Not wäre es möglich, die Hieroglyphe für das Auge, koptisch ⲉⲓⲁ < *ỉr.t*, mit dem darvon abgeleiteten ptolemäischen Lautwert *y* zu lesen und so für die Schreibung des meroitischen Namens *Msye* in Anspruch zu nehmen. Wie dem auch sei, das Element *Mš* ist in jedem Fall möglich, und sei es in der Form *ỉr.t-Mš „Sonnenauge“*.

Eine andere und sehr elegante Lesung wäre die Annahme des meroitischen Lautwertes für das Augenzeichen, nämlich */d/*, der sich letztendlich vom *wḏꜣ.t*-Auge ableitet. Man denke auch an die Schreibung des Gottesnamens *Apedemak* als *pꜣ-ỉr-mkỉ*. Denn damit eröffnet sich eine weiterere Interpretation des Namens unter der Prämisse, daß dieses <*d*> für */t/* steht. Damit läge das Element *-t* vor,[69] das aus einer Assimilation von „Genitivsuffix“ *-s* + Prädikationssufffix *-lo* entstanden ist. Nach dieser Leseart ergibt sich für den vorliegenden Personennamen die Bedeutung *„Der des Masa“*, womit sich der Namensträger als besonderer Anhänger des Sonnengottes *Masa* ausweist.

---

[66] B.G. Trigger, Meroitic and Eastern Sudanic. A linguistic relationship?, in: Kush 12, 1964, 189.

[67] I. Hofmann, Material für eine Meroitische Grammatik, Beiträge zur Afrikanistik 13, Wien 1981, 86.

[68] Siehe bei L. Török, Meroitic religion: Three contributions in a positivistic manner, in: Meroitica 7, 1984, 169.

[69] Diese Interpretation verdanke ich einem freundlichen Hinweis von K. Zibelius-Chen.

Sucht man nach Parallelen im meroitischen Onomastikon,[70] so muß man feststellen, daß dieser Name in dierer Form nicht belegt ist. Bezeugt sind lediglich *Msdoye* und *Msidd*.[71] Der ptolemäische Lautwert *m* für das Auge paßt auf den Namen *Mseme*, *y* auf den Namen *Mseye*.[72] Steht in der Inschrift <*ṭ*> anstelle von <***s***>, käme auch *Mdeye* in Frage.[73]

Wer aber war nun dieser obskure *Masat* (<**Masaslo*)? Er tritt an ziemlich prominenter Stelle in Erscheinung und dürfte demnach keine allzu unwichtige Person gewesen sein. Wie de Meulenaere gezeigt hat, ist sein Titel eher von untergeordneter Bedeutung[74] und erlaubt keinesfalls, in ihm den ἐπιστρατηγος Oberägyptens zu sehen, besonders, da der Amtsinhaber aus den Jahren 185–176/5 v.Chr. bekannt ist.[75] Sehr überzeugend erscheint mir sein Hinweis auf die Ähnlichkeit mit der Beschreibung eines gewissen Φοι[. . .], der nach Ausweis einer Inschrift aus Assuan (149/8 v.Chr.) über die Äthiopen herrschte:

> [. . . τὸν τότε ὄν]τα τῶν Αἰθιόπων ἐπάρχοντα Φοι[. . .].[76]
> *„Phoi, der zu dieser Zeit die Aithiopen beherrschte. . . .“*

Leider ist die Stele sehr fragmentarisch, sodaß die genaue Funktion und der Rang dieses Funktionärs unklar bleibt. Immerhin können wir so viel erkennen, daß die Nubier des Gebiets südlich von Philae einem Einheimischen unterstanden. Verwaltungstechnisch war der Tricontaschoinos an die Thebais angeschlossen und unterstand dem dortigen στρτηγος.[77] Ein solcher wäre die autorisierte Person gewesen, eine Inschrift wie die der Hungersnotstele in Auftrag zu geben, wenn sie wirklich zur Legitimation des ptolemäischen Königs gedient hat.

So spricht vieles dafür, in *Masat* (<**Masaslo*) eher einen der Meroiten zu sehen, die von 196–186 v.Chr. Elephantine besetzt hielten.

Aus dieser Warte besehen, war der Zweck der Hungersnotstele die Bekräftigung *meroitischer* Ansprüche auf den Dodekaschoinos. Vielleicht erklärt sich dadurch die geringe Qualität des Textes.

Als Autor des Textes käme so kein gut ausgebildeter königlicher

[70] Auch für die Auskunft zu den weiteren meroitischenn Belegen und die Diskussion darum möchte ich mich herzlich bei K. Zibelius-Chen bedanken.
[71] REM 0525/1/2A und REM 0324/5/36.
[72] REM 0238/2/2A.
[73] REM 0235/2/2A.
[74] H. de Meulenaere, in: BiOr 14, 1957, 33f.
[75] E. Van't Dack, Notes concernant l'épistratégie ptolémaique, in: Aegyptus 32, 1952, 441f.
[76] Siehe Anm. 62 und T. Eide, T. Hägg, R.H. Pierce & L. Török, Fontes Historiae Nubiorum (FHN), Bergen 1996, Vol. II, 631–635, Nr. 140.
[77] Siehe vorige Anm.

Schreiber in Betracht,[78] sondern nur ein wenig versierter Verfasser aus der Umgebung, möglicherweise mit aramäischem Hintergrund.

Literaturverzeichnis

P. Barguet, *La Stèle de la Famine à Séhel*, BdE 24, 1953.
H. Barth, *Reisen und Entdeckungen in Nord- und Central-Afrika*, Gotha 1858.
H. Beinlich, *Die Nilquellen nach Herodot*, in: ZÄS 106, 1979, 11–14.
K. Beyer, *Die aramäischen Texte vom Toten Meer*, Göttingen 1984.
J.-B. Chabot, *Recueil des inscriptions libyques*, Paris 1940.
J.-F. Champollion le jeune, *L'Égypte sous les Pharaons ou recherche sur la géographie, la religion, la langue, les écritures et l'histoire de l'Égypte avant l'invasion de Cambyse.* Description géographique. Paris, De Bure, juillet 1814, I, 115.
B. Couroyer, *Termes égyptien dans les papyri araméens du Musée de Brooklyn*, in: RB 61, 1954, 555–559.
S. Dalley, *Myths from Mesopotamia. Creation, the flood, Gilgamesh and others*, Oxford 1989.
Ch. de Foucauld, *Dictionnaire touareg-français*, Paris 1951–1952.
G. Dreyer, in: LÄ III, 356f. s.v. Katarakt(e).
T. Eide, T. Hägg, R.H. Pierce & L. Török, *Fontes Historiae Nubiorum* (FHN), Bergen 1996, Vol. II.
A. Erman, *Geschichtliche Inschriften aus dem Berliner Museum*, in: ZÄS 38, 1900, 114–121.
J. Friedrich, AOF 20, 1963, 102.
J.C. Garcia, *Études sur l'administration, le pouvoir et l'idéologie en Égypte de l'Ancien au Moyen Empire*, Aegyptiaca Leodiensia 4, 1997.
A.H. Gardiner, *The House of Life*, in: JEA 24, 1938, 157–179.
W. Gesenius, *Hebräisches und Aramäisches Handwörterbuch über das Alte Testament*, Berlin [18]1987.
H. Goedicke, *Comments on the „Famine Stela"*, San Antonio 1994.
F.L. Griffith, Karanòg. *The meroitic inscriptions of Shablûl ans Karanòg*, Philadelphia 1911.
W. Hallo et al. (Hg.) T*he Context of Scripture, Vol. I, Canonocal Compositions from the Biblical World*, Leiden 1997.
H. Halm, *Ägypten nach den mamelukischen Lehensregistern*, II. Das Delta, TAVO Beih. B 38/2, Wiesbaden 1982.
W. Helck, *Die Beziehungen Ägyptens zu Vorderasien im 3. und 2. Jahrtausend v. Chr.*, ÄA 5, Wiesbaden 1962.
J. Hoch, *Semitic Words in Egyptian Texts of the New Kingdom and Third Intermediate Period*, Princeton, New Jersey 1994.
I. Hofmann, *Material für eine Meroitische Grammatik*, Beiträge zur Afrikanistik 13, Wien 1981.
J. Hoftijzer, K. Jongeling, *Dictionary of the North-West Semitic Inscriptions*, HdO I, 21, Leiden 1995.
L. Kákosy, in: LÄ I, 1221, s.v. Elephantine.
F. Kammerzell, in: LingAeg. 2, 1992.
E. Kautzsch, Gesenius' *Hebräische Grammatik*, Leipzig [28]1909.
B. Kienast, *Historische Semitische Sprachwissenschaft*, Wisbaden 2001.

---

[78] Es gibt keinerlei Hinweise darauf, daß die ptolemäische Inschrift der Endpunkt einer kuschitenzeitlichen Umarbeitung eines älteren Textes ist, dessen Vorläufer bis in die 3. Dynastie zurückgehen, wie Wildung meint (D. Wildung, Die Rolle ägyptischer Könige im Bewußtsein ihrer Nachwelt I, MÄS 17, 1969, 85–91.).

L. Koehler und W. Baumgartner, *Hebräisches und Aramäisches Lexikon zum Alten Testament*, Leiden [3]1967.
W. Kornfeld, *Onomastica Aramaica aus Ägypten*, SÖAW 333, Wien 1978.
J. Leibovitch, *Quelques égyptianismes contenus dans les textes araméens d'Égypte*, in: BIE 18, 1935f., 19–29.
W. Leslau, *Comparative Dictionary of Ge'ez*, Wiesbaden 1987.
M. Lichtheim, *The Famine Stela*, in: W. Hallo, K. Lawson Younger, Jr., Hrsg., *The Context of Scripture I, Canonical Compositions from the Biblical World*, Leiden 1997, 130–134.
A.B. Lloyd, *Herodotus Book II*, Commentary 1–98, EPRO 43, Leiden 1976.
H. de Meulenaere, in: BiOr 14, 1957.
L.D. Morenz, *Versorgung mit Getreide: Historische Entwicklung und intertextuelle Bezüge zwischen ausgehendem Alten Reich und Erster Zwischenzeit in Achmim*, in: SAK 26, 1998, 81–117.
Y. Muchiki, *Spirantization in fifth-century BC north-west semitic*, in: JNES 53, 1994, 125–130.
M. Noth, *Ramses II.* in Syrien, ZDPV 64, 1941, 39–74.
C. Peust, *Egyptian Phonology*, Göttingen 1999.
——, Das Napatanische, Göttingen 1999.
J.F. Quack, *Ein demotischer Ausdruck in aramäischer Transkription*, in: WdO 23, 1992, 15–20.
D.B. Redford, *A Study of the Biblical Story of Joseph*, VT Suppl. 20, 1970.
W. Schenkel, *Einführung in die altägyptische Sprachwissenschaft*, Darmstadt 1990.
——, *Wie das ägyptische Labyrinth zu seinem Namen kam*, in: GM 159, 1997, 87–90
T. Schneider, O. Rössler. *Gesammelte Schriften zur Semitohamitistik*, AOAT 287, Münster 2001.
S. Segert, *Altaramäische Grammatik*, Leipzig 1975.
K. Sethe, *Dodekaschoinos. Das Zwölfmeilenland an der Grenze von Ägypten und Nubien*, UGAÄ 2, 1901.
H. Shirun, in: LÄ I, 362–670 s.v. *Aramäische Texte aus Ägypten.*
L. Török, *Meroitic religion: Three contributions in a positivistic manner*, in: Meroitica 7, 1984, 156–182.
B.G. Trigger, *Meroitic and Eastern Sudanic. A linguistic relationship?*, in: Kush 12, 1964.
E. Van't Dack, *Notes concernant l'épistratégie ptolémaique*, in: Aegyptus 32, 1952, 441f.
G. Vittmann, *Zu den ägyptischen Entsprechungen aramäisch überlieferter Personennamen*, in: OrNS 58, 213–229.
——, *Ägyptisch-Aramäische Kleinigkeiten*, in: WZKM 83, 1993, 233–246.
J.v. Beckerath, in: LÄ I, 1111–1112, s.v. Djoser.
——, *Handbuch der ägyptischen Königsnamen*, MÄS 49, [2]1999.
W.v. Soden, *Grundriss der Akkadischen Grammatik*, AnOr 33, Rom [3]1995.
H. Wehr, *A Dictionary of Modern Written Arabic*, Wiesbaden [3]1971.
W. Westendorf, *Koptisches Handwörterbuch*, Heidelberg 1965–77.
D. Wildung, *Die Rolle ägyptischer Könige im Bewußtsein ihrer Nachwelt I*, MÄS 17, 1969.
J. Yoyotte, *Les principeautés du delta*, in: Mélanges Maspero I: Orient Ancien Bd. 4, Paris/Kairo 121–179.
K.-Th. Zauzich, *Ägyptologische Bemerkungen zu den neuen aramäischen Papyri aus Saqqara*, in: Enchoria 13, 1985, 115–118.
K. Zibelius, in: LÄ III 84, s.v. Hungersnotstele.

THIRD CONSONANTS IN ANCIENT EGYPTIAN

Christopher Ehret
(University of California, Los Angeles)

The problem

In two publications I have argued at length from large bodies of supporting data for a particular theory of the root in Semitic and in Afrasan (Afroasiatic) as a whole.* This theory posits that the basic root structure in pre-proto-Semitic and still earlier in Afrasan history was CVC-, with a smaller number of C- roots, and that third and fourth consonants in nouns and verbs could normally be explained as having originated as morphological extensions of the root. The first of these works (Ehret 1989) used the method of internal reconstruction to support the case, drawing on more than 1200 examples from Arabic. The second (Ehret, 1995) followed this up with an additional 400-plus internal reconstructions based on sets of related roots from Arabic. But more important, the second work builds a comparative historical case for this theory of root structure. It identifies on this basis numerous examples from Semitic as well as from elsewhere in Afroasiatic—another 700-plus cases from Semitic; approximately 420 verb examples from ancient Egyptian, along with many more examples of the proposed old nominal suffixes; 170 cases of the proposed verb extensions from the Chadic division, and a similar number from the Cushitic division of the family, along again with much larger numbers of the proposed nominal suffixes; and around 180 cases altogether from Omotic.

What I propose to do here is to test the ancient Egyptian data further, applying the method of internal reconstruction specifically to these materials. To the Egyptian examples cited in Ehret 1995 I

* I prefer the term "Afrasan" over either "Afrasian" or "Afroasiatic" for this family, and so I am trying it out for the first time in this article. The reason for my preference is that its particular pronunciation, better than either of the other two names, properly emphasizes the African origins and locations of the great majority of the family.

will add a considerable number of further Egyptian examples, primarily from Middle Egyptian and the Pyramid texts. Two questions need to be answered. Can we make the case for a similar theory of root structure using just the Egyptian data by themselves? Do the proposed morphemic meanings attributed in the theory seem sufficiently close to what internal reconstruction from the Egyptian data implies, so that a common history is implied; or are they so different as to indicate a distinct explanation?

Root extensions still productive in ancient Egyptian

The origins of a number of third-consonants raise no particular problems for their interpretation. They consist of nominal and verbal suffixes widely productive still today in various branches of the Afrasan family, including Semitic, and visibly productive in ancient Egyptian. These are well known already to scholars, and we will cite only a representative sample of the numerous Egyptian attestations of each.

1. *t noun suffix
This noun formative is productive still in a great number of the Afrasan languages today. We can quickly find convincing Egyptian examples. Several different varieties of meaning attach to this suffix, illustrated by the examples list under the subcategories a–f:

a. noun complement of adjectives;
b. tangible or abstract noun complement of a noun;
c. deverbative object of action;
d. deverbative attributive;
e. deverbative instrument/agent; and
f. deverbative complement, forming *inter alia* abstract nouns.

The last of these usages (three cases of which are cited here) may have been the most productive in ancient Egyptian. The linking sense seems to be "thing characterized by or characteristic of the action, condition, or thing denoted by" the root to which the *t suffix attaches. Similar ranges of meanings attach to this suffix in other branches of the Afrasan family.

a.	*bin*	"bad, evil (adj.)"	*bint*	"evil (noun)"
	dḥr	"bitter"	*dḥrt*	"bitterness"

	mḏ	"deep"	*mḏt*	"depth"
	ẖ3b	"crooked"	*ẖ3bt*	"curl; crookedness"
b.	*ṯbw*	"sole of foot"	*ṯbwt*	"sandal"
	mk	"protector"	*mkt*	"protection"
	ẖnm	"basin (?) for irrigation"	*ẖnmt*	"cistern, well"
c.	*pḏ*	"to draw bow"	*pḏt*	"bow"
	tw3	"to support; hold up, set (crown on head)"	*tw3t*	"temple roof"
	ḳnb	"to bend, bow"	*ḳnbt*	"corner, angle"
d.	*dm*	"to pierce (sky); sharpen; be sharp"	*dmt*	"knife"
e.	*zf*	"to cut up, cut off"	*zft*	"sword, knife"
	šc	"to cut off"	*šct*	"knife"
	mnc	"to nurse"	*mnct*	"nurse"
f.	*sf*	"to be mild, merciful"	*sft*	"clemency"
	mn	"to hurt"	*mnt*	"malady"
	cḏ	"to hack up, destroy"	*cḏt*	"slaughter, massacre"

2. *y noun and adjectival suffix

A suffix in *y functions widely in the family as a deverbative and as a formative of attribute nouns. The productive ancient Egyptian cases of this suffix seem, in contrast, most often to derive agent nouns from other nouns (a). This suffix also widely has adjective- or adverb-forming functions in the Afrasan family, as it did also in Egyptian (b). An interesting example, deriving a noun from a noun by the addition of both the *t and the *y nominal suffixes, appears in (c):

a.	*pḏt*	"bow"	*pḏty*	"bowman"
	cḥt	"farmland"	*cḥty*	"cultivator"
	sḥy	"council; counsel"	*sḥyt*	"man of good council"
b.	*tp*	"head; headman"	*tpy*	"being upon, principal first"
	i3b	"east wind"	*i3by*	"east, eastern; left"
c.	*rw*	"lion"	*rwty*	"lion's den"

3. *w noun suffix

This suffix functioned, more generally than *y, as a deverbative. It commonly forms

(a) agent nouns;
(b) less commonly, instrument nouns;
(c) attribute nouns, including nouns derived from adjectives; and
(d) noun complements.

Here are some examples:

a.	*sf*	"to be mild, merciful"	*sfw*	"gentle man"
	mtr	"to testify concerning"	*mtrw*	"witness"
	nḏ	"to grind"	*nḏw*	"miller"
	ḏ3i	"to oppose"	*ḏ3iw*	"opponent"
	bh3	"to flee"	*bh3w*	"fugitive"
b.	*spḥ*	"to lasso"	*spḥw*	"lasso"
	ḥtr	"to bind together"	*ḥtrw*	"lashings"
	ḳ3s	"to bind, tie"	*ḳ3sw*	"bonds"
c.	*tnm*	"to disappear"	*tnmw*	"darkness, gloom"
	ṯbb	"to step on" (gemin. as iter.)	*ṯbw*	"sole of foot"
	t3	"hot"	*t3w*	"heat"
	dšr	"red"	*dšrw*	"blood"
	wbn	"to rise, shine (sun)"	*wbnw*	"eastern; the East"
d.	*sf*	"to mix"	*sfw*	"muddle"
	gs	"to anoint"	*gsw*	"ointment"
	dw3	"to rise early"	*dw3t*	"dawn, morning; tomorrow"
	nhp	"to rise early in morning"	*nhpw*	"early morning"

4. *y verb extension

The verb extension in *y has several recurrent functions wherever it is or has been productive in the Afrasan family:

(a) as a denominative;
(b) as an inchoative; and
(c) as a marker of extended action.

Egyptian presents examples of all of these outcomes:

a.	*mk*	"protector"	*mki*	"to guard, protect"
	šf	"respect, honor (?)"	*šfi*	"to respect"
b.	*dw3*	"to rise early"	*dw3-y-t*	"morning": stem plus *y as inchoative i.e., "become morning," plus *t n. suff.
	ṯbw	"sole of foot" (see 3c);	*ṯbi*	"to be shod"
	ṯbwt	"sandal" (see 1b)		
	w3	"far; long ago"	*w3i*	"to become distant"
	ḳn	"fat (adj.); fat (n.)"	*ḳny*	"to become fat"
	mn	"sick man"	*mni*	"to be ill, suffer"
	gb	"deficiency, deprivation	*gbi*	"to be weak, deprived, deficient"
	i3w	"old man"	*i3wi*	"to be aged, attain old age"
c.	*hbhb*	"to traverse" (redup. stem) travel"	*hbi*	"to tread out; tread;

cḫt	"to swoop" (see 14)	*cḫi*	"to fly"
fdḳ	"to divide, split" (see 27)	*fdi*	"to pluck, pull up, uproot, pull out"

A number of further examples, especially of category c, will appear in subsequent comparative data, including instances of *y as a verb extension of little or no semantic content, a not uncommon outcome elsewhere in the family. Widely in Afrasan, *y can have a durative effect or is added to verbs whose meanings already inherently convey an extended action.

Formerly productive root extensions inferred from internal reconstruction

A second and much large body of root extensions seems to have been either rarely productive or no longer so at all in ancient Egyptian. Their former existence can be discovered through the techniques of internal reconstruction. Unless specifically cited as a sample, the examples include most of the identified cases (in Ehret 1995 and the writer's research work in progress).

Several noun suffixes are so strongly apparent in the comparative Afrasan evidence that the presence of their proposed reflexes in Egyptian is not surprising.

5. *r (> Eg. *3* word-final) noun suffix, or *ʔ noun suffix (> Eg. *3*)
A noun suffix in *r is attested all through the family in the comparative data, and it has remained productive in some languages down to the present. There are two problems for establishing its presence in ancient Egyptian. First, PAA *r fell together with PAA *ʔ in most word-final positions in Egyptian, and PAA *ʔ itself can be argued to have been a separate old nominal suffix, most often adjectival in implication, in Afrasan, so that the suffixes would usually have merged word-finally in their realizations. Second, although the comparative evidence yields a significant number of cases of either the suffix in *r or the suffix in *ʔ in ancient Egyptian (Ehret 1995; Ehret in preparation), the examples suggested on the basis of internal reconstruction are close to nil. Just two cases are presented here. The first is straightforward; the second we will consider again later in this article:

nḏ	"to grind"	*nḏ3w*	"chips (of stone)" (with *-w* pl.)
ḳmd	"to devise, invent" (see 18)	*ḳm3*	"appearance, form" (also "to create, produce")

6. *n adjective suffix

An adjective-forming suffix in *n is widely present in Afrasan, as well as a noun-forming suffix in *n. Quite a few lexicalized cases of both adjectival and noun usages of *n suffix can be argued from the comparative evidence of Afrasan root reconstructions to occur in the Egyptian reflexes of old Afrasan roots. But the evidence for this suffix based solely on internal reconstruction is not extensive:

sf	"to be mild, merciful"	*sfn*	"to be kindly, merciful" (proposed earlier adj., "kindly, merciful," converted to essive verb)
ṯbhn	"to leap, prance (of animals" (see 15 and 34)	*ṯbn*	"to be quick" (proposed earlier adj. "quick," converted to essive verb "to be quick")

7. *m noun and adjective suffixes

Noun and adjective suffixes in *m are also very widely attested in the Afrasan family. Both have remained productive, for example, in a several Cushitic languages right down to recent times. Several examples of the *m noun suffix and a couple of cases of the *m adjective suffix can be proposed from the comparative evidence for ancient Egyptian (Ehret 1995: 22). Just two good examples can as yet be proposed from the internal reconstruction data, but both the noun- (a) and adjective-deriving (b) functions of the posited Afrasan suffixes can be seen in these two:

a. *ẖnw*	"brook" (see 13 for *w*)	*ẖnm*	"basin (?) (for irrigation)"
b. *nḳc*	"to scrape, incise; polish (?)" (see 23)	*nḳm*	"to be bald" (proposed underlying adj. converted to essive verb)

8. *l (> Eg. r word-final) noun and adjective suffix

A suffix in *l has been a prominent noun and adjective formative in several branches of the Afrasan family. Since according to the author's findings PAA *l > Eg. *r* /_#, its reflexes should appear as *r* in most cases in ancient Egyptian. Examples of both noun (a) and adjective (b) derivation can be cited:

a.	*ḳ3b*	"to fold over";	*ḳ3r*	"bundle"
	ḳ3	"to bind, tie"		
	ḥt	"to become entangled"	*ḥtr*	"yoke of oxen"
	ḥtr	"to bind together" (see 22)		
	bcbc	"to bubble" (redup. stem)	*bcr*	"fountain"
b.	*m3ct*	"ideal state of things, proper ordering of life" (*mc root plus *t n. suff.)	*mcr*	"fortunate, successful, without fault"
	wš	"to fall out (hair); lack; be destroyed; desolate (a place)"	*wšr*	"to be despoiled; be barren (woman)" (proposed derivation: adj. "despoiled, lacking" converted to essive verb)

9. *s noun-forming suffix

This suffix can be argued to be present in the Chadic, Semitic, and Egyptian branches of Afrasan, but not in the earlier diverging Cushitic and Omotic branches. The comparative evidence suggests that this suffix may have originated as a deverbative complement formative

ḏ3i	"to oppose" (see 3a)	*ḏ3is*	"dispute, argument; civil war" (also converted to v. "to dispute, argue (with)")
ḫ3b	"to be bent" (see 19)	*ḫ3s*	"curl (on front of Red Crown)"
ḫ3m	"to bow down" (see 16)		

10. *b animate noun suffix

As Diakonov and others have noted, there is an old animate noun suffix *b to found in Semitic and other branches of Afrasan. One neat example is the following, but it is certainly not the only such instance in ancient Egyptian:

ḳ3b	"to fold over";	*ḳ3b*	"intestines" (from the twisting shape of the small intestines)
ḳ3s	"to bind, tie";		
ḳ3r	"bundle" (see also 8a)		

11. *s causative as a verb suffix

The causative in *s, of proto-Afrasan provenance, was still productive in ancient Egyptian, but in its productive version was prefixed to the verb root, as it is in the Semitic branch. The evidence from the rest of the family, in which it is also a still generally productive marker, shows that it originated as a suffix. The shift of this item to prefixal position appears thus to be one of several shared innovations tying Egyptian and Semitic together in their own closer-related subgroup of the family. In keeping with this solution, the comparative Afrasan evidence indicates fossil, suffixed occurrences of this extension in ancient Egyptian, left over from a much earlier period before it moved to a prefixal location. Examples can also be identified by internal reconstruction, comparing verbs with final *s* to semantically relatable verbs differing in their third consonants:

ḳ3b	"to fold over, double over"	*ḳ3s*	"to bind, tie"
ḳ3r	"bundle" (see 8a);		
ḳ3b	"intestines" (see 10)		
ḥtm	"to perish, be destroyed" (see 16)	*ḥts*	"to bring to an end"

12. *s verb extension, non-causative

In a variety of instances, Egyptian roots include a final *s* where a causative meaning is not indicated. In general, such *s* appears to accompany an implication of extended action. In the last four cases cited here, final *s* is not likely to be a fossilized causative because it attaches to a root already transitive in meaning.

ẖ3r	"to bolt (?) (of horses)"	*ẖ3s*	"to scramble (?)"
ẖ3ẖ	"to be speedy; hurry" (see 29)		
dg3	"to walk" (see 20)	*dgs*	"to walk"
ẖbẖb	"to pierce; kill" (redup. *ẖb*)	*ẖbs*	"to hack up the earth"
wḥ3	"to hew (stone)" (see 20)	*wḥs*	"to cut off (hair)"
wgp	"to triturate" (see 25)	*wgs*	"to cut open"

13. *w verb extension

In the Afrasan family as a whole, the *w extension had virtually the same range of functions as those noted for *y (5). Instances of it are of relatively rare occurrence in Egyptian, although common in both Cushitic and Semitic examples. In Cushitic languages it is still often a productive suffix. A number of Egyptian cases can be adduced in the comparative data (Ehret 1995 and Ehret in preparation), and several more cases will be noted when we get on to other sections below. Just one example is given at this point—an instance of *w with durative effect—so that, in contrast to the verb extension in *y, it is unlikely still to have been productive in ancient Egyptian:

zwn	"to perish"	*zwnw*	"to suffer"

14. *t verb extension

The *t extension, which is still productive in many Afrasan languages, all across the family conveys a continuing action, and the examples in Egyptian fit right in with that meaning:

cẖi	"to fly"	*cẖt*	"to swoop"
nwd	"to vacillate";	*nwtwt*	"to totter" (partially redup. *nw)
nwr	"to shake" (see 20b);		
nwḏ	"to deviate" (see 17a);		
nwn	"to let hair hang loose over forehead" (see 15)		
nfnfn	"to unroll" (partially redup. stem as iter.);	*nft*	"to loosen, detach"
nfc	"to remove" (see 23b)		
ḥpgt	"leaping dance" (*t n. suff., see 1; for *g*, see 32a)	*ḥpt*	"to travel, hurry"

15. *n verb extension

In ancient Egyptian, as widely elsewhere in the family, verbs with a third consonant in *n are associated with action that has duration.

si	"to shuffle"	*sin*	"to run"
sysy	"to hasten, hurry" (redup. stem as intens.)		
nwd	"to vacillate" (see 14 for the rest of this set of verbs)	*nwn*	"to let hair hang loose over forehead"
pšš	"to straddle; spread oneself; spread out"	*pšn*	"to separate" (combatants)"
ṯbn	"to be quick" (see 6 for explanation of final *n* here)	*ṯbhn*	"to prance, leap (of animals)" (for *h*, see 34)
nft	"to loosen, detach" (see 14)	*nfnfn*	"to unroll" (partially redup. *nfn)
nfc	"to remove" (see 21)		
wbẖ	"to be bright" (see 29)		
cw3	"to look after, care for (?)" (see 20)	*cwn*	"to covet"

16. *m verb extension

Verbs in ancient Egyptian with *m* as the third consonant tend to denote

(a) action with duration or done repetitively or
(b) action of ongoing effect:

a.	*sḥr*	"to strike" (see 22)	*sḥm*	"to crush, pound"
	w3i	"to roast (?) (grain)";	*w3m*	"to bake (?)"
	w3w3t	fiery one (?)" (redup. stem plus *t noun suff.);		
	w3w3w	"sheen" (redup. stem plus *w n. suff.)		
	ḫnp	"to breathe" (see 25)	*ḫnm*	"to breathe; smell (odors)"
	ḫ3b	"to be bent (of arm)" (see 19)	*ḫ3m*	"to bow down; bend (arm, in respect)"
	ḫ3s	"curl on front of Red Crown" (see 9)		
	ẖ3b	"crooked" (see 19)	*ẖ3m*	"to bend down (arms in respect)"
	nhd	"to rage, act fiercely" (see 18)	*nhm*	"to shout" (also *nhmhm* "to yell" (stem partially redup. as intens.)
	nhp	"to mourn" (see 15)		
	ḥtp	"to be at peace; be peaceful (after storm); occupy (throne); rest (in tomb)" (see 25)	*ḥtm-t*	"chair" (stem *ḥtm "to stay seated")
	ḥ3ḳ	"to plunder; capture (towns); carry off (captives) (see 31);	*ḥ3m*	"to catch (fish)"
	ḥ3d	"fish trap" (see 18);		
	ḥ3b	"to fish" (see 19)		
b.	*ḥts*	"to bring to an end" (see 11)	*ḥtm*	"to perish"
	šni	"to enclose, surround"	*šnm*	"to enclose, incorporate; join together, join"
	ḥtp	"offerings; altar" (see 25)	*ḥtm*	"to provide"
	tnbẖ	"to turn aside, swerve" (see 19, 35)	*tnm*	"to turn aside; go astray; deflect (of balance); be confused (of roads)"

17. *dl (Eg. *ḏ*) verb extension

Proto-Afrasan (PAA) in the writer's reconstruction had a verb extension in *dl, which is still productive in the Eastern Cushitic languages. PAA *dl regularly yielded Eg. *ḏ* (Ehret 1995). Following

Hayward's (1984) work, we can understand this extension as having functioned like the Indo-European middle voice. It probably basically served as a marker of reciprocal or associated action (a), but with inchoative outcomes as well (b). Both these effects appear in Egyptian verbs ending in *ḏ* as the third consonant:

a.	*dmi*	"to touch, be joined"	*dmḏ*	"to assemble; associate; join; accumulate"
	nwd	"to vacillate" (see 18)	*nwḏ*	"to deviate (?)" (underlying root *nw "to turn")
b.	*wrš*	"to spend the day, spend time" (see 24)	*wrḏ*	"to grow weary, tire"
	mnc	"to nurse" (see 23)	*mnḏ*	"breast" (proposed derivation: noun < former verb with sense, "to get sucked"; i.e., breast is that which is sucked)

18. *d verb extension

Egyptian verbs with *d* as the third consonant usually have one of two connotations, either of extended or ongoing action (a) or of stativeness (b). The latter connotation can give rise as well to intransitive formations (c). Exactly these three outcomes can be argued for the PAA verb extension in *d on the basis of the comparative evidence (Ehret 1995) and can be argued from internal reconstuction in Semitic (Ehret 1989).

a.	*ḫnz*	"to traverse a region" (see 28)	*ḫnd*	"to tread"
	ḳm3	"appearance, form" (see 8)	*ḳmd*	"to devise, invent"
	ḳm3	"to mourn" (see 20)	*ḳmd*	"to mourn"
	nwr	"to shake" (see 20)	*nwd*	"to vacillate"
	nb	"to tie"	*nbd*	"to plait"
	nhm	"to shout"	*nwd*	"to rage, act fiercely"
	nšnš	"to tear up (documents)" (redup. *ns & as iterative)	*nšd*	"to tear up"
	wš3	"to utter (plaudits), recite (praises)" (see 20)	*wšd*	"to address"
b.	*ḥ3b*	"to fish" (see 19)	*ḥ3d*	"fish-trap" (proposed derivation: noun from former verb meaning "to

				be caught (of fish)": trap is that in which the fish is caught)
c.	*wbḫ*	"to be bright" (see 29)	*wbd*	"to burn; be scalded"
	wbn	"to rise, shine (of sun)" (see 15)		

19. *b verb extension

A verb extension in *b, with the same range of effects as *d (18 preceding), can be proposed from both the comparative Afrasan and internal Semitic evidence. The Egyptian verbs with *b* as their third consonant show just the same range of connotations,

(a) extended action;
(b) stativity; and
(c) intransitiveness:

a.	*tnm*	"to turn aside; go astray," etc. (see 16)	*tnbẖ*	"to turn aside, swerve; run at random" (for *ẖ*, see 35)
	zny	"to pass"	*znb*	"to overstep (boundary); overthrow (landmark)" (i.e., *continue on* beyond some point)
	ḥsḳ	"to decapitate" (see 27)	*ḥsb*	"to break up"
	tš	"to split (wood); smash (heads); grind (corn)";	*tšb*	"to smash"
	tštš	"to crush" (redup. as intens.)		
	ḥ3m	"to catch (fish)" (see 16)	*ḥ3b*	"to fish"
	ḫšḫš	"rubble" (redup. *ḫs & as intens.)	*ḫšb*	"to mutilate"
	ḥn	"to provide"	*ḥnb*	"to convey"
b.	*ḫ3m*	"to bow down, bend (arm in attitude of respect)" (see 16)	*ḫ3b*	"to be bent (of arm)"
	ẖ3m	"to bend down (arms in respect)" (see 16)	*ẖ3b*	"crooked; crookedness; crookedly"
c.	*ḳni*	"to surround"	*ḳnb*	"to bend, bow, incline oneself"
	ḳ3s	"to bind, tie" (see 11);	*ḳ3b*	"to fold over, double over"
	ḳ3r	"bundle" (see 8)		

20. *r (> Eg. *3* / _#) verb extension
Another widely lexicalized verb extension (proposed in Ehret 1989 and supported with comparative evidence in Ehret 1995) had *r as its consonant. PAA *r fell together in most word-final positions with the glottal stop *3* in Egyptian. The proposed *r extension is associated generally in Afrasan with action having duration and a diffuse scope of action, and so has been called a "diffusive." Most Egyptian *3* in third consonants fit this profile: they occur in verbs connoting

(a) extended activity and, very commonly,
(b) action that is diffuse or scatters outward in its effects:

a	*ḳmd*	"to mourn" (see 18)	*ḳm3*	"to mourn"
	cwn	"to covet" (see 15)	*cw3*	"to look after, care for (?)"
	ngi	"to break open, break up"	*ng3*	"to slaughter (ritually)"
	dgs	"to walk" (see 12)	*dg3*	"to walk"
	wḏi	"to depart; stray (of cattle)"	*wḏ3*	"to go, set out, proceed"
	wḥs	"to cut off (hair)" (see 12)	*wḥ3*	"to hew (stone)"
b.	*sṯi*	"to strew, sow"	*sṯ3*	"to sow"
	nft	"breath, wind" (stem *nf plus *t noun suff.)	*nf3*	"to blow (out the nose)"
	wšd	"to address" (see 18);	*wš3*	"to utter (plaudits), recite (praises)"
	nwd	"to vacillate" (see 14 for the rest of this set of verbs)	*nwr*	"to shake" (PAA *r stays Eg. *r* /w_#)

21. *ʔ verb extension
In a few instances, however, *3* in third-consonant position is associated with a quite opposite verb meaning, a narrowly focussed action carried to completion. There is another proposed fossil extension, in PAA *ʔ, which has been argued to give just such a focus to the action of a verb root. It has been called a "concisive." Since PAA *ʔ also yields Egyptian *3*, the plausible solution is to attribute these rare instances to the proposed *ʔ concisive:

dm	"to pierce (sky); be sharp; sharpen"	*dm3*	"to cut off (heads)"
mni	"to moor (ship)";	*mnṯ3*	"to fasten"
mnḫ	"to string (beads)" (see 29)		

22. *l (> Eg. *r* /_#) verb extension
Another proposed widely lexicalized PAA extension had the shape *l. It is recurrently associated with verbs that convey

(a) an action carried to completion or
(b) an action abruptly carried out.

For that reason it has been called (in Ehret 1989, 1995) a "finitive." PAA *l went to Egyptian *r* word-finally, so we need to look specifically at instances of *r* in third-consonant position. Precisely the same two kinds of connotations are repeatedly conveyed by the Egyptian examples:

a.	*ḥt*	"to become entangled (of hair)"	*ḥtr*	"to bind together"
	ḥwtf	"to rob, plunder" (see 14, 33)	*ḥwrc*	"to steal" (for *c* here, see 23)
	ṯ3w	"to take up, seize, snatch; don; rob, steal"	*ṯ3r*	"to make fast; take possession of"
b.	*ḫ3s*	"to scramble" (see 12)	*ḫ3r*	"to bolt (?) (of horses)"

23. *ʕ verb extension
A proposed PAA extension in *ʔ has been given the name "sunderative" (Ehret 1989) or "partive" (Ehret 1995) because it repeatedly occurs as the third consonant in verbs bearing three related connotations:

(a) action directed away from or out of something;
(b) action that separates one thing from another; and, less often,
(c) itive, that is, action directed toward something else.

Ancient Egyptian verbs with ʕ (conventionally transliterated as *c*) in the third-consonant (in one instance below, fourth-consonant) position cover the very same range of senses:

a.	*mnḏ*	"breast" (see 17)	*mnc*	"to nurse" (i.e., to suck *out* milk)
	šni	"to dispel (strife)"	*šnc*	"to turn back, repulse, repel"
	ḫ3ḫ	"to spear (fish)" (see 29)	*ḫ3c*	"to throw; thrust; harpoon (hippo)"
	pnḳ	"to bail out" (see 27)	*pnc-yt*	"cataract" (stem plus *y, *t noun suff.)
b.	*nft*	"to loosen" (see 14)	*nfc*	"to remove"
	wḏḥ	"to wean" (see 26)	*wḏc*	"to cut (cords), cut off (head); be parted (of lips of wound); open (door); distinguish; remove"
	nḳm	"to be bald" (see 7)	*nḳc*	"to scrape, incise; polish (?)" (proposed original sense: to scrape off)
	ḥwtf	"to rob, plunder" (see 14, 33)	*ḥwrc*	"to steal"
c.	*cmcm*	"to smear" (redup. stem as iterative or extended action)	*cmc*	"to smear" (i.e., spread fluid *on something else*)

24. *ɬ verb extension

Another consonant, PAA *ɬ, has been proposed to have originally denoted ventive direction of movement. In Ancient Egyptian *ɬ became *š*. So what can we say about Egyptian verbs with *š* as the third consonant? There is a consistent connotation to such verbs: open-ended, ongoing action (a). Just one case noted so far in the internal reconstruction evidence has a potentially venitive connotation (b): *prš* "to rend, tear, break open." Rending or tearing something open usually involves grasping and pulling (toward oneself) to separate something into pieces, and even it could be considered to imply an ongoing or at least extended action. The difference between the previous proposals (Ehret 1989, 1995) suggests that the previously reconstructed function of this fossil extension may need to be revised.

a.	*ḫnz*	"to traverse a region";	*ḫntš*	"to walk about freely"
	ḫnd	"to tread" (see 18)		

wnwn	"to move about" (redup. stem as iterative)	*wnšnš*	"to walk, proceed"
wrḏ	"to grow weary, tire" (see 17)	*wrš*	"to spend the day, spend one's time"
g3p	"to lance (?) (infection)" (see 25)	*g3š*	"to spill"

25. *p extension
Ancient Egyptian verbs ending in *p* as the third consonant can be associated with three categories of action:

(a) intensive;
(b) intensive, in particular in its effects on the thing acted upon; and
(c) extended action or condition without intensiveness.

The first two connotations fit the pattern elswhere in the Afrasan family of a proposed *p extensive, conveying intensive senses, including intensives of effect (b below). Whether the extensive senses (c) reflect the same underlying marker is not clear at this point, but the evolution of an intensive int an extensive—i.e., into a marker of, essentially, more action—seems not implausible.

a. *nhzi*	"to wake" (see 28, 4)	*nhp*	"to rise early in the morning" (i.e., rise up *early* as opposed to rising at the usual time)
nhm	"to shout" (see 16)	*nhp*	"to mourn" (mourning, we can suggest, probably required much public wailing)
b. *sti*	"to shoot (arrow); thrust (into); spear (fish)"	*stp*	"to cut up (animal); cut off (limbs)"
wgs	"to cut open, gut (fish, etc.)"	*wgp*	"to triturate"
ḥt	"to become entangled" (see 8)	*ḥtp-t*	"bundle (of herbs)" (verb plus *t noun suffix)
c. *ḥtm*	"to provide" (see 16)	*ḥtp*	"offerings; altar"
wdd	"to be cooked"	*wdpw*	"butler, cook" (verb plus *w noun suff.)

ḥtmt	"chair" (stem *htm plus *t noun suff.: underlying *ḥt "to sit, stay"; see 16)	*ḥtp*	"to be at peace; be peaceful; become calm (after storm); occupy (throne); rest (in tomb)"
ḫnm	"to breathe" (see 16)	*ḫnp*	"to breathe"

Suggested additional cases of lexicalized root extensions in ancient Egyptian

There remain a further ten Egyptian consonants that occur as alternative third consonants in pairs or triplets of roots that are alike in their first two consonants and have relatable meanings. For five of these consonants, just three or four cases allowing internal reconstruction have been identified, making it more difficult to judge their validity.

26. **ḥ* verb extension
The Egyptian verbs cited here with *ḥ* as their third consonant each appear to have (a) iterative or (b) durative connotations. These meanings conform to those attributed to the proposed **ḥ* extension, posited to have been in origin an iterative (Ehret 1989, 1995).

a. *ptt*	"broken up"	*ptḥ*	"to form" (meaning of the Coptic eflex of this verb, *pōth* "to chisel, sculpt," suggests the original meaning was "to form from stone by breaking off pieces")
b. *wd̲c*	"to cut (cords), cut off (head); be parted (of lips of wound); open (door); distinguish; remove"	*wd̲ḥ*	"to wean"
bcbc	"to bubble up"	*bcḥ*	"inundated land" (i.e., land with water continually or repeatedly flowing onto it)
bcr	"fountain" (see 8)		

27. *ḳ (< PAA *k') as third consonant
Egyptian verbs with *ḳ* as their third consonant, in three of the four cases available to us for internal comparison, convey a sharp or intensive action (a). The fourth (b) attaches to a verb implying repetitive, extended action or, alternatively, action away from ("to bale *out*": bailing involves throwing the water away from oneself, out of the boat).

Intensive is the meaning reconstructed for the proposed *k' extension of early Afrasan. A second extension, posited as *kʷ', has been proposed to have been an itive/andative (Ehret 1989, 1995), one of the two possible connotations of the fourth item *pnḳ* "to bale out."

a. *fdi*	"to pluck, pull up, uproot, pull out"	*fdḳ*	"to divide, split"
ḥsb	"to break up" (see 19)	*ḥsk*	"to decapitate"
b. *pncyt*	"cataract"	*pnḳ*	"to bale out"

28. *z as a third consonant

Two of the three Egyptian verbs we can cite here with *z as the third consonant convey extended action. What effect *z* had in the third case (b) is obscured by the addition of the *i* extension, which apparently was still productive in ancient Egyptian.

a. *ẖnd*	"to tread" (see 18)	*ẖnz*	"to traverse a region"
b. *nhp*	"to rise early in the morning" (see 25)	*nhzi*	"to wake"

29. *ẖ as a third consonant

Two very different kinds of action characterize the three verbs cited here with *ẖ* as their third consonant:

(a) single sudden or strong action; and
(b) complementive action (consequence or attribute of the action of underlying verb).

So the Egyptian evidence does not make a good case for a single, now lexicalized extension in *ẖ*.

On the other hand, these two functions are very like those of two separate extensions imputed to PAA (Ehret 1995), which, because of the loss of the feature labial in pre-ancient Egyptian, would have merged as Egyptian *ẖ*. The proposed PAA *ɣ intensive of effect fits well the kind of action represented in (a) in the verb "to spear (fish)." The second extension, PAA *ɣʷ complementive, has been attributed just the kind of semantic effects evident in the two verbs of (b). So the cases individually are very weak; they amount to one and two examples respectively for each connotation. But their parallel connotations with those of the two extensions proposed elsewhere from more evidence are striking.

a. *ḫ3c*	"to throw; thrust; harpoon (hippo)" (see 23)	*ḫ3ḫ*	"to spear (fish)"
b. *ḫ3r*	"to bolt (?) (of horses)" (see 22)	*ḫ3ḫ*	"to be speedy, hurry"
wbd	"to burn; be scalded" (see 18)	*wbḫ*	"to be bright" (proposed underlying "continue to burn brightly," hence, "be bright" as a characteristic or lasting feature)
wbn	"to rise, shine (of of sun" (see 15)		

30. *ṯ as a third consonant

Egyptian *ṯ* can be reconstructed as deriving from PAA *tl', and it has been proposed that early in PAA there existed a verb extension of the shape *tl' that connoted a narrow focus of action. At least two of the three examples we are able to cite here can be argued to convey an action with a narrow locus (b) or a single action (b). The third example (c) could also be understood as a narrowly focussed action if by "slaughter" was originally meant the particular action of killing the animal, accomplished by cutting the neck or spearing the beast, before the actual butchering takes place.

a. *mni*	"to moor (ship)";	*mnṯ3*	"to fasten"
mnḫ	"to string (beads)" (see 29)		
b. *zf*	"to cut up, cut off"	*zfṯ*	"to slaughter"

Another five Egyptian consonants appear for now in only one or two pairings of roots that allow us to apply internal reconstruction techniques. The most we can say in these cases is that the few instances we have either do or do not fit in with the proposed meanings of early Afrasan extensions made up of the same reconstructed source consonants in PAA.

31. *k as a third consonant

In one instance of *k* as a third consonant (a), the action has duration ("inhale"). In the other (b), *k* is attached to a verb that conveys an intensive meaning ("plunder, capture, carry off") when we compare it with its partner ("to catch (fish)"). The first (a) fits the specifications of the proposed old PAA *k durative extension. There is, however, a second proposed extension in *k^w (Ehret 1995) that is pertinent here. This extension is posited to have been a "finitive," that is, a morpheme connoting an action that is not open-ended but is bounded. As an example, to attack a town is open-ended, but capturing a town is a bounded action. To capture something is to complete the process of trying to take possession of it. Since PAA *k^w yields E.g. *k*, example (b) here could be cited as possible support for the *k^w finitive.

a. *sryt*	"cough" (stem plus *y ext. plus *t noun suff.)	*srḳ*	"to inhale"
b. *ḥ3m*	"to catch (fish)" (see 16)	*ḥ3ḳ*	"to plunder; capture (towns); carry off (captives)"

32. *g as a third consonant

The two verbs cited here with *g* as a third consonant have opposing connotations: (a) repetitive and perhaps intensive action versus (b) a finitive or perhaps single action. Again, as for *k* preceding, two alternative extensions have been proposed for early Afrasan, *g^w as a durative and *g as a "finitive fortative," that is, a bounded action that is strongly carried out. Since *g^w and *g merged as E.g. *g*, each could plausibly be argued to be an example of one of the two proposed extensions, (a) as repetitive action and (b) as completed strong action:

a. *ḥpt*	"to travel, hurry" (see 14)	*ḥpg-t*	"leaping dance" (verb plus *t noun suff.)
b. *brḳ*	"to shine, glitter, flash" (see 27)	*brg*	"to light up"

33. *f as a third (or fourth) consonant

The one instance we are able to cite here of *f* as a final consonant (in fourth position) can be taken as indicating a repetitive action if we focus on the second meaning "plunder." To plunder is to steal many things. In that case final *f* would fit the specifications of the proposed old PAA *f extension, which the comparative and internal reconstruction suggest to have originally have been an iterative (Ehret 1989, 1995).

ḥwrc	"to steal"	*ḥwtf*	"to rob, plunder"

34. *h as a third consonant

Another pair of verbs relatable in meaning differ in their lacking or having an additional consonant *h*. The verb without *h* means simply "to be quick." The verb with added *h* means, in contrast, "to prance, leap," connoting quick movement, but with enhanced motions and flourishes. If this is indeed the correct implication here, *h* in this instance would fit with the *h extension proposed for early Afrasan (Ehret 1989, 1995). This extension has been called an amplificative, that is, a marker of increased quantity of action.

ṯbn	"to be quick" (see 6 for *n* here)	*ṯbhn*	"to prance, leap (of animals)" (see 15 form final consonant *n*)

35. **ẖ* as a final consonant

In the first example we cite here of *ẖ* (a) is the last consonant of four in a word. We have already viewed the third consonant, *b*, as a marker of extended action (see 19 above). That connotation is implied in this instance in the meaning "to swerve." What is additional in here and not explained by the presence of *b* is the sense "to run at random." The consonant *ẖ* seems associated, in other words, with an undirected swerving about, done rapidly, i.e., by running. It attaches to a verb of forcefully or vigorously repetitive action. In the set of proposed ancient verb extensions of PAA, *x^w is reckoned to have been an extendative fortative (Ehret 1995), that is, a proposed marker of an action that has duration and is strongly carried out. And that fits the case here well: running at random is an action both extended and strongly carried-out, and it involves turning, the underlying meaning that connects the two words.

Seemingly more problematic is the attribution of the second item to this set, because it shows *ḫ* instead of *ẖ*. This item fits, however, because of a regular sound shift in ancient Egyptian: PAA *x^w merged with Egyptian *ḫ* in the environment of a preceding sonorant (Ehret 1995: 529, Egyptian rule 12), exactly the environment present in example (b) below. Elsewhere *x^w went to *ẖ*, just as we see in the proposed reflex of *x^w after *b* in citation (a). As for attributing *ḫ* in (b) to the posited *x^w extendative fortative, the action "to string (beads)" is certainly an extended action. It cannot be called "fortative" in the sense of being vigorously performed, but it is an amplified action in the sense that it involves very long-term repetitive activity.

a. *tnm*	"to turn aside; go astray" (see 16)	*tnbh̠*	"to turn aside, swerve; run at random"
b. *mni*	"to moor (ship)" (see 21)	*mnḫ*	"to string (beads)"

Interim conclusions

The evidence of internal reconstruction in Egyptian, it seems, produces many of the same results as internal reconstruction in Arabic (Ehret 1989) and comparative reconstruction in the Afrasan (Afroasiatic) family (Ehret 1995). Most of the same nominal suffixes appear, several of them still visibly productive in ancient Egyptian. In addition, a considerable number of verb extensions can be postulated for the earlier ancestry of ancient Egyptian, although nearly all of these would have become non-productive by the time of ancient Egyptian itself. Some of these are very strongly attested; some, very weakly. But time and again, whenever we can internally reconstruct their connotations, they are very much the same as those of the phonologically regularly corresponding extensions proposed for pre-proto-Semitic and for Afrasan (Afroasiatic) as a whole.

Bibliography*

Ehret, C.
1989 "The Origins of third consonants in Semitic roots: An internal reconstruction (applied to Arabic)," *Journal of Afroasiatic Languages* 3 (1989).
1995 *Reconstructing Proto-Afroasiatic (Proto-Afrasian): Vowels, Tone, Consonants, and Vocabulary.* Berkeley: University of California Press.

Hayward, R.
1984 "A reconstruction of some root extensions of the Eastern Cushitic verb." In J. Bynon (ed.), *Current Progress in Afro-Asiatic Linguistics*, pp. 33–67. Amsterdam: Benjamins.

* Similar ideas on root extension affixes have been suggested by Gertrud Thausing in WZKM 68 (1941), 5–34, another prominent figure of "Wiener" Egyptology along with Werner Vycichl, which Ch. Ehret apparently failed to consider. The fact, however, that both authors independently arrived at quite similar results, makes this paper still actual. This is why I decided to include the paper by non-Egyptologist Ehret in the Egyptological section even in spite of some of his suggestions which will be probably debated in Egyptology. Editor's remark.

"OH KOMM GUTER ZWERG, KOMM . . ." ÜBER DEN RELIGIÖSEN HINTERGRUND DER PATÄKEN-AMULETTE IM NEUEN REICH

Hedvig Győry
(Museum of Fine Arts, Budapest)

Um die Mitte der 18. Dynastie erschienen unter den Zwerg-Amuletten die in der Literatur oft Patäken genannten eigenartigen Figuren, und sie wurden in den nachfolgenden Zeiten immer mehr und mehr populär. Auf Grund der Ikonographie entwickelten sich zwei verschiedene Gruppen noch bis zum Ende dieser Dynastie,[1] und beide wurden während der ganzen Produktionszeit hergestellt. Die einfache Patäken haben nur ein zusätzliches Element, nämlich die sich an den Kopf schmiegende Kappe. Diese erweckt entweder den Eindruck von Kahlheit, wie es bei den Zwerg-Dämonen schon früher oft üblich war, über eine Furche an der Stirn oder den Eindruck der Kappe von Ptah, dem Schöpfergott aus Memphis. Andere Zusätze scheinen nur in der ausgehenden Ramessiden-Zeit aufzutauchen, wiederum nur auf dem Kopf: der Skarabäus—der die Verbindung zu Ra, dem Sonnengott betont, oder die Straußenfeder mit der Sonnenscheibe, wiederum ein solarer Kopfputz, besonders dem memphitischen Sokaris eigen. Die komplexen Patäken-Amulette ähneln den Horus-Sched-Tafeln und den späteren Horus-Stelen durch ihre Anordnung und Ausstattung, und beherrschen gewöhnlich auch Inschriften, die auf Atum oder Amon (-Ra) deuten. All diese Phänomene zeigen, dass schon zu Beginn der Entwicklung der Patäken-Ikonographie—neben den zwei Grundtendenzen—auch andere religiöse Konzeptionen mitwirkten, d. h. sich komplizierte Vorstellungen an den Gott knüpften, und sein Imago war schon damals nicht ganz einheitlich.

Die geographische Verteilung der Amuletten weist auf ziemlich allgemeine Vorstellungen hin, denn das Kopieren der Typen ist in Ägypten unvorstellbar ohne die Annahme des religiösen Inhalts, natürlich mit den lokalen Kulten harmonisiert. Die Fundkomplexe suggerieren, dass

[1] H. Győry, Über die Patäken-Amulette im Neuen Reich, in: Fs. Satzinger, 2002, im Druck.

die Figuren mit Vorliebe Kindern und Frauen mitgegeben wurden—vor allem sie trugen sie also. Über den einfachen Patäken erzählt visuell nur seine Gestalt, die an Babys erinnert, und der Kopf, der wie der eines Erwachsenen bzw. manchmal eben eines Greises aussieht. Das macht wahrscheinlich, dass er etwas mit Kindern zu tun hat, nämlich, dass er den allgemeinen Schutz während Geburt und Kindheit gegen alle Arten von Missgeschick gibt. Das wurde auch durch die Darstellungen der Apotropaia bestätigt, die in gewissem Maße als Vorläufer dienten in beiden Funktionen und ikonographischen Bereichen. Die komplexen Patäken machen mit ihren zusätzlichen Elementen die Verteidigung gegen schädliche Tiere wahrscheinlich.

Im Folgenden möchte ich mich damit beschäftigen, wer genauer dieses Wesen sein konnte, und was für eine Funktion seine Statuetten auf Grund beider, bildlicher und schriftlicher Quellen im Neuen Reich repräsentieren.

Die selbständige ikonographische Gruppe von Patäken-Amuletten ist in Texten nicht eindeutig aufspürbar. Seine einfache Form heißt als Hieroglyphe nmw "*Zwerg*", aber derselbe Name konnte auch komplexe Mischgestalten mit Zwergenzügen benennen, wie z. B. eine Gestalt auf der Vignette des Spruches 164 in einem saitischen Totenbuch wird mit "*Zwerg*" angeredet, doch die Beschreibung unterscheidet sich von den oben besprochenen Gestalten: "*A dwarf (nmw) stands before her, another behind her, each facing her and wearing plumes. Each has a raised arm and two heads, one is the head of a falcon, the other a human head.*"[2] Also, obwohl zwei verschiedene ithyphallische Zwerggestalten (eine mit menschlichen eine mit zwei Köpfen) in der Vignette gezeichnet wurden,[3] beide haben die gleiche *nmw* Bezeichnung. Diese ikonographischen Gestalten bilden aber nur einen Teil der Zwergbegriffe in ägyptischen Texten.

An anderen Stellen wird die als Zwerg beschriebene Gestalt Bes, Re oder Horus genannt.[4] Auf Horus-Stelen, mit Schlangen in den Händen bekommt er auch das Beischrift Ptah.[5] Und damit sind noch nicht alle Exemplare der ägyptischen Erklärungen erschöpft. Da die oben genann-

[2] R.O. Faulkner, The Ancient Egyptian Book of the Dead, London 1985, S. 160.

[3] R. Lepsius, Todtenbuch der Ägypter nach dem Hieroglyphischen Papyrus in Turin, Leipzig 1842, Tf. LXXVIII.

[4] Siehe Meeks, Génies, anges et démons, Sources Orientales 8, Paris 1971, S. 55–56. O. El-Aguizy, Dwarfs and Pygmies in ancient Egypt, ASAE 71, 1987, S. 57–59.

[5] BM 36.250, E.A.Th.W. Budge, The Mummy, chapters on Egyptian funereal archaeology, Chambridge 1893, Tf. 33.

ten Götter ihre gewöhnliche, eigene, unabhängige Darstellungsweise haben, müssen die durch die Namen manifestierten Annäherungsversuche einen gemeinsamen Aspekt von diesen in der Zwergengestalt ergeben.

Der *nmw* wird auch im Neuen Reich oft auf Papyri erwähnt. Der Magische Harris Papyrus gibt eine ausgezeichnete Beschreibung des Patäken Typs: "*Oh, Du Zwerg (nmj) da, der Du im Himmel bist, zweimal; Du Zwerg mit dem großen Gesicht (ˁ3 ḥr), mit dem hohen Rücken und den kurzen Beinen, Du große Säule, die im Himmel anfängt, und bis zur Unterwelt (reicht)*".[6] Die Beschreibung enthält auch einen Widerspruch, wie klein und hoch, ebenso wie ein Spruch von Deir el-Medineh, der ihn mit Ra identifiziert: "*Oh Ra, dessen eine Hälfte ist der Zwerg der Himmel, (die andere Hälfte) ist der Zwerg der Erde. . . . Oh dieser Zwerg, der Mann in Heliopolis, der kleine, dessen Beine zwischen Erde und Himmel sind*".[7] Diese Sätze beschreiben nicht nur seine Gestalt, sondern knüpfen ihn auch noch an Schu. Gleichzeitig wird er auch als solarer Osiris aufgefaßt, als er "*der König der Unterwelt, der Herr der beiden Länder, Herr des Leibes in Heliopolis*" ist,[8] und dieser solare Charakter manifestiert sich auch in anderen Göttergestalten in seiner Form, wie z. B. Amon-Ra,[9] Atum[10] oder Kheper.[11]

---

[6] H.O. Lange, Der Magische Papyrus Harris, Copenhagen, 1927, S. 72–74, Spruch (18=)U, VIII. 9–10: Pmag Harris, VIII, 9–10. Verg. J.F. Borghouts, The Magical Texts of Papyrus Leiden I. 348, Leiden, 1971, S. 146, Anm. 347. Auch später: F.Ll. Griffith – H. Thompson, The Demotic Magical Papyrus of London and Leiden, I., London, 1904, 82–83. Vgl. S. Sauneron, BIFAO 53, 1953, 70 viii (Réharahti); Wien, Kunsthistorisches Museum 270 = Dasen, Dwarfs, S. 52, Abb. 5.4 (Bes als er den Himmel stüzt).

[7] J. Černý – G. Posener, Papyrus hiératiques de Deir el-Médineh, I, Cairo 1978, DFIFAO 8, 9–10.

[8] J. Černý – G. Posener, Papyrus hiératiques de Deir el-Médineh, I, Cairo, 1978, DFIFAO 8, S. 9, und ebenso in Mag. pHarris VIII, 10: "*Du Herr des grossen Leichnams, der in Heliopolis ruht, du grosser lebender Herr, der in DD.t ruht!*"

[9] Z.B. Brussels, E. 5866 (Auskunft von Dirk Hughe), oder J. Vercoutter, *Objets égyptiens et égyptisants du mobilier funéraire Carthaginois*, Paris 1945, Nr. 809, 814, 815—Statuetten mit Inschrift mit der gewöhnlichen Schreibweise von Amon-Re. J. Sliwa, *Egyptian Scarabs, Scaraboids and plaques from the Cracow Collections. Zeszyty Naukowe Uniwersytetu Jagiellonskiego DCCLX*, Prace Archeologiczne, Zeszyt 38, Studia z Archeologii Sródziemnomorskiej, Zeszyt 8, Crakow, S. 54, Nr. 78, Tf. XIII, Chryptographie für die Name Amon-Ra.

[10] Die Verbindung existierte schon im Mittleren Reich: der Feld der Zwergen gehörte wohl Atum, sehe CT II. 153, Sp. 132a, CT.II. 161, Sp. 136c.

[11] Z.B. Auf einem mythologischen Papyrus ist er in der Sonnenscheibe, an der Stelle des Skarabäus: The Hague, Dyn. 21—siehe M. Heerma van Voss, Zwei ungewöhnliche Darstellungen des ägyptischen Sonnengottes, Visible Religion 4–5, 1985–86, S. 73–75 = V. Dasen, Dwarfs in Ancient Egypt and Greece, Oxford,

Die schützende Rolle des Zwerges läßt sich unleugbar auch in schriftlichen Quellen finden. Nach dem Magischen Papyrus 1993 von Turin wurde Geb von ihm geschützt, und Neit hatte Angst vor ihm.[12] Dies deutet also noch auf neue göttliche Beziehungen hin, die bis zur 22. Dynastie so weit gingen, dass die Zwerge von Neit damals schon eine Priesterschaft hatten,[13] also die Zwerge unter der Kontrolle der Göttin standen. Die andere Folgerung aus diesen Texte ist, dass auch Götter spätestens von der 20. Dynastie an ihre schützende Hilfe brauchten, eben durch Amulette.[14]

Konnte er mit irgendeinem Gott in Zusammenhang stehen, stand er immer auf der positiven Seite, neben Maat. Die Leute durften auf seine Hilfe hoffen. Seine schützende, verteidigende Funktion steht immer im Vordergrund: "*Komm und rette N, die Tochter von M, wie du den Erstickenden* (= Osiris) *gerettet hast an jenem Tag des Begräbnisses*"— wurde er in dem Papyrus Nr. 4 in Deir el-Medineh gebeten.[15] Die

1993, S. 49, Abb. 49. Später z.B. Tb 165. Verg. die Zusammenschmelzung von Bes und des Skarabäus: G. Roeder, Ägyptische Bronzefiguren, Berlin 1956, S. 101, par. 147a, S. 102–3, par. 148a.

[12] W. Pleyte—F. Rossi, Papyrus de Turin, Leiden 1869–76, Taf. 124,14: pTurin 1993, rt. 4,14 = R. el-Sayed, La déesse Neith de Sais, Cairo 1982, BdE 86, Bd. I., S. 131, Bd. II. S. 372, Doc. 381: "*N, Sohn des NN, ist der Fisch ꜣbt, der auf dem Bug der Barke von Ra ist. Er ist der Zwerg aus Faience (nmw n ṯḥnt), der am Halse des Geb ist; Neith fürchtet sich vor ihm.*" (s. J.F. Borghouts, The Magical Texts of Papyrus Leiden I. 348, Leiden, 1971, S. 154, n. 370; D. Jankuhn, Das Buch "Schutz des Hauses" (*sꜣ-pr*), Bonn 1972, S. 88. Auch auf einem Horus-Stele von 21–22. Dyn. = G. Daressy, Description des monuments épigraphiques trouvés a Karnak en 1921–1922, ASAE 22, 1922, S. 268, Zeile 10–11.

[13] W. Spiegelberg, Neue Schenkungsstelen über Landstiftungen an Tempeln, ZÄS 56, 1920, 59–60, Tf. VI. = V. Dasen, Dwarf, S. 51, Tf. 3,1. Verg. die Zwerge von Neit später auf Horus-Stelen: z.B. R. el-Sayed, La Déesse Neith de Sais, Cairo 1982, BdÉ 86, Bd. I. S. 131, Bd. II. S. 468, Doc. 640; Borghouts, pLeiden I. 348, S. 154, Anm. 370; K.C. Seele, Horus on the Crocodiles, JNES 45, Tf. 1A, rechts (Z6), links (Z1); D. Meeks, in E. Lipinski (ed), State and Temple Economy in the Ancient Near East, II., Louvain 1979, S. 674, Nr. 26.0.6; Ramadan el-Sayed, Deux aspects nouveaux du culte a Sais, BIFAO 76, 91–100. Pl. XVIb.

[14] Es blieb bis ins hellenistische Periode so. Siehe "*die Verteidigung dieses Fayence Zwerges, der den Hals von Neit schützt*" an der westlichen Innenseite des Umfassungsmauer, oben: PM VI. S. 162, (312) = E. Chassinat, Le Temple d'Edfou, vol. VI, MMAF 23, Cairo 1931, S. 149, 7–8, 1.43 = E. Chassinat, Le Temple d'Edfou, vol. X.2, MMAF 27, Cairo 1960, Tf. 149 = el-Sayed, Neit, Bd. I. 131, Bd. II. 592, Doc. 950. Verg. Edfou Mammisi 173, 15; CG 9403 = G. Daressy, Textes et dessins magiques, Cairo 1903, S. 10–11; CG. 9431bis = G. Daressy, Textes et dessins magiques, Cairo 1903, S. 40–41, links: 48–51 = R. el-Sayed, La Déesse Neith, 1982, Bd. I. S. 131, Bd. II. S. 468, Doc. 640; s. J.F. Borghouts, The Magical Texts of Papyrus Leiden I. 348, Leiden, 1971, S. 154, Anm. 370.

[15] J. Černý – G. Posener, Papyrus hiératiques de Deir el-Médineh, I., Cairo 1978, DFIFAO 8, S. 9. Verg. Pmag.Harris U.VIII.11–12. Verg. Tb 164; G. Roeder, Der Ausklang der ägyptischen Religion, Zürich 1961.

schützende Funktion hatte während der gesamten Pharaonenzeit Bestand—sie wurde auch ein wichtiges Element der Horus-Stelen.[16]

Es gibt auch ein Ostrakon aus Deir el-Medineh, wo unter dem Bett der säugenden Wöchnerin ein Zwerg in Grätschstellung—wegen der Löwenmähne wohl Bes—Schlangen hält.[17] Unter den Amuletten findet sich eine ähnliche Komposition, die komplexen Patäken, schon vor der Ende der 18. Dynastie.[18] Die Funktion der beiden Zwerg-Aspekte, Bes und Zwerg ohne Löwenmähne, könnte also zu dieser Zeit nicht nur mit Schlangenbissen sondern auch mit Entbindung in Zusammenhang stehen. Eben in pLeiden I.343 und I.345 steht Schlange und schwere Entbindung nebeneinander: "*And how does she give birth? It means that she is suffering and weaping/ because of the snake, the one which the god (i.e. Seth) has assigned to you*"—as Borghouts translated.[19] Es ist also ganz verständlich, dass der Schlangen vernichtende Zwerg, ohne besonderer Beschreibung, in einem Papyrus in Leiden der kreißenden Frau zu Hilfe kommt: "*Anderer Spruch—für den Zwerg: Oh komm guter Zwerg, wegen ihm, der dich geschickt hat, dass du sagst: 'er ist Ra, der steht, während Thot sitzt; seine beide Beine sind am Boden, den Nun umgibt, und die Hand ist an dem Balken. Komm runter Plazenta, komm runter Plazenta, komm runter! Ich bin Horus, der beschwört. Und der Gebärende geht es gut, sie wurde als ob sie schon gebar. Oh Sepertusenet—die Frau von Horus, Nechbet—die nubische und die östliche, Unu—Herrin von Aschmunein! Kommt bitte, handelt für den, der in eurer Macht steht! Seht, Hathor wird ihre Hand auf ihn legen, ein Gesundheits-Amulett. Ich bin Horus, der sie rettet (Sdj).' Viermal sagen über einem Tonzwerg, der auf der Schläfe deren Frau gelegt ist, die eben am Kreißen leidet.*"[20]

---

[16] Vergl. "*die Verteidigung von Horus ist der große Zwerg, der die Unterwelt im Abendgrauen durchquert*" wurde auf dem Béhague Heilstatuenbasis in Leiden geschrieben: A. Klasens, A Magical Statue Base (Socle Béhague) in the Museum of Antiquities at Leiden, Leiden 1952, OMRO 33, S. 56, 94: Spruch IV. f 9–10.; Rev Eg. Anc 2, 1929, S. 189–190. Verg. C.E. Sander-Hansen, The Texte der Metternichstele, Copenhagen 1956, S. 72, Z. 223.

[17] E. Brunner-Traut, Die altägyptischen Scherbenbilder (Bildostraca) der deutschen Museen und Sammlungen, Wiesbaden 1956, S. 69, Nr. 65, Tf. 25; G. Pinch, Childbirth and Female Figurines at Deir el-Medina and el-Amarna, Orientalia 52 (1983), S. 406–407; E. Brunner-Traut, Die Wochenlaube, MIO 3, 1955, 11–30, usw.

[18] H. Győry, Über die Patäken-Amulette im Neuen Reich, in: Fs. Satzinger, 2002, im Druck.

[19] Borghouts, Papyrus Leiden I. 348, S. 158, Anm. 382.—. . . *jw.s ḥr šn.t ḥr rmyt/ n pꜣ ḥfꜣw pw* . . . in Publ. von A. Massart, The Leiden Magical Papyrus I 343 + I. 345, S. 105, Vs. 5,1–2, steht da: "I made your mother who was pregnant with thee. How does (she) bring forth? She readeth an incantation weeping because of the serpent which the god hath given thee . . ."

[20] Borghouts, pLeiden I. 348, Vs. 12,2–6 (Sp. 30).

Dieses Papyrus Leiden I. 348 enthält magische Sprüche wahrscheinlich aus der Zeit Ramses II.[21] Auf Grund des Leiden Inventarbuches stammt es aus Memphis. Wie sich auch aus dem Titel des Kapitels ergibt, der zitierte Spruch bezieht sich auf den Zwerg: er wird um Hilfe gebeten. Wie wir aber herausfinden können, steht dieser Zwerg im Dienst des Sonnengottes Ra,[22] eben so wie Bes und Toeris in der Gebärszene in Luxor Tempel.[23] Über Ra hält es aber der Spruch hier für wichtig zu bemerken, dass er in einem besonderen Aspekt seinen Bot geschickt hat: er ist der Sieger über Apophis d. h. des Chaos, und noch dazu der Kapitän der Tagesbarke. Ra ist also die schon aufgestandene Mittagssonne.[24] Diese Aspekte sollten nur durch diesen steht-sitzt Gegensatz angedeutet sein. Ein anderer wichtige Zug dieses Ra ist seine Himmel und Erde trennende Rolle, womit er sich als mit Shu verschmolzen zeigt, als ein Schöpfer. Insgesamt zeigen sich indirekt seine das Chaos vernichtende, und Maat behaltende Ra-Schu-Aspekte. Er ist ein Kosmokrator, der gleichzeitig eine Genesung hervorbringende Gottheit ist. Die Zwerge vermittelten seinen Willen. Diese Aspekte wurden auch ungefähr tausend Jahre später in der Edfu-Theologie, die die ältere Traditionen gesammelt, systematisiert und weiterentwickelt hat, als ein poetisches Bild formuliert: "*Ein Lotus ragt heraus, und in ihm ist ein schönes Kind, das die Erde mit seinem Strahlenglanze beleuchtet . . . eine Sprosse, in welcher der Zwerg war, den Schu gern ansieht.*"[25]

Wie der oben zitierte magische Spruch in Leiden, so zeigt auch der darauf folgende in ganz anderer Hinsicht ähnlichen Begriffe. "*Ein anderer Spruch—für die Vulva. Ich bin Horus, der über der Wüste heruntergekommen ist. Ich war durstig wegen des Schreies. Ich habe einen Wehklagenden gefunden, der weinend dastand. Seine Frau war am Kreißen(?) (ḥr sjꜣt).*[26] *Ich habe das Wehklagen und das Weinen gestillt. Die Frau des Mannes hat wegen einer Tonzwergen-Statuette (šsp nmjt n sjn) gerufen. Komm, komm runter zu*

[21] Borghouts, pLeiden I. 348, S. 3.

[22] Vergl. Griffith-Thompson, The Demotic Magical Papyrus of London and Leiden, S. 82–83, Kol. XI. 6–7: "*Ich bin das heilige Kind, das im Haus des Ra ist, der heilige Zwerg, der in der Höhle ist . . .*"

[23] "*wir sind aus dem Himmel gekommen mit Re/und geben*"—H. Brunner, Die Geburt des Gottkönigs. Studien zur Überlieferung eines altägyptischen Mythos, Wiesbaden 1964, Tf. 9, Szene IXLc, S. 102.

[24] Verg. pTurin 1993, vs. 4,6–8 = Borghouts, pLeiden I. 348, S. 148, Anm. 351.

[25] Le Marquis de Rochemonteix, Le Temple d'Edfou I (Paris 1897) rev. B.S. Cauville – D. Devauchelle, Cairo, 1984, IFAO X, S. 289, Tf. XXIXb, Nordwand, 4.

[26] Vielleicht *beim "Erkennen" ihres Kindes*—dann würde später die Plazenta und damit das Kind angeredet: "*Komm runter . . .*"

Hathor, Herrin von Dendera! Ihr Gesundheits-Amulett wurde dir gebracht! Sie gibt es, die Entbindung der kreißenden Frau. Dieser Spruch soll . . . mal gesprochen werden . . . über den Blättern des . . . Baumes, die auf den Kopf der Frau gelegt wurden, die daran leidet." (Sp. 31)[27] Der Magier-Medizinmann ist wieder Horus,[28] der wiederum Hathor darum bittet, die Zwergenstatuette zu beschaffen, weil deren "*Gesundheits-Amulette*" bei der Entbindung helfen.

Ziemlich bekannt ist Hathors helfende Rolle im Bezug auf die Geburt,[29] weniger ihr hier verwendetes Instrument. Die Geste erinnert an manche Horus-Stelen, wo eine Göttin ihre Hand auf das Horus-Kind legt.[30] Obwohl die spätere Darstellungen sind, ist der Zusammenhang der gleiche. Die Methode, das Hand Auflegen, besprochen im Spruch 30, kommt auch in anderen zeitgenössischen Texten als schützende Geste vor.[31] Deren Bedeutung als *wḏ꜡ snb*—"*Gesundheits-Amulett*" wäre jedoch ungewöhnlich. Dies berücksichtigte die Bewegung nicht nur als absichtliches medizinisches Instrument, sondern benötigte dazu auch eine gegenständliche Manifestation, die als Amulett aufgefasst wurde. Das Instrument könnte auch als ein Hand-Amulett aufgefasst werden. Hand-Amulette[32] begegnet man tatsächlich in ziemlich großer Menge, aber es gibt bei ihnen keine Hinweise auf konkrete Götter. Sie weisen eher auf eine allgemeine Schutzgeste hin. So kann es hier nur etwas anderes sein.

Der Begriff "*Gesundheits-Amulett*" war keine Rarität. Mehrere iatromagische Texte erwähnen Statuetten während des Heilung-Prozesses.

---

[27] Borghouts, pLeiden I. 348 Vs. 12,6–9 (31).

[28] Verg. O. Strassburg H 111 (= W. Spiegelberg, Horus als Arzt, ZÄS 57, 1922, 70–71, 6– = Pleyte-Rossi, pTurin 1993, rt. 6,3 = Tf. 131,1–3; vs. 2,1 = Tf. 134,1; vs. 3–5 = Tf. 135,5; pVatican 19a, rt. 1,2 = Orientalia, nova series III, 1923, S. 63–87.

[29] Z.B. Borghouts, pLeiden I. 348, Nr. 28, rt. 13,10: "*Hathor, the Mistress of Dendera, who lifts up in order that she may give birth! Hathor, the mistress of Dendera, is the one who is giving birth!*"; Brunner, Geburt, Szene VIL: S. 73, Szene VIIILc, S. 87, XDd, S. 110, XIDd, S. 118. Verg. D. Müller, Ägypten und die griechische Isisare-talogien, Berlin 1961, S. 46.

[30] Z.B. G. Daressy, Textes et dessins, Tf. 3, Zeile 2, letzte Szene rechts.

[31] Z.B. MuK vs. 3,2 und 3,6 und 4,2 und 4,5 Z.B. MuK vs. 3,2 und 3,6 und 4,2 und 4,5 (*ḏr.t ḥr*), rt. 2,10 (*ʿ.wy ḥr*). Siehe H. Győry, "The Seal is your protection", RRÉ 2–3 (1998–1999), 36–52; A. Massart, The Leiden Magical Papyrus I 343 + I. 345, S. 78, Anm. 12, rt. 8,14: *w꜡ḥ ḏr.t ḥr*; und Eb 171 = Eb 194. Später: mag. pLondon-Leiden, S. 52–53, Kol. 6,16; Socle Behague Nr. 1 = Metternich Stele S. 58 (*w꜡ḥ ʿwyḥr*).

[32] Cl. Müller-Winkler, Die Ägyptischen Objekt-Amulette. Orbis Biblicus et Orientalis—Series Archeologica 5, Freiburg 1987, S. 179–189; Cl. Sourdive, La main dans l'Égypte pharaonique, Berne-Francfort-New York 1984, S. 437–460.

Zu dieser Zeit spricht auch Chnum von seinem Gesundheits-Amulett, aber da sind wir wirklich unsicher. Obwohl es detailliert beschrieben wurde, wissen wir nichts darüber. Nur seine Schnur wird bekannt gegeben: "*Hnum, lord of Elephantine, writes to Hnum, lord of Hwt-wrt: let there be bought to me your health-amulet, (that I can) fasten it to the neck of NN, son of NN. Its string which is (attached) to it is like something which Isis spun, as something which Nephthys has wrought, as something which Hedjhotep has wowen, as a work of Ptah, as something which Isis and Uadjet have made in Resenet and Mehenet, as something which Neith has knotted for its forepart.*"[33] Das Amulett selbst ist also ganz und gar unbekannt.

Im Leiden Spruch 31 bezieht sich Hathor's Gesundheits-Amulett auf das Zwergen-Amulett: der Mann wollte es bekommen, und der Horus-Medizinmann hat nach Hathors Gesundheits-Amulett geschickt. Es ist logisch, beide gleichzusetzen. Diese Interpretation ist auch gut möglich im Fall von Spruch 30, denn Hathor soll hier ihre Hand auf den Patient legen, und danach lesen wir in den Anweisungen, dass eine Zwergenstatuette auf die Schläfen der kreißenden Frau gelegt wird. Die Zwergenstatuetten haben ja eine ähnliche Form wie ein Baby, können es also magisch repräsentieren, d. h., das Ereignis der Geburt darstellen. Als Vorbilder könnten die Zwergenstatuetten aus dem Mittlerem Reich dienen, die—obwohl sie keine Götterstatuetten sind—eindeutige Fruchtbarkeitsaspekte haben. Es kommt noch hinzu, dass einige davon wahrscheinlich schon damals für Fruchtbarkeitsmagie verwendet oder als Schlangen vertreibendes Mittel genutzt wurden.[34]

Was für eine Zwergenstatuette die Frau brauchte, wird im Text nicht geklärt. Funktion, Zweck und Zugehörigkeit sind gegeben, ikonographische Anweisungen gar nicht. Es kann nur heißen, dass sie nicht erwähnenswert waren, weil sie ganz trivial waren, d. h. jeder, der damit zu tun hatte, kannte sie, oder aber ganz egal waren, nur die Zwergengestalt war wichtig. Nach den Statuetten, die erhalten geblieben sind, können die beiden Bes und Patäken sein—diese wurden sogar meist in Frauen- oder Kindergräbern gefunden, erfüllten also deren Bedürfnisse. Die Erklärung liegt auf der Hand: die Kindersterblichkeit war sehr hoch und die Komplikationen bei Entbindungen vielfältig.[35]

[33] Pleyte-Rossi, pTurin 1993, rt. 2,1–2,3, übersetzt von J. F. Borghouts.

[34] M. J. Raven, A Puzzling Pataekos, OMRO 67, 1987, Abb. 1, Tf. 1, S. 7–17; Dasen, Dwarfs, S. 89–90.

[35] H. Győry, Providing Protection, Orvostörténeti Közlemények 170–173, 2001, S. 106–108.

Viele Frauen und Kinder brauchten also Schutz, um am Leben bleiben zu können. Da die Patäken-Amulette aber zu dieser Zeit zu zwei großen ikonographischen Gruppen gehören, und beide nah miteinander verwandte Exemplare haben, scheint es wahrscheinlich, dass die dahinterstehenden Konzeptionen, obwohl sie miteinander eng verknüpft sind, sich ebenso in zwei große, aber genau bestimmbare Einheiten trennen lassen. Die einfachen Patäken sollen in erster Linie das Baby als solches heraufbeschwören, wie es in den oben genannten Texten hieß, wahrscheinlich mit einem Hinweis auf das jeden Morgen neu geborene Sonnenkind und das Horus-Kind. Die komplexen Patäken erinnern in erster Linie an die Schlangen/Skorpionen-Gefahr, was ja auf der mythischen Ebene auch das Horus-Kind heraufbeschwört, das im Sumpfgebiet gebissen und geheilt wurde, und dem alt gewordenen Sonnengott, dessen heimlichen Name Isis mit der Hilfe ihrer Schlange gelernt hatte. Die Zusammenhörigkeit beider Funktionen ist nicht unbegründet. Für das hilflose Kleinkind (und den Greis) bedeuteten die Schlangen, Skorpione und schädliche Tiere eine besonders große Gefahr.

Diese Interpretation des komplexen Patäken wird nicht nur durch die Konstruktionselemente der Patäken-Siegelamuletten[36] unterstützt, sondern auch durch einige zeitgenössische magische Texte gegen Schlangenbisse, worin der Zwerg auch oft vorkommt. In einem Papyrus in Kairo, geschrieben im Neuen Reich, erreichte das Gift den Bauch des Patienten in der Form der Göttin Bastet. Es wird dann mit der Hilfe der analogen Magie ausgetrieben: wie es aus dem Bauch des Zwerges verschwindet, so wird von hier auch entfernt werden. "*Falle ins Feuer, Gift! Das in dein Herz aufgestiegen ist als Bastet, denn sie ist mächtig! Das im Bauch des Zwerges und des Mannes! Komm heraus, Gift! Komm heraus aus dem Bauch des Zwerges und des Mannes, vom Leib des N, geboren von N! Wenn du nicht herauskommst aus dem Herz, Bastet, vom Leib des N, geboren von N, werde ich verhindern, dass die Götter und Göttinnen an dem ersten Fest der Sonnenscheibe, am Fest des Mannes und seiner Neunheit gelobt werden.*"[37]

Eine andere Frage ist, was das Gift mit dem Zwerg zu tun hat. Die Ikonographie der komplexen Patäken-Amulette deutet auf ein

[36] H. Győry, To the Interpretation of Pataikos standing on crocodiles, BMHBA 94, 2001, S. 27–40.
[37] Y. Koenig, Le Papyrus Boulaq 6, Cairo 1981, BdE 1981, S. 68–72, rt. VI,3–VII,1.

eventuelles Moment des Schlangen Fressens hin, indem die Schlange aus dem Mund hängt, als ob er sie in zwei Teile beiße oder esse. Die Amulette lenken aber auch die Aufmerksamkeit auf andere Schlangen vernichtende Methoden, wie den Kopf abschneiden—durch das Messer in beiden Händen—, oder zertreten. Das Zertreten der zwei Krokodile zeigt aber auch eine Verallgemeinerung. Auch die verkörpern die negativen Mächte, ihre Besiegung heißt also die Herstellung der Ordnung, das ägyptische Maat. Das gleiche Motiv wird in der Königideologie auch durch das Zertreten—diesmal der menschlichen Feinde—dargestellt. Da der König ja ideologisch Horus ist, und die heilende Person, die die Feinde besiegt, identifiziert sich auch magisch mit Horus, ist die Transplantation der Ikonographie gut verständlich. Auf der anderen Seite, da der Zwerg oft mit gleicher Ikonographie dargestellt wird und er die Genesung in den Texten bringt, ist die Gleichsetzung des Zwerges mit einem Horus-Aspekt ganz natürlich. Es ist manchmal auch in den Texten greifbar.

Während der 18. Dynastie tauchen auch die Horus-Sched-Stelen auf,[38] die wiederum gegen Schlangenbisse verwendet wurden, und wo der Gott Horus mit Beinamen "*Retter*" (*Ḥr šd*)[39] wiederum mit den schädlichen Tieren auf zwei Krokodilen dargestellt wird. Diesmal schreitet er, wie die Götter im Allgemeinen dargestellt wurden, und hält er mehrere Tierarten in seinen Händen, ebenso wie es später nicht nur die Harpocraten auf den Horus-Stelen, sondern auch einige komplexe Patäken-Figuren machen. Diese Ikonographie ist letztendlich auch von den Darstellungen der Apotropaia abzuleiten, die vom Mittleren Reich bis in die Zeit der 18. Dynastie benutzt wurden.[40] Solche Bilder dienten dazu, die schädlichen Tiere magisch unschädlich zu machen, also mit der Visualisierung der Vernichtung dieser Tiere wurde die Wirkung des Giftes aufgehoben. Auf einer höheren Ebene wird damit die Vernichtung der Mächte der Dunkelheit und Chaos ausgedrückt, die ja an den Unterwelttoren auch manchmal durch zwergenhafte Dämonen mit vergleichbarer Ikonographie dargestellt

[38] B. Bruyere, Rapport sur les fouilles de Deir el-Medineh (1935–1940), FIFAO 20/3, Le Caire 1952, S. 138–170; A. Eggebrecht (Hrg.), Suche nach Unsterblichkeit, Hildesheim 1990, S. 76–77, Nr. T24. = A. Eggebrecht (Hrg.), Pelizäus Museum Hildesheim. Die Ägyptische Sammlung, Mainz 1993, S. 68, Nr. 62; LÄ, V. Kol. 547–549.

[39] Verg. S. Sauneron, Représentation de l'Horus-ched a Karnak, BIFAO 53, 1953, S. 53–55; E. Jelínková Reymond, Les inscriptions de la statue guérisseuse de Djed-Her-Le-Saveur, Le Caire 1956, S. 62. + Anm. 4.

[40] H. Altenmüller, Die Apotropaia und die Götter Mittelägyptens, Diss. München 1965.

sind.[41] Somit wird auch der tägliche Kampf des Sonnengottes gegen die Schlange Apopi miteinbezogen.

Wie Horus schon Seth besiegt hat,—nicht nur im Kampf um das Erbe, sondern auch mit seiner Geburt oder durch die Genesung nach dem Skorpionenbissen—wird der mit Horus identifizierte Medizinmann oder Patient den Gesetzen der analogen Magie folgend den in der Krankheit manifestierten Seth und das Chaos durch die solare Hilfe des Zwerges besiegen und damit die Genesung erreichen. Diese ramessidische Konzeption wird später weiterentwickelt—der Zwerg und Horus scheinen ineinander zu verschmelzen, und diese Verschmelzung der zwei positiven Akteure wird auf manchen späten Patäken-Figuren durch die Jugendlocke auch visuell ausgedrückt.[42]

Wenn wir uns den Inschriften dieser Amulette die auf dem Rückenpfeiler während der 18–20. Dynastie vorhanden sind, zuwenden, können wir feststellen, dass die Darstellungen inhaltlich auf diesen Sieg hinweisen. Die kryptographische Gruppen auf den Statuetten,[43] die schon am Ende der 18. Dynastie feste Trigramme zu sein scheinen, sind zwei verschiedene Götternamen. Da die Amulette, die sie tragen, ikonographisch vollkommen gleich sind, ist es anzunehmen, dass sie verschiedene Ausdrücke der gleichen Konzeption sind, oder verschiedene Kennzeichen des gleichen Gottes ausdrücken. Ihre Zusammengehörigkeit ist auch dadurch offensichtlich, dass später beide Trigramme, die auf dem Rückenpfeiler vorhanden sind, auch nebeneinander, als Siegel-Inschrift, vorkommen.[44] Die eine Kryptographie kann als die Name des Gottes Atum entziffert, die andere als "*älteste*" gelesen werden, das ein ständiges Epitheton der Schöpfergötter ist, und eine gewöhnliche Beiname des Atum oder des Horus, der eine Missgeburt erlitten hatte. Es heißt also, dass am Beginn die Schöpferfunktion

---

[41] Z.B. A. Piankoff, The Litany of Re, New York 1964, ERT 4, S. 69, Nr. 6–7; A. Piankoff-Rambova, Mythological Papyri, Bollinger Series XL.3, New York 1957, P. Dirpu: Nr. 6, Szene 7, P.P. Khonsu-renep: Nr. 11, Szene 4 (mit Schlangen in der Mund und Messer in den Händen); auf dem Papyrus der Henuttaui: Dasein, Dwarfs, S. 91, Abb. 7.2.

[42] Vgl. "*Ich bin das heilige Kind, das im Haus des Ra ist, der heilige Zwerg, der in der Höhle ist*...", Klasens, The Socle Behag, Sp. IV, f 9–10, oder noch später Griffith-Thompson, The Demotic Magical Papyrus of London and Leiden XI. 6–7—1. Jh. n.Chr.

[43] H. Győry, Über die Patäken-Amulette im Neuen Reich, in: Fs. Satzinger, 2002, im Druck.

[44] Z.B. V. Dasen, Dwarfs, S. 95, Abb. 7.3a (Berlin); M.L. Ryhiner, A propos de trigrammes panthéistes, *RdÉ* 29, 1978, S. 125–137; Y. Koenig, Les Pateques inscrits du Louvre, *RdÉ* 43, 1992, S. 123–132.

und der Regenerationscharakter des Zwerges am wichtigsten war,[45] und diese Eigenschaft ermöglichte ihm, die Leben spendende Kraft und die Fähigkeit zu retten bei Schlangenbissen auszuüben.

Der Schöpfer-Aspekt wird an den komplexen Patäken-Figuren von Anfang an auch mit dem Skarabäus auf dem Kopf betont, der aber zugleich seinen solaren Aspekt zeigte, und zwar den der aufgehenden Sonne. Das wurde mit der Inschrift für Atum mit der untergehender Sonne, und mit der Statuette, also dem "Mann", wie Re im Mag. pHarris heißt,[46] auch mit der Mittagssonne ergänzt. Die Statuette war aber auch ein magisches Siegel. Der omnipräsente Reichsgott, der so verbreitet auf magischen Siegelamuletten war,[47] durfte auch nicht fehlen. Er war oft auf der Basis in kryptographischer Form. Allerdings, meistens in seinem solaren Aspekt, als Amon-Ra. Somit war das Amulett in der Entstehungszeit ein viele symbolhafte Deutungen innehabendes solares Objekt, das seine Wurzel in der Sonnentheologie von Heliopolis, mit Ergänzungen der Horusmythen hatte. Diese Assoziationen scheinen später weiterentwickelt worden zu sein, zuerst mit einem (Ptah-)Sokaris(-Osiris) Aspekt, wie die Federkrone zeigt. Die passt mit der Regenerationsidee auch gut zusammen.

Die Sonnenideologie in Verbindung mit dem Zwerg zeigt einen engen Kontakt zu der heliopolitanischen Theologie, die eine hiesigen Ursprung dieser Zwerg-Konzeption wahrscheinlich macht. Dieser Zwerg hatte aber spätestens in der 20. Dynastie einen offiziellen Kult in Memphis. Da sollte man ihm ein Naos von 1/2 Ellen machen.[48] Er saß darin mit Affengesicht.[49] Freilich, spätestens noch in der Zeit der Ramessiden gibt es eine Verschmelzung auch mit dem memphitischen Ptah, der nicht nur mit Sokaris identifiziert wird und ein Schöpfer- und starker solarer Gott war,[50] sondern auch einige Eigenschaften von Schu und Ra, wie z. B. die Beschreibung "*deine beide Beine auf*

[45] Diese Konzeption der Wiedererwachen und Regeneration wurde durch die Darstellungen, die ihn mit verschiedenen Götter, wie Horus, Khonsu, Amon, Osiris zusammenschmelzt, ausgedrückt.

[46] Z.B. Lange, Mag. pHarris, V (19), IX.8, oder siehe oben in pDeir el Medineh (Anm. 7.) und pBoulaq (Anm. 36).

[47] Z.B. B. Jaeger, *Essai de classification et datation des scarabées Menkheperré.* OBO, Series Archeologica 2, Fribourg—Göttingen 1982, und E. Hornung – E. Staehelin, Skarabäen und andere Siegelamulette aus Basler Sammlungen, Mainz 1976, passim.

[48] Lange, Mag. pHarris U (18), IX.1–2, S. 73–74.

[49] Lange, Mag. pHarris U (18), IX.4–5, S. 73–74 und V (19), IX. 7–10, S. 80–81.—Später kennen wir z.B. mehrere Statuetten wo der Pavian von Zwergen getragen wird.

[50] W. Wolf, Der Berliner Ptah-Hymnus, ZÄS 64, 1929, (pBerlin 3048) S. 21, Z. 6–7: "*Es erwacht der Aton des Himmels . . . für sein Auge, der die beiden Länder mit seinen*

der Erde, dein Kopf im Himmel" bestätigt, hatte.[51] Und eben durch Ptah würden die 7 Falken entstehen, die den Verstorbenen nach einem Skorpionenbiss ins Leben zurückrufen konnten.[52] So liegt die Vermutung nahe, dass die Bewohner der Ramessidischen Handelsstadt Memphis sich schon früh die wichtigsten Elemente des heiligen Zwerges nicht nur zu eigen gemacht haben, sondern sie auch in den Populärkult des Ptah eingebaut haben.[53] Dieser Vorgang wurde ikonographisch durch die Kappe erleichtert, die beide, der Zwerg und Ptah, trugen, und dadurch, dass unter den Handwerkern vermutlich mehrere Zwerge arbeiteten.[54] Dieser Aspekt des Zwerges konnte sich leicht in ganz Ägypten verbreiten, denn Memphis war ja eine maßgebliche Stadt des Neuen Reiches.

Die Patäken-Figuren garantierten so ursprünglich die ständige Wiederholung der Schöpfung und die Erhaltung der Weltordnung. Sie repräsentierten in erster Linie den Sonnengott und seine Wille mitsamt der Horustheologie, die immer stärker herausragte, wurden aber langsam auch mit anderen Göttern in Zusammenhang gebracht. Ihre schützende Rolle konzentrierte sich auf zwei Spezialgebiete, auf die Geburt und Schlangenbisse. In Anbetracht dessen, dass die Täter, also die Mächte der Dunkelheit und des Chaos, des Bösen in der Götterwelt durch Apopi oder Seth verkörpert werden, gibt die Szene der komplexen Patäken-Amulette die Möglichkeit das Überwältigen des Bösen symbolisch darzustellen, dem die magische Realisation folgt. Diese Vorstellung knüpft sich aber auch eng an die Entbindung und das Wochenbett. Dies ist doch die Zeit, in der Mutter und Kind der größten Gefahr ausgesetzt sind.[55] Ihre Zusammenhörigkeit manifestiert

---

Strahlen erleuchtet, in Frieden." S. 27, Z. 57–59: "*Wenn Du untergehst, entsteht Finsternis, Deine beiden Augen sind es, die Licht machen. Du leuchtest mit Deinem funkelnden Auge.*" Verg. Wadi Hammat, Dyn. 30. in: M. Sandman Holmberg, The god Ptah, Lundi 1946, S. 105–7.

[51] W. Wolf, ZÄS 1929, pBerlin 3048, 5,4. Vgl. J. Berlandini, Ptah démiurge et l'exaltation du ciel, *RdÉ* 46, S. 9–41, Abb. 5, Tf. 4; M.S. Holmberg, Ptah, Lundi 1946.

[52] A. Massart, The Egyptian Geneva Papyrus MAH 15274, MDAIK 15, 1967, S. 180, Tf. 31, Rt. V.7. Verg. auch die spätere komplexe Patäken Figuren mit Falken auf den Schultern.

[53] Verg. M.S. Holmberg, Ptah, S. 184–185: die sind ursprunglich Amulette gegen schädlichen Demonen, und wurden später mit den grössen Götter in Zusammenhang gebracht.

[54] S. Montet, Ptah-Pateque et les orfevres nains, BSFE 11 (1952), 73–74.

[55] H. Győry, "*Providing protection to the new-born on the day of birth*"—Extra- and Intrauterine complications and Abnormalities in Ancient Egypt, Orvostörténeti Közlemények 170–173, 2001, 106–108.

sich noch dazu auch darin, dass giftige Bisse auch den Gesichtsausdruck beeinflussen. Die Ägypter, die sich ans Gebären erinnerten, benutzten es als Gleichnis für die Beschreibung der Wirkung des Schlangenbissens, wie z. B. in pGeneva steht: "*his face being in the manner of (the face of) a woman who gives birth* (msy)".[56] Es ist auch nicht unmöglich, dass dieser groteske Gesichtsausdruck auch die Vorstellung eines Affengesichts hervorrufen sollte.

Zusammenfassung

Von mythologischer Seite gehören die Patäken-Amulette im Neuen Reich also in den Kreise der Weltschöpfung und zeigen stark solare Züge, womit sie gegen die böse Mächte, besonders in Moment der Entbindung und bei Schlangenbissen während des Genesungsprozesses verwendet werden konnten. Sie standen in Zusammenhang mit mehreren Göttern, am dominierendsten war aber Ra. So kann man die Patäken-Amuletten als verschiedene Manifestationen oder Aspekte des heliopolitanischen Sonnengottes auffassen,[57] was durch lokal-memphitischen Anschauungen mit Ptah in seinem solaren Aspekt in Zusammenhang gebracht wurde. Die Amulette beherrschen gleichzeitig strenge Horus-Züge, die wahrscheinlich aus in der Iatromagie oft verwendeten populär-magischen Gründen herrühren.

[56] A. Massart, The Egyptian Geneva Papyrus MAH 15274, MDAIK 15, 1957, S. 178, Tf. 29, rt. IV.1–2.

[57] El-Aguizy, Dwarfs and Pygmies in Ancient Egypt, ASAE 71, 1987, 53–60, V. Dasen, Dwarfs in Ancient Egypt and Greece, Oxford 1993, S. 84–98.

BEITRÄGE ZUR LEXIKOGRAPHIE 1: MÖGLICHE PHANTOMWÖRTER IM HL1

Rainer Hannig
(University of Göttingen)

Wörterbücher gehören meist zu den "lebenden", nicht abgeschlossenen Büchern ähnlich wie Enzyklopädien und Lexika.[1] Sie weisen dann keine festgefügte, unveränderliche Form und festen Inhalt auf, sondern wachsen mit dem Fortschritt der Wissenschaft. Der Wörterbuchmacher ist also dazu gezwungen, alle Entwicklungen in allen Teilbereichen zu beobachten. So wird auch der ägyptologische Lexikograph, der sich mit der Semantik der Wörter beschäftigt, gezwungen sein, alle Ergebnisse der ägyptologischen Teildisziplinen in der Hinsicht auszuwerten, inwieweit sie für die Wortforschung von Bedeutung sind. Im Grunde arbeitet somit die gesamte Ägyptologie an der Gestaltung von Wörterbüchern, Enzyklopädien und Lexika. Umgekehrt verläßt sich die gesamte Ägyptologie auf eben diese Buchsorten, um einen ersten Überblick über die Problematik zu gewinnen. Vielfach prägen sie die Wissenschaft für einen längeren Zeitraum; so wirken das alte Berliner Wörterbuch und Faulkners Dictionary bis heute nachhaltig fort und bilden indirekt noch heute Generationen von Ägyptologen aus. Alle ägyptischen Wörterbücher haben etwas gemeinsam: Sie verlangen eine mehr oder minder lange Eingewöhnungszeit, bis man den angemessenen Gebrauch und die Vor- und Nachteile jedes dieser Bücher erlernt hat. Der Benutzer sollte aber zumindest einige Grundsätze kennen, die für alle ägyptologische Wörterbücher gelten:

- Kein Wörterbuch ist vollständig. Obwohl ich selbst HL1 für nahezu vollständig hielt—natürlich für den vorgesehenen Zeitraum von 2850–950 v.Chr.—sind mittlerweile mehrere Hundert neue Lemmata in das Wörterbuch aufgenommen worden.
- Kein Wörterbuch ist übersichtlich genug. Die vokallose Schrift erschwert die Anordnung der Lemmata.

[1] Ich danke Matthias Müller für einige Informationen und die Diskussionen zu hieratisch geschriebenen Wörtern und Albrecht Endruweit für einige sprachliche Korrekturen.

- Jeder Lexikograph hat eine differenzierte Meinung zu den einzelnen Lemmata, die er aus Platzgründen nicht verbalisieren, allenfalls annotieren kann. Im HL1 ist dies durch Asteriskus und Ähnlichem non-verbal notiert. Hoch hingegen führte ein Zahlensystem ein, um die Wahrscheinlichkeit der Etymologie zu kennzeichnen.
- Kein Wörterbuch kann bislang genaue Bedeutungsangaben machen, da die semantische Analyse erst in den Anfängen steckt.[2]
- Die meisten Wörterbücher nehmen auch Problemfälle in die Lemmaliste auf, was dazu führt, dass gelegentlich sogar nichtexistente Wörter aufgenommen werden, die auf Fehllesungen (durch den Ägyptologen verursacht) oder -schreibungen (durch den ägyptischen Schreiber verursacht) beruhen. Diese Phantomwörter nannte man früher gern vox nihili.[3]

Die nachfolgende Liste enthält die meisten der im HL1 als "[Existenz des Wortes nicht gesichert]" gekennzeichneten Lemmata, die somit vox nihili bzw. Phantomwörter sein können. Jede Listennummer enthält den Wörterbucheintrag im HL1, in eckigen Klammern den Fundort in den Wörterbüchern und dann den oder die Belege, wonach die kurzgefasste Erörterung der Problematik folgt. Zuletzt wird mit einer Empfehlung (Status) darauf hingewiesen, wie das Lemma meiner Meinung nach zum gegenwärtigen Zeitpunkt zu bewerten ist.

Liste:

1.  **ꜣ** [interj] he! ≈ **js r=k!** he, geh doch!
[WB ø; HL1, 1] Beleg: EAG §859
Problematik: Edels Kommentar zur Interjektion in seiner Grammatik hat noch heute Gültigkeit. Status: Abwarten, bis neue Belege die Ausgangslage verbessern.

2. , det.  **ꜣt** *f* 'Pantherhelm', 'Leopardenhelm' (*e. Kopfschmuck *mit Uräus*) **mr** ≈ mit schlimmem Pantherhelm

[2] Am deutlichsten auf den transitorischen Charakter des Berliner Wörterbuches—und somit eigentlich auf alle anderen Wörterbücher ebenfalls—hat Gardiner in JEA 34, S.17, hingewiesen: "to sum up, out of the 20 words on the first two pages of Wb., I have found all but three urgently calling for further elucidation".

[3] Für manche Wörterbücher außerhalb der Ägyptologie ist bezeugt, dass absichtlich Phantomwörter in die Lemmaliste aufgenommen wurden. An das Phantomlemma Ombalophobie "Angst vor dem Bauchnabel" vermag ich mich zu erinnern, nicht aber in welchem deutschen Wörterbuch es vorkam.

[WB I, 1.11; HL1, 1] Belege (nach Wb): Pyr 297; 940; 973; 1032; Urk. IV 246. Beleg für **mr ꜣt :** CT III 206n
Problematik: Gardiner in JEA 34 (1948), S. 13, möchte das Wort eliminieren und die Belege der Bedeutung "Kraft" bzw. "readiness to strike" zugewiesen haben. Gardiners Einwände sind noch immer gültig und lassen starke Zweifel an der Existenz des Wortes aufkommen. Status: Das Wort nicht sofort eliminieren, sondern neue Belege und Interpretationen abwarten.

3. **ꜣjw** e. Stab
[WB ø; HL1, 2] Beleg: Hassan (1976), S. 6
Problematik: Wort stammt aus einem späten Totenbuch. Status: Streichen in HL1.

4. *ꜣꜥ *zögern; *ängstlich sein
[WB ø; HL1, 2] Beleg: Habachi (1972), S. 39f.
Problematik: Aleph-Zeichen nicht sicher (Kopf leicht gebogen), überdies ist das Zeichen links am Rand zerstört. Status: Noch abwarten.

5. **ꜣw** [Musik] *Trommeleinheit ("Länge")
[WB ø; HL1, 4] Beleg: mCairo JE 49566 (2 Belege)
Problematik: Zur Diskussion: JEA 72 (1986), S. 43 N.m. Vom Kontext her geurteilt, ist kaum auszuschließen, daß das Wort tatsächlich existiert, obwohl die genaue Bedeutung noch nicht bestimmt werden kann. Status: Abwarten.

6. **ꜣwẖ** *dienen (**n** *jdm*)
[WB I, 5.19; HL1, 5] Beleg: CT IV 365a (Spruch 343)
Problematik: Stabile Schreibung, von 7 Textzeugen hat nur einer die Variante **ꜣẖ**. Status: Abwarten.

7. **ꜣwd** e. Körperteil
[WB ø; HL1, 5] Beleg: Assmann (1991), Textband, S. 155; Tafelband, Tf. 66
Problematik: Das Wort **jbḥ** "Zahn" geht voraus, deshalb ist das Wort wegen des Zahndeterminativs richtig **nḥdt** "Zahn" zu lesen. ist zu verlesen worden, obwohl es die Brustfeder hat. ist offensichtlich der Kopf des , dessen Rest in der Zerstörung ist. Status: Streichen, weil eindeutig nicht-existent.

8.  **ꜣbꜣb** *entzückt sein [cf. **ꜣbj** spaßen]
[WB I, 8.3; HL1, 6] Beleg: Quack (1994), B 22,5 und B 22,19
Problematik: Handschriften B und G haben deutlich **ꜣbb**. Status: Streichen, weil eindeutig nicht-existent.

9.  **ꜣḥyt** *f* [coll] Äcker [cf. **wḥyt**]
[WB I, 12.19; HL1, 11] Beleg: Davies (1903–8) Bd. VI, 27.11
Problematik: Von der Schreibung ist zu wenig erhalten. Status: Streichen.

10.  **ꜣḥs** (?)
[WB ø; HL1, 11] Beleg: gNecro 1372
Problematik: Unklarer Beleg; viell identisch mit **rḥs** [WB II, 442.4; HL1, 474]. Status: Abwarten.

11.  **ꜣtj** *erleuchten
[WB ø; HL1, 17] Beleg: CT VI, 363o
Problematik: Graefe (1971), P.47 schlägt die Bedeutung vor und verweist auf den Namen des Sonnenschiffes **ꜣtj**. Der Kontext ist schwierig und nicht sehr hilfreich. Status: Abwarten.

12.  **jwt-jb** "Kommen des Herzens" (*Gier)
[WB ø; HL1, 28] Beleg: CT III.82
Problematik: de Buck führt 5 Textzeugen mit durchaus stabilem und verständlichem Kontext an. Bedeutung bleibt unklar trotz der Abgrenzung zu **ꜣwt-jb** und den beiden benachbarten Oppositionspaaren, die das Prinzip erkennen lassen. Status: Wort wohl existent, weshalb die Markierung "[Existenz . . . nicht gesichert] entfällt.

13. 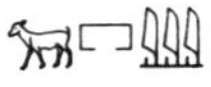 **jbw-sẖt** e. Pflanze ["Schutzhütte des Feldes"]
[WB ø; HL1, 40] Beleg: Edel (1961–3), S. 252
Problematik: Die wörtliche Bedeutung läßt eher an einen geographischen Namen denken als an eine Pflanze. **jbw-sẖt** steht in einer Reihe von Bezeichnungen, die ebenfalls mit **sẖt** "Feld" gebildet sind. Die dazugehörigen Baumdarstellungen sind aneinander ähnlich, was gleichfalls auf eine Bezeichnung einer Feldmark weisen könnte. Status: Als Bezeichnung einer Pflanze streichen, allenfalls als Eigenname aufnehmen.

14. ***jmj-ḥsww** *Leiter der Sänger
[WB ø; HL1, 66] Beleg: Ward (1982), S. 54 (Schimmel Nr. 183)
Problematik: Vermutlich ist **rꜣ** ausgefallen, so daß eigentlich das gut belegte **jmj-rꜣ ḥsww** "Vorsteher der Sänger" zu lesen ist. Status: Streichen.

15. **jmsy** [subst]
[WB I, 88.7; HL1, 73] Beleg: Griffith/Newberry (1895) Bd. II, T. 21 oben L. 8
Problematik: Text stand im heute zerstörten Teil. Die Rekonstruktion erfolgte durch Photo. Status: Abwarten, obwohl das Wort wenig vertrauenserweckend wirkt.

16. **jn** e. Gefäß
[WB ø; HL1, 75] Beleg: oDeM 579,3
Problematik: Die Diskussion in Janssen (1975), S. 434, A. 177 ist noch immer gültig. Status: Abwarten.

17. **jn** e. Metallobjekt
[WB ø; HL1, 75] Belege: Peet (1930), T. 27, L. 12 (pBM10403); pMayer A, 1.16 (korrigiert in Peet (1982), T. 24)
Problematik: Obwohl offenbar zwei Belege angeführt werden können, ist Existenz und Bedeutung noch unklar. Status: Abwarten.

18. **jrrt**.*f* [coll] Übeltäter ≈ **nbt r=s** alle Übeltäter gegen sie
[WB I, 113 (?); HL1, 91] Beleg: Gardiner / Sethe (1928), VIa, Zeile 10
Problematik: Wegen der Fehlschreibung **ḥnꜥ** "mit" statt "von . . . (retten)" ist die Stelle nicht sicher. Cf. auch Zeile 3 und 4. Status: Abwarten.

19. **jhꜣw** [pl] *Knospen
[WB ø; HL1, 95] Beleg: Helck (1970), L. 67 (oDeM 1675)
Problematik: Das erste Zeichen des Wortes ist nach Posener und Fischer-Elfert unsicher; kann aber wie ein **j** verstanden werden. Zu Fischer-Elferts (1986: 2), S. 52 (L. 67), Anm. a) Kommentar ist im Moment nichts hinzuzufügen. Status: Abwarten.

20. **dbwjj** "der von den Beiden Ufern" (*epit König Ägyptens*)
[WB ø; HL1, 117] Beleg: Helck (1977), S. 72; Merikare P X.10 = C III. 11

Problematik: Das Verständnis von **jdbwjj** als Wort stammt von Scharff (1936), S. 55, Anm. 5. Helck (1977), S. 72, emendiert zu **nb jdbwj**, was Scharff wegen des doppelt gesetzten Götterdeterminativs in seinen Überlegungen bereits ablehnte. Cf. Burkard (1977), S. 262–3. Status: Abwarten.

21.  **ʿḫ-pt** e. Fest
[WB ø; HL1, 157] Beleg: Luft (1992), S. 140 (2 Belege)
Problematik: unsichere Ergänzung, weil die Hieroglyphe in keinem Fall erkennbar ist. Status: Abwarten.

22.  **ʿš** e. Mahlzeit (*d. Soldaten*)
[WB I, 227.17; HL1, 159] Beleg: pAn I 17,2
Problematik: Fischer-Elfert (1986), S. 144, Anm. g) vergleicht offenbar **ʿš** mit dem **šʿyt** -Gebäck (femininer Genus), doch ist die Identifizierung wegen des maskulinen Possessivartikels schwierig. Die einzige Variante schreibt **šʿ**. Status: Abwarten.

23. 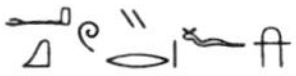 **ʿqrf** [ext, syll, näg] e. *Korb [viell identisch mit **ʿqr** *od.* **nqr=f**]
[WB ø; HL1, 163] Beleg: Gardiner/Černý (1957), T. 50,1 rt 10
Problematik: An der hieroglyphischen Übertragung und Lesung ist nicht zu zweifeln. Zur Diskussion cf. Janssen (1975), S. 148 und Anm. 73. Status: Ziemlich sicher nicht-existent; trotzdem im HL1 belassen und abwarten.

24.  **ʿḏꜣt** *f* e. Stock (Zu verbessern in: "e. Szepter")
[WB ø; HL1, 167] Beleg: Montet (1941), Bd. II, T. 94
Problematik: In der Liste steht **ʿḏꜣt** in Wort und Bild neben den Szeptern **wꜣs** und **ḏʿm**. Status: Abwarten, bis neuer Beleg vorhanden ist.

25. 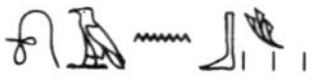 **wꜣnb** e. Pflanze [Existenz nicht gesichert]
[WB I, 251.16; HL1, 173] Beleg: pEbers 533
Problematik: Die Diskussion in v. Deines/Grapow (1959), S. 124 ist noch immer gültig. **wꜣnb** sieht wie eine Schreibung für **wꜣb** "Wurzel" aus. Status: Abwarten, obwohl von der Nicht-Existenz auszugehen ist.

26. **wʿbw** *Appell
[WB ø; HL1, 185] Beleg: CT VII, 393b
Problematik: Faulkner (1973–8): Bd. III, S. 154, übersetzt "priestly service", van der Molen (2000), s.v., versieht diese Übersetzung mit Fragezeichen. Ich schließe mich der Erklärung an und ordne den Beleg unter Priesterdienst ein. Der Vorschlag "Appell" von Schott (1990), S. 43, ist unwahrscheinlich. Status: In HL1 streichen.

27. **wḏʿwj sḫt** (?)
[WB ø; HL1, 234] Beleg: Edel (1961–3), Bd. 1, S. 252
Problematik: Cf. Erklärung oben unter **jbw-sḫt**. Status: Streichen.

28. **bwt** *f* *Bynnibarbe (Barbus bynni) [nur in Personennamen belegt]
[WB I, 453.4; HL1, 251] Beleg: Berlin 14108 (Ranke (1935–77), Bd. 1, S. 95.1)
Problematik: Unter dem Einfluß von Montet in Kemi 1, 16 wurde im ersten Manuskript des HL1 das Lemma eliminiert, später allerdings wegen Ranke wieder aufgenommen. Status: Abwarten.

29. **bḥwt** **f* *e. Vogel (**vergöttlicht*)
[WB ø; HL1, 258] Beleg: Borghouts (1971), rt 2.4
Problematik: Das Wort an sich und der Kontext sind wenig vertrauenserweckend, z.B. steht ein als Determinativ nach dem Genitiv-**n**, was Borghouts mit einem *sic* versieht. Allerdings ist Borghouts hieroglyphische Übertragung des hieratischen Papyrus nicht zu verbessern. Vielleicht ist eine Verschreibung von **bjk** "Falke" zu denken, in einer "ähnlichen" hieratischen Schreibweise wie rt. 3.5 (nicht aber wie rt 1.5). Trotzallem wäre dann das für ungewöhnlich. Status: Abwarten.

30. **bḫn** ② "Burg" (*ein Gefäß in der 'Burg'-Form*)
[WB ø; HL1, 259] Beleg: ChB V rt 8.11
Problematik: Cf. pBM III, Txb S. 49, Anm. 4. Der Kontext ist so eindeutig, daß **bḫn** tatsächlich nur ein Gefäß sein kann. Status: Als eigenes Lemma aufnehmen, ohne den Vermerk [Existenz . . . nicht gesichert].

31.  **bẖh** [*vb]
[WB ø; HL1, 259] Beleg: Faulkner (1969), § 1855c
Problematik: Anfang und Ende des Wortes unbekannt. Die wahrscheinliche Inkompabilität der Laute, die mit dem Zeichen  und  wiedergegeben werden, legt die Nicht-Existenz nahe. Status: Abwarten.

32.  **bḏt** **f* e. Metallwerkzeug
[WB ø; HL1, 267] Beleg: Junker (1925–55) Bd. IV, T. 9
Problematik: Drenkhahns Interpretation (1976, S. 38), daß der Metallklumpen nicht als Determinativ zum Wort gehört, schließe ich mich an. Das im übrigen klar geschriebene **bḏt** könnte eine Variante von **bḏ** "Schmelztiegel" sein. Sicher ist das freilich nicht. Der Lemmaeintrag im HL1 heißt jetzt:  **bḏt** *f* *Schmelztiegel; *e. Metallwerkzeug. Status: In HL1 belassen, mit Eintrag wie oben beschrieben.

33. 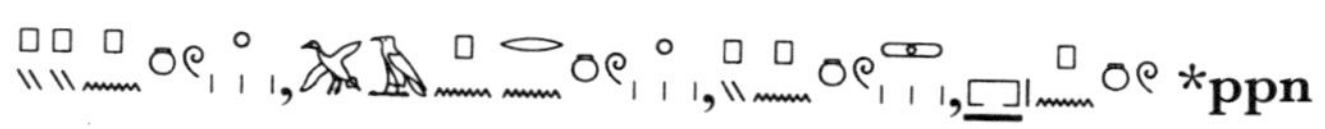 ***ppn** [syll, näg, subst] (*Pfeffer, Piper nigrum) [Transkription nicht gesichert]
[WB ø; HL1, 276] Beleg: oDeM 350 rt I 3, II 1 (2 Belege); oDeM 350 vs 2 + 9 (2 Belege); oDeM 554 vs 6; mehrere unpublizierte Belege aus Černýs Notizbüchern.
Problematik: Das Wort ist sicher belegt, wenn auch die Transkription wegen der unterschiedlichen Schreibungen nicht sicher ist. Es ist bislang nur auf den Deir-el-Medina Ostraca gefunden worden. Die Bedeutung ist nur geraten, obwohl ich davon ausging, daß das Gewürz und das Wort "Pfeffer" internationale Verbreitung hatte. Das Gewürz findet man meines Wissens zuerst unter Ramses II. Es muß sehr kostbar gewesen sein, da es eingeführt wurde. Ob aber die Menge so wichtig war, daß man zwölf Körner abzählte (wie in oDeM 554 vs 6), ist nicht sehr wahrscheinlich. Die tentative Identifizierung ist somit mit aller Vorsicht zu betrachten. Status: In HL1 belassen, nur mit dem Vermerk [Transkription noch nicht gesichert].

34. 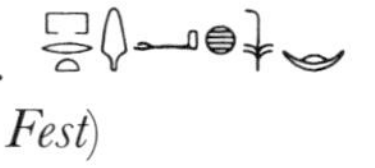 ***prt-jmꜣ-ꜥ-Ḫnsw** Auszug des "Ima-o-Chonsu" *(e. Fest)*
[WB ø; HL1, 284] Beleg: mPhiladelphia E 13540
Problematik: Cf. Fisher (1924), S. 153. Die Belegstelle ist für mich durch ein Photo nicht nachprüfbar. Status: Abwarten.

35.  **psdw** e. Kleidungsstück
[WB ø; HL1, 295] Beleg: oDeM 86
Problematik: Cf. Janssen (1975), S. 257. Status: Abwarten, bis neue Belege bekannt werden.

36.  **pḏ** e. Teil des Fischnetzes
[WB ø; HL1, 300] Beleg: CT VI 25j
Problematik: Nur ein Textzeuge (B1Bo). Der Kontext ist nicht aufschlußreich. Faulkner (1973–8) Bd. II, S. 116, übersetzt mit "Bogen" mit Hinweis auf das Wort **pḏt**. Status: Abwarten.

37. 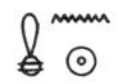 **mjn** ② der Zeitgenosse
[WB II, 43.10; HL1, 325] Beleg: Edel, in: MIO 1, S. 213–7
Problematik: Edel übersetzt **mjn** mit "Ehrung", was m.E. die Erklärung des Wortes nicht verbessert. Auf keinem Fall kann von einer Widerlegung der gängigen Meinung im Sinne Quacks (BiOr 54, 1997, C. 331) gesprochen werden, wenn an Stelle einer bekannten Wurzel eine bis dato unbekannte Wurzel mit der Grund bedeutung "Ehren" ersetztwird.[4] Der dritte Beleg Edels  **jw=j m mjn ḫr jmj-rꜣ ḥmw-nṯr** traditionell (nach Erman) übersetzt mit "ich war/ bin ein Zeitgenosse beim Priester-Vorsteher", wird von Edel mit folgenden Worten abgetan: "Der Sinn . . . ist recht dünn; nachdem sich der Mann eines mehr oder weniger verantwortungsvollen Postens im Hause zweier aufeinanderfolgender Hoherpriester gerühmt hat, sollte er sich damit bescheiden, bei den nachfolgendem Hohenpriester nur 'Zeitgenosse' gewesen zu sein? Wenn er gesagt hätte, er sei auch bei dem letzten Hohenpriester 'geachtet', 'geschätzt' oder 'geehrt' gewesen, so wäre das eine sinnvolle biographische Notiz." Weiterhin schreibt er "'Gleichzeitigkeit' zu einem Herrscher ist eben kein besonderes Privileg, dessen man sich schicklich rühmen könnte, da auch die ärmsten Untertanen 'Zeitgenossen' sind." Meiner Ansicht nach kann jemand aus mehreren Gründen herausstellen, daß er ein "Zeitgenosse", der "Jetztgenosse" jemandes ist. Zum einen kann er damit betonen, daß er unter mehreren Herrschern lebte und jetzt zum Zeitpunkt

[4] In diesem Artikel neigt Quack bei einigen Lemmata zu apodiktischen Urteilen, wenn er einigen Autoritäten aufs Wort glaubt. Viele von seinen Anregungen habe ich zwar in meine neue Version der Wörterbücher aufnehmen können; andere aber mußte ich zurückweisen oder -stellen, da sie einer genaueren Prüfung nicht standhielten.

der Schriftabfassung unter dem gegenwärtigen Herrscher lebt und wirkt. Zum anderen ist es deutlich vorsichtiger, wenn man in den Anfangsjahren eines neuen Machthabers von "Zeitgenössigkeit" schreibt statt von Ehrungen, die eventuell noch gar nicht stattgefunden haben. Zum dritten gibt man zu verstehen, daß man seines Amtes beim Machtwechsel nicht enthoben worden ist. Mag es im Einzelfall sein wie es will, bei Edels Interpretation muß von *zwei* Nomina ausgegangen werden: von "Ehrung" (in den Beispielen, wo nach Edel das wie **mjn=j** mit unterdrücktem Personalpronomen zu lesen ist) und von "Geehrter" im obigen Beispiel. Auch Ermans "Zeitgenosse" ist nicht ohne Bedenken, wenn man Edels Beispielliste durcharbeitet. Rein gefühlsmäßig erwartet man in einigen Fällen ein Abstraktum à la "Gleichzeitigkeit" oder "Zeitgenössigkeit". Status: Abwarten.

38. **mꜥr** [pl, *allg] wertvolle Steine
[WB II, 49.3; HL1, 328] Beleg: pTurin CG 54301 rt 21.4
Problematik: Unklare Lesung, cf. Condon (1978), S. 104. Status: Abwarten.

39. **mm** *transportieren (*Vieh über Fluß*)
[WB ø; HL1, 332] Beleg: BM 1671 (Stele des Heqa-ib)
Problematik: Cf. Polotsky in JEA 16, S. 197 (pro) und die Diskussion von Fischer in Kush 9, P.51 (contra). Status: Abwarten.

40. **mny** *e. Schmuckstück [cf. **mnj** Rötel]
[WB ø; HL1, 338] Beleg: oDeM 579.16
Problematik: Janssen (1975), S. 309f.; Janssen weist darauf hin, daß der Preis des **mny** zu niedrig sei, um als Preis für ein Menit zu gelten; andererseits ist es immer möglich, daß ein Amulett-Menit diesen geringen Preis erfordert. Status: Abwarten.

41. **mnḫt** *f* [subst] [wohl irrtümliche Schreibung für **mnḫt** Gewand]
[WB II, 88.3; HL1, 341] Beleg: Griffith (1889), T. 11, L. 23
Problematik: Brunner (1937), S. 22, Anm. 50, übersetzt das Wort wohl richtig mit "Kleidern/Gewand", was wohl richtig ist, wenn auch der Kontext keinen Aufschluß gibt. Status: Abwarten.

42. **mnk** (***mnkꜣ**) [subst] (*Fürsorger)
[WB ø; HL1, 343] Beleg: Brüssel E 4985
Problematik: Polotsky (1929), S. 52; Lichtheim (1988), S. 41; Schenkel (1965), Nr. 72–73 übersetzt ohne Anmerkung mit "Versorger"; Clère/Vandier (1948), nos. 18–19, S. 14; Limmé (1979) S. 19 (Photo). Status: Abwarten.

43. **mrt** *f* *Mörser
[WB ø; HL1, 347] Beleg: Jéquier (1921), S. 297f. (F. 781)
Problematik: Für Jequier ist die hieroglyphische Transkription des unklar; diese Meinung kann ich nicht teilen. Status: In HL1 belassen.

44. ***msḥm** [subst]
[WB ø; HL1, 364] Beleg: ZÄS 63, S. 64
Problematik: Das Zeichen ist auf dem Photo nicht sicher identifizierbar. Cf. auch JEA 52, S. 173. Status: Abwarten.

45. **mš** *f* [näg, subst, syll] [viell identisch mit **mšt** Ente
[WB ø; HL1, 367] Beleg: gTheb IV 2157
Problematik: Das Graffito ist grob übersetzbar mit: "Die **mšt** der Leute von der Königsgräberverwaltung ist auf der Holzkohle." Status: Abwarten.

46. **mkbrs** [syll, näg] (?)
[WB ø; HL1, 371] Beleg: Bakir (1966), T. 48
Problematik: In dieser Kolumne sind nur zwei Wörter untereinander angeführt, deren Bedeutung unklar bleibt. Das zweite Wort **gw** ist vermutlich identisch mit dem Wort **gwꜣt** Kleiderkasten (HL1.897). Das vorausgehende **mkbrs** ist ohne Determinativ geschrieben, was die Einordnung in eine semantische Klasse unmöglich macht. Nicht ganz auszuschließen ist die Lesung **m-ʿ kbrs** oder **Kbrs**. Status: Abwarten

47. **mḏꜣt** *f* *Holztafel
[WB ø; HL1, 381] Beleg: pCairo 58053 rt 7 (2 Belege); pCairo 58054 rt 13
Problematik: Das Determinativ ist im Vergleich zum in Zeile 1 nicht sicher, da es am oberen Astende eingerollt ist. Andererseits

ist die Umschreibung mit  ebenfalls nicht sicher, wenn man L. 10 von pCairo 58054 rt heranzieht. Status: Nur neue Belege können die Existenz der **mḏꜣt**-Holztafel sichern.

48.  **nj-ẖnw** *Flußschiffer
[WB ø; HL1, 386] Beleg: Junker (1925–55), Bd. IV, S. 59
Problematik: Junkers Darstellung kann zur Zeit nichts hinzugefügt werden. Status: Abwarten.

49.  **nj-sw** [math] *Volumen [viell als **nj-sw** "er gehört zu" zu übersetzen]
[WB ø; HL1, 386] Beleg: pMoskau E 4676 rt 28.6 (Pyramidenstumpf-Aufgabe); pRhind (= BM 10057–8) 45.2, 46.2.
Problematik: Offenbar haben wir es hier mit einer erstarrten Nisbe-Konstruktion zu tun, die Wortrang erreicht hat. Wegen der Ähnlichkeit mit einer Nisbe ist es bislang nicht als selbständiges Lexem verstanden worden. Für die Auffassung des **nj-sw** als Substantiv (Nomen) spricht, daß hinter **mk** in dem mathematischen Papyrus ein Substantiv folgt (meist allerdings in Begleitung von **pw**). Auch die Belege im math. pRhind geben das Volumen an, doch nicht als Gesamtsumme, sondern als Rechenformel. Status: Nur die Kollegen mit mathematischer Ausrich-tung können eine Entscheidung treffen, ob das Lemma zu Recht existiert.

50.  **nmꜥw-n=k** dein Parteigänger ("einer der dir gegenüber positiv voreingenommen ist")
[WB ø; HL1, 413] Beleg: Gardiner/Sethe (1928), T. IV, L. 2; JEA 52, S. 39ff., T. 9 rt L. 2
Problematik: Gegen das von mir favorisierte "einer, der . . ." bzw. "der (üblicherweise) parteiisch ist in deinem Interesse" wendet Fecht (MDIK 24, S. 122ff. (Exkurs)) ein, daß **nmꜥ** nicht ethisch neutral begünstigen heißt, sondern stets eine ethisch zu mißbilligende Handlung sei. Solche aus allgemeinen Erwägungen heraus gezogenen Schlüsse haben keine entscheidende Beweiskraft. Status: Abwarten.

51.  **nmḥyw** *Freilassung (*von Sklaven*)
[WB ø; HL1, 413] Beleg: Urk IV 1344.13
Problematik: Gegen die Übersetzung von Helck (1961) "Diener *eines kleinen Mannes*" spricht die Schreibung. Status: Die Existenz des Wortes scheint gesichert zu sein, die genaue Bedeutung muß aber noch eruiert werden, wenn neue Belege angeführt werden können.

52. **nrwt** e. Körperteil (*e. Tieres*)
[WB ø; HL1, 1] Beleg: Kitchen (1968ff.), Bd. I, P.94, C. VII.10
Problematik: Obskur, sicherlich nicht-existent. Cf. Kitchen (1993: 2), S. 76. Status: Abwarten.

53. **nsbt** *f* e. Gebäck
[WB II, 334.15; HL1, 424] Beleg: Nelson (1930–64), Bd. III, T. 158, Nr. 1014
Problematik: Vermutlich eine Verschreibung für ein Gebäck. Nelson (1930–64), Bd. III, T. 158, Nr. 1014 weist statt dem ein (mit *sic* gekennzeichnet) auf. Vermutlich ist **dpt** zu lesen. Status: Sicher nicht-existent, deshalb streichen.

54. **ngꜣyt** (**ngyt**) *f* Defloration, Entjungferung
[WB II, 349.10; HL1, 432] Beleg: Amunshymnus Leiden I 350 5.2
Problematik: Quack in BiOr 54 (1997), C. 331, verweist auf Zandee (1947), S. 92, wo statt **ngꜣyt** das Wort **nḏmyt** gelesen wird. Weil mir kein Photo dieses Papyrus zur Einsicht zur Verfügung steht, wird eine Entscheidung vertagt. Status: Abwarten.

55. **rꜣ-wnmw** Futter **smw m** ≈ Gras als Futter
[WB ø; HL1, 439] Beleg: Kitchen (1968ff.), Bd. I, S. 49.11 (Nauri 22)
Problematik: Kitchen (1993), S. 43 übersetzt **rꜣ-wnmw** mit "fowl-reserves", versteht es also ebenfalls als Kompositum. Seine Übersetzung begründet er nicht. Status: Abwarten.

56. **rꜣ-ḏꜣwt** [subst]
[WB ø; HL1, 457] Beleg: CT II 76a
Problematik: Faulkner (1973–8), Bd. 1, S. 95, N.3, bemerkt, daß die Variante aus Meir (M3C) eine Emendation einer korrupten Textstelle, die auf den Särgen von Bersheh noch geschrieben wird, sein könnte. Dem kann man entgegenhalten, daß die bersheanische Sondersammelstelle für Sargtexte vermutlich eher Emendationen vornehmen würde, als die Ortstradition aus Meir.[5] Status: Abwarten.

[5] Cf. Jürgens (1995), S. 83f.

57.  **rw** e. Örtlichkeit
[WB ø; HL1, 460] Beleg: JEA 54, T. VIa, L.1 (Privatsammlung)
Problematik: Obwohl das hieratische Zeichen "liegender Löwe" beschädigt ist, läßt sich eine andere Lesung kaum rechtfertigen. Status: Abwarten.

58.  **hꜣdt** *f* e. Gefäß
[WB ø; HL1, 489] Beleg: oDeM 28
Problematik: Das Wort ist nur durch einen unvollständigen Beleg bekannt, wo das erste Zeichen beschädigt ist. Status: Abwarten, obwohl die Existenz unwahrscheinlich ist.

59. * **ḥꜣ** *Monster, Ungeheuer
[WB ø; HL1, 501] Beleg: Blackman (1914–53), Bd. V, T. 30 (links unten)
Problematik: Für mich ist dieser Beleg nicht durch Photo nachprüfbar; die Bedeutung ist möglich und sinnvoll, aber von Blackman erraten. Status: Abwarten.

60.  **ḥꜣwtj** Protome (*Antlitz Gottes auf Barke oder Gefäßen*) **mꜣꜣ** ≈ die Protome (fig. Antlitz) anschauen
[WB III, 29.1–3; HL1, 508] Beleg: Habachi (1977), S. 58
Problematik: Quacks Einlassung in BiOr 54 (1997), C. 332, ist überzeugend und wird durch den Beleg bei Habachi sehr schön bestätigt. An dem Gefäßrand prankt eine Protome der Göttin Hathor. Status: Existenz ist gesichert.

61.  **ḥwt** *f* Schwein [nur in Ortsnamen belegt; viell **ḥwt-rrj** zu lesen]
[WB ø; HL1, 518] Beleg: Jacquet-Gordon (1962), S. 438, Nr. 14
Problematik: In JEA 14, S. 225, wird der Domänenname als "pig-destroyer" verstanden. Ich selbst dachte an ein durch Einkonsonantenzeichen ausgeschriebenes , was aber bei den bei Jacquet-Gordon aufgelisten Namen als Schreibung nicht belegt ist. Status: Abwarten.

62.  **ḥmyw** [pl] Matrosen, Ruderer [cf. **jrj-js, jrj-qd**]
[WB ø; HL1, 530] Beleg: PT 711a.c
Problematik: Quack in BiOr 54, C. 332, möchte, mit Fischer, ZÄS 93 (1966), S. 56–69, den hinteren Teil dieses Wortes selbständig als

jrj-js lesen. Die beiden Pyramidentextstellen passen nicht recht zu dieser Auffassung: Es ist doch sehr unwahrscheinlich, daß die (göttlichen[6]) "Grabbauer" (**jrj-js**) den Gott Re rudern (PT 711a). Faulkner (1973–8) §711 übersetzt dementsprechend: "It is the sailors who row Re . . .; it is the sailors who convey Re round about the horizon . . .". Wie Kaplony (1966), S. 163, Anm. 215, zu Recht vermerkt, haben wir es hier doch eher mit einer Schreibung für **ḥmyw** "Ruderer" bzw. "Steuerleute" zu tun. Die Frage bleibt offen, inwieweit **ḥmyw** mit **jrj-js** vereinbar ist; denn die Analyse von Fischer ist durchaus überzeugend. Status: Abwarten.

63.  ***ḥr** e. Spiegel (*Bez.*)
[WB ø; HL1, 545] Beleg: Louvre E 10779A
Problematik: Aufgeführt von Liliquist (1979), S. 71. Vermutlich Kurzform von **mꜣꜣ-ḥr/mꜣw-ḥr**. Status: Abwarten, ob sich noch andere Belege für die Kurzform finden.

64.  **ḥst** *f* erhobener, angewinkelter Unterarm [Existenz des Wortes in der Zeit AR-NR nicht gesichert]
[WB III, 160.1; HL1, 559] Beleg: TB (nach Naville), 172.29
Problematik: GM 44, S. 58. Status: Abwarten.

65.  **ḥsꜣ** e. Vogel/Insekt
[WB ø; HL1, 560] Beleg: CT IV 53a
Problematik: Faulkner (1973–8), Bd. I, S. 221, Anm. 2; 782813; 772843. Ich folge in der Analyse Faulkners; die neue alternative Bedeutungseinengung auf "Insekt" basiert auf der Parallele zu **jbꜣyt**. Jedoch ist es durchaus nicht sicher, daß wir es mit einem Substantiv zu tun haben. Status: Abwarten.

66.  **ḥss** [syll, subst]
[WB ø; HL1, 562] Beleg: oDeM 667.6
Problematik: Freistehendes Wort, das gut lesbar ist und wo nichts zu fehlen scheint. Status: Abwarten.

[6] Das Wort wird bei Teti mit dem Horus auf der Standarte determiniert.

67. ***ḥkwn** *e. Käfer
[WB III, 178.1; HL1, 565] Beleg: pEbers 94.21–22
Problematik: Der Diskussion in v. Deines/Grapow (1959), S. 383, ist nichts hinzuzufügen. Status: Abwarten.

68. **ḥknwt** *f* *Salbung; *gesalbte Stelle [var. mit]
[WB ø; HL1, 565] Beleg: CT II, 74c
Problematik: Faulkner (1973–8), Bd. I, S. 94, Anm. 7; van der Molen (2000), s.v., übersetzt wie **ḥknw** "praise". Status: Abwarten.

69. **ḥḏt** *f* [subst]
[WB III, 211.20–21; HL1, 575] Beleg: LD II, S. 119 (Obelisk von Abgig); pHearst 11.8
Problematik: Der Diskussion in v. Deines/Grapow (1959), S. 385, ist nichts hinzuzufügen. Status: Abwarten.

70. **ẖꜣw** *Perücke [wahrscheinlich identisch mit **ẖꜣw** Kräuter]
[WB ø; HL1, 580] Beleg: CT VI, 5a
Problematik: Faulkner (1973–8), Bd. II, S. 110, N.13. Bidoli (1976), S. 59–60, vermerkt richtig, daß das Wort **ẖꜣw** "Kräuter" vorliegt. Das Determinativ "Haar" wird dem Wort beigegeben, weil die theologische Sinngebung die Kräuter als die "Haare von Osiris" interpretieren will. Status: Streichen.

71. **ẖꜣb** e. Stoff *od.* Kleidungsstück
[WB ø; HL1, 582] Beleg: Pendlebury (1951), S. 173, Nr. 12; Tfb. T. 85
Problematik: Die Schreibung ist nicht nachprüfbar. Es wurde keine Ähnlichkeit zu anderen Wörtern in den verschiedenen Sprachstufen erkannt. Status: Abwarten.

72. **ẖꜣn** e. Fleischstück
[WB ø; HL1, 583] Beleg: Pendlebury (1951), S. 173, Nr. 217; Tfb. T. 93
Problematik: Die Schreibung ist nicht nachprüfbar. Es wurde keine Ähnlichkeit zu anderen Wörtern in den verschiedenen Sprachstufen erkannt. Status: Abwarten.

73. **ẖwtj** [vb] (*füllen *Topf*)
[WB ø; HL1, 589] Beleg: pBM III, Txb S. 17, Tfb T. 7a (rt 8.8)
Problematik: Lesung ist nicht zu bezweifeln, selbst wenn das Verb eine ungewöhnliche Bauweise aufweist, was auf einen Fehler hinweist. Für die angenomme Bedeutung liegt aber keine ausreichende Begründung vor. Status: Abwarten.

74. **ẖnrtt** *f* *Verschwörung (**Haremsverschwörung*)
[WB IV 296.9; HL1, 605] Beleg: Urk. IV 139
Problematik: Quack (BiOr 54, 1997, C. 332) lehnt die Existenz des Wortes mit Hinweis auf Posener (RdE 10, S. 92f.) ab. Posener sieht in der Stelle eine Verschreibung des ersten für und möchte sie verstehen in etwa wie **wꜣj=f r tr n rqt** "il est entré dans une période de dissidence." Meines Erachtens ist die Emendation dieser Stelle nicht begründet genug und eher unwahrscheinlich. Das doppelte ist kein Hindernisgrund, wenn wir ein Nomen auf der Basis einer weiblichen Nisbe annehmen. Status: Abwarten.

75. **ẖnr** (**ẖl**) [näg, syll] *verweigern, zurückziehen *in:* ≈ **ḏrt=f** *seine Hand verweigern [viell identisch mit **ẖnr** zerstreuen]
[WB III, 298.15; HL1, 605] Beleg: Ani 4,9 (nach Quack)
Problematik: **ẖnr** im Sinne von "verweigern" könnte durchaus eine abgeleitete Bedeutung von "zerstreuen" sein. Das Verständnis und die Übersetzung unserer Stelle in Quack (1994), S. 99, Anm. 51, ist aber deutlich besser: "Verschleudere nicht mit deiner (eigenen) Hand (dein Habe) an unbekannte Leute". Status: Zu streichen.

76. **ẖnẖ** [näg, syll] e. Ackergerät
[WB III, 299.3; HL1, 606] Beleg: pAnast II 7.1
Problematik: Nach Fischer-Elfert in SAK 10, S. 149, ist das Wort im Zusammenhang mit oDeM 4.4 und 14.6 zu sehen. Die Schreibungen pChB IV vs 3.12, pChB IV vs 6.2 und pChB V rt 7.10 seien vermittelnde Schreibungen eines Wortes, dessen Konsonantenbestand noch nicht eindeutig bestimmt werden kann. Der neue Eintrag in HL1 wird heißen:
***ẖnẖ** [näg, syll] e. *Ackergerät; *Riemen(schaft) Status: Abwarten.

77. **ḫrpr** [syll, näg, subst *f*]
[WB ø; HL1, 618] Beleg: pBM 10298 rt II.2 (JEA 54, T. 18a, L. 4)
Problematik: Die hieroglyphische Umschreibung ist noch nicht zu verbessern, obwohl das Wort ein verdächtiges Aussehen aufweist. Inhaltlich könnte es sich in L. 1–7 um einen grammatischen Kommentar handeln. Status: Abwarten.

78. **ẖʿw** e. Gefäß [cf. **ẖpʿw**]
[WB ø; HL1, 632] Beleg: Gardiner/Peet/Černý (1952–5), Bd. II, S. 128, N.p.; Gardine/Peet/Černý (1952–5), Bd. I, T. 46 (123B.4)
Problematik: Vermutlich ist **kꜣpw** "Räuchergerät" zu lesen, wobei das das -Zeichen repräsentiert. Merkwürdigerweise wurde das angeblich nachher durch einen Vergleich mit dem Photo hineingebracht. In der Aufzählung folgt **snṯr** "Weihrauch". Status: Zu streichen.

79. **ẖms** (**šms**) e. Räucherwerk [Existenz wegen der Schreibung im MR nicht gesichert]
[WB III, 367.7; HL1, 633] Beleg: CT VI 122a, VI 370k
Problematik: 783200. In CT VI 122a, wo **ẖms** (**šms**) parallel nach sncr "Weihrauch" folgt, ist die Bedeutung "Räucherwerk" sicherlich überdenkenswert. Status: Abwarten.

80. **sꜣḥw** [pl] *Lehnsarbeiter
[WB ø; HL1, 661] Beleg: pRam D vs
Problematik: Der Beleg von Quirke (1990), S. 193, für **sꜣḥw** "estate workers (?)" (cf. Anm. 11) ist in HL1 verarbeitet worden. Der Hinweis auf S. 146 mit Anm. 31 habe ich aber übersehen. In Anm. 31 wird auf den besten Beleg Helck (1995), S. 62, L. 8, hingewiesen, der als einziger sicherer Beleg gelten darf. Insgesamt sind nun drei Belege bekannt: Helck (s.o.); pRam D vs 7; pBrooklyn 35.1446 (Hayes (1972), T. VI (Insertion C, L. 4) verbessert in Quirke (1990), S. 145.). Quirke bemerkt zur Übersetzung "donated people (?)", es seien vielleicht besonders Personen, die einer Domäne zugewiesen werden, die durch eine Stiftungsurkunde ins Leben gerufen wurde. Status: Existenz gesichert, wenn auch die Bedeutung noch unklar bleibt.

81. , , det. **swnw** (**zwnw**) Arzt **ḥrj** ≈ **w m pr-Ptḥ** Chefarzt im Ptahtempel
[WB ø; HL1, 677] Beleg: Ghalioungui (1983), S. 27 (Nr. 76)
Problematik: Diskussion des Titels in RdE 25, S. 77. Status: Abwarten.

82. **sbẖt** *f* *e. Mineral
[WB ø; HL1, 689] Beleg: pChB IV vs. 8,4
Problematik: Existenz möglich. Status: Abwarten.

83. **spwt** (***sprwt**) Art Rinder
[WB ø; HL1, 691] Beleg: ASAE 52, S. 331; Kitchen (1968ff.), Bd. IV, S. 28.9
Problematik: Das obere Drittel des Zeichenquadrats zerstört; unklar. Status: Abwarten.

84. **spks** [näg, syll] e. Tier (*mit Fell*)
[WB ø; HL1, 695] Beleg: oDeM 1575. 6
Problematik: Nicht durch Photo nachprüfbar; offenbar in Liste mit seltenen Tieren. Status: Abwarten.

85. **sm** Sem-Priester ≈ **Skr** Sem des Sokar [Existenz und/oder Abgrenzung zu **sm/stm** nicht gesichert]
[WB IV, 121.4–7; HL1, 700] Beleg: passim
Problematik: JARCE 3, S. 28: Nach H.G. Fischer sollte **sm** nicht mit dem **stm** verwechselt werden. Status: Abwarten.

86. **smꜣ** e. Götterbarke
[WB IV, 124.12+121.15; HL1, 700+703] Beleg: pTur (P/R) T. 86.4
Problematik: Condon (1978), S. 36, hat plausibel nachgewiesen, daß das Wort **smꜣ** in Wirklichkeit (**m**)**sktt** zu lesen ist. Status: Streichen.

87. **smj** peitschen, züchtigen
[WB IV 130.10; HL1, 705] Beleg: Urk. VII, S. 54.15
Problematik: Die Beurteilung der Stelle in Quack (1992), S. 127, Anm. 20, können wir uns nicht anschließen. Die Belegstelle (Urk. VII, S. 54.15) (+Nomen) wird transkribiert als **jnk smj ḫwj ḫꜣw m rqww**, was mit "ich bin ein Prügel, der Tausende von Aufrührern schlug." übersetzt wurde. Die traditionelle Lesung wäre **jnk smj ḫꜣw m rqww** mit der Übersetzung "ich bin einer, der Tausende von Aufrührern peitscht." Das Zeichen wird hierbei als Determinativ zu **smj** verstanden und nicht als Abbreviation des Wortes **ḥwj**. Die Lesung **ḥwj** für alleinstehendes wäre ungewöhnlich, allerdings vermutet Montet in Kemi 3, S. 49, Anm. 2, unter dem Zeichen ein kleines oder ein Pfahl. Auf der anderen

Seite wäre die Übersetzung "Prügel" für **smj** neu (dann besser schon "Peitsche"). Der wichtigste Einwand gegen die Lösung von Quack ist folgender: Die Struktur der anderen mit **jnk** eingeleiteten Sätze in unmittelbarer Umgebung (Zeilen 12, 19 und 21) ist vom Typ **jnk** +Partizip + Objektnomen + Adverbialphrase eingeleitet mit **m**. Die Wahrscheinlichkeit, daß wir es hier mit einem Partizip des Verbs **smj** "peitschen" zu tun haben, wird durch diese Parallelität der Umgebung sogar noch gestärkt. Status: Abwarten.

88.  **smsmtj** e. Tier [cf. **snmmtj**]
[WB IV 130.10; HL1, 710] Beleg: CT V 89e
Problematik: Cf. unten unter **snmmtj**. Status: Abwarten.

89.  **snww** Papyrusglätter
[WB ø; HL1, 715] Beleg: Steindorff (1896/1901), T. 5, S. 30; Weber (1969), S. 56, Anm. 337–8.
Problematik: Die hieroglyphische Lesung ist nicht sicher. das  versieht Steindorff mit einem Fragezeichen, aber auch die beiden  sehen eher wie  aus, die aus Platzmangel gequetscht wurden. Status: Abwarten.

90.  **snꜣ** (?)
[WB ø; HL1, 716] Beleg: Brunner (1986), S. 110
Problematik: Nach Brunner Meinung ist eine sichere Lesung möglich, ihr kann ich mich nicht anschließen. Status: Die Existenz des Wortes ist eher unwahrscheinlich. Abwarten.

91.  **snm-rnpt** *Jahresübel [Schreibung aus 2 Varianten zusammengesetzt]
[WB ø; HL1, 720] Beleg: GM 49, S. 81f.
Problematik: Die Diskussion von Westendorf hat Bestand. Das Wort **snm-rnpt** könnte eine Korruption des richtigeren **jꜣdt-rnpt** "Jahresseuche" sein. Status: Das Wort sollte primär als ein Phantomwort verstanden werden, das durch Mißverständnis von ägyptischen Schreibern in den ägyptischen Text hineingekommen ist. Doch ist die Angleichung so gut gelungen, daß die Nicht-Existenz nicht bewiesen werden kann. Die vorsichtigere Vorgehensweise ist sicherlich die, es zunächst im HL1 mit dem üblichen Vermerk zu belassen.

92.  **snmtj (snmmtj)** e. Tier [cf. **smsmtj**, *viell* cf. **snbtt**] [WB IV, 165,13; HL1, 720] Beleg: CT V 89e.
Problematik: Der Schwanz dieses Tieres soll am Heck das Schiff bewachen. Status: Abwarten.

93.  **snsnt** *f* *Duft
[WB ø; HL1, 723] Beleg: CT V 115l—m, CT VII 221n, CT VII 155h
Problematik: Rößler-Köhler (1979), S. 166 (L. 104), S. 209. Status: Abwarten.

94.  ***sḥ-ḫ3j-sẖt** *e. Pflanze ("Laube hinterm Feld")
[WB ø; HL1, 734] Beleg: Edel (1961–3), Bd. I, S. 251+254
Problematik: Cf. Erklärung oben unter **jbw-sẖt**. Status: Vermutlich als Pflanzenname nicht-existent, deshalb im HL1 streichen.

95.  **sẖmẖm** [*vb]
[WB ø; HL1, 746] Beleg: PT 1950c (Spruch 667B, nach Faulkner)
Problematik: Hinter dem Wort ist eine Zerstörung, so daß die Umgebung unklar zu bestimmen ist. Status: Abwarten.

96.  **ssnj** [*kaus*] *ähnlich sein
[WB ø; HL1, 755] Beleg: CT I, 289b
Problematik: Faulkner (1973–8), Bd. I, S. 64, Anm. 32, übersetzt mit "ähnlich sein", während van der Molen (2000), S. 546 "conceal, make unknowable" aufführt. Eine Entscheidung vermag ich nicht zu treffen. Status: Abwarten.

97. 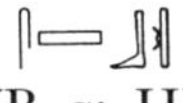 **sšb** *erleuchten (*besser*: [subst])
[WB ø; HL1, 762] Beleg: Roeder (1938), S. 22, §75.2, T. 23
Problematik: Die Übersetzung im HL1 ist falsch, da wir es mit ziemlicher Sicherheit mit einem Nomen zu tun haben. Die Umgebung lautet:  "du bist wie Re, der auf . . . des Horizontes ist. Die Lesung des u scheint mir nicht sicher. Andererseits vergleiche das Wort **sbš** *klar sein (*Himmel*) (HL1, 689). Status: Abwarten.

98. **sšm** *schützen (*Gesicht, Augen vor zu starker Sonneneinstrahlung*)
[WB IV, 285,4; HL1, 763] Beleg: Sonnenlitanei I 42 und II 40 (37)

Problematik: 783827:  (lect. douteuse) dans tous le cas on pourrait comprendre <abriter> (le visage, les yeux) d'une lumière trop violente. Status: Abwarten.

99. 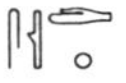 **sqd** schlafen lassen
[WB ø; HL1, 771] Beleg: CT V 211c
Problematik: Von Zandee (1960), S. 84 stammt der Beleg und die Übersetzung. Die Übersetzung von Faulkner (1973–8) "who conveys away souls" ist aber überzeugender. Status: In HL1 streichen.

100.  **skk** (?)
[WB ø; HL1, 775] Beleg: Davies/Gardiner (1915), T. 15
Problematik: Die Diskussion in Caminos (1956), S. 10, ist noch immer gültig. Das Wort **skk** steht am Zeilenbeginn und der Ende der vorausgehenden Zeile ist zerstört. Status: Abwarten.

101.  **stꜣy** *siegeln
[WB ø; HL1, 779] Beleg: CT VI, 195d
Problematik: Faulkner (1973–8), Bd. II, S. 183 (Sp. 580), Anm. 3. Status: Abwarten.

102.  **sṯntf** [vb] [cf. **sṯftn**]
[WB ø; HL1, 786] Beleg: CT VII 421c
Problematik: Faulkner (1973–8), Bd. III, P 157, Anm. 3 (Sp 1101) erläutert die Probleme dieser Stelle. Status: Abwarten.

103.  **sdp** [subst]
[WB IV, 393.8; HL1, 789] Beleg: oMicha T. 38, Z.1
Problematik: Erwartet wird **skꜣp** "räuchern lassen", doch läßt sich das hieratische Zeichen kaum als  identifizieren, wenn man nicht eine starke Deformierung des Facsimiles annehmen möchte. Status: Abwarten.

104.  **sḏr** (?) (*in Zshg mit Arbeit an Holzsarg*)
[WB IV, 415.9; HL1, 796] Beleg: oPetrie 4 (= Gardiner/Černý (1957), 62, 3r4)
Problematik: Wahrscheinlich handelt es sich um das Wort **srḏ** "mit Dächsel/Meißel arbeiten" (HL1, 732) mit Lautumstellung oder Lautwandel. Status: Abwarten.

105. **šjp (šp)** [näg, *syll] (?)
[WB ø; HL1, 805] Beleg: oPetrie 28 (= Gardiner/Černý (1957), 8, 7vs1)
Problematik: Das Wort steht frei ohne Zusammenhang mit anderen Wörtern. Status: Abwarten.

106. **šw** *m* [näg, subst]
[WB ø; HL1, 811] Beleg: pBM 10373 vs 6
Problematik: Cf. Janssen (1990), S. 45, Anm. 18. Es könnte sich um das Wort **šw** "(leerer) Papyrus" handeln. Status: Abwarten, obwohl das Wort vermutlich nicht-existent ist.

107. **šbb** *Röhrenperle [viell identisch mit **šbw**]
[WB ø; HL1, 813] Beleg: oCochrane (Coll)
Problematik: Schreibung in Ordnung. Cf. JEA 49, S. 173 Anm. 5; JEA 3, S. 195, Janssen 307. Status: Abwarten, aber wohl sichere Variante des älteren **wšbyt**.

108. ,det. , det. **šdw** *Floß
[WB ø; HL1, 845] Beleg: JEA 50, S. 27 (Admonitions)
Problematik: Helck hat mir mündlich die Nicht-Existenz dieses Wortes versichert und eine Ersatzbedeutung angegeben, die mir leider entfallen ist. Status: Abwarten.

109. **qꜣqꜣ** e. Spiel (*besser*: *Gewichtheben)
[WB ø; HL1, 850] Beleg: Decker (1994), T. 346 (P5.5)
Problematik: Nach Touny/Wenig (1969), S. 36, handelt es bei diesem Spiel um Gewichtheben. Status: Abwarten, da der Beleg für mich nicht nachprüfbar ist.

110. **qfꜣt** **f* [subst] (*in Zshg mit Türschloß*)
[WB V, 32.8; HL1, 855] Beleg: pH500 rt 2,12 (pBM 10060)
Problematik: Die Lesung mit an Stelle von zu verwerfen. Die Identifzierung mit **qrꜣt** "Riegel" wird im allgemeinen favorisiert, was m.E. die beste Erklärung darstellt. Status: Abwarten.

111. **tsm** e. (kleineres) Schiff
[WB V, 328.15; HL1, 939] Beleg: pTurin 1972.5 (= LRL 7, 12)
Problematik: Spiegelbergs Idee, in dem Wort eine Schreibvariante von **rms** zu sehen (cf. LRL 7a), ist nicht zwingend, weil rms offenbar eine Art "Floß" ist, welches man kaum schicken kann, um jemandem abzuholen.[7] Allenfalls müßte man dann an dieser Stelle mit Sarkasmus, Ironie oder Argot rechnen. Status: Abwarten.

112. **ttm** [näg, syll] e. Pflanze
[WB ø; HL1, 942] Beleg: pLeiden I 343+345 vs VI.10 (Massart (1954), S. 63, Anm. 319)
Problematik: Lesung nach Massart nicht sicher. Status: Abwarten, obwohl das Wort vermutlich nicht existiert.

113. **ṯꜣt** *f* weiblicher junger Vogel
[WB ø; HL1, 943] Beleg: Brunner (1986), S. 110
Problematik: Das Wort wurde offensichtlich eigens für die Königin Hatschepsut gebildet, so daß die Existenz wohl als sicher gelten kann, wenn auch das Wort selbst nur in einem eingeschränkten Gebrauch verwendet wurde. Status: Im HL1 belassen, aber mit dem Hinweis auf Hatschepsut und eventuell der Klassifizierung als [Kunstwort].

114. **ṯjst** *f* Flamme
[WB ø; HL1, 950] Beleg: CT III, 52a
Problematik: Faulkner (1973–8), Bd. I, S. 149, Anm. 12. Status: Abwarten.

115. **ṯsw** [pl] Teile von der Tür
[WB ø; HL1, 963] Beleg: Vandier (1950), S. 232
Problematik: Die Existenz des Wortes scheint sicher zu sein, nur ist es fraglich, ob das Wort ein gängiger Begriff, ein terminus technicus der Handwerker oder eher eine ad hoc Bildung ist, um dem Gott Neheb-kau einzubringen. Status: Das Wort ist im HL1 zu belassen, wenn auch der Status des Wortes und die Bedeutung noch unklar sind.

[7] Das Wort rms ist vom Neuen Reich bis zur griechisch-römischen Zeit durchgängig belegt. Auch im Demotischen gibt es aufschlußreiche Belege. Im modernen Arabisch ist die hocharabische Form rmc und eine Dialektform *ramus* bei Winkler (1936), S. 18, T. 87.1 zu nennen. Eine Bearbeitung aller Belege steht noch aus.

116. **dwd** tragen (*jdn*)
[WB ø; HL1, 973] Beleg: CT II, 40b
Problematik: Faulkner (1973–8), Bd. I, S. 87, Anm. 34; ZÄS 79, S. 45 Anm. 3; ZÄS 101, S. 64, L. 36b; van der Molen (2000), S. 787. Die Bearbeiter dieser Textstelle sind sich darin weitgehend einig, daß es sich zuvörderst um eine Verschreibung oder Variante des Verbs **wdj** "setzen" handeln muß. Status: Abwarten.

117. **ḏnḏd** Flamme, Hitze [viell cf. **ḏnḏnt**]
[WB ø; HL1, 1009] Beleg: CT IV 328g
Problematik: Faulkner (1973–8), Bd. I, S. 271 (Sp. 336), Anm. 13. Vermutlich ist das Wort als zu begreifen, das eine Variante zu bilden dürfte. Status: Existenz eher unwahrscheinlich, doch ist es besser abzuwarten.

118. **ḏḥꜣ** *Abgabe
[WB V, 605.8; HL1, 1014] Beleg: Urk. I 211.14+17 (2 Belege)
Problematik: Die noch immer geltende Diskussion findet sich in MDIK 16, S. 133, Anm. 7. Status: Abwarten.

119. **ḏsr** rufen [cf. **ḏsw**]
[WB ø; HL1, 1015] Beleg: CT VI 104f.
Problematik: Faulkner (1973–8), Bd. II, S. 147 (Sp 516), Anm. 8. Sichere Variante zu **ḏsw** "rufen"; eine dialektale Variation ist jedoch eher unwahrscheinlich. Status: Als Lemma streichen, ein Verweis von **ḏsr** zu **ḏsw** sollte genügen.

120. ***ḏtn** (***ḏt**) e. Götter-Barke [Existenz und Lesung des Wortes nicht gesichert]
[WB ø; HL1, 1016] Beleg: CT VII 488f.
Problematik: Die Schreibung der Särge B5C und B1Be erinnert an eine Schreibung für **ḏt** "Ewigkeit", die seit den Pyramidenzeiten belegt ist. Der Name "Ewigkeit" für eine Götterbarke scheint passend zu sein. Die Schreibung des Wortes bei B1P läßt an dieser Erklärung freilich Zweifel aufkommen, so daß doch von einer Dreiradikalität auszugehen ist. Status: Abwarten.

Lemma zu streichen

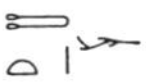 **ṯt** *f* [subst] [HL1, 943] ist zu streichen, da die Belege es als Schreibung für **ṯt** "Tisch" ausweisen.

Literaturverzeichnis

EAG • Edel, Elmar, Altägyptische Grammatik, 2 Bde, AnOr 34 u. 39, 1955 u. 1964 EAG.

HL1 • Hannig, Rainer, Großes Handwörterbuch Ägyptisch-Deutsch: d. Sprache der Pharaonen (2800–950 v. Chr.). Kulturgeschichte der antiken Welt 64, 1995 HL1.

77xxxx • cf. Meeks, Dimitri, Année lexicographique I (1977), Paris 1980.

78xxxx • cf. Meeks, Dimitri, Année lexicographique II (1978), Paris 1981.

79xxxx • cf. Meeks, Dimitri, Année lexicographique III (1979), Paris 1982.

Assmann (Jan): 1991 Assmann, Jan/Barthelmeß, Petra, Das Grab des Amenemope (TT 41) [Textband] Theben 3.

Bakir (Abd el Mohsen): 1966 The Cairo Calendar (N. 86637).

Barns (John W. B.): 1956 Five Ramesseum Papyri, Oxford.

Bidoli (Dino): 1976 Die Sprüche der Fangnetze in den altägyptischen Sargtexten, ADAIK 9, Glückstadt.

Blackman (Aylward M.): 1914–53 The Rock Tombs of Meir IVI, 6 Bde, ASE 22–25, 28–29.

Borghouts (J.F.): 1971 The Magical Texts of Papyrus Leiden I 348: Oudheidkundige Mededelingen uit het Rijksmuseum van Oudheden te Leiden: N.R. 5.

——: 1978 Ancient Egyptian Magical Texts: Religious Texts Translation Series NISABA 9.

Brunner (Hellmut): 1937 Die Texte aus den Gräbern der Herakleopolitenzeit von Siut mit Übersetzung und Erläuterungen, AF 5.

——: 1986 Die Geburt des Gottkönigs, Studien zur Überlieferung eines altägyptischen Mythos, AA 10, 2. Auflage.

Burkard (Günter): 1977 Textkritische Untersuchungen zu ägyptischen Weisheitslehren des Alten und Mittleren Reiches, AA 34.

Caminos (Ricardo A.): 1956 Literary Fragments in the Hieratic Script, Oxford.

Clère/Vandier: 1948 Textes de la Première Periode Intermédiaire et de la XIème Dynastie, fasc. I, BAe 10.

Condon (Virginia): 1978 Seven Royal Hymns of the Ramesside Period. Papyrus Turin CG 54031. München-Berlin.

Davies (Norman de Garis): 1903–08 The Rock Tombs of El Amarna, 6 Bde, ASE 13–18.

Davies/Gardiner: 1915 The Tomb of Amenemhet (No. 82), TTS I.

Decker (Wolfgang): 1994 Bildatlas zum Sport im alten Agypten: Corpus der bildlichen: Quellen zu Leibesübungen, Spiel, Jagd, Tanz und verwandten Themen; Teil 1: Text; Teil 2: Abbildungen Handbuch der Orientalistik: Abt. 1: Der Nahe und der Mittlere Osten; Bd. 14.

v. Deines/Grapow: 1959 Wörterbuch der ägyptischen Drogennamen. Grundriss der Medizin der Alten Agypter VI. Berlin.

Drenkhahn (Rosemarie): 1976 Die Handwerker und ihre Tätigkeiten im alten Agypten, AA 31.

Edel (Elmar): 1961–3 Zu den Inschriften auf den Jahreszeitenreliefs der "Weltkammer" aus dem Sonnenheiligtum des Niuserre, I–II, 8, NAWG.
Faulkner (Raymond O.): 1969 Supplement of Hieroglyphic Texts, Oxford 1969 AEPT Suppl.
——: 1973–8 The Ancient Egyptian Coffin Texts. 3 Bde, Warminster.
Fischer-Elfert (Hans-Werner): 1986 Die satirische Streitschrift des Papyrus Anastasi I. Übersetzung und Kommentar. AgAb 44. Wiesbaden.
Fischer-Elfert (Hans-Werner): 1986:2 Literarische Ostraka der Ramessidenzeit in Übersetzung, KAT. Wiesbaden.
Fisher (Clarence Stanley): 1924 The Minor Cemetery at Giza, Philadelphia.
Gardiner (Alan H.): 1931 Description of the Hieratic Papyrus Chester Beatty n. 1, Oxford.
——: 1935 Hieratic Papyri in the British Museum, 3. Series: Chester Beatty Gift, Ed. Alan H. Gardiner, 2 Bde, London.
——: 1947 Ancient Egyptian Onomastica, 3 Bde, London.
Gardiner/Sethe: 1928 Egyptian Letters to the Dead. London.
Gardiner/Peet/Černý: 1952–5 The Inscriptions of Sinai, 2 Bde, EEF 45, 2.Auflage
——: 1957 Hieratic Ostraca, Bd I, Oxford.
Ghalioungui (Paul): 1983 The Physicians of Pharaonic Egypt. Kairo.
Goedicke/Wente: 1962 Ostraka Michaelides, Wiesbaden.
Graefe (Erhart): 1971 Untersuchungen zur Wortfamilie bj3. Diss Köln.
Griffith (Francis Llewellyn): 1889 The Inscriptions of Siut and Der Rifeh, London.
Griffith/Newberry: 1895 El Bersheh, Band 2, ASE IV.
Habachi (Labib): 1972 The Second Stela of Kamose, ADAIK 8, Glückstadt Habachi, Kamose.
——: 1977 Tavole d'offerta, are e bacili da libagione, n. 22001–22067, Torino.
Hassan (Ali): 1976 Stöcke und Stäbe im pharaonischen Agypten, MAS 33.
Hayes (William C.): 1972 A Papyrus of the Late Middle Kingdom in the Brooklyn Museum, BMI 5, New York 1955, 1972.
Helck (Wolfgang): 1961 Urkunden der 18. Dynastie: Übersetzung zu den Heften 17–22 Urkunden des ägyptischen Altertums.
——: 1970 Der Text des "Nilhymnus", KAT.
——: 1977 Die Lehre für König Merikare: KAT.
——: 1995 Historisch-biographische Text der 2. Zwischenzeit und neue Texte der 18. Dynastie: Nachträge. KAT 6, 2. Auflage.
Hornung (Erik) Das Amduat. Die Schrift des verborgenen Raumes, Wiesbaden, AA 7,2 (Kommentar).
Jacquet-Gordon (H.K.): 1962 Les Noms des domaines funéraires sous l'Ancien Empire Egyptien, BdE 34.
Janssen (Jac J.): 1975 Commodity Prices from the Ramessid Period, Leiden.
——: 1990 Late Ramesside Letters and Communications: Hieratic Papyri in the British Museum 6.
——: 1921 Les Frises d'Objets des Sarcophages du Moyen Empire, MIFAO 47.
Junker (Hermann): 1925–55 Bericht über die von der Akademie der Wissenschaften in Wien auf gemeinsame Kosten mit Dr. Wilhelm Pelizäus unternommenen Grabungen auf dem Friedhof des AR bei den Pyramiden von Giza, 12 Bde, DAWW 69–75.
Jürgens (Peter): 1995 Grundlinien einer Überlieferungsgeschichte der altägyptischen Sargtexte: Stemmata und Archetypen der Sprachgruppen 30–32 + 33–37, 75(–83), 162 + 164, 225 + 226 und 343 + 345 GOF 31.
Kaplony (Peter): 1966 Kleine Beiträge zu den Inschriften der ägyptischen Frühzeit, AA 15.
Kitchen (Kenneth A.): 1968ff. Ramesside Inscriptions, 7 Bde, Oxford.

——: 1993 Ramesside inscriptions, translated and annotated, Translations: Vol. 1: Ramesses I, Sethos I and contemporaries.
——: 1993:2 Ramesside inscriptions, translated and annotated, Translations: Notes and comments; Vol. 1: Ramesses I, Sethos I and contemporaries.
Lichtheim (Miriam): 1988 Ancient Egyptian Autobiographies Chiefly of the Middle Kingdom: A Study and an Anthology. OBO 84.
Liliquist (Christine): 1979 Ancient Egyptian Mirrors from the Earliest Times through the Middle Kingdom. MAS 27.
Limme (Luc): 1979 Stèles Égyptiennes: Guides du Département Égyptien 4.
Luft (Ulrich): 1992 Die chronologische Fixierung des Mittleren Reiches nach dem Tempelarchiv von Illahun: [Österreichische Akademie der Wissenschaften; phil.-hist. Klasse: Sitzungsberichte; 598] Veröffentlichungen der Ägyptischen Kommission der Österreichischen Akademie.
Massart (Adhémar): 1954 The Leiden Magical Papyrus I 343 + I 345: OMRO: N.R. 3.
van der Molen (Rami): 2000 A Hieroglyphic Dictionary of Egyptian Coffin Texts, Leiden.
Montet (Pierre): 1941 Tanis, Paris.
Nelson (Harold Hayden): 1930–64 Medinet Habu, 7 Bde, OIP 8, 9, 23, 51, 83, 84, 93, Chicago.
Osing (Jürgen): 1992 Das Grab des Nefersecheru in Zawyet Sultan: AV 88.
Peet (Thomas Eric): 1930 The Great Tomb Robberies of the Twentieth Egyptian Dynasty, 2 Bde, Oxford.
——: 1970 The Rhind mathematical papyrus.: British Museum 10057 and 10058. Introduction, transcription translation and commentary.
Pendlebury (J.D.S.): 1951 The City of Akhenaten III. The Central City and the Official Quarters 1926/27 and 1931/36, EEF 44.
Polotsky (Hans Jakob): 1929 Zu den Inschriften der 11. Dynastie, UGAA XI, Leipzig.
Quack (Joachim F.): 1992 Studien zur Lehre für Merikare: GOF 23.
——: 1994 Die Lehren des Ani: e. neuägyptischer Weisheitstext in seinem kulturellen Umfeld. OBO 141.
Quirke (Stephen): 1990 The Administration of Egypt in the Late Middle Kingdom.
Ranke (Hermann): 1935–77 Die altägyptischen Personennamen. Glückstadt.
Roeder (Günther): 1938 Der Felsentempel von Bet El-Wali, Temples Immergés, Kairo.
Rossi/Pleyte: 1869–76 Papyrus de Turin, Facsimilés par Francesco Rossi et publ. par Willem Pleyte, Leiden 1981.
Rößler-Köhler (Ursula): 1979 Kapitel 17 des ägyptischen Totenbuches, GOF 10.
Scharff (Alexander): 1936 Der historische Abschnitt der Lehre für König Merikarê, SBAW.
Schenkel (Wolfgang): 1965 Memphis—Herakleopolis—Theben: Die epigraphischen Zeugnisse der 7.–11. Dynastie Agyptens. AA 12.
Schott (Siegfried): 1990 Bücher und Bibliotheken im alten Agypten: Verzeichnis der Buch- und Spruchtitel und der Termini technici:/von Siegfried Schott. Aus d. Nachlass niedergeschr. von Erika Schott, mit e. Wortindex von A. Grimm.
Steindorff (Georg): 1896/1901 Grabfunde des Mittleren Reiches in den Königlichen Museen Berlin.
Struve (V.V.): 1930 Mathematischer Papyrus des Staatlichen Museums der Schönen Künste in Moskau, Quellen und Studien zur Geschichte der Mathematik, Abt. A, Bd 1, Berlin.
Touny/Wenig: 1969 Der Sport im Alten Agypten, Leipzig 1969.
Vandier (Jacques): 1950 Mo'alla, La Tombe d'Ankhtifi et la Tombe de Sebekhotep, BdE 18.

Ward (William A.): 1982 Index of Egyptian Administrative and Religious Titles of the Middle Kingdom. American University of Beirut.
Weber (Manfred): 1969 Beiträge zur Kenntnis des Schrift- und Buchwesens der alten Agypter.
Winkler (Hans Alexander): 1936 Ägyptische Volkskunde. Stuttgart.
Zandee (Jan): 1947 De Hymnen aan Amon van Papyrus Leiden I 350, OMRO 28.
——: 1960 Death as an Enemy: Studies in the History of Religions 5.

TIME PARADOXES IN RELIGIOUS LITERATURE

† László Kákosy
(ELTE, Budapest)

Werner Vycichl's many-sided and comprehensive scholarly activity comprised even recent Egyptian folklore. In *Mélanges Adolphe Gutbub*[1] he published an article entitled *Un royaume dans un pot de lentilles. Une histoire de magie copte recuillie en 1936 à Farchout (Haute Égypte). L'origine du mot* hik "*magie*". The story relates that an old monk, who had practised magic in his younger years, heard a knocking on the door in the desert monastery where he was living. He saw a deacon standing at the entrance, and the visitor implored the former sorcerer to instruct him in magical arts. After some hesitation the monk seemed to agree but first of all he wanted to put the deacon to a test. He had to go to the kitchen and look after a pot of lentils on the fireplace lest it run over.

While watching the boiling water and the lentils dancing in it, the deacon obviously fell in a kind of hypnotic state. He found himself in a town he had never seen before. The people there acclaimed him king of the country and he married the daughter of the former ruler. His happiness was, however, embittered by the lack of children. He sent for the magician-monk and asked for his help. The magician promised him to help on condition that he would come into possession of half of his future descendants. When a son was born to the ruler's wife, he forgot his pledge to the magician. One day, however, the latter appeared in the royal palace and summoned the king to keep his word. The king tried in vain to reason with him to accept an extension of time until he would receive another child, the magician handed over him a knife to cut his son in two. When the king gave the order to throw him in prison, all of sudden, everything changed and he became again a deacon and saw the lentils having run out. He had to realise that his brilliant career was nothing more than imagination or a dream. Furthermore, as he was not able to stand the test, he lost the opportunity to have instruction in magic.

[1] Montpellier 1984, 233–7.

The nature of *time* and particularly its duration was always a favoured subject not only of philosophy, religion and science but also of popular imagination. In this tale we are confronted with a case of dilation of time based upon the commonly accepted conception that God has the power to make a whole lifetime or, as in the present case, a long period of years to pass in a twinkling of an eye. The famous passage of the Bible "For a thousand years in thy sight are but as yesterday when it is past, and as a watch in the night."[2] was well-known in Christian communities. The duration of time is not uniform in different spheres of the cosmos, it is not equivalent on earth and in heavens. In the story above an instant of earthly reality corresponds to a long period of an imaginary sphere of existence.

The story-teller of the recent Upper-Egyptian tale is likely to have drawn, through intermediaries unknown to us, from other contemporary or ancient sources too. According to a Moslem legend, a saint in Cairo named Taštūši (or Daštūti, 16. cent.) gave a severe rebuke to a Sultan for his incredulity concerning Mohammed's ascension to heaven on the horse Burāq in one night time. They agreed to play a game of chess with the bet that the Sultan must plunge into a water basin if he loses the game. When the Sultan actually lost, he had to keep his word and merge himself in the water. When he did so, he felt himself to be transformed into a woman. His female form was living in a palace and gave birth to three children. When one day he stepped out from the palace in his imaginary world, he actually emerged from the water and realised that what he experienced as a period of many years was in reality no longer than several seconds. This experience made him believe that the ascension of the Prophet could actually have taken place in a single night.[3]

An analogous tale occurs in one of the versions of the Thousand and One Nights wherein the protagonist is Sultan Mahmoud who comes to be cured of his melancholy in a radical way by a sheikh from the Maghreb. The sheikh instructed him to stare into the water in a basin and when he did so, the sheikh suddenly pushed his head into the water. Like in the stories treated before, the Sultan imagined to encounter many strange adventures (he was dethroned, he took the shape of an ass, etc.), the main point being again that the

---

[2] Psalm 90, 4.

[3] R. Kriss – H. Kriss Heinrich: Volksglaube im Bereich des Islam. I. Wiesbaden 1960, 78.

imaginary long time corresponded to an instant in the material world.[4]

The legend of the Seven Sleepers was undoubtedly widely known in Coptic hagiography. It was translated in several independent versions from the Greek original.[5] Told in a nutshell, it recounts the martyrdom of seven noble youths in Ephesos during the persecution of Christians under Emperor Decius (249–251). When they took refuge from the men of the Emperor in a cave near the city, Decius ordered the entrance of the cave to be walled up with large stones. There they sank into a deep death-like sleep for more than hundred and fifty years. Christ raised them to life under Theodosius II (408–450). When they evoke they thought to have slept no more than one night. One of them went to Ephesos to find that it became a Christian city. When he wanted to pay with the coins of Decius, the people of the city charged him of having discovered a treasure. Later, when the full truth came to light, even Emperor Theodosius came to Ephesos to pay reverence to the resurrected saints. Soon after their waking up, they died again.

Remarkably, the legend of the Christian saints had exercised attraction to the popular mind to such an extent that it became part of Islamic theology and piety and it is treated at great length in *sura 18* of the Qurān. The names of the Aṣḥāb el-Kahf (Companions of the Cave) became words of power in magic and popular piety and were inscribed on drinking cups and trays.[6] They can be read even on a Turkish sword from 1810[7] and still appear on recent amulets.[8]

The motif has been elaborated in modern Egyptian literature by Taufiq el-Ḥakīm in a novel (Ahl el-Kahf) adding a romantic love story to the religious theme.

As seen, the legend was popular in the Middle East and may have been an important agent in inspiring stories with time paradoxes. If compared with the stories related above, one substantial difference must be yet noted. It lies in the inverse relation of real and imaginary time. In the history of the Seven Sleepers—while many years

[4] J.C. Mardrus: Les Milles et une Nuits, Paris 1927 tome 13, 41–53. My thanks are due to Prof. A. Fodor for drawing my attention to this story.

[5] J. Drescher, Three Coptic Legends. Hilaria * Archellites * The Seven Sleepers. Le Caire 1948 VII–VIII.

[6] E.W. Lane: Manners & Customs of the Modern Egyptians, London 1908, 255.

[7] A. Fodor: Amulets from the Islamic World (The Arabist. Budapest Studies in Arabic 2) 1990, pp. 53–4 (no. 94–95. Amulet on white sheet of plastic, metal pendant).

[8] *Ibid.* p. 54 (no. 96).

had come and gone in the real world—, the span of the time of sleeping or death seems to be one night, in contrast to the long fantasy-periods in the tale about Taštūši and the others. The legend of the Seven Sleepers has one of its famous prototypes in the life of the Greek thaumaturge Epimenides. One day when he was looking for a stray sheep, he went into a cave, where he slept for fifty-seven years. When he awoke he thought he had rested for a short time and was perplexed to find a fully changed world.[9]

The scope of this article does not permit to deal with other parallels[10] like the legend of the monk Felix, the tale of a noble youth in the Hungarian Codex Érdy up to Rip Van Winkle. Still an interesting recent example from India is worth quoting.

"There is a local legend that when the engineers were digging to determine the cause of the instability of the terrain (of the temple of Shiva in Benares <Varanasi> at the Manikarnikã Ghat) here they unearthed a yogi seated in an underground cavern. Awakened from his meditation, the yogi was shocked to discover that the golden era of King Rāma and Queen Sitā of Ayodhyā had long passed away, and that the Kali Age had arrived. He leaped up from his long-held seat, plunged into the Ganges, and disappeared."[11]

In Egypt conceptions concerning anomalies of time have a long history. The reversibility of time is first attested as early as in the Pyramid texts,[12] a phenomenon naturally salutary to the deceased causing his rebirth. The fear of confusion of seasons and time units also occurs.[13] Time is far from being constant and the conception of divine time reflects the same notions which underlie Psalm 90,4. Amun is praised in a hymn of Dyn. 18 as follows: "A moment is each day to you, it has passed when you go down."[14] We read again in a Ptolemaic hymn to Sobek: "Eternity (*d̲.t*) is with you as yesterday which passed away."[15] The difference in time units appears in the funerary beliefs too, and the author of the Instruction Addressed

---

[9] Diogenes Laertius I. 109. Augustine tells of apocalyptic fears of the return of Nero in his age. There were people who believed that he did not die but had withdrawn in concealment and would return as the Antichrist. (De Civ. Dei XX.19)

[10] Cf. Handwörterbuch des deutschen Aberglaubens I. 1067.

[11] D.L. Eck, Banaras City of Light, London 1983 (edition in India 1993), 247)

[12] Pyr. 705.

[13] E.g. pAnastasi IV. 10,1ff. (A.H. Gardiner, LEM p. 45.)

[14] Urk. IV 1944, 13–4. Translation of M. Lichtheim: Ancient Egyptian Literature II, Berkeley, Los Angeles, London, p. 87.

[15] P. Bucher: Les hymns à Sobek-Ra. Kêmi I. (1928) col. II. 17, p. 50.

to King Merikaré—probably King Khety—advises his reader not to have trust in the length of the years of his life because the tribunal of the gods in the world beyond views lifetime as an hour.[16] In an inscription in Edfu Horus is addressed with the words "your year gave birth to our years"[17] that is divine years have a preexistence and they differ in quality from earthly time.

The same idea manifests itself in the Coptic gnostic Pistis Sophia when Jesus reveals to Mary Magdalene that one day in the realm of light is the equivalent of a thousand year in the material world (cosmos).[18] Similar ideas seem to underlie Augustin's difficult argumentation on the creation of angels. As he expounds, this could have taken place in a time before measured time came into existence.[19] His reasoning involves that time cannot be supposed to be a homogenous entity.[20]

Returning now to the starting-point of this article, we do not intend to suggest that even a fraction of the literary material quoted above was familiar to the narrators who entertained their audience in Southern Egypt with tales about heroes who somehow dropped out from normal everyday life to have strange adventures in another realm of time. Nevertheless, such ideas, wide-spread all over the world and particularly deep-rooted in Egypt, created an atmosphere favourable to the birth of new stories that centre on this fascinating subject.

[16] W. Helck: Die Lehre für Merikare (Kleine Ägyptische Texte), Wiesbaden 1977, p. 31, J. Fr. Quack, Studien zur Lehre für Merikare (GOF IV/23) Wiesbaden 1992, p. 35.

[17] Edfou VI 307 line 6 (line 16 of the inscription).

[18] Chapter 99. W. Till: Koptisch-gnostische Schriften I, Berlin 1962, p. 156.

[19] De civitate dei XII. 16.

[20] Augustin on time see De Civitate Dei XI. 4,6,7; Confessiones XI. 11ff.

JOH 2_4 IN KOPTISCHER SICHT

Ulrich Luft
(ELTE, Budapest)

Jesus, zu Gast auf der Hochzeit von Kana, antwortet seiner Mutter, die ihn darauf hinweist, daß dem Gastgeber der Wein ausgegangen sei, in einer nach den Übersetzungen unfreundlichen Weise: «Weib, was geht's dich an, was ich tue?»[1] Der griechische Text ist tatsächlich als Frage formuliert, enthält aber offensichtlich nicht den Tonfall der Lutherschen Version: τί ἐμοὶ καὶ σοί, γύναι; Die Vulgata hat fast die gleiche Formulierung, fügt aber noch das Hilfsverb *esse* hinzu: *Quid mihi, et tibi est mulier* ?

In einer modernen deutschen Übertragung werden weder die Frage noch die Anrede beachtet und eine Textauslegung anstelle einer Übersetzung gegeben: «Was ich zu tun habe, ist meine Sache, nicht deine.»[2] Wenn auch gemildert, ist der Ton nicht weniger abweisend. Aus den zitierten Übersetzungen wird ersichtlich, daß der Text heute noch auf Verständnisschwierigkeiten stößt. Denn solche werden auch aus der Übersetzung der Formel im griechischen Alten Testaments, der sog. Septuaginta, deutlich, der zum größten Teil ein hebräischer Originaltext zugrunde liegt.

Die neutestamentliche Forschung muß, um Jesus nicht dem Verdacht auszusetzen, daß er das fünfte Gebot nicht einhalte, die scheinbare Unhöflichkeit, die vor allem in der Anrede "Weib" manifest wird, interpretieren. Strack—Billerbeck verweisen in ihrem etwas

---

[1] In der drastischen Sprache von Martin Luther. Die Zürcher Bibel gibt ebenfalls eine nicht gerade freundliche Version: *Weib, was habe ich mit dir zu schaffen?* Tillmanns Übersetzung lautet etwas anders, weicht im Grundton nicht ab: *Frau, was habe ich mit dir zu tun?* Die Übersetzung der New English Bible interpretiert und sieht den Handelnden in der Mutter: *Your concern, mother, is not mine.* Die englische Übersetzung übersieht die eindeutige Frage und interpretiert γυνή als Mutter. Die drei deutschen Übersetzer nehmen den ersten Dativ für den Handelnden, aus der englischen Version geht dies nicht eindeutig hervor. Die vier Versionen sind zu finden in Tetrapla 1964. Das Neue Testament in der Übersetzung Martin Luthers, der Zürcher Bibel, Fritz Tillmanns und der New English Bible,[2] Berlin: Evangelische Haupt-Bibelgesellschaft, 1967.

[2] Die Bibel im heutigen Deutsch[4], Berlin-Altenburg: Evangelische Haupt-Bibelgesellschaft, 1987. Dabei wird die vielleicht anstößige Anrede «Frau» weggelassen.

älteren Kommentar auf die semitische Formung des Verses[3] und bemühen sich, den abweisenden Ton der Antwort zu mildern. Mit dem Ausdruck τὶ ἐμοὶ καὶ σοί grenze sich Jesus nicht gegen seine Mutter ab, sondern es sei auf eine Gemeinsamkeit der beiden Personen gegenüber einer konkreten Angelegenheit angespielt. Die semitische Grundlage des in Jo 2_4 gebrauchten Ausdrucks, auf die sich Strack—Billerbeck in ihren Kommentar berufen, findet sich in Ri 11_{12}, 2Sam 16_{10}, 2Kg 9_{18} in der sprachlichen Form מה־לי ולך oder מה־לי ולכם. Den Ausdruck führen Köhler—Baumgartner als Redensart «was habe ich mit dir/euch zu tun?»[4] innerhalb des Lemmas מה gesondert auf.

Es ist interessant den hebräischen Text der griechischen und koptischen Übersetzung gegenüberzustellen:

Ri 11_{12}	מה־לי ולךְ כי־
	Τί ἐμοὶ καὶ σοί ὅτι ...
	ⲟⲩ ⲡⲉ ⲡⲉⲕϩⲱⲃ ⲛⲙ̄ⲙⲁⲓ ϫⲉ ...[5]
2Sam 16_{10}	מה־לי ולכם בני צריה
= 2Reg	Τί ἐμοὶ καὶ ὑμῖν, υἱοὶ Σαρουιας ;
	ⲁϩⲣⲱⲧⲛ̄ ⲛⲙ̄ⲙⲁⲓ ⲛⲉϣⲏⲣⲉ ⲛⲥⲁⲣⲟⲩⲉⲓⲁⲥ[6]
2Kg 9_{18}	מה־לך ולשלום
= 4Reg	Τί σοι καὶ εἰρήνη ;
	ⲉⲕⲟ ⲛ[ⲟⲩ] ⲙⲛ̄ ⲉⲓⲣⲏⲛⲏ[7]

Ich füge noch hinzu:

1Kg 17_{18}	מה־לי ולךְ איש האלהים
= 3Reg	Τί ἐμοὶ καὶ σοί, ἄνθρωπε τοῦ θεοῦ ;

Das letzte Beispiel könnte in folgenderweise ins Saidische übertragen worden sein:

ⲉⲕⲟⲩⲉϣ ⲟⲩ ⲛⲙ̄ⲙⲁⲓ, ⲡⲣⲱⲙⲉ ⲙ̄ⲡⲛⲟⲩⲧⲉ ;

---

[3] Strack, H.L. – Billerbeck, P.: Das Evangelium nach Markus, Lukas und Johannes, und die Apostelgeschichte, erläutert aus dem Talmud und Midrasch[7], München: Beck, 1978, 401.

[4] 498b.

[5] Thompson, H.: A Coptic Palimpsest containing Joshua, Judges, Ruth, Judith and Esther, in the Saidic dialect, Oxford, 1911, 198. Die koptischen Text aus dem Alten Testament verdanke ich fast ausschließlich der freundlichen Hilfe von Herrn Nagel, Bonn.

[6] Drescher, J.: Coptic (Sahidic) Versions of Kingdoms I, II (Samuel I, II) (CSCO), Louvain, 1970, 313.

[7] Browne, G.M. – Papini, L., in: Orientalia 51 (1982) 202.

Denn die bohairische Version lautet: ⲁϧⲟⲕ ⲛⲉⲙⲏⲓ ϩⲱⲕ,[8] was bedeutet, daß das Fragewort nicht besonders betont worden muß wie in einer Formulierung ⲉⲕⲟ ⲛⲟⲩ.[9]

Die Struktur der Formel ist in der hebräischen und griechischen Sprache eindeutig: Auf das Fragewort מה, griechisch τί, folgt ein erster Dativ, die Konjunktion ו, griechisch καί, und ein zweiter Dativ. Köhler—Baumgartner wie auch die deutschen Übersetzer des Neuen Testaments sehen in dem ersten Dativ den Handelnden.

Die koptischen Übersetzungen der Stellen zeigen demgegenüber eine auffällige Vielfältigkeit und Klarheit. Keineswegs übernimmt der Kopte die auffällige semitische Struktur mit den beiden Dativen, sondern transponiert den Sinn in seine Sprache, übersetzt also nicht wörtlich, sondern sinngemäß. Eine erste Variante ist der Nominalsatz, in dem das Fragewort als erstes Glied des Nominalsatzes gesetzt ist, also an betonter Stelle stehend, wie das von einem Fragewort zu erwarten ist.[10] Eine zweite Variante bettet das Fragewort in eine emphatische Konstruktion, hier das Präsens II, ein. Spätestens seit Polotsky wissen wir, wozu diese emphatischen Konstruktionen auch gut sind.[11] Die dritte Variante verwendet das suffigierte Fragewort ^{S}ⲁϩⲣⲟ=, ^{B}ⲁϧⲟ=,[12] bei dem der Handelnde mit dem Suffix ausgedrückt wird. Damit ist auch die notwendige Betonung gesetzt.

Eines ist jedoch den koptischen Übersetzungen der alttestamentlichen Beispiele bis auf eine Ausnahme gemeinsam: Wenn zwei Dative, mit

---

[8] CD 25b. Der koptische Übersetzer hat an dieser Stelle den Handelnden durch ein nachgesetztes ϩⲱⲕ herausgehoben, was nach dem vorliegenden griechischen Text nicht notwendig gewesen wäre. Die saidische Übersetzung ist eine Vermutung aufgrund Joh 2_4 nach PPalau Rib.183 ed. Quecke, wo die gleiche Formulierung im Saidischen und im Bohairischen entsprechend übertragen worden ist. Doch kann auch folgende Möglichkeit nach dem Vorbild von 2Sam 16_{10} in Betracht gezogen werden: ⲁϩⲣⲟⲕ ⲛⲙ̄ⲙⲁⲓ ⲡⲣⲱⲙⲉ ⲙ̄ⲡⲛⲟⲩⲧⲉ.

[9] Siehe 2Kg 9_{18}.

[10] Zum Nominalsatz, der logisch bedingt zweigliedrig sein muß, vgl. die deutlichen Ausführungen von Westendorf, W.: Beiträge zum altägyptischen Nominalsatz (NachrGöttingen, 1981/3), Göttingen: Vandenhoeck & Ruprecht, 1981. Alle Diskussionen zu der vorgeblichen Kopula *pw* scheinen am Thema vorbeizulaufen, weil sie alle von der Ebene der lateinischen Sprachen aus geführt werden. Der Grundbestand eines Nominalsatzes sind zwei Glieder. Alles andere ist nominale oder adverbiale Erweiterung.

[11] Les temps seconds (Études de syntaxe Copte), Le Caire, 1944, 32–33.

[12] Etymologie bei Černý, J.: Coptic Etymological Dictionary, Cambridge: University Press, 1976, 19: *jḥ* + *r* + Suffix; vgl. auch Vycichl, W.: Dictionnaire étymologique de la langue Copte, Leuven: Peeters, 1983, 22–23 ohne eigentliche Etymologie. Vycichl verweist auf die arabische Formulierung: ما لك, doch scheint dies nur eine verkürzte Form der hier besprochenen Formel.

Personen verbunden, aufeinander folgen, sieht der koptische Übersetzer nur in der erstgenannten Person einen Dativ, d.h. den Betroffenen, während die zweite Person nach dem ו oder dem καί, ebenfalls im Dativ konstruiert, als "Handelnder" verstanden wird. Ist der zweite Dativ mit einem Begriff verbunden, nimmt er die Person des ersten Dativs als "Handelnden", und aus dem Begriff wird der Betreff.

Anders müsse nach Strack—Billerbeck die Trennung inbezug auf eine Sache oder eine Person ausgedrückt werden, wofür sie als Beispiele 2Sam 20_{1}, Neh 2_{20}, Jos 22_{24} und Jer 23_{28} anführen. Das Muster sei מה ל׳ את. Diese Formulierung habe ich jedoch nur in Jer 23_{28} gefunden.

Jer 23_{28} מה־לתבן את־הבר
Τί τὸ ἄχυρον πρὸς τὸν σίτον ;[13]
ΟΥ ΠΕ ΠΤ]ѠϨ Μ[Ν ΠΕ C]ΟΥΟ.

Die Vulgata ändert den Nominativ der LXX in einen Dativ, doch wird der Sinn dadurch nicht variiert: *quid paleis ad triticum.*

In 2Sam 20_{1} sowie Neh 2_{20} wird die Trennung durch die Präposition ב ausgedrückt:

Neh 2_{20} אין־חלק וצדקה וזכרון בירושלם
= 2Esdr 12_{20} καὶ ὑμῖμ οὐκ ἔστιν μερὶς καὶ δικαιοσύνη καὶ μνημόσυνον ἐν Ιερουσαλημ
2Sam 20_{1} אין־לנו חלק בדוד
= 2Rg Οὐκ ἔστιν ἡμῖν μερὶς ἐν Δαυιδ
ΜΝ̄ ΜΕΡΙC ϢΟΟΠ ΝΑΝ ϨΜ̄ Δ̄Ā Δ̄[14]

Folgerichtig benutzt die LXX hier die Präposition ἐν und der Kopte **ϨΝ** (mir nur aus 2Sam 20_{1} bekannt), in Jer 23_{28} die Präposition πρός für die hebräische את Präposition der Abgrenzung. Die koptische Formulierung von Jeremias lautet demgegenüber ganz anders. Zwei Nominalsätze werden durch **ΜΝ** verbunden, das gleichzeitig das Fragepronomen **ΟΥ** mit dem zweiten Satz verbindet, der somit nur scheinbar unvollständig ist. Jos 22_{24} folgt jedoch dem oben besprochenen Schema:

Jos 22_{24} מה־לכם וליהוה אלהי ישראל
Τί ὑμῖν κυρίῳ τῷ θεῷ Ισραηλ ;
ΕΤΕΤΝΟ ΝΟΥ ΜΝ ΠϪΟΕΪC Π̄ΝΟΥΤΕ ΜΠΙCΡΑΗΛ[15]

---

[13] «Wie reimen sich Stroh und Weizen zusammen?» (nach Luther).
[14] Drescher: CSCO 313, 167.
[15] Thompson, H.: A Coptic Palimpsest containing Joshua, Judges, Ruth, Judith and Esther, in the Saidic dialect, Oxford, 1911, 112.

Auch an dieser Stelle wird wie oben im Zitat 2Kg 9_{18} der Handelnde im ersten Dativ erkannt, wobei schon in der LXX die Konjunktion καί vor dem zweiten Dativ ausgefallen ist, während der hebräische Text die korrekte volle Form zeigt. Dieser Befund untermauert, daß die oben aufgestellte Regel nur für den pronominalen Fall gilt und nicht allgemein auf Personen übertragen werden darf.

Der etwas modernere Kommentar zum Johannesevangelium von Brown verzeichnet die Stelle Joh 2_4 ebenfalls als Semitismus unter Verweis auf 2Sam 16_{10} als einzigen Beleg.[16] Diesen Semitismus zeigt auch die arabische Übersetzung der Stelle: ما لي ولك يا امراة. Während jedoch LXX den Semitismus solcher Aussagen nachahmt, geht der Kopte auch bei der Übersetzung des Johannes-Evangeliums einen anderen Weg. Nach der guten saidischen Handschrift PPalau Rib.Inv.-Nr. 183,[17] die Quecke mit den Texten 813 und 814 der Chester Beatty Library und dem Text Michigan 569 verglichen hat, finden wir folgende Übersetzung: ⲧⲉⲥϩⲓⲙⲉ ⲉⲣⲉⲟⲩⲉϣ ⲟⲩ ⲛ̄ⲙ̄ⲙⲁⲓ,[18] im bohairischen Dialekt jedoch lesen wir ⲁϧⲟ ⲛⲉⲙⲏⲓ ϩⲱⲓ ϯⲥϩⲓⲙⲉ.[19] Die Anrede wird im sahidischen Dialekt an den Beginn der Frage gesetzt, die Frage selbst durch das Präsens II eindeutig gemacht. In dieser Formulierung verliert das Fragewort ⲟⲩ die dominierende Position in der Frage und die Betonung fällt auf den adverbialen Ausdruck ⲛ̄ⲙ̄ⲙⲁⲓ. Die Übersetzung entspricht etwa der folgenden griechischen Wendung τί θέλεις αὐτόν; «Was möchtest dú?», im Koptischen mit der Betonung auf dem adverbialen Ausdruck «von mir».[20] Es dürfte damit deutlich sein, daß die griechische Version tatsächlich einem aus den semitischen Sprachen übernommenen Muster folgt.

---

[16] The Gospel according to John (I–XII), New York: The Anchor Bible. Doubleday, 1966, 99.

[17] Quecke, H.: Das Johannesevangelium saïdisch. Text der Handschrift PPalau Rib.Inv.-Nr. 183 mit den Varianten der Handschriften 813 und 814 der Chester Beatty Library und der Handschrift M 569 (Papyrologica Castroctaviana, 11), Roma – Barcelona, 1984.

[18] Horner, G.: The Coptic Version of the New Testament in the Southern Dialect, etc., vol. III: The Gospel of S.John, Oxford, 1911, 22, die gleiche Formulierung. Eine Variante dazu findet sich bei von Lemm, O.: Bruchstücke der sahidischen Bibelübersetzung nach Handschriften der kaiserlichen öffentlichen Bibliothek zu St.Petersburg, Leipzig: Hinrichs, 1885, 19.

[19] Horner, G.: The Coptic Version of the New Testament in the Northern Dialect, etc., vol. II: The Gospels of S. Lucas and S.John, Oxford, 1898, 345; CD 25b F: ⲁϩⲁ ⲛⲉⲙⲏⲓ.

[20] CD 501a.

Die gleiche Formulierung wie in Joh 2_4 findet sich auch in Mt 8_{29}: τί ἡμῖν καὶ σοί, υἱὲ τοῦ θεοῦ; Die Frage wird in den saidischen Dialekt nach dem Schema von Joh 2_4 übersetzt: ⲉⲕⲟⲩⲉϣ ⲟⲩ ⲛⲙ̄ⲙⲁⲛ; In der bohairischen[21] und mittelägyptischen[22] Version wird eine abgewandelte Version gebraucht: ⲁϩⲣⲁⲕ ⲛⲉⲙⲉⲛ ⲡϣⲏⲣⲉ ⲙⲡⲛ̄ϯ (Codex Scheide), doch erreichen beide Versionen das gleiche Ziel, die Betonung der Adverbialbestimmung. Die beiden Versionen können so übersetzt werden: «Was hast du mit uns, Sohn Gottes?».

Aus den oben vorgestellten koptischen Varianten kann eine Erklärungsmöglichkeit für die griechische Formulierung gewonnen werden. Somit ist auch deutlich geworden, warum der koptische Übersetzer in Joh 2_4 die zweite Person sg.f. als Handelnden auffassen kann. Die deutsche Übersetzung der koptischen Version des Verses dürfte etwa so lauten: «Was hast du mit mir zu schaffen, Frau?».

Die Formulierung wird auch an anderen Stellen gebraucht, wo wir ebenfalls nicht unmittelbar nachprüfen können, ob die Formulierung dem hebräischen מה לי ולך entspricht. In den Apophtegmata patrum, dessen griechische Version bekannt ist, hat die Frage ⲁϩⲣⲟⲓ ⲁⲛⲟⲕ ⲙⲛⲡⲣⲱⲙⲉ in der griechischen Sprache folgende Gestalt: Tί θέλω ἐγὼ μετὰ τοῦ ἀνθρώπου; «Was habe ich mit dem Menschen zu tun?».[23] In den Acta martyrum findet sich folgende Frage: ⲁϧⲟⲕ ⲛⲑⲟⲕ ⲛⲉⲙⲡⲁⲓⲣⲁⲛ ϫⲉ ⲓ̄ⲏ̄ⲥ̄; «Was hast du mit diesem Namen Jesus zu schaffen?».[24] Obwohl die Übersetzung des Zitats aus den Apophtegmata zur Vorsicht mahnt, könnte das griechische Original eine solche Gestalt gehabt haben: Tί σοὶ καὶ ὀνόματι τοῦ Ἰησοῦ.[25] Schenutes Frage mag ein wenig kräftiger ausgefallen sein: ⲏ ⲁϩⲣⲟⲓ ⲙⲛ(ⲛ)ⲣⲱⲙⲉ ϫⲉⲉⲩⲟⲩⲱⲙ ⲛⲁϣ ⲛϩⲉ; «Oder was geht es mich an, wie die Menschen essen?».[26]

Im Licht der eindeutigen koptischen Übersetzungen, in denen bei zwei mit Personalpronomen verbundenen Dativen dem zweiten der

---

[21] CD 25b.

[22] Schenke, H.-M.: Das Matthäus-Evangelium im mittelägyptischen Dialekt des Koptischen (Codex Scheide) (Texte und Untersuchungen, 127), Berlin: Akademie, 1981, Text S.70.

[23] Zoega, G.: Catalogus codicorum copticorum manu scriptorum qui in Museo Borgiano Velitris adservantur, Roma, 1810, 290.

[24] Balestri, I. – Hyvernat, H.: Acta martyrum II (CSCO, 86), Louvain, 1924 (21)–(22).

[25] Ich habe den bestimmten Artikel vor ὀνόματι nach dem Vorbild von 2Kg 9_{18} ausgelassen.

[26] Leipoldt, J.: Sinuthii archimandritae vita et opera omnia IV (CSCO, 73), Paris: Gabalda, 1913, 156 (27)–(28).

Vorrang vor dem ersten eingeräumt wird, kann das bisherige Verständnis der Stellen aus dem Alten Testament in Frage gestellt werden. In allen Fällen, wo die LXX die Übersetzung τί + ersten Dativ + καί + pronominalen zweiten Dativ bietet, muß die Person des zweiten Dativs als Handelnder angesehen werden. Somit sind folgende Übersetzungen vorzuziehen:

1Kg 17_{18}: «Was hast du mit mir zu schaffen, Mann Gottes?»
Ri 11_{12}: «Was hast du mit mir zu tun, daß (du zu mir kommst)?».
2Sam 16_{10}: «Was habt ihr mit mir zu tun, Kinder der Zeruja?».

Sicher haben auch die Kopten Verständnisschwierigkeiten gehabt und deshalb die beiden eindeutigen Übersetzungen gefunden. Doch aus diesen geht hervor, daß in dem zweiten Dativ der Handelnde zu erkennen ist, falls Personen genannt sind, was aufgrund der griechischen Formulierung nicht zu entscheiden war.

REMARQUES SUR QUELQUES ÉTYMOLOGIES COPTES

Dimitri Meeks
(CNRS, Aix-en-Provence)

1. ⲂⲰⲦⲈ *(S.A) «haïr» (Crum 1939, 45b)*

Il est généralement admis que le copte ⲂⲰⲦⲈ (S. A.) a pour origine l'ancien verbe *ft* «éprouver de l'écœurement, être dégoûté» qui, selon Černý, serait encore attesté en démotique sous la forme *bty*.[1] Toujours selon le même auteur, il y aurait eu contamination entre ⲂⲰⲦⲈ et ⲂⲞⲦⲈ < *btꜣ* «faute, crime». Toute-fois, Vycichl a bien souligné que ⲂⲞⲦⲈ < *btꜣ* et ⲂⲰⲦⲈ < *bty* (démot.), *ft* (hiérogl.) étaient deux termes bien distincts.[2] Cette dérivation n'est pas sans soulever quelques problèmes. D'abord l'ancien verbe *ft* «éprouver de l'écœurement, être dégoûté» semble bien être un bilitère et non un 3ae inf. Dans ce cas la voyelle finale en copte ne s'explique guère. Ensuite, la forme *bty*, en démotique, paraît difficilement pouvoir être issue de l'ancien *ft*. Si l'on se reporte au dictionnaire de Erichsen, on constate que la forme démotique invoquée () est classée sous l'entrée *btꜣ* «Abscheu, Verbrechen» mais présente une graphie particulière, bien différente de toutes les autres enregistrées dans la notice. Elle comporte le signe du poisson comme déterminatif et, de ce fait, paraît devoir être sémantiquement liée à l'ancien *bw.t* «abomination, tabou». Ce dernier terme dérive cependant d'un verbe *bwi* «haïr, détester» qui ne saurait, sous cette forme,[3] être l'ancêtre du copte ⲂⲰⲦⲈ.

On peut se demander, dès lors, si le démotique *bty* n'a pas été classé abusivement sous l'entrée *btꜣ* et s'il n'y a pas lieu d'en faire un verbe *b(w)ty* «haïr, détester» que l'on aurait manqué à identifier jusqu'à présent. Que c'est là la bonne solution est confirmé par un

[1] Černý 1976, 28 avec renvoi, pour le démotique, à Erichsen 1954, 126 en bas. Westendorf 1977, 28 se rallie à cette opinion.

[2] Vycichl 1983, 32.

[3] Pour *bwi* comme 3ae inf. voir Osing 1976 II, 566.

exemple, au moins, tiré des textes hiéroglyphiques du temple d'Edfou. Des dieux sont censés protéger le sanctuaire «contre le mâle du serpent *nây* 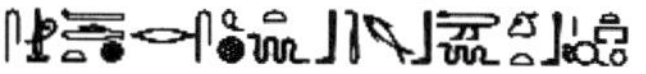 préservant Edfou du serpent *seftekh*, abominant le serpent *betch* dans le Lieu-de-Rê».[4] Nous avons bien affaire ici à une forme *b(w)ty* de l'ancien verbe *bwi*. De telles extensions verbales en *-ty* ont été signalées par Osing qui en cite nombre d'exemples.[5] Dans notre cas, celle-ci se serait développée à partir de l'infinitif, comme le montre un autre texte, du temple de Dendara cette fois. Le roi, est-il dit, trône dans le palais «les  mains lavées, les doigts purs, détestant la tristesse de l'Œil de Rê».[6]

Le *Wörterbuch* avait déjà signalé que le verbe *bwi* avait assez tôt pris la forme *bwt*,[7] sans que cette évolution ait, à ma connaissance, reçu d'explication. En fait, si les graphies du type *bwt* apparaissent dès le Moyen Empire au moins, *bwt* et *bwi* continuent à coexister.[8] La façon dont ces deux formes s'articulent entre elles n'est pas clair pour l'instant. L'exemple démotique confirme, en tout cas, que la forme *bwty* était bien employée à l'époque tardive.

Spiegelberg avait déjà bien séparé, dans son lexique du *Mythus*, les graphies démotiques *bty* «verabscheuen, hassen», *bty.t* «Abscheu» déterminés tous deux par le poisson, d'une part, de *btw* «Abscheu» (provenant de l'ancien *btꜣ*) qui ne comporte pas ce déterminatif, d'autre part.[9] Il avait donc bien perçu que ces mots appartenaient à des familles différentes.

---

[4] *Edfou* IV, 128, 7–8.

[5] Osing 1976 I, 333–338; II, 874 n. 1435.

[6] *Dendara* IV, 246, 10. Tournures *ḥr* + inf. fréquentes dans les textes tardifs, voir E. Winter, *Untersuchungen zu den ägyptischen Tempelreliefs der griechisch-römischen Zeit* (Vienne, 1968), 48.

[7] *Wb* I, 453, 5: «Alt III. Inf.; anscheinend früh durch bwt ersetzt».

[8] Les exemples anciens ont été étudiés, dans leurs contextes, par E. Edel, *Beiträge zu den Inschriften des Mittleren Reiches in den Gräbern der Qubbet el Hawa* (Berlin, 1971), 22–23. La grande procession géographique d'Edfou, lorsqu'elle traite des interdits de chaque province, emploie concurremment les formes *bwi* et *bwt*, cette dernière étant la moins fréquente; voir: *Edfou* I, 335, 11 et 342, 12.

[9] W. Spiegelberg, *Der ägyptische Mythus vom Sonnenauge* (Strasbourg, 1917), 125 n° 249; 126 n° 250 et 251.

2. ⲕⲉⲗⲗⲟϫ *(B.) «jeune chien, jeune animal»* *(Crum 1939, 104a)*

Tous les ouvrages de référence s'accordent pour dire que ce mot, antérieurement au copte, n'est attesté que comme nom propre.[10] Crum, lui-même, avait consacré un article détaillé sur la question.[11] Il y montrait que ⲕⲉⲗⲗⲟϫ était abondamment connu dans l'onomastique sous sa forme hellénisée Κολλουθε, Kolluthe (et var.) et reconnaissait quelques antécédents en démotique. Herman De Meulenaere réexaminait et complétait, par la suite, le dossier onomastique en classant, entre autres, les différentes graphies hiéroglyphiques du nom, mettant bien en évidence la série de genre féminin.[12] Il remarquait notamment que des graphies hiéroglyphiques très similaires pouvaient rendre aussi bien le nom propre Kolluthe que le nom du dieu enfant Κολάνθης, la relation entre les deux formes restant alors inconnue. Crum avait montré que ⲕⲉⲗⲗⲟϫ désignait le jeune d'un animal, d'un quadrupède précisait-il. L'emploi du déterminatif de la peau d'animal () dans certaines graphies en hiératique et en démotique, pour Kolluthe d'une part, du déterminatif de l'enfant (), pour Kolanthes d'autre part, confirme l'existence de deux séries distinctes. Quaegebeur a produit les arguments pertinents montrant qu'elles doivent être soigneusement différenciées et le dictionnaire démotique des noms propres, en cours de publication, ne les confond pas.[13]

Une fois le dieu Kolanthes écarté de ce dossier, il convient d'examiner quelques documents peu utilisés dans l'étude du terme qui nous intéresse. Le dictionnaire démotique des noms propres s'était déjà demandé si ⲕⲉⲗⲗⲟϫ ne pouvait pas trouver son origine dans un terme attesté uniquement dans un passage des poésies du papyrus Harris 500 où le bien-aimé se compare à un oiseau pris au piège par son amante:  «je suis une jeune oie», dit-il.[14] Ici *krṯ* est un qualificatif s'appliquant à *gb* «oie».[15] De plus, la

[10] Cerny 1976, 56; Westendorf 1977, 508; Vycichl 1983, 78.

[11] *Byzantinische Zeitschrift* 30 (1929–1930), 323–325.

[12] *BIFAO* 55 (1956), 143–146.

[13] J. Quaegebeur, *Kolanthes*, dans *LÄ* III, 671–672. E. Lüddeckens; H.-J. Thissen et al., *Demotisches Namenbuch* I/13 (Wiesbaden, 1995), 990–991 (*Qlwḏꜣ*/Kolluthe); 994–995 (*Qlnḏꜣ*/Kolanthes).

[14] En dernier lieu voir B. Mathieu, *La poésie amoureuse de l'Égypte ancienne* (Le Caire, 1996), 57 et pl. 9 (r° 2, 1) dont la transcription du hiératique peut être légèrement améliorée.

[15] Le mot *gb(w)* semble être un terme générique pour l'oie. En effet, les représen-

graphie du mot s'apparente de près avec quelques-unes des graphies de *Krṯ*/*Qrḏ* relevées par Herman De Meulenaere,  par exemple. Il s'agit du même mot, ancêtre du copte ⲕⲉⲗⲗⲟϫ. Le contexte, en effet, laisse bien supposer que *krṯ* désigne ici un animal fragile et inexpérimenté. James Hoch était parvenu à une conclusion similaire sans faire, toutefois, référence au copte.[16] On ne le suivra peut-être pas lorsqu'il associe *krṯ* du pHarris 500 au nom propre *Qḏr* (), considérant qu'il s'agit du même mot dans les deux cas. Ce nom propre n'étant attesté qu'à deux reprises dans le corpus des 'Tomb Robberies', il n'est pas possible de connaître sa signification. Du point de vue morphologique, l'identification des deux termes supposerait une métathèse dans le cas de *krṯ*. Or le nom propre *Krṯ* ne montre jamais ce type de métathèse (*Krṯ* > **Kṯr*), dans ses formes hiéroglyphiques ou démotiques. Si le nom propre *Qḏr* s'explique, pour sa part, aisément comme un emprunt au sémitique et s'apparente à une série de termes désignant, en effet, un jeune oiseau *krṯ*, en revanche, comme l'admet d'ailleurs James Hoch, il poserait quelques problèmes, sur le plan phonologique, si l'on veut en faire une graphie métathésée de ce même mot d'emprunt. On considérera, pour l'instant, qu'il s'agit de deux termes différents.

Reste à examiner encore le nom propre *Ḥr-pꜣ-krḏ* connu par quelques documents démotiques. Les graphies du dernier élément du nom, *krḏ*, sont très semblables à celles du nom *Krḏ*/*Ql(w)ḏ*, Kolluthe.[17] Il ne peut s'agir que du même terme dans les deux cas. Le nom peut se traduire «Horus-le-petit». La similitude des graphies n'autorise pas à voir dans *krṯ* une graphie aberrante de *ẖrd* «enfant» qui aurait été influencée par le grec -κρατ. Il ne s'agit pas, non plus, de graphies renvoyant à Kolanthès. La structure même du nom propre impose de voir dans *krṯ* un substantif. En fait, tous les documents démotiques où apparaît ce nom propre proviennent d'une région bien circonscrite, Éléphantine et ses environs immédiats, au nord. De ce fait *Ḥr-pꜣ-krṯ* ne peut se référer qu'à un aspect local du dieu

---

tations précises et en couleur de l'oiseau montrent des espèces différentes selon les cas, même si statistiquement l'oie rieuse (*Anser albifrons*) domine. Voir P.F. Houlihan, *The birds of Ancient Egypt* (Warminster, 1986), 59. La traduction «sarcelle» proposée autrefois par P. Montet, *Scènes de la vie privée dans les tombeaux égyptiens de l'Ancien Empire* (Strasbourg, 1925), 144 et reprise par B. Mathieu, *o.c.* ne peut être retenue.

[16] J. Hoch, *Semitic words in Egyptian texts of the New Kingdom and Third Intermediate Period* (Princeton, 1994), 311–312.

[17] Voir E. Lüddeckens; H.-J. Thissen et al., *o.c.* I/11, 806 à comparer avec I/13, 990–991.

enfant, «Horus-le-petit», dont on ne peut, pour l'instant, savoir s'il était de forme animale ou non.

3. ⲟⲩⲁⲥϥⲉ *(S) «oisiveté» (Crum 1939, 493a)*

Alors que le verbe ⲟⲩⲱⲥϥ (S) «être inactif, inoccupé» trouve son antécédent dans *wsf* de même sens, comme l'indiquent les ouvrages de référence,[18] le substantif féminin n'a curieusement pas d'ancêtre reconnu, le substantif masculin *wzf* «inactivité, absence» ne pouvant prétendre à ce statut. En fait, seules des formes théoriques reconstruites ont été proposées.[19]

Ce substantif féminin (), absent des dictionnaires, est en fait employé une fois dans le Rituel d'Abattre le Mauvais pour parler de «l'oisiveté, la paresse» de celui-ci.[20]

4. ϣⲱⲛϥ, ϣⲱⲛⲃ *(S) «joindre, lier» (Crum 1939, 573b–574a)*

L'étymologie de ce vocable semble reconnue depuis fort longtemps. Erichsen, reprenant une ancienne idée de H. Brugsch, l'avait rapproché de l'ancien *šbn* «mélanger, mêler», certaines graphies démotiques de ce mot offrant, en apparence, une forme métathésée *šnb*.[21] Il a été suivi en cela, sans hésitation, par Černý, Westendorf et Vycichl.[22]

Quelques équivalents grecs signalés par Crum συναρμολογοῦσθαι ou συνζευγνύναι par exemple suggèrent, si l'on s'en tient aux emplois concrets, des choses qui s'imbriquent, s'ajustent entre elles ou sont jointes l'une à l'autre par un lien. Or il existe bien un verbe *šnb* qui répond précisément à cet emploi dans un texte relativement banal inscrit sur une statue trouvée à Tolmeita, Ptolémaïs de Cyrénaïque, et conservée dans le musée de cette même ville.[23] Le propriétaire de la statue se vante d'avoir rénové un temple d'Osiris et précise:  «les portes (étaient) en pin excellent *šnb* de

[18] Černý 1976, 217; Westendorf 1977, 278; Vycichl 1983, 238.
[19] Osing 1976 I, 84; Vycichl 1983, 238.
[20] S. Schott, *Urkunden mythologischen Inhalts* (Leipzig 1939), 29, 18.
[21] Erichsen 1954, 499.
[22] Černý 1976, 247; Westendorf 1977, 320; Vycichl 1983, 267.
[23] A. Rowe, *New light on ægypto-cyrenæan relations. Two ptolemaic statues found in Tolmeita* (Le Caire, 1948), 74 et pl. XIV–2; M. D'Este, dans: *La Cirenaica in età antica. Atti del Convegno internazionale di studi, Macerata, 18–20 Maggio 1995*, a cura di E. Catani e S.M. Marengo (Macerata, 1998), 181–2 et pl. IV.

cuivre d'Asie». Le verbe *šnb* est un hapax absent des dictionnaires, mais on connaît nombre de ces textes où il est fait mention de la rénovation des portes d'un sanctuaire dans une tournure identique à la nôtre. Le verbe qui s'y trouve le plus communément employé, à la place de notre *šnb*, est  *nbd*. Ce dernier s'applique aussi couramment au travail de la sparterie. Or, comme le remarque Jac. Janssen, les paniers égyptiens n'étaient généralement pas tressés mais faits d'enroulements de boudins de fibres végétales.[24] C'est donc ce mouvement d'enroulement que désigne le verbe *nbd*. Employé à propos des cheveux, on le traduira par «boucler». S'agissant de vantaux de porte, constitués de planches ou de lattes jointives, on comprendra «cercler». Le cerclage des portes à l'aide de bandes métalliques servait ici à assurer la cohésion entre les éléments et leur stabilité.

Le verbe *šnb* décrivait donc une opération similaire sans être nécessairement identique. On pensera à des barres métalliques «liant, maintenant» entre eux les éléments de la porte, à la façon des pentures modernes. L'idée de «lier» différentes parties se retrouve peut-être dans le substantif *šnb.t* qui désignerait un conteneur de kohl à tubes multiples accolés les uns aux autres.[25]

À l'issue de cet examen, il convient donc de se demander si, en démotique, la forme *šnb* doit bien être purement et simplement assimilée à *šbn* comme le fait Erichsen dans son *Demotisches Glossar*. Une métathèse *šbn* > *šnb* est, bien sûr, envisageable et c'est la solution qui a été généralement adoptée, comme on l'a vu. Toutefois l'extrême rareté de la forme *šnb* dans les textes hiéroglyphiques et démotiques ne favorise pas cette option. L'exemple hiéroglyphique, de plus, dans son emploi particulier, invite à distinguer *šbn* de *šnb* et à faire de ce dernier seulement le prototype du copte ϣⲱⲛϥ, ϣⲱⲛⲃ.

Bibliographie

Černý (Jaroslav) 1976: *Coptic Etymological Dictionary* (Cambridge, 1976).
Crum (Walter E.) 1939: *A Coptic Dictionary* (Oxford, 1939).
Erichsen (Wolja) 1954: *Demotisches Glossar* (Copenhague, 1954).
Kasser (Rodolphe) 1964: *Compléments au dictionnaire copte de Crum* (Le Caire, 1964).
Osing (Jürgen) 1976: *Die Nominalbildung des Ägyptischen* (Mainz/Rhein, 1976).
Vycichl (Werner) 1983: *Dictionnaire étymologique de la langue copte* (Louvain, 1983).
Westendorf (Wolfhart) 1977: *Koptisches Handwörterbuch* (Heidelberg, 1977).

[24] Jac. J. Janssen, *Commodity prices from the Ramessid Period* (Leyde, 1975), 136 et suiv.
[25] J. Malek, *JEA* 77 (1991), 185–6.

BEITRÄGE ZUR KOPTISCHEN ETYMOLOGIE

Joachim Friedrich Quack
(Freie Universität, Berlin)

Werner Vycichl hat sich unter anderem auf dem Gebiet der koptischen Etymologie ausgezeichnet. Sein „Dictionnaire étymologique de la langue copte" (Vychicl 1983) zählt neben den älteren Publikationen von Westendorf 1965–77 und Černý 1976 sowie dem auch mit reichen Erörterungen zur Etymologie versehenen Werk über Nominalbildung von Osing 1976b zu den Standardwerken. Im Folgenden möchte ich einige neue Beiträge auf diesem Gebiet bringen. Der Schwerpunkt liegt dabei im Bereich des Demotischen, das bisher noch zu stark vernachlässigt worden ist. Einerseits ist das Demotische lexikalisch bisher vegleichsweise schlecht aufbereitet, andererseits stand keiner derjenigen modernen Forscher, die sich um koptische Etymologien bemüht haben, der demotistischen Forschung nahe. Vergleichsweise am meisten geleistet hat hier Černý 1976, der allerdings durch seine Benutzung von Glanvilles Zettelkästen neben einigen guten Beiträgen etliche Fehllesungen und -übersetzungen eingebracht hat, die seitdem allzuoft übernommen worden sind. Es genügt, das Glossar bei Thissen 1984 durchzusehen, um zu bemerken, an wievielen Punkten Černý 1976 Lesungen und Übersetzungen gibt, die von der Forschung überholt sind.

Jedoch ist das Demotische gerade deshalb von besonderer Bedeutung, weil von ihm als sprachgeschichtlich direktem Vorläufer des Koptischen vergleichsweise größere Ähnlichkeit im Wortschatz als im älteren Ägyptisch zu erwarten ist. Schließlich ist das Demotische auch dadurch von großem Potential, weil sein Wortschatz bisher alles andere als vollständig erfaßt ist. Unter diesem Gesichtspunkt sind die von Westendorf 1978: 42 aufgestellten Statistiken nicht als Abbild der Realität anzusehen, sondern rein durch den Forschungsstand bedingt. Die scheinbar hohe Zahl koptischer Wörter mit nur hieroglyphisch/hieratischen, nicht auch demotischen Vorläufern ist ein Phantom. Fast jede Publikation eines umfangreicheren demotischen literarischen Textes bietet derzeit Bereicherungen im bekannten Wortschatz, und viele davon sind direkt aus dem Koptischen erklärbar. Auch Editionen inhaltlich ungewöhnlicher nichtliterarischer Quellen können wertvolle etymologische Informationen geben, wie etwa die spätrömischen Ostraka aus Medinet Madi (Narmouthis), auf deren Publikationen (Bresciani/Pernigotti/Betrò 1983; Gallo 1997) hier generell verwiesen sei. Dies wird sich in absehbarer Zeit wohl nicht ändern, und ich kenne aus unpublizierten Texten zahlreiche etymologische Vorläufer bislang nur koptisch bekannter Wörter. Hier soll jedoch bewußt unter Konzentration auf bereits zugängliche Quellen einiges Material präsentiert werden. Ergänzend verweise ich ferner auf eine Reihe etymologischer Deutungen, die in den philologischen Anmerkungen einer von Friedhelm Hoffmann und mir bearbeiteten Anthologie der demotischen Literatur erscheinen und für manche koptischen Wörter erstmals demotische Entsprechungen liefern werden. Neben den Beiträgen aus dem demotischen Bereich, die den Hauptteil meiner Ausführungen ausmachen, sind auch einige Ergänzungen für die älteren Sprachstufen genannt. In einigen Fällen habe ich es ferner als sinnvoll angesehen, fehlerhafte Etymologien explizit zu streichen, auch wenn ich keinen positiven Gegenvorschlag machen kann.

ⲁⲓⲃⲉ „Fleck, Makel“: Die bisher üblichste etymologische Verbindung mit der Wurzel *ꜣb* „brandmarken“ (Westendorf 1965–77: 2; Černý 1976: 3) ist bereits von Vycichl 1983: 5 zu Recht angezweifelt worden. Die von ihm stattdessen erwogene Verbindung zu *ꜥb.w* „Unreinheit“ kann inzwischen abgesichert werden, da es ein verbindendes Glied in Form des demotischen *ꜥyb* gibt, das im pBM 10507 2, 14 bezeugt ist (M. Smith 1987: 69, wo das Wort zu Unrecht für eine einfache Variante von *yꜥb.t* „Krankheit“ gehalten wird, das kopt. **ⲉⲓⲁⲁⲃⲉ** entspricht).

ⲁⲙϩⲣⲏⲣⲉ „Käfer“: Die Etymologie dieses Wortes wurde bisher als problematisch eingeschätzt, relativ sicher schien nur demotisch *mẖrr* „Skarabäus“ (Westendorf 1965–77: 7 u. 486; Černý 1976: 7; Vycichl 1983: 11). So mag es nicht unnütz sein, einen bisher übersehenen Vorschlag in Erinnerung zu rufen, nämlich eine Verbindung mit der Bezeichnung *ꜥnḫ-mrr* (WB I 203, 10) für ein käfergestaltiges Amulett (Lexa 1947–51: 107).

ⲁⲡⲉ „Kopf“: Sicher ist nur die Verbindung mit dem im Spätdemotischen belegten *ꜥpe.t*. Darüber hinaus wird dieses Wort generell von *tp.t* abgeleitet, indem das vordere *t* von den Sprechern als femininer Artikel aufgefaßt und abgetrennt worden wäre. Dies wird jedoch bereits von Vycichl 1983: 14 zu Recht bezweifelt. Tatsächlich gibt es im Demotischen neben *ꜥpe.t* auch noch *tp* als Wort für „Kopf“, während *tp.t* nicht mehr existiert, was die bisherige Theorie nicht gerade stützt. Die korrekte Etymologie für ⲁⲡⲉ ist vielmehr, wie ich bereits bemerkt habe, eher ägyptisch *ỉp.t* „Scheitel“ mit einer semantisch plausiblen leichten Bedeutungserweiterung (Quack 1999b: 461).

ⲁⲥ „zugehörig zu“: Dieses Wort ist in den bisherigen koptischen Wörterbüchern nicht verzeichnet, findet sich jedoch im altkoptischen Horoskop (Černý/Kahle/Parker 1957), Z. 123. Dort lautet der Text ⲁϥⲁϣⲏ ⲁⲍⲧⲁϩ ⲁⲥ ⲡⲣⲱ ⲛⲕⲉ ⲡⲛⲟⲩⲧⲉ, und dies deute ich als *ỉw=f r šm r ḏtḥ is pr-ꜥꜣ n-ge pꜣ nčr* „er wird in die Haft Pharaos oder des Gottes gehen“ (d.h. Staats- oder Tempelhaft). Das Wort ⲁⲥ ist somit das alte *ni-sw* > *ns* „zugehörig zu“, das im Demotischen üblicherweise unetymologisch als *ỉ(w=)s* geschrieben wird (Spiegelberg 1925: § 66). Das Auftreten dieses koptisch sonst nicht belegten Wortes kann schon insofern nicht überraschen, als das „altkoptische“ Horoskop seinem Sprachzustand nach nicht Koptisch, sondern Demotisch in frühkoptischer Schrift ist. Die Vokalisation mit *a* entspricht dabei dem, was auch in dem Namen Ase(n)neth (Josephs ägyptische Frau) bekannt ist, deren Namen ungeachtet gelegentlich geäußerter Zweifel (Muchiki 1999: 208f., dagegen Quack 2000c) doch sicher auf ägyptisch *(n)s-Nỉt* „sie gehört zu Neith“ zurückgeht (so auch Vycichl 1983: 17).

ⲁϭⲛⲓ „Fleck, Makel“. Hier wird allgemein auf demotisch *ꜥčn(.t)* „Narbe o.ä.“ verwiesen, was ungeachtet der Zweifel von Devaud 1923: 89 auch sicher richtig ist (Černý 1976: 19). Darüber hinausgehende Verbindungen mit dem Wort *ꜥčn.t* zur Bezeichnung des Zustandes von gegossenem Kupfer (Westendorf 1965–77: 19) oder dem Krankheitsdämon *ꜥčn* (Vycichl 1983: 23) blieben bisher relativ unsicher. Inzwischen hat sich die Basis allerdings insofern verändert, als ich nachweisen konnte, daß das Zeichen 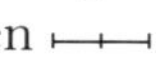 nicht *ḳn*, sondern *ꜥčn* zu lesen ist (Quack 2000a). Ergänzend zu den dortigen Ausführungen kann ich noch darauf hinweisen, daß das Wort *ꜥčn* „Matte“ als Sitz des Königs mehrfach in eindeutiger alphabetischer Ausschreibung belegt ist, nämlich Dendera Mammisis 53, 11 sowie Edfou VII 98, 2; 258, 7: 260, 16. Den Hinweis auf die Edfu-Belege (erwähnt auch Budde/Kurth 1994: 8 und Wilson 1997: 188) verdanke ich J. Osing. Gleichzeitig als Nachtrag zur Demonstration des Lautwertes und für die koptische Etymologie kann ich die Oracular Amulettic Decrees der dritten Zwischenzeit heranziehen. In ihnen findet sich L_6 vs. 30 ein Wort , T_2 rt. 104 ein Wort  als

Bezeichnung für etwas, vor dem der Träger des Amulettes geschützt werden will. Es ist bereits bemerkt worden, daß der generelle Zusammenhang dieser beiden Stellen sehr ähnlich ist (Edwards 1960: 66 Anm. 61). Somit hindert nichts daran, einerseits die beiden Worte für identisch zu erklären und in der Variation der Schreibung einen zusätzlichen Beleg für die Lesung von  zu sehen, andererseits hier den etymologischen Vorläufer von demotisch *ʿq̣n(.t)* „Narbe" und koptisch ⲁϭⲛⲓ „Makel, Fleck" zu sehen, dessen (bohairische) Lautform exakt dazu paßt.

ⲃⲏ „Grab": Bisher schon ist generell demotisch *b.t* als Vorläufer erkannt worden. Allerdings gilt es hier, genauer zu trennen. Zweifelsfrei feminines *be.t* „Grab" liegt im pMag. LL 15, 2 vor. Mythus Leiden 2, 5, wo man bisher auch „Grab" verstanden hat, ist dagegen angesichts der Schreibung *bʿwy.t*, die auf eine Aussprache **bowy* o.ä. hindeutet, sicher ein anderes Wort zu erkennen, nämlich altes *bwꜣ.t* „Hügel" WB I 454, 17. Dafür sehe ich Harfner 3, 19 keinen Grund, das dortige *b.t* nicht als „Grab" aufzufassen. Der abweichende Vorschlag von Thissen 1992, vielmehr altes *bw* „Ort" wiederzuerkennen, ist orthographisch nicht zu halten. Im Demotischen signalisiert ein hinter dem Determinativ stehendes *t* unzweideutig feminines Genus, während die hieroglyphische Schreibung  auf die sich Thissen beruft, lediglich die in der Spätzeit häufige Verwendung der Gruppe 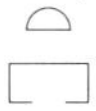 insgesamt als Determinativ zeigt und am maskulinen Genus von *bw* nichts ändert. Eine über das demotische zurückreichende etymologische Ableitung von ⲃⲏ geben nur Westendorf 1965–77: 492 und Osing 1976b: 248 u. 819 Anm. 1081, die darin altes *bꜣy* „Loch" wiedererkennen. Dieses, bzw. genauer das feminine *bꜣ.t* u.ä. ist in der Tat in der Bedeutung „Erdgrube" u.ä. im Ägyptischen zu finden und korrespondiert zweifelsfrei mit koptisch ⲃⲏ (Ward 1977: 271–274; Ward 1978: 49f.)

ⲃⲱⲧⲉ „verabscheuen; besudeln": Hier ist teilweise sicher zu Recht demotisch *bty* „verabscheuen" vorgeschlagen (Westendorf 1965–77: 28, Černý 1976: 28), teilweise darüber hinaus auch eine Verbindung zu *ft* „sich ekeln" ins Auge gefaßt worden (Černý 1976: 28; Vycichl 1983: 32). Letzteres ist sicher nicht zutreffend, schon aufgrund der demotischen Form mit *b*, denn im Demotischen wechseln, anders als im Koptischen, *b* und *f* noch nicht miteinander. Tatsächlich ist hier ein gewisses „Aufräumen" bei den demotischen Formen nötig (s. dazu

Hughes 1968: 181; H. Smith 1980: 150 Anm. cb), das auch Folgen für die koptische Etymologie hat. Es gibt 1. ein maskulines Wort *btw* „Verbrechen, Bestrafung", das auf altes *btꜣ* zurückgeht und im Koptischen nicht mehr belegt ist. 2. ein feminines Wort *bty.t* „Abscheu, Tabu", das koptisch **ⲃⲟⲧⲉ** (feminin!) „Abscheu" entspricht. Dies stellt eine Weiterbildung von altem *bw.t* „Tabu" dar, dessen Wurzel sich bereits in alter Zeit von einer 3ae infirmen Form *bwy* zu einer starken Form *bwt* gewandelt hat (WB I 453, 5). D.h. das Verb **ⲃⲱⲧⲉ** geht auf die Wurzel *bwi̯* > *bwt* > *bty* zurück, das Substantiv **ⲃⲟⲧⲉ** auf *bw.t* > *bwt.t* > *bty.t*. Besonders handgreiflich kann man diesen Prozeß am Buch vom Tempel demonstrieren, in dem ein hieratisches  „Frevel verabscheuen" demotisch als *bṱ bṱy.t* wiedergegeben wird (zur Stelle s. Quack 1999a).

ⲃⲏⲩ „Frevel": Gesichert ist hier die Verbindung zu demotisch *bw(ꜣ)*. Die übliche Ableitung von *bw.t* „Tabu" (Westendorf 1965–77: 29; Vycichl 1983: 33) kann aber angesichts der obigen Ausführungen nicht zutreffen. Tatsächlich korrekt ist die von Černý 1976: 28 vorgeschlagene Verbindung mit ägyptisch *bꜣ.w* „Macht, Zorn", die inzwischen dadurch abgesichert werden kann, daß im Demotischen *bw n nčr* belegt ist, das kaum von älterem *bꜣ.w n nčr* zu trennen ist (M. Smith 1987: 119).

ⲉⲓⲁⲁⲃⲉ „Krankheit, Eiter": Die Verbindung mit demotisch *yꜥb(y).t* „Krankheit" war nie ein Problem. Abgelehnt werden muß jedoch die allgemein angenommene etymologische Verbindung mit einem angeblichen Wort *ỉꜥb* „übel riechen" in den Pyramidentexten. Dieses Wort ist nämlich zum einen in seiner Bedeutung nicht gesichert, d.h. bisher immer aufgrund der vorgeblichen Etymologie geraten worden, zum anderen kommt es schon deshalb gar nicht in Frage, weil im Demotischen *yꜥb(y).t* auch in solchen Handschriften mit *ꜥ* geschrieben wird (z.B. demotische Chronik), die *ꜥ* ausschließlich etymologisch korrekt verwenden. Zudem dürfte das angebliche *ỉꜥb* als spezielles Lexem in der geratenen Bedeutung gar nicht existieren, sondern lediglich das AR-Pendant zum jüngeren *ꜣbi̯* „fernhalten, verhindern" sein (Allen 1984: 552).

ⲕⲛⲟⲥ „verfaulen": Hier ist eine gewisse Klärung der demotischen Formen nötig. Heutzutage hat man seit Černý 1976: 59 die alte Idee von Brugsch 1888: 33 wieder aufgegriffen, der im demotischen Gedicht vom Harfner 4, 5 das Wort *ḳns.t* als „(stinkender) Leichnam" verstehen und mit dem koptischen Wort **ⲕⲛⲟⲥ** „verfaulen" verbinden wollte. An der betreffenden Textstelle ist aber eher *ꜣtp.t ḳns.t* als „üble Last" aufzufassen (vg. Thissen 1992: 53). Prinzipiell ist demotisches *ḳns* als Metathese von altem *ḳsn* „übel, schlecht" aufzufassen (Quack 2000d: 170). Diese Annahme kann inzwischen durch einen wertvollen zusätzlichen Beleg gestützt werden, nämlich das Tebtunis-Onomastikon, Fragm. B, 2, 12; 4, 6 und FA 30, das zu hieratischem *ḳsn* die demotische Glosse *ḳns* angibt. Hier ist von Osing 1998: 70f. und 213 die demotische Glosse als *gns* gelesen worden, tatsächlich ist nach Überprüfung der Phototafeln jedoch zweifelsfrei alphabetisch geschriebenes *ḳns* zu erkennen. Demotisches *ḳns* geht somit sicher auf altes *ḳsn* zurück und dürfte teilweise die alte Bedeutung „schlecht" beibehalten, teilweise auch eine Spezialbedeutung „faul sein" angenommen haben, die sich noch im Koptischen als **ⲕⲛⲟⲥ** gehalten hat. Zu klären ist allerdings noch die bohairische Form **ϫⲱⲛⲥ**, die bisher der Grund dafür war, die koptische Form von einem hypothetischen **kns* abzuleiten (Osing 1976b: 37 u. 503 Anm. 197; Vycichl 1983: 83). Das anlautende **ϫ**, das eher für altes *k* spricht, ist in der Tat ein Problem. Jedoch ist z.B. auch ᴮ**ϫⲟⲥ** „Rülpsen" mutmaßlich von äg. *ḳìs* abzuleiten (Westendorf 1965–77: 511; Vycichl 1983: 247). Im vorliegenden Fall könnte man vermuten, daß im Bohairischen eine ursprünglichere Form ***ϫⲛⲟⲥ**, in der die Lautform regulär ist, sekundär nach dem Muster der „ersten Infinitive" zu **ϫⲱⲛⲥ** abgewandelt wurde. Von dem demotischen alphabetisch geschriebenen *ḳns* „übel, faul" unbedingt abzutrennen ist aber ein anderes Wort *gns* „Unrecht, Buße", das meist mit einer historischen Gruppe, gelegentlich auch alphabetisch als *gns* oder *kns* geschrieben und von Erichsen 1954: 542 zu Unrecht als *ḳns* transliteriert und mit den wenigen echten Belegen für *ḳns* zusammengeworfen wurde. Dieses *gns* entspricht bekanntermaßen kopt. **ϭⲟⲛⲥ** „Gewalt, Unrecht", für das auch schon eine syllabische Schreibung *gns* als neuägyptischer Vorläufer bekannt ist. Gerade im Lichte der beiden deutlich verschiedenen demotischen Formen ist jedoch zu betonen, daß dieses *gns* nicht auf altes *ḳsn* zurückgeführt werden kann.

ⲕⲱⲕ „abschälen, abschaben": Bislang ist nur die hieroglyphische Entsprechung *ḳḳ* habhaft gemacht worden. Das Wort existiert aber auch im Demotischen, nämlich Mythus Lille A 9, wo es heißt [. . . *n pꜣ y]ʿr ìw=f ḳḳ ḥr tꜣy=f ʿmy*[*.t*] „[. . . aus dem F]luß, indem er an seiner Kehle abgeschabt ist". Obgleich der Satz schlecht erhalten und die Übersetzung deshalb wenig abgesichert ist, spricht nicht nur die Lautgestalt, sondern auch die Determinierung von *ḳḳ* mit den Gruppen für  und  für die Verbindung mit kopt. ⲕⲱⲕ. Ein weiterer demotischer Beleg desselben Wortes ist wohl Mythus Leiden 19, 25, wo die Lesung von Jasnow 1984: 9 zutreffend ist.

ⲗⲟⲓϭⲉ „Vorwand, Klage Schuld“: Dieses im Koptischen recht häufige Wort ist bisher ohne Etymologie geblieben. Es läßt sich aber eine demotische Entsprechung finden, nämlich Mythus Lille A 47, wo es heißt: *ḫr gmi̯=t ryky n pꜣ nti č̣ṭ i͗w=y* „Du findest (sogar) einen Vorwand (oder: eine Klage) gegen den, der ‘Ja’ sagt“ (Vgl. de Cenival 1985: 102, wo aber das Wort irrig als *ryḳy* statt des paläographisch sicheren *ryky* gelesen wird). Das Wort *ryky* ist dabei als Enstprechung zu ⲗⲟⲓϭⲉ (bzw. genauer ᶠⲗⲁⲓϭⲓ, da die Handschrift aus dem Fayum stammt) zu erkennen, da demotisches alphabetisches *k* koptischem ϭ, nicht ⲕ entspricht, so verführerisch auch der koptische Ausdruck ϭⲛ-ⲁⲣⲓⲕⲉ im Vergleich sein mag, an den de Cenival 1985: 104 wohl gedacht hat—aber auch ⲗⲟⲓϭⲉ kann mit ϭⲛ—konstruiert werden. Mutmaßlich ist generell das von Erichsen 1954: 265 ohne Etymologie mit der Bedeutung „Hindernis o.ä.“ angeführte Wort *lgy(.t)/lyg.t* mit kopt. ⲗⲟⲓϭⲉ zusammenzubringen und als „Vorwand u.ä.“ zu verstehen.

ⲙⲡⲉ „nein“: Sicher korrekt ist die Deutung als absolut gebrauchtes Präfix des negierten Vergangenheitstempus (Westendorf 1965–77: 97). Zu streichen ist dagegen das angebliche demotische *i͗n pꜣi͗*, da es sich an seiner vorgeblichen Belegstelle nur um den hinteren Bereich der Negation *bn . . . in pꜣi* des Substantivalsatzes handelt, der von Spiegelberg 1931: 38 irrig abgetrennt worden ist.

ⲙⲁⲧⲟⲓ „Soldat“: An sich bereitet die Etymologie keine Schwierigkeit, da die Ableitung von dem Wort für „Meder“ bekannt ist, und dies sowohl hieroglyphisch als auch demotisch sicher belegt ist. Ein klärendes Wort scheint aber notwendig, da ungeachtet der beherzigenswerten Ausführungen von Sethe 1916: 124–131 und Černý 1976: 93, die ⲙⲁⲧⲟⲓ ausschließlich auf *mty* „Meder“ zurückgeführt haben, die Ansicht unausrottbar scheint, dieses Wort sei von den Ägyptern mit der afrikanischen Volksbezeichnung *mč̣ꜣy* verquickt worden (Westendorf 1965–77: 105; Vycichl 1983: 125; zuletzt Meeks 1999: 581). Demgegenüber sollte man betonen, daß die Schreibung *mč̣ꜣy* mit dem  -Zeichen im Neuen Reich eindeutig zeigt, daß der Dental *nicht* zu *ṯ* geworden ist, die Verbindung also bereits lautlich unmöglich ist. Ferner ist im Demotischen das Wort *mty* „Meder, Perser“ recht häufig, dagegen das angebliche *mč̣ꜣy* „Soldat“ nach neueren Ergebnissen eindeutig nicht existent (Ritner 1990: 105f.; Zauzich 1990: 161f.). Zusammengenommen kann man somit nur nochmals deutlich sagen, daß kopt. ⲙⲁⲧⲟⲓ „Soldat“ ausschließlich auf „Meder“ zurückgeht und auch spätzeitliche hieroglyphische Belege der Schreibung *mty* oder *mṯy* stets als „Meder“ zu verstehen sind, einschließlich der Form 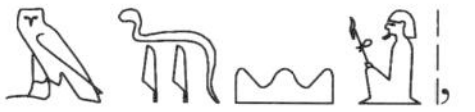, in der mit Sethe 1916: 128 das *č̣* nur pseudoarchaisch für *ṭ* steht.

ⲙ̅ϫⲉⲧ „Pech“: Dieses Wort ist nur im Lykopolitanischen bekannt, und auch dort erst kürzlich durch die Publikation neuer Abschnitte der Kephalaia bekannt geworden. Belegt ist die Form Kephalaia 298, 11 u. (schlechter erhalten) 15. Seine Bedeutung erschien bislang unsicher (Nagel 1999: 298). Der dortige Zusammenhang ϩⲙ̅ ⲡϣⲁϩ ⲙ̅ⲡⲣⲏⲧⲉ ⲙ̅ⲡⲥⲁⲛⲧⲉ ⲙⲛ̅ ⲡⲙ̅ϫ[ⲉⲧ] „in der Flamme wie das Harz und das ⲙ̅ϫⲉⲧ“ spricht jedoch dafür, daß es sich um eine brennbare Substanz handelt. Ich halte dieses Wort für eine neue Form des bislang als ⲗⲁⲙϫⲁⲧⲡ, ⲗⲁⲙϫⲁⲡⲧ, ⲗⲁⲙϫⲁⲧ u.ä. bekannten Wortes „Pech“, was inhaltlich guten Sinn ergibt. Das Fehlen des ⲡ ist bereits im Koptischen selbst nicht ohne Parallele, für die Form ohne ⲗⲁ kann ich auf eine kürzlich identifizierte demotische Form *nčpt* verweisen (Quack 2000b: 292), bei der das Fehlen des *l* umgekehrt durch die neue koptische Form verständlicher wird.

ⲡⲛⲛⲏ „Türschwelle“: Nachdem man früher das Wort von *bnn.t* ableiten wollte (Westendorf 1965–77: 149), hat sich inzwischen ein Meinungsumschwung zugunsten von *pnꜥy.t* ergeben (Černý 1976: 126; Westendorf 1965–77: 531; Vycichl 1983: 160). Diesen kann man noch zusätzlich absichern, indem man auf einen zusätzlichen demotischen Beleg Mythus Lille A 28 verweist, wo *pnꜥꜥy[.t]* geschrieben ist. Die eindeutige Schreibung mit ꜥ zeigt deutlich, daß nur *pnꜥ.yt* als etymologischer Vorläufer relevant ist.

ⲣⲓⲛ „Namen“: Diese in den Wörterbüchern noch nicht verzeichnete Form, die NH II 11, 26 belegt ist, kann als bisher einziger Beleg eines echten Plurals des Wortes ⲣⲁⲛ verstanden werden. So wie im Singular *rn̄* regulär koptisch ⲣⲁⲛ ergibt, so wird im Plural lautgesetzlich regulär *rn̄.w* zu ⲣⲓⲛ.

ⲥⲱⲙⲧ „spannen, ausstrecken“: Dieses Wort ist meist ohne Etymologie gelassen worden. Lediglich Westendorf 1965–77: 538 gibt im Anschluß an Osing 1976b: 526 Anm. 317 ein demotisches *sꜥmt* „sich erstrecken“ an. Diese angebliche Etymologie ist zu streichen, da sie auf einer simplen Fehllesung beruht. An der angeblichen demotischen Belegstelle pStraßburg 3 vs. „1, 7“ (korrekt nach heutiger Zählung 5, 7) ist gegen Lexa 1947–51: 772 keineswegs *sꜥmṱ* zu lesen, sondern *sḥṱ*, „erleuchten“ (M. Smith 1993: 79).

ⲥⲙⲁⲟⲩ „Wimper“: Zusätzlich zu dem von mir bereits Quack 1999b: 461 genannten unveröffentlichten Beleg kann ich als zumindest in Photographie zugängliche Stelle noch pBerlin 6750 B, 7 angeben, wo *smwe* geschrieben ist (Spiegelberg 1902: T. 76).

ⲥⲟⲟⲩⲧⲛ̄ „ausstrecken“. Als unmittelbarer Vorläufer ist demotisch *swtn* gut bekannt. Da für hieroglyphische Equivalente bisher nur Formen der Art *sṭwn* oder *stwn* vorgeschlagen sind, mag der Hinweis auf eine tatsächliche Schreibung *swṭn* in einem hieratischen Text nicht unwillkommen sein. In einer Beschreibung von Göttertypen (bzw. Statuen) (Cauville 1995) heißt es im pBerlin 10472 A, 2, 19 *iꜣbi=f*  *ẖr iwn.t* „sein linker (Arm) ist ausgestreckt mit einem Bogen“. Hier ist offensichtlich das bisher nur demotisch und koptisch bekannte Wort zu erkennen.

ⲧⲉϩⲉⲛ „grünen“: Dieses bislang nur im mittelägyptischen Dialekt bezeugte Wort hat Gabra 1988 besprochen und mit ägyptisch *čḥn* „strahlen“ verbunden. Nachzutragen ist zunächst einmal das demotische *tẖn* „funkeln, glänzen“ Mythus Leiden 6, 26 (Erichsen 1954: 655) in einer Handschrift, in der bereits gelegentlich *ẖ* für ursprüngliches *ḥ* eintritt. Noch näher an der koptischen Bedeutung dürfte eine andere Belegstelle liegen, nämlich *ṱḥn ṱ=k =y m-ḳṭ pꜣ nti rṭ ẖn pꜣ mw* „ich werde dich grünen lassen wie das, was im Wasser wächst“ Mythus Lille A 41 (bei de Cenival 1985: 102, 104 u. 114 nicht korrekt gelesen und verstanden, das Suffix steht hier graphisch hinter dem enklitischen Personalpronomen, was auch sonst belegt ist).

ⲟⲩⲱ in dem Ausdruck **ϯ-ⲟⲩⲱ** „erlösen, befreien“: Während sonstige koptische Formen **ⲟⲩⲱ** mit Recht von *wꜣḥ* oder *wḥꜥ* abgeleitet werden, dürfte dieser Ausdruck, bei dem das zusätzliche **ϯ** „geben“ sonst relativ unverständlich wäre, etymologisch völlig abzutrennen sein. Es handelt sich nämlich um das alte Wort *wꜣi̭.t* „Weg“, das gerade im Demotischen in der Verbindung *č̭i̭.t w* und der Bedeutung „freilassen“ sehr gebräuchlich ist. Die Lesung des demotischen Ausdruckes, der lange als *č̭i̭.t wtn* „ein Boot geben“ verkannt worden war, hat Hoffmann 1996: 41f. geklärt, der auch die hieroglyphische Entsprechung *č̭i̭.t wꜣi̭.t* gibt, die in der Tat „den Weg freigeben“ bedeutet. Gerade die koptische Form, die ich hier noch hinzufügen kann, hilft auch, die von Hoffmann besprochene unetymologische Schreibung dieses Ausdruckes mit dem Wort *w(ı͗ꜣ)* „Barke" zuverstehen. Da für das Wort Barke anhand des Dekans *ḥrı͗-ı͗b-wı͗ꜣ*, der bei Hephaistion I, 1 als ῥηουω belegt ist und von Firmicus Maternus, Mathesis 4, 21—für das hier allein interessierende Ende gleichartig—als *eregbuo* gegeben wird, die Lautform ***ⲟⲩⲱ** erschließbar ist, war das Wort „Barke" in der Spätzeit vollständig mit dem Ausdruck „freier Weg" zusammengefallen und konnte deshalb unetymologisch dafür eintreten. Dies führt übrigens zu einer interessanten Konsequenz bei einer anderen Etymologie. Allgemein wird das Wort **ⲟⲩⲟⲉⲓ** „Ansturm, Lauf", auch im Ausdruck **ϯ-ⲟⲩⲟⲉⲓ** „sich hinbegeben" belegt, mit ägypt. *wꜣı͗.t* „Weg" zusammengebracht. Dies ist schon deshalb problematisch, weil ägyptisch *ꜥḳ.t wꜣı͗.t* eben nicht „sich hinbegeben", sondern „den Weg freimachen" bedeutet. Deshalb ist die gerade aus diesem Grund von Vycichl 1983: 231 vorgeschlagene Verbindung mit dem Ausdruck *wꜣy*, der ägyptisch bisher vom Wind „*m wꜣy=f*" belegt ist, zu befürworten (Osing 1976b: 69 u. 529 Anm. 336)—beim Wind kann nach den Belegstellen tatsächlich sehr gut „in seinem Ansturm" gemeint sein. Auch das maskuline Genus des koptischen Wortes **ⲟⲩⲟⲉⲓ** „Ansturm" spricht übrigens eher gegen eine Verbindung mit dem femininen *wꜣı͗.t* Weg". Nochmals abzutrennen ist übrigens, ungeachtet des identischen Konsonantengerüstes, *wꜣı͗.t* „Seite", kopt. [B]**ⲟⲩⲟⲓ**, wobei das koptische Wort bereits angesichts seines femininen Genus und ebenso der abweichenden Bedeutung eindeutig ein anderes Lexem darstellt.

ⲟⲩⲟⲉⲓⲉ „Bauer": Eindeutig und allgemein anerkannt ist die Verbindung mit dem. *wyꜥ* „Bauer". Zweifelhaft erscheint dagegen die weitere Verbindung mit äg. *ꜥwꜣı͗* „abreißen, ernten" (Westendorf 1965–77: 268; Černý 1976: 209; Osing 1976b: 169; Vycichl 1983: 231). Ich möchte einen Gegenvorschlag unterbreiten. In den Ackerdokumenten des Neuen Reiches und der Dritten Zwischenzeit ist einer der allerhäufigsten Titel der jeweiligen Feldbesteller , also das Wort *wꜥ(.w)* „Infanterist, Soldat" (Gasse 1988: 206; Vleeming 1993: 57). Historisch ist dies darauf zurückzuführen, daß die einfachen Soldaten ein kleines Stück Land erhielten und von dessen Bestellung sich und ihre Familie ernähren konnten. Sachlich ist es dann aber recht wahrscheinlich, daß die Häufigkeit des Titels *wꜥ.w* bei Feldbestellern dazu geführt hat, daß dieses Wort zum generellen Begriff „Bauer" geworden ist. Als einziger Hinderungsgrund gegen diesen Vorschlag steht scheinbar die Vokalisation, denn für *wʿ.w* sind aus den Amarna-Texten Formen belegt, die für eine Aussprache *weʿu* o.ä. sprechen (Ranke 1910: 19) und mit der Vokalisation von **ⲟⲩⲟⲉⲓⲉ** nicht vereinbar sind. Allerdings kann man festhalten, daß es im Koptischen auch Nebenformen **ⲟⲩⲉⲓⲉ**, **ⲟⲩⲁⲉⲓⲉ**, **ⲟⲩⲁ** oder **ⲟⲩⲉ** gibt, die sehr gut zur keilschriftlichen Vokalisation passen, und andererseits die keilschriftlichen Formen eventuell wenigstens teilweise auf die Pluralformen bzw. Kollektivbildungen zurückgehen dürften, die koptisch als **ⲟⲩⲉⲉⲓⲏ**, **ⲟⲩⲓⲉ**, **ⲟⲩⲁⲓⲉ**, **ⲟⲩⲓⲏ** u.ä. bezeugt sind. Teilweise kann man nach den Möglichkeiten der Keilschrift auch ins Auge fassen, die ersten Zeichen des Wortes als *wa-i* zu lesen, da das Zeichen PI nicht auf einen Vokalwert festgelegt ist, sondern *w* mit jedem beliebigen Vokal bezeichnen kann.

ϣⲟⲩⲣⲏ „Weihrauchgefäß": Dies Wort wird, sofern nicht ohne Etymologie gelassen, üblicherweise von ägyptisch *ḫꜣ.wt-rʿ* „Altar des Re" abgeleitet (Černý 1976: 258; Westendorf 1965–77: 560). Diese bisher seit Spiegelberg 1930: 38 Anm. 2 nur anhand zweier hieroglyphischer Bezeugungen angegebene Verbindung kann inzwischen auch im Demotischen nachgewiesen werden. Im demotischen Traumbuch pBerlin 15683, Z. 12 gibt es innerhalb einer Liste von Metallobjekten, aus deren Traumerscheinung Vorhersagen abgeleitet werden, auch den Eintrag *ḫwy-Rʿ*, wobei das Wort zuerst mit dem Gottesdeterminativ (für den Gott Re), anschließend mit dem Metalldeterminativ für den Gesamtausdruck versehen wird (vgl. Zauzich 1980: 93, 95 u. Abb. 7, wo aber der hintere Teil des Wortes nicht erkannt worden ist). Da *ḫwy* die übliche demotische Form von *ḫꜣ.wt* „Altar" darstellt, kann hier also die Verbindung realiter und zwar mutmaßlich bereits in der koptischen Bedeutung nachgewiesen werden.

ϣϫⲉ „Spreu": Generell wird hier ein angebliches demotisches *šky* angeführt, dessen Lesung allerdings schon Erichsen 1954: 524 und in seinem Gefolge Vycichl 1983: 277 angezweifelt haben. Tatsächlich ist die Lesung auch eindeutig falsch. Es handelt sich nämlich um das in demotischen Ackerpachtverträgen sehr häufige Wort, das ursprünglich als *šb* gelesen wurde (Sethe 1920: 172f., wo bereits die Lesung *šky* korrigiert wird), nach neueren Untersuchungen aber eindeutig *šw* zu lesen ist und „Leere" im Sinne von nicht bestellten Ackerflächen bezeichnet (Quack 1992; Felber 1997: 140f.). Eine Verbindung zu dem koptischen Wort ist somit ausgeschlossen; dessen Etymologie wird von Grund auf neu angegangen werden müssen.

ϥⲟ „Kanal": Gesichert ist als etymologischer Vorläufer demotisches *fꜥ* „Kanal". Darüber hinaus hat Černý 1976: 265 unter Berufung auf Dévaud zweifelnd vorgeschlagen, das Wort mit neuägyptisch *bꜣy* „ein Platz mit Wasser" zu verbinden. Dies wurde von Vycichl 1983: 280 abgelehnt, der eine Ableitung von *fꜣy* „tragen" befürwortete. Unabhängig davon, ob letzterer Vorschlag zutrifft, kann man zumindest sagen, daß aufgrund des demotischen Beleges der erste Laut als *f* gesichert, Černýs Etymologie somit ausgeschlossen ist, da *f* und *b* weder im Mythus Leiden (aus dem der Beleg stammt) noch überhaupt im Demotischen miteinander wechseln.

ϩⲱⲱⲕ „sich rüsten": Hier ist immer schon mit Recht auf demotisch *ẖ(ꜥ)ḳ* verwiesen worden. Gänzlich unglaubwürdig ist jedoch die weitere Verbindung mit ägypt. *ẖkr* „schmücken", zumal das Kausativum davon als *sẖkr* auch im Demotischen Erhaltung des *r* zeigt. Gerade angesichts des mindestens fakultativ ausgeschriebenen *ꜥ* bietet es sich vielmehr an, eine übertragene Bedeutung von *ẖꜥḳ* „(sich) rasieren" anzunehmen, das im Koptischen als ϩⲱ(ⲱ)ⲕ(ⲉ) auch eine eng vergleichbare Form aufweist. Diese übertragene Bedeutung ist tatsächlich sogar bereits im Mittleren Reich in einer recht bekannten Passage nachzuweisen, nämlich im pReisner II E, 3 u. 5. Die erste Stelle sei als Beispiel zitiert. Dort heißt es *ἰri̯ n=ṯn rḏi̯.t ẖꜥḳ.tw=ṯn ḥnꜥ ꜥꜣꜥꜣ=ṯn m šꜣ.tn=ἰ n=ṯn nb.t* „Macht euch ein Veranlassen, daß ihr ausgerüstet werdet, sowie, daß ihr euch anstrengt(?) bei allem, was ich euch bestimmt habe!" Mit der Ansetzung „ausrüsten" als übertragene Bedeutung von „rasieren" läßt sich hier gegenüber bisherigen Interpretationen (Derchain-Urtel 1966; Müller 1967: 353) ein besserer Sinn erzielen.

ϩⲛⲁ= „wollen": Dieses Wort wird gerne als ein Relikt des alten *sḏm=f* angesehen, wobei es für die Vokalisation der Verbalformen herangezogen wird (Osing 1976a: 176f.). Eine spezielle Theorie sieht in ihm sogar ein Relikt des ursprünglichen Kasusvokals *i* des Genitivs (Callender 1975; Ray 1991: 245f.). Tatsächlich sind diese Annahmen jedoch zu korrigieren. Schon der syntaktische Gebrauch von ϩⲛⲁ= schließt aus, daß es sich um ein altes *sḏm=f* handelt, auch die von Vycichl 1983: 303 ins Spiel gebrachte Ableitung aus einem passiven Partizip wird gerade der Konstruktion des koptischen Ausdrucks im Relativsatz mit ⲉⲧⲉ kaum gerecht. Genaue Klärung der realen Ableitung verschaffen die demotischen Quellen. In einem spätdemotischen (römerzeitlichen) Papyrus, nämlich pBerlin 7056, Z. 3 findet sich der Satz *pꜣ rmṯ n.ἰm=n ntἰ.iw ḥn n=f sṯ=f* „der Mann unter uns, der sich fortbegeben möchte", und hierbei ist *ntἰ.iw ḥn n=f* die Entsprechung zu kopt. ⲉⲧⲉ ϩⲛⲁϥ, wie Zauzich 1977: 152 erkannt hat, der damit die theoretisch bereits von Černý 1971: 46 vorgeschlagene

Ableitung (Černý 1976: 288 nicht erwähnt) aus einem Verb mit anschließender Präposition *n* bestätigen kann, allerdings unter Korrektur des anzusetzenden Verbs. Die Tendenz zur Univerbierung zeigt sich bereits im Demotischen selbst, das in sonstigen Belegen in Handschriften des späteren 1. und 2. Jhds. n. Chr. bereits *nti.iw ḥn=t* und *mtw ḥn=k* für „was du willst" schreibt (M. Smith 1994: 259).

ϩⲣⲓ „Endivie": Teilweise wird hier eine Verbindung zur hieratisch belegten Pflanzenbezeichnung *hri͗* gezogen (Osing 1976b: 193 u. 721f. Anm. 846; Westendorf 1965–77: 383). Zweifel äußert jedoch Vycichl 1983: 307. Diese dürften auch berechtigt sein. Im medizinischen Text pWien D 6257, 9, 34 erscheint nämlich eine demotische Pflanzenbezeichnung *ẖry* (Reymond 1976: 273 Nr. 121), die lautlich fast sicher mit dem koptischen Wort zu verbinden ist, aufgrund des *ẖ* aber nicht zu *hri͗* mit einfachem *h* paßt.

ϩⲱϣϥ „zerstören, zerreiben": Bisher ist nur der hieroglyphische Vorgänger *ḫšb* identifiziert worden, in genau dieser Schreibung *ḫšb* ist das Wort aber auch im Demotischen pBerlin 8278, 2, 21 belegt. Der betreffende Text ist noch nicht bearbeitet (Edition durch F. Gaudard in Vorbereitung), jedoch ist bei Spiegelberg 1902: T. 95 eine Photographie publiziert.

ϫⲡ „(genaue) Stunde": Allgemein ist in den Nachschlagewerken bisher keine gute Etymologie ausgemacht worden (Westendorf 1965–77: 428; Vycichl 1983: 329). Der Vorschlag von Černý 1976: 317, darin ein (unbelegtes!) feminines *ⲧ-ϣⲡ zu sehen, arbeitet mit sehr unsicheren Hypothesen. Demgegenüber gibt es aber eine ebenso einfache wie plausible Lösung, die auch schon längst vorgeschlagen worden ist, da sie keinen Eingang in die etymologischen Wörterbücher gefunden hat, jedoch hier nochmals in Erinnerung gebracht sei. Im Demotischen wird zur Angabe der genauen Stunden standardmäßig der Ausdruck *pꜣ č̣ṱ wnt.t* bzw. mit Schreibvariante *čꜣi̯ wnw.t* verwendet. Daß diese Ausdrucksweise mit koptisch ϫⲡ zusammenhängt, haben bereits Griffiths/Thompson 1904: 35 Anm. zu L. 15 richtig gesehen, Sauneron 1969: 66 bietet zusätzlich ein hieratisches Beispiel und gibt explizit an, der koptische Ausdruck sei durch Metathese aus dem demotischen entstanden. Ohne Berücksichtigung der demotischen und koptischen Formen hat auch Grimm 1994: 192 (zu G 35, j) eine Reihe hieroglyphischer Beispiele der Schreibung *pꜣ č̣ṱ* aufgeführt.

ϫⲱϩⲙ „beflecken": Hier ist als demotische Entsprechung bisher ein Ausdruck *č̣ṱ ḫm* im „Late Demotic Gardening Agreement" A15 angegeben worden (Parker 1941: 93; Černý 1976: 323). Diese Stelle ist jedoch sowohl orthographisch als auch in ihrer tatsächlichen Bedeutung mit großen Problemen behaftet, da dort ein *byr n č̣ṭ ẖm* mutmaßlich einen Korb zum Transport von Erde bezeichnet. M.E. liegt dort vielmehr eine unetymologische Schreibung für *čꜣi̯ ẖm* „Staub (WB III 277, 15–278, 2) aufnehmen“ vor; *čꜣi̯* und *č̣ṭ* wechseln im Demotischen gerade im *status constructus* oft in der Schrift und das Determinativ paßt hervorragend zum Erdklumpen. Ein sehr viel klarerer und eindeutig korrekter etymologischer Vorläufer des koptischen Wortes ist dagegen *č̣ẖm* Mythus Lille A 4 in *pꜣy=y sẖw č̣ẖm n nmy ỉw=f ẖr snf* „mein Schlachthof ist befleckt von einem blutigen Schlachtblock“ (de Cenival 1985: 98 u. 102).

ϭⲱⲧϩ „durchlöchern“: Generell wird ein angebliches demotisches *ḏth* „durchbohren, eindringen“ zitiert. Dagegen spricht aber, daß die Korrespondenz von demotischem *ḏ* zu saidischem ϭ irregulär ist. Zudem ist im Textzusammenhang die angebliche Bedeutung des Wortes alles andere als sicher. Dort heißt es nämlich *n md.t r pꜣ rmṯ ỉw wn ḳs č̣the ḥr tꜣy=f šnbe.t* „zum Sprechen über den Mann, wenn ein Knochen in seiner Kehle steckt“, wobei das Wort zunächst eindeutig Qualitativ sein muß und im Zusammenhang kaum etwas anderes als eine Form von *č̣tḥ* „verhaften, festsetzen“ sein kann—eine Übersetzung „wenn ein Knochen durchlöchert in seiner Kehle ist“ dürfte kaum einen Sinn ergeben, da es darum geht, einen im Hals steckengebliebenen Knochen (bzw. eine Gräte) zu entfernen. Auch die semitische Etymologie *ḳdḥ* ist mit der demotischen Form nicht zu vereinbaren, die deshalb als etymologische Entsprechung zu streichen sein wird.

ϭⲟⲩⲏⲗ „Heuschrecke“: Für dieses Hapax hat Meeks 1994: eine Verbindung mit dem nur in der Wiedergabe eines vorderasiatischen Ortsnamens belegten hieroglyphischen Wortes  vorgeschlagen. Diese Theorie ist nicht auszuschließen, übermäßig plausibel ist sie aber nicht, da die Gruppe *ỉn-ỉw* sonst standardmäßig für *nu* gebraucht wird und kaum mit dem nachfolgenden *r* zusammen insgesamt für ein *l* stehen kann (Hoch 1994: 391f.). Hier soll auf einen möglichen demotischen Beleg hingewiesen werden, der leider aufgrund des schlecht erhaltenen Zusammenhangs unsicher bleibt. Mythus Lille B 8 findet sich eine Schreibung *gwꜥre* mit dem Determinativ des Tierfelles, das im Demotischen nicht nur für Säugetiere, sondern auch für manche Gliedertiere (Ameisen, Skorpione) gebraucht wird. Sofern das dem Wort im Text vorangehende *y* noch zum vorherigen Wort gehört, hätte man eine zumindest lautlich passende Entsprechung zu koptisch ϭⲟⲩⲏⲗ gefunden.

ϭⲟϫϭϫ „schlagen, massakrieren" Die übliche etymologische Verbindung mit *ktkt* scheint mir schon rein semantisch falsch, zumal *ktkt* gegen WB V 146, 13f. tatsächlich durchaus nicht „schlachten" bedeutet, sondern nur die Bedeutung „zittern, wackeln" hat (Quack 1997: 333). Zudem ist die phonetische Entsprechung von altem *t* zu ϫ irregulär, die bohairische Form ϭⲟⲧϭⲉⲧ ist im Vergleich zu allen anderen Dialekten sicher als Dissimilation zu erklären. Es dürfte aber einen besseren Kandidaten geben, nämlich hierogylphisches *kčkč*, das in dem Satz *n pꜣ.w wḏ.n=f kčkč* „er befahl nichts Mangelhaftes" (oder „er befahl kein Massaker"?) bezeugt ist (vgl. Drioton 1944: S. 116f., wo das Wort zu Unrecht mit *ktkt* „zittern, beben" zusammengeworfen worden ist, das schon aufgrund seiner demotischen Form *ḳtḳt* Chascheschonqi 21, 4 unbedingt abzutrennen ist). Die „hyperkorrekte" Konstruktion statt des eigentlich im klassischen Ägyptisch richtigen *n pꜣw=f wḏ* spricht übrigens für eine relativ späte Entstehung der hieroglyphischen Passage.

Bibliographie

Allen (James P.): 1984 The Inflection of the Verb in the Pyramid Texts, BiAe 2, Undena Publications, Malibu.

Bresciani (Edda)/Pernigotti (Sergio)/Betrò (Maria Carmela): 1983 Ostraca demotici da Narmuti I, Giardini, Pisa.

Budde (Dagmar)/Kurth (Dieter): 1994 „Zum Vokabular der Bände Edfou V–VIII", S. 1–24 in: D. Kurth (Hrsg.), Die Inschriften des Tempels von Edfu, Beiheft 4. Edfu: Studien zu Vokabular, Ikonographie und Grammatik, Harrassowitz, Wiesbaden.

Brugsch (Heinrich): 1888 "Das Gedicht vom Harfner. Eine demotische Studie", ZÄS 26, S. 1–52.

Callender (John Bryan): 1975 "Afroasiatic Cases and the Formation of Ancient Egyptian Constructions with Possessive Suffixes", Afroasiatic Linguistics 2/6, S. 95–112.

Cauville (Sylvie): „Un inventaire de temple: Les papyrus Berlin 10.472 A et 14400", ZÄS 122, S. 38–61.

de Cenival (Françoise) 1985: „Les nouveaux fragments du mythe de l'œil du soleil de l'Institut de Papyrologie et d'Égyptologie de Lille", CRIPEL 7, S. 95–115.

Černý (Jaroslav): 1971 "Coalescence of Verbs with Prepositions in Coptic", ZÄS 97, S. 44–46.

——: 1976 Coptic Etymological Dictionary, Cambridge University Press, Cambridge u.a.

——/Kahle (P.E.)/Parker (Richard A.) 1957: "The Old Coptic Horoscope", JEA 43, S. 86–100.

Dévaud (Eugène): 1923 „Notes de lexicologie copte", Le Muséon 36, S. 83–99.
Derchain-Urtel (Marie-Thérèse): 1966 „Faire l'impossible en Égyptien", CdE 41, S. 100–101.
Drioton (Étienne): 1944 „Les dédicaces de Ptolémée Évergète II sur le deuxième pŷlone de Karnak", ASAE 44, S. 111–162.
Edwards (I.E.S.): 1960 Hieratic Papyri in the British Museum, Fourth Series. Oracular Amuletic Decrees of the Late New Kingdom, The British Museum, London.
Erichsen (Wolja): 1954 Demotisches Glossar, Ejnar Munksgaard, Kopenhagen.
Felber (Heinz): 1997 Demotische Ackerpachtverträge der Ptolemäerzeit. Untersuchungen zu Aufbau, Entwicklung und inhaltlichen Aspekten einer Gruppe von demotischen Urkunden. Harrassowitz, Wiesbaden.
Gabra (Gawdat): 1988 ⲧⲉϩⲉⲛ „grün" und ⲧⲉϩⲛⲏ „Saat (junges Getreide?)", GM 105, S. 11–13.
Gallo (Paolo): 1997 Ostraca demotici e ieratici dall'archivio bilingue di Narmouthis II (nn. 34–99), Editione EES, Pisa.
Gasse (Annie): 1988 Données nouvelles administratives et sacerdotales sur l'organisation du domaine d'Amon XXe–XXIe dynastie à la lumière des papyrus Prachov, Reinhardt et Grundbuch (avec édition princeps des papyrus Louvre AF 6345 et 6346–7), BdE 104, IFAO, Kairo.
Griffith (Francis Llewelyn)/Thompson (Herbert): 1904 The Demotic Magical Papyrus of London and Leiden, Vol. 1, H. Grevel & Co, London.
Grimm (Alfred): 1994 Die altägyptischen Festkalender in den Tempeln der griechisch-römischen Epoche, ÄAT 15. Harrassowitz, Wiesbaden.
Hoch (James E.): 1994 Semitic Words in Egyptian Texts of the New Kingdom and Third Intermediate Period, Princeton University Press, Princeton.
Hughes (George R.): 1968 "A Demotic Plea to Thoth in the Library of G. Michaelides", JEA 54, S. 176–187.
Jasnow (Richard): 1984 "Three Notes on Demotic Lexicography", Enchoria 12, S. 7–13.
Lexa (František) 1947–51: Grammaire démotique, Selbstverlag, Prag.
Meeks (Dimitri): 1994 „Étymologies coptes. Notes et remarques", S. 197–212 in: S. Giversen, M. Krause, P. Nagel (Eds.), Coptology. Past, Present, and Future, OLA 61, Peeters, Leuven.
——: 1999 „Dictionnaires et lexicographie de l'Égyptien ancien. Méthodes et résultats", BiOr 56, Sp. 569–594.
Muchiki, (Yoshiyuki): 1999 Egyptian Proper Names and Loanwords in North-West Semitic. SBL Dissertation Series 173, Society of Biblical Literature, Atlanta.
Müller (Dieter): 1967 „Neue Urkunden zur Verwaltung im Mittleren Reich", Or 36, S. 351–364.
Nagel (Peter) 1999: Kephalaia I, zweite Hälfte. Lieferung 13/14, Kohlhammer, Stuttgart.
Osing (Jürgen): 1976a Der spätägyptische Papyrus BM 10808, ÄA 33, Harrassowitz, Wiesbaden.
——: 1976b Die Nominalbildung des Ägyptischen, SDAIK 3, Philipp v. Zabern, Mainz.
Parker (Richard A.): 1941 "A Late Demotic Gardening Agreement", JEA 26, S. 84–113, T. XVII–XX.
Quack (Joachim Friedrich): 1992 „Ein demotischer Ausdruck in aramäischer Transkription", WdO 23, S. 15–20
——: 1997 „Rezension zu R. Hannig, Die Sprache der Pharaonen", BiOr 54, Sp. 328–334.
——: 1999a „Der historische Abschnitt des Buches vom Tempel", S. 267–278 in: J. Assmann, H. Blumenthal (Hrsg.), Literatur und Politik im pharaonischen und ptolemäischen Ägypten, BdE 127, IFAO, Kairo.

——: 1999b „Rezension zu W. Westendorf, Handbuch der altägyptischen Medizin", OLZ 94 (1999), Sp. 455–462.
——: 2000a „Zur Lesung von Gardiner Sign-List Aa 8", LingAeg 7, S. 219–224.
——: 2000b „Rezension zu E. Lüddeckens, Demotische Urkunden aus Hawara", LingAeg 7, S. 289–292.
——: 2000c „Rezension zu Y. Muchiki 1999", Review of Biblical Literature 2000 www.bookreview.org.
——: 2000d „Kollationen und Korrekturvorschläge zum Papyrus Carlsberg 1", S. 165–171 in: P.J. Frandsen, K. Ryholt (Eds.), The Carlsberg Papyri 3. A Miscellany of Demotic Texts and Studies, CNI Publications 22, Museum Tusculanum Press, Kopenhagen.
Ranke (Hermann): 1910 Keilschriftliches Material zur altägyptischen Vokalisation, Königl. Akademie der Wissenschaften, Berlin.
Ray (John): 1991 "An approach to the *sḏm-f.* Forms and Purposes", LingAeg 1, S. 243–258.
Reymond (Eve Anne Elisabeth), From the Contents of the Libraries of the Suchos Temples in the Fayyum, Part I. A Medical Book from Crocodilopolis. P. Vindob. D. 6257, MPER NS 10, Brüder Hollinek, Wien.
Ritner (Robert Kriech): 1990 "The End of the Libyan Anarchy in Egypt: P. Rylands IX. cols. 11–12", Enchoria 17, S. 101–108.
Sauneron (Serge): 1969 „La notion de l'heure dans les textes d'Esna", RdE 21 (1969), S. 63–69.
Sethe (Kurth): 1916 „Spuren der Perserherrschaft in der späteren ägyptischen Sprache", Nachrichten der K. Gesellschaft der Wissenschaften zu Göttingen, Phil.-hist. Klasse 1916, S. 112–133.
——: 1920 Demotische Urkunden zum ägyptischen Bürgschaftsrechte vorzüglich der Ptolemäerzeit, B.G. Teubner, Leipzig.
Smith (Harry S.): 1980 "The Story of ʿOnchsheshonqy", Serapis 6, S. 133–157.
Smith (Mark): 1987 Catalogue of Demotic Papyri in the British Museum, Third Series. The Mortuary Texts of Papyrus BM 10507, The British Museum, London.
——: 1993 The Liturgy of Opening the Mouth for Breathing, Griffith Institute, Oxford.
——: 1994 „Rezension zu P.J. Frandsen (Ed.), The Carlsberg Papyri 1", JEA 80, S. 258–260.
Spiegelberg (Wilhelm): 1902 Demotische Papyrus aus den königlichen Museen zu Berlin, Giesecke & Devriebt, Leipzig/Berlin.
——: 1930 „Die ägyptischen Namen für das Rote Meer", ZÄS 66, S. 37–39.
——: 1931 Die demotischen Papyri Loeb, C.H. Beck, München.
Thissen (Heinz Josef): 1984 Die Lehre des Anchscheschonqi (P. BM 10508). Einleitung, Übersetzung, Indices, Dr. Rudolf Habelt, Bonn.
——: 1992 Der verkommene Harfenspieler. Eine altägyptische Invektive (P. Wien KM 3877), DeSt 11, Gisela Zauzich Verlag, Sommerhausen.
Vleeming (Sven): 1993 Hieratische Papyri aus den staatlichen Museen zu Berlin Preussischer Kulturbesitz, Lieferung II. Papyrus Reinhardt. An Egyptian Land List from the Tenth Century B.C., Akademie-Verlag, Berlin.
Vycichl (Werner): 1983 Dictionnaire étymologique de la langue copte, Peeters, Leuven.
Ward (William A.): 1977 „Lexicographical Miscellanies", SAK 5, S. 265–292.
——: 1978: The Four Egyptian Homographic Roots *B-ꜣ*. Studia Pohl, Series Maior 6, Pontificio Istituto Biblico, Rom.
Westendorf (Wolfhard): 1965–77 Koptisches Handwörterbuch, C. Winter, Heidelberg.
——: 1978 „Bemerkungen zum Abschluß des koptischen Handwörterbuches", Enchoria 8/2, S. 41–44.

Wilson (Penelope): 1997 A Ptolemaic Lexicon. A Lexicographical Study of the Texts in the Temple of Edfu. OLA 78, Peeters, Leuven.
Zauzich (Karl-Theodor): 1977 „Spätdemotische Papyrusurkunden IV", Enchoria 7, S. 151–180.
——: 1980 „Aus zwei demotischen Traumbüchern", Archiv für Papyrusforschung 27, S. 91–98, Abb. 7–8.
——: 1990 „Noch eine Versteigerung", Enchoria 17, S. 161f.

OMOFONI

Alessandro Roccati
(University of Rome, La Sapienza)

Premessa

La componente fonetica nella scrittura egizia ebbe sempre grande peso nello sviluppo della stessa, sia a livello di sistema (ad esempio nelle varianti provocate da motivi superstiziosi), sia per fenomeni causati dalla pronuncia effettiva. L'importante edizione dell'Onomasticon di Tebtunis, ad opera di J. Osing, ha messo in evidenza come gli Egizi dell'età romana (e sicuramente anche prima) trasmettessero la pronuncia delle parole mediante l'accostamento ad altre (divenute) omofone. Questo procedimento non è estraneo, nella sua origine, a giochi stilistici fondati sull'allitterazione e affinità di pronuncia, che si ritrova fin da tempi remoti. E' conveniente notarne una sua applicazione anche in funzione della spiegazione dei significati, fondata però sui suoni e non sulle immagini, in particolare per casi di omofonia, di cui vorrei qui presentare due esempi significativi in onore di Werner Vycichl.

1. *Omeopatia lessicale*

La ricostruzione del vocalismo dei verbi monosillabici fornisce l'indicazione base CāC' per il nome d'azione e CūC' per lo stativo (esempio copto inf. ⲙⲟⲩⲛ < mān, qual. ⲙⲏⲛ < mūn). Questo dato è verificabile con congetture fondate su procedimenti di assonanza in testi antichi, che erano anzitutto proposti a livello orale.

In questo caso rientra l'espressione *mtwt mt.ti* «il veleno è morto», usata in testi magici del Nuovo Regno (es. Pleyte e Rossi tav. 77,2), che poteva suonare **mútwa mút(t)a* in base alle nostre conoscenze attuali sulla fonetica del tempo. Il vocabolo *mtwt* rende insieme «seme» e «veleno», e il suo esito copto ⲙⲁⲧⲟⲩ si può far risalire ad un prototipo ricostruito **mútwat*, con caduta della desinenza femminile *-t* dalla pronuncia alla fine del III millennio. Lo stativo di *mt* «morire» nella terza persona femminile del singolare non interponeva invece alcuna vocale tra il tema e la desinenza, come suggerisce la frequente aplografia delle due consonanti dentali, sicché se ne può postulare una pronuncia effettiva **mutta* o **muta* (Schenkel 1999). Si veda anche la grafia 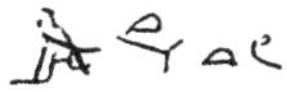 *mttw* in neoegizio; inoltre tale verbo è usato in assonanza anche con altri termini, P. D. e. M. I vs. (tav. 13,4 dell'edizione di Černý 1978) *ink mwt.k ꜣst, nn mt.k* "io sono tua madre (*anàk mutàk* ?) Isi, non morirai (*na mutàk* ?). Se ne deduce la quasi identità di resa dei vocaboli «veleno» ed «è morto» durante tutto il II millennio a.C., che poté generare un procedimento esorcistico di natura lessicale nei confronti del veleno dei rettili. L'identità può essere addirittura totale sulla base della grafia del termine *mtwt* «veleno» che è attestata nel papiro BM EA 9997 (Leitz 1999), passim : *mtty* , e specialmente tav. 3, 7 : *tꜣ mtty mt*[. . .), fr. Orientalia 70 (2001) 194.

L'assonanza valeva qui probabilmente da mezzo di annientamento.

2. *Omografia provocata da omofonia*

Nell'obelisco lateranense le iscrizioni geroglifiche aggiunte da Thutmosi IV riportano un'espressione  *m innt.f* (Urk. IV 1550,3), che a prima vista si comprenderebbe nel senso di «come cosa che egli deve apportare», con un participio passivo reduplicato, o una forma verbale relativa con raddoppiamento (secondo la terminologia del Gardiner). Il riscontro puntuale del testo richiede invece che l'espressione sia analizzata come *m in.n (i)t.f* «come quello (obelisco) che suo padre (Thutmosi III) aveva portato». Lo stile epigrafico e la somiglianza delle due espressioni potrebbero da soli bastare a spiegare la grafia ambigua; nondimeno si possono addurre ragioni di ordine fonetico in favore di una identità tra le due espressioni anche a livello di pronuncia.

Per una pronuncia **aninatVf* del participio passivo con raddoppiamento della seconda radicale provvedono indicazioni giochi di allitterazione (Roccati 1988). La forma *sḏm.n.f* del verbo *ini* «portare» può egualmente esser ricostruita come **anina* (Roccati 1988). Richiede invece una spiegazione il lemma *it.f* «suo padre», poiché la resa copta **ⲉⲓⲱⲧ** presuppone un antetecedente **iāti* o **iāta*. La semivocale *j* iniziale non è però certa in base all'etimologia che collega il vocabolo ad un termine mediterraneo *atta*. La mia impressione è che la *j* iniziale presente nella forma copta sia secondaria e che derivi in particolare dall'uso vocativo : **ja āti*, o simili «o padre mio», come in arabo *ja-bū-ia*. Si può confrontare anche la grafia  per *pꜣy(.ỉ) it* in una tomba tebana della XVIII dinastia (Polz 1997, p. 34), copto ⲡⲁⲉⲓⲱⲧ.

Una indicazione in tale senso è provveduta dalla Stele del Sogno di Tanutamon (Urk.III 60 [11]) *ỉty ỉt tꜣ nbt* «sovrano che ha vinto ogni terra», in cui *ỉty* e *ỉt tꜣ* giocano sugli stessi suoni : **at(t)a at ta (nibi)*, ed è molto probabile una identità originaria tra i termini per «padre» e «sovrano».

Se si accetta la ricostruzione della pronuncia **atVf* per «suo padre», si può allora pensare ad una crasi tra la *a* finale di **anina* e la *a* iniziale di **atVf*, ottenendo la forma **aninatVf*, che è appunto identica al participio passivo suddetto.

Bibliografia

J. Černý, Papyrus hiératiques de Deir el-Médineh, tomo I (Doc. de Fouilles VIII), Cairo 1978.

Chr. Leitz, Magical and Medical Papyri of the New Kingdom, Hieratic Papyri in the British Museum VII, London 1999.

J. Osing, Hieratische Papyri aus Tebtunis, Copenhagen 1999.

W. Pleyte e F. Rossi, Papyrus de Turin, Leiden 1869.

D. Polz, Das Grab des Hui und der Kel (Theben Nr. 54), Mainz 1997.

A. Roccati, Scritture ellittiche in egiziano: Vic.Or. 7 (1988) 35–38.

W. Schenkel, Haplographie von *t* als scheinbares morphologisches Indiz: GM 171 (1999) 103–111.

HURRISCH ḪIAROḪḪE "GOLDENES" ALS FACHTERMINUS IM ÄGYPTISCHEN

Thomas Schneider
(University of Basel)

Die Terminologie der Bestandteile des ägyptischen Streitwagens umfaßt zahlreiche nichtägyptische Fachtermini. Bei der Beschreibung des Wagenkastens erscheint in Pap. Anastasi IV (Schulman 1986) 16, 8 in besonders ungewohnter Notation der Begriff  ḫtrḫt: *jw nꜣy-śn ʿ-m-d-j-y bꜣk.w m nbw nꜣy-śn ḫtrḫt m nbw* "ihre Stützen [semit. ʿmd] sind aus Gold gearbeitet, ihre ḫtrḫt sind aus Gold". Mit den 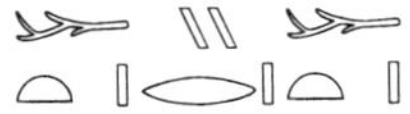 sind allem Anschein nach die Brüstungsstangen des Wagenkastens (upper framework of the chariot box; Schulman 1986, 42f. [21.], Hoch 1994, 252f. und Fuhrmann 1989, 231 [35.]) gemeint, die mit Gold überzogen bzw. beschlagen gewesen sein dürften (zu den Techniken vgl. Reiter 1997, 437–464; Nicholson/Shaw 2000, 165f.). In der Notation des Ausdrucks liegt offenbar eine sogenannte Wortschreibung unter zweifacher Verwendung von ägyptisch *ḫt* "Holz" vor. Da das (grundsätzlich stammhafte) <t> des ägyptischen Lexems letztlich aber wie die Endung <t> des Femininums nicht mehr gesprochen wurde (*ḫit > kopt. ϣⲉ, s. Osing 1976, 294.409), erwog Hoch neben einer Lesung <ḫtr> alternativ auch <ḫir> oder <ḫirḫi> (Hoch 1994, 252f.; auch <ḫtrḫt> kann nicht a priori ausgeschlossen werden). Eine überzeugende etymologische Herleitung des Lehnwortes konnte bisher aber nicht gefunden werden; weder Hochs Anschluß an semitisch ḫṭr "Stab" noch mein eigener Vergleich mit hethitisch ḫattalu "Riegel" (Schneider 1996, 176) sind überzeugend.

Notation und Bedeutung scheinen mir jetzt aber eine Interpretation als hurritisch *ḫiaroḫḫe* "golden, Goldenes, Gold" zu befürworten, das eine Ableitung mit dem Eigenschaftssuffix -ḫḫe (stimmloser velarer Reibelaut, vgl. Wegner 2000, 40) von *ḫiari* "Gold" (ḫiar=o=ḫḫe; Wegner 2000, 48) darstellt. Für Belege von *ḫiaroḫḫe* s. Laroche 1972, 105; Haas 1984, Index S. 367f.; Haas 1988, II, Index S. 22; vgl.

Haas 1998, 219 mit Anm. 200. Der vorliegende Terminus wäre damit ein weiterer Beleg für die erst in sehr geringem Umfang nachgewiesenen hurritischen Lehnwörter im Ägyptischen (dazu Schneider 1999, 679f.). Gleichzeitig würde diese Etymologie den Abfall des stammhaften <t> von *ḫt* schon für das Neue Reich erweisen. Da auch für intervokalisches /r/ (VrV) Verwendung findet (vgl. Hoch 1994, 126 und 406), kann als wünschenswert deutliche ägyptische Näherungsschreibung für hurr. /ḫiaroḫḫe/ betrachtet werden.

Bibliographie

Fuhrmann 1989: M. Fuhrmann, Fuhrwesen und Pferdehaltung im Alten Ägypten, Diss. Bonn 1989.

Haas 1984: V. Haas (Hg.), Die Serien itkaḫi und itkalzi des AZU-Priesters, Rituale für Tašmišarri und Tatuḫepa sowie weitere Texte mit Bezug auf Tašmišarri, Roma 1984 (Corpus der hurritischen Sprachdenkmäler. Abteilung 1: Die Texte aus Bogazköy; Bd. 1).

—— 1988: V. Haas/I. Wegner (Hgg.), Die Rituale der Beschwörerinnen sal SU.GI, Roma 1988 (Corpus der hurritischen Sprachdenkmäler. Abteilung 1: Die Texte aus Bogazköy; Bd. 5).

Hoch 1994: J.E. Hoch, Semitic Words in Egyptian Texts of the New Kingdom and Third Intermediate Period, Princeton 1994.

Haas 1998: V. Haas (Hg.), Die hurritischen Ritualtermini in hethitischem Kontext, Roma 1998 (Corpus der hurritischen Sprachdenkmäler. Abteilung 1: Die Texte aus Bogazköy; Bd. 9).

Laroche 1972: E. Laroche, Glossaire de la langue hourrite, Paris 1972.

Nicholson/Shaw 2000: P. Paul T. Nicholson/I. Shaw (eds.), Ancient Egyptian Materials and Technology, Cambridge 2000.

Osing 1976: J. Osing, Die Nominalbildung des Ägyptischen, 2 Bde, Mainz 1976.

Reiter 1997: Karin Reiter, Die Metalle im Alten Orient unter besonderer Berücksichtigung altbabylonischer Quellen (AOAT 249), Münster 1997.

Schneider 1996: T. Schneider, Rez. von James E. Hoch, Semitic Words in Egyptian Texts of the New Kingdom and the Third Intermediate Period, 1994, in: Orientalia 65 (1996), 174–177.

—— 1999: Eine Vokabel der Tapferkeit. Ägyptisch *tl-* hurritisch *adal*, in: UF 31 (1999) [2000], 677–723.

Schulman 1986: A.R. Schulman, The So-called Poem on the King's Chariot, JSSEA 16(1986), part 1, 19–35; part 2, 39–49.

Wegner 2000: I. Wegner, Einführung in die hurritische Sprache [Cover: Hurritisch. Eine Einführung], Wiesbaden 2000.

SECTION TWO

SEMITIC LINGUISTICS

FOR AN INTERPRETATION OF EBLAIC *NE-SI-IN*

Pelio Fronzaroli
(University of Firenze)

The Eblaic text TM.75.G.2561 ends with a speech addressed by the king of *ʾÀ-du*^{ki} to the assembly of the dignitaries in order to persuade them on the utility of an alliance with Mari:

ù-ḫu-wa-du/Ib-la^{ki}/nu sa$_6$/ap/*ù-ḫu-wa-du/Ma-rí*^{ki}/sa$_6$/*ne-si-in* (rev. VI 6–10) "The alliance with Ebla is not good whereas the alliance with Mari is good . . .".

> *ù-ḫu-wa-du*: This phonetic writing, in construct state position, can be interpreted as an abstract /ʾuḫūw-at-um/, derived from *ʾaḫum* "brother". The pattern is well attested in Arabic with nouns denoting parentage both standing in the plural and in abstract use (e.g., *ʾuḫuwwa* "brotherhood"; cf. also thamud. *ʾbwt* "fatherhood"). The same writing is attested in one of the sources of the bilingual lexical list (*ù*-[*ḫu-wa**]-*t*[*um*], = ma-du$_{10}$, D) and in an excerpt (*ù-ḫu-wa-tum*, = mu-du$_{10}$, TM.75.G.1734+12678 obv. II 1–2), next to the gloss *a-ḫu-tum/du-um* of the other sources (= ma-du$_{10}$, A, B, C); on the interpretation of the two sumerograms, see Krebernik (1983: 32, Verbalformen mit den Präfixen ma- bzw. mu-: "hat (mir) gut getan").

The writing of the last case (*ne-si-in*), of difficult interpretation, has given rise to different suggestions. On commenting this passage in an article on the study of the Eblaic conjunction *ap* (Fronzaroli 1981: 174), I had thought to a verbal form to compare with NI-*si-in* (*ARET* II 33 obv. VII 8; TM.75.G.1444 obv. II 2, rev. IV 2). The latter writing had been analyzed by D.O. Edzard as a 1st person singular without suggesting any interpretation (Edzard 1981a: 136, s.v.; 1981b: 47: NI = *ʾa*$_x$, now *ʾa*$_5$, according to von Soden – Röllig 1991: 10*, 146). In the article mentioned above I noticed also the existence of a verbal theme in the Semito-Hamitic area, phonetically consistent with those writings (**swn* "to know", cf. Greenberg 1966: 58, 42; also Diakonoff 1965: 48), but left *ne-si-in* without translation. In Eblaic texts it is in fact attested both the Semitic verb **w/ydʿ* "to know" (Krebernik 1988: 40 and 97, s.v. *mu-da-a*; Pagan 1998: 185ff.) and *lmd* "to get informed" (e.g., *lu-ma-du-ma*, /lu-yilmad-ū/, TM.75.

G.2237 rev. IV 18) and appears quite unlikely that a verb which does not seem to be elsewhere attested in Semitic languages is here found.

Later on G. Pettinato, in a preliminary edition of the text TM.75.G.2561, interpreted NE-*si-in* as *li*$_9$-*ši-in* "si stabilisca", giving the explanation that it were a "forma ottativa del verbo *šyn*" (Pettinato 1987: 35 and n. 54). The difficulties of this proposal are evident, starting from the reading *li*$_9$ of the sign NE, which seems a rather dubious attestation at Ebla (Krebernik 1982: 196; 1985: 57, n. 11), as well as for the existence of a Semitic verb **šyn* "to fix".

More recently J.G. Dercksen (1990: 444) and M.C. Astour (1992: 45) have indipendently suggested to consider the writing *ne-si-in* as a form of the dative of a independent pronoun of the 1st person singular, /nēšin/ (corresponding to the Akk. *niāšim*). However this hypothesis, accepted also by L. Milano (1999: 143, n. 38), does not seem consistent with the rest of the Eblaic corpus. Indeed a contraction in the first syllable is not compatible with the other forms of the independent pronoun attested at Ebla. Let us compare/niāši(m)/ (šu mu-"tak$_4$"/*ne-a-si*, TM.76.G.235 obv. II 11–12) and /niāti/ (*mi-ne-iš*/ḫi-mu-túm ḫi-mu-túm/*ne-a-ti*/*si-in*/Má-NE^{ki}/*na-ni*, TM.75.G.2237+ rev. V 24–VI 4; *wa*/gi$_4$/*wa*/kur$_6$/*ne-a-ti*/*wa*/kéš-da/*ne-*[ ], TM.76.G.233 obv. V 2-rev. I 1; al$_6$-èn-tar/*ne-a-ti*, TM.76.G.271 rev. I 2'–3'). Furthermore it is to recall that nunation, just seldom written at Ebla, is so far limited to dual endings alone.

The various hypotheses put forward do not seem to take into consideration the fact that the writing *ne-si-in* occurs also in some chancery texts written in epistolary style, such as TM.75.G.1531 (rev. VI 15; left edge 4), TM.75.G.1583 (obv. IV 2, 14), TM.75.G.2039 (obv. II 1). Besides, an interpretation of such writing cannot be offered separately from that of the writing NI-*si-in* (*ARET* II 33 rev. I 8; TM.75.G.1444 obv. II 2, rev. IV 2; TM.75.G.2094 rev. II 7), and perhaps also that of *ne-si-da-an* (TM.75.G.1583 obv. II 10).

Provided the meaning results suitable for all contexts, the three writings could be traced back to the verb **š'n* "to be quiet", attested in Ugaritic and Hebrew (as to Ugaritic, see Dietrich – Loretz 1979: 191f., "ruhig, ungestört, friedlich sein"; as for the reading *mlk tnšan*, instead of *mlktn šan*, in *KTU* 1.103+145 47, see Dietrich – Loretz 1999: 143, with bibliography). The same verb could be still found in Ethiopic languages as **sn'w* "to be in peace, harmony" (for a different opinion, Leslau 1987: 505, s.v.); for the difficulties of Syr.

**šyn*, perhaps a loan from Avestic, see recently Koehler – Baumgartner 1967–1996: 1279f. The three writings could be interpreted as /niš'in/, /'aš'in/, /ništān/.

In the speech of the king of *'À-du*[ki] then, the use of the 1st person plural in the verbal form concluding his words could be a rhetorical device. The king pretends to believe that the dignitaries shared his opinion thus trying to make the assembly agree on his proposal of overturning of alliances: "The alliance of Ebla is not good! The alliance of Mari instead is good, we agree!".

Bibliography

Astour (Michael C.): 1992 "An Outline of the History of Ebla (Part I)", Eblaitica 3, pp. 3–82.

Edzard (Dietz Otto): 1981a Verwaltungstexte verschiedenen Inhalts (aus dem Archiv L.2769). Archivi Reali di Ebla. Testi—II, Missione Archeologica Italiana in Siria, Roma.

——: 1981b "Der Text TM.75.G.1444 aus Ebla", Studi Eblaiti 4, pp. 35–59.

Dercksen (J.G.): 1990 Review of Ebla 1975–1985, a cura di Luigi Cagni; M. Krebernik, Die Personennamen der Ebla-Texte, Bibliotheca Orientalis 47, pp. 433–445.

Diakonoff (I.M.): 1965 Semito-Hamitic Languages, "Nauka" Publishing House, Moscow.

Dietrich (Manfried) – Loretz (Oswald): 1979 "Einzelfragen zu Wörtern aus den ugaritischen Mythen und Wirtschaftstexten", Ugarit-Forschungen 11, pp. 189–198.

——: 1999 Mantik in Ugaritic, Ugarit Verlag, Münster.

Fronzaroli (Pelio): 1981 "La congiunzione eblaita *ap*", Studi Eblaiti 4, pp. 167–176.

Greenberg (Joseph H.) 1966 The languages of Africa[2], Mouton & Co., The Hague.

Koehler (L.) – Baumgartner (W.): 1967–1996 Hebräisches und aramäisches Lexikon zum Alten Testament[3], E.J. Brill, Leiden.

Krebernik (Manfred): 1982 "Zu Syllabar und Orthographie der lexikalischen Texte aus Ebla. Teil 1", Zeitschrift für Assyriologie 72, pp. 178–236.

——: 1983 "Zu Syllabar und Orthographie der lexikalischen Texte aus Ebla. Teil 2 (Glossar)", Zeitschrift für Assyriologie 73, pp. 1–47.

——: 1985 "Zur Entwicklung der Keilschrift im III. Jahrtausend anhand der Texte aus Ebla", Archiv für Orientforschung 32, pp. 53–59.

——: 1988 Die Personennamen der Ebla-Texte. Eine Zwischenbilanz, Dietrich Reimer Verlag, Berlin.

Leslau (Wolf): 1987 Comparative Dictionary of Ge'ez (Classical Ethiopic), Otto Harrassowitz, Wiesbaden.

Milano (Lucio): 1999 "Le dossier éblaite sur l'affaire de 'Adu", Eothen 10, pp. 133–148.

Pagan (Joseph Martin): 1998 A Morphological and Lexical Study of Personal Names in the Ebla Texts. Archivi Reali di Ebla. Studi—III), Missione Archeologica Italiana in Siria, Roma.

Pettinato (Giovanni): 1987 "Dieci anni di studi epigrafici su Ebla", Ebla 1975–1985. Dieci anni di studi linguistici e filologici, a cura di Luigi Cagni, pp. 1–35, Istituto Universitario Orientale. Napoli.

von Soden (Wolfram) – Röllig (Wolfgang): 1991 Das akkadische Syllabar[4], Editrice Pontificio Istituto Biblico, Roma.

NEW ETYMOLOGIES FOR COMMON SEMITIC ANIMAL NAMES

Leonid Kogan and Alexander Militarev
(Russian State University for the Humanities, Moscow)

During their work on the second volume of the Semitic Etymological Dictionary the authors of the present contribution detected a considerable amount of animal names more or less reliably reconstructible for the Proto-Semitic level and, apparently, not yet treated by other scholars. Some of such terms, belonging to different fields of the faunistic lexicon, are listed below. Broader comparison has not originally been intended, but a few Afrasian (Afroasiatic) glosses are scattered throughout the article, especially when they support in some way the reconstructions proposed. A twofold notation for the Proto-Semitic reconstructions containing sibilants and interdentals is adopted: the traditional one is followed by the so-called "affricate" one (for more details cf. SED LXX–LXXI).

Mammals

1. ***tVrbal- ~ *bVrtal-*** 'wild bull, aurochs': Jud. *turbālā, torbəlā* 'aurochs' (Ja. 1656); Tgr. *bärtäl* 'bull (of rhinozeros)' (LH 277).

The Arm. term is traditionally explained as an example of word-composition with the first element *tōr* 'bull'. *bālā* is explained either as a dissimilation from *bārā* 'field, steppe' (Levy IV 634, Talshir 1981 252) or as *bālā* 'prairie, pasture ground' (Ja. 135). Both explanations are clearly folk-etymological.

Of interest is Amh. *tərbe* 'baby elephant' (K 966) which can go back to **tVrbäl* with a weakening of *l* through palatalization.

The variant ***tVrbal-*** is perhaps the original one since it can be compared to Egyptian *ˀirbꜣ* 'Nashorn' (Old Kingdom, EG I 115) with *ꜣ* < *l* in Egyptian and a prefixed **tV-* Semitic. Some anatomic terms with this prefixed element are listed in SED CXLII, most probably to be complemented by a number of animal names in the near future. Tgr. *tärḳoba* 'heel' vs. Proto-Semitic **ˁarḳūb-* '(Achilles') tendon' (discussed *ibid.*) is particularly instructive for the present case since it also exhibits a loss of the laryngeal after this prefixed element.

2. ***tāˀ/y-*** 'kind of antelope': Hbr. *təˀō* (constr. *tō(ˀ)*; Samaritan version *tʔy* [tāˀi]) 'antelope' (KB 1673); Tgr. *tay* (pl. *tayatat*) 'young of gazelle' (LH 320).

Hbr. *təˀō* is a rare word attested only twice in the Bible: the dietary list of Dt 14 (v. 5) where it is listed among wild hoofed animals allowed for food and Is 51.20 (*tō(ˀ) mikmār* 'a snared antelope'). Its meaning is disputed, suggestions under discussion being 'antelope', 'wild goat', 'wild bull' (cf. KB 1673 and a full-range discussion in Talshir 1981 252).

Note Amh. *təw(w)* 'small elephant' (K 994).

An alternative Tgr. etymology for the Hbr. word may be *wäˀat* 'cow' (LH 441) implying a metathesis **taˀaw-* ~ **waˀat-*. Cf. also Gog. *wətəññä*, Muh. Msq. *wəttəññä*, Cha. *wətənä*, Eža *wəttənnä* 'the young (male) of a goat or a sheep, ram' (LGur. 670).

3. ***ˀa(n)z/ḏar-*** ◊ ***ʔa(n)ʒ/ǯar-*** 'wild cat': Akk. *azaru* (*azzaru*) 'lynx' OB on (CAD a2 527, AHw 92); Gez. *ˀanzar* 'wild cat' (LGz. 34).

On a more exact identification of *azaru* as *Lynx chaus* cf. (Landsberger 1934 87, Salonen 1951 186).

Comparative evidence (the Akk. by-form with *-zz-* in particular) speaks against Leslau's supposition that Gez. *ˀanzar* is a misprint for *ˀanar*.

This PS term is certainly cognate of Cushitic terms meaning 'wild cat, viverra' (reconstructed as *[ˀ]*aǯaHar-* in Dolgopolsky 1973 300) so that a PS reconstruction with **ḏ* is preferable.

Har. *adurru* 'cat' (LHar. 19) and Zwy. *adurru* id. (LGur. 18) are most probably Cushitic loanwords. Cf. further HSED No. 2643 where a number of Cushitic, Chadic and Omotic forms close to the present ones are united under Proto-Afrasian **ǯaˀir-* (or **ˀaǯir-*). Akk. *azaru*, however, is compared by the authors of HSED to Egyptian *ḥḏr* 'hyena' (under **ḥaǯar-* No. 1258) which is unlikely: Egyptian *ḏ* does not correspond to Proto-Semitic **ḏ*.

4. ***gVr(-at)-*** 'kind of hoofed animal': Akk. *gurratu*, *agurratu* 'ewe' MA (CAD a1 160, AHw 299); Tgr. *gärwa* 'kudu (antelope)' (LH 576).

Here may also belong Tna. *gahret*, *gahrät* 'antilope femmina' (Bass. 807).

To be compared to Cushitic, Chadic and Omotic forms yielding Proto-Afrasian **gar-*/ **gawar-* 'antelope' according to HSED No. 898.

Birds

5. ***ˁarw/y-/*ˁawr-*** 'bird of prey': Akk. *erû* (*arû*) 'eagle' OB on (CAD e 324, AHw 247; according to Salonen 1973 104, 161 also 'Geier' and 'Lämmergeier'); Jud. *ˁar* 'a bird of prey, perhaps Lammergeyer' (Ja. 1109), *ˁaryā* id. (ibid. 1116), Off. *ˁr* 'bearded vulture' (HJ 884; uncertain); Arb. *ˀaˁwar-*, dim. *ˁuwayr-* 'corbeau' (BK 2 406).

The Akk. term has been repeatedly identified with PS *ʕarwiy- 'lion' (Salonen 1973 104, Fronzaroli 1968 292, AHw 247, KB 87 and many others) which is semantically difficult. On the other hand, comparison of Akk. *arû* to Chadic forms reconstructed as **war-* proposed in HSED No. 15 is not *a priori* impossible but should most probably be abandoned in view of the Semitic cognates with *ˁV-* listed above. More convincing Sem. parallels to these Chadic forms can be found below under No. 15.

In Akk. cf. also *urinnu* 'ein Adler' MB on (AHw 1430) considered a diminutive of *a/erû* in Salonen 1973 286.

In Arb. cf. also *ˁuwwār-* 'hirondelle' (BK 2 405).

Note Tgr. *ˁəwira lila* 'bat' (LH 477).

6. ***ṣaḳ(ʷ)āt-*** ≬ ***caḳ(ʷ)āt-*** 'kind of bird': Akk. *saḳātu* 'a wading bird' SB (CAD s 168), 'Langfussvogel' (AHw 1027); Tna. *šäḳʷat* 'cingallegra; uccelino dalla coda' (Bass. 228).

The Akk. word is found in lexical lists only, equated to Sum. GÌR.GÍD.DA and Akk. *šēpšu arik* 'its-foot-is-long' (see discussion in Salonen 1973 172). Note that the difference in meaning between the terms under comparison is considerable.

7. ***ḫVl-*** 'kind of bird': Hbr. *ḥōl* 'phoenix' (KB 297); Arb. *ʔaḫyal-* 'faucon blanc de bon nid; oiseau à plumage bigarré, et regardé comme de mauvais augure' (BK 1 657).

The Hbr. term is a Hapax in Job 29.18: *wāʔōmar ˁim ḳinnī ʔägwāˁ // wəkaḥōl ʔarbǟ yāmīm* 'And I said: I will dye at my nest // but as the phoenix will I prolong my days'. This interpretation, going back to the Rabbinic authorities ('name of a fabulous bird (Phoenix)' is the translation proposed in Ja. 433), is by far not the only possible one (cf. discussion in Pope 1973 189–90) but is attractive in view of the mention of 'nest' in the first part of the verse and seems now to be etymologically confirmed (derivation of the Hbr. term from Proto-Dravidian *kol* 'bird' suggested in KB is unlikely).

8. ***gVmgVm-*** 'kind of bird': Akk. *gamgammu* 'a bird' SB (CAD g 32, AHw 278); Gez. *gumgumā* 'pelican' (LGz. 194), Tgr. *gumguma* 'esp. d'oiseau' (LH 570). For a possible non-reduplicated prototype cf. Tna. *guma* 'avvoltoio molto grande che ha il collo quasi pelato e divora le carogne' (Bass. 819).

The Akk. term is found almost exclusively in lexical texts (plus one passage from the *šumma ālu* omen series) and its meaning is disputed (cf. discussion in Salonen 1973 166–7). Salonen (as well as CAD and, with a question mark, also AHw) assumed that *gamgammu* is a loanword from Sum. GÀM.GÀM.MUŠEN which is questionable in view of the present comparison; a reverse development (an Akkadism in Sumerian) is at least equally plausible.

To be compared to Egyptian *gm.t* 'Ibis religiosa' (from the Old Kingdom, EG V 166).

9. ***ṣVl-** ◊ ***çVl-** 'bird of prey': Akk. *ṣallalu* 'a nocturnal bird' SB (CAD ṣ 73, AHw 1077); Syr. *ṣalṣūlā* 'avis quae pisces venatur' (Brock. 631); Gez. *ṣilat* (in *ʿofa ṣilat*) 'kite (bird)' (LGz. 556), Amh. *çululle* 'kite, bird of prey' (K 2200) (also *č̣əlat* 'sparrow hawk', *ibid.* 2201), Har. *č̣ulullu* 'kind of bird of prey' (LHar. 51, also *ṭilli* 'hawk', *ibid.* 153), Sod. Zwy. *č̣ululle*, Gog. *č̣ulule*, Msq. *č̣uləlle* 'kind of hawk' (LGur. 180).

Likely a biconsonantal stem with different ways of development in particular languages.

Akk. *ṣallalu* was identified with 'long-eared owl' in Salonen 1973 168, 232, 262 and is therefore well comparable with terms denoting various birds of prey. Interpretation of *ṣallalu* as a "(während des Tages) schlafender Vogel" (< *ṣalālu* 'to sleep') most probably belongs to the domain of folk etymology, though clearly a very old one as the Sumerian (from Pre-Sargonic period on) name of this bird, NÁ.(A.)MUŠEN shows (NÁ = *eršu* 'bed', *nâlu* 'to sleep').

Ethiopian cognates were compared to each other in LGz. 556, all considered Cushitisms.

Note another bird name with the same set of consonants but a different meaning in Hbr. pB. *ṣōṣāl* 'dove' (Ja. 1270); Jud. *ṣōṣəlā, ṣōṣiltā, ṣōṣaltā* 'a species of small little doves' (Ja. 1270), Syr. *ṣūṣəlā* 'columba torquata' (Brock. 636), Mnd. *ṣiṣlia* 'small doves' (DM 394); Arb. *ṣulṣul-* 'ramier, pigeon sauvage' (BK 1 171). These Central Semitic forms were compared to each other in Brock. 636. Akk. *ṣililītu* 'a bird' LL (CAD 1 188, AHw 1100) may also belong here (according to Salonen 1973 262 *ṣ/silīlītu* is *passer domesticus*).

10. ***sVmVm(-at)-** ◊ ***cVmVm(-at)-** 'kind of bird': Akk. *summu* 'dove' OB on (CAD s 380, AHw 1058), *summatu* (*simmatu*) id. OAkk. on (CAD s 378, AHw 1058; more details on both terms—of unknown origin according to von Soden—cf. in Salonen 1973 254–8); Arb. *samāmat-* 'sorte de petit oiseau semblable à l'hirondelle' (BK 1 1134).

Arb. *sumānat-, sumānā* 'espèce de caille' (BK 1 1143) may eventually be related to the present root (note further Egyptian *smn* 'Gans', from the texts of Pyramids on, in EG IV 136).

11. ***kVs(Vs)-** ◊ ***kVc(Vc)-** 'a bird of prey': Akk. *kasūsu* 'a falcon' OB on (CAD k 256, AHw 454: *kassūsu* '(Jagd-)Falke'; cf. also Salonen 1973 207–8); Hbr. *kōs* 'small owl' (KB 466).

The meaning of the Hebrew word is uncertain because of the scarcity of contexts; it is listed among the unclear birds in Lv 11.17 and Dt 14.16 (position in the list apparently not significative) and in Ps 102.7 as a bird frequenting ruins (*hāyītī kə-kōs ḥŏrābōt* 'I have become like a *k.* of the ruins); more details for its identification can be found in Talshir 1981 64–5.

12. ***waw-at-*** 'kind of bird': Jud. *wāwətā* 'stork' (Ja. 376); Gog. Sod. Muh. Msq. *wawat* 'crow' (LGur. 673).

While the difference in meaning is considerable, the phonetic similarity of the terms under comparison is striking (note in particular the atypical *w-* in Jud.) though their independent onomatopoetic origin is also plausible. Note that the Gurage terms were identified by Leslau with (Ethio-) Semitic verbal roots meaning 'to shout'.

Cf. possibly Egyptian *w* 'Wächtel' (als Schriftzeichen) in EG I 243.

13. ***wVˁ-*** 'kind of bird': Syr. *yaˁˁā* 'avis quaedam, expl. Qaṭā i.e. pterocles, al. coturnix' (Brock. 304); Tgr. *wiˁa* 'sorte de passereau' (LH 442).

Note Tna. *ˁaˁa* 'specie di oca selvatica, e voce onomatopeica' (Bass. 701). Possibly related with metathesis is Egyptian *ˁw* 'Kränich' (from the Old Kingdom, EG I 170).

14. ***ḳVr(Vl)l-*** 'kind of bird': Syr. *ḳurlā* 'grus' (Brock. 696); Arb. *ḳirillā* 'espèce d'oiseau' (BK 2 723); Gog. *ḳarulle* 'kind of bird' (LGur. 497; thought to be a Cushitic (Oromo) loanword).

Brockelmann's somewhat vague reference to Greek *grúllos* in connection with Syr. *ḳurlā* seems strange since this word is translated as 'Karikatur' in Frisk 329. A certain phonetic similarity to the Indo-European words for 'crane' (Latin *grūs* and cognates quoted in WH 624) is hardly sufficient to postulate a borrowing (thus, none of these forms exhibit a *-l-*). While an onomatopoetic origin of the Syr. form is tenable (cf. Russian курлыкать said of sounds produced by cranes), its similarity to the remaining forms under comparison is striking.

15. ***ˀarVr-*** 'bird used for decoy': Akk. *arru* 'bird used for decoy' MB on (CAD a2 305, AHw 71); Tna. *ˀirir* 'passeraceo che ha l'istinto di guidare il cacciatore dove vi è il mielle' (Bass. 494).

Realia connected with the use of *arru* (in particular those species which were used as decoy-birds) are discussed in Salonen 1973 29–31. Aramaic forms like Syr. *ˀarrā* 'avis illicebra' (Brock. 45) are most probably Akkadisms (cf. Kaufman 1974 36).

Of interest are Syr. *warwārā* 'merops' (Brock. 186; unless an Arabism), Arb. *warwār-* 'guépier (oiseau)' (BK 2 1526). A non-reduplicated prototype—though with a somewhat different meaning—see perhaps in Tna. *wari* 'specie di merlo' (Bass. 639), Amh. *wari* 'a kind of blackbird' (K 1500). On possible Chadic cognates cf. above under No. 5.

16. ***ˀVbbVl-*** 'kind of bird': Akk. *ibbiltu* 'a bird' SB (CAD i 1, AHw 363; cf. also ibid. 147); Arb. *ˀabābīl-* 'nom d'oiseaux fabuleux' (BK 1 5).

Akk. *ibbiltu* seems a suitable parallel to the misterious birds mentioned in the Qur'ān (105.3), especially from the view of its vocalic shape (a singular like *^{ʔ}*ibbīl-at-* is easily conceivable for a broken plural ^{ʔ}*abābīl-* in Arabic). On unsuccessful attempts of interpreting the Qur^{ʔ}ānic term by both traditional and modern philologists cf. Jeffery 1938 43–4. An exact identification of the Akk. term is difficult, however, cf. Salonen 1973 137, 193 ("ein schwalbenähnlicher Vogel").

Gez. *bābil* 'name of a fictious bird' (LGz. 85) is clearly an Arabism.

A number of other bird names based on biconsonantal **bVl-* and therefore comparable to the present root are attested throughout Semitic: Akk. *bulīlu* 'a species of crested bird' SB (CAD b 310, AHw 137, compared by von Soden to Arb. *bulu^{ʕ}lu^{ʕ}-* 'langhalsiger Wasservogel'); Arb. *bulbul-* 'rossignol' (BK 1 157; most probalbly borrowed into Mnd. *bulbul,* var. *bulul* 'nightingale', cf. DM 55; the alleged Iranian origin of this well-known term is strongly rejected in Eilers 1971 609); Tgr. *bäla* 'a small brown bird' (LH 268), Amh. *bullal* 'dove' (K 862, compared to Arb. *bulbul-* in DRS 68); Msq. Gog. Sod. Wol. *bullal,* Muh. *bulle,* Eža *bunnəyät,* Cha. Gyt. *bunyät,* Gyt. *bunwät,* Enm. Gyt. *bunār,* Enm. *bunəyäd,* End. *bunnarä* 'pigeon' (LGur. 141; compared to Akk. *bulīlu* in the Addenda, p. 728).

To be compared to a number of similar terms in non-Semitic Afrasian (reconstructed as Proto-Afrasian **bul-* 'dove' in HSED No. 300).

Reptiles, Worms, etc.

17. ***gVdVr-*** 'kind of worm': Tna. *g^{w}ändära* 'vermi intestinali, che diconsi' (Bass. 879), Amh. *g^{w}ändära, g^{w}ändora* 'a kind of intestinal worm, hookworm' (K 2012); Mhr. *gədərēt* 'worm' (JM 114), Hrs. *gederēt* 'woodworm' (JH 38), Jib *əẑdírə́t* 'small insect (which eats clothes, wood)' (JJ 71).

Any connection with ***garad-*** 'kind of insect' (No. 21)?

18. *^{ʔ}**aṯ(h)al-** ≬ ***ʔač(h)al-*** 'mythical reptile, dragon, crocodile': Syr. ^{ʔ}*ātalyā* 'draco; stella, quae solem tegens eclipsim efficit' (Brock. 55), Mnd. *talia* 'fictive dragon causing eclipse' (DM 479); Tgr. ^{ʔ}*ashalät* 'dragon' (LH 361), Tna. ^{ʔ}*asälät,* ^{ʔ}*ashalät* 'animale favoloso, di smisurata grandezza e della specie del coccodrilla' (Bass. 493).

Syr. and Mnd. terms are traditionally considered loanwords from Akk. *attalû* 'eclipse' (cf. Kaufman 1974 40 with previous literature). However, there is no reference to any mythical creature producing eclipse in the extant Akkadian literature so that a loan hypothesis is plausible for the astronomical meaning only. The similarity of Arm. and Eth. terms both in form and meaning is striking and it is tempting to suppose a borrowing. However, an Aramaic loanword in Neo-Ethiopian (without being attested in Geez!) is an incredible rarity.

Of interest is Gez. *nestāli* (*nesātāli, nəstāle*) 'serpent-idol of bronze; field snake' (LGz. 403). It is considered a transcription of Greek *neesthan* (< Hbr. *nəḥuštān*) by Leslau, but this interpretation does not explain the word-final *-le/-li*. A contamination with the present root would seem a plausible solution even though **ʔaṯ(h)al-* is not reflected in the extant Classical Ethiopic sources.

The Sem. term has parallels in other Afrasian, cf. Berb.: Hgr. *âššel*, Ayr *aššel*, pl. *aššel-ăn*, Mzab *t-iššəl-t* 'snake, viper' (see Kossmann No. 681; all < **Haššil* < **ʔaččVl*); North Cush.: Beja *sáala* 'big snake, Boa constrictor' (Rein, 198; < **čaʔal*, with metathesis?); South Cush.: Dah. *ṯáʔala* 'puff adder' (Ehr., Eld. & Nur. 8; metathetic it *ṯ* is < **č*).

Here may also belong one of the two Eg. terms: *swy*, crocodile image, in B.D. (EG IV 65), possibly < **swl* < **čwl*; and *sry.w* 'snake' in Pyr. (*ibid.* 193), possibly < **sly* < **čly*.

19. ****ḏVr-*** ≬ ****ǯVr-*** 'kind of parasite worm/insect': Jud. *dīrā* 'name of a grain worm' (Ja. 305); Arb. *ḏarr-* 'très-petites fourmis' (BK 1 766); Mhr. *ḏərḏēr* 'flea' (JM 81), Hrs. *ḏerḏīr* id. (JH 29; also *ḏarr* 'ants' *ibid.* 28), Jib. *ḏɛrḏér* 'flea' (JJ 47).

Not without semantic difficulties.

Hbr. pB. *dūrā* (*dawwārā*) 'a parasite worm in the bowels' (Ja. 289) is probably an Aramaism.

Cf. possibly the Afrasian parallels united under **ǯaʔar-* 'insect' in HSED No. 2641.

Insects etc.

20. ****hatVtVw/y-at-*** 'spider': Akk. *ettūtu* (*ettītu, uttūtu*) 'spider' OB on (CAD e 396, AHw 263); Tgr. *hatatit* 'spider' (LH 17).

The pl. *et-tu-wa-tum* once attested in Akk. suggests that *-t* is, at least synchronically, not part of the root in this language. Both Akk. and Tgr. point to a combination of a "weak" radical and the fem. marker in *Auslaut* (**-Vw-at-* > *-ūt-*, **-Vy-at-* > *-it*). At the same time, the Tgr. form looks very much like a broken plural from a non-attested form like **hVttVt-* with final *-t* forming part of the root. **ha-* > *e-* in Akk. is unusual though not without precedent.

The Akk. form can by no means be connected with PS **ʕankabVṯ-* 'spider' (cf. Landsberger 1934 137 where this comparison is admitted as "möglich").

21. ****garad-*** 'kind of insect': Arb. *ǯarād-* 'sauterelle' (BK 1 276), *ǯardam-* 'espèce de sauterelle noire et à tête verte' (*ibid.* 278); Tna. *gärädo* 'ragno di colore molto oscuro, il cui morso dicono sia mortale' (Bass. 820); Jib. *gérɔ́d* 'locusts' (JJ 78).

An Arabism in Jib. cannot be ruled out.

22. ***sVḥ/ḫVṭ-** ◊ ***cVḥ/ḫVṭ-** 'kind of insect': Akk. *saḫṭu* 'a locust' SB (CAD s 67, AHw 1010); Gez. *səhiṭ, səḥiṭ* 'fly' (LGz. 492).

Not quite certain as the Akk. term is a hapax in a lexical list and the reading of the first sign is not entirely clear ([*s*]*a*?-*aḫ-ṭu*).
Cf. Amh. *suṭi* 'tapeworm' (K 590), *šuṭi* id. (*ibid.* 664).

23. ***ḫVnz(iz)-** ◊ ***ḫVnʒ(iʒ)-** 'kind of insect': Akk. *ḫanzizītu* (*ḫazzizētu*) 'a green winged insect' SB (CAD ḫ 83, AHw 321); Arb. *ḫunzuwānat-* 'mouche qui s'attaque au chameau, s'introduit dans son nez et le tourmente' (BK 1 639); Tna. *ḥənǯiǯ* 'specie di calabrone' (Bass. 58), Amh. *ənzəz, ənziz* 'beetle' (K 1228), Cha. Eža Enn. End. Gye. *ənzəz*, Muh. Msq. Gog. Sod. *ənzizza* 'May bug' (LGur. 78).

Sel. *zīzo*, Wol. *zizo* 'May bug' (LGur. 78) are connected by Leslau with the Eth. forms quoted above, but should rather be separated from these and united with such terms as Hbr. *zīz* 'the small creatures that ruin the fields' (KB 268) and Arb. *zīz-* 'cigale' (BK 1 1032).
Akk. *anzūzu* 'a spider' SB (CAD a2 155, AHw 56, see also Landsberger 1934 138–9) comes close both phonetically and semantically, but precludes a reconstruction with **ḫ-* based on Arb. *ḫunzuwānat-*. Note, however, *ḥ-* in Arb. *ḥuwwāz-* 'grands scarabées' (BK 1 513) which may be also eventually related to the present root.
Of interest is Tgr. *ḥənǯur* 'wasp' (d'Abb.: 'scarabée')' (LH 86).

24. ***gVg-** 'kind of insect': Syr. *gəwāgay* 'aranea' (Brock. 108); Gez. *gugā* 'flea' (LGz. 184).

25. ***mVšVṭ-** ◊ ***mVsVṭ-** 'kind of insect': Syr. *māšoṭā* 'locusta non alata; teredo; erucae' (Brock. 407); Gez. *mâsəṭ* 'termite, white ant' (LGz. 369; according to Leslau, an Amharism), Amh. *misṭ, məsṭ* 'termite, white ant' (K 222).

Jud. *šāmōṭā, šāmūṭā* 'name of a species of locusts' (Ja. 1592) is obviously related with metathesis.

26. ***ṣVlVm-** ◊ ***çVlVm-** 'kind of insect': Syr. *ṣlmwḥ*?, *ṣlmwny*?, *ṣlmwnt*? (all unvocalised) 'tarantula' (Brock. 630); Arb. *ˀal-ˀaṣlam-* 'puce' (BK 1 1364); Tna. *ṣällam ṭel* 'ragno di colore oscuro, velenoso' (Bass. 948).

The Tna. word means literally 'black goat', perhaps a folk-etymological interpretation of an original faunistic term.
Probably related with metathesis is Akk. *lamṣatu* 'a fly' SB (CAD l 68, AHw 533).

27. ***bukay-** 'kind of insect': Akk. *bukānu* (*bukannu*) 'an insect' SB (CAD b 308, AHw 136: translated as 'ein Wurm'); Hbr. pB. *bukyā* 'the spider' (Ja. 145), *bīkay* 'name of a spider' (*ibid.* 161); Zwy. *bōke*

'gnat' (LGur. 135, considered a Cushitism and compared to Tna. *bəkʷ*, not found in Bass.).

Akk. *bukānu* is identified in both sources with *bukānu* 'pestle' which is hardly convincing (see a cautious remark in Landsberger 1934 130).

28. ***nVṣVr-* ◊ *nVçVr-*** 'cricket': Hbr. pB. *nēṣär* 'cricket' (Ja. 930); Syr. *nāṣorā* 'fritinnitor, gryllus' (Brock. 444); Tgr. *ˀənṣərar* 'cricket' (LH 375), Tna. *ˁənč̣ərar* 'grillo che di notte fa un gridio assordante; si sente solanunte nella stagione delle pioggie' (Bass. 697), Amh. *ənč̣ərar* 'a kind of cricket' (K 1252), *ənč̣ərarit* 'a kind of grasshopper' (*ibid.*).

Possibly connected with PS **ṣVrṣVr-* 'cricket' (for a provisional list of cognates cf. KB 1031). Eth. forms are treated here as having the consonantal root **nṣr* with *ˀ/ˁV-* prefixed, but their analysis as **ṣVrVr-* with *ˀ/ˁVn-* prefixed is equally possible.

Abbreviations of Languages and Linguistic Periods

Akk.	Akkadian	Jud.	Judaic Aramaic
Amh.	Amharic	MA	Middle Assyrian
Arb.	Arabic	MB	Middle Babylonian
Arm.	Aramaic	Mhr.	Mehri
Berb.	Berber	Mnd.	Mandaic
Cha.	Chaha	Msq.	Masqan
Cush.	Cushitic	Muh.	Muher
Dah.	Dahalo	OAkk.	Old Akkadian
Eg.	Egyptian	OB	Old Babylonian
End.	Endegeñ	Off.	Official Aramaic
Enn.	Ennemor	PS	Proto-Semitic
Eth.	Ethiopian Semitic	SB	Standard Babylonian
Gez.	Geˁez	Sel.	Selti
Gog.	Gogot	Sem.	Semitic
Gye.	Gyeto	Sod.	Soddo
Har.	Harari	Sum.	Sumerian
Hbr. (pB.)	Hebrew (post-Biblical)	Syr.	Syriac
Hgr.	Ahaggar	Tgr.	Tigre
Hrs.	Harsusi	Tna.	Tigriña
Jib.	Jibbali	Zwy.	Zway

Abbreviations of Lexicographic Sources

AHw	W. von Soden. Akkadisches Handwörterbuch. Wiesbaden 1965–1981.
Bass.	F. da Bassano. Vocabolario tigray-italiano e repertorio italiano-tigray. Roma, 1918.
BK	A. de Biberstein-Kazimirski. Dictionnaire arabe-français. Paris, 1860.
Brock.	C. Brockelmann. Lexicon Syriacum. Halle, 1928.
CAD	The Assyrian Dictionary of the Oriental Institute, the University of Chicago, 1956–.
DM	E.S. Drower, and R. Macuch. A Mandaic Dictionary. Oxford, 1963.
DRS	D. Cohen. Dictionnaire des racines sémitiques ou attestées dans les langues sémitiques. Paris, 1970–.
EG	A. Erman, H. Grapow. Wörterbuch der aegyptischen Sprache. I–V. Berlin, 1955.
Ehr., Eld. & Nur.	C. Ehret, E.D. Elderkin, D. Nurse. Dahalo lexis and its sources. Afrikanistische Arbeitspapiere, 1989, N. 18 (pp. 1–49).
Frisk	H. Frisk. Griechisches Etymologisches Wörterbuch. Heidelberg, 1960.
HJ	J. Hoftijzer, K. Jongeling. Dictionary of the North-West Semitic Inscriptions. Leiden – New York – Köln, 1995.
HSED	V. Orel and O. Stolbova. Hamito-Semitic Etymological Dictionary. Leiden – New York – Köln, 1995
Ja.	M. Jastrow. A Dictionary of the Targumim, the Talmud Babli and Yerushalmi, and the Midrashic literature. N.Y., 1926.
JH	T.M. Johnstone. Ḥarsūsi Lexicon. Oxford, 1977.
JJ	T.M. Johnstone. Jibbāli Lexicon. Oxford, 1981.
JM	T.M. Johnstone. Mehri Lexicon. London, 1987.
K	T.L. Kane. Amharic-English Dictionary. Wiesbaden, 1990
KB	L. Koehler and W. Baumgartner, revised by W. Baumgartner. The Hebrew and Aramaic Lexicon of the Old Testament. Leiden – New York – Köln, 1995.

LGur. W. Leslau. Etymological Dictionary of Gurage. Wiesbaden, 1979.
LGz. W. Leslau. Comparative Dictionary of Geˁez (Classical Ethiopic). Wiesbaden, 1987.
Levy J. Levy. Wörterbuch über die Talmudim and Midraschim. Wien – Berlin, 1924.
LH E. Littman und M. Höfner. Wörterbuch der Tigre-Sprache. Wiesbaden, 1956.
LHar. W. Leslau. Etymological Dictionary of Harari. Berkeley and Los Angeles, 1963.
Rein. L. Reinisch. Wörterbuch der Bedauye-Sprache. Wien, 1895.
SED A. Militarev, L. Kogan. Semitic Etymological Dictionary. Vol. 1. Anatomy of Man and Animals. Münster, 2000.
Sok. M. Sokoloff. A Dictionary of Jewish Palestinian Aramaic. Jerusalem, 1990.
WH A. Walde, J.B. Hoffmann. Lateinisches etymologisches Wörterbuch. Heidelberg, 1938.

Bibliography

Dolgopolsky (Aharon): 1973 Сравнительно-историческая фонетика кушитских языков. /Comparative-Historical Phonetics of Cushitic. Moscow/ (in Russian).
Eilers (Wilhelm): 1971 Iranisches Lehngut im Arabischen. Actas do IV Congresso de Estudos Árabes e Islâmicos (Coimbra-Lisboa, 1 a 8 de setembro de 1968), pp. 581–659. Leiden.
Fronzaroli (Pelio): 1968 Studi sul lessico comune semitico. V. La natura selvatica.—Accademia Nazionale dei Lincei. Rendiconti della Classe di Scienze morali, storiche e filologiche. Serie VIII, Vol. XXIII, fasc. 7–12 (pp. 267–303).
Jeffery (Arthur): 1938 The Foreign Vocabulary of the Qurʾān. Baroda.
Kaufman (Stephen): 1974 The Akkadian Influences on Aramaic. Chicago and London.
Kossmann (Marten): 1999 Essai sur la phonologie du proto-berbère. Köln.
Landsberger (Benno): 1934 Die Fauna des Alten Mesopotamien. Leipzig.
Pope (Mervin): 1973 Job (Anchor Bible). New York.
Salonen (Armas): 1951 Jagd und Jagdtiere im Alten Mesopotamien. Helsinki.
——: 1973 Vögel und Vögelfang im Alten Mesopotamien. Helsinki.
Talshir (David): 1981 The Nomenclature of the Fauna in the Samaritan Targum. PhD thesis. Hebrew University of Jerusalem.

AN EGYPTIAN COGNATE FOR UGARITIC *ḤWY* (II)?

Wilfred G.E. Watson
(University of Newcastle upon Tyne)

Abstract

Evidence is provided for a Ugaritic verb *ḥwy* II, "to strike" (a homonym of the verb *ḥwy* I, "to live") from context and from comparison with Egyptian *ḥwi*, "to strike, etc.". Wordplay may be a factor. However, some uncertainty remains since proof is by no means conclusive.

This note is by way of an experiment to see whether in Ugaritic *ḥwy* may have another meaning besides "to live".[1] Accordingly, some texts are examined here to see the outcome of such a proposal. The meaning suggested for *ḥwy* (II) is "to strike", as in Egyptian,[2] but the suggestion itself is by no means new. Some time ago, Gordon had explained the difficult verb forms *yšthwy* (etc.) as an Št form of *ḥwy*, "to strike": "The root is Eg.-Sem." . . . *ḥwi* 'to strike'. Thus Ug./Heb. *ḥwy* Št means 'to throw oneself down,' tying in perfectly with the addition of 'earthward' in Heb." (Gordon 1965 § 847; cf. § 856). However, although the proposal is mentioned in Halot (I, 295) it has been rejected by Ugaritic scholars[3] in favour of the explanation by Kreuzer.[4] Here, instead only texts using the G and D forms of *ḥwy* (II) are discussed, not *yšthwy* (etc.), whether or not they are Št forms of *ḥwy*.

[1] The verb *ḥwy* (II) Št "postrarse" recorded in DLU, 186a (cf. also Verreet 1988: 50.111.118, etc.; Smith 1994: 168 n. 95) really belongs to *ḥwy* (I), "to live", as proposed by Kreuzer 1985 and accepted by Tropper 1990: 72–75. Some support for this proposal comes from Arab. *taḥīya*, *taḥāyā*, "greeting, salutation; salute; cheer (= wish that God may give s.o. long life)" (Wehr-Cowan 1971: 221) from the root *ḥayiya* (etc.), "to live" (see also Marcus 1972: 82).

[2] Wb. III 46; Middle Egyptian *ḥwy*, "[t]o hit, strike, smite"; with object of place "[to] visit" (Allen 2000: 463a); *ḥwi*, "to beat, strike, smite" (CDME 165); "**ḥw** is a verb mainly used for dealing with enemies and hostile forces . . . It can be used of the action of weapons" (Wilson 1997: 623–624). Cf. also EDE I, 102. It also occurs in West Chadic (HSED § 1282—though there the *-w-* is considered to be vocalic).

[3] Emerton 1977: 46f. rejects Gordon's proposal on the grounds that "the absence of a convincing cognate in a Semitic language is a disadvantage to the theory that the verb in queston is derived from *ḥwy*".

[4] See previous note; Kreuzer (1985), who suggests "hoch leben lassen" as a "Huldigungsakt" (ibid. 85) a št of ḥwy "to live".

All the occurrences of *ḥwy* (II), "to strike, etc." occur in the "Tale of Aqhat" (KTU 1.17–1.19).[5] There are two clear examples:

(1) KTU 1.18 iv 12–13

at ʿ[l qšth] *tmḫṣh*	You, fo[r[6] his bow], should strike him,
qṣʿth hwt l tḥ[wy]	(for) his arrows you should truly cl[ub] him.

Verreet (1988:109) notes: "Die Verneinung *l* = *lā* bei einem Juss. statt *al* = *ʾal*, ist sonderbar".[7] This problem disappears if the *l* in the second line is asseverative, as in the translation proposed here.

(2) KTU 1.19 i 10–16

kapʿ il bgdrt	like an enormous viper in the sheepfold,
<k>*klb lḫth imḫṣh*	<like> a dog for his stick I struck him,
kd ʿl qšth imḫṣh	thus[8] for his Bow I struck him,
ʿl qṣʿth hwt l aḥw	for his arrows I truly clubbed him.

In both these texts there is clear parallelism between the verbs *mḫṣ*, "to strike"[9] and *ḥwy*. Similar parallelism occurs between *mḫṣ* and *kly*, D stem, "to destroy, wipe out",[10] in KTU 1.5 i 1–2 (and par.) and in KTU 1.19 iv 39–40. Furthermore, the usual translations such as "you should not let him live", in (1) and "I did not let him live", in (2) are very feeble given the context.[11] In fact, it is apposite to say that they lack the punch expected in a climactic line. Note that in the fourth line the *l* is again asseverative.

A third example is less obvious:

(3) KTU 1.18 iv 21–27

bn nšrm arḫp ank	Among the raptors I myself shall hover,
ʿl aqht ʿdbk	over Aqhat shall I station you,
hlmn ṯnm qdqd	hit him twice on the skull,
ṯlṯid ʿl udn	thrice over the ear!
špk km šiy dm	pour out (his) blood like a falcon,
km šḫṭ l brkh	like a hawk on his knees
tṣi km rḥ npšh	Let his life go out like the wind,

[5] Here the transcription is in simplified form for clarity.

[6] "for", literally, "on account of".

[7] Based on the translation "you should not let him live" or the like.

[8] See DLU, 210b.

[9] Or "to slay (by striking down)", Held 1959: 170.

[10] DLU, 216.

[11] See, for example, the translations in Parker 1997: 65 and 67, and Pardee 1997: 350 and 351.

km iṯl brlth	like saliva his verve,
km qṭr baph	like smoke from his nose
u ap mprh ank l aḥwy	and even his very pulse shall I hit!

Here the 10-line stanza is framed by the opening and closing lines,[12] both with redundant and therefore emphatic *ank*, "I", used with a first person verb (*arḫp, aḥwy*). Once again the verb is used with an asseverative *l* (in the last line). And the last line corresponds to [wtʿn] *ʿnt bṣmt mp̀rh*, "[And] Anat [watched?] as his pulse stopped", if correctly restored.[13]

However, in KTU 1.17 vi 32–33, after offering Aqhat immortality like Baal, Anat had said (using the verb *ḥwy* "to live"):[14]

ap ank aḥwy aqht [ǵ]*zr* I shall also make hero Aqhat live![15]

But Aqhat had immediately rejected the promise as a pack of lies, stating that he would die like all men, which proved to be the case.

Conclusions

The following conclusions can be suggested:

1. It is very likely—though not absolutely proved—that there is a second verb *ḥwy* in Ugaritic meaning "to strike, hit, etc." which occurs at least threee times.[16]
2. The closest cognate to the Ugaritic verb is Egyptian *ḥwy* with the same meaning.[17] There may be further cognates in Chadic.
3. Recognition of this verb in Ugaritic shows that *l* is positive or asseverative rather than negative in the three passages discussed.
4. In the *Aqhat* text there seems to be a play on words:[18] having promised Aqhat life (with the verb *ḥwy*, D stem: "to give life")

---

[12] Forming an "envelope figure".

[13] Wyatt 1998: 287, following Margalit 1989: 156 and Wright 1994. For a different solution cf. Pardee 1997: 350 and nn. 75–76.

[14] See Wyatt 1998: 273 n. 112, for discussion of who is speaking here; it would seem to be Anath.

[15] See Verreet 1988: 54–55.

[16] There may be occurrences elsewhere, e.g. KTU 1.4 i 42; 1.10 ii 20 and 1.82: 6.19.34, but they remain very uncertain.

[17] As Emerton (1977: 47) had previously noted "The absence of a known and suitable Semitic cognate does not, of course, disprove a derivation of the Ugaritic verb from a root *ḥwy*, for it is possible that all other traces of the root with a suitable meaning have been lost."

[18] For other plays on words in Ugaritic see Watson 2000.

Anat then threatens him with death because he spurned her offer, and in the execution of her threat she uses the homonymous verb *ḥwy*, "to strike, hit".[19]

Abbreviations

CDME	Faulkner (Raymond O.): 1962—*A Concise Dictionary of Middle Egyptian*, Oxford
CS	Hallo (William W.) with Younger Jr. (K. Lawson): 1997—*The context of scripture.* Vol. 1 *Canonical compositions from the biblical world*, Leiden
DLU	del Olmo Lete (Gregorio)—Sanmartín (Joaquín) *Diccionario de la lengua ugarítica.* Vol. I, Aula Orientalis Supplementa 7; Sabadell, Barcelona 1996; Vol. 2 Aula Orientalis Supplementa 8; Sabadell, Barcelona 2000
EDE I	Takács (Gábor): 1999—*Etymological Dictionary of Egyptian* Vol. I, HdO I 48; Leiden
HALOT	*The Hebrew and Aramaic Lexicon of the Old Testament* I–V, translated by Mervin E.J. Richardson, Leiden 1994–2000
HdO	Handbuch der Orientalistik
HSED	Orel (Vladimir. E.) – Stolbova (Olga V.): 1995—*Hamito-Semitic Etymological Dictionary. Materials for a Reconstruction*, HdO I 18, Leiden
KTU	Dietrich (Manfried) – Loretz (Oswald) – Sanmartín (Joaquín): 1995—*The Cuneiform alphabetic texts from Ugarit, Ras Ibn Hani and other places*, Abhandlungen zur Literatur Alt-Syrien-Palästinas und Mesopotamiens 8, Münster
JSOTSS	Journal for the Study of the Old Testament, Supplement Series, Sheffield
Wb	Erman (Adolf)-Grapow (Herrmann): 1926–1963—*Wörterbuch der ägyptischen Sprache*, vols. *1–7*, Berlin

[19] It may be significant that the composite bow is Egyptian in origin This would explain the choice of at least two Egyptian words (*mpr* and *ḥwy*) much as *iht* is used in KTU 1.3 vi 8–15 which mentions *np*, "Memphis", *ḥkpt*, "Egypt" (twice), since it was a practice in ancient Near Eastern texts to use words from the language of the country in question. See the comments by Machinist 1983 (on Assyrian), Israelit-Groll 1998 (on Egyptian), and Lubetzki – Gottlieb 1998 (also on Egyptian).

Bibliography

Allen (James P.): 2000 *Middle Egyptian. An Introduction to the Language and Culture of Hieroglyphs*, Cambridge.

Emerton (John A.): 1977 "The Etymology of *hištaḥ^a^wāh*", *Oudtestamentische Studien* 20 pp. 41–55.

Gordon (Cyrus H.): 1965 *Ugaritic Textbook*, Analecta Orientalia 38, Rome.

Held (Moshe): 1959 "*mḫṣ/*mḥš* in Ugaritic and Other Semitic Languages (A Study in Comparative Lexicography)", *Journal of the American Oriental Society* 79 pp. 169–176.

Israelit-Groll (Sarah): 1998 "The Egyptian Background to Isaiah 19.18", Lubetski – Gottlieb – Keller, eds, 1998, pp. 300–303.

Kreuzer (Siegfried): 1985 "Zur Bedeutung und Etymologie von *hištaḥ^a^wāh / yšthwy*", *Vetus Testamentum* 35 pp. 39–60.

Lubetzki (Meir) – Gottlieb (Claire): 1998 "Isaiah 18: The Egyptian Nexus", Lubetski – Gottlieb – Keller, eds, 1998, pp. 364–384.

Lubetzki (Meir) – Gottlieb (Claire) – Keller (Sharon), eds: 1998 *Boundaries of the Ancient Near Eastern World. A Tribute to Cyrus H. Gordon*, JSOTSS 273; Sheffield.

Machinist (Peter): 1983 "Assyria and its Image in first Isaiah", *Journal of the American Oriental Society* 103, pp. 720–724.

Marcus (David): 1972 "The Verb 'To Live' in Ugaritic", *Journal of Semitic Studies* 17 pp. 76–82.

Margalit (Baruch): 1989 *The Ugaritic Poem of Aqht*, BZAW 182; Wiesbaden.

Noegel, (Scott B.) ed.: 2000 *Puns and Pundits. Word Play in the Hebrew Bible and Ancient Near Eastern Literature*, Bethesda MD.

Pardee (Dennis): 1997 "West Semitic Canonical Compositions", CS pp. 239–375.

Parker (Simon B.): 1997 "Aqhat", in Parker, ed. 1997 pp. 49–80.

—— ed.: 1997 *Ugaritic Narrative Poetry*, SBL Writings from the Ancient World Series 9; Atlanta GA.

Smith (Mark S.): 1994 *The Ugaritic Baal Cycle. Volume I. Introduction with Text, Translation and Commentary of KTU 1.1–1.2*, Supplements to Vetus Testamentum 55; Leiden.

Tropper (Josef): 1990 *Der ugaritische Kausativstamm und die Kausativbildungen des Semitischen*, Abhandlungen zur Literatur Alt-Syrien-Palästinas 2; Münster.

Verreet (Eddy): 1988 *Modi ugaritici: eine morpho-syntaktische Abhandlung über das Modalsystem im Ugaritischen*, OLP 27, Leuven.

Watson (Wilfred G.E.): 2000 "Puns Ugaritic Newly Surveyed", in Noegel, ed. 2000, pp. 117–134.

Wehr (Hans) – Cowan (J. Milton): 1961 *A Dictionary of Modern Written Arabic*, Wiesbaden.

Wilson (Penelope): 1997 *A Ptolemaic Lexikon. A Lexicographical Study of the Texts in the Temple of Edfu*, Leuven.

Wright (Robert M.): 1994 "Egyptian *np3p3*: a cognate for Ugaritic *mpr* «convulsion»", *Ugarit-Forschungen* 26, pp. 539–541.

Wyatt (Nicolas): 1998 *Religious Texts from Ugarit. The Words of Ilimilku and his Colleagues*, The Biblical Seminar 53; Sheffield.

TRACES OF *IPTARAS* IN ARABIC

Andrzej Zaborski
(Jagellonian University of Kraków)

The fact that some Arabic verbs of the iqtatala i.e. no. VIII class have the same meaning as the forms of the class no. I has been known since a long time but it has been seriously underestimated. E.g. Fleisch (1990, vol. 2, 309–315), Chouemi (1966, 200) and Kropfitsch (1991, 63: "In einigen w e n i g e n [spacing A.Z.] Fällen bestehen Doppelformen") mention only a couple of examples. Only Wright (1906–1898, t. 1, 42) says that "In not a few words the first and the eighth forms agree, like the Greek active and middle voices, so closely in their signification, that they may be translated by the same word" but he gives only three verbs. On the other hand, Tropper (2000, 532) emphasizes that most verbs with infixed *-t-* are not reflexive but rather transitive, intensifying, durative and iterative-habitual while sometimes no clear semantic difference can be established between *Gt* and *G* forms.

As I said already in 1998, 283, the verbs with identical meaning in the I and the VIII class are traces of *iptaras* "Perfect" (< periphrastic passive) which is attested in Akkadian and which has a cognate in Berber as well as in Beja. The number of such verbs is very big and amounts to over one third at least. Here are the examples found in Baranov's *Arabic-Russian Dictionary* (2nd edition) which combines Classical and Post Classical vocabulary and it has been compared with the English version of Wehr's *Dictionary of Modern Written Arabic* (edited by M. Cowan) and partially with the *Dictionary of Classical Arabic* by Lane.

I. There is a big number of transitive verbs with the same meaning in class I and class VIII, many of them not occuring in other derived classes:

aḫaḏa = VIII to take
bada'a = III = VIII to begin
bada'a = VIII to invent
baḏala to give generously = VIII, cf. V to be overgenerous; cf. baḏara to sow, II to waste = bazara to sow
bazza to take away, steal = VIII

basara (1) to tell too early = VIII
baʿaṯa (1) to send = VIII
baʿaṯa (2) to incite = VIII
balaʿa to swallow = VIII
balawa to try, to test = VIII
banaya to build = VIII
tabiʿa to follow, pursue = VIII = III
tajara to trade = VIII
jaḏaba to attract = VIII
jaraʿa to swallow = VIII; cf. V to drink
jarafa to sweep away = VIII; VII pass.
jarama to commit a crime = IV = VIII
jazza to cut off = VIII; cf. jazaʾa, jazara
jassa to touch = VIII; cf. jasara (?)
jasara to span, cross
jalaba to attract, to get = VIII = X
jalawa/jalaya to reveal, to clear up = II = VIII = X, also VII which is 1. medium, 2. transitive
janaya to gather, harvest = VIII
ḥabasa to block, detain = VIII; VIII also passive = VII
ḥaḏawa to imitate = VIII
ḥazza to notch, incise, cut = II = VIII
ḥasaba to reckon, take into account = VIII
ḥaḍana to incubate = VIII to bring up, raise (child)
ḥaṭṭa to put down = II = VIII; cf. VII
ḥaṭaba to gather firewood = VIII (denom.)
ḥaffa to surround = II = VIII
ḥafara to dig = VIII
ḥafiẓa to preserve, protect = III = V = VIII, cf. X
ḥafila = ḥafawa/ḥafiya to recive kindly = VIII
ḥaqura to despize = VIII = X
ḥakara to buy up = VIII
ḥakama to decide = VIII
ḥalaba to milk = VIII = X
ḥamala to carry = VIII
ḥawaza to possess, own, have = VIII = X
ḥawaša to round up = VIII; cf. ḥawaṭa
ḥawaṭa to guard, protect = VIII trans.; VIII also medium
ḥawaya to encompass, embrace, have = VIII
ḫabara to try, test = VIII
ḫabaza to bake bread = VIII (denom.); VII pass.
ḫatala to cheat, deceive = VIII
ḫatama to finish, conclude = VIII (denom.)
ḫaraqa to pierce, break = VIII; VII pass.; cf. ḫarama (?)
ḫazala to cut off = VIII
ḫazana to store, lay up = II = VIII (denom.)
ḫaṣā to distinguish = VIII, also VIII to be distinguished

ḫaṭṭa to mark, outline, trace out = VIII
ḫaṭifa to snatch, seize = VIII = V; VII pass.
ḫalaba (1) to seize with claws = VIII (denom.)
ḫalaba (2) to cajolate, bewitch, enchant (trans.)
ḫalasa to steal = VIII
ḫalaʿa to take off = VIII
ḫalaqa to create, make, shape = VIII
ḫayara to choose, prefer = VIII
adġama IV to insert, incorporate = VIII, VII pass.
ḏaḫara to keep, preserve, save = VIII; cf. ḏakara
ḏakara to mention = VIII
rašafa/rašifa to suck = V = VIII
rakiba to commit crime, to pursue = VIII
rawada to look, search = VIII to explore
zarada to swallow = VIII, cf. sariṭa id.
zaraʿa to sow = VIII
zaraya to rebuke, scold VIII = X to slight, think little of, defy
zalafa to flatter = VIII = V
sabaya to take prisoner, capture = VIII
saḥawa to shave = VIII
sariṭa to swallow = V = VIII, cf. zarada id.
saqaya to draw water = VIII
salla to pull out, remove = VIII
salaba to take away, steal = VIII, cf. salla, salata
samiʿa to hear, listen = V, VII to listen
sanna to prescribe, establish a law = VIII (denom. ?)
sawaqa to drive (herd) = VIII
šaraṭa to impose as a condition = VIII, cf. III and V
šaraʿa to enact laws = VIII = II (denom.)
šamma to smell (trans.), sniff = VIII, cf. V, šamšama id.
šamila to contain, comprise = VIII; VIII also refl.
šahawa/šahiya to desire, wish = VIII
ṣanaʿa to make, produce = VIII
ṣayada to catch, hunt = VIII = V
ṣayafa to spend summer = II, V, VIII (denom.)
ḍahada to oppress, persecute = VIII; cf. ḍaġaṭa id.
ṭaraḥa to throw = VIII
ṭarada to drive away = VIII, cf. II
ʿadda to look at, consider, deem = VIII
ʿarafa to recognize, acknowledge, concede = VIII
ʿarawa to befall, grip, seize, strike = VIII
ʿasafa to oppress = VIII to force, compel; cf. II = IV
ʿaṣara to press, squeeze = II = VIII; V = VII pass.
ʿaqaba to follow = II = IV = V = VI = VIII
ʿaqala to detain, arrest = VIII
ʿamada to support = VIII to employ, use, confirm, authorize
ʿawiza to need = VIII

ʿawaqa to hinder, prevent = II = IV = VIII
ġaraza to insert, stick, stab = VIII; VIII also: to be inserted, cf. VII and cf. ġazza
ġarafa to ladle, scoop = VIII
ġazala to spin = VIII
ġaṣaba to take by force, rob = VIII
ġamara to cover, bury = VIII; cf. ġamma (?)
ġanima to take as booty = VIII
fataḥa to open = VIII = II = X; V = VII to open (intr.)
fatana to subject to temptations = VIII, VIII also: to be subjected to temptations
fadaya ransom, sacrifice = VIII; VIII also refl.
farasa to kill, tear = VIII
faraša to spread = VIII
faraḍa to impose, suppose, prescribe = VIII
faraya to invent lyingly, calumniate = VIII
faḍḍa to deflower = VIII
faʿala to do = VIII to concoct, invent, forge
fakka to separate, destroy = VIII, cf. faraqa (?)
falaya to scrutinize = VIII
fahima to understand = VIII
qabba to cut off = VIII
qabasa to take over = VIII
qabila to receive = VIII = V = X
qaḥafa to swallow, gulp down = VIII
qadda to cut into strips = VIII
qadaḥa to strike fire = VIII
qaraša to earn money = II = VIII (denom.)
qasama to divide, distribute = VIII = VI, V = VII be divided
qaṣṣa (1) to tell, narrate = VIII
qaṣara/qaṣala/qaṣṣa to cut off, shear = VIII
qaḍaya to demand, recquire = VIII = X
qaṭṭa/qaṭaʿa to cut off, tear apart = VIII, cf. qaṭala, qaṭama id.
qaṭafa to pick, gather, harvest = VIII
qafara to follow tracks = VIII
qalaʿa to pluck out, tear out = VIII
qanaṣa to hunt, shoot = VIII
qanawa/qanaya to acquire, get = VIII
qawada to lead = VIII, IX also: to be led
qayasa to measure = VIII = II
kataba to write = VIII; VIII also: to be recorded
katama to hide, conceal = II = III = VIII
kaḥala to paint with kohl = II = V = VIII (denom.)
kasaba to gain, acquire, get = V = VIII
kasaḥa to sweep = VIII
kašafa to uncover, demonstrate, detect = VIII = X, cf. III
kanaza to amass, gather = VIII

kanafa to surround = VIII
laḥiqa to overtake, reach = VIII
laqaṭa to gather, collect, pick up = II = V = VIII
laqifa to seize, snatch = V = VIII
laqima to devour, swallow = VIII; cf. lahima, V = VIII id.
laqiya to meet = VI = VIII
maḥana to try, test = VIII
madaḥa to praise = VIII
mašaqa to draw out = VIII
maṣaqa to suck = VIII; maṣmaṣa id.
mala'a to fill = VIII; cf. mali'a to be full = VIII
malaja to suck = VIII
malaḫa to pull out = VIII
malaka to take in possession, to have = V = VIII = X
mahana to humble, degrade = VIII
najawa to entrust a secret = VIII to whisper = III
naḫaba to select, choose = VIII
naḫala to sift, sieve out = VIII = V
nadaba to appoint, assign = VIII
nadawa to get together, assemble = VIII = VI
naḏara = VIII to promise
naza'a to remove, pull out = VIII = II
nasaḫa to abolish = VIII
nasafa to blow up = VIII; cf. nasama, nafaḫa and tanaffasa
našala to save = VIII
naḍawa to undress = VIII to unsheathe (a sword)
naẓara to look, expect = VIII to wait = V = X
nafa'a to be useful; II = VIII = X to utilize, put to use
naqada to criticize = VIII
nahaba/nahiba to take by force = VIII to grip, seize
nahara to drive away = VIII
nahaka to wear out = VIII
haḍama to oppress = VIII

II. There is also a considerable number of medium verbs with the same meaning in the I and the VIII class:

barada/baruda to become cold = VIII
basara (2) to begin too early = VIII
basama to smile = V = VIII; cf. bašša and bašara
baġaya to seek, desire = VIII
taḫima to suffer from indigestion = VIII
jaru'a to dare, venture = V = VIII
jaza'a to be content = VIII; cf. jazaya to please
jaluda to be resistant = VIII
jahada to strive, endevour = III = VIII; cf. IV
jawaba to travel = VIII

jawaza to pass, come through = VIII = VI
ḥaḏira to be cautious, to beware = III = V = VIII, cf. ḥaraza/ḥarasa (?)
ḥarra to be hot; cf. VIII to be heated
ḥaḍara to be present = VIII
ḥaḍana to clasp in one's arms = VIII
ḥafala (1) to pay attention = VIII
ḥafala (2) to gather (intr.) = VIII
ḥalla to setttle down = VIII
ḥalama to attain puberty = VIII
ḫabba to trot (horse) = V = VIII
ḫasafa to sink, go down = VIII
ḫaṭawa to step, pace, walk = VIII
ḫafiya to be hidden = VIII = X
ḫalawa to be alone = VIII
danawa to be near, to come near = VIII = VI = IV (sic!)
raʾasa to be at the head = V, VIII to become the head (denom.)
raʾaya to see, consider, be of the opinion = VIII
rajaʿa to come back = VIII = III = V
rajafa to be shaken = VIII to tremble; cf. rajja I and med. VIII
rajawa to hope, expect = VIII
raḥala to set out, move away = VIII
raḫuṣa to be cheap = VIII
raḫuwa/raḫiya to slacken, slump = VIII = X
zalafa to approach = VIII, cf. dalafa (?)
raqiya to ascend, climb = VIII = V
rakaḍa to race, run = VIII to move (?)
zahara to shine, be radiant = VIII
zahara (2)/zahawa to blossom = III = IV = VIII (denom.)
zawaḥa/zayaḥa to go away = VIII
zayada to grow, become greater = VIII
sakka to be deaf = VIII
sawaya to be equal = VIII
šubiha (pass.!) to be doubtful = VI, cf. VIII to be in doubt, to suspect; cf. šakka/šakala (?) id.
šarika to share, participate = VIII = III = VI
šaṭṭa to go to extremes = VIII (denom.)
šakawa to complain = V = VIII
ṣabara to be patient = V = VIII
ḍajaʿa to lie = iḍṭajaʿa/iḍḍajaʿa, cf. VII = I
ḍarima to catch fire, burn = VIII = V
ḍaġina to resent, bear a grudge = VIII = VI
ʿaraḍa to happen = VIII
ʿazama to decide, resolve = VIII
ʿaṭiba to perish, be destroyed = VIII, cf. V
ʿakafa to devote o.s. = VIII
ʿalla/ʿulla to be or fall ill = VIII
ʿalana to be known, evident = VIII = X

ʿalawa/ʿalaya to be high, rise, ascend = VIII = V = VI = X
ʿamada to intend, purpose = V = VIII
ʿamila to act. operate, work = VIII
ʿaniya/ʿuniya to be concerned, anxious = VIII
ġubiṭa (pass.) to be happy = VIII
ġadawa to go away early in the morning = VIII (denom.)
ġaṣṣa to be overcrowded, congested = VIII
ġaniya to be rich = VIII to become rich = X
ġawala to snatch, grab = VIII
faḫara to boast = VIII = VI, cf. V
faqada to miss = VIII = X
faqura to be/become poor, needy = VIII to become poor, need
fakara to reflect, meditate II = V = VIII
qadara to possess ability, be able = VIII
qaruba to come near = VIII = V = III = VI
qaṣada to adopt a middle course = VIII
qaʿada to sit down = VIII
qaniʿa to content o.s., be content = VIII
kaʾiba to be sad = VIII
kamala/kamula to be perfect = VI = VIII
kahula/kahala to be middle-aged
lajaʾa/lajiʾa to take refuge = VIII; cf. lawaḏa id. (?)
laḥada to deviate, abandon one's faith = VIII
lazija/laziqa/laṣiqa to stick, cling = VIII iltazaqa/iltaṣaqa; cf. lazima, lawaṭa
lamaḥa/lamaʿa to gleam, shine = VIII
lahiba to flame, burn = V = VIII
lahawa/lahaya to amuse o.s. = V = VI = VIII
maʿiḍa to be annoyed = VIII
manna to be kind = VIII
manaʿa to stop doing something = VIII = V
naʾaya to be faraway = VI = VIII
nabiha to mind, observe; to wake = V = VIII
naḥawa to turn = VIII = V
nazaḥa/nazaʿa to emigrate = VIII
našiqa to inhale = VIII; cf. istanšaqa id.
našawa/našaya to become intoxicated = VIII
naṣafa to reach its midts (day) = VIII
nafaja to spring, jump = VIII
naqaṣa to decrease, become less = VIII
naqama to revenge o.s. = VIII
naqaha to convalesce = VIII
nahaja to take a road = VIII
nahaḍa to stand up, rise = VIII
nawaya to propose, intend = VIII
hamma to worry, be concerned = VIII
hayaba to fear, be afraid = VIII = V; also V trans. (?)

waḫima to suffer from indigestion = VIII
wazuna to be balanced = VIII = VI = VIII
wasiḫa to be dirty = V = VIII ittasaḫa
wasuʿa to be wide, extensive = V = VIII to be extended, cf. X
waṣala to arrive = VIII
waḍaḥa to become clear = V = VIII
waḍuʿa to abase o.s., humble o.s. = VI = VIII

Some medium verbs occur in class VIII only:

iktaraṯa to care, pay attention, take an interest
iltajja to be noisy, roar
imtarā to doubt cf. III (?)
imtaṭā to mount (an animal) = IV
ihtāja to be, to get excited, agitated = V; cf. hayaša/hawiša id.
ittaʾada (w-ʾ-d) = V to be slow
ittajaha (w-j-h) to tend, be directed; cf. V; (denom.)
ittasaqa (w-s-q) to be in good order

III. Another group consists of non-medium verbs which occur in class VIII but not in class I:

iʾtanafa to start; cf. X to start again, renew
ibtadara = III to do promptly
ibtadaha to improvise
ibtakara to invent (trans.!), also: to be the first
ibtahara to present in a dazzling light
ijtarra to ruminate = IV
ijtaraḥa to commit
iḥtabala to ensnare (denom.)
iḥtajja to advance as an argument, plea; cf. V
iḥtajjana to snatch up, grab
iḥtarama to honor, revere, esteem
iḥtāja to have need, to need (?)
iḥtāla to deceive, cheat, cf. I
iḫtaraʿa to invent, devise, create
iḫtarama to destroy, annihilate
ḫazza to pierce = VIII, cf. ḫazaqa id.
iḫtaṣara to shorten, abridge (trans.)
irtajala to improvise
istalama to touch; to receive, get, take over
iṣtafawa to choose, select = X
iṣtabaḥa to light (trans.)
iḍṭarra to force, compel = IV, uḍṭurra pass. to be forced, cf. I to harm
iṭṭalaʿa to look, see, inspect, detect = V = III, also VIII to be informed, acquained
iʿtabara to look at, esteem, respect
iʿtajana to knead = I = II (denom.)

i'tamara to visit (denom.)
i'tanaqa to embrace (denom.) = II
i'tawara to befall, affect; to shape
iġtabaqa to drink in the evenning
iġtamaza to belittle, disparage
iġtawala to assasinate
iġtayaba to slander, calumniate
ifta'ana to tell lies; to violate
ifta'ada to make fire
iftarra to reveal, show; farraja id.
iftara'a to deflower
iftawata to belie, betray
iqtatta to uproot, extirpate
iqtadawa to imitate, copy
iqtaraḥa to invent; to propose, suggest
iqtara'a to vote, elect
iqtarafa to commit crime
iktadda to urge, drive, rush = X (cf. kadaḥa!)
iktaraya to rent, hire = III = IV = X
iktanaha to fathom, sound
iltamasa to request, ask
intajaba to choose, select = X (denom. ṭ)
intaqaša to extract, pull out
intaqawa to pick up, select
ihtabala (1) to intrigue, to scheme, to cheat; cf. I = II
ihtabala (2) to earn = II = V

IV. There are also transitive and causative verbs of the X class which have nothing to do with medium and must be interpreted as *iptaras* "perfect" forms:

ista'ṣalata to uproot, to eradicate
ista'nafa to resume, renew
istabdala to exchange = I = III = VI
istab'ada to single, set aside
istabqā to make stay = IV
istabkā to make cry = II = IV
istabāna to explain, also: to be clear, evident
istaṯbata to verify
istaṯnā to except, exclude
istajadda to make new = II; also: to be new
istajma'a to gather, collect = I, cf. V = VIII medium
istajāba to answer
istajwaba to interrogate, examine, question
istaḥabba to like, to prefer
istaḥadda to sharpen
istaḥdaṯa to renew; to invent, create

istaḥḍara to call, get, send, prepare, bring etc.
istaḥfaẓa to entrust
istaḥaqqa to demand, make requisite
istaḥlafa to make swear
istaḥmasa to fill with enthusiasm (trans.!)
istaḫaffa to carry away, transport
istaḫlaṣa to extract, copy, excerpt
istadraja to promote
istadraka to correct, repair
istadʿā to call, appoint = I
istadāma to make last, to continue
istadarra to withdraw (trans.)
istaraqqa to make a slave (denom.)
istašʾama to perceive an evil omen = IV
istašʿara to feel, notice, perceive = I
istašfaʿa to plead, intercede = I (?)
istašhada to call upon as a witness = IV
istaṣdara to bring about, issue = IV, cf. also II
istaṣfaya to confiscate
istaṣlaḥa to make arable = IV
istaṣnaʾa to have sg. made, produce
istaṭyara to make fly = IV
istaẓhara to show, demonstrate = IV, cf. VI
istaʿbada to enslave (denom.) = II = VIII
istaʿjala to urge, drive, expedite = IV, X also medium
istaraʾa to inspect, review
istaʿrafa to discern, recognize
istaʿazza to overwhelm; also: to become powerful
istaʿṣaya to resist, oppose = I; cf. VI to refuse
istaʿlana to bring to light
istaʿmala to use, employ
istaʿhada to have s.o. sign a contract
istaʿāda (ṭ) to regain, recover, cf. IV
istaġarra (ṭ) to come unexpectedly, surprise
istaġwaya to misguide, lure, bait = I = II = IV
istaġyaba to slander, calumniate = VIII
istaftaḥa to begin, start
istafrada to isolate, cf. faraza id.
istafraġa to empty
istafazza to startle; cf. faziʿa to be frightened, IV to startle
istafayada to make use
istaqṭara to distill
istaktaba to make write
istakṯara to increase (trans.) = IV
istakraba to force, compel = IV
istakrā to hire, rent = III = IV = VIII
istakmala to complete

istaḫlaqa to annex
istamsaka to grab, seize = IV
istanbata to plant, to grow (trans.) = IV (denom.)
istanbaṭa to find, discover = IV
istanzaʿa to drain off, extract = IV
istanzala to make descend = IV
istanšaʾa to search; cf. našada id.
istanfada to consume, use up = IV
istanfaqa to spend, waste (money)
istahalla to begin start, open (trans.), also intrans.
istahlaka to waste, consume; cf. pass. ustuhlika to perish, die
istahwaya to atttract, seduce, charm
istawdaʿa to lay down, deposit = IV
istawrada to have supplied, buy, procue = IV
istawzara 1. to appoint a minister, 2. to be appointed as minister (denom.)
istawqafa to bring to a stop

Conclusion: all of these examples prove that *iptaras* existed in Arabic and actually even survived in the historical period. Medieval Arab linguists and philologists who had a strictly synchronic approach (cf. Fleisch 1990, vol. 2, 314–315) put them together with medium verbs derived from nom-medium class I forms into the synchronically derived VIII class. There must have been a number of back formations i.e. of non-medium class I forms derived from forms with the infixed (originally prefixed) *t-*. As I indicated in 1999, 44, this *ta-/-ta-* prefix/infix (suffix in Egyptian and in Cushitic!) was originally an auxiliary with the meaning "to be, to become" parallel to another "to be, to become" auxiliary viz. *-n-* which still occurs as independent verb e.g. in Beja and Afar but which survives only as a derivational prefix in Semitic and Berber while in Egyptian it occurs in the *sḏm-n-f* form being usually misinterpreted as *nota genetivi*. At least in Proto-Semitic, Proto-Berber and Proto-Egyptian (thus clearly in the majority of proto-Hamitosemitic dialects) *-t-* was used as an auxiliary making passive and reflexive or simply medium forms (cf. Diem 1982). Already in Proto-Hamitosemitic these forms were used also as "Perfect" which survived fully in Akkadian and in Berber. Due to assimilations (and also incompatibility!) in a number of cases the forms with two preposed prefix-conjugated auxiliaries were ambiguous morphologically since e.g. **iqqatala* could go back either to **in-qatala* or **it-qatala*, similarly in the prefix conjugation, cf. Berber, Akkadian, Ugaritic, Hebrew etc. where derivational *n-* and/or *t-/-t-* assimilate to the first radical consonant.

Bibliography

Chouemi M. 1966. *Le verbe dans le Coran*. Paris: Klincksieck.

Diem W. 1982. *Die Entwicklung des Derivationsmorphems der t-Stämme im Semitischen.*= Zeitschrift der Deutschen Morgenländischen Gesellschaft 132, 29–84.

Fleisch H. 1990. *Traité de philologie arabe*, vol. 1–2. Beyrouth: Dar el-Machreq.

Kropfitsch L. 1991. *Zur semantischen Struktur der Verbalstämme im Neuhochara-bischen*. In: M. Forstner (ed.), *Festgabe für Hans-Rudolf Singer*, part 1, 55–65. Frankfurt am Main: Peter Lang.

Tropper J. 2000. *Ugaritische Grammatik*. Münster: Ugarit-Verllag.

Wright W. 1896–1898. *A Grammar of the Arabic Language*. T. 1–2. Cambridge: Cambridge University Press.

Zaborski A. 1998. *The Problem of archaism in Classical Arabic*. In: H. Jankowski (ed.), *From Mecca to Poznan,* 269–283. Poznan: Adam Mickiewicz University.

—— 1999. *Remarks on derived verbs in Hamitosemitic*. In: L. Edzard, Mohammed Nekroumi, (eds.), *Tradition and innovation—norm and deviation in Arabic and Semitic Linguistics*, 44–51. Wiesbaden: Otto Harrassowitz.

SECTION THREE

BEJA LINGUISTICS

BEJA AS A CUSHITIC LANGUAGE

David Appleyard
(SOAS, London)

1. *Introduction*

The mythology of Beja as somehow having a special relationship with Ancient Egyptian was long ago dispelled by Vycichl [1960], and in the same article he demonstrated that the closest relatives of Beja were the Cushitic languages of Ethiopia and Eritrea. The general acceptance of Beja as a Cushitic language, however, has not in the meantime gone completely unquestioned. Linguists working in the field of Cushitic will be familiar with Hetzron's [1980: 78–101] arguments for setting Beja apart from Cushitic: 'Beja, even though obviously Afro-asiatic, cannot be proven to have any special genetic affinity with Cushitic' [*ibid.*, 101]. Hetzron's arguments, prompted by what Zaborski famously called a 'classical rumour' [1997a: 49, also 1987: 133, 1989: 574], have not generally been accepted, and most linguists today are content to include Beja in the Cushitic family, albeit as a distinct branch. Nonetheless, the classificatory position of Beja does not remain without its problems, and there has been some debate in the academic press in the years since Hetzron's study appeared between two scholars in particular, Voigt [1988, 1996, 1998] and Zaborski [1988, 1997a, 1997b], centring around one particularly important question: the origin of the stem of the [New] Present of prefix-inflecting verbs of the type *ʔa-danbíil*. Voigt essentially sees the nasal infix in the stem of the singular of these verbs as an archaism, a dissimilation from an inherited pre-Cushitic geminate consonant. Zaborski, however, sees this stem pattern as an innovation arising from the incorporation of an auxiliary verb in **Vn*. The question is seen as a very relevant one for the classification of Beja [Tosco 2000: 91–92], as the dissimilation theory would at most place Beja on a lateral branch to Cushitic "proper", whilst the auxiliary theory simply implies that Beja innovated at a later stage than "Proto-Cushitic". In fact, as both Voigt and Zaborski themselves have shown, the question is not as simple as outlined here, and I will return to it below. However, I want to move away from a discussion of this particular feature and try and look at a wider bundle of factors that argue for the inclusion of Beja within Cushitic, and not as a parallel branch to Cushitic.

In addition, therefore, there are both several other morphological features in which Beja differs, or appears to differ from what has been termed "nuclear" Cushitic, namely Central Cushitic (or Agaw) and East Cushitic (Lowland and Highland),[1] and, equally, there is also a couple of important morphological features which Beja shares with nuclear Cushitic. If these are to be diagnostic in the classification of Beja, we have to determine what are innovations proper to Cushitic and what are archaisms retained from an earlier stage within the history of Afroasiatic. This is by no means an easy task as the discussion of the internal groupings of the phylum is still in a fluid state. One picture that does seem to be emerging, based on morphological criteria, is the relative closeness of the Semitic, Berber and Cushitic families within Afroasiatic. If this is a real construct, then features that Beja shares with nuclear Cushitic that are also found in either or both Berber and Semitic cannot, of course, be used as decisive factors in the argument. Since my intention here is to examine the arguments for including Beja within the Cushitic family, the first step will be to identify those features which mark Cushitic as distinct from the other members of the phylum, in the first place, and then from Berber and Semitic. I shall focus on morphological features, not only for reasons of space, but also because I am convinced of the primacy of morphology—not merely patterns but actual morphemes—as the major diagnostic tool in classification. Phonology is in this context too small a field, and indeed Beja lacks some of the principal segmental phonological features that are often thought of as typical of Cushitic, especially East Cushitic: pharyngeals (*ħ, ʕ*) contrasting with glottals (*h, ʔ*), a special series of coronal and velar obstruents with originally probably glottalised articulation (*t', k', p', s', č' . . .*)[2] constrasting with simple ones. Syntactic patterns are also not the best criteria to use in classification because of the relatively greater ease of borrowing and the effect of contact between lan-

[1] I shall retain the term "nuclear Cushitic" here, simply as shorthand to describe Cushitic without Beja, in particular to denote the construct for which "Proto-Cushitic" reconstructions have usually been made.

[2] Beja voiced retroflex *ɖ* and its rarer voiceless pair *ʈ* are the correspondents of some of the glottalised coronals in East Cushitic.

guages: syntactic patterns may be borrowed, as may even occasionally be syntactic markers and particles, so Beja has borrowed Arabic *wa* as a nominal connector. Syntactic patterns may also be areal rather than genetic indicators: so, for example, SOV order, clause-chaining mechanisms, and focus systems often with relative clause (cleft construction) origins are widespread in the Horn of Africa. The final area of linguistic analysis is, of course, lexicon and lexical material is often used in ascertaining the relatedness of languages and thus in classification. Lexicon is, of course, famously open to borrowing, but generally less so in fields of basic or 'core' vocabulary. To date scholars have generally paid little attention to using lexical cognates as a means of quantifying the "Cushitic-ness" of Beja; an exception is Zaborski [1989], and now also the on-going work of Blažek on an etymological dictionary of Beja. Whilst I want to concentrate on morphological features in this discussion, I will, therefore, add at the end of the discussion a few remarks on some major lexical isoglosses that link Beja to the rest of Cushitic.

2. *Morphological features*

There follows an inventory of the principal morphological features that distinguish Cushitic from its closest relatives in the Afroasiatic phylum, Berber and Semitic. The features are framed in terms of what is reconstructable for a Proto-Cushitic stage, and are not of course recorded in this form for any modern language. Likewise, not all individual Cushitic languages show reflexes of these features.

- gender-marking pronominals masc. **ku*, fem. **ti*; these may variously appear as elements in demonstratives and possessive pronouns, deictics, definite markers, adnominal subordinate phrase heads, etc.
- "marked nominative" system in masculine nouns in **-i* (variant **-u* ?):

	masculine	feminine
absolute case	**-a*	**-a*
subject case	**-i*, **-u* ?	**-a*
genitive case	**-i*	**-a-t-i*, or **-V-t-i*

Figure 1

- heterogeneous noun plural formation with a wide range of morphemes, both suffixes (*-*Vt*, *-*Vw*, *-*Vn*), which are not gender specific, and internal modification (typically partial reduplication).[3] Other factors involved in the category of number may also be reconstructed at the Cushitic level, such as gender/number interaction or polarity, the existence of categories of singulative and collective, etc.
- loss of gender distinction in the 2nd person, pronouns and verbal inflexion. Traces of originally masc. **ku* and fem. **ki* occur across Cushitic, and together with this, the fact that so-called South Cushitic languages (Iraqw, Alagwa, Burunge) preserve gender distinction in the 2nd person pronouns suggests that gender neutralisation here is actually a later, post-Proto-Cushitic development.
- two basic classes of verb subject inflexion: an archaic inherited prefix-inflecting pattern ("*ʔ–t–y–n* block pattern"), alongside an innovative suffix-inflecting pattern involving an original prefix-inflecting auxiliary (perhaps vocalic *-*V[V]*) suffixed to an invariable verb base.
- two fundamental aspects in verbs (perfective v. imperfective); in the suffix conjugation aspectual contrast is shown by the vowels: perf. **i* ~ **u*): impf. **a*, which also underlies the formal aspectual marking in the prefix conjugation.[4]

2.1. *The Cushitic deictic *ku : *ti and the Beja article*

Similar in function to the various reflexes of Cushitic **ku* : **ti* is what is in Beja usually called the "article". This is both a true definite marker prefixed to nouns and noun phrases and a marker of gender/number/case concord in possessive pronoun suffixes, and the near demonstrative: *ʔuu-gáw* 'the house', *ti-kaam-tuú-k* 'your she-camel', *ʔaá-n ʔi-gawà* 'these houses', and note also as a definite marker to a whole adjectival clause: *ti-ʔár tí-ʔanè rihan-eè-t* 'the girls that I saw'. The Beja article has the following long forms, which occur with pos-

[3] The wide range of Semitic internal or "broken" plurals seen for example in Arabic is not now generally reconstructed for the Proto-Semitic stage. Some internal plural patterns are, however, reconstructable for Proto-Semitic, as for Proto-Berber.

[4] The *a*-vowel is of course also a mark of the imperfective aspect in Proto-Semitic, but is there also associated with the stem shape *-*parVs* in contrast to perfective *-*prVs*.

sessive pronoun suffixes, the near demonstrative element *-n*, and before monosyllabic nouns that do not begin with a glottal (*ʔ* or *h*):

	masc.sg.	fem.sg.	masc.pl.	fem.pl.
nominative	*[ʔ]uu*	*tuu*	*[ʔ]aa*	*taa*
accusative	*[ʔ]oo*	*too*	*[ʔ]ee*	*tee*

Figure 2

Before nouns beginning with a glottal, and polysyllabic nouns the following forms occur:

	masc.sg.	fem.sg.	masc.pl.	fem.pl.	
nom/acc	*wi-*	*ti-*	*yi-*	*ti-*	noun with a glottal initial
nom/acc	*ʔi-*	*ti-*	*ʔi-*	*ti-*	elsewhere

Figure 3

The short *i* vowel of the forms in figure 3 is explained as a reduction of the long vowels in the primary set, and indeed in Reinisch's grammar forms with the full vowels are used everywhere 'wenn jemand in getragener rede spricht und jedes wort klar und deutlich hervorheben will.' [1893: 60]. We may therefore take the long forms (figure 2) as original and the short forms as secondary, although the question remains whether the semivowels *w/y* of the pre-glottal masculine forms are also in some sense original, or are also secondary, the *w* retaining the rounded quality of the underlying long vowels *uu* and *oo*, and the *y* perhaps merely a homorganic glide before the following short *i* instead of *ʔ*. The Beja article is usually described as a reduction of the near demonstrative, from something like **wuun*, **tuun*, etc. [Vycichl 1953, Voigt 1998: 312, Zaborski 1986a, 1997: 52], thus presupposing not only original *w-* in the masc., but also loss of final *-n*. The latter is prompted by the small number[5] of nouns in Beja beginning in an obstruent that insert a homorganic nasal before the article: *dè* 'mother' : *tuu-ndè* 'the mother'; *gerab* 'evening' : *ʔi-ngerab* 'the evening'; *da* 'men' : *ʔaa-nda* 'the men'; *bʔe* 'day' : *ʔi-mbʔe* 'the day'. In some instances comparative evidence suggests that the nasal element is part of the noun root: *[n]da* 'men' if this is connected (as a loan?) with Tigrinya *ʔənda* 'family, household' and *[n]dè* 'mother' if this is cognate with Somali *hiindo* 'mamma' and a widespread

[5] There are 23 such nouns listed in Roper's vocabulary [1928].

Omotic root for 'mother', e.g. Zayse *indo*, Shinasha *inda*, Yem *into*, etc. It would seem odd that only a few nouns should retain the nasal if the article is in origin the same as the near demonstrative, and all the more so that no glottal initial nouns are included here where we might suppose the context would have been suitable for the retention of the nasal. Rather, I think it is more likely that the near demonstrative is itself a compound of the article and the Cushitic demonstrative **-nV*. Indeed, in much of East Cushitic this combines with the **ku* : **ti* article in the same way: e.g. Somali *kun, kan* : *tun, tan*, Oromo *kuni, kana* : *tuni, tana*, Darasa *kunni* : *tinni*, etc. [see Zaborski 1986b for details.] The Beja article must therefore derive from **wuu*, **tuu*, etc.[6] The initial *w-* as masculine marker, rather than Ø or *ʔ-*, as currently occurs in all but the pre-glottal form, is also suggested by the accusative case vowel *oo*, since this is best explained as developing from some such as **wa*, i.e. masculine marker *w-* + inherited Cushitic accusative case vowel **-a* (cf. the East Cushitic accusative demonstratives, *kan, tan*, etc. above.) Proceeding from this point, the earliest recoverable pre-Beja forms for the article in the singular would be:

	masculine	feminine
nominative	**wu*	**tu*
accusative	**wa*	**ta*

Figure 4

Nom. **wu-* > **wuu-* > *ʔuu-* /–CV[V][C], > *wi-*[7] /–HV . . ., > *ʔi-* elsewhere.
Acc. **wa-* > **woo-* > *ʔoo-*, etc.

The vocalic patterns *uu/oo/i* would then have been copied on to the feminine base *t-*.

If this hypothesis is correct, then Beja has a different masculine deictic element *w-* from the rest of Cushitic, which has *ku-*, later re-analysed in East Cushitic as *k-* + subject case *-u*, hence absolute forms in *-a*. The originality of the *u*-vowel in Proto-Cushitic is confirmed by Agaw, which has masc. gender suffix **-ɣ*^{w} < **ku* as

[6] Vycichl's suggestion [1988: 415] that the accusative form of the Beja article *woo, too*, etc., is the more original and that the nominative form derives from this plus the case suffix *-i* (**woo* + *i* > *wuu*, etc.) is untenable.

[7] Phonemic wi- is realised as *wʊ-*, *ʔʊ-*, *wə-* according to dialect.

the reflex of this deictic. Hetzron [1980:] suggested that Beja *w-* derived from Proto-Cushitic *k^w-, but as far as there is available evidence to say, k^w remains in Beja, cf. *k^wa* 'sister', which is probably cognate with Proto-Agaw **ʔəγ^w-Vna* 'woman' or Bilin *k'^{w}i* 'wife'.

So far, we have only looked at the singular article. In the plural different vocalisations occur, as can be seen from figure 2, and there is no evidence whatsoever of the masculine marker in *w-*. Furthermore, the vocalisations nom. *-aa*, acc. *-ee* seem to show a different case marking system from the singular. I will return to this question briefly in section 2.2.

Looking across the Afroasiatic spectrum, there is no single consonantal element associated with masculine gender marking, unlike feminine **t-*. Only in Berber is *w-* contrasted with *t-* in the prefix of the annexed state: Proto-Berber **wă* : **tă* [Prasse 1974: 14–15], and in the basic deictics or "pronoms d'appui" **wā* : **tā* and **wī* : **tī* [Prasse 1972: 185–186]. There is a pronomianl base in *k-* in Beja, used in the interrogative *kak* 'how?' and probably in the defective verb *kee-* 'be where?'. It is an innovation of nuclear Cushitic to employ *k-* as a deictic of masculine gender. Incidentally, not all nuclear, non-Beja Cushitic languages use *k-* in this sense. In Saho-Afar gender marking in demonstratives has been lost, and forms without overt original gender markers are used alongside forms with initial *t-* apparently as free variants: Afar *a, ama, woo*[8] : *ta, tama, too.*

2.2. *Primary case marking in Cushitic and Beja*

By "primary case" here I refer to subject-object (or absolute)-genitive cases only. Subject and object case marking in Beja is for the most part carried out only by the article and is not otherwise marked on the noun phrase. The exception is the suffix *-b* which is added only to non-definite nouns or noun phrases and their modifiers, but only where the noun is non-definite, is in the accusative case and ends in a vowel: *haḍaà-b rihán* 'I saw a lion'; note also *ʔoo-yàas wí-ʔoón ʔi-takiì-b rihán* 'I saw this man's dog' where *-b* is added at the very end of the noun phrase on the following, modifying genitive. The same suffix also appears on a small number of pronominal

[8] The initial *w* here is probably an onset feature before the vowel *oo*, as it does not occur in the other demonstratives.

forms: *-heè-b* 1st sg. object suffix, *ʔaa-b* 'whom?' acc., *beé-b* 'that' masc.sg. acc., *balií-b* 'those' masc.pl. acc. This suffix *-b* is something of a mystery; attempts have been made to connect it with the base of the far demonstrative *beén*, etc., or the emphatic or focusing particle *baa* in Somali, or even the masculine deictic base *p-* in Ancient Egyptian, none of which seems especially convincing, for the Beja suffix *-b* specifically encodes both the category of masculine gender and accusative case, which none of these does.

If the reconstruction of the single article proposed above (figure 4) is correct, then Pre-Beja had a (singular) nominative in **-u* and an accusative in **-a*, at least in the deictic. There is no means of knowing from Beja evidence whether the same system applied to nouns, but given that the same endings occur in Semitic and are thus Pre-Cushitic (if not Common Afroasiatic) it would not seem unlikely. However, the relevant point here is that this system is not quite the same as has been reconstructed for Proto-(Nuclear) Cushitic. It is probable that an earlier masc. nom. ending **-u* can be assumed for Proto-Cushitic in so far as East Cushitic was able to re-analyse the final vowel of the masculine deictic **ku* as a case marker and so create an accusative form **ka*. There is no trace of masculine subject case marking in *-i* in Beja, nor is there any direct evidence for the absence of specific subject case marking in the feminine (see figure 1). The feminine article, as we have seen, follows exactly the vocalisation of the masculine forms, and thus maximally differentiates subject and object cases (nominative and accusative). However, there are two interesting clues to suggest that perhaps Beja did not always originally distinguish these two cases in the feminine: a suffix *-t* is added to non-definite feminine nouns and their modifiers, with certain structural restraints,[9] in both subject and object function: *ʔoó-t dawrií-t rihán* 'I saw a pretty girl', *ʔoó-t dawrií-t rihti-heèb* 'a pretty girl saw me'. Secondly, the far demonstrative does not distinguish the two cases in the feminine, unlike the masculine: sg. *beét*, pl. *baliít*. This suffix *-t* is, of course, a gender marking suffix and has no case marking function, but it is, I think, interesting that in non-definite phrases Beja distinguishes subject and object only in the masculine.[10]

[9] See Hudson [1974: 119] and Appleyard [forthcoming (b)] for details. This suffix *-t* does not of course carry any case marking, and its current partial paralleling of masculine *-b* may simply be a coincidence.

[10] There are, of course, phonological constraints on the appearance of masc. *-b* and it does not occur everywhere [Hudson, *op. cit.*, and Appleyard [*op. cit.*].

The plural article suggests a different subject-object case marking system with vocalisations in nom. *-aa*, acc. *-ee*, which of course immediately reminds one of Semitic duals, nom. *-*aa*, acc./gen. *-*ay*. There is nothing resembling this in nuclear Cushitic.

The genitive case in Beja, however, is clearly cognate with what has been reconstructed for Proto-Cushitic (see figure 1). The structure of the possessive phrase in Beja is extremely complex, involving often multiple conconcord marking between the noun head and the possessive phrase: *tuu-ndè tí-wi-ʔoor-iì-t* 'the mother of the boy', where both *tí-* and *-t* mark feminine gender agreement of the possessive *wi-ʔoorii-* 'of the boy' with the head noun *tuu-ndè*. Concord between a modifying genitive and its noun head also exists in some nuclear Cushitic, for instance in Bilin *k'ʷi gərw-i-ri* 'the man's wife', but here only when the genitive is postposed. A further complexity arises from the fact that Beja treats the possessive as an accusative case from the point of case concord. Thus, in a phrase like *ʔoón ʔi-tak-ì yàas* 'the dog of this man', the demonstrative *ʔoón* is in the accusative form "in agreement" with the genitive *ʔi-takì* 'of the man'. From a purely descriptive point of view, therefore, the genitive in Beja can be described as a derivative of the accusative, formed by means of an adjectival or modifier suffix *-i* (sg.). One is reminded of diptotic nouns in Classical Arabic, as well as the fact that in Semitic plural and dual nouns do not distinguish the accusative from the genitive.

The genitive suffix in Beja is *-i* (sg.) and *-e* (pl.). The latter presumably derives from the context of noun pl. *-a[a]* + *-i*, which then was re-analysed as a distinct plural genitive *-*ai* > *-e[e]* and then spread to all contexts as a Beja innovation. Feminine nouns insert the marker *-t-* between the noun and the genitive suffix: *ti-ʔoo-t-ì baabà* 'the father of the girl', *ti-ʔa-t-è baabà* 'the father of the girls'. In principle, therefore, the Beja genitive in the singular is formally similar to the Proto-(nuclear) Cushitic *-*i* (masc.), *-*Vti* (fem.), but the evidence of Semitic indicates that the genitive formative *-i* is an inheritance and not a specifically Cushitic innovation. However, what is a Cushitic innovation, and one shared by Beja, is the presence of the feminine marker *-t-* before *-i* only in the genitive. In Semitic, of course, feminine *-t-*, where present, occurs in all three cases, and feminine nouns without *-t* in the nominative and accusative, such as Akkadian *umm-u-m* 'mother', etc., do not add it in the genitive.

2.3. *Noun plural formation in Beja*

Noun plural formation in Cushitic is so heterogeneous, involving a wide range of devices, all of inherited Afroasiatic origin, that it is probably not a useful area to employ for classification. Beja noun plurals are of four types: (i) suffixation of *-à* to some consonant-final nouns: *ragád* : *ragadà* 'foot, leg'; (ii) shortening of a long vowel in the final syllable of other consonant-final nouns: *miitaát* : *miitát* 'bone'; (iii) shift of accent-type in both vowel-final nouns and some consonant-final nouns: *baabà* : *baabá* 'father'; (iv) no difference between singular and plural: *haḍà* 'lion(s)'. None of these formative devices has an exact correspondent in nuclear Cushitic. The suffix *-à* is reminiscent of the plural article (nominative) vocalisation *-aa-*, especially when one considers that the short vowel of the ending is lengthened before suffixes in accordance with the general morphophonemic rule: *ʔi-gawà* 'the houses' but *ʔi-gawaa-(y)aá-k* 'your houses', where the *y* is the required glide between two vowels.

Beja does not appear to have special number categories such as singulatives or collectives that are so widespread in nuclear Cushitic.

2.4. *Gender distinction in the 2nd person*

Most nuclear Cushitic languages do not retain a gender distinction in the 2nd person, either in the pronouns or in the inflexion of the verb. As indicated above, there are however traces of original masculine **ku* and feminine **ki* in the (originally) non-subject independent pronouns, and such forms are retained with their original gender contrasting function in languages of the so-called South Cushitic sub-branch (Iraqw, Alagwa, Burunge) of East Cushitic.[11] In Beja much of the necessary evidence has however been lost in the complete reorganisation of the independent pronoun series, where only the old 1st person pronouns are retained (sg. *ʔanè*, pl. *hinìn*) and all the 2nd and 3rd persons are rebuilt on a base *bar-*, which is of nominal origin and evidently derived from the verb root meaning 'to have' [Bechhaus-Gerst 1985, Zaborski 1998: 73ff.]: *bar-uú-k* 'you' (masc.sg.), *ba[r]-t-uú-k* 'you' (fem.sg.), *bar-aá-k* 'you' (masc.pl.), *ba[r]-t-aá-k* 'you'

[11] See Tosco [2000:99ff.] for a discussion of the new classification of these languages and Dahalo as a sub-branch of East Cushitic.

(fem.pl.), etc., which are possessive constructs meaning perhaps 'your owner', i.e. 'yourself'.

The dependent pronouns of the 2nd person are posessive *-k* (sg.) : *-kna* (pl.) and object *-hook* (sg.) : *-hookna* (pl.). To the singular object forms[12] may be added optionally the allocutive clitics *-a* (masc.) : *-i* (fem.), which refer to the gender of the person addressed and thus create a gender distinction in the 2nd person sing. dependent pronouns: *-hooka* : *-hooki*. They may also be added after the 1st sg. object suffix, not to define the gender of that person, but again to refer to the gender of the addressee: *ʔuu-yaàs tamì-heeb-a* 'the dog bit me' said by a woman to a man [see Roper 1928: 29]. These same clitics are also regularly added to the 2nd sg. persons of the verb when no object pronoun suffix is added: *tam-taà* (< *tam-tà* + *-a*) 'you (masc.sg.) ate' : *tam-taà-i* > *tamtaày* 'you (fem.sg.) ate'; *tí-dbil-a* : *tí-dbil-i* 'you collected', etc. Superficially this makes Beja 2.fem.sg. forms like *tídbili* look like Semitic **ta-qtul-ii*. However, the corresponding masc. sg. form in Semitic has Ø ending **ta-qtul*, indicating that the feminine is there derived from the masculine, whereas in Beja the behaviour of the *-a* : *-i* suffixes on verbs with object pronouns suggests that they were originally free clitics. A contrary view is, however, expressed by Voigt [1998: 312–313], who rather sees the Beja forms as an Afroasiatic archaism, whilst in Semitic the masculine *-a* is lost in the prefix conjugation (see footnote 17). Hetzron [1980: 80–82] also contests any connection with Semitic here. Whichever is the more likely explanation, the fact again remains that nothing similar is found in nuclear Cushitic. It is worth repeating, however, that in Beja this gender distinction occurs only in the singular, and there is no such distinction made in the plural.

2.5. *Prefix and suffix conjugations in verbs*

A lot has been written about the competing theories of the origins of the tenses (or aspects) of the Beja prefix conjugation [see especially Zaborski 1975, 1988, 1997a, Voigt 1988, 1998: 313ff., and also Hetzron 1980: 82ff.]. Zaborski's theory of a "push chain" in the development of the Beja tenses, whereby the current affirmative present is a new

[12] Also the possessive suffixes in some dialects [Reinisch 1893: 103].

formation, which allowed for the shift of the "Old Present" into past-tense function, and the "Old Past" into a tense or modal with a variety of functions[13] is very convincing and is supported not only on internal Beja evidence—the current negative present employs the current past: *tam-íiní* 'he eats', *tam-yà* 'he ate' but *ká-tam-yà* 'he doesn't eat'—but also on comparative evidence. The question then arises, what is the origin of the "New Present"? As has been said earlier, the question can be seen as a very relevant one for the classification of Beja, as the dissimilation theory of Voigt would at most place Beja on a lateral branch to nuclear Cushitic, whilst the auxiliary theory of Zaborski simply could imply that Beja innovated at a later stage than "Proto-Cushitic". The question of the origin of the "New Present" is more complex than is sometimes presented, as Voigt [1998: 313ff.] has pointed out, in that the type of verb that forms its (singular) present stem by means of an *n*-infix (the "dissimilation" from a geminate) is only part of the story. There are other patterns followed by different classes of verbs. It seems to me that no single origin can be proposed for the current situation that exists in Beja. For reasons of space, I do not want to get into the discussion here, particularly as Zaborski [1997b: 53–57] has already written about the possibility of a multiple origin, which the heterogeneity of the tense would alone suggest. There are numerous irregular forms of this "New Present" even amongst the verbs that form their singular stem by the insertion of *-n-*: biliteral basic stems regularly place the nasal before the first radical: *ʔa-mbíis* 'I bury' and triliterals place it before the medial: *ʔa-danbíil* "I collect", but there are many triliterals, especially those with glottal medial radicals, which, in some dialects at least, place the nasal before the first radical: *ʔa-mbʔiir* 'I wake', *ʔa-mbʔiis* 'I turn over', *ʔa-nkhiin* 'I love', *ʔa-ngwăhiir* 'I steal', etc. [all from Roper 1928], but note also *ʔa-nfiriid* 'I speak' and *ʔa-nkiriif* 'I go to meet' [from Hudson's unpublished dictionary]. These irregularities make it more difficult to see how the nasal might have arisen from the dissimilation of a geminate (medial) consonant.

An equally important feature of verbal inflexion, and one that in

[13] This is the tense Reinisch calls "plusquamperfect", Roper "conditional", and Hudson "past" (what he calls "preterite" I am here calling past). Hudson's glosses indicate a tense referring variously to a remote or anterior past event, a continuous or on-going past event, or a doubtful event, whilst in Roper the same form seems to be used mainly in the apodosis of unreal conditions. In the oldest grammar of Beja, Almkvist's informants were apparently unfamiliar with such a tense.

many ways is more definitive, is the presence of a suffix conjugation in Beja, the evidence of which alone is often taken as sufficient proof for the inclusion of Beja within Cushitic [Tosco 2000: 92]. The present, i.e. the "New Present" of the suffix conjugation is transparently formed by means of the suffixation of the present of the irregular prefix-inflecting verb *-Vn*, which Reinisch records as a "verbum substantivum" and Roper as an incomplete paradigm of 'say'. This would seem to be a Beja innovation, which incidentally also supports Zaborski's theory of a shift in tense forms.[14] The "Old Present" and the "Old Past" forms, on the other hand, do appear to be directly cognate with the nuclear Cushitic suffix conjugations. The "Old Present" has vocalisation in *a* throughout, like the Lowland East Cushitic present and the imperfective base of many subordinate forms, especially the relative, in Agaw, where a new conjugation involving a different suffixed "auxiliary" has supplanted the older forms in main-verb function [Appleyard 1993]. Comparable developments also occur in Highland East Cushitic.

A "Old Present"	Beja	Proto-Agaw	Proto- L. East Cush.
1sg.	*-án*	**-ʔa*	**-aa*
2sg.	*-taà* *-taà-y*	**-ta*	**-taa*
3sg.m.	*-yà*	**-a*	**-aa*
3sg.f.	*-tà*	**-ta*	**-taa*
1pl.	*-nà*	**-na*	**-naa*
2pl.	*-taàna*	**-tan*	**-taani*
3pl.	*-yaàn*	**-an*	**-aani*

Figure 5

The only problem with matching the Beja form with the Cushitic forms is the final *-n* in the 1st sg., and more importantly the occurrence of this *-n* in all persons when this tense is used with the embedding suffix *-e*: *rih-yà* 'he saw' but *rih-yan-eé-k* 'if he saw'.[15] The question is

[14] The "New Present" of the suffix conjugation is transparently an innovation and has as its formant the verb *-Vn* 'be, say', causing the shift in function of the older present and past. This process required a parallel step in prefix conjugation verbs, where the "New Present" was created, possibly out of diverse forms, but also interestingly in one common basic stem involving again a nasal consonant.

[15] The full set of endings is: *-an, -taan* (masc. & fem.), *-yan, -tan, -naan, -taan, -yaan* [Roper 1928: 45 under "Subjunctive Mood"].

whether both *-n*'s are original to the paradigm or not. In the basic paradigm 1st sg. *-n* may simply represent a reduced form of the independent personal pronoun *ʔanè* 'I'. In the northerly Agaw languages, Bilin and Khamtanga, the 1st persons, singular and plural, of the main verb paradigms also have a final *-n*, which is not found in the other Agaw languages, and here, too, this is probably a reduced form of the independent pronoun used as a clitic. With regard to the *-n-* before the embedding suffix *-e*, there is evidence of (sporadic ?) loss of absolute final *-n* in the history of Beja (cf. *ʔa* 'milk' and Afar *ħan*, Somali *ʕaano*, Oromo *aannan*,[16] etc.). The extended forms like *rihyan-do* seem to occur before some other suffixes: *tam-yán-hoob* 'when he ate' and *ʔuu-yaàs tam-yan-oók-hoob* 'when the dog bit you' [Roper 1928: 47–48], though the whole picture is not clear because of the paucity of satisfactory data: thus, the suffix *-àayt* 'because' appears to combine with the past ("Old Present") without this intermediary *-n*, but the forms given by Roper [1928: 88] are difficult to interpret: *irhánai͡t* 'because I saw' but *irhī́ai͡t* 'because he saw' in his transcription. If this *-n* is original to the "Old Present", then the Beja paradigm cannot be compared directly with the nuclear Cushitic forms. I am, however, inclined to think that it is not original to the paradigm, but is a secondary development. For one thing, parity with the "Old Past" conjugation would be lost as the latter does not show any added *-n* (figure 6). Of course, this argument presupposes that the two tenses are formally linked, which is both the natural assumption and what would be expected for a Cushitic language.

The "Old Past" has vocalisation in *i* throughout. It's Agaw cognate, which again has been supplanted in main-verb function by a new paradigm and is employed now only as the base of a number of subordinate forms, and as a base in some compound tenses, has vocalisation in *ə*, or in Awngi partly in *u* (< **uu*). These probably represent varying vocalisations at the Proto-Cushitic level, i.e. a high vowel **i* or **u* as perfective aspect marker [Sasse 1980: 157]. Lowland East Cushitic has vocalisation, however, in a diphthong **ay*, typically resolved to *e[e]* in most languages. This may be an innovation, or may just reflect a variant vocalisation of the prefixes of the original auxiliary **ʔa-yi* instead of **ʔi-yi* [Appleyard forthcoming (a)].[17]

---

[16] The Somali and Oromo forms are in origin plurals, hence the endings *-o* and *-an*, respectively.

[17] Hetzron's [1980: 41] suggestion that the diphthong respresents a different aux-

B "Old Past"	Beja	Proto-Agaw	Proto- L. East Cush.
1sg.	*-ì*	*-*ʔə* / *-*ʔu*	*-*ay*
2sg.	*-tiìya* *-tiì*	*-*tə* . . .	*-*tay*
3sg.m.	*-ì*	*-*ə* . . .	*-*ay*
3sg.f.	*-tì*	*-*tə* . . .	*-*tay*
1pl.	*-nì*	*-*nə* . . .	*-*nay*
2pl.	*-tiìna*	*-*tən* < *-*tin* ? *-*tun*	*-*teeni*
3pl.	*-iìn*	*-*ən* < *-*in* ? *-*un*	*-*eeni*

Figure 6

The Beja form is thus most closely related to the Agaw, where the vowel **ə* is the regular outcome of both short high vowels in Proto-Cushitic, **i* and **u*.

One further point of structural and formal similarity between the Beja and nuclear Cushitic suffix conjugations concerns the position of the morphemes of the derived stems in the verbal morpheme chain, such as simple causative *-s-*, double causative *-siis-*, passive-reflexive *-am-*, and combinations of these. Just as in nuclear Cushitic, these occur between the root and the inflecting element: *raat-am-eèn* 'they asked themselves', *baroó ʔibaab-s-án* 'I sent him on a journey'. In prefix inflecting verbs, of course, the morphemes of verbal derivations are prefixed to the root and come between it and the personal prefix: *ʔi-moo-maàn-na* 'they shaved one another', *ʔi-too-maàn-na* 'they have been shaved', *baroó ti-s-dabìl-a* 'you made him collect it'.

The reservations about the *-n* suffix in present aside, therefore, it is apparent that the Beja and nuclear Cushitic suffix conjugations are of the same origin, and this is one of the strongest morphological arguments for classifying Beja as a Cushitic language.

iliary **hay* 'be' can be discounted as the supposed reflexes of this root (e.g. Somali *ahay*, etc.) are actually from Proto-Cushitic *-*k-y* 'be', which incidentally also occurs in Beja.

3. *Lexical comparisons*

Having examined the major morphological comparisons between Beja and nuclear Cushitic, I would like to close this survey by looking at some of the major lexical isoglosses which link Beja with Cushitic. There is a fair number of items of Beja lexicon that have cognates in various Cushitic languages, sometimes apparently only in Agaw: e.g. *harro* 'millet': Proto-Agaw **ʔar* 'grain'; *gáw* 'house': Proto-Agaw **käw* 'village';[18] *ʔamna* 'guest': Proto-Agaw **ʔabən-*; sometimes a really (Agaw, Saho-Afar): e.g. *ɓoy* 'blood': Proto-Agaw **bər*, Saho *búlo* 'blood price'; *ʔandiirho* 'chicken': Proto-Agaw **dirw-a*, Afar *dorrahi*;[19] *ʔoor-* 'son': Awngi *ira* 'son', *-[y]íri* 'children', Bilin *ʔər-t-* 'be pregnant', Afar *úrru*, Saho *irro* 'children'; and sometimes in East Cushitic only: *šʔa* 'cow': Proto-E. Cushitic **šaʕ-*; *raba* 'male': Proto-E.Cushitic **lab-/*leb-* 'male, big'; *ḍahalaay* 'charcoal': Proto-E. Cushitic **č'ulħ-/*č'ilħ-*; *hayuuk* 'star': Proto-E. Cushitic **ħizk-/*ħuzk-*; *win* 'big': Proto-E. Cushitic **wayn-*; *maykʷa* 'righthand': Proto-E. Cushitic **mizg-*; *ʔa* 'milk': Afar *ħan*, Somali *ʕaan-o*, Oromo *aann-an*; *miitaát* 'bone': Oromo *mita* 'joint', Arbore *mittá*, etc.; *gʷadaáb* 'chest, breast': Proto-H.E. Cushitic **godob-* 'belly'. Indeed, there appear to be more cognates with East Cushitic than with Agaw, though the different states of comparative lexicography may be as much of an explanation here as anything else.

What is of particular interest in this discussion, however, is a number of lexical isoglosses that Beja shares with both Agaw and East Cushitic. Some of these do have cognates elsewhere in Afroasiatic, but not always with precisely the same form or meaning which Beja and other Cushitic share. The following brief list is far from exhaustive, and there are doubtless others that could be added to it. The point is, rather, that core items like 'two', 'ten', 'be', 'know', 'give', 'head', etc., are alone compelling lexical evidence for classifying Beja as a Cushitic language.

'two' Beja *-rama* in *ʔasaráma* 'seven'. Beja 'six' to 'nine' are formed by prefixing *ʔas[a]-* to roots meaning 'one' to 'four', respectively. This is immediately reminiscent of the Agaw unit number system, where 'six' to 'nine' are formed by the

---

[18] Blažek [unpublished] relates the Beja term to Somali *góob* 'place'.

[19] Also in the northern Ethiopian Semitic languages: Geʿez *därho*, Amharic *doro*, etc.

suffix *-*ta* added to 'one' to 'four'. Beja 'two' proper, *mhalò*, may conceivably be a metathesised form of this root which is found elsewhere in Cushitic: Proto-Agaw **läŋa*, Proto-E. Cushitic **lama*.

'ten' Beja *támin*: Proto-Agaw *-*täŋən* as a formative in the tens; Proto-E. Cushitic **tomman-*/**tomn-*.

'be' Beja *-k-y* (irregular verb): Proto-Agaw *ʔ*ak-*/*ʔ*äx-*; Proto-E. Cushitic *-*ik[k]*/*-*ak[k]*.

'know' Beja *-k-n* (irregular verb): Proto-Agaw **kan-*/**kin-* (Awngi *kan-t-* 'see', Bilin *kən-t-*, Kemant *kin-š-* 'learn', etc.); Proto-E. Cushitic *-*k'aan*/*-*k'iin*.

'give' Beja *-hii[w]*: Proto-Agaw *ʔ*əw-*; Proto-E. Cushitic *-*hiw*/ *-*huw*.

'go' Beja *baay-*: Proto-Agaw **ba-t-* 'leave'; Proto-E. Cushitic **baħ-* 'go out'.

'eat' Beja *ʔaam-*: Proto-Agaw *ʔ*əŋ-* 'bite'; Proto-E. Cushitic *-*ʕum*/*-*ʕam*. The Beja term is glossed by Roper [1928: 148][20] as 'eat, devour'; the usual Beja term for 'eat' is, of course, *tam-*, which has cognates in Agaw (Bilin, Kamtanga, Kemant) *tam-* 'taste' [v.tr].

'head' Beja *mat* 'top of the head, crown': Proto-E. Cushitic **matħ-* 'head' and a possible Proto-Agaw **ŋat-a* (Awngi *ŋarí* 'head', Kemant *nara* 'brain').

'nipple' Beja *nug*^{w}: Proto-Agaw *ʔ*əng*^{w}/*ʔ*ang*^{w} 'breast'; Saho-Afar *angu* (probably a loan from Agaw), and Proto-E. Cushitic **nuug-* 'suck'.

'tooth' Beja *k*^{w}*ire*: perhaps Proto-Agaw *ʔ*ərk*^{w}*-*; Proto-E. Cushitic *ʔ*ilk-*, by metathesis.

'eye' Beja *liili*: Proto-Agaw *ʔ*əl-*; Proto-E. Cushitic *ʔ*il-*. This presumes that the Beja form is a reduplication of the basic root, perhaps like verbal forms in E. Cushitic such as L.E. Cushitic *ʔ*ilaal-* 'look, watch', Sidamo *lell-* 'appear', and Afar *lilli hee-* 'look behind, look at'.

[20] *ʔaam-* 'eat, devour' is not found in Hudson's unpublished dictionary.

4. *Conclusions*

The evidence proposed in this paper, principally morphological but also lexical, is enough to justify the classification of Beja as a Cushitic language. More than that, the weight of the morphological evidence indicates that Beja represents a separate branch distinct from the other Cushitic languages, not sharing a couple of important innovations: the **ku* masculine deictic, masculine subject case marking in *-i*, and innovating in other areas: the "New Present", new independent pronouns and possibly the allocutive clitics *-a* and *-i*, if these are not archaisms from an earlier stage in Afroasiatic.[21] The principal morphological feature that identifies Beja as a Cushitic language remains the suffix conjugation in verbs. The classification of Beja as the earliest off-shoot of the family, distinct from all the other Cushitic languages, that can be drawn from this discussion is the same conclusion that Voigt [1998] reached using essentially an analysis of the prefix conjugation and aspect marking as his argument. Whilst I do not fully agree with some of the arguments presented there, particularly the much-discussed question of the present of prefix conjugation verbs, the picture of Beja's separateness from nuclear Cushitic that emerges is the same. A possible re-drawing of the internal classification of Cushitic is presented in figure 7, adapted from Tosco [2000: 108], where the details of the subdivisions of Lowland East Cushitic are also given according to the most recent analysis. Beja is obviously a very important language for the history of Cushitic, and whilst some new data (essentially Hudson's) and much discussion of existing data has appeared since Vycichl first worked on the language, there is a pressing need for the complexities of the language to be looked at anew with fresh data filling in the gaps of our current knowledge.

[21] This is what Voigt [1998: 312] argues, though in the Semitic example of the independent pronoun masc. **ʔanta*, fem. **ʔantii*, which he cites, the *-a* of the former is not so much a suffix pairing with the the *-ii*, as the *-ii* is a suffix added to the (unmarked) base **ʔanta*, as is borne out by the fact that the verbal prefix of the 2nd person is simply the prefix **ta-*, whilst gender and number s suffixes fem. sg. **-ii*, masc.pl. **-uu*, etc.

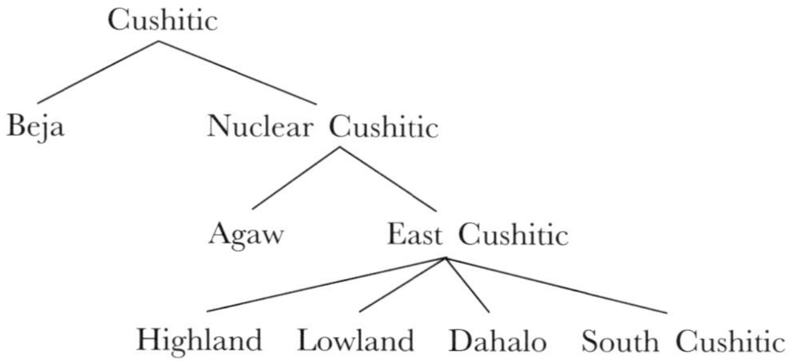

Figure 7

Bibliography

Appleyard (David): 1993 "Vocalic ablaut and aspect marking in the verb in Agaw." *Journal of Afroasiatic Languages* 3: 126–150.

——: forthcoming (a) "The verb 'to say' as a "recycling device" in Ethiopian languages." To appear in Andrzej Zaborski (ed.), Memorial volume for Robert Hetzron.

——: forthcoming (b) "Beja morphology." To appear in Alan Kaye (ed.), *Morphologies of Africa and Asia.*

Bechhaus-Gerst (Marianne): 1985 "'Du bist, was du hast'—Zur Entstehung neuer Personalpronomen im Tu Bedawie (Beja)", *Afrikanistische Arbeitspapiere. Schriftenreie des Kölner Instituts für Afrikanistik* 1: 125–129.

Blažek (Václav): unpublished "Fragments of a comparative and etymological dictionary of Beja."

Hetzron (Robert): 1980 "The Limits of Cushitic", *Sprache und Geschichte in Afrika* 2: 7–125.

Hudson (Richard A.): 1974 "A structural sketch of Beja," *African Language Studies* 15: 111–142.

——: unpublished *A Dictionary of Beja.* Database version prepared by Roger Blench (1996).

Prasse (Karl G.): 1972 *Manuel de grammaire touarègue I–III Phonétique—Ecriture—Pronom.* Copenhague: Editions de l'Université de Copenhague.

——: 1974 *Manuel de grammaire touarègue IV–V. Nom.* Copenhague: Akademisk Forlag.

Reinisch (Leo): 1893 *Die Beḍauye-Sprache in Nordost-Afrika. II. (Sitzungsberichte der kaiserlichen Akademie der Wissenschaften in Wien. Philosophisch-historische Classe. Bd CXXVIII).* Wien: in Kommission bei Alfred Hölder.

Roper (E.M.): 1928 *Tu Beḍawiɛ. An Elementary Handbook for the Use of Sudan Government Officials.* Hertford: Stephen Austin and Sons, Ltd.

Sasse (Hans-Jürgen): 1980 "Ostkuschitische und semitische Verbalklassen." In Werner Diem & Stefan Wild (eds.), *Studien aus Arabistik und Semitistik*, pp. 153–174. Wiesbaden: Harrassowitz.

Tosco (Mauro): 2000 "Cushitic overview," *Journal of Ethiopian Studies* 33: 87–121.

Voigt (Rainer): 1988 "Zur Bildung des Präsens im Beḍauye." In Marianne Bechhaus-Gerst and Fritz Serzisko (eds.), *Cushitic-Omotic. Papers from the International Symposium on Cushitic and Omotic Languages. Cologne, January 6–9, 1986*, pp. 379–407. Hamburg: Helmut Buske.

——: 1996 "Zur Gliederung des Kuschitischen: die Präfixkonjugationen." In Catherine Griefenow-Mewis & Rainer Voigt (eds.), *Cushitic and Omotic Languages. Proceedings of the Third International Symposium. Berlin, March 17–19 1994*, pp. 101–131. Köln: Rüdiger Köppe Verlag.

——: 1998 "Zur Gliederung des Kuschitischen: das Beḍauye und das Restku-schitische." In Ines Fiedler, Catherine Griefenow-Mewis & Brigitte Reineke (eds.), *Afrikanische Sprachen im Brennpunkt der Forschung*, pp. 309–324. Köln: Rüdiger Köppe Verlag.

Vycichl (Werner): 1953 "Der bestimmte Artikel in der Bedja-Sprache," *Le Muséon* 66:373–379.

——: 1960 "The Beja language Tū Beḍawīye. Its relationship with Old Egyptian", *Kush* 8: 252–264.

——: 1988 "Beja—a language with seven seals." In Marianne Bechhaus-Gerst & Fritz Serzisko (eds.), *Cushitic-Omotic. Papers from the International Symposium on Cushitic and Omotic Languages. Cologne, January 6–9, 1986*, pp. 411–430. Hamburg: Helmut Buske.

Zaborski (Andrzej): 1975 *The Verb in Cushitic. Studies in Hamito-Semitic I. (Zeszyty Naukowe Uniwersytetu Jagiellońskiego CCCXCVII. Prace Językoznawcze, Zeszyt 48).* "Beja", pp. 13–28. Warszawa: Panstwowe Wydawnictwo Naukowe.

——: 1986a "The Cushitic article." In H.L.J. Vanstiphout, K. Jongeling, et al. (eds.), *Scripta Signa Vocis. Studies about Scripts, Scriptures, Scribes and Languages in the Near East, Presented to J.H. Hospers by his Pupils, Colleagues and Friends*, pp. 317–331. Groningen: E. Forsten.

——: 1986b "A note on Cushitic demonstrative pronouns", *Orientalia Suecana* 35: 505–511.

——: 1987 "Reinisch and some problems of the study of Beja today." In Hans G. Mukarovsky (ed.), *Leo Reinisch. Werk und Erbe*, pp. 125–139. Wien: Verlag der österreichischen Akademie der Wissenschaften.

——: 1988 "Remarks on the Verb in Beja." In Y.A. Arbeitman (ed.) *Fucus—a Semitic/Afrasian gathering in Remembrance of Albert Ehrman*, pp. 491–498. Amsterdam: J. Benjamins.

——: 1989 "Der Wortschatz der Bedscha-Sprache—eine vergleichende Analyse." In Einar von Schuler (ed.), *XXIII. Deutscher Orientalistentag vom 16. bis 20. September 1985 in Würzburg. Ausgewählte Vorträge*, pp. 573–591. Stuttgart: Franz Steiner Verlag.

——: 1997a "Problems of the Beja present seven years later," *Lingua Posnaniensis* 39: 145–153.

——: 1997b "The position of Cushitic and Berber within Hamitosemitic dialects." In Alessandro Bausi & Mauro Tosco (eds.), *Afroasiatica Neapolitana. Contributi presentati all'8º Incontro di Linguistica Afroasiatica (Camito-Semitica). Napoli, 25–26 Gennaio 1996*, pp. 49–59. Napoli: Istituto Universitario Orientale.

——: 1998 "Personal pronoun systems and their origin in some languages of Ethiopia," *Language and Linguistics* I: 65–86.

BEJA IDENTITY IN TU BEḍAWIƐ*

Marianne Bechhaus-Gerst
(University of Köln)

1. *Introduction*

When he contributed to the Cushitic—Omotic Symposium in 1986 the late Werner Vycichl spoke of Beja as 'A Language with seven seals' (Vycichl 1988), thus calling to our attention everything we don't know about the language and its speakers. The Beja and their language (tu beḍawiɛ, s. map) have in fact been largely neglected by linguistic and anthropological research of the last century. The question of its position within the Cushitic or Afroasiatic language family still remains open, studies of linguistic problems (in phonology, morphology, syntax as well as semantics or discourse) are missing, our knowledge of Beja culture, of the way the Beja conceptualize and organize their world is in its infancy. Its the last topic which seems to be the most urgent to deal with in the near future. During the last centuries the Beja society has undergone rapid changes due to a variety of causes. Ongoing drought which resulted in loss of livestock and famine, attempts by the Sudanese government to settle down the pastoralists, and the warlike conflicts of recent years led to massive migrations of Beja to Port Sudan, Kassala, Tokar and other towns in the Sudan as well as to Saudi Arabia. The inevitable consequence of these migrations is the disruption of the traditional way of life. When I did my field research with the Beja in 1984, I was under the impression, that it had almost disappeared and that in consequence the main motivation for retaining tu-beḍawiɛ was also dwindling. Monolingual tu-beḍawiɛ speakers were hardly found. Especially in mixed marriages where one of the partners only spoke Arabic, the children could at best be regarded as semi-speakers of tu-beḍawiɛ.

* The linguistic data were collected in the course of a four month stay in the northeastern Sudan between Port Sudan and Kassala. I thank my informants who have been extremely cooperative and helpful, in particular I am grateful to Mohamed Mahjoub Saliḥ Shōf, Hamid Mohamed Habib, Jafar Bamkar, Mohamed Tāhir Īsa, Hussein Hassan Mohamed Faid, and finally Mohammed Daitak for his music.

Most of them had no knowledge of the language other than a few greetings or other phrases. It may well be that as a result of massive cultural loss tu-beḍawiɛ has to be regarded as an endangered language in Sudan.

Latest figures speak of 1.148.000 Beja in the three countries Egypt, Sudan and Eritrea (Ethnologue 2000), their largest number being found in north-east Sudan. The Beja are divided into several sub-groups, and although a common Beja identity is confirmed by members of each of these groups, a common, non-Arabic ethnonym does not exist. Most of the Beja groups still speak mutually intelligible dialects of *tu-beḍawiɛ*, but nowadays there seem to be no monolingual Beja-speakers left. Most speakers are bilingual in Arabic (Egypt and Sudan) or Tigre (Sudan and Eritrea) and an increasing number completely shifts to one of these languages. Some sub-groups like the Ababda in the north and others in Eritrea are still to be regarded as Beja socially and culturally, but are monolingual speakers of either Arabic or Tigre.

Although in the last years the Beja language has been promoted in Eritrea as a consequence of a new language policy, it appears to be inevitable at least for the Sudanese speech area that the aforementioned cultural change and cultural loss will lead to a linguistic loss, which means more language shifts which are preceded by language decay. Especially in those parts of the language which are closely related to the traditional Beja identity, as e.g. the cultural specific vocabulary, the motivation for maintenance ceases to exist with the loss of the corresponding cultural characteristics. It's a trivial observation that their is a close relationship between a culture and its vocabulary. For the Beja this observation, however, gains new significance, because due to the massive changes parts of what once constituted Beja culture and identity can nowadays only be reconstructed through the lexicon of tu beḍawiɛ.

2. *Beja identity in tu beḍawiɛ*

The relationship between lexical elaboration and cultural interest has been noted by almost every writer on ethnography and linguistic anthropology. One of the most comprehensive list of elaborated vocabulary in the language of the pastoralist northern Beja was found with regard to camel husbandry (Bechhaus-Gerst 1991/1992). Equally

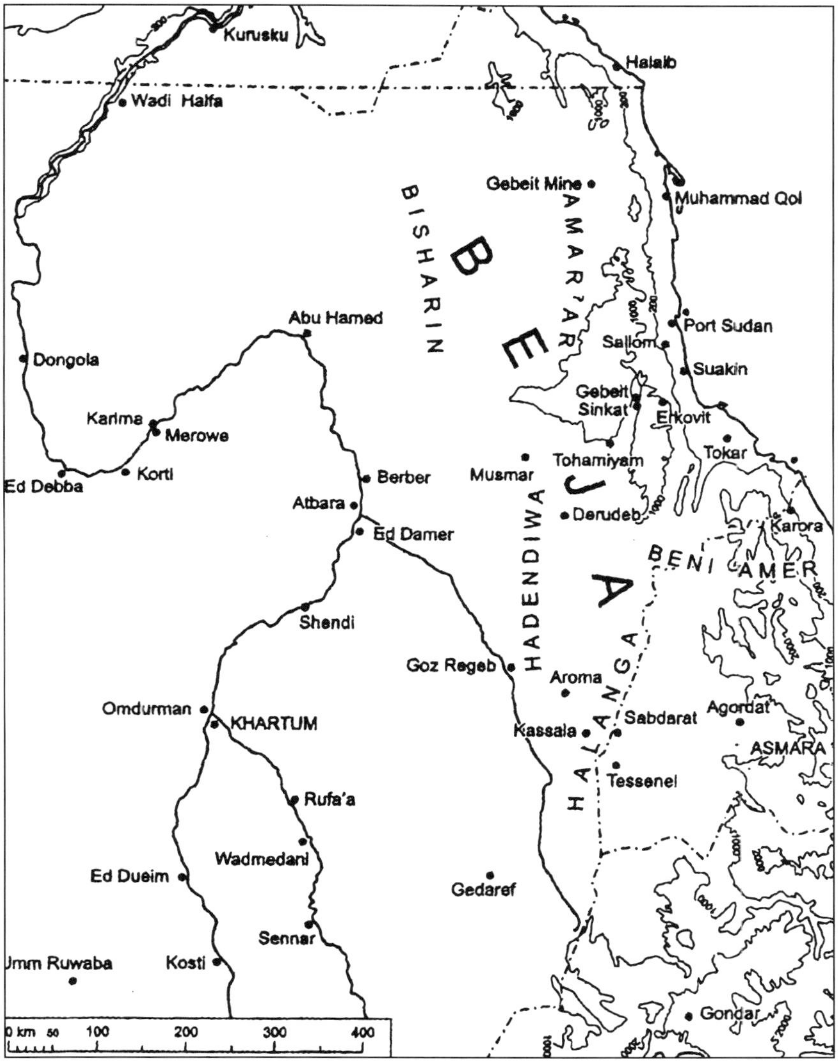

Figure 1 Tu Beḍawiε

differentiated is or was the part of the tu-beɖawiɛ lexicon which concerns the perception and conceptualization of the Beja environment, which was vital for the Beja who were on the move searching for pasture. The northern part of the Beja territory mainly consists of desert, where rain seldom falls and the ground is dry and barren. There are no permanent rivers in the north; small wadis, called *khor* in the northern Sudan, carry water after the very rare rains. The southern part of the area has a significant rainy season and therefore more favourable conditions with regards to drinking water and pasture. Only during the rainy season the Gash river carries water, a precondition for the transformation of the otherwise dry ground into fertile soil. The wadi or khor is a dry river and a central element of the landscape in the northeastern Sudan. After the very rare rains the wadis carry water which is indispensable to the Beja who live or move around the wadis. The following expression concerning the wadi environment were recorded:

1. general terms

malal	khor and surroundings
ʔaba	khor

2. special terms

kár	steep khor
dhi	narrow khor
ɖau	khor with trees
irʔóo	small khor
birga	small khor opening into a big one
shuuga	wide khor between mountains
rhaab	wide khor in plain

3. parts of the *khor*

herbuub	bed of khor
dirbani	steep bank of khor

4. water found in *khor*

birka	pool
hagir	pool in bed of khor
magwil	shallow pool in bed of khor made by digging
ʃia	water-hole dug at the edge of khor

ḍai	shallow pool with stagnating water
kwan	rain water brook, flooding water in khor
kalatanai	small stream, running water

Although the Beja area is bound by the River Nile in the west and the Red Sea in East and although we know from classical sources about Beja groups occupying the Nile valley abou 2000 years ago, this is not reflected in an elaborated vocabulary with regard to river and sea environment. It is thus easy to conclude that their is a lack of cultural focus comparable to other Cushitic groups of northeast Africa. River and sea are designated by the Arabic loanword *bahar* which is accompanied by the tu beḍawiɛ adjectives *nafir* 'sweet' and *hami* 'bitter'.

bahar nafir	river, Nile (lit.: 'sweet water')
bahar hami	sea (lit.: 'bitter water')

Of particular importance for the survival of the nomadic Beja was thorough meteorological observation as prerequisite for weather forecast and optimal adaptation to changing weather conditions. The question of whether and when it would be raining was central, because the rare rainfalls supplied water and subsequently new vegetation. This cultural focus is reflected by an elaborated vocabulary referring to clouds, rains, and wind:

5. clouds

afrat	cloud (cumulus)
baal	rain-cloud
gemberis	rain-cloud
shiwao	small tall cloud
lasso	deep cumulus
háfani	small cloud before rain starts
pʔaluk	thick and deep rain-cloud
ároiniut	distant rain-cloud

6. types of rain

birɛ	rain
mitwai	rain at the end of winter
wiit	rain at the beginning of winter
wiya	rainy season, winter

hibe, hubi	rainy season (July–midst of September), rain falling during that period
hibɛb	spend the rainy season
siif	drizzle
tɛɛwi	heavy rain (October–November)
kulinfe	lasting rain
ţab	constant drizzle

7. wind and weather

baram	wind, climate
ɛlogáni	whirl-wind without rain
moog	storm with rain
ɖʔaʃ	cold wind
ʔakil	piercing cold weather

The ways and roads which had to be traveled were named relating to their position and condition.

8. ways and paths

lági	way, road, road through the wood
garábi	footpath through the desert
sálal	way, path
miʔat	trail, beaten track
katʔai	difficult path between hills
doy	beaten track (trodden by camels)
fara	road across the mountains
agab	pass
gálel	camel road

Concerning the actual movements of people and animals verbs denoting time and direction of travelling can be found.

9. travelling

moyʔi	to travel through the heat of the day (without looking for shadow and without taking a rest)
ʔáyim	to pass the noon-time in a shadowy place
libás	to travel in the cool of the nighti
nagee	to drink at a well and pass on to rest

ʔawil	to move westwards from the Red Sea Hills i.e. in an westerly direction generally'
ɖʔ(a)	to move towards the Red Sea, i.e. in an easterly direction generally

Only few informants still remembered the whole range of terms which once was available to the Beja speakers. With the end of pastoralism the knowledge of a differentiated vocabulary in the field of weather and climate becomes less and less important.

The typical dwelling of the pastoralist Beja was the *baʔaɖaigau* or *biɖaigau*, a hut or tent which consisted of a wooden frame covered with plaids of goat's hair and straw mats. Other less solid types of huts and shelters were used whenever quick and temporary accommodation had to be set up.

10. matting-hut, temporary huts and shelters

baʔaɖaigau/biɖaigau	lit.: 'house of mats', hut which is constructed of a frame of poles which are covered with mats
lake	temporary hut when halting somewhere
ʃafat	temporary hut, esp. for guests build beneath a tree
bekkar	hut made of mats
ʃʔoba	pole
hummar/hammar	curved upper parts of the frame which carry the roof
hilʔe	pole which forms the backbone of the biɖaigau
gasane	tent-peg
bal	mat used to cover the door of the biɖaigau
ʃamalɛ	plaid made of goat's hair which lines the biɖaigau and functions as back and side-wall

Turning from the sphere of the outside world as it is conceptualized in the Beja lexicon to the Beja people itself, we find the Beja men constructing their identity with the help of a rather differentiated vocabulary with regard to hair and arms. Their tradition as warriors as well as their striking hair-style earned the Beja a rather effusive hymn by Rudyard Kipling and the name 'Fuzzy-Wuzzy'. Sha'aban writes in her book 'Die Hadandawa-Bedscha' (1970) about the Beja man who is never seen without three objects: a sword for his defense, a dagger, which is carried in a leather belt and which is used for different daily tasks, and a stick to fend off snakes and dogs. What seems to have been everyday life in the mid-sixties, when Sha'aban conducted her field-work, was an rather exceptional occurrence only twenty years later, when the author stayed in the Beja area. Especially the sword, the original symbol of full manliness, given by a father to his son, had lost significance. Only the stick seemed to dominate the appearance of the Beja men on the road. The erstwhile importance of the sword and the shield still reflected and preserved in the vocabulary:

10. arms

baɖaɖ, mʔaɖaɖ	sword
bɛrsham	guard of sword
gaim	handle of sword
kar	central flute on blade
mitakwerri	sword with three flutes
nagash,	runes on blade
mhawi, nʔafa, mishmam	sheath of sword
limmi	rings on sheath
gubɛ, gwibɛ (Am)	shield
agaba	shield made of buff-skin
isin	shield made of hippopotamus leather
kurbia	shield made of elephant leather
annur	boss
dooma	crossbar
adala	grip of shield
balas	peep hole
ʔadare	dance with sword and shield
biiboo	dance jumping with both feet holding sword and shield
kolɛy	stick
bilbil	throwing stick
fina/fɛna	spear

hanjar	dagger, curved knife carried in belt
huus	knife
sotʔal/ʃotʔal	dagger or knife with curved end

The Beja traditionally spent considerable time with hygiene and beauty culture. The Beja men's care concentrated upon their hair, which was never washed, but was regularly anointed. Only every two years the hair was cut. Wooden combs or hairpins with one to five teeth which on one side were often decorated were regarded as not dispensable and stuck into the hair. Only those Beja men who lived under a religious leader or who belonged to a chief's or local authority's family, always cut their hair and wore a turban. During the last decades, however, Islam considerably gained in significance among the Beja, a process which had the consequence of an decreasing acceptance of the traditional hair-style. More and more men decided to cut their hair and to wear the turban as is the custom in other parts of the northern Sudan. In 1984 terms for the different parts of the typical Beja-coiffure were remembered, but designations for grease, oil and perfume were no longer parts of the general lexicon.

11. hair-style

haŋkwila	down hanging part of the hair-style
yawad	down hanging part of the hair-style made of little plaits
tirra, tilla	part of the hair-style which stands erect on the head
ḍifi	shorter hair, not divided into *tilla* and *haŋkwila*
fetit	to dress men's hair, to part the men's hair with a wooden comb or pin
hadugw	to plait the hair
hɛlal	hairpin
magargaf	comb with several teeth
lʔas	to grease the hair
lʔam	to grease the hair
darir	special perfume for hair
kwati	special grease or oil for the lower part of the coiffure
wadak	special grease or oil for the upper part of the coiffure

These examples from tu-beḍawiɛ lexicon may demonstrate one of the many ways the study of vocabulary can be useful to the ethnographer. Although the Beja belong to the numerically largest ethnic groups of Sudan their culture and language seem to be endangered. Traditional pastoralism which once was characteristic of the northern Beja groups is dwindling. The increasing role of Islam as well as the rapid cultural and social change expedites language shift towards Arabic. Long before the shift has taken place these changes result in language decay, which becomes apparent in loss of e.g. cultural vocabulary. With the massive loss of those parts of the lexicon which constructed the traditional Beja identity, however, an important motive for the maintenance of tu-beḍawiɛ as a symbol of this identity seems to become void.

Bibliography

Bechhaus-Gerst (Marianne): 1991/92 "The Beja and the Camel,. Camel related lexicon in tu-beḍawiɛ", Sprache und Geschichte in Afrika (SUGIA) 12/13, pp. 41–62.

——: 2000 "A Study of Beja Place-Names", Afrikanistische Arbeitspapiere (AAP) 61, pp. 145–170.

Hess (J.J.): 1918 "Geographische Bennenungen und Pflanzennamen in der nördlichen Bischari-Sprache", Zeitschrift für Kolonialsprachen 9,1, pp. 209–225.

Shaʿaban (S.): 1970 "Die Hadandawa-Bedscha" Ph.D. thesis, University of Bonn.

Vycichl (Werner): 1988 "Beja—A Language with Seven Seals", in: M. Bechhaus-Gerst & F. Serzisko (eds.), Cushitic—Omotic. Papers from the International Symposium on Cushitic and Omotic Languages, Cologne, January 6–9, 1986, pp. 411–430, Helmut Buske Verlag, Hamburg.

QUELQUES OBSERVATIONS SUR LES CORRESPONDANCES VOCALIQUES DANS LES THÈMES VERBAUX SÉMITIQUES ET DU BÉDJA

Anna G. Bélova
(Oriental Institute, Moscow)

Au cours de la recherche comparative sur le vocalisme thématique des verbes sémitiques [Bélova 1993] nous nous sommes intéressée aussi aux données de certaines langues couchitiques de l'Afrique de l'Est.

En comparant des formes verbales du bédja dans le dictionnaire de L. Reinisch un phénomène a attiré notre attention. L'auteur présente au verbe 1.5 (« starke Verben ») trois formes thématiques auxquelles il attribue des termes « Perfect—Plusquamperfect—Präsens » [Reinisch, Bd. 130, Abh. 7, § 224]. Plus tard ces formes sont nommées « Past-Old, Past-Present » [Zaborski 1975, § 367], « Prétérit—Habitatif—Présent » [Dolgopol'ski, 1991, p. 54]. Sans discuter leurs valeurs grammaticales en synchronie nous bornons à considérer les deux formes premières *à*=$C_1C_2VC_3$ (« Perfect »-Perf) et *i*-=$C_1C_2VC_3$ (« Plusquamperfect »-Plq) ; par exemple : *áktib : īktib* [Reinisch, 1895, p. 151]. Au point de vue de leur structure et de leur origine toutes les deux sont les plus anciennes [Zaborski, 1975, §§ 3, 7 ; Dolgopol'ski, 1991, p. 48] et sont identifiables aux thèmes afroasiatiques communs [Diakonoff, 1988, pp. 85–86].

En présentant trois formes thématiques du verbe 1. dans son dictionnaire L. Reinisch construit aussi un thème verbal primaire, par exemple—pour le verbe à trois consonnes—le thème $C_1eC_2iC_3$. Ce thème semple invariable (à l'exception de cas prosodiques et de l'influence des laryngales/pharyngales) dans Perfect et Plusquamperfect. Ainsi cette forme est traitée en table de formes et conjugaison du Bédja [Dolgopol'ski, 1991, pp. 123–124].

Néanmoins nous avons trouvé dans ce dictionnaire des formes du Plusquamperfect (Old Past/Habitatif) dont la voyelle thématique n'est pas =*i*=, mais =*e*=, par ex. : *fedig* v. 1, Perf. *áfdig*—Plq. *ī́fdeg*—Präsens *afandig* « défaire » [R, p. 75]. Ce phénomène n'est expliqué ni par les règles phonétiques du bédja (v. [Reinisch 1893, Bd. 128, (84), (85)],[1]

[1] Cf. *áktib*—*iktib* "écrire".

ni par sa valeur grammaticale. Il faut souligner aussi que L. Reinisch qui indique dans son dictionnaire tous ces cas, ne les explique pas et ne fait aucun commentaire à leur propos dans sa grammaire du Bédja (cf. § 199, § 231). A. Zaborski insiste tout spécialement sur la question de l'apophonie *i : a* dans des thèmes verbaux tels que *a=dir : e=dar* « tuer » [§ 10, § 17], mais il ne mentionne pas quelques autres variantes de l'apophonie thématique.

Ayant relevé des cas du Plusquamperfect comportant la voyelle thématique *=e=* nous essayons de comparer ses formes avec celles des verbes sémitiques dont le vocalisme est établi.

Dans l'exposition suivante des exemples nous marquons la voyelle thématique du verbe arabe à l'Imparfait comme (*u*), (*i*), (*a*),[2] les deux voyelles des deux thèmes verbaux accadiens du Présent/Prétérit (*a/u, a/i* etc.),[3] du thème verbal en hébreu comme (*o*) ou (*a*).

À plusieurs reprises des thèmes sémitiques parallèles allégués par L. Reinisch sont pris en considération et en comparaison.

1. *Les thèmes verbaux Béd =e= : Sém =*u=*

1) Bédja *betik* [R-53] «schneiden» Perf. *ábtek*—Plq. *ī́btek* (Präs. *abantīk*): Sém Acc *btq/bdq (a/u)* Hbr *btq(o)* Arab *btq/btk (u)* Gz *btk (yəbtək)* «couper, retrancher» < Sém **=btuq/btuk*;
2) Bédja *bis* [R-52] « bergen, den Leichram begraben, bestatten » Perf. *abis*—Plq. *ī́bes* (Präs. *ambīs*) : Sém Arab *bwṣ (u)* [BK, I, 178] « se cacher, rester caché ».
3) Bédja *tebōk* [R-221] « übereinander legen, aufhäufen ; mit den Händen Korn in den Sack füllen » Perf. *adbṓk*—Plq. *ī́-dbūk* : Sém (?) Acc *tbk/tpk (a/u)* « hin/schütten, vergiessen » Arab *tbq (u)* [BK, II, 55] « couvrir, envelopper » ;
4) Bédja *tūf/tuff di* [R-223] « spucken, ausspeisen » Perf. *tūf ádi*—(Präs. *tūf ándi*) Sa ʿAfar *tuf dah* : Afras **təf* II > Sém Hbr *topet* (hapax) Arab *tff (u)* Eth Tna *tuff bälä* Amh *əttəf balä* « cracher » [HCVA, N 152].
5) Bédja *t̲uk̲uk* [R-225] « fertig machen, vollbringen, vollenden » Bil *dun* Perf. *átk̲uk/át̲uk̲úk*—Plq. *ī́-tkuk* (Präs. *atankuīuk*) : Sém Arab *dnq*

[2] Si le thème arabe du Parfait a une voyelle *=i=* ou *=u=*, nous l'installons devant celle de l'Imparfait (par ex. *i—a*).

[3] C'est la voyelle deuxième en Prétérit accadien qui est pertinente.

(u) « entrer dans les petits détails, être absorbé par les minuties » [BK, I, 738–739] Gz *tnqq* « be exactly, do sth accurately, with precision » [Leslau, p. 594] ;

6) Bédja *gŭʾad* [R-86] « wachen, bewachen » Perf. *agŭʾad*—Plq. *ī́gŭʾed* [Präs. *agŭʾanīd*) : Sém Arab *qʿd (u)* [BK, II, 776] « être en embuscade et guetter qn ; être assis et prêt pour le service de qn ; attendre » ;

7) Bédja *hakur* [R-115] « binden, zubinden, verbinden » Perf. *ahakur*—Plq. *ihukur* (Präs. *ahankuī́r*) : Sém Hbr *ḥgr (o)* [KB, 276] « etwas als Gürtel, Gurt anlegen » Arab *kwr (u)* « rouler en spirale (le turban) » [BK, II, 942]. Cf. aussi *qawr=* [BK, II, 833] « corde de coton nouvelle et forte » Gz *ʿäqʷara (yəqʷər/yəʿqʷar)* [Leslau, 68] « roll up, wrap up, bind up, knot . . . ». Cf. chez W. Leslau la comparaison de C. Brockelmann *ʿqʷr* avec Arab *ʿqd (i)*. Nous y préférons de voir la base primaire **k/qʷr* (> *ḥ/ʿ* = (complément) = *k/qʷr*) selon la thèse des compléments dans les racines afroasiatiques [Diakonoff 1988, pp. 43, 51, 54 ; Bélova 1992, pp. 15–16] ;

8) Bédja *debil/ḍebil* [R-60] « raffen, sammeln, anhäufen » Perf. *ádbil*-Plq. *īdbel* (Präs. *adambīl*) : Sém Arab *dbl (u)* [BK, I, 668] « réunir, rassembler » Gz *dbl (yədbəl)* « bring together, gather » [Leslau, 120] ;

9) Bédja *demim* [R-67] « umschliessen, zusammenpressen, mit beiden Händen ausdrücken » Perf. *ádmim*- Plq. *ī-dmem* (Präs. *adammīm*) : Sém PbHbr (?) *ṣamīm* « noeud » Arab *ḍmm (u)* [BK, II, 36] « rassembler les bouts d'une chose, rapprocher, serrer » Gz *ḍmm (yəḍməm)* [Leslau, 150] « bind, tie around, patch up » (> Couch. Bil *čamam* « enclose, surround ») [Leslau, 150] ;

10) Bédja *din* [R-67] « meinen, dafürhalten, glauben » Perf. *adín*—Plq. *īdin/īden* (Präs. *andīn*) : Sém Arab *ẓnn (u)* [BK, II, 142] « croire, juger, penser » ;

11) Bédja *dūr* [R-70] « besuchen »—Sém Arab *zwr (u)* [BK, I, 1025] « visiter » ;

12) Bédja *remig* [R-192] « betteln, als Schmarotzer von Haus zu Haus Visiten machen » Perf. *ármig*—Plq. *īrmeg* (Präs. *arammīg*) : Sém Arab *rmq (u)* [BK, I, 92] « regarder, toujours furtivement ; attendre » (cf. *rāmiq=* « envieux, pauvre, misérable » ;

13) Bédja *remid* [R-192] « feindlich überfallen ; in ein fremdes Land in räuberischer Absicht einfallen » Perf. *ármid*—Plq. *īrmed* (Präs. *arammīd*) : Sém Arab *rmd (u)* « attaquer, faire une invasion, commettre une agression contre une tribu ». Cf. *mrd (u)* (métathèse) « s'être rebellé avec préméditation » (?) Gz *rmd : ʾrmd* « stamp the ground, strike, hit » [Leslau, 470] ;

14) Bédja *setir* [R-206] « ein=/verhüllen, =bergen, =stecken » Perf. *ástir*—Plq. *īster* (Präs. *asantīr*) : Sém Hbr *str* (nif.) « sich verbergen/hide » Arab *str (u)* [BK, I, 1049] « couvrir, cacher » Gz *str (yəstər)* > couch. Bd., Bil. *satar* [Leslau, 518]

15) Bédja *serid* [R-204] « wahrsagen durch Muschelwerfen » Perf. *ásrid*—Plq. *īsred* (Präs. *asanrīd/asarrīd*) : Sém Arab *srd (u)* « arranger avec art et agencer toutes les parties d'un discours ; réciter, raconter » ;

16) Bédja *sekŭ* [R-197] « ziehen » Perf. *asúḵ*—Plq. *īsuḵ* (Präs. *ansīuḵ*) : Sém Arab *ḏḥw (u) / zğw (u) / zḥḥ (u) / zḫḫ (u)* [BK, I, 766, 976, 977, 980] « pousser, repousser ; faire marcher devant soi » ;

17) Bédja *selih* [R-199] « streicheln » Perf. *áslih*—Plq. *īsleh* (Präs. *asanlīh/asallīh*) : Sém Arab *zlq (u)* [BK, I, 358] « glisser à la surface du sol, la glace » ; cf. *ṣlğ (u)* « frotter » ;

18) Bédja *semim* [R-202] « fetten, schmalzen, mit Fell übergiessen die Speise » Perf. *ásmim*—Plq. *īsmum* (Präs. *asammīm*) : Sém Hbr *šmn* (Imperf. *wa yišman*) [KB, 989] « grow, be fat » Arab *smn (u)* [BK, I, 1143] « graisser un mets en y mettant du beurre fondu, de la graisse » ;

19) Bédja *sim/sum* [R-201] « nennen, bennennen » Perf. *asím/asúm*—Plq. *īsem/īsum* (Präs. *ansīm*) : Sém Arab *smw (u)* [BK, I, 1144] « nommer, appeler qn d'un nom » ;

20) Bédja *šehŭar/šehar* [R-212] « schnarchen » Perf. *ášhar*—Plq. *īšhur* (Präs. *ašankŭīr*) : Sém Arab *šḫr (i)* [BK, I, 1201], *ḫrr (u)* [BK, I, 554], *ḫrḫr* [BK, I, 556], *nḫr (u)* [BK, II, 1220] « ronfler, renifler, renâcler » (tous < **X^wr*) ;

21) Bédja *šehak* [R-212] « verschollen gehen » Perf. *ášhak*—Plq. *īšhuḵ* (Präs. *ašanhīuḵ*) : Sém Arab *sḥq (u)* [BK, I, 1061] « effacer les traces de qch sur la terre (du vent) ; perdre, faire disparaître » ;

22) Bédja *ḍim* [R-74] « ausfüllen einen Rum » Perf. *aḍím*—Plq. *īḍem* (Präs. *anḍīm*) : Sém Arab *ṭmm (u)* [BK, II, 105] « remplir » ;

23) Bédja *ḍin* [R-74] « anfangen, beginnen » Perf. *aḍín*—Plq. *īḍen* (Präs. *anḍīn*) : Sém Gz *wṭn (yəwṭən/yəṭan)* « begin, commence, set forth » [Leslau, 623] ;

24) Bédja *fedig/fetig/fetik* [R-75] « auflösen, losbinden, öffnen, befreien » Perf. *áfdig*—Plq. *īfdeg* (Präs. *afandīg*) : Sém (?) Acc *ptq (i/i)* « formen, bilden » Arab *ftq (u)* [BK, II, 535–536] « fendre, rompre, séparer, défaire, découdre » ;

25) Bédja *fekik* [R-78] « öffnen die infibulierte Jungfrau, entjungfern » Perf. *áfkik*—Plq. *ī́fkek* (Präs. *afankīk*) : Sém Arab *fkk/fqq (u)* [BK, II, 623] « dégager, défaire, séparer, disjoindre, ouvrir » Gz *fqq* « split,

cleave » [Leslau, 164] (Cf. [HCVA 1994, N 15 : **pVk* « to open »]) ;
26) Bédja *fenin* [R-80] « aus=, strecken, dehnen » Perf. *áfnin*—Plq. *ı́fnen* (Präs. *afannı̄́n*) : Sém Arab *fnn (u)* [BK, II, 635] « prolonger à qn le délai pour le payement de la dette » ;
27) Bédja *kib* [R-135] « giessen, aus=, ein=, giessen » Perf. *akib*—Plq. *īkeb* (Präs. *ankīb*) : Sém Arab *kbb (u)* [BK, II, 850], *n=kb (u)* [BK, II, 1336], *s=kb (u)* [BK, I, 1112] « verser, incliner qch pour verser » (< **=kub*) ;
28) Bédja *kŭbib* [R-135] « schneiden » Perf. *ákbub*—Plq. *īkbub* (Präs. *akŭambīb*) » Sém Arab *kwf (u)* « couper » [BK, II, 944] *ǧbb/ǧwb (u)/(ū)* [BK, I, 245, 348] « couper, fendre, déchirer » ;
29) Bédja *kil* [R-139] « kreisen, fliegen » Perf. *akíl*—Plq. *īkel* (Präs. *ankīl*) : Sém Ug *gyl* Hbr *gwl=n* « im Kreis gehen / go around [KB, 175], *gyl (i-)* [KB, 180] « sich umdrehen / go around » Arab *ǧwl (u)* [BK, I, 358] « tourner, voltiger en cercle ; tourner autour de » ;
30) Bédja *mekir* [R-167] « raten, einen Rat geben ; kaufen » Perf. *ámkir*—Plq. *īmker* (Präs. *amankīr*) : Sém Acc *mkr (a/u)* Hbr *mkr (o)* [KB, 522] « Handel treiben/ trade; verkaufen/ sell » Arab *mkr (u)* [BK, II, 1138] « tromper qn » Gz *mkr (yəmkar/yəmkər)* « advise, exhort, recommend, take counsel » (> Couch) [Leslau, 340] ;
31) Bédja *melit* [R-169] « rupfen, ausreissen die Haare/Feder » Perf. *ámlit*—Plq. *īmlet* (Präs. *amanlīt/amallīt*) : Sém Acc *mrṭ (a/u)* « einreiben » Hbr *mrṭ* [KB, 566] *(o)* « raufen/ pull of (hair)[4] Arab *mrṭ (u)* [BK, II, 1092], *mlṭ (u)* [BK, II, 1148] Gz *mlṭ/mrṭ* « uproot, pull out » [Leslau, 346, 361] ;
32) Bédja *negil* [R-181] « öffnen, aufdecken, enthüllen, bekannt machen » Perf. *ángil*—Plq. *īngel* (Präs. *anangīl*) : Sém Arab *nǧl (u)* [B-807] « manifester, montrer » Gz *ngl (yəngəl)* « be visible, adorned » [Leslau, 329] ;
33) Bédja *nefik* [R-180] « furzen » Perf. *ánfik*—Plq. *īnfek* (Präs. *ananfīk*) : Sém Arab *nfḫ (u)* [BK, II, 1306] « souffler, lâcher un pet » (Cf. aussi *nfǧ (u)* « souffler, gonfler » [BK, II, 1304] Acc *npḫ (a/u)* « anblasen, aufgehen », mais Hbr *npḥ (a)* [KB, 708] Gz *nfḫ/nfḥ (yənfāḫ/ḥ)* [Leslau, 388] ;
34) Bédja *temu̲k* [R-229] « zusammenpressen, auspressen » Perf. *átmuk*—Plq. *ītmuk* (Präs. *atammīuk*) : Sém Gz *ṣmq (yəṣməq)* « squeeze out, wring out » [Leslau, 558].

[4] Cf. aussi **Hbr** *mlṭ* (hit.) « sich kahl erweisen / prove bald, hairless [KB, 529].

2. *Certains cas de la divergence entre des voyelles thématiques du bédja et des thèmes sémitiques*

35) Bédja *bedil* [R-42] « ändern, verändern, austauschen » Perf. *ábdil*—Plq. *ībdil* (Präs. *abandīl*) : Sém Arab *bdl (u)* « remplacer, changer qch » [BK, I, 97] ;
36) Bédja *tib* [R-220] « anfüllen, voll machen » Perf. *atīb*—Plq. *ītib* (Präs. *antīb*) : Sem Arab *ṯwb (u)* [BK, I, 240] « couler de différants points dans un réservoir, bassin » ;
37) Bédja *gid* [R-89] « niederwerfen, zu Boden strecken » Perf. *agīd*—Plq. *īgid* (Präs. *angīd*) : Sém Arab *ǧẓẓ (u)* [BK, I, 298] « renverser, jeter à terre » (Cf. aussi *ǧʿb*) ;
38) Bédja *gedil* [R-91] « spinnen » Perf. *ágdil*—Plq. *īgdil* (Präs. *agandīl*) : Sém Arab *ǧdl* (*i*, parfois *u*) [BK, I, 265] « rendre fort, solide en tressant et en tordant fortement une corde » ;
39) Bédja *demin* [R-67] « Bürgschaft leisten, bürgen, haften, gutstehen » Perf. *ádmin*—Plq. *īdmen* (Präs. *adammīn*) : Sém Arab *ḍmn (i—a)* « assurer, garantir qch » [BK, II, 40] ;
40) Bédja *selib* [R-199] « berauben » Perf. *áslib*—Plq. *īslib* (Präd. *asanlīb*) : Sém Acc *šalāp*= *(a/u)* Hbr *šlp (o)* Arab *slb (u)* [BK, I, 1118] « arracher qch de vive force ; piller ; dégainer (le sabre) / herausziehen, zücken/draw out » Gz *slb (yəsləb)* « take off, plunder » [Leslau, 498] ;
41) Bédja *šemim* [R-216] « verbinden, zubinden » Perf. *ášmim*—Plq. *īšmim* : Sém Arab *ḍmm (u)* [BK, II, 36] « rassembler les bouts d'une chose, réunir, serrer » Gz *ḍmm (yəḍməm)* « bind, tie around » [Leslau, 150] ;
42) Bédja *fetit* [R-84] « zerteilen » Perf. *áftit*—Plq. *īftit* : Sém Hbr *ptt (o)* [KB, 789] Arab *ftt (u)* [BK, II, 531] « écraser, broyer, casser, fendre » Gz *ftt* (> Couch Béd *fetit* « divide ») [Leslau, 171].
43) Bédja *fetik/fetig* [R-84] « ent=, wegziehen, abtrennen » Perf. *áftik*—Plq. *īftik* : Sém Arab *ftq (u)* [BK, II, 535] « fendre, rompre ; défaire, découdre » ;
44) Bédja *ferik* [R-83] « graben einen Brunnen, ein Grab » Perf. *áfrik*—Plq. *īfrek* : Sém Arab *ḥfr (i)* [BK, I, 457],[5] mais en Syr. dial. *ḥfr (o)* 'creuser (la terre) » ;
45) Bédja *ketib* [R-151] « screiben » Perf. *áktib*—Plq. *īktib* : Sém Hbr *ktb (o)* [KB, 459] Arab *ktb (u)* « écrire ».

[5] Si la forme du bédja est traitée comme métathèse pour **Sém** *ḥfr*.

3. *Les thèmes verbaux Béd =i= : Sém =i=*

46) Bédja *tebik* [R-221] « an eine Beschäftigung gehen, ein Geschäft beginnen, die erste Hand anlegen an eine Arbeit » Perf. *ádbik*—Plq. *īdbik*: Sém Arab *ṭfq (i)* [BK, II, 89] « aborder, commencer qch, entamer » (de la correspondance Béd *b*=C_2: Sém **p* v' [Dolgopol'ski, 1973, p. 329]) ;
47) Bédja *gerib* [R-100] « siegen, besiegen im Kriege, im Process gewinnen » Perf. *ágrib*—Plq. *īgrib* : Sém Arab *ġlb (i)* [BK, II, 489] « vaincre qn » (de la correspondance Béd *r* = C_2: Sém =*l*=C_2 v' [Dolgopol'ski, p. 337]) ;
48) Bédja *gelid* [R-95] « schwören, eidlich geloben » Perf. *áglid*—Plq. *īglid :* Sém Arab *ǧlṭ (i)* [BK, I, 316] « jurer, faire un serment » ;
49) Bédja *genif* [R-98] « biegen, krümmen » Perf. *ágnif*—Plq *īgnif*: Sém Arab *ǧnf (i)* [BK, I, 339], *knf (i)* [BK, II, 936] « s'écarter, dévier de la voie droite » ;
50) Bédja *hadim* [R-111] « zerstören »—Perf. *ahadim*—Plq. *īhadim* : Sém Arab *hdm (i)* [BK,II, 1402] « démolir, abattre, faire crouler (un édifice) » ;
51) Bédja *harid* [R-124] « schlachten » Perf. *aharíd*—Plq. *iherid* : Sém Arab *ḥrd (i)* [BK, I, 405] « percer, perforer » Gz *ḥrd (yəḥrəd)* « slaughter, sever, slay, destroy » [Leslau, 241] ;
52) Bédja *hasib* [R-127] « denken, meinen, aussinnen, zählen, rechnen » Perf. *ahasíb*—Plq. *ihesíb* : Sém Hbr *ḥšb (o)* [KB, 339] « zählen, beachten, für wertvoll halten / account, regard, value » Arab *ḥsb (i, u, a)* [BK, I, 423] « compter, croire, penser » Gz *ḥsb* « think, beliwe, consider » [Leslau, 244] ;
53) Bédja *hakif/hakib* [R-114] « umarmen » : Sém Arab *ʿkf (i)* [BK, II, 330] « entourer, cerner qn ». Cf. aussi en Gz *ḥqf (yəḥqəf/yəḥqaf)* « hug, embrace, brood, fold (hands) [Leslau, 239] ; et aussi en Acc (avec une métathèse) *epēq= (i)* [Riemschneider, 258] « umfassen » ;
54) Bédja *hamir* [R-121] « gären, sauer werden » : Sém Arab *ḫmr (i, u)* « faire lever la pâte en y mettant du levain » [BK, I, 630] ;
55) Bédja *hayid* [R-133] « nähen » Perf. *ahayíd/aháyd*—Plq. *īhayd* : Sém Arab *ḫyṭ (ī)* [BK, I, 655] « coudre, recoudre qch » ;
56) Bédja *defir* [R-61] « flechten die Haare » Perf. *ádfir*—Plq. *īdfir :* Sém Arab *ḍfr (i)* [B, 436] « tresser les cheveux en larges tresses » Gz *ḍfr (yəḍfər)* « braid, plait, interlace, plait, twist, weave » [Leslau, 148] ;
57) Bédja *rib* [R-188] « widerstreben, zurückweisen ; verweigern, abgenutzt sein, hassen » Perf. *aríb*—Plq. *īrib* : Sém Arab *ryb (ī)*

[BK, I, 959] « jeter qn dans le doute ou dans l'embarras ; inspirer à qn des doutes, soupçons, mécontenter qn, inquiéter qn ». Cf. aussi Sém Hbr *ryb (i-)* [KB, 888] « mit Worten, Anklagen, Behauptungen, Vorwürfen einen Rechtsstreit führen ; rechten/ with words complaints, assertions contestins, reproaches contend, conduct a (legal) case, auit »

58) Bédja *redid* [R-189] « stumpf, abgenützt sein » Perf. *árdid*—Plq. *īrdid* : Sém Arab *rṯṯ (i)* [BK, I, 819] « être vieux, usé, rapé (habit) » ;

59) Bédja *refif* [R-189] « einwickeln » Perf. *árfif*—Plq. *īrfif* : Sém Arab *rff (i)* [BK, I, 892] « entourer, cerner » (Cf. aussi Arab *lff (u)* « plier, rouler, envelopper, entourer » [BK, II, 1007], Gz *lff (yəlfəf)* « write, roll around, cover » [Leslau, 306], Acc *lpp (a/u)* « umwickeln) ;

60) Bédja *refit* [R-189] « in kleine Stücke zerbrechen, zerschneiden » Perf. *árfit*—Plq. *īrfit* : Sém Arab *rft (i, u)* [BK, I, 893] « casser, briser en petits morceaux » ;

61) Bédja *šetit* [R-218] « zerreißen, zerschneiden » Perf. *áštit*—Plq. *īštit* : Sém Arab *štt (i)* [BK, I, 1189] « séparer, jeter ça et là, êrre séparé, jeté » ;

62) Bédja *šerim* [R-217] « zerreissen, abreissen ein Stück vom Ganzen » Perf. *áširim*—Plq. *īšrim* : Sém Arab *šrm (i)* [BK, I, 1222] « fondre légèrement, déchirer légèrement »/*zrm (i)* [BK, I, 987] « interrompre » ;

63) Bédja *šenig* [R-216] « erdrosseln, erwürgen » Perf. *ášnig*—Plq. *īšnig* : Sém Arab *šnq (i)* [BK, I, 1277] « étrangler (un homme), étouffer » ;

64) Bédja *fegir* [R-77] « bedecken, bedachen » Perf. *áfgir*—Plq. *īfgir* : Sém Acc *apār=/epēr= (i)* Bed *(i/e)*, M-nA *apir=* [Soden, p. 57] Arab *ġfr (i)* [BK, II, 482], *kfr (i)* [BK, II, 913] « couvrir, cacher » Gz *ʿfr (yəʿfər)* « cover, put sth » [Leslau, 58] ;

65) Bédja *fetir* [R-84] « frühstücken » Perf. *áftir*—Plq. *īftir* : Sém Arab *fṭr (i, u)* [BK, II, 611] « déjeuner » ;

66) Bédja *kedim* [R-136] « dienen » Perf. *ákdim*—Plq. *īkdim* : Sém Arab *ḫdm (i, u)* « servir qn, être au service de qn » ;

67) Bédja *kerir* [R-147] « meuchlings überfallen, feindlich angreifen » : Sém Arab *ḫrr (i, u)* [BK, I, 551] « sortir tout à coup, on ne sait d'où, et fondre sur qn » ;

68) Bédja *terib* [R-231] « teilen, spalten » Perf. *átrib*—Plq. *ītrib* : Sém Arab *tbr (i)* [BK, I, 190] avec métathèse « briser, se séparer, séparer ».

4. *Les thèmes verbaux Béd =a= : Sém =a=*

4.0

Les thèmes du Béd à =*a*= thématique présentent deux groupes (autant qu'en sémitiques) : des thèmes à valeur grammaticale—valeur intransitive ou valeur d'état, de qualité etc. [Dolgopol'ski, 1991, pp. 48–54]—(4.1.) ; des thèmes dont la voyelle est conditionnée par les laryngales et pharyngales [Zaborski, 1975, § 17]—(4.2.).

4.1

69) Bédja *gerāk* [R-101] « untersinken, versinken, untergehen im Wasser » Perf. *agrāk*—Plq. *egrāka* : Sém Arab *ġrq (i—a)* [BK, II, 459] « être plongé tout entier dans l'eau, submergé ; se noyer, périr à la mer » ;

70) Bédja *gŭmād* [R-97] « lang, hoch, tief sein » Perf. *agmād*—Plq. *īgmeda* : Sém Arab *qmd (u—a)* [BK, II, 810] « avoir le cou long » ;

71) Bédja *kesál* [R-148] « träge, faul, lässig sein » Perf. *aksāl*—Plq. *éksila* (Präs. *aksalī/áksali* : Sém Arab *ksl (i—a)* [BK, II, 899] « être paresseux, négligent, fainéant » ;

72) Bédja *hadāl* [R-110] « schwarz, dunkel, trübe, finster sein » Perf. *ahadāl*—Plq. *ehédla* (Präs. *áhdali*) : Sém Arab *ġṯl (i—a)* [BK, II, 480] « être très sombre » (Cf. aussi *ġtš* [BK, II, 553] « être sombre », où =*š* < **ŝ*) ;

73) Bédja *harāf* [R-125] « dumm, beschränkt sein » Perf. *aharáf*—Plq. *ehárfa* (Präs. *ahárfi*) : Sém Arab *ḫrf (i—a)* [BK, I, 561] « avoir le cerveau troublé, avoir le délire ».

4.2

74) Bédja *gedah* (R-91] « schöpfen » Perf. *ágdah*—Plq. *īgdah* : Sém Arab *qdḥ (a)* [BK, II, 68] « tirer avec une cuiller de la soupe ; curer un puits en tirant l'eau bourbeuse » Gz *qdḥ (yəqdaḥ)* « draw water, pour out » [Leslau, 420] ;

75) Bédja *lehas* [R-156] « lecken » Perf. *álhas*—Plq. *īlhas* (Präs. *alanhīs*) : Sém Hbr *lḥś (a)* Arab *lḥs (a)* [BK, II, 973] Gz *lḥs (yəlḥas)* « lécher qch/ lick » [Leslau, 311].

La voyelle =*a*= apparaît aussi dans des verbes dont les thèmes n'ont pas de correspondants en sémitique et ne sont par des emprunts aux langues sémitiques : Bédja *šeʾag* [R-209] « aufhängen » Perf. *ášʾag*—Plq. *īšʾag* « suspendre » ; Bédja *feraʾ* [R-81] « aus=/herausziehen, hervorbringen » Perf. *áfraʾ*—Plq. *īfraʾ* « arracher, extraire, tirer » ; Bédja *kehan* [R-138] « befreundet sein, lieben, verehren » Perf. *ákhan*—Plq. *īkhan* « aimer, estimer, être amical, bienveillant ».

5. *Le problème des emprunts*

Il paraît évident qu'en bédja il y a un grand nombre de racines à trois consonnes empruntées à l'arabe ou aux langues éthiopiennes [Reinisch 1894, Bd. 130, Abh. 7, § 197], bien que cette opinion soit contestée jusqui'à un certain point [Zaborski, 1975, p. 12].

Si nous supposons que les racines verbales empruntées aux sémitiques conservent leurs voyelles thématiques dans la forme conjuguée préfixale, une autre question s'impose : pourquoi la trace de la voyelle sémitique (*u*) ne se retrouve-t-elle qu'en une forme, le « Plusquamperfect » ?

Par ailleurs, il existe des verbes en bédja d'origine nonsémitiques ou bien d'origine couchitique qui forment leur « Plusquamperfect » avec =*e*=, p.ex. : *beḍif* [R-43] « ausbreiten, ausstrecken » Perf. *ábḍif*—Plq. *ībḍef ; gif* [R-92] « anstossen, an etwas stromcheln » Perf. *agíf*—Plq. *īgef ; kemis* [R-142] « sitzen » Perf. *ákmis*—Plq. *īkmes ; nefir* [R-180] « vergnügen, an etwas finden, genießen, süß sein » Perf. *ánfir* Plq. *īnfer.*

Par contre certains emprunts (ils semblent être culturels et plus avancés) directs ont une voyelle =*i*= dans toutes les formes : cf. NN 35, 37–43, 45 ; ou bien encore : *rejim* [R-190] « verwünschen, schmähen, fluchen » perf. *árjim*—Plq. *īrjim* : Sém Acc *rgm (a/u ; u/u)* « rufen, gerichtlich klagen » Hbr *rgm (o)* [KB, 873] « mit e. Steinhaufen bedecken / cover with a heap of stones » Arab *rǧm (u)* « lancer des pierres contre qn et le lapiderl ; maudire » [BK, I, 832] Gz *rgm (yərgəm)* « curse, insult, execrate » [Leslau, 465].[6]

En même temps l'emprunt *ketib* (N 45) en bédja présente le thème en =*i*=. Dans ce cas on pourrait penser à un emprunt au dialecte

---

[6] Il faut prêter attention à un autre cas : **Bédja** =*e*= : **Sém** **a* dans un exemple unique *lemid* [R-159] « lernen » Perf. *álmid*—Plq. *īlmed* : **Sém Acc** *lmd (a/a)* **Hbr** *lmd (a)* [KB, 482] « kennenlernen, erfahren » **Gz** *lmd (yəlmad/yəlməd)* « be accustomed to, be trained, learn » [Leslau, 315] ; ce fait peut être expliqué comme un reflet phonétique direct du **Gz** *yəlməd.*

soudanais où l'on prononce *yiktib*.[7] Mais cf. en afar le vocalisme thématique de la même racine : *uktube* « write/écrire » [P/H, 203].

Si nous nous tournons vers le guèze, nous pouvons dire, que la voyelle thèmatique =*ə*= de la forme *yə*=$C_1C_2əC_3$ étant le résultat de la réduction *u/i*, elle ne donnerait pas en bédja de nouveau *ə* > *i/e*. Il nous reste à envisager deux possibilitées :

1) La forme « Plusquamperfect » conserve et reflète le vocalisme *u/i/a* qui a été emprunté avec des verbes arabes à la forme d'Imperfect =$C_1C_2VC_3$. Cependant il paraît difficile d'admettre l'influence directe du vocalisme thématique des verbes arabes, qui seraient empruntés, uniquement sur l'une des formes verbales du bédja lesquelles entrent dans le paradigme régulier. De toute façon ce phénomène devrait être expliqué.
2) La forme « Plusquamperfect » avec ses =*i*=/=*e*=/=*a*= conserve les reflets du vocalisme plus ancien qui remonte au vocalisme afro-asiatique.

En effet, si l'on prend en considération le fait que les thèmes verbaux intransitifs du bédja ont =*a*= comme en sémitiques, on peut supposer aussi que le vocalisme *i/e* du « Plusquamperfect » correspond à celui du protosémitique : *i/u*. En plus, l'influence des laryngales et pharyngales dans la racine peut changer la voyelle thématique primaire de la forme préfixale =$C_1H_2VC_3$/=$C_1C_2VH_3$ > =$C_1H_2aC_3$/=$C_1C_2aH_3$ comme cela se passe en hébreu et arabe.

Bibliographie

B—Belot I.: 1955. Al-Faraïd arabe-français. Beirouth.
Belova (Anna): 1993. K voprosu o rekonstruktsii semitskogo kornevogo vokalizma.—Voprosy yazykoznaniya, N 6, pp. 28–56.
——: 1992. La structure de la racine afroasiatique. Le cas d'extension phonétique.—Komparative Afrikanistik. Sprach-, Geschicht- und Literaturwissenschaftliche Aufsätze zu Ehren von Hans G. Mukarovsky. Hrsg. von E. Ebermann, E.R. Sommerauer und K.E. Thomanek. Wien.
Cohen (David): 1974. Alternance vocaliques dans le système verbal couchitique et chamito-sémitique.—Actes du I-er Congrès Chamito-Sémitique.
Diakonoff (Igor): 1988. Afrasian Languages. Moscow.
——, Militarev A., Porkhomovsky V., Stolbova O.: 1993. On the Principles of Afrasian Phonological Reconstruction.—St. Petersburg Journal of African Studies. N 1.

[7] Cette forme m'est communiquée par l'arabisant Boris Romanoff auquel je suis bien reconnaissante.

Dolgopol'sky (Aharon): 1991. Kushitskiye yazyki.—Yazyki Azii i Afriki. T. IV, kn. 2. Moscow.
——: 1973. Sravnitel'no-istoritcheskaya fonetika kushitskih yazykov. Moscow.
HCVA—Historical Comparative Vocabulary of Afrasian. I. Diakonoff (Head of Team), A. Belova, A. Chetverukhin, A. Militarev, V. Portkhomovsky, O. Stolbova.—St. Petersburg Journal of African Studies, NN 2–6, 1994–1997.
Hudson R.A.: 1973. An Item-and Paradigm Approach to Beja Syntax and Morphology.—Foundations of Language. Vol. 9, N 4.
——: 1974. A Structural Sketch of Beja.—Afrasian Language Studies. Vol. 15.
BK—Kazimirski A. de Biberstein. 1860. Dictionnaire arabe-français. T. I–II. Paris.
KB—Lexicon in Veteris Testamenti Libros. L. Koehler, W. Baumgartner. Leiden, 1958.
Leslau (Wolf): 1987. Comparative Dictionnary of Geʿez. Wiesbaden.
P/H—Parker E.M., Hayward R.J. 1985. An Afar-English-French Dictionary. London.
Reinisch (Leo): 1893–1895. Die Beḍauye-Sprache in Nordost-Afrika.—Österreichische Akademie der Wissenschaften. Philosophisch-historische Klasse. Sitzungsberichte. Bd. 128, Abh. 3 ; Bd. 130, Abh. 7 ; Bd. 131, Abh. 3.
——: 1895. Wörterbuch der Beḍauye-Sprache. Wien.
Riemschneider K.K.: 1973. Lehrbuch des Akkadischen. Leipzig.
Acc—Soden (Wolfram): 1962. Akkadisches Handwörterbuch. Wiesbaden.
Voigt (Reiner): 1987. The two prefix-conjugations in East-Cushitic, East Semitic and Chadic.—Bull. of School of Oriental and African Studies. Vol. 50, pt. 2. London.
Vycichl (Werner): 1960. The Language Tu-Bedawiye : its relationship with Old Egyptian.—« Kush », Vol. 8 (Khartoum).
Zaborski (Andrzej): 1989. Der Wortschatz der Bedscha-Sprache. Eine vergleichende Analyse.—XXIII. Deutscher Orientlistentag. Stuttgart.
——: 1975. Note on Biconsonantal and Triconsonantal Roots in Cushitic.—Folia Orientalia. Vol. XVI, Warszawa-Kraków.
——: 1965. Notes on the Medieval History of the Beja Tribes.—Folia Orientalia, T. 7.
——: 1987. Reinisch and Some Problems of the Study of Beja Today.—Reinisch Leo. Werk und Erbe. Hrsg. von Mukarovsky H.G. Wien.
——: 1975. The Verb in Cushitic.—Studies in Hamito-Semitic. I. Kraków-Warszawa.

BEJA PRONOUNS AND GLIDES: DIALECTS IN SEARCH OF OPTIMA

Klaus Wedekind
(Ministry of Education of Eritrea, Asmara)

1. *Studies of Beja pronouns*

This brief study focuses on puzzles posed by glides in Beja (Bidhaawyeet)[1] pronouns—a word class which—starting with Almkvist and down to today—has attracted the interest of various linguists, including especially Werner Vycichl.

Beja has a comparatively rich set of "possessive pronouns", and over the last 120 years, they have been documented extensively and repeatedly—in spite of their low textual frequencies. The full sets of these pronouns were recorded (1) 1881 by Almkvist, pp. 102–104 for the Bisharin dialect, (2) 1893 by Reinisch pp. 101–102 for the Gash-Barka dialect, and (3) 1928 by Roper p. 28 for the Port Sudan dialect. Later, Vycichl (1953), Hudson (1976), Bechhaus-Gerst (1985) and Zaborski (1989) have commented on various other features of this word class—features which however are not in focus in this brief note.

Table I (below) presents the basic set of pronouns in the two forms which for Beja have been called the "subject" and "object" cases—a distinction accepted for Cushitic languages.[2]

[1] The self-name for this language is "Bidhaawiyéet", an indefinite fem. noun in its "citation" form. The definite form would be "Tuu-Bdháawiyee". Note that (1) the acute accent indicates pitch-accent—which is contrastive but not used in the orthography; (2) the "i" functions as a "schwa mobile"; (3) the double vowels are long vowels, and (4) the "dh" stands for a retroflex d. The spelling "Bidhaawiyeet" reflects the official Eritrean orthography.

[2] But starting with Almkvist (1881:64, 89), linguists have wondered why Beja speakers are nonchalant about using case "correctly". Our text studies—which use Valin's "RRG" approach—have convinced us that textual functions rather than "case" must be considered here.

Table I Basic pronouns

	"Object" (citation form)	"Subject"
Sg. 1	ánee(b)	áni
Sg. 2 masc.	baróok	barúuk
Sg. 2 fem.	batóok	batúuk
Sg. 3 masc.	baróo(h)	barúu(h)
Sg. 3 fem.	batóo(h)	batúu(h)
Pl. 1	hinéen, hinín	hinín
Pl. 2 masc.	baréekna	baráakna
Pl. 2 fem.	batéekna	batáakna
Pl. 3 masc.	barée(h)	baráa(h)
Pl. 3 fem.	batée(h)	batáa(h)

Note: Double vowels stand for long vowels, accent aigu stands for pitch-accent.

Table II (below) presents the pronouns in one-word-clauses which could be glossed as follows:

Sg.M.: *"he is mine, he is yours" etc.*
Pl.M.: *"they (masc.) are mine, they are yours" etc.*
Sg.F.: *"she is mine, yours" etc.*
Pl.F.: *"they (fem.) are mine, they are yours" etc.*

The data in the column "Asmara 2001" of Table II (below) are based on text studies with speakers from Eritrea and Port Sudan.

Table II Possessive pronouns

Possessor	Item	Almkvist 1881	Reinisch 1893	Roper 1928	Asmara 2001
Sg. 1	*Sg.masc.*	aníibu	aníibu	aníibi	aníibu
Sg. 2 masc.		barióoku*	baryóoku	barióki	bariiyóoku
Sg. 2 fem.		batióoku	batyóoku	batióki	batiiyóoku
Sg. 3 masc.		barióo**h**u	baryóo**s**u	bári**h**iyi	baríiyoo**h**u
Sg. 3 fem.		batióo**h**u	batyóo**s**u	báti**h**iyi	batíiyoo**h**u
Pl. 1		henéebu	hannéebu	hinéebi	hinéebu
Pl. 2 masc.		baréeoknáayu	bareeyóoknaayu	bareeóki	bareeyóoknaayu**
Pl. 2 fem.		batéeooknáayu	bateeyóoknaayu	bateeóki	bateeyóoknaayu**
Pl. 3 masc.		baréeoo**h**náayu	bareeyóo**s**naayu	barée**h**iyi	barée**h**oonaayu**
Pl. 3 fem.		batéeoo**h**náayu	bateeyóo**s**naayu	batée**h**iyi	batée**h**oonaayu**
Sg. 1	*Pl. masc.*	aníiba	aníiba	ániiba	ániiba
Sg. 2 masc.		bariéeka	baryéeka	bariéeka	bariiyéeka
Sg. 2 fem.		batiéeka	batyéeka	batiéeka	batiiyéeka

Table II (cont.)

Possessor	Item	Almkvist 1881	Reinisch 1893	Roper 1928	Asmara 2001
Sg. 3 masc.		barié e***h***a	baryée***s***a	bári***h***iya	baríiyee***h***a
Sg. 3 fem.		batiée***h***a	batyée***s***a	báti***h***iya	batíiyee***h***a
Pl. 1		henéeba	hannéeba	híneeba	híneeba
Pl. 2 masc.		baréeeknáya	bareeyéeknaaya	bareeéeka	bareeyéeknaaya**
Pl. 2 fem.		batéeeknáaya	bateeyéeknaaya	bateeéeka	bateeyéeknaaya**
Pl. 3 masc.		baréee***h***náaja	bareeyée***s***naaya	baréе***h***iya	baréе***h***eenaaya**
Pl. 3 fem.		batéee***h***náaja	bateeyée***s***naaya	batée***h***iya	batée***h***eenaaya**
Sg. 1	*Sg. fem.*	aníitu	aníitu	aníiti	aníitu
Sg. 2 masc.		báriitóoktu	baritóoktu	baritókti	bariitóoktu
Sg. 2 fem.		bátiitóoktu	batitóoktu	batitókti	batiitóoktu
Sg. 3 masc.		báriitóo***h***tu	baritóo***s***tu	baríit***h***iti	barii***h***tootu
Sg. 3 fem.		bátiitóo***h***tu	batitóo***s***tu	batíit***h***iti	batii***h***tootu
Pl. 1		henéetu	hannéetu	hinéeti	hineetu
Pl. 2 masc.		baréetooknaatu	bareetóoknaatu	bareetókti	bareetooknaatu***
Pl. 2 fem.		batéetooknaatu	bateetóoknaatu	bateetókti	bateetooknaatu***
Pl. 3 masc.		baréetoo***h***naatu	bareetóo***s***naatu	baréet***h***iti	baree***h***toonaatu***
Pl. 3 fem.		batéetoo***h***naatu	bateetóo***s***naatu	batéet***h***iti	batee***h***toonaatu***
Sg. 1	*Pl. fem.*	aníita	aníita	ániita	ániita
Sg. 2 masc.		báriitéekta	baritéekta	baritéekta	bariitéekta
Sg. 2 fem.		bátiitéekta	batitéekta	batitéekta	batiitéekta
Sg. 3 masc.		báriitee***h***ta	baritée***s***ta	baríit***h***ita	baríi***h***teeta
Sg. 3 fem.		bátiitée***h***ta	batitée***s***ta	batíit***h***ita	batíi***h***teeta
Pl. 1		henéeta	hannéeta	híneeta	híneeta
Pl. 2 masc.		baréteeknáata	bareetéeknaata	bareetéekta	bareetéeknaata
Pl. 2 fem.		batéteeknáata	bateetéeknaata	bateetéekta	bateetéeknaata
Pl. 3 masc.		barétee***h***náata	bareetée***s***naata	baréet***h***ita	b~~arée***h***tee~~enaata
Pl. 3 fem.		batétee***h***náata	bateetée***s***naata	batéet***h***ita	batée***h***teenaata

The 4 transcriptions have been harmonized as follows: Double letters stand for length, accent aigu for pitch-accent, y for the palatal semivowel.

* *The variant spelling* baar *in Almkvist's tables has been ignored. (The norm is* "bar", *a form which Bechhaus-Gerst comments on.)*

** *Instead of* bar**eeyoo**knaayu, bar**eeyee**knaaya *etc.*, bar**iiyee**knaayu, bar**iiyee**knaaya *etc. are also used.*

*** *Instead of* ***too***, ***tee*** *is also used.*

2. *Puzzling power play: phonology vs. morphology*

Concerning the interplay of phonological and morphological forces, the following three points should be noted first:

(1) The non-onset "h" in a syllable can be realized in any of the following ways:

- as a fricative "feature" of the word, hardly audible,
- as a fricative "lenis" consonant, hardly audible,
- as a fricative "h" coda consonant, audible.

All of these variations can be heard where the "h" is not clearly the onset of a new syllable. Some speakers will reject a forceful articulation of a syllable final "h": Yes it is there—but it should be articulated delicately and with taste. For this reason, the "h" in Table I has been put in parentheses.

(2) The "h" in a syllable onset does not exhibit these variations. In the onset, the "h" always is a clear consonantal segment, pronounced with the same force as any other consonant. For this reason, no parentheses are used for the onset "h".

(3) Concerning the canonical form of Beja morphemes, it should be remembered that in their "citation form" (usually identified as "object"), all nominals—not just the pronouns—require a word final consonant. So the coda of a word final syllable will either have to be "t" in those cases where the nominal is feminine (even if this results in a double coda Ct)—or will have to be "b" if the nominal is masculine and does not happen to end in a consonant already. See, for instance, the pronoun anee(b) "me", in Table I, where the "b" is attached to make the pronoun presentable.

Actually, as far the (h) in the basic pronoun set is concerned, it is the absence of this "b" suffix which proves that the place has already been taken by some other consonant, namely (h).

2.1 *Puzzles and differences*

It would appear that the Beja possessive pronouns have received a disproportionate amount of attention already. After all, the textual frequencies of these pronouns are rather low. In a Beja corpus of about 14000 words (based on the rather representative text collection in the thesis of Mohammed Ohaj, 1985), a frequency ranking shows that, as usual, the most frequent pronoun is "I" (34th rank of all words, 1st rank among pronouns). This is followed by "we" (44th rank, 2nd rank among pronouns—etc., see Table III in the Appendix). But even the most frequent possessive pronoun does not occur more than twice in the entire corpus, ranking 12th behind most other pronouns, and ranking only 1528th among all words.

It is a healthy exercise to be reminded of the low frequency of high profile words such as these. So the reason why they have received much attention must be the high incidence of complexities and "interesting" features.

There are several puzzles which call for explanations.

When Table II is read from the left to the right, the variations are striking. Some of them are dialectal, and they go along with other dialectal variations such as the difference "i" vs. "u" for "3rd ps. sg. copula", and the different sources of loan words, such as Tigre vs. Arabic. But it should be noted that, considering the geographical spread, the dialect differences are comparatively few. It can be observed again and again that the ease of communication is not affected by them.

The very two items which make for the most noticeable and most frequent incidence of "dialect difference" are the two items which are prominently displayed in the Tables below:

(1) The fricative "h" has a variant "s" in the closing syllables of the 3rd person pronouns. This "s" happens to characterize Western dialect areas.
(2) The vowel "u" has the variant "i" in the masculine and feminine copula forms of the singular. This "i" happens to characterize Gash Barka dialect areas, but also the dialect of Roper's data.

The differences between the pronoun sets cannot be explained as difference in the phonological representations, or different preferences of the different scholars who presented them.

Like the dialect variations, the differences between the transcriptions are not serious. While Roper's transcription (the most "deviant") is of a "narrow" or "phonetic" and "non-systematic" character and somewhat unreliable, the transcriptions of Reinisch and especially the careful transcription of Almkvist are on the "broader" or more "phonological", systematic end of the scale. Hudson's, Morin's and the present transcription are systematically phonological. (The latter are very close to the official "Hidareb" orthography of Eritrea, except for the accent marking.)

2.2 *Two messages in one signal*

One puzzling "non-symmetry" in these pronoun sets is the merger of different morphological signals in the same few phonological elements. Although such merging (telescoping, fusion) is common especially in possessive pronouns, on the first encounter it is puzzling:

- The vowel "ii" in the 2nd syllable—does it signal the genitive case for masculine gender of the possessor, or the singular of the possessor, or both?
- The vowel "ee" in the 2nd syllable—does it signal the genitive case for the plural of the possessor, or the masculine gender of the item possessed, or both?
- The vowel "oo" in the 3rd syllable—does it signal the singular number of the item possessed—or its masculine gender, or both? Different Beja linguists have focused on different aspects of these ambivalent signals.

2.3 *Two signals for one message*

In addition to those phonological signals which carry two messages, it is also true that some of the meanings are signalled twice by two discrete phonological items in the same word.

This clearly is the case for the "t" which stands for the feminine gender of the possessed item: It is consistently signalled twice in all 2nd and 3rd persons.

3. *Floating liquids and semivowels*

The most puzzling item, however, is the place of the "h" (or "s", its dialectal variant). It consistently signals "*3rd ps*"; but it is not consistently found where it "should" be, i.e., where it "was" in the "basic" pronoun set (Table I).

The main question of this brief study is: Why does the "h" shift away from its "proper" place, and when, and where to? And how does this relate to the incidence of "y"?

It is true that Beja does offer several morphological surprises as far as the sequencing of affixes is concerned. E.g., the place of derivational vs. inflectional affixes is "negotiable" in the sense that some inflectional affixes are closer to the root than inflectional affixes. And there are affixes such as the suffix -ka "*any, more, than*" which seem to upset any orthodox suffix sequencing.

But presently, only one of these shall be considered: the optional 3rd ps. signal "h".

In the basic pronoun set (see Table I, 3rd ps.), this "h" is the word final consonant of the basic pronouns for the 3rd person, and in this set, the "h" solidly holds the same position throughout the paradigm.

In the possessive pronoun set however (see Table II, 3rd ps. sg. m.), the "h" moves to the onset of the final syllable. Similarly, in Almkvist's and Reinisch's data the "h" (or the corresponding "s") is found at the coda of the 3rd syllable rather than the 2nd. In some pronouns, the "h" even moves to the 4th syllable.[3]

Actually, not only the pronouns, but also the Beja verbs and their object affixes allow for similar movements of the "h".

However, for the sake of convenience the focus will be narrowed down to pronouns—and presently to the pronouns "bariiyoo***h***u" and "batiiyoo***h***u": Why did the "h" shift to the onset of the last syllable in these words? (With a very lenis pronunciation, but definitely there. Actually, the glottal stop behaves very similarly, as will be shown in a study of "strong" Beja verbs.)

In terms of some non-segmental phonology, the following explanation might be offered:

- The "h" (3rd. ps.) is a feature of the entire nominal. Depending on the speaker or the dialect,
- It will affect the degree of "spirantization" of the word,
- It will spread to the right and crystallize as "h" (or "s") in the first syllable which is not already occupied by some other consonant.

But this does not explain all cases. Neither does the interplay with other suprasegmentals—such as vowel lengths or stress—offer any explanation.

4. *In search of an optimal place for glides*

In terms of an optimality theory, the movement of "h" would reflect the interplay of various forces—possibly in the following order:

[3] Obviously the "h" is not predicable like the "-k" "2nd ps". About the "h", Roper says, "[it] is usually quite inaudible, so I have not printed it". (1928:111)

(1) Once the speaker has decided to refer to a "3rd ps." explicitly—rather than leaving it implicit—a place must be found for the "h". The "h", after all, is the only distinct signal for "3rd ps."[4]
(2) The "original place" or the "origin" of this "h" is at the end of the basic pronoun form of the 3rd ps. pronoun.
(3) But the "h" will move from this place as other forces come into play. It will move to the right and settle on that syllable which (a) is closest to the "origin" of the "h", and (b) which otherwise would have no full consonantal onset.
(4) In this search, the formation of CC Clusters (the demotion of onsets to codas) will be avoided—but it seems to be acceptable when there is no other place for the "h" to settle.

So far so good. This reasoning explains the form of some pronouns—but it does not explain why the "y"—rather than the "h"—gets the right of way in cases such as baríiyoo***h***u. Here, the "y" carries no meaning. It is the dummy onset[5] of the singular genitive "ii". (The "y" in "yii" is not an integral part of the morpheme "genitive". It is true that Reinisch transcribes the genitives as "y" rather than "i", and he explicitly rejects Almkvist's correct suggestion that this consonant is "euphonic". But in actual fact, the signal for the "genitive" is "ii"—as Reinisch recognizes elsewhere, and the "y" only turns it into an acceptable syllable.)

So concerning our question why the actual form is baríiyoo***h***u rather than baríi***h***ooyu, we are left without an explanation.

---

[4] Like elsewhere in this area so also in Beja, the unmarked possessive and object pronoun is the 3rd person. But with 3rd ps. object suffixes of verbs, with 3rd ps. possessive suffixes of nouns, and with 3rd ps. possessive pronouns, the speaker has a choice: The choice is between (a) expressing the 3rd ps. explicitly as a suffix, (b) leaving it implied and without any morphological marker, and (c) making the pronoun affix a (barely audible) feature of the entire word.

But there is one alternative which Beja does not offer, namely: Expressing the object both as pronoun word *and* verb suffix. Thus, *Hineen rhi-ta-hoon "us saw-she-us" ("She saw us.") is ungrammatical. Pronouns *must* be dropped.

[5] Actually, the "y" isn't always as "dummy" as here: For instance, in the definite masc. article of nouns, the "y" serves as phonological alternative to "hamza" when prefixed to nouns which start with "hamza" or "h". Likewise, in the 3rd ps. masc. subject prefix of verbs, the "y" also serves as alternative to "hamza" when prefixed to verbs which start with "hamza" or "h".

This is an interesting kind of "laryngeal" dissimilation which seems to be an area feature: E.g. Saleh M. found that it characterizes the Tigre verb morphology—a feature not recognzied by Raz, but described by Saleh M., forth.

Appendix

Table III

The frequency ranks of all Beja pronouns and possessive pronouns occurring in a text collection of 14290 words

Rank, counting pronouns (Rank, counting all words)	Frequ.	Form and Gloss
1st (34 th)	*27*	ani *I Subj.*
2nd (44 th)	*20*	hinin *we Subj.*
3rd	*19*	baruu(h) *he Subj.*
4th	*17*	baruuk *you M Subj.*
5th	*14*	baraa(h) *they M Subj.*
6th	*10*	barook *you M Obj*
7th	*10*	baree(h) *they Pl M Obj*
8th	*10*	batuu(h) *she Subj.*
9th	*9*	batoo(h) *she Obj.*
10th	*8*	baroo(h) *he Obj*
11th	*4*	baraakna *you Pl M Subj*
12 th (1518 th)	***2***	**batiiyoo(h)** ***her / M Item***
13th	***2***	**batiiyee(h)** ***her / M Item***
14th	*2*	batook *you F Obj*
15th	*2*	batuuk *you F Subj*
16th	***2***	**bariiyook** ***your M Obj / M Item***
17th	***2***	**bariiyoo(h)** ***his Obj / M Item***
18th	*2*	bareek *you Pl M Obj*
19th	***2***	**aniib** ***mine M / M Item***
*20**th***	*1*	hineet *them Obj*
21st	*1*	hineen *us Obj*
22nd	***1***	**hineeb** ***ours M***
23rd	***1***	**bariiyook** ***your Sg / M Item***
24th	***1***	**bariiyee(h)** ***his / M Item***
25th	***1***	**bariituuk** ***your M / F Item***
26th	***1***	**bariitoo(h)** ***his M / F Item***
27th	***1***	**bareetoo(h)** ***their / F Item***
28th	***1***	**bareetee(h)** ***their / F Item***
*29**th***	*1*	bareekna *you Pl M Obj*

Bibliography

Almkvist, Herman N., 1881, "Die Bischari-Sprache in Nord-Ost Afrika", vol. 1–2, Uppsala: Koenigl. Societaet der Wissenschaften.

——, 1885, "Bishari-deutsches und deutsch-bischarisches Woerterbuch" (vol. 2); Uppsala: Koenigliche Societaet der Wissenschaften (pp. 1–113).

Bechhaus-Gerst, Marianne, 1985, "Du bist, was du hast"; Zur Entstehung neuer Personalpronomen im Tu Bed'awie (Beja); Afrikanistische Arbeitspapiere AAP no. 1 1985 pp. 125–128 [Focuses on "bar"].

Hudson, Richard A., 1974, "A Structural Sketch of Beja". African Language Studies 15, 111–142.
——, 1976, "Beja". In: M.L. Bender (ed.), The Non-Semitic Languages of Ethiopia, 97–132. Carbondale. [Revised reprint of Hudson 1974].
Mohammed Adaroob Ohaj, 1971, "Min taraath albijaa althacabaa", Thesis, Khartum.
Morin, Didier, 1995, "Des paroles douces comme la soie", Paris: Peeters.
Reinisch, Leo, 1893, "Die Bedauyesprache in Nordostafrika", Wien: Hoelder.
——, 1895, "Woerterbuch der Bedauyesprache", Wien: Hoelder.
Roper, E.M., 1928, "Tu Bedawiɛ: An Elementary Handbook for the Use of Sudan Government Officials", Hertford: Stephen Austin.
Saleh Mahmud, forth., "Some Neglected Features of the Tigre Verb System".
Van Valin, Robert, and Randy LaPolla, 1997, "Syntax: Structure, Meaning and Function", Cambridge University Press.
Vycichl, Werner, 1953, "Das persoenliche Fuerwort im Bedja und im Tigre", Museion 66, 157–161.
Zaborski Andrzej, 1989, "Cushitic Independent Pronouns". In: Taddese Beyene (ed.), Proceedings of the Eighth International Conference of Ethiopian Studies 2, 649–672. Addis Ababa.

SECTION FOUR

CHADIC LINGUISTICS

PRÉLIMINAIRES À UNE ÉTUDE DE LA LANGUE[1] KAJAKSE D'AM-DAM, DE TORAM DU SALAMAT, D'UBI DU GUÉRA ET DE MASMAJE DU BATHA-EST (TCHAD)[2]

Khalil Alio
(Université de N'Djamena)

I. *Kajakse*

1. *Les hommes*

Les Kadjakse se disent venir de la Mecque. Leur ancêtre qui aurait quitté avec cinq fils serait parti en *hijra* ou *mahjar* en quête de connaissance islamique. Dans leur migration, ils traver-sèrent le Soudan actuel et arrivèrent au mont *Mira* à l'intérieur des frontières tchadiennes actuelles. Ces cinq enfants sont: Kidjam et Djoumo issus d'une même mère et Abissa, Karare, et Djangala issus également d'une autre mère. Le pays était entretemps occupé par les For. Ils ont dû livrer bataille avec ses occupants trois années durant avant de les chasser, en les poussant plus à l'est, c'est-à-dire au Soudan. Avant de s'implanter, définitivement, les cinq frères s'éparpillèrent dans la région. C'est ainsi que Djoumo se dirigea vers le village Kadjaske dans la region de Dar-Sila et y fonda le clan des Kadjakse de Dar-Sila. Les quatre autres frères se dirigèrent chacun dans le village de son choix. Kidjam se rendit à Am-Talaata, Abissa à Baara, Karare à Bineedir et Djangala à Iddal-Assad. Après avoir été maîtres du terrain, les cinq frères retour-nèrent à *Mira* pour amener le reste de leurs familles qui y seraient restées. Les Kadjakse occupent le pays depuis 324 années, c'est-à-dire depuis 1678. Une autre bataille que les Kadjakse se remémorent encore aurait eu lieu en 1792, il y a 210 ans.

Le premier sultan des Kadjakse à être installé s'appellait Khaddam. Ensuite vint Djaar, puis Haroun qui a eu maille à partir avec le colonisateur. Suite à son refus de recouvrer l'impôt pour le compte du

[1] Ces données ont éte recueillies le 21 mars 2001 auprès de Monsieur Abdel-Aziz Adam Mahamat, Chef de race de la communauté Kadjakse à N'Djamena.

[2] Cette étude a été rendue possible grâce à l'intervention du Prof. Dr. Herrmann Jungraithmayr.

colonisateur, il fut exilé à Moundou à dos de taureau. Après quelques années de prison, il fut réhabilité et même reconduit dans ses fonctions de sultan où il régna encore pendant 20 ans, puis confia le pouvoir à son serviteur Moustapha, avec l'intention de le reprendre plutard. Celui-ci occupa le trône pendant deux ans et le remit à son fils Hamit Moustapha qui régna pendant six ans et mourut. Outman Moustapha, l'autre fils alors prit les rênes du pouvoir et les conserva pendant 24 ans. Le fils de Outman, Adoum a également régné pendant 22 ans. Avec l'avènement de la démocratie Adoum Outman fut déposé par les habitants du canton et son frère Awad Outman fut démocratiquement élu à sa place, chef de canton, appellation officielle adoptée par les Français à leur arrivée, le terme de Sultan étant désormais réservé uniquement aux trois royaumes du Tchad, à savoir, le Baguirmi, le Kanem et le Ouaddai.

Les Kadjakse sont tous musulmans et comptent de grands marabouts dans leur rang. Néanmoins il leur arrive de célébrer de temps à autre, dans les montagnes, des sacrifices à la mémoire de leurs ancêtres. Ils sont agro-pastoraux. Ils cultivent le petit mil, le sorgho, l'arachide, le sésame et pratiquent le jardinage. Ceux qui habitent au sud du canton s'adonnent quelquefois à la chasse.

2. *Le pays*

Il existe deux groupes de Kadjakse: Les kadjakse Kinaane ou Kadjakse I de la Sous-préfecture d'Am-Dam du Département du Ouaddai et les Kadjakse II de la sous-préfecture de Goz-Beida du Département du Dar-Sila nouvellement érigé selon le nouveau découpage géographique de la République du Tchad, conformément à la politique de décentralisation entrée en vigueur en 2000. Le pays Kadjakse est limité à l'est par le *Ouadi Kadja*, à l'ouest par la sous-préfecture de Mangalmé, au nord par la sous-préfecture d'Ab-Goudam et au sud par la sous-préfecture d'Abou-Deia du Département du Salamat ayant comme chef-lieu de préfecture Am-Timan. Le Chef lieu de canton de Kadjakse I est Hawich (haawish). Les autres villages du canton sont:

1. - Ab-Dourta
2. - Ab-Niiran
3. - Afzaoona
4. - Adji Atash
5. - Adji Iyaal Ab-Djouda
6. - Adji Hidjer

29. - Dabkaraaye
30. - Direyte
31. - Djakhdjakhaaye
32. - Djoukha
33. - Gana
34. - Gadoum

7. - Aliili Kabir
8. - Aliili Kadama
9. - Alo
10. - Am Charamiit
11. - Am Damanya
12. - Am-Digeemaat (Birgit)[3]
13. - Am-Dokhon
14. - Am-Kashwaaye
15. - Am-Talaata Kabir
16. - Am-Talaata Skhair
17. - Am-Tchakeene
18. - Ardeebe
19. - Arshooye
20. - Askaniite
21. - Attawiil
22. - Baara
23. - Badao
24. - Bineedir
25. - Bineediriyye
26. - Bouloum Boutou
27. - Boochinkin (Birgit)
28. - Choukhaara
35. - Goufo
36. - Hawich
37. - Iddal-Assad
38. - Kayaw
39. - Khoummi
40. - Koorya
41. - Kourdila
42. - Laabid
43. - Makakou
44. - Mirer
45. - Miyeele
46. - Samasim
47. - Sangafout
48. - Saraf Kouro
49. - Saraf Lugmaan
50. - Shaamir
51. - Siref
52. - TaffeWizziine
53. - Tarma (Bakkha)[4]
54. - Zamaan
55. - Wizziine

3. *La langue*

3.1 *Classification*

Westermann et Bryan (1952) sont les premiers linguistes à mentionner la langue kadjakse au sein du groupe "Sokoro-Mubi" parmi les langues dites "Tchado-Hamitiques" qu'ils placent sous la langue moubi, considérée peut-être au même titre que le masmaje et le birgit comme des dialectes de la langue moubi. Jungraithmayr (1981) reclasse la langue kajakse dans le sous-groupe Mubi-Toram. Les Kadjakse eux-mêmes se nomment Mìnyaawò masc. Sg., Mìnyaawè fém. sg., pl. Mìnyì. Ex.: ʔíntè ʔín máll̀iyà mìnyaawè "je parle la langue kajakse" ou ʔíntè ʔín máll̀iyà kàawí tát mìnyì "je parle la langue des Kadjakse.

[3] Villages kadjakse se trouvant à l'intérieur du canton Birgit.
[4] Villages kadjakse se trouvant à l'intérieur du canton Bakha(bakkha).

Le kajakse figure sur une liste de Swadesh de 100 mots que Doornbos et Bender (1983) ont appliquée au "Mubi group of Chad" auquel appartiennent, en plus du mubi, le kajakse, le kujarke et le minjile.

3.2 *Phonologie*

3.2.1 Les voyelles

Il existe en kajakse cinq voyelles orales courtes et cinq voyelles orales longues qui se distinguent par leur aperture et leur localisation. Les cinq voyelles orales sont:

i		**u**
e		**o**
	a	

Les unités lexicales suivantes peuvent servir d'illustration:

/sin/ "dent"
/ley/ "plume"
/fàn/ "bouche"
/kôr/ "haut"
/lùk/ "ventre"

Les cinq voyelles longues sont:

ii		**uu**
ee		**oo**
	aa	

Les unités lexicales suivantes nous permettent d'illustrer les phonèmes vocaliques longs:

/liisi/ "langue"
/fòoso/ "main"
/bùutù/ "sol"
/táakà/ "jour"
/reeɓe/ "mensonge"

3.2.2 Les consonnes

Le kajakse possède vingt trois consonnes:

	bilab.	alvéol.	alv-pal.	palat.	vélaires	laryng.
occlus.	b	t			k	ʔ
occlus.	p	d			g	
glottal.	ɓ	ɗ		ɗy		
affriq.				c		
affriq.				j		
fricat.	f		s			
fricat.			z			
nasales	m	n		ny	ŋ	
contin.	w		l	y		
vibrant.			r			

3.2.3 Les tons

Dans l'état actuel de nos connaissances sur la langue nous ne pourrions retenir que l'hypothèse de l'existence de trois tons en kajakse, notamment haut (´), moyen, non marqué graphiquement ici, et bas (`). Exemples:

sin	"dent"
sún	"penser"
fàn	"bouche"
fúká	"chien"
liisi	"langue"
ʔàbàr	"sang"
sigàr	"long"
fársò	"cheval"
ɗùbal	"homme"
kòrci	"anus"

3.3 *Morphologie*

3.3.1 Les adjectifs possessifs

Les possessifs dépendants sont suffixés au nom singulier ou pluriel. L'adjonction du suffixe ne modifie pas la structure tonale ou segmentale du déterminé: Exemples avec le lexème fàn "bouche":

fàn-co	"ma bouche
fàn-dam	"ta (masc. sg.) bouche"

fàn-ke	"ta (fém. sg.) bouche"
fàn-de	"sa (masc. sg.) bouche"
fàn-ki	"sa (fém. sg.) bouche"
fàn-ca	"notre bouche"
fàn-kun	"votre bouche"
fàn-ko	"leur bouche"

3.3.2 Les pronoms possessifs substantifs

Les pronoms possessifs substantifs ou indépendants s'ac-cordent en genre et en nombre avec le déterminé. Le déterminé féminin ou masculin donné en exemple ici est au singulier. Ces pronoms se présentent comme suit:

déterminé	masculin	déterminé	féminin
kèedjo	"le mien"	tèejo	"la mienne"
kèedam	"le tien"	tèedam	"la tienne"
kijìge	"le tien"	tijìge	"la tienne"
kìyèedam	"le sien"	tìyèedam	"la sienne"
kijìgi	"le sien"	tijìgi	"la sienne"
kèeja	"le nôtre"	tèeja	"la nôtre"
kèejan	"le vôtre"	tèejan	"la vôtre"
kùjùgo	"le leur"	tùjùgo	"la leur"

3.3.3 La formation du pluriel des noms

Le kajakse fait partie des langues tchadiques de l'est qui possèdent une riche morphologie nominale, en particulier dans le domaine de la formation du pluriel où il existe plusieurs façons d'obtenir le pluriel des noms. Présentement six types de formation de pluriel ont été identifiés. Ce sont:

Type 1: Pluriel interne se caractérisant par le changement de voyelles internes ou finales suivies des modifications tonales. Ce type comporte trois sous-types, à savoir:

1.1.

luy	lày	"femme"
sin	sàn	"dent"
liisi	liyàs	"langue"
fòoso	fàs	"main"
sàrfi	siràf	"côte"
kôymi	kuyòm	"oreille"
culɗimi	cúlɗòm	"barbe"

còlgòm	cùloogùm	"menton"
guugumí	gigàami	"hibou"
càrà	cèrè	"racine"
fooca	fuuci	"fleur"
ʔíiwò	ʔéèwe	"caillou"

1.1.1.

fúká	fikè	"chien"
rùgrùga	rùgrige	"nuage"
kùmaayò	kìme	"viande"

1.2.

márɗyà	màraaɗyì	"jeune homme"
ɗúrkùl	ɗìrakìli	"âne"
tàwò	tàwù	"peau"
fársò	fársù	"cheval"
tùmàaʔì	tùmàaʔu	"mouton"
ʔiiso	ʔiise	"oeuf"
fàafo	fàafe	"sein"
kaawo	káàwè	"serpent"
ʔòora	ʔòorè	"ver de terre"
njo	nji	"personne"
daayò	daayi	"hôte
màrfo	màrfi	"puits"
jìngiɗà	jíngìɗi	"clitoris"
tirenygo	tirenygi	"fourmi magnant"
nyabùlo	nyabìli	"pintade"

Type 2: Modification tonale uniquement. Exemples:

ɗùbal	ɗùbàl	"homme"
sìmè	sime	"nom"

Type 3: Ce type comporte plusieurs procédés en même temps: augmentation du radical du singulier par voie de réduplication, allongement vocalique interne, ou adjonction d'un élément différent à l'initiale mais généralement à la finale. Ce type se compose également de trois sous-types qui sont:

3.1.

gìf	gàgìf	"genou"
lùk	làlùk	"ventre"
ʔáàra	ʔàarurom	"dos"
ʔagaw	ʔàgaagàw	"danse"
ʔàaso	ʔáasìsàk	"penis"

3.2.

kàc	kàɗyúk	"tête"
kúrí	kurak	"jarre"
ʔariiri	ʔàràaràk	"scorpion"

3.3.

táakà	fáatàk	"jour"
saaro	sàarát	"corde"
ʔátò	ʔàtây	"arbre"
fàn	fàbundaŋ	"bouche"

Type 4: Restructuration interne des sons vocaliques surtout, généralement par insertion et allongement de la voyelle **-i-** modifiant ainsi la structure tonale du mot pluriel obtenu. Exemples:

ɗiwèy	ɗíiwì	"marche"
gùtòr	gùtirì	"potier"
ʔàjum	ʔajíìmi	"épine"

Type 5: Réduction de quantité vocalique et/ou consonantique de la deuxième syllabe du radical singulier provoquant une modification tonale. Exemples:

ʔàriinì	ʔarìn	"oeil"
ʔataan	ʔátìn	"nez"
tìwiyyo	tiwiy	"mouche"

Type 6: Syncope accompagnée d'une réduction de quantité vocalique de la deuxième syllabe ou insertion de la voyelle du pluriel—**a-**. Exemples:

kunoono	kunon	"os"
ɗeeɗuwo	ɗèeɗàw	"oiseau"
ʔataaɗi	ʔataɗ	"pou"
ʔáatìɗa	ʔaataɗ	"intestin"

bòngòoso	bòngòs	"poisson"
wàagirì	waagàr	"chèvre"
wássàya	wassa	"fil à coudre"
sisiiwi	síisàw	"étoiles"
kùrófò	kùròf	"griffes, serres"
ʔinyàwe	ʔínyàw	"queue"
kùróocì	kòròc	"fesses"
gùròoli	gùròl	"testicules"

3.3.4 Pronoms sujets préposés[5]
Avec le verbe "manger"

ʔintè	ʔin	tuwà	"je"
kamtè	kam	tuwà	"tu"
kintè	kin	tuwà	"tu"
ʔakàr		tuwà	"il"
tirte		tuwà	"elle"
ʔantè	ʔan	tuwà	"nous"
ʔeetè	ʔee	tuwà	"vous"
ʔayar	ʔee	tuwà	"ils"

3.3.5 Pronoms objets directs préposés
Avec le verbe "voir"

ʔín	ʔoomù	"me"
kam	ʔoomù	"te" (m.)
kin	ʔoomù (e)	"te" (f.)
-	ʔoomù	"le"
-	ʔooman	"la"
ana	ʔoomù	"nous"
kann	ʔoomù	"vous"
ʔèè	ʔoomù	"les

3.3.6 Pronoms objets indirects postposés
Avec le verbe maliya "parler"

maliya	ʔo	"me"
maliya	ʔam	"te"
maliya	ʔe	"te"

[5] La morphologie verbale proprement dite sera traitée ultérieurement.

maliya	ʔi	"lui" (m.)
maliya	digi	"lui" (f.)
maliya	ʔa	"nous"
maliya	ʔun	"vous"
maliya	dugo	"leur"

Inaccompli / ***Accompli***

verbe	tiya	"manger"	verbe	tiya	"manger"
ʔíntè	ʔín	tuwà	ʔíntè	ʔín	ti
kamtè	kam	tuwà	kamtè	kam	ti
kintè	kin	tuwà	kintè	kin	ti
ʔakàr	-	tuwà	ʔakàr	-	ti
tirte	-	tuwà	tirte	-	ti
ʔantè	ʔan	tuwà	ʔantè	ʔan	ti
ʔeetè	ʔee	tuwà	ʔeetè	ʔee	ti
ʔayar	ʔee	tuwà	ʔayar	ʔee	ti

verbe	siya	"boire"	verbe	siya	"boire"
ʔíntè	ʔín	suwà	ʔintè	ʔin	si
kamtè	kam	suwà	kamtè	kam	si
kintè	kin	suwà	kintè	kin	si
ʔakàr	-	suwà	ʔakar	-	si
tirtè	-	suwà	tirtè	-	si
ʔantè	ʔan	suwà	ʔantè	ʔan	si
ʔeetè	ʔee	suwà	ʔeetè	ʔee	si
ʔayar	ʔee	suwà	ʔayar	ʔee	si

3.4 *Les nombres*

1.	un	fine
2.	deux	sìr
3.	trois	sóòp
4.	quatre	faat
5.	cinq	fíɗɗyà
6.	six	ʔìstàlà
7.	sept	mùryúk
8.	huit	mártá
9.	neuf	dooso
10.	dix	kúryì
11.	onze	kúrúk dí fine
20.	vingt	kúrwì kúrwì sìr
100.	cent	ʔàm kàrsà fine

3.5 *Liste des mots*

N° lexème sg.	pl.	Sens
1. - ʔàaʔa	-	youyou des hommes
2. - ʔaadan	-	mordre
3. - ʔaambìri	-	antilope
4. - ʔàame	-	eau
5. - ʔáàra	ʔaarurom	dos
6. - ʔàasó	ʔáasìsàk	penis
7. - ʔáatìɗa	ʔaatàɗ	intestin
8. - ʔàbàr	-	sang
9. - ʔàbìndùran	-	araignée
10. - ʔàbìr	-	grand-père
11. - ʔàbkornok	-	lézard
12. - ʔabo	-	ici
13. - ʔàboodan	-	singe
14. - ʔagaw	ʔàgaagàw	danse
15. - ʔàgeel	-	babouin
16. - ʔagìli	-	haricot
17. - ʔàjum	ʔàjíìmi	épine
18. - ʔákà	-	ce
19. - ʔale	-	y'en a
20. - ʔàlòl	-	sel végétal
21. - ʔàloolo	-	sel
22. - ʔàmbajala	-	faucille
23. - ʔàmbarwì	-	chauve-souris
24. - ʔàmɗàrcà	-	natte
25. - ʔàmùy	-	bouillon
26. - ʔangara (ar.)	-	nuque
27. - ʔànyiinyà	-	nager
28. - ʔàràari	ʔàràaràk	scorpion
29. - ʔarapte	-	saison de récolte
30. - ʔàrbiyè	-	hache
31. - ʔàriinì	ʔarìn	oeil
32. - ʔàsày	-	excréments
33. - ʔàtàaɗi	ʔàtat	pou
34. - ʔàtaan	ʔátìn	nez
35. - ʔátò	ʔàtây	arbre
36. - ʔàwàn	-	sommeil
37. - ʔawmì	-	miel

38. - bàatìke	-	habit
39. - bállè,		
bállìlà (inacc.)		
ballà (acc.)	-	vomir
40. - bàngirì	-	sentier
41. - bargi	-	sorgho
42. - bòngòoso	bòngòs	poisson
43. - booge	-	rhinocéros
44. - bòoge	-	bataille
45. - bògoogà (inacc.)		
búugì (acc.)		se battre
46. - bûg	-	cor
47. - bùr	-	vagin
48. - bùrmà	-	lion
49. - bùrúurù	-	tourbillon
50. - bùsùn	-	semences
51. - bùutù	-	sol
52. - ɓàake	-	peur
53. - ɓáakì (acc.)	-	avoir peur
54. - ɓáakúwò	-	peureux
55. - ɓìtàr	-	varan
56. - caabúk	-	lance
57. - càabúrbúr	-	courant d'eau
58. - càra	cèrè	racine
59. - cárú	-	creuser
60. - cìbil	-	sésame
61. - còlgom	-	mâchoire
62. - còlgòm	cùloogùm	menton
63. - cómmà	-	vert
64. - cooba		
cùbóobà (inacc.)		
cúubì	-	laver
65. - cornàaɗa	-	sale, mauvais
66. - córnà	-	bien
67. - culɗimi	cúlɗòm	barbe
68. - cùwáawì		léger
69. - dàarà	-	le soir
70. - daayò	daayi	hôte
71. - dàhaabìre	-	nouveau

72. - dàraabà (ar.)	-	gombo
73. - dàrɓòk	-	bouillie
74. - dàrɗyà (vn)	-	serrer
75. - dárɗyé (pp)	-	sérré
76. - díngìɗi	jìngíɗà	clitoris
77. - dìrim	-	hyène
78. - dirsù (impér.) dìreesà (inacc.) dirsì (acc.)	-	s'agenouiller
79. - dìyà (vn) duwà (inacc.) díyén (acc.)	-	tuer
80. - domʔol	-	rond
81. - dòodò	-	talon
82. - dúggìyà	-	écouter
83. - dùlùmdùlùm	-	tiède
84. - dumbur	-	melon
85. - dumbùr kat ʔátò	-	tronc d'arbre
86. - ɗàaɗà (vn) ɗaaɗù (impér.) ɗìɗaaɗà (inacc.) ɗaaɗì (acc.)	-	tirer
87. - ɗáará	-	debout
88. - ɗáarù (impér.)	-	se tenir debout
89. - ɗáày	-	dedans
90. - ɗa (négation)	-	pas[6]
91. - ɗáskà	-	court
92. - ɗaywà	-	marcher
93. - ɗèeɗúwò	ɗèeɗàw	oiseau
94. - ɗeefal	-	tourner
95. - ɗiisì (acc.)	-	tirer, viser
96. - ɗiwèy	ɗíiwì	marche
97. - ɗùbal	ɗùbàl	homme
98. - ɗúrkùl	ɗìràakìli	âne
99. - ɗyaakde	-	doux, tranquille
100. - ɗyamkù (impér.)	-	coudre

[6] ʔintè ʔín siirà ɗa "je ne pars pas"

101. - ɗyàrwi	-	déchiré
102. - ɗyìmbarbírè	-	source
103. - ɗyúuɗyù (impér.) ɗyúuɗyùwà (inacc.)	-	sucer
104. - fàaʔan	-	brûler
105. - fàa-co	-	père-mon
106. - fàafè	-	lait
107. - fàafo	fàafè	sein
108. - fàara	-	dehors
109. - fàati	-	soleil
110. - faatiri tá kàc	-	visage
111. - fácú	-	cracher
112. - fàn	fábúndàŋ	bouche
113. - fàr	-	donner
114. - fársò	farsu	cheval
115. - fátú (impér.) faati (acc.)	-	diviser
116. - fâwta	-	tenir
117. - fidi	-	saison de pluie
118. - fiɗic	-	urine
119. - fiisi	-	moustique
120. - fineere	wùrunko	autre
121. - finnyá	-	plein
122. - firaaca	-	large
123. - fitàatàw	-	cendres
124. - fitàayi	-	secko
125. - fo	-	plaie
126. - fooca	fuuci	fleur
127. - fòoso	fas	main
128. - forlan	-	souffler
129. - fúká	fikè	chien
130. - fundùk	-	toit
131. - fùudì	-	cuisse
132. - fùufine	-	poumon
133. - gàaci (acc.) gicaw (inacc.) gícà (vn.)	-	essayer
134. - gàaɗùfù (impér.)	-	compter
135. - gaaɗyika	-	épaule

136. - gàagà	-	poitrine
137. - gàlfoofo	-	écorces
138. - gàmburò	-	souris
139. - gargaaji (ar)	-	chasseur
140. - gàywàn	-	éléphant
141. - gìf	gàgìf	genou
142. - gìndam	-	courge
143. - gòoɗi	-	couteau
144. - gòrgùro	-	saison sèche
145. - gúggùm	-	joue
146. - gùroolì	gùròl	testicules
147. - gùtòr	gùtirì	potier
148. - guugumí	gígàamí	hibou
149. - ʔica	-	toux
150. - ʔìiri	-	route
151. - ʔiiso	ʔiise	oeuf
152. - ʔíiwò	ʔéèwe	caillou
153. - ʔìlaag	-	année
154. - ʔimmi (ar.)	-	oncle paternel
155. - ʔinèy	-	grand
156. - ʔinyàawe	ʔínyàw	queue
157. - ʔìnyàl	-	herbe
158. - ʔìrìn	-	sentir
159. - ʔìwawgà	-	frapper
160. - ʔìyat (inacc.)	-	
ʔayɗì. (acc.)		dormir
161. - jòffé	-	déféquer
162. - jóòn (inacc.)		
júùn (acc.)	-	s'asseoir
163. - kàaɗyaw	-	maladie
164. - kàaɗyi	-	sec, vide
165. - kaaɗyiɗi	-	sécher
166. - kàawi	-	language
167. - kaawo	káàwe	serpent
168. - kaaye	-	qui
169. - kàc	kaɗyúk	tête
170. - kàɗi	-	bas
171. - kàdiiràm	-	à côté
172. - káfàk (ar.)	-	peu

173. - káfú	-	crâne
174. - kàlɗàŋ	-	grenouille
175. - kàlgi	-	aile
176. - kàri	-	chaleur, travail
177. - kàri	-	chaud
178. - kàrleele	-	épervier
179. - kàrsà	-	attacher
180. - kàsinyà	-	loin
181. - kàwi	-	feu
182. - kèet-àm		
kèet-ungo	-	poignarder
183. - kembò	-	hier
184. - khiddimà (ar.)	-	travailler
185. - kìɗaaɗì	-	fort
186. - kìfiré	-	blanc
187. - kìlàw	-	citrouille
188. - kìlíìmi	-	charbon
189. - kìlelɗà (inacc.)		
kalɗì (acc.)		tomber
190. - kìlíìmi	-	charbon
191. - kinàw	-	lancer, jeter
192. - kìraamì	-	petit
193. - kìraanì	-	crapaud
194. - kìrìiri	-	grêle
195. - kiriiri	-	rosée
196. - kìrsà (vn)		
kìréesà (inacc.)		
kírsì (acc.)		géler
197. - kìyà ták khalà	-	"vache de la brousse" (buffle)
198. - koosa	-	pourri
199. - kôr	-	haut
200. - kòrke (vn)		
korkiywa (impér.),		
kókìkà (inacc.)		
korkà (acc.)	-	frotter
201. - kòrka	-	coude
202. - kòrlò	-	coeur
203. - kòrnyí	-	anus
204. - kôymì	kuyòm	oreille

205. - kùnun ka kàc	-	corne
206. - kùnoonò	kùnòn	os
207. - kùfkìre	-	noir, sombre
208. - kùkùrre	-	poussière
209. - kúllìrè (ar.)	-	tout
210. - kùmac	-	ami
211. - kùmàasì	-	rire
212. - kùmaayò	kìme	viande
213. - kùrɗi	-	lièvre
214. - kúrí	kurak	jarre
215. - kùrkùr	-	le matin
216. - kùrófò	kùròf	serres, griffes
217. - kùróocì	kòròc	fesse
218. - kòrnyí	-	anus
219. - kúsúk	-	vent
220. - kùukì	-	aisselle
221. - láàdi	-	animal
222. - làwyè tát ʔàame	-	fleuve
223. - lày	-	cheveux
224. - leɗɗiŋat	-	mouillé
225. - ley	-	plume
226. - lì	-	chose
227. - liisi	liyàs	langue
228. - lùk	làlùk	ventre
229. - lùwirè	-	épouse
230. - luy	lày	femme
231. - màabi	-	esprit, ancêtre
232. - màabi	-	grand-mère
233. - màagar	-	oncle maternel
nàabu kee fàaco	-	"le frère de mon père"
234. - maare	-	fille
235. - màatà (vn)	-	mourir
236. - màɗi/mèeɗi	-	beaucoup
237. - màlà	-	quoi
238. - màlì/kàawi	-	langage
239. - mâr	-	enfant, garcon
240. - mâr ki ràamar	-	"petit enfant" (bébé)
241. - marɗya	màraaɗyì	jeune homme
242. - màrfo	màrfi	puits

243. - mbur	-	vautour
244. - meela	-	lourd
245. - mòkòròg	-	bérbéré (sol)
246. - monsòono	-	arachide
247. - moota	-	près
248. - nàabú	-	frère
249. - námmà	-	gros
250. - nàwaatì	-	demain
251. - ndìye	-	rien, pas
252. - ndon	-	la nuit
253. - ngá	-	quand
254. - njàw (impér.)	-	aller
255. - njo	nji	personne
256. - nyáa-cò	-	mère-ma
257. - nyabùlo	nyabili	pintade
258. - nyàlànlàŋ	-	faible
259. - nyaamɗì nyamguuɗì (inacc.) nyamganɗì (acc.)	-	pousser
260. - nyìlìili	-	youyou des femmes
261. - nyooɗyàm	-	sourire
262. - nyùgoolò	-	gauche
263. - ʔòllà	-	trou
264. - ʔòlle kát ʔàame	-	mare (trou de l'eau)
265. - ʔoome	-	voir
266. - ʔòora	ʔòorè	ver de terre
267. - ràafi	-	argile
268. - ràazìr	-	fumée
269. - rànnyà	-	rouge
270. - ráwwà	-	froid
271. - reeɓe	-	mensonge
272. - rèɓeeɓà (inacc.) riiɗì (acc.)	-	mentir
273. - réekò	-	flûte
274. - rìiwi	-	chant
ruwaw (inacc.) raaw (acc.)	-	chanter
275. - roki	-	mari

276. - rùgrùga	rùgrìge	nuage
277. - rùumi	-	jeune femme
278. - saaɓat	-	essuyer
279. - saaŋa	-	pointu
280. - sàarò	sàarát	corde
281. - sàatì	-	foie
282. - sáká	-	venir
283. - sámà (ar.)	-	ciel
284. - sigàr	-	long, grand de taille
285. - sàrfi	siràf	côtes
286. - sawni	-	graisse
287. - sáyyà	-	mince
288. - seeʔat (inacc.)		
siiʔiddè (acc.)	-	avaler
289. - shalluufa (ar.)	-	lèvre
290. - siʔinò	-	respiration
291. - sìk	-	corps
292. - sìmè	sime	nom
293. - sisiiwi	síisàw	étoiles
294. - sin	sàn	dent
295. - sín	-	jambe
296. - síwín	-	huile
297. - súfány	-	panthère
298. - sún	-	penser
299. - sùnnyo	-	sable
300. - súunùwa (inacc.)		
súunùwà (acc.)	-	rêver
301. - suuto	-	tamarin
302. - sùwa	-	calebasse
303. - tàafà (vn)	-	planter
304. - tàagar	-	après-demain
305. - taakà	-	aujourd'hui
306. - táakà	fáatàk	jour
307. - tàanà	-	bon
308. - tàawu (impér.)	-	se coucher
309. - tàgdìka	-	chasser
310. - tàwò	tàwù	peau
311. - tiiri	-	lune
312. - tírènygo	-	fourmi-magnant

313.	- tìtíirà	-	voler
314.	- tìwiyyo	tiwiy	mouche
315.	- tòlɗà (vn)	-	préparer la boule
316.	- tòtka	-	couper
317.	- tùban	-	houe
318.	- tuggu	-	termitière
319.	- tùlle	-	lit
320.	- tùmàaʔi	tùmàaʔu	mouton
321.	- tundoŋ	-	la nuit (cf. ndoŋ)
322.	- turor	-	colline
323.	- tùujù	-	millet
324.	- tùwàaye	-	droite
325.	- ʔujbi (pp)	-	pourrir
326.	- ʔùr	-	transpiration, sueur
327.	- wàaʔul	-	semer
328.	- wàagirì	waagàr	chèvre
329.	- wàaɗyko	-	se lever
330.	- wássàya	wassa	fil
331.	- warwìra	-	préparer la sauce
332.	- wáwù (impér.) wòwáw (inacc.) wáawù (acc.)	-	accoucher
333.	- wìlè	-	crachat, salive
334.	- wísàk (inacc.) wàsiki (acc.)	-	s'enfler
335.	- yaa ŋani	-	comment
336.	- yawandi	-	savoir
337.	- yaaŋanì	-	humide
338.	- zaaɗì	-	usé
339.	- zòrʔìrà	-	gorge
340.	- ?		rein
341.	- ?		nombril
342.	- ?		caméléon
343.	- ?		écureuil

II. *Toram*[7] *du Salamat*

1. *Classification*

La langue toram apparaît pour la première fois dans la classification de Westermann et Bryan (1952) parmi les langues dites "Tchado-Hamitiques". Dans sa classification, Jungraithmayr (1981) la place dans le sous-groupe Mubi-Toram.

Le toram est parlé dans le canton Toram au sud d'Abou-Deia, sous-préfecture du Département du Salamat, ayant comme Chef-lieu de Département Am-Timan, au centre-est de la République du Tchad. Il est parlé par environ 7.000 personnes (Beauvilain 93).

2. *Phonologie*

2.1 *Les voyelles*

L'inventaire vocalique du toram compte cinq voyelles orales courtes et cinq voyelles orales longues qui se distinguent par leur aperture et leur localisation. Les cinq voyelles orales sont:

i		**u**
e		**o**
	a	

Les unités lexicales suivantes peuvent être citées à titre d'exemples:

/hibir/ "girafe"
/geteŋ/ "mangouste"
/bara/ "chacal"
/lòkòm/ "chameau"
/bùrshù/ "signe, trace"

Les cinq voyelles longues sont:

ii		**uu**
ee		**oo**
	aa	

[7] Cette étude s'inscrit dans le cadre de recherche sur les langues tchadiques orientales en voie de disparition, initiée par le Prof. Dr. Herrmann Jungraithmayr.

Les unités lexicales suivantes peuvent être citées à titre d'exemples:

/diibi/ "termite"
/ɗeeɗà/ "sac en peau"
/jàanà/ "guerre"
/fooɾo/ "jour"
/tuuru/ "haricot noir"

2.2 *Les consonnes*

La langue toram possède vingt cinq consonnes:

	bilab.	alvéol.	alv.-pal.	palat.	vélaires	laryng.
occlus.	b	t			k	ʔ
occlus.	p	d			g	h
glottal.	ɓ	ɗ		ɗy		
affriq.				c		
affriq.				j		
fricat.	f		s	sh		
fricat.			z			
nasales	m	n		ny	ŋ	
contin.	w		l	y		
vibrant.			r	ɾ		

2.3 *Les tons*

Dans l'état actuel de l'étude sur la langue nous ne pouvons que retenir l'existence de trois tons en toram, notamment haut marqué par un accent aigu (´), moyen non marqué graphiquement ici et bas marqué par un accent grave (`). Exemples:

kíllú "chenille"
garɗyi "éléphant"
jòorè "phacochère"
kèbin "buffle"
bóokok "margouillat"
ɗyíirò "pintade"
kòkóre "poule"
ʔérŋa "tonnerre"
harɗò "fer"
fàde "gombo"

3. *Morphologie*

Pour marquer le pluriel des noms, le toram emploie les procédés morphologiques suivants:

a. - Alternance vocalique en finale de nom

bùróngòogú(wo)	bùrongòoguwí	"grande fourmi noire"
bóokok(ò)	bóokókè	"margouillat à tête rouge"
tángáraaɗò	tángáraaɗì	"petite fourmi noire"
kèbin(o)	kebine	"buffle"
bèreera	bèreere	"papillon"
kíllú(wo)	kíllúwí	"chenille"
gàyàm(o)	gàyàmi	"civette"
nyògòl	nyògòole	"anguille"
hireeɗò	hireeɗì	"gecko"
nyòlòoluwo	nyòlòoluwi	"ver"

b. - Syncope ou chute de la voyelle finale du singulier

kùmò	kòm	"rat"
hìlaalè	hìlal	"aigle"
gòokìneenè	gòokìnen	"centipède"
ʔirindeeɗà	ʔirideɗ	"scorpion"
kòkóre	kokor	"poule"
táfàre	tafar	"feuilles"
njamò	njàm	"épine"

c. - Modification tonale

ʔàŋe	ʔàŋè	"fourmi rouge"
gòròŋ	gòríŋ	"phacochère"
kòkór	kokor	"coq"

d. - Pluriel interne avec insertion de **-a-** ou **-aa-** selon le cas

ɗungum	ɗungàame	"singe"
ɗurkuk	ɗurkàake	"âne"
shigila	shìgaalè	"pot à eau"
min-	mane	"propriétaire"

4. *Liste des mots toram*

N° Lexème	Sens
1. - ʔaan	retourner
2. - ʔàbtíkkà (ar.)	pantalon
3. - ʔàbut	arrondir
4. - ʔac	anneau
5. - ʔaɗa	cicatrice
6. - ʔaɗy	sec
7. - ʔàfil	payer
8. - ʔàfilke	rachat
9. - ʔafut	tante
10. - ʔàga	flamme
11. - ʔàgàɗo	gommier rouge
12. - ʔagant	chaud
13. - ʔàgay	mouvoir, remuer
14. - ʔàgìdak	ensorceler
15. - ʔàgiy	branler
16. - ʔàjankà	guêpe
17. - ʔákkà	natron
18. - ʔàkkú	perroquet
19. - ʔandeŋi	obscurité
20. - ʔanɗì	pâte de mil
21. - ʔàndìgèelo	canne à marcher
22. - ʔàndiheene (ar.)	arbre à beurre
23. - ʔanfoʔe	journée
24. - ʔàŋe	fourmi rouge
25. - ʔàngùmmà	couscous
26. - ʔàngumaajì (ar.)	pagne de femme
27. - ʔàrju	suie
28. - ʔàtik	filer
29. - ʔàtoonà	teinture
30. - ʔàttik	tisser
31. - ʔàwàk	chèvre
32. - ʔàwàko	bouc
33. - ʔàwiiɗo	bouillie
34. - bàarût (ar.)	poudre
35. - bàɗye	belle fille
36. - bàɗyeet	belle soeur

37. - bàɗyiti		beau frère
38. - bàgarnà		cravache
39. - bàgas		diminuer, manquer
40. - bage		sauterelle
41. - bàlbût (ar.)		sillure
42. - bàlnyant		bleu, vert
43. - bàlʔûm (ar.)		sac
44. - bàngàw		patate douce
45. - bara		chacal
46. - bárkey		neuf (9)
47. - bársubà		sept
48. - bàrtù		brins de paille
49. - be		bouche
50. - bèedya		cinq
51. - bèeta		clan
52. - bèreeera		papillon
53. - bi		moustique
54. - biidì (ar.)	pl. bayadà	étalon
55. - biitim		grand tambour
56. - biliw		arc
57. - bìkuk		rôtir, griller
58. - bòkon		pièce, chambre
59. - bondor		hutte, lieu des rites
60. - bookok		margouillat à tête rouge
61. - bookont		ventre
62. - bòot		soeur
63. - bòota		ferme, champ
64. - bòr		évaser
65. - borom		lion
66. - bùhaw		graine de céréale
67. - buik		cuire la chaux
68. - bujùr (ar.?)		savonnier
69. - bùŋ		Dieu
70. - bùróngòogú		grande fourmi noire
71. - bùrshù		signe
72. - bùt		farine
73. - bùutì		cendre
74. - ɓele		flèche

75. - dàbbaal (ar.)		sentier
76. - dahab (ar.)		or
77. - dalny-		désherber
78. - dànàgà		rocher, colline
79. - dàngàlic		tambour
80. - darnut		co-épouse
81. - delet		fille
82. - digilo		canot
83. - digin		montrer, enseigner
84. - diibi		termite
85. - dirwin		écrire
86. - doòm		dômier
87. - dùbaal (ar.)		étrier
88. - dungilo		tronc d'arbre
89. - dùufáàt		filet de pêche
90. - duugin		dresser un piège
91. - ɗa		sentir mauvais
92. - ɗayìg		vendre
93. - ɗawɗaw		chevreuil, daim
94. - ɗeeɗa		sac en peau
95. - ɗénɗilwin		se rouler par terre
96. - ɗìkin		couper
97. - ɗikimin		cueillir
98. - ɗikim		fondre
99. - ɗihaag		cicatrices, scarifications
100. - ɗòkin		battre, forger
101. - ɗokoɗit		petit
102. - ɗook		hacher
103. - ɗonk		passer
104. - ɗùm		marais, marécages
105. - ɗungum	pl. ɗungàame	singe
106. - ɗurkuk	pl. ɗúrkàake	âne
107. - ɗyangum		pois de terre
108. - ɗyèw		ouvrir, fendre
109. - ɗyiirò		perdrix
110. - ɗyíirò		pintade
111. - ɗyìm		abeille, miel
112. - ɗyolom		le matin

113. - ʔeɗ		pêcher
114. - ʔeeɗ		moudre, pétrir
115. - ʔeeɗo	pl. ʔeeɗi	canne à sucre
116. - ʔeete		bois à brûler
117. - ʔete		acacia, tanier
118. - ʔeteŋ		nez
119. - faanà		hache
120. - fàde		gombo
121. - falgin		tresser une corde
122. - fardè		pagne de femme
123. - fartal		déployer
124. - fàtalgà		tissage
125. - felletuwe		flûte
126. - fideetìr		saison pluvieuse
127. - fihash		se disperser
128. - fihe		jument
129. - fiho		cheval
130. - fishirgin		séparer
131. - fòo		soleil
132. - fòoɗa		quatre
133. - foolin		cultiver
134. - fòolò		grande houe
135. - fóoɾe		jarre à eau
136. - fooɾo		pot à bière
137. - fòosh		défendre, interdire
138. - fòotu		bras
139. - fòta		manche
140. - fòto		massue
141. - fuddà (ar.)		argent (métal)
142. - gàbàare		figuier
143. - gàdarbe		caroubier
144. - gajùbe		gauche
145. - gàlin		plonger
146. - gardyi	pl. gàràadye	éléphant
147. - gàyàm	pl. gàyàami	tigre, civette
148. - gayin		labourer, cultiver
149. - gè		gens
150. - gèder		être capable, pouvoir

151. - geegàr		ville
152. - gemè (ar.)		blé
153. - geteŋ		mangouste
154. - gifitu		genou
155. - gìlàabe		fromager
156. - gìme		vache
157. - gìmo		boeuf, animal dom.
158. - gín		avoir
159. - gìn		faire, construire
160. - gìna		métier, travail
161. - gìrìntiyyé (ar.)		hyppopotame
162. - girjabo	pl. girjabe	varan terrestre
163. - goɗor		captif
164. - gokok		ancêtre
165. - gòmorkò		panier, corbeille
166. - gondi		bébé
167. - goobà		roussette
168. - gòokineenè	pl. gòokinen	centipède
169. - gookureedà	pl. gooreedè	crapaud
170. - goorò (Hausa)		kola
171. - gootin		creuser
172. - gooyu		frire
173. - gòre		épaule
174. - gorom		gruau
175. - gòròŋ	pl. gòríŋ	phacochère
176. - gub		petite houe
177. - gùlal		testicules
178. - gure/gèekireeɗà		coquille
179. - gurgùr		bousier
180. - gushàd		taille, ceinture
181. - gùwaarò	pl. gùwaarè	vautour
182. - haalo		pipe
183. - hamaam		pigeon
184. - harɗò		fer
185. - he		boire
186. - hibir		girafe
187. - hiɗ		récolter
188. - hiɗik		abattre un arbre
189. - hijáàb		grigri

190. - hìlaalè	pl. hilal	aigle, faucon
191. - hinyo		sable fin
192. - hint		frère
193. - hir		examiner
194. - hìràafe		rivière
195. - hireeɗo	pl. hireeɗi	gecko
196. - hògòre		porc-épic
197. - hogúnà		âtre, foyer, cuisine
198. - hoom		ramasser, collecter
199. - hoon		rêver
200. - hòore		jujubier
201. - hòorúmò		arme, fusil
202. - hootu		descendre
203. - hòy		apprivoiser
204. - huun		grossir
205. - huraagu		cor
206. - ʔihil		annau de pied
207. - ʔirindeeɗà	pl. ʔirindeɗ	scopion
208. - ʔishag		dresser les oreilles
209. - ʔìtaare		meule
210. - jaam		recevoir
211. - jàanà		guerre
212. - jàasûs (ar.)		espion
213. - jàrge		pois de terre
214. - jenne (ar.)		paradis
215. - jòŋe		manioc, tubercule
216. - joor		suspendre
217. - jòorè		héron garde-boeuf
218. - jòorin		billonner
219. - jòre		source, fontaine
220. - juga		hamecon, crochet
221. - jùuji		millet
222. - kaali		dent
223. - kaalo		étoile
224. - kaat		partir, émigrer, germer
225. - kàata		tête
226. - kàdi		habit d'homme
227. - kaɗaɗo		chaine

228. - kàjàngane		haricot sp.
229. - kanjàr (ar.)		faucille
230. - karbal		tamiser
231. - kàrtaayà		harnais
232. - katkat		tisserand
233. - kèbin	pl. kèbine	buffle
234. - kèlem		garder, rester
235. - kerɗew		panthère
236. - kew		champ
237. - kìiri		bracelet
238. - kiituk		mettre de côté
239. - kib		découdre
240. - kiɗa		sol
241. - kìlaama		charbon de bois
242. - kìlgà		créer
243. - kíllú	pl. kíllúwi	chenille
244. - kilma		ombre
245. - kìntàawo		bêlier castré
246. - kirdì		grêle
247. - kirt		puiser de l'eau
248. - kitirfil		antilope
249. - koɓele		fesses
250. - koɗi		rosée
251. - kòɗògonay		pendantif
252. - kojogor	pl. kojogore	hyène
253. - koko		grand-mère
254. - kòkór	pl. kokore	coq
255. - kòkóre		poule
256. - kòle		figuier
257. - kòngà		clôture, haie
258. - kòrɗe		boisson alcoolique
259. - korɗyò		sorgho
260. - korgol		cloche
261. - korkòɗy		gravier
262. - kòrnò		cuillère
263. - korome		doigt
264. - korroori		bulbe, oignon
265. - kot		belle-mère
266. - kòy		fin, bout, finir
267. - kuuku		citouille, potiron
268. - kuffaàr		masque

269. - kúlúl		autruche
270. - kulmo		tamarinier
271. - kùmò	pl. kòm	rat
272. - kùngùrù		tortue
273. - kùrtaalà		carquois
274. - kùrum		rônier
275. - la		couleur
276. - laʔarɗo		multicolore
277. - laawa		cheveux
278. - làhug		mouiller
279. - lehewe		mais
280. - lettu		chauve-souris
281. - li		chose, outil
282. - liho		langue
283. - liiko	pl. liike	branche
284. - lòkòm		chameau
285. - loog		descente
286. - looki		coude
287. - lùkkak		éperon
288. - lùw		semer, planter
289. - maagìr		oncle
290. - maawà		village
291. - màayi		saison chaude
292. - madaame		marché
293. - mafirsha (ar.)		natte
294. - màgàr		pot
295. - màgayno		cultivateur
296. - màgidifà		piège
297. - màgootà		plantoir
298. - màlànɗa		pauvre
299. - mangà		fourmi
300. - marɗyo		garcon
301. - màriye		chanteuse
302. - màrnye		sorgho
303. - màrta		huit
304. - martì		voyage
305. - màrto	pl. màrti	hôte, étranger
306. - màteera		apiculteur
307. - màtèerà		chasseur
308. - màwaara		danseuse

309. - màwiyàye		accoucheuse
310. - màyhuke		cache-sexe masculin
311. - mèɗye		filtre à boisson
312. - mèeko		orphelin
313. - meetit		mâle, mari
314. - mele		puits
315. - mèlèm		sorcier
316. - méta		manche
317. - mìde		droite
318. - mihit		fils ainé
319. - mìito		homme
320. - míkkà		six
321. - min-	pl. mane	propriétaire, maître
322. - mish		termite
323. - moʔorbe		aiguille
324. - mòʔòrè		drap, tissu
325. - mòʔoore		cassolette
326. - moɗoki		potier
327. - mogot		grand-père
328. - mohe		tombe
329. - mohog		pilon
330. - molge		cailcédrat
331. - molom		sorcière
332. - mòonà		fourager
333. - morfi		sentier
334. - mòsòono (ar.?)		arachide
335. - mòtògòl		riche
336. - mòtook		mendier
337. - mòy		fumer
338. - mùhigaag		enterrement
339. - mùnshaak		nord
340. - múro	pl. mure	gazelle
341. - muse	pl. mùsì	lièvre
342. - mùt		mourir
343. - mutaal (ar.)		fuseau
344. - muube		clitoris
345. - na		mûrir
346. - nàhas (ar.)		cuivre, bronze
347. - nayyàl		teindre
348. - ndaawut		chat

349. - ndafaaye (ar.)		chapeau de paille
350. - ndooro		veau
351. - niir		grossir
352. - njamò	pl. njàm	épine
353. - njelfe		melon
354. - nèngere		couteau
355. - nùngaarà		tambour
356. - nussatì		côté, moitié
357. - nyaŋarooma		grand koudou
358. - nyìri		coton
359. - nyògòl	pl. nyògòole	anguille
360. - nyòlòoluwo	pl. nyòlòolúwi	ver
361. - nyoore		peau de bête
362. - nyòorò	pl. nyóore	chaussure
363. - ŋal		instruire
364. - ŋaamùsh		éclairer
365. - ʔooh		éventer
366. - ʔooʔit		poitrine
367. - ʔookut		bassin
368. - ʔoolant		froid
369. - ʔoom		front
370. - ʔooy		maudire
371. - ʔooyug		mettre dans
372. - ʔoh		calculer
373. - ʔok		feu
374. - ʔòle		sec
375. - ʔony		entrer
376. - ʔòrrò		dix
376. - ʔòt		atteindre
377. - ràabo		argile
378. - raamant		jalousie
379. - raami		lune
380. - ratùl (ar.)		livre (mesure)
381. - reer		courir
382. - rihew (ar.)		tourterelle
383. - riis (ar.)		riz
384. - riya		forêt
385. - riy		chanter
386. - riye		chanson

387. - rùgàw		combat
388. - run		enfant
389. - ruum		kapokier
390. - sàabûn (ar.)		savon
391. - sàba (ar.)		est
392. - saddaàr (ar.)		chemise
393. - sàllá (ar.)		prier
394. - sandàl (ar.)		arbre sp.
395. - sariimè (ar.)		bride
396. - sarìj (ar.)		selle
397. - see		deux
398. - seèf (ar.)		sabre, épée
399. - shaari		racine
400. - shakale		hernie
401. - shelŋe		sésame
402. - shigile	pl. shigaale	canari
403. - shil		dune
404. - shimim		cauri
405. - shòbòoba		poumon
406. - sìndaalà		forge
407. - sìta		poivre, piment
408. - soom		fonio
409. - suuba		trois
410. - suusi		ordures
411. - ta		manger
412. - tàbàga (ar.)		tabac
413. - tàbaldì (ar.)		baobab
414. - táfàre	pl. tafar	argent
415. - tàhuurà (ar.)		circoncision
416. - tàmàgo	pl. tàmági	mouton
417. - tambàl (ar.)		tambour
418. - tángáraaɗò		fourmi magnant
419. - tát-		père
420. - teer		chasser
421. - tegel		beurre, graisse
422. - tegen		huile
423. - tewe		nourriture
424. - teewù		sauce
425. - tiif		arracher
426. - tiifug		enlever, ôter

427. - tikir	mesurer
428. - ting	protéger
429. - tirkil	vipère
430. - tìrmàaɗo	bouclier
431. - tíwínjú	mouche tsé-tsé
432. - tòore	oseille de Guinée
433. - tòoro	cerveau
434. - tuggàl	caillou
435. - tùkkíyè	lileur
436. - tùlò	abcès
437. - tùmbure	python
438. - tun	planter
439. - tung	se retourner
440. - tuureeny	rhinocéros
441. - tuuru	haricot noir
442. - tùwàaw	collier
443. - ʔùbaalà	brasier, braise
444. - ʔùdò	oeil
445. - ʔudurt	diable
446. - ʔúnt-	habiter
447. - ʔunuw	envelopper
448. - ʔurb	coudre
449. - ʔúrde	grenier
450. - ʔurumta	écorce
451. - ʔush	se lever, bouillonner
452. - ʔuskur	ongle
453. - ʔuug	aiguiser
454. - waahu	éléphantiasis
455. - waar	danser
456. - wa	accoucher
457. - waidaro	poule des rochers
458. - want	beau
459. - war	clarté
460. - waragà (ar.)	grigri
461. - watì (ar.)	ouest
462. - wer	terre, lieu
463. - were	cou
464. - werket	égaliser
465. - zaagiye (ar.)	jardin

III. *Ubi du Guéra (Tchad)*

1. *Classification*

Du point de vue de la classification le ubi n'a à aucun moment été mentionné dans les différentes classifications. Il a été d'abord considéré comme un dialecte de la langue bidiya. Mais lors de nos enquêtes en 1983, nous avions constaté qu'il présentait des divergences linguistiques importantes par rapport au bidiya, au point de devenir une langue à part entière. Il demeure certes une langue tchadique sur le plan lexical et du fait de son genre grammatical.

Le ubi est parlé dans le canton Bidiyo situé dans le Département du Guéra, ayant comme Chef-lieu de Département Mongo. Il est parlé dans sept villages.

2. *Phonologie*

2.1 *Les voyelles*

Il existe en ubi cinq voyelles orales courtes et cinq voyelles orales longues qui se distinguent par leur aperture et leur localisation. Les cinq voyelles orales sont:

i		**u**
e		**o**
	a	

Les unités lexicales suivantes peuvent être citées à titre d'exemples:

/ciri/ "cervelle"
/meyè/ "femme"
/bàla/ "panier"
/ʔòsò/ "vent"
/mugù/ "éléphant"

Les cinq voyelles longues se présentent comme suit:

ii		**uu**
ee		**oo**
	aa	

Les unités lexicales suivantes peuvent être citées à titre d'exemples:

/biigì/ "viande"
/beere/ "mauvais"

/ʔààrà/ "lui"
/cóogo/ "faim"
/buuzè/ "poisson"

2.2 *Les consonnes*

La langue ubi compte vingt-deux consonnes:

	bilab.	alvéol.	alv-pal.	palat.	vélaires	laryng.
occlus.	b	t			k	ʔ
occlus.	p	d			g	
glottal.	ɓ	ɗ		ɗy		
affriq.				c		
affriq.				j		
fricat.			s			
fricat.			z			
nasales	m	n		ny	ŋ	
contin.	w		l	y		
vibrant.			r			

2.3 *Les tons*

Dans l'état actuel de nos connaissances sur la langue, nous ne pouvons qu'émettre l'hypothèse de l'existence de trois tons en ubi, notamment haut (´), moyen non marqué graphiquement ici et bas (`). Exemples:

ɗíiɗé "oiseau
ɗeenya "salive"
cùwà "arbre"
kokilà "coude"
kákìlà "aile"
laaginyá "branche"
gésà "lance"
ʔákò "feu"
ʔàko "ici"

3. *Morphologie*

3.1 *Formation de pluriel*

En matière de morphologie nominale et en particulier la formation du pluriel, le ubi est particulier s'il faut le comparer aux langues tchadiques voisines tel que le bidiya. Il ne possède qu'une seule forme pour marquer le pluriel. Le formatif employé est, au singulier **-rum** pour les noms de type **CVV** et **-um** pour les noms se terminant par une consonne, **-reetì** est la forme commune pour le pluriel. En ce qui concerne les unités lexicales disyllabiques et autres, le suffixe du pluriel remplace la voyelle finale et s'adjoint directement à la consonne de la dernière syllabe. Bien entendu la suffixation du morphème du pluriel peut donner lieu à des procédés morphologiques tels que assimilation, réduction de quantité vocalique ou modification tonale. Exemples:

bùu-rùm	búu-reetì "bouche"
bòg-ùm	bòg-reetì "nuit"
ʔooɗ-ò	ʔor-reetì "chèvre"
dumil-à	dumilreetì "nez"
goon-a	gonreetì "tête"
mòt-a	mòtreetì "homme"
pìny-à	pìnyreetì "peau"
sìin-à	sìnreetì "dent"

3.2 *Les pronoms possessifs*

indépendants		dépendants	
donò	"le mien"	-nò	"mon"
dunkà	"le tien"	-kà	"ton"
denkè	"le tien"	-kè	"ton"
diikà	"le sien"	-díikà	"son"
dentì	"le sien"	-déntì	"son
dénnè	"le nôtre"	-dénnè	"notre"
dénkum	"le vôtre"	-kum	"votre"
dénkin	"le leur"	-kin	"leur"

3.3 *Les pronoms sujets*

Forme absolue/forme raccourcie:

naara/naa	"moi/je"
cira/ci	"toi/tu"
kerke/ke	"toi/tu"
ʔàarà/a	"lui/il"
ʔàtàarà/ʔàti	"elle"
ʔìnanì/nì	"nous"
kunàŋ/ku	"vous"
ʔanàŋ/ʔan	"eux/ils"

3.4 *Les pronoms objets directs*

-nò	"me"
-kà	"te"
-kè	"te"
-ki	"le"
-kiya	"la"
-ne	"nous"
-kum	"vous"
-kin	"les"

3.5 *Les pronoms objets indirects*

dónò	"me (à moi)"
dúnkà	"te m. (à toi)"
dénkè	"te f. (à toi)"
díikà	"lui (à lui)"
déntì	"lui (à elle)"
dénè	"nous (à nous)"
dénkùm	"vous (à vous)"
dénkìn	"leur (à eux)"

4. *Liste des mots ubi*

N° Lexème	sens
1. - ʔaagigùm	crépuscule
2. - ʔàanin	prendre, tenir
3. - ʔàarà	lui
4. - ʔàdû	droit
5. - ʔaɗinyin	diviser
6. - ʔagè	là
7. - ʔagilgà	lourd
8. - ʔake	avec
9. - ʔàko	ici
10. - ʔákò	feu
11. - ʔàmjalpè	melon
12. - ʔàmmàraarà (ar.)	bile
13. - ʔàmyò	eau, pluie
14. - ʔànam	celui-là
15. - ʔànaŋ	ils
16. - ʔànin	geler

17. - ʔàpʔurùp (ar.)		antilope sp.
18. - ʔasŋin		compter
19. - ʔatà/ʔatùm		ventre
20. - ʔatàs (ar.)		soif
21. - ʔàtoonà		boue
22. - ʔàwin		goûter
23. - (ʔay) yé		qui
24. - bahar (ar.)		mer
25. - bàla		panier
26. - beemuɗù		sept
27. - beere		mauvais
28. - beyò		haricot
29. - biigì		viande
30. - bigboorì		animal sauvage
31. - birìn		donner
32. - bìziyò		moustique
33. - bò		personne
34. - bògin		dire, parler, langue
35. - bòogin		rotir
36. - bògùm		nuit
37. - bòjìrà		aveugle
38. - boolè		hyène
39. - bòlù		petit mil
40. - bónnà		hier/soir
41. - borbilà		queue
42. - boorgà		large
43. - bòrgò		cor
44. - bòrgù		vache
45. - bòori		dehors
46. - bòoyìn		souffler
47. - bòyin		fleur
48. - bùu-rùm	pl. búu-reetì	bouche, lèvre
49. - búuze		poisson
50. - bumìn		sentir
51. - bùrà		aigre
52. - càcàllàkí		pointu
53. - càɗin		laver
54. - ce		calebasse
55. - ceccewì		léger

56. - cempiyò	mensonge
57. - cèrù	racine
58. - cìlìlìm	charbon
59. - cílmà	pleine lune
60. - cìlmìŋ	noir, sombre
61. - cirà	grêle
62. - cirì	cervelle
63. - cóogo	faim
64. - coorà	poule
65. - còmín	soulever, porter
66. - coŋin	écouter
67. - còrgà	vessie
68. - còrgòlò	fleuve
69. - còrin	uriner
70. - còriyò	urine
71. - cúlmà	araignée
72. - cùwà	arbre
73. - da	maison
74. - dàalà	tam-tam
75. - dàarímà	guerre
76. - dàrmuudì (ar.)	pot
77. - deenya	salive
78. - dèbinà	grand
79. - dendiyò	rire
80. - dèrŋílà	genou
81. - dèyin	tuer
82. - díiɗé	oiseau
83. - dibrà	nombril
84. - dìmbil	ver de terre sp.
85. - dìnà	place, endroit
86. - doolè	jeune femme
87. - dooyìn	déféquer
88. - dòbìsin	s'agenouiller
89. - dongòm	lion
90. - dòwa	mouche
91. - dumilà	nez
92. - ɗeenà	jambe
93. - ɗéenà	pied
94. - ɗeezè	oeuf

95. - ɗektà	au milieu
96. - ɗîn	marcher
97. - ɗìnyin	jouer
98. - ɗìpìn	fermer
99. - ɗìsse	colline
100. - ɗooyìn	demander
101. - ɗokìn	frapper
102. - ɗuuzà	faucille, couteau
103. - ɗu	aller
104. - ɗungìyà	mâchoire
105. - ɗùrgù	pierre
106. - ɗùrkul	âne
107. - ʔèebin	venir
108. - ʔebinì	sel
109. - ʔejewìn	tousser, toux
110. - ʔepìn	respirer
111. - ʔèrwa	nouveau
112. - ʔèsà	os
113. - ʔeygù	écureuil
114. - ʔeyin	apporter
115. - gaayìm	cuisse
116. - gaayìn	accompagner
117. - gabgà	montagne
118. - gajìn	pousser
119. - galìn	cuisiner
120. - gambò	singe
121. - gàngàŋé	dur
122. - gàpà	corne
123. - garpà	forgeron
124. - gèɗín	courir
125. - gésà	lance
126. - gèyin	chasser
127. - goolè	oseille
128. - goonà	tête
129. - goɗolà	testicule
130. - gol-um bòone	ciel (tête de Dieu)
131. - gon ʔùte	toit
132. - gonkònìyò	griffes, serres
133. - gòrdè	lézard

134. - gòrgiyò	puce
135. - gòygòyà	bêlier
136. - gòyòl	à gauche
137. - guugùm	hibou
138. - gùjumà	barbe
139. - gurɓò	bouillon
140. - gùwin	vomir
141. - ʔiigiro	chaud
142. - ʔìnà	bien
143. - ʔìnanè	nous
144. - ʔìrì	oeil
145. - ʔisò	défécations
146. - ʔìyin	secher
147. - ʔìyo	sec
148. - jaggà	long
149. - jàttò	cent
150. - jèndà	vagin
151. - jèpà	plaie
152. - jereyà	cou, gorge
153. - jeygà	peu
154. - jilà	penis
155. - jìnín	sortir
156. - joorìn	source
157. - jobilà	épaule
158. - jùɗùm	pou
159. - kàalè	fer
160. - kabila	feuille
161. - kákìlà	aile
162. - kàlòotòoyè	carquois
163. - karaatitì	tout
164. - kecìŋey	grenouille
165. - keckecì	froid
166. - kèebin	entrer
167. - kèelin	réunir
168. - kèepà	lièvre
169. - keesè	flèche
170. - kòogin	gratter
171. - koomò	amer

172. - kòbùnò	buffle
173. - kògiyò	serpent
174. - kokilà	coude
175. - kòlgín	déposer
176. - kòlgò	sol
177. - kònyà	orteil
178. - kòppa	court
179. - kòrŋa	courge
180. - kosiɗò	chaleur
181. - kòtòŋ	crapaud
182. - kòyà	main
183. - kòymòtà	à droite
184. - kuumè	souris
185. - kùmbà	dans
186. - kùmiyò	citrouille
187. - kùnìiyà	doigt
188. - kùtì	nuque
189. - kùtùwé	poussière
190. - kuyù	chien
191. - laaginyá	branche
192. - léwà	scorpion
193. - lèyìn	revenir
194. - liilù	peur
195. - lin	chanter
196. - liyò	chanson
197. - lobinà	semences
198. - lòkúɗò	gombo
199. - lòwà	cheveux
200. - lòwin	insulter
201. - maagì meyè	tante
202. - maagìr mòtà	oncle
203. - màna gum	comment
204. - maryà	jeune homme
205. - màtá	quand
206. - màyìn	voler, dérober
207. - mayyè	voleur
208. - mèedèega	pancréas
209. - meejè	feuilles de haricot
210. - meejù	vert

211. - mèetà		hôte
212. - meyè		femme
213. - mèynè		épouse
214. - mìibirò		arachide
215. - miɗinyè		dedans
216. - mòotá		homme
217. - moozà		hanche
218. - mò		quoi
219. - mòlin		fatigue
220. - momonna		chose
221. - mombì		mouillé
222. - mòrmìn		blanc
223. - mòrsò		jaune
224. - mòysò		faible
225. - muuɗù		mort
226. - mugù		éléphant
227. - mùn-		mari
228. - munnà		plein
229. - mùlkúm		colombe
230. - murgamà		sorgho
231. - mùrulò		intestin
232. - mùrzò		vingt
233. - naarà		moi, je
234. - nayìn		voir
235. - nerrà		gras, gros
236. - neygà		à côté
237. - niiniyò		ombre
238. - nigirò		demain
239. - nìgìrtìye		matin
240. - nìyín		entendre
241. - noogà		faire
242. - nubbal		arc
243. - nyaggà		mince
244. - nyèɗeyín		avaler
245. - nyùunyù		panthère
246. - ʔooɗò	pl. orreetì	chèvre
247. - ʔòogin		brûler
248. - ʔoomìn		mordre

249. - ʔoonò	visage
250. - ʔoorà	route
251. - ʔòowin	nager
252. - ʔooyà	poitrine
253. - ʔòoyin	flotter, nager
254. - ʔòozò	herbe
255. - ʔògibà	année
256. - ʔoniyà	oreille
257. - ʔoŋilà	coeur
258. - ʔòpìn	creuser
259. - ʔòròkì	dix
260. - ʔòsin	tirer vers soi
261. - ʔòsò	vent
262. - ʔòwìlin	fièvre, maladie
263. - paanè	hache
264. - paawò	lait
265. - paynà	sein
266. - peɓinyìn	sucré
267. - pécò	humide
268. - pìɗi	nouvelle lune
269. - piɗimòtà	lune, mois
270. - pijìn	cracher
271. - pindarì	un
272. - pinyà	peau
273. - pìriikà	écorce
274. - pooyà	brouillard
275. - poɗà	quatre
276. - porpoɗà	huit
277. - puɗiyò	soleil
278. - pùggà	fourmilière
279. - pùrgum	saison des pluies
280. - ràabìn	rouge
281. - raagà	natte
282. - reemin	jeter
283. - reetì	beaucoup, plusieurs
284. - reezè	crâne
285. - rèyò/reeyò	bâton, bois
286. - riyò	travail
287. - rooɗiyè	pourri

288. - roomò	garçon
289. - rooyà	chaussure
290. - ròdyè	usé
291. - rom, lèbinyò, loyya	bébé
292. - rub	cendres
293. - rub ʔigirà	cendres chaudes
294. - rugumìn	bouillir
295. - rum	enfant
296. - rumò meyè	fille
297. - rumò mòtà	fils
298. - saakùrè	chambre en bois
299. - sàawin	essuyer
300. - sayin	boire
301. - sèemò	nom
302. - seɗè	sang
303. - sèpà	corde
304. - sìinà	dent
305. - siinè cùwe	tronc d'arbre
306. - siirùm	corps
307. - sìgin	descendre
308. - sìlínyò	langue
309. - sinò	frère
310. - siyò	fumée
311. - sobilà	pintade
312. - sògònin	rêve
313. - soyò	abeille
314. - sùba	trois
315. - suunè	huile
316. - tàarà	dos, derrière
317. - tèetu	muet
318. - te-	père
319. - tèbrin	tourner
320. - teɗeekì	petit
321. - telpìn	toucher
322. - tergà	loin
323. - tèyelgà	épais
324. - tezeyin	enterrer
325. - tímyò	étoile
326. - tîn	manger

327. - tìndìro	fourmi blanche
328. - tìrŋayò	fourmi-magnant
329. - tìsirò	rosée
330. - tòoɗín	monter
331. - toogà	acéré, tranchant
332. - tòoziyò	foie
333. - tògínì	vrai
334. - tòliyò	lit
335. - tòrbín	coudre
336. - tuulè	mare
337. - turgà	secko
338. - tupìn	penser
339. - ʔùunin	attacher
340. - ʔùdùmin	savoir
341. - ʔulè	trou
342. - ʔulnyà	beau
343. - ʔunìn	s'asseoir
344. - ʔuntà	vivre, rester
345. - ʔùrgin	chasser
346. - wàajin	poignarder
347. - waanyìn	ouvrir
348. - wàske	fil à coudre
349. - wòorin	se tenir debout
350. - wò	où
351. - wòl ʔìsìrò	anus
352. - wòlà	fesse
353. - wòya	champ
354. - wosìn	s'enfler
355. - wuyù	dormir, sommeil
356. - yiimìn	couper
357. - yi-	mère
358. - yoogìn	viser
359. - yoolè	sable
360. - yum koyum	aujourd'hui
361. - zèeyin	voler (oiseau)
362. - zilŋàm	habit, vêtement
363. - zom-no	ami
364. - zùmzùm	tiède
365. - zùrre	courant d'eau

IV. *Masmaje du Batha-Est (Tchad)*

1. *Liste des villages Masmadje*

1. - Abdjidad
2. - Allibeydad
3. - Amkoofa
4. - Amlammeena
5. - Amlammeena Amzi'eef
6. - Amriiri
7. - Amchag
8. - Amshalkhti
9. - Amsideere I
10. - Amsideere II
11. - Birkit Fatime
12. - Birren
13. - Birren gardaaye
14. - Dalme
15. - Daramde
16. - Giree'iine
17. - Gireewit
18. - Hajaalic
19. - Karkajo
20. - Kileege
21. - Kiwweeke
22. - Kolkol
23. - Kulga
24. - Mirey
25. - Mirey Hileele
26. - Mour (Ammur, Mireere)
27. - Nabaawa
28. - Raamo
29. - Saafig
30. - Seheeba
31. - Shi'eerin
32. - Shu'ran
33. - Sila
34. - Sila Hijeer
35. - Sila Kadaade
36. - Tarwane
37. - Tawaayil

2. *Classification*

Le masmaje a été cité pour la première fois par Westermann et Bryan (1952) au sein du groupe "Sokoro-Mubi" parmi les langues dites "Tchado-Hamitiques". Il est intégré dans le sous-groupe de la langue moubi, considérée peut-être au même titre que le kajakse et le birgit comme des dialectes de la langue moubi. Le masmaje reapparaît justement dans le sous-groupe Mubi-Toram dans la classification de Jungraithmayr (1981).

Le masmaje est parlé dans le canton Masmadje dans le Département du Batha-Est, ayant comme Chef-lieu de département Oum-Hadjer. Il est parlé par 6.000 personnes (Beauvilain 93).

3. *Phonologie*

3.1 *Les voyelles*

Le masmaje possède cinq voyelles orales courtes et cinq voyelles orales longues qui se distinguent par leur aperture et leur localisation. Les cinq voyelles orales sont:

i		**u**
e		**o**
	a	

Les unités lexicales suivantes peuvent être citées à titre d'exemples:

/finì/ "un"
/fèytè/ "autre"
/sáaŋà/ "tranchant"
/jòrgò/ "rônier"
/kúrúk/ "dix"

Les cinq voyelles longues sont les suivantes:

ii		**uu**
ee		**oo**
	aa	

Les unités lexicales suivantes peuvent être citées à titre d'exemples:

/fiisi/ "moustique"
/beece/ "tubercule"
/faat/ "quatre"
/soob/ "trois"
/buuk/ "cor"

3.2 *Les consonnes*

Le masmaje possède vingt trois consonnes:

	bilab.	alvéol.	alv-pal.	palat.	vélaires	laryng.
occlus.	b	t			k	ʔ
occlus.	p	d			g	h
glottal.	ɓ	ɗ		ɗy		
affriq.				c		
affriq.				j		
fricat.	f		s			

Table (*cont.*)

	bilab.	alvéol.	alv-pal.	palat.	vélaires	laryng.
fricat.			z			
nasales	m	n		ny	ŋ	
contin.	w		l	y		
vibrant.			r			

3.3 *Les tons*

Dans l'état actuel de nos recherches sur la langue nous postulons l'existence de trois tons en masmaje, notamment haut marqué par un accent aigu (´), moyen qui n'est pas graphiquement marqué ici et bas (`) marqué par un accent grave. Exemples:

tíwí	"mouche"
haawa	"large"
ɓàakò	"peur"
káàkò	"serpent"
kìɗí	"terre"
nùwáawí	"être mûr"
ʔúrdè	"grenier"
kaatù	"partir"
gùuri	"pilier"

4. *Morphologie*

Le masmaje utilise plusieurs procédés morphologiques pour la formation du pluriel. En voici quelques-uns:

a. - Pluriel interne

bògòs	bùgùuso	"poisson"
farsò	firaasù	"cheval"
fèysìne	fìyàasùnu	"lance"
ʔilgi	ʔilaag	"année"

b. - Changement vocalique en fin de mot

gìyàayi	giyaayè	"tesson de poterie"
káàkò	káàkè	"serpent"

5. *Liste des mots masmaje*

N° Lexème sens

1.	- ʔàaɗyò		être enrhumé
2.	- ʔaaya		dur
3.	- ʔàbàr		sang
4.	- ʔabdiweekh		urne de polypore
5.	- ʔaggàw		danse
6.	- ʔàmbargì		sorgho rouge
7.	- ʔàmbìtìnytìny		oiseau sp.
8.	- ʔàmbirtìtooye		grenouille
9.	- ʔàmdabbò		barbe
10.	- ʔàmfarraara (ar.)		biceps
11.	- ʔàmʔuloole		fontanelle
12.	- ʔàngakkò/ʔàmhakkò		jeu sp.
13.	- ʔàmkuurùm		anguille
14.	- ʔànjirè		culture remunérée
15.	- ʔaràsh		ramures (puits)
16.	- ʔasìlè		boisson non fermentée
17.	- ʔassìrgitàr		étreindre
18.	- ʔawaanà		causer
19.	- bàayok		jeu de pois de terre
20.	- bàarà		mare
21.	- baba		père
22.	- bákkàl		avaler des aliments
23.	- bàlàngà		bâton de soutien
24.	- baskà		mouiller
25.	- beece		tubercule sp.
26.	- boori		hyène
27.	- bògòs	pl. bùguuso	poisson
28.	- buuk		cor
29.	- ɓàakò		peur
30.	- ɓarè		tige d'épis de mil
31.	- ɓeerungo		esclave
32.	- ɓìreetì		concourir
33.	- ɓirti		s'évader
34.	- ɓo		aller

35. - cagil		cacher
36. - calak		oiseau
37. - carak		haricot
38. - celli		éplucher
39. - ciboobi		faire la vaisselle
40. - ciiri		devenir rouge
41. - ciriwkitàr		fendiller
42. - comma		devenir vert
43. - coy		sauce
44. - cukka		côtiser
45. - cupkà		laver
46. - dalù		gourde
47. - dàr		porte, route
48. - dàrangàl		hangar
49. - deetè		rien, personne
50. - ɗàagínyì		bâton à boule
51. - ɗaara		apparaître (lune)
52. - ɗaarù		s'arrêter, freiner
53. - ɗyágìlkà		chercher
54. - ʔelèl		voyant
55. - fàafé		lait
56. - faat		quatre
57. - faɗyuŋ		faire boire le bébé
58. - fàn		bouche
59. - fàn hi kere		clan
60. - far		donner
61. - farsò	pl. firaasù	cheval
62. - fèysìne	pl. fiyàasùnu	lance
63. - feyte		autre
64. - fiɗyaŋ		urine
65. - fiɗa		arène de lutte
66. - fiisi		moustique
67. - finì		un
68. - fitaato		cendres
69. - fòrlà		allumer le feu
70. - gàali		disparaître
71. - galbì		hameçon

72. - gìyàayi	pl. giyaayè	tesson de potereie
73. - gongoŋ		hache
74. - gòròmbe		fissure
75. - gùuri		pilier
76. - gùutu		descendre
77. - haawa		large
78. - haaya		se rassasier
79. - habbat		glaner
80. - hale		peut-être
81. - hanìn		goûter
82. - heegel		dépasser
83. - hifirkítàr		dénouer
84. - hiigul		se frayer un passage
85. - ʔìbín		soif
86. - ʔìgaalò		cynocéphale
87. - ʔiiba		avoir honte
88. - ʔìjà		poussière
89. - ʔilgà		passer l'année
90. - ʔilgi	pl. ʔilaag	année
91. - ʔilgità		cette année
92. - ʔinyoolay		buche
93. - ʔístàlà		six
94. - ʔìtaanò		nez
95. - jii-co		parents
96. - jò		épouvantail
97. - jòrgò		ronier
98. - jùnguɗò		clitoris
99. - kàaɗyàw		fièvre
100. - káàkò	pl. káàkè	serpent
101. - kaatù		sortir
102. - kàc		payer graduellement la dot
103. - kàdabdè		mentir
104. - kalman-co		beau-frère
105. - kállù		plonger
106. - kàmgaarè	pl. kamgerre	grand
107. - kàrany		hyène rayée
108. - kárdàlà		bassine

109. - khàlbítkìtàr	malaxer
110. - kì/kìyà	vache
111. - kìɗí	terre
112. - kìʔeb	faucille
113. - kìfikámà	rugueux
114. - kiiri	terrier
115. - kimkime	cauris
116. - kíráanì	crapaud
117. - kìrì	maison
118. - kòllàka	fruit du savonnier
119. - kòllók	savonnier
120. - kombò	hier soir
121. - kùlkùlây	arbre sp.
122. - kùrrí	poule sp.
123. - kúrúk	dix
124. - kusuk	puanteur
125. - láddà	sarcler
126. - leci	fleurir
127. - loog	épouse
128. - lúkùk	ganglion
129. - lútkìtàr	déraciner
130. - màabó	vieux
131. - màaní	gouffre
132. - martak	huit
133. - mùbbáakà	muselière
134. - mùró	gombo vert
135. - múryúk	sept
136. - náakù	monter
137. - náddà	sécher
138. - nágsíkìtàr	diminuer
139. - nàp-co	soeur
140. - nefki	pétiller
141. - nùwáawí	mûrir
142. - réeréwà	léger
143. - ròmbóoyè	puisette
144. - sáaŋà	tranchant
145. - sàarí	guide

146. - sàfiifitè	crinière
147. - sèegírì	long
148. - séyyà	moribond
149. - síitòm	voix, gorge
150. - sìrráarà	lutter
151. - sìrrì	deux
152. - sìyyà	boire
153. - soob	trois
154. - súugù	venir, arriver
155. - súunúwà	rêver
156. - súutì	tamarinier
157. - súksúgò	rat
158. - sùráarà	lutte
159. - súrrò	escargot
160. - tàbán	mettre en jachère
161. - tàcí	frapper, éteindre
162. - tàɗíkà	couper
163. - tàgíldì	fermer
164. - tàkíkìtàr	tisser, renvoyer
165. - tàngàará	lézard
166. - tássàny	bataille
167. - tímdà	disconvenir, opposer
168. - tíssàaséiny	se battre
169. - tíwí	mouche
170. - tìyà	manger
171. - túlwàagì	champignon polypore
172. - tùujùŋ	millet
173. - ʔúumì	voir
174. - ʔùlóolò	salé
175. - ʔúrdè	grenier
176. - ʔùwéenì	préparer les bagages
177. - wáagàr	chèvre
178. - wàagírì	bouc
179. - wàalà	semence, graine
180. - wáalí	l'an dernier
181. - wàayó	criquet
182. - wál kàrá	l'an prochain

183. - wèenà	ouvert
184. - wìráarì	aboyer
185. - yín	vouloir

Bibliographie

Beauvilain, A., 1993. *Tableau de la population du Tchad des années 20 à 1993*. Centre National d'Appui à la Recherche (CNAR), N'Djamena.

Doornbos, P. & Bender, L., 1983. "Languages of Wadai-Darfur" in *Nilo-Saharan Language Studies*. Markus, H.G. and Hudson, G. (eds.). African Studies Center, Michigan State University, Ann Arbor.

Jungraithmayr, H., 1981. "Inventaire des langues tchadiques" in *Les Langues dans le monde ancien et moderne*. Ouvrage publié sous la direction de Jean Perrot, CNRS, Paris.

Westermann, D. & M.A. Bryan, 1952. *The Languages of West Africa*, Handbook of African Languages, Part II. Oxford University Press, London, New York, Toronto.

GENITIVE CONSTRUCTIONS IN SOUTH BAUCHI (WEST CHADIC) LANGUAGES, ZUL AND POLCHI, WITH COMPARISONS TO ANCIENT EGYPTIAN[1]

Ronald Cosper[2]
and
Garba Mohammed Gital[3]

Abstract

A distinctive construction found in many Chadic languages (and others—e.g., Ancient Egyptian) is the direct genitive, i.e., the juxtaposition of two nouns without a genitival particle. These Chadic languages make use of both the direct genitive and the linked genitive constructions. It has been suggested in the literature that these constructions differ semantically, according to the alienability of possession. Our research shows that in these South Bauchi languages, as well as Egyptian, the direct and marked genitives do occur, but the relevant semantic distinctions are not primarily focussed on alienability. Semantic distinctions coded by these types of genitive constructions include location, possession, specificity of referent, animal/human/material, and degree of lexicalization. It appears that we cannot make the generalization that alienability is the key semantic distinction coded into genitival constructions.

Introduction

The universality of grammatical constructions and associated semantic distinctions has been the subject of much research and discussion. It has been proposed that a widespread semantic distinction in north-

---

[1] An earlier version of this paper was presented at the 30th Annual Conference on African Linguistics (ACAL), University of Illinois at Urbana-Champaign, U.S.A., July 5, 1999.

[2] Saint Mary's University, Halifax, Canada and Bayero University Kano, Nigeria.

[3] Bauchi State Polytechnic, Bauchi, Nigeria.

ern Africa is that between alienable and inalienable possession. Schuh (1981) illustrates this contrast with an example from Kanakuru (Newman, 1974):

(1)

a. ɓil kimne "the buffalo's horn" (inalienable)
   horn buffalo

b. ɓil -i ma lowo -i "the boy's horn" (alienable)
   horn the of boy the

Inalienable possession implies that the *nomen regens* is an inherent and inseparable attribute of the *nomen rectum*, whereas in alienable possession, the *nomen regens* can be merely temporarily associated with the possessor.

Schuh observes that syntactically "the alienable construction requires some sort of overt genitival 'linking' morpheme between N1 and N2, whereas the inalienable construction involves mere juxtaposition of the nouns . . ." He identifies these construction types specifically with Chadic languages, but in a 1989 paper, Claudi and Heine suggest that this pattern is characteristic of many northern African languages, and give examples from Kabiye (Gur) and Acholi (Western Nilotic). Theoretically, Schuh is interested in the development of the genitival linker from demonstratives, while Claudi and Heine show the grammaticalization of the linker from a locative noun and preposition, and discuss the metaphorical shift in semantics from location to possession.

Genitive Constructions in Zul

Zul is a South Bauchi West Chadic language of the Afro-Asiatic family mainly spoken in Zul village near Zaranda Mountain in Nigeria.[4] Like the languages discussed above, Zul has two types of genitive

[4] The languages is also spoken in four Zulawa settlement areas (houses) around Tashan-Durmi, Zaranda, Tintin and Wom villages in Toro Local Government Area of Bauchi State in Nigeria. It is one of the South Bauchi group of languages (i.e., Geji, Polci, Buli, Jimi, etc.), many of which are endangered due to the spread of Hausa and their small numbers of native speakers. Data were collected in Zul village in 1995. Research was funded by the Social Science and Humanities Research Council of Canada.

construction: the Direct Genitive (the juxtaposed nouns) and the Linked Genitive. Two linkers are used in Zul: *gə* for possessive pronouns and *kə* to link nouns.

In the following examples, the genitival linker is required:

(2)
a. pə́rsí kə Binta "Binta's horse"
horse(s) GL Binta

b. yer kə bom --í "dog of the house"
dog(s) GL house Det

c. am kə yaali "right hand"
hand GL right

d. kaptilan kə Bala "Bala's shoes"
shoes GL Bala

e. wod kə bagaala "ram's intestine"
intestine GL ram

In some cases, however, the GL is expressed optionally (examples in 3), while it is obligatorily omitted in the surface structures of the examples in (4):

(3)
a. gul (kə) tlá "cow's bone"
bone (GL) cow

b. kəm (kə) kóorí "hen's ear"
ear (GL) hen

c. bom (kə) jiirí "grass house"
house (GL) grass

d. sírdí (kə) pə́rsí "horse saddle"
saddle (GL) horse

e. tlərti (kə) kíiní "tree root"
root (GL) tree

(4)
a. máal doomí "honey"
water bee

b. mír tlá "butter"
oil cow

c. wátli bagere "tribal mark"
mark face

d. bom lipe "farm house"
house bush

e. kur tlá "leather"
skin cow

f. tat shimí "cooking pot"
pot food

In its genitive constructions, Zul partially confirms Schuh's conclusions about Chadic: both the direct genitive and the linked genitive exist. Semantic distinctions do not appear to follow neatly the typology of alienable/inalienable possession. The examples in (2) of genitivally linked phrases do in some cases appear to be situations of alienable possession: "Binta's horse" and "Bala's shoes" are clearly examples of alienable possession. On the other hand, the phrases meaning "right hand" and "ram's intestine" would normally not convey a sense of alienability.

In the examples of (4), phrases are given in which the presence of the genitival linker would be grammatically unacceptable. In some instances the phrase has undergone partial lexicalization, in which the sense of the head noun is specialized or changed. For example, *máal doomí* "honey" is not really water, and *mír tlá* "butter" is not really oil. The obligatory direct genitive, however, does not so much indicate inalienable possession as it does a special sense of the head noun. Perhaps these phrases could be considered compounds, but there is no consistent phonological marking of such compounds, if they exist. *kur tlá* might be an instance of inalienable possession, since body parts are traditionally assigned to this class in some other languages, but in this case the meaning "leather" again is an example of a specialized or extended meaning of the head noun. In the other phrases using direct genitive, the relationship between the two nouns cannot really be considered one of possession, but rather a relationship of location or purpose.

The examples in (3) were rated as grammatically acceptable by our informants with or without the genitival linker, but the meanings also differ depending on the presence of the genitival linker. That is, *gul kə tla* can refer to a (specific) bone of a (specific) cow, while *gul tla* can refer to any bone of a cow or to cow bone as a substance (to be carved, for example.) Likewise, *tlərti kə kíiní* can denote a specific root and/or tree, while *tlərti kíiní* can refer to tree root as a material, for example. Phrases 3 (c and d) in their direct genitive forms may likewise reflect some degree of lexicalization: *bom jiirí* "grass house", and *sírdí pə̀rsí* "horse saddle". That is, the direct genitive phrases refer to a certain type of house and a certain type of saddle, whereas the phrase using the linker can denote specific objects.

Genitive Constructions in Polci

There are three genitive constructions in Polci: Noun + Noun, Noun + *kə* + Noun, Noun + *ghə* + Noun. The first one is the Direct Genitive, and is similar in form to the construction noted for other Chadic languages. However, the use of this construction is rather different from the presumed inalienable possession. This construction is of the form Head + Modifier, where the modifier is a noun that represents a place where the Head object is found, or a larger whole to which the head object belongs.

(5)

a. ɗiin tlaa — "butter"
fat cow

b. wál pət — "tree leaf"
leaf tree

c. leetə maar — "the raising of goats"
raising goat

d. miir aam — "fingers"
children hand

e. tloo bən — "domestic animal"
animal town

f. rəp mvaaɓə — "workplace"
place work

g. been yaadli — "bird nest"
shelter bird

h. been shugop "shop for smithing"
shelter blacksmithing

i. tlóò kóoro "chicken meat, mushroom"
meat chicken

j. tlóò tláa "beef"
meat cow

Examples in (5) illustrate the range of meaning the direct genitive construction conveys. Phrases a. and b. show instances where the head can be seen as a part of a whole, represented by the modifying noun. Examples (5) e. and f. show how place can be conveyed by this construction. There is sometimes a degree of lexicalization in these phrases as illustrated by (5) a, d, g and i. That is, children are not really fingers, nor is butter really oil. A sense of inalienable possession may be conveyed by (5) a. and d. The direct genitive can be also used to refer to animals, although i. also is an interesting instance of lexicalization.

(6)

a. tler kə pət "root of tree"
root IG tree

b. a bí kə Musa "according to Musa"
at mouth IG Musa

c. pət kə lə́ə̀p "tree of the forest"
tree IG bush

d. bukata -gəm kə bən "our needs in the town"
needs 1PlPos IG village

e. Jaami'a kə Jos "the University of Jos"
university IG Jos

f. mbaaɓə́ kə príntiŋ "the work of printing"
occupation IG printing

g. asəm (kə) pərsə "the horse's foot"
foot IG horse

The examples in (6) show the use of *kə*, the second type of genitive in Polci. This construction could perhaps more properly considered prepositional, with meanings of "in the place of", or "from".

However, because of its range of uses, it will be called the Independent Genitive. *kə* is optionally used with body parts of animals, as in (6) g. *asəm kə pərsə* "the horse's foot". It can be used when the possessor is non-human.

The third type of genitive construction in Polci can be called the Bound Genitive. Its basic form is /-Vghə/, where V is the final vowel of the noun base, or an epenthetic schwa. Alternate phonological representations are: /-ŋə after a nasal consonant, and /-kə/after a voiceless consonant.

(7)

a. rəpci -ghə goŋ — "the king's food"
food BG king

b. tloo -ghə bən — "livestock"
animal BG village

c. gaam -ŋə Audu — "Audu's head"
head BG Audu

d. sirdə -ghə pərsə — "the saddle of the horse"
horse BG horse

e. nyap -kən -ŋə tát — "the hardness of the stone"
hard Nom. BG stone

f. bii -ghə goŋ — "the king's mouth"
mouth BG king

g. mbátl -kə tloo -ghə goŋ — "the heart of the king's animal"
heart BG animal BG king

The examples in (7) illustrate the Bound Genitive of Polci. This form is used for body parts and possession by humans and for certain properties of inanimate things and animals. It cannot be used in the locative way that *kə* can be used: **bən -ŋə Baazali* "the town of Bazali" was rejected as ungrammatical by informants.

Genitive Constructions in Egyptian

Ancient Egyptian, another Afroasiatic language, had more than one type of genitive construction. The direct genitive, as in Chadic, involved the juxtaposition of two nouns, the nomen regens, or head, preceding the nomen rectum. Examples, from Gardiner (1982: 65) are:

(8)

a. imy r pr "overseer of the house, steward"
within mouth house

b. nb im3ḫ "venerable"
possessor veneration

c. z3 ibn "son of Yeben"
son Yeben

d. rḫ ḫrt -ib nb -f "knowing the desire of his lord"
knowing state heart lord 3SgPos

Of these four examples of the direct genitive from Egyptian, only (8) c. "son of Yeben" could be considered to have an inalienable sense. The others pertain to states of mind or location. There were also noun compounds in Egyptian, which differed from the direct genitive in having stress on the first syllable (Loprieno, 1995: 6–7). Gardiner does suggest that the direct genitive is used when the connection between the nouns is "especially close, as in titles, set phrases, etc." It seems that the direct genitives may manifest a degree of lexicalization, as well. Loprieno observes that the direct genitive is an early form, going back to the time of the Old Kingdom.

The so-called indirect genitive makes use of an interposed marker, between the nominal constituents. The linker used was *n* "to, for", often expanded to *ny* "belonging to".

(9)

a. nsw n kmt "the king of Egypt"
king GL Egypt

b. niwt nt nḥḥ "the city of eternity"
city GL eternity

c. '3 -w n sḫty pn "the asses of this peasant"
ass Pl GL peasant this

d. inw nb nfr n sḫt "all good produce of the field"
produce all good GL field

The examples in (9) illustrate the uses of the indirect genitive in Egyptian. (9) c. is clearly possessive and alienable. (9) a. and b. are locative and partially lexicalized. (9) d. is locative perhaps more so than genitive in sense.

Conclusions

The thesis has been put forward by previous writers (Schuh, Nichols, 1992: 116–123) that an important dimension cross-linguistically of genitives is alienability/inalienability. Specifically, it has been argued that direct genitives tend to be inalienable in Chadic and in North Africa, while marked genitives tend to be alienable. Our research on genitives of two South Bauchi languages, Zul and Polci, as well as Ancient Egyptian, does not confirm this hypothesis.

In Zul direct genitives tend to be partially lexicalized or perhaps compounds, whereas the marked genitive has a greater degree of specificity in its referent. Contrary to expectation, Polci has three, rather than two, genitive constructions. The Direct Genitive is used for lexicalization, part-whole relationships, and animals, as well as inalienability. The Independent (marked) Genitive is used for animal body parts, location, purpose and provenance. The Bound Genitive is never locative, but is used for body parts and possession by humans, as well as sometimes for inanimate things and animals. In Egyptian, the Direct Genitive is used for location and titles and can be partially lexicalized. The Indirect (or marked) Genitive is not dissimilar in meaning and can also refer to location and possession, and be partially lexicalized.

Our conclusion is that the Direct Genitive does indeed occur in these languages in contrast to the marked genitive(s). However, the meanings attributed to these genitive constructions do not concur with previous conclusions about the importance of alienability. It would be our suggestion that future research on genitive universals should concentrate on syntax and not on semantics.

In our view constructions develop in language, through ritualization, and they also develop meanings, but the meanings of the constructions vary considerably from language to language.

Bibliography

Claudi, U. and B. Heine 1989 "On the Nominal Morphology of 'Alienability' in Some African Languages." Pp. 3–19 in Paul Newman and Robert D. Botne (editors), *Current Approaches to African Linguistics (Vol. 5)*. Dordrecht, Holland: Foris Publications.

Gardiner, Sir Alan 1982 *Egyptian Grammar. Being an Introduction to the Study of Hieroglyphs.* Oxford: Griffith Institute, Ashmolean Museum.

Newman, P. 1974 *The Kanakuru Language.* West African Language Monographs, 9. Leeds: Institute of Modern English Language Studies.

Nichols, J. 1992 *Linguistic diversity in space and time.* Chicago: University of Chicago Press.

Schuh, R.G. 1981 "Types of Genitive Constructions in Chadic." *Studies in African Linguistics.* December, suppl. 8, pp. 117–121.

A GRAMMATICAL SKETCH OF GOEMAI: WORD CLASSES

Birgit Hellwig
(Max-Planck-Institut für Psycholinguistik, Nijmegen)

1. *Introduction*

Goemai is a Chadic language spoken by an estimated 200.000 speakers in the Great Muri Plains, located between the Jos Plateau and the river Benue of Central Nigeria. It is classified as a member of the Southern Angas-Goemai sub-group of West Chadic A (Hoffmann 1975, Newman 1977a). There is very little linguistic documentation on languages of this Southern group (but cf. Jungraithmayr 1964a). However, grammars have been written on some closely related languages of the Northern group, notably on Angas (Burquest 1973, Foulkes 1915, Jungraithmayr 1964b), Mupun (Frajzyngier 1993) and Mwaghavul (Jungraithmayr 1963a). The information available suggests that languages of both sub-groups are closely related. In addition, it has been noted that the Jos Plateau and its adjacent regions constitute a language area, in which languages of both Chadic and Niger-Congo origin share lexical and structural properties (Gerhardt 1983, Gerhardt and Wolff 1977, Hoffmann 1970, Jungraithmayr 1963b).

On Goemai itself, there is some phonological material available (Kraft 1981, H. Wolff 1959). In addition, several unpublished manuscripts exist: a comparative phonological study (Hoffmann 1975), a grammatical sketch (Sirlinger 1942) and two dictionaries (Sirlinger 1937, 1946). These three latter manuscripts are of historic interest, as they constitute an excellent document of the language as it was spoken around 1930. The present paper attempts to fill a gap in the descriptive literature, presenting a concise grammatical description of Goemai as it is spoken today.[1]

---

[1] I am grateful to Felix Ameka for his helpful comments and suggestions on an earlier version of this paper.

The data was collected over 10 months of fieldwork conducted between 1998 and 2001, funded by the MPI für Psycholinguistik, Nijmegen. My thanks go to the people of Kwande village, Qu'an Pan LGA, and especially to Mr. Louis Longpuan,

It concentrates on the word classes, focussing on the noun phrase and its elements, and on the elements of the verbal clause. Briefly, Goemai has SVO word order (and related features such as prepositions, noun-genitive ordering) and is a serializing language. It does not have any verbal extensions. Number is marked on the verb; it does not have nominal plurals. And TAM categories are expressed periphrastically.

This sketch does not include a discussion of the phonology, as such material is available in the studies mentioned above. Note that for the purposes of the present paper, I adopt a modified version of the practical orthography developed in Sirlinger (1937). This orthography does not mark tone; as a consequence I will only mark tone whenever it is grammatically relevant. The following notation is used:

Consonants:

	labial	alveolar	palatal	velar	glottal
stops					
voiceless aspirated	p	t		k	
voiceless non-aspirated	p’	t’		k’	
voiced	b	d		g	
implosive	d’	d’			
fricatives					
voiceless aspirated	f	s	sh		h
voiceless non-aspirated	f’	s’	sh’		
voiced	v	z	j		
nasals	m	n		ng	
liquids					
lateral		l			
trill		r			
glides	w		y		
Vowels:	i	û (= /ʉ/)	u		
	e	oe (= /ə/)	o		
		a			

without whose invaluable help this grammatical sketch could not have been written. The sketch is based to a large extent on the Kwo dialect. But whenever possible, data was crosschecked with speakers of other dialects (Duut, East Ankwe/Derteng, Dorok). These dialects are very similar and differ mainly on the phonological and the lexical level.

2. *Nominals and the noun phrase*

2.1 *Noun phrase*

Nominals can be identified on the grounds of their ability to occur as the head of a noun phrase. A noun phrase consists of a head that can be accompanied by (quantifying and qualifying) modifiers and by determiners. The order of these constituents is fixed:

Table (1): The structure of the noun phrase

(Modifier)	Head	(Modifier)	(Determiner)
Quantifier Plural		Possessive Numeral Nomz. verb Nomz. clause	Demonstrative Locative anaphor Definite

All constituents above can co-occur in the order depicted, both within (examples 1a to 1c) and across (1d) columns, e.g.:

(1a)	War	**d'u**	**gwen**	*d'a* (. . .).
	remove(pl)	**many**	**PL**	*calabash*
		quantifier	plural	head

'He removed the **many** *calabash***es** (. . .).' [LIIT, 28/12/99][2]

[2] The elements in square brackets refer to the texts and fieldnotes, from which the examples were taken. A backslash in an example represents an intonation break. And the abbreviations used in the interlinear glosses are as follows:

ADVZ	adverbializer	LogB	addressee-logophoric
ANT	anterior	m	masculine
BEN	benefactive	NEG	negation
DEF	definite article	NOMZ	nominalizer
DEM.DIST	distal demonstrative	OBL	obligative
DEM.PROX	proximal demonstrative	ORD	ordinal number
CL	classifier	PAST.REM	remote past
COM	comitative	PAST.CL	close past
COMP	complementizer	PERM	permissive
COND	conditional	PL	plural
CONJ	conjunction	POSS	possessive
EMPH	emphasis	PROGR	progressive
f	feminine	PROH	prohibitive
FOC	focus	PUR	purpose
FUT.CL	close future	RED	reduplication
HAB	habitual	RESULT	resultative
INTERR	interrogative	SG	singular

(1b)	A /	*pe*	**goe-f'yer** / (. . .)	**goe-d'ik**	**G.**
	FOC	*place*	**NOMZ(sg)-become_big(sg)**	**NOMZ-build**	**G.**
		head	nominalized verb	nominalized clause	

'It is a **big** *place* (. . .) **that G. built**.' [MIL_AS]

(1c)	goe	eep	*fridge*	**n-d'e-nnoe**	**hok**
	2Sgm	open	*fridge*	**ADVZ-Cl:exist-DEM.PROX**	**DEF**
			head	demonstrative	definite

'open **the/this existing** *fridge*' [WITCH2]

(1d)	goe	nak	**ndoe**	*haas*	**goe-n-d'ek**	**hok.**
	2Sgm	fetch	**some**	*flour*	**NOMZ-ADVZ-winnow**	**DEF**
			quantifier	head	nominalized clause	definite

'you fetch **some** (**of**) **the** *flour* **that was winnowed**.' [CROP]

The existence of the phrasal unit 'noun phrase' can be shown with respect to clitics, which attach to the final element of a noun phrase (e.g., clitic *hoe* 'exactly' in the example below). In addition, the whole noun phrase can occur in the syntactic direct object slot, i.e. preceding syntactic boundary morphemes such as the morpheme *yi* (cf. 3.1.1), e.g.:

(2a)	d'e	t'ong	mûûr /	
	exist	PROGR	steal	
	oerem	**ji**	**nnoe**-*hoe*	*yi*?
	beans	**Sgm.LogA.Poss**	**LOC.ANAPH-exactly**	*PROGR*

'(He$_1$ said who) is stealing **these his$_1$** very **beans**?' [FUAN]

Note that this criterion excludes quantifying adverbs as constituting part of the noun phrase (as *dip* 'all' in the example below). They can co-occur with a noun phrase, in which case they are in apposition to each other, referring to the same entity. Syntactically, they thus occur in different slots. This criterion, by contrast, includes complex heads, such as the nouns in a genitive construction (as *long lwa* 'chief of animals' in the example below).

IRR	irrealis	SEQ	sequential
LOC	locative	SUB	subordinating particle
LOC.ANAPH	locative anaphor	TH	theme
LogA	speaker-logophoric		

(2b)	Liit	a	toe	**long**	**lwa**	*yi*	**dip**	n-s'et.
	lion	FOC	EMPH	**chief**	**animal**	*SUB*	**all**	LOC-bush
				noun phrase			adverb	

'So it is the lion (who is) the chief of the animals, (of) all in the bush.' [LIIT]

2.2 *Modifiers in the noun phrase*

A noun phrase can include both quantifying and qualifying modifiers. There are distinct subgroups among them, whereby members of one subgroup cannot co-occur.

With the exception of numerals, all quantifiers precede the head noun. One subgroup consists of the quantifiers *ndoe* 'some', *nde* 'one/other', *d'em* 'remainder', *la* (sg)/*jap* (pl) 'little/few', and *d'u* 'many/much'. They occur as modifiers in the first slot of the noun phrase (3a). In addition, they can occur as the lexical head (3b).

(3a)	See	**nde**	**la**	**liit**	gok	muut.
	then	**one/other**	**child(sg)**	**lion**	become_ill	die(sg)

'Then **one child of the lion** became ill (and) died.' [LIIT]

(3b)	To /	**nde**	d'e	d'i	zak.
	okay	**one/other**	exist	LOC.ANAPH	again

'Okay, **(another) one** is there again.' [DIALECT]

Quantifiers thus behave like nouns, and, in fact, the quantifier *la* (sg)/*jap* (pl) 'little/few' has a corresponding noun (cf. *la* 'child (sg)' in example 3a above). They probably originated in genitive constructions (cf. below), but have undergone semantic bleaching in the meantime. Now, they belong to a distinct slot of quantifiers.

Like quantifiers, numerals occur both as modifiers and as heads of noun phrases. The following forms exist:

Table (2): Numerals

	Cardinal numbers	Ordinal numbers
1	*(goe)me*	*goeme*
2	*vel*	*goevel*
3	*k'un*	*goek'un*
4	*fer*	...
5	*paat*	
6	*poemo* (give 1)	
7	*poevel* (give 2)	
8	*poek'un* (give 3)	

Table (2) (*cont.*)

Cardinal numbers		Ordinal numbers
9	*poefar* (give 4)	
10	*s'ar* (< *s'a* 'hand')	
11	*s'ar k'a goeme* (10 plus 1)	
. . .		
20	*ya gurum* ('catch person')	
21	*ya gurum shik'a goeme* (20 plus 1)	
. . .		
30	*ya gurum shik'a s'ar* (20 plus 10)	
40	*ya gurum vel* (20 twice)	
50	*ya gurum vel shik'a s'ar* (20 twice plus 10)	
. . .		

Goemai makes use of a base 20 system,[3] while the numerals below twenty are based on five (from 6 to 9) or ten (from 11 to 19). However, speakers usually resort to Hausa loans for the numerals above twenty.

Finally, Goemai has an associative plural morpheme *gwen* that occurs preceding the head noun (and following the quantifiers), and which refers to one person and all people associated with him/her, e.g.:

(4)	**gwen**	Naan	yok	n-zam
	PL	God	return(pl)	LOC-field

'God **and his people** returned from the farm' [GOELONG]

It is extended to cover objects of the same kind, e.g., several calabashes as in example (1a) above. Note, however, that it cannot be used to refer to entities of different kinds. In fact, Goemai does not have any general and obligatory plural morpheme.[4]

In most cases, a noun phrase is left unmarked for number. There are several loci for marking number, both in the noun phrase and in the clause: quantifiers, associative plural *gwen*, numerals, modifying morphology (cf. 2.5), classifying elements (cf. 2.3), lexical form of some nouns (cf. 2.4) and lexical form of some verbs (cf. 3.1.2). But none of them triggers the use of the plural morpheme *gwen*. Note

[3] A vigesimal system is not very common, either in Chadic or on the Plateau; it is more common in Jukun and the old Kororofa empire of which Goemai was a part (Gerhardt 1987, Ibriszimow 1988).

[4] This is strikingly different from many Chadic languages, which have an elaborate system of nominal plural marking (e.g., Frajzyngier 1977, Newman 1990). It is more common on the Plateau, where languages have developed one general plural morpheme that occurs (obligatorily) within the noun phrase (Gerhardt and Wolff 1977).

also that this is in line with a general phenomenon in the language: number tends to be marked only once. Compare the following two examples:

(5a)	Takarda	**goe**-n-d'e-nnoe-hoe.	
	paper	**NOMZ(sg)**-ADVZ-Cl:exist-DEM.PROX-exactly	

'This very existing paper.' [COLOR_AS/LL_15]

(5b)	**la**	takarda	n-d'e-nnoe-hoe.
	little(sg)	paper	ADVZ-Cl:exist-DEM.PROX-exactly

'this very existing small paper.' [COLOR_AS/LL_16]

The demonstrative form can optionally contain the prefixes *goe-* (sg) and *moe-* (pl) (cf. 2.3). Their presence coincides with the absence of number marking elsewhere in the noun phrase or the clause: it is thus present in example (5a), but absent in (5b), where number is already marked in the quantifier *la* 'little (sg)'. Number marking in the noun phrase is thus not an agreement phenomenon, but actually adds semantic information.

A set of qualifying modifiers occurs following the head noun. These are first the set of possessive modifiers. Today, these are free forms, but there are some indications that Goemai originally made use of possessive suffixes bound to the head noun. Remnants of this older pattern are found in the lexemes 'body' and 'self/own'. All three forms are given in the table below.

Table (3): Possessive modifiers

	Possessive	'Body'	'Self/own'
1Sg	*noe*	*san*	*mmaan*
2Sgm	*goe*	*sak*	*mmak*
2Sgf	*yoe*	*shik*	*mmik* ~ *mmit*
3Sg	*muk*	*sek* (*muk*)	*mmuk*
1Pl	*men*	*sem*	*mmen*
2Pl	*gwen*	*suk*	*mmuk* (< **mnuk*)
3Pl	*mûep*	**shak*	(*mmûep*)
Sgm.LogA	*ji*	*sûûn*	*mmûûn*
Sgf.LogA	*doe*	*sat*	*mmat*
Pl.LogA	*d'wen*	*sut*	(*mmûep*)
Sgm.LogB	*gwa*	(*sek gwa*)	(*mmak*)
Sgf.LogB	*pa*	(*sek pa*)	(*mmik* ~ *mmit*)
Pl.LogB	*nwa*	(*sek nwa*)	(*mmûep*)

The lexemes for 'body' and 'own/self' apparently go back to the proto forms *s- and *m- respectively, accompanied by old possessive suffixes. These are formally similar to (possessive) pronouns found in other Chadic languages (Blažek 1995, Dolgopolsky 1988, Kraft 1974). Today, however, they are only found in these two lexemes, both of which are mainly used in grammatical contexts: 'body' as the reflexive pronoun, and 'self/own' as the independent possessive pronoun. In the latter case, the prefix *m-* probably goes back to an adverbializing prefix *N-* (cf. 4.1).

The present-day possessive modifiers immediately follow the head noun. And the order noun-possessor mirrors that of genitive constructions, where two nouns are juxtaposed without any formal markings, e.g.:[5]

(6a)	mûaan	**lu**	**muk**	
	go(sg)	**house**	**3Sg.Poss**	

'he went to **his house**' [ABST_SM]

(6b)	mûaan	**lu**	**la**	hok.
	go(sg)	**house**	**child(sg)**	DEF

'he went to the/a **house of the child**.' [LA]

Note that genitive constructions constitute a complex head of a single noun phrase. There is some independence of the two nouns in that they can occur with separate quantifiers and associative plural morphemes. However, all other modifiers and all determiners can occur only once, modifying the possessor.

Goemai does not have a form class of adjectives. However, it has a nominalizing mechanism by which it turns property verbs into modifiers. These derived forms are used both as modifiers and as heads (cf. 2.5).

In addition, a separate mechanism exists that nominalizes clauses and thereby allows them to occur within the noun phrase. Either, only a nominalizing prefix *goe* 'NOMZ' is added, in which case the original clause structure is preserved and all arguments are expressed (7a). Or the adverbializing prefix *N-* 'ADVZ' is added, in which case the direct object is not expressed and a passive-like reading develops (7b) (cf. 3.1.3).

[5] Only few Chadic languages seem to form the genitive through juxtaposition of nouns (Schuh 1990).

(7a)	Shim	**goe-d'an**	**muk**	hok.
	yam	**NOMZ-boil**	**3Sg.Poss**	DEF

'The yam **that she boiled**.' (lit. 'of her boiling')[6] [LIGYA, LL, 12/10/00]

(7b)	Fûan	lap	shim	**goe-n-d'an.**
	rabbit	receive	yam	**NOMZ-ADVZ-boil**

'The rabbit received the yam **that was boiled**.' (lit. 'of being in a boiled condition') [LIGYA]

Such nominalized clauses follow all modifiers and precede all determiners, e.g. the determiner *hok* 'definite' in the example below (cf. also example 1d above). As such, they function in a way similar to complement clauses, which provide another means of 'relativizing' a clause. However, the latter follow all noun phrase elements (as the clause introduced by the complementizer *goepe* in the example below). In fact, they occur in the syntactic adjunct position, following the boundary morphemes (cf. 3.1.1).

(7c)	p'en	bi (. . .)	**goe-t'o**	**d'i**	hok /
	remove(sg)	thing	**NOMZ-lie(sg)**	**LOC.ANAPH**	DEF

goepe	*ni*	*nyet*	*nd'ûûn*	*boega.*
COMP	*3Sg*	*leave*	*INSIDE*	*well*

'he removed the thing (. . .) **that lay there**, *which he had left in the well.*' [MOESHAR]

It is not possible to have two nominalized clauses co-occurring in a noun phrase. But it is possible to have a nominalized clause followed by a complement clause as in the above example.

2.3 *Determiners in the noun phrase*

A bare noun phrase can be interpreted as being either definite or indefinite, but definiteness can be marked explicitly. Goemai has three sets of determiners dedicated to this purpose: the demonstratives, the locative anaphor and the definite article.

[6] Note that if the head noun does not correspond to the subject of the nominalized clause, this subject follows the verb in possessive form, e.g., *muk* '3Sg.Poss'. In this case, it refers to the subject ('her boiling') and not to the head noun (*'her yam').

The Goemai demonstrative modifiers are complex forms, containing an optional nominalizing prefix, an adverbializing prefix, a classifier, and a deictic root.

Table (4): The demonstrative forms

Nominalizer	Adverbializer	Classifier	Deictic root
goe- (sg) *moe-* (pl)	*n-*	*d'e-* 'exist' *lang-* (sg), *leng-* (pl) 'hang/move' *t'ong-* (sg), *t'wot-* (pl) 'sit' *d'yem-* (sg), *d'yam-* (pl) 'stand' *t'o-* (sg), *t'oerep-* (pl) 'lie'	*nnoe* 'proximal' *nang* 'distal'

Demonstratives can be used both as modifiers and as heads of noun phrases. In the latter case, the nominalizing prefix is obligatory.

(8a) **Hoos** (**goe-**) **n-d'e-nnoe** la.
tooth (**NOMZ(sg)-**) **ADVZ-Cl:exist-DEM.PROX** hurt(sg)

'**This existing tooth** hurts.' [DQ_LL/SM_1]

(8b) **Goe-n-d'e-nnoe** la.
NOMZ(sg)-ADVZ-Cl:exist-DEM.PROX hurt(sg)

'**This existing one** hurts.' [DQ_LL_1]

The demonstratives are used exclusively in the spatial domain, referring to physically present and identifiable objects. Moreover, they are only used to draw attention onto a referent. Once attention has been established, reference to its location makes use of the locative anaphor *nnoe* (cf. Hellwig, in prep. a), e.g.:

(9) K'epmang ndoe **goe-n-d'e-nang**-hoe.
different CONJ **NOMZ(sg)-ADVZ-Cl:exist-DEM.DIST**-exactly

Tep nkyat ndoe **goe-nnoe** ba.
become_black equal CONJ **NOMZ(sg)-LOC.ANAPH** NEG

'It is different **from that existing one**. It is not as black as **that one**.' [COLOR_AS_8]

Finally, the definite article *hok* explicitly marks a referent as being identifiable from previous discourse. When referents are mentioned for the first time in discourse, they are marked by either a bare noun phrase or by a quantifier (*ndoe* 'some', *nde* 'one/other') (in the non-spatial domain), or a demonstrative form (in the spatial domain). Subsequent reference then makes use of the definite article.

(10)	Sai	**ndoe kaam**	t'a	nd'ûûn (. . .)	lu	k'us	mûep.
	then	**some festival**	fall(sg)	INSIDE	house	near	3Pl.Poss

'Then **some festival** came close to their town.

(. . .) mûep	goe	mûen	goe	pe	**kaam**	**hok**.
(. . .) 3Pl	OBL	go(pl)	SPACE	place	**festival**	**DEF**

(. . .) they should go to the place of **the festival**.

(. . .) mûep	yin	d'u	wul	a	**kaam**	**hok**.
(. . .) 3Pl	SAY	Pl.LogA	arrive	FOC	**festival**	**DEF**

'(. . .) they$_1$ said that they$_1$ had arrived for **the festival**' [LIGYA]

The three sets of determiners thus have clearly different functions, which explains their co-occurrence possibilities. This phenomenon is cross-linguistically rare as languages tend to unite different functions such as exophoric use, anaphor and previous mention within a single morpheme or within a single form class (Diessel 1999, Lyons 1977). Similar patterns, however, are attested in the closely related language Mupun (Frajzyngier 1993).

2.4 *Nominal subclasses*

Nominals function as heads of noun phrases. This comprises the subclasses of numerals (cf. 2.2), quantifiers (cf. 2.2), pronouns and common nouns. Nouns and pronouns differ from numerals and quantifiers in that they cannot occur as modifiers. There is no formal category that would be marked directly on the noun: nouns do not differentiate number, gender, or noun class. However, there are remnants of old non-productive number and class marking morphology.

First of all, the following five nouns are marked for number in that they have suppletive singular/plural forms:

singular	*plural*	*gloss*
k'a	*k'ek*	'head'
la	*jap*	'child, little'
mat	*sh'arap*	'woman, female'
mis	*daas*	'man, male'
reep	*zarap*	'girl'

Note that two of the plural forms, *sh'arap* 'women' and *zarap* 'girls', contain a -VrV- sequence. This is a common formative for deriving verbal plurals (cf. 3.1.2), both in Goemai and in Plateau languages in general (Gerhardt and Wolff 1977). In addition, Goemai has a large number of nouns that formally exhibit this sequence, and that semantically refer to collectives, e.g.:

***guru**m*	'person/people'	***ara**ng*	'ashes'
*shy**ara**p*	'fish'	***oere**m*	'beans'

It is very likely that these are remnants of an older productive pattern of plural formation.

In addition, a process is taking place whereby the overt number marking associated with derived nouns (cf. 2.5) is gradually extended to non-derived nouns. In the example below, a form *gurum* 'person' is marked with the 'nominalizing' plural morpheme *moe-*, which does not have any derivational function here: the unmarked form is already a noun, and could occur in the same slot as the marked form.

(11)	**moe-gurum**	muk /	mûep	mûarap	dip.
	NOMZ(pl)-person	3Sg.Poss	3Pl	die(pl)	all

'his **people,** they have all died.' [WITCH2]

It is conceivable that such a process may eventually develop into the overt morphological marking of number on the noun.

Nouns are generally neutral with respect to gender. The only exceptions are the following kinship terms:

mat 'woman, wife, female'	*mis* 'man, husband, male'
reep 'girl, daughter'	*yam* 'son'
nûûn 'mother'	*nda* 'father'

With all other nouns referring to humans, gender can be differentiated through adding the modifiers 'male' or 'female', which are derived from the nouns for 'man' and 'woman' respectively, e.g.:

(12) Mûep yong jap **moe-daas**.
3Pl call children(pl) **NOMZ(pl)-men(pl)**

'They call the **male** children.' [LU_LL]

Unlike in many Chadic languages, gender is not marked in the 3rd person pronoun (cf. below). Pronominal reference thus does not differentiate gender either. However, gender is marked in the 2nd person pronoun.

Finally, nouns referring to small animals, birds, and kinship relations often contain an initial prenasalized consonant, e.g.:

nf'et 'mosquito' *ngum* 'insects'
nkya 'vulture' *ndeng* 'bird species'
nda 'father' *nsh'ik* 'grandson'

This seems to be an areal feature in Plateau languages, which can be traced back to an old Niger-Congo noun class prefix (Frajzyngier and Koops 1989).

Pronouns are treated like nouns in that they can head a noun phrase and can occur with all modifiers, e.g.:

(13) (...) de goe mûaan goe p'en **ni** **nnoe**.
(...) PUR go(sg) SEQ remove(sg) **3Sg** **LOC.ANAPH**

'(He wanted) to go and remove **this/it**.' [LIIT]

They occur in all syntactic slots where a noun can occur: as independent pronouns (in a non-verbal clause, following a preposition), as subjects and as direct objects. The following pronominal categories are distinguished:

Table (5): The pronouns

	Independent/object	Subject
1Sg	*hen*	*hen* ~ *n*
2Sgm	*goe*	=
2Sgf	*yoe* ~ *yi*	=
3Sg	*ni*	=
1Pl	*men*	*moe*
2Pl	*gwen*	*gu*
3Pl	*mûep*	=
Sgm.LogA	*ji*	=

Table (5) (*cont.*)

	Independent/object	Subject
Sgf.LogA	*doe*	*doe*
Pl.LogA	*d'wen*	*d'u*
Sgm.LogB	*gwa*	=
Sgf.LogB	*pa*	=
Pl.LogB	*nwa*	=

As can be seen from the table above, the forms are nearly always identical across syntactic contexts. And although there are tonal differences, these are not restricted to the pronouns but are a property of the syntactic slot.

Some specific features of the pronoun system are of general interest. First, Goemai distinguishes gender in the 2nd person singular only. This differs from other Chadic languages, where gender tends to be differentiated in both the 2nd and the 3rd person singular (Blažek 1995, Dolgopolsky 1988, Kraft 1974). And cross-linguistically, languages that have a gender distinction in the 2nd person, generally also have it in the 3rd person (Claudi 1985).

Secondly, Goemai has two sets of logophoric pronouns. One set specifies co-reference with the speaker (set A), the other with the addressee (set B).[7]

(14)

Yin /	to / (. . .)	**ji**	goe	ndoe	ûen
SAY	okay	**Sgm.LogA**	COM	some	medicine

goepe	t'ong	**ji**	poe	*pa*	ba.
COMP	IRR	**Sgm.LogA**	give	*Sgf.LogB*	NEG

'(**He**$_1$ said to *her*$_2$) that, okay, (. . .), **he**$_1$ does not have any medicine that **he**$_1$ could give *her*$_2$.' [MATWO]

The logophoric pronouns are used in clauses introduced by speech act verbs and/or the complementizer *yin* 'SAY'. Their use reflects not only elements of indirect speech, but also of direct speech (such as interjections and the use of absolute tenses that were true at the

[7] The terminology 'set A' (co-reference with speaker) and 'set B' (co-reference with addressee) is borrowed from Frajzyngier (1993). Similar logophoric systems are found in some other Chadic languages, including the closely related languages Mupun and Mwaghavul. See Frajzyngier (1985a, 1985b, 1993) for details.

time of the direct speech, but not at the time of the reported speech). In addition, the gender distinction in the logophoric pronouns of set A mirrors that of the 2nd person pronouns, but not the 3rd person pronouns.

The main function of the logophorics is reference tracking, and as such they can occur outside the speech act context to indicate co-reference with the subject. This use is restricted to possessive forms, though. Compare the following example, where the possessive uses the logophoric form, whereas the direct object uses the non-logophoric form.

(15) goe-k'oon n-k'a **ji** /
NOMZ-face_down(sg) LOC-head(sg) **Sgm.LogA.Poss**

t'ong goe wakaam goepe liit t'ong t'an *ni.*
sit(sg) SPACE road COMP lion IRR pursue *3Sg*

'after covering **his$_1$** head, (he$_1$) sat on the road where the lion$_2$ would pursue *him$_1$*.' [LIIT]

Thirdly, the pronouns can be divided into two sets depending on their position relative to the verbs in a serial construction:

Set 1	**Set 2**
1Sg	2Sg
3Sg	1Pl
3Pl	2Pl
LogB	LogA
Nouns	

In all serial constructions, pronouns of set 1 precede the first verb (16a), while those of set 2 follow the first and all subsequent verbs, except for the last (16b). The latter can additionally precede the first verb to focus on the pronoun. In this case, it appears either in its independent or in its subject form (16c).

(16a) **Mûep** *buk* *d'yam* t'ong pil sek mûep yi.
3Pl *return(pl)* *stand(pl)* PROGR watch body 3Pl.Poss PROGR

'They returned (and) stood watching each other.' [STAGE_AS_46]

(16b) *Buk* **gu** *t'wot* **gu** *shin* bi goe-d'emen n-ni.
return(pl) **2Pl** *sit(pl)* **2Pl** *do* thing NOMZ(sg)-good COM-3Sg

'You return (and) you sit (and) you do something good with it.' [YOUTH]

(16c) Goemai / **gu** *buk* **gu** *t'wot* / gu rang nye yi.
Goemai **2Pl** *return(pl)* **2Pl** *sit(pl)* 2Pl think word SUB

'Goemai, you return (and) you sit, so that you think (about) it.' [YOUTH]

It is possible that pronouns of set 1 are, in fact, nominal forms. In terms of their syntactic position, they behave like nouns. And there is some evidence that the logophoric B pronouns derive from nouns (cf. Frajzyngier 1993: 118 for an analysis of the cognate forms in Mupun).

Nouns, pronouns, numerals and quantifiers are the only elements that occur as non-derived nominals. In addition, the demonstratives and the nominalized verbs can occur both as modifiers and as head nouns. However, both contain nominalizing morphology, and thus have to be analyzed as derived forms (cf. 2.5).

2.5 *Derived nominals*

Goemai has a mechanism that nominalizes property verbs. The approximately 50 property verbs are a distinct sub-class of state-change verbs that encode the inchoative concept of entering a state. They form a semantically coherent group that encodes adjectival concepts such as dimension (*f'yer* 'become big'), physical property (*shyoon* 'become heavy'), color (*b'ang* 'become red') and age (*gya* 'become old') (following the semantic types laid out in Dixon 1982), e.g.:

(17a) Hangoed'e d'e t'ong **b'ang** yi.
water exist PROGR **become_red** PROGR

'The water is **getting red**.' [DPP_LL_83] (said while water was in the process of turning red)

(17b) Mûep **nan** t'ei ba.
3Pl **become_big(pl)** already NEG

Mûep la **nan** (. . .) / dang hok **b'ang**.
3Pl COND **become_big(pl)** tail DEF **become_red**

'They (= fish species) have not yet **grown big**. When/After they have **grown big** (. . .), the tails will have **become red**.' [DIALECT]

Formally, property verbs are the only state-change verbs that can be nominalized through the addition of the prefixes *goe-* (sg) and *moe-* (pl), e.g.:

(18)	goepe	**moe-b'ang**	rwo	goe	yil	Duut/
	COMP	**NOMZ(pl)-become_red**	enter(pl)	SPACE	country	Duut

goe-b'ang	nnoe	na	ndoe	mat
NOMZ(sg)-become_red	LOC.ANAPH	see	some	woman(sg)

'when the **red ones** (= Europeans) entered the country of Duut, this **red one** saw some woman' [SHENDAMW]

The nominalized forms function like simple nouns, i.e., they can occur in all syntactic positions for nouns and they can co-occur with all modifiers. In addition, they convey a stative reading: the inchoative property verbs cannot be used in reference to a state, whereas their nominalized counterparts can.

The same morphology is used to derive agent nouns from activity verbs (19a), and pronouns from determiners (19b).

(19a)	A	gya	**moe-shyang**	toe.
	FOC	song/dance	**NOMZ(pl)-hunt**	EMPH

'It is the dance of the **hunters**.' [HAND_AS/LL] (from the verb *shyang* 'hunt')

(19b)	**Goe-nnoe**	rang.
	NOMZ(sg)-LOC.ANAPH	become_mad

'**This one** has become mad.' [SHAAR]

The two prefixes do not have only a nominalizing function, they also have a modifying function. In which case the nominalized property verb occurs within the noun phrase, following the head noun (20a).[8] They agree in number with the head, and this agreement feature justifies analyzing them as modifiers. They cannot be analyzed as nouns in a genitive construction, because the two nouns refer to

[8] It is likely that the nominalized uses preceded the attributive uses as the same prefixes are used to derive nominals from determiners (i.e., modifiers in Goemai). Such processes are attested cross-linguistically for, e.g., demonstratives, where demonstrative pronouns being in apposition with a noun become re-interpreted as demonstrative modifiers (Diessel 1999).

Furthermore, although Goemai has a mechanism for deriving adjective-like attributive forms from verbs, this cannot be taken as evidence for the existence of a form class of adjectives. Following Dixon (1982), I assume that any adjective class has to have a core of non-derived forms, which is not the case in Goemai. But cf. Lyons (1977) who argues against such a position. I rather assume that Goemai has a specific modifying construction, within which various elements (verbs, nouns, modifiers) can occur, thereby receiving a qualifying reading. Cf. below for further explanations.

different entities in the world, and thus do not show any agreement (20b).

(20a)

la	**goe-f'yer** /	t'ong	goe	zem
child(sg)	**NOMZ(sg)-become_big(sg)**	IRR	OBL	like

de-goe	n-bi	wakaam	Naan	ba.
PUR	PUR-follow	road	God	NEG

'the **grown** (sg) *child* (sg), (he) would not want to follow the ways of God.' [PEOPLE]

(20b)

Goelong	t'ong	tang	shyep	wa	n-ni
Goelong	IRR	seek	wood	return(sg)	COM-3Sg

doe	poe	**sh'arap**	**Naan**.
come	give	**women(pl)**	**God**

'Goelong would look for wood (and) return with it (and) give it here to the **wives** (pl) **of God** (sg).' [GOELONG]

These two prefixes also derive modifiers from nouns, provided they are semantically compatible with fulfilling a qualifying function, e.g. descriptive color terms, which are based on nouns (21a). In addition, all determiners and numerals can be optionally marked with the two prefixes whenever they occur in modifying positions (21b).

(21a)

lu	**moe-haam-haas-ke**
house	**NOMZ(pl)-water/color-egg-chicken**

'**yellow** houses' [TL_99]

(21b)

Gurum	**moe-k'un**	n-d'e-nnoe-hoe
person	**NOMZ(pl)-three**	ADVZ-Cl:exist-DEM.PROX-exactly

'These existing **three** people' [CLOTH_LL]

Recall that determiners and numerals do not need derivational morphology in order to occur within the noun phrase (cf. 2.2 and 2.3). In the last example, the prefixes therefore do not have a derivative function. It rather seems that Goemai is in the process of developing a unique modifying construction, in which the modifying function is overtly marked. However, this is a recent phenomenon: the manuscripts of Sirlinger (1937, 1942, 1946) do not contain any evidence of such a construction. In present-day Goemai, both the marked and unmarked forms are used, and speakers differ as to whether they consider the marked forms to be grammatical.

The distribution between the marked and the unmarked forms within the noun phrase correlates partly with another function of the nominalizing morphology: the marking of number. In the case of determiners, the presence of number marking elsewhere correlates with the absence of the nominalizing prefix (cf. examples 5a/b above). Cf. also example (11) above, where the 'nominalizing' prefix is used to overtly mark number in a noun. It is possible that these prefixes will eventually turn into agreement markers that obligatorily occur in every modifier within the noun phrase and mark (a) its modifying function and (b) its number.

In addition to the nominalizing prefixes *goe-* (sg) and *moe-* (pl), there are some other ways of deriving nominals from verbs. First, some verbs occur with cognate objects. These act like nouns and can take on all modifiers. However, they can only occur in direct object position, following their respective verbs (cf. example 24b below). And secondly, a prefix *nye-* 'word/kind' derives abstract nouns from mental verbs, e.g.:

Verb	**Nominalized verb**
rang 'think'	*nye-rang* 'thought'
tal 'ask'	*nye-tal* 'question'
k'a 'doubt'	*nye-k'a* 'doubt'

3 *Verbs and verbal clauses*

Verbs are identified by their ability to occur as predicates of verbal clauses. As such they follow pronominals of the subject pronoun set (cf. table 5 above), and they occur with specific TAM morphemes whose occurrence is restricted to verbal clauses (cf. 3.2).

The structure of a simple verbal clause maintains SVO word order. The position of a subject pronoun relative to a TAM morpheme depends on (a) the set the pronoun belongs to (cf. 2.4), and (b) whether or not the TAM morpheme grammaticalized from a verb or a preposition (cf. 3.2). Note that there are no bound pronouns nor are there any TAM inflections; these categories are all encoded in free forms. Generally, verbs do not carry any inflectional or derivational morphology. However, a subgroup of verbs mark number on the verb stem (cf. 3.1).

3.1 *Transitivity*

In Goemai, core arguments of a verb can be omitted under certain conditions. And since these are not cross-referenced on the verb, determining the basic valence of a verb is far from trivial. However, there are a number of criteria that help to determine it. The evidence comes from the syntactic position of noun phrases (cf. 3.1.1), from number marking on the verb (cf. 3.1.2), and from nominalization (cf. 3.1.3).

3.1.1 *Syntactic position*

A syntactic criterion helps to determine whether the element following a verb is a direct object or an adjunct. Certain boundary morphemes, such as the morpheme *yi*, only allow direct objects to precede them (22a), while adjuncts follow (22b and 22c).

(22a)	Kan	goe-bi	t'ong	b'em	**yil**	*yi*.
	incline	like	IRR	touch	**ground**	*SUB*

'It is inclined as if it would touch the ground.' [DIS_NK/SM_15.4]

(22b)	de	hen	sam	*yi*	**n-yil**.
	COMP	1Sg	descend	*SUB*	**LOC-ground**

'so that I descend onto the ground.' [ANIMAL1]

(22c)	de	yi	ru	*yi*	**lu**	**men**.
	COMP	2Sgf	enter(sg)	*SUB*	**house**	**1Pl.Poss**

'so that you enter our house/home.' [LU_SM]

This criterion is especially relevant in the case of unmarked adjuncts. Since there is no formal marking to indicate their syntactic status (neither on the verb nor on the adjunct), they could be mistaken for direct objects, and the verb could be mistaken for a transitive verb. In the last example above, the phrase *lu men* 'our house' could equally well be a direct object following a transitive verb *ru* 'enter'. However, its syntactic position shows its adjunct status (comparable to 'home' in English), thus allowing for the possibility that *ru* 'enter' is an intransitive verb.

3.1.2 *Number marking*

A subset of verbs have different singular and plural forms. The following formatives are attested:

Formative	**Example**
suppletion	*f'yer* > *nan* 'become big'
-a-, *-^{w}a-*, *-^{y}a-*	*f'yer* > *f'yar* 'become big/important'
-ara-, *-ar*	*tap* > *tarap* 'snap'
-aba-	*k'oon* > *k'aban* 'face down'
-a-ap (*t* > *r*)	*muut* > *mûarap* 'die'
-e-	*mûaan* > *mûen* 'go'
-oere-p, *-oere-*	*gep* > *goerep* 'cut'
-oe-eng	*d'al* > *d'oeleng* 'swallow'
-wo	*ru* > *r(u)wo* 'enter'
-t	*twam* > *twat* 'cause standing'

Many other Chadic languages mark number overtly on the verb stem; and some of the morphology employed in Goemai, especially the infix *a*, is very likely to be of Chadic origin (Frajzyngier 1977, Newman 1990). Other formatives, e.g. the *-r-* infix, or the *-ng* suffix, are common in both Chadic and Niger-Congo languages spoken on the Jos Plateau. These can be traced back to Niger-Congo verbal extensions (Gerhardt and Wolff 1977). The form a plural stem would take is not predictable on the basis of its phonological form. And, in fact, the largest group are the suppletive forms.

Around 10% of the collected verb lexicon is marked for number. And although number marking is to be found in almost every semantic domain, it occurs predominantly with verbs of posture, motion, caused motion, and destruction. While it is totally absent with verbs of cognition, perception, speaking, and consumption.

Number marking correlates with the basic valence of the verb. An intransitive verb agrees with the subject (23a), and a transitive verb with the direct object (23b). This pattern holds even when the direct object is not overtly expressed (23c).

(23a)

Kafin	*ni*	**muut**	dai (. . .).
before	*3Sg*	**die(sg)**	indeed

Jap	*muk* (. . .)	d'e	t'ong	**mûarap**	yi.
children(pl)	*3Pl.Poss*	exist	PROGR	**die(pl)**	PROGR

'Before he died (. . .). His children are dying.' [TIME_LL]

(23b)

Ima (. . .)	**tu**	*goeme.* (. . .)	Ni	**two**	*mûep*	dip.
Ima	**kill(sg)**	*one*	3Sg	**kill(pl)**	*3Pl*	all

'Ima (. . .) killed one. (. . .) He killed them, all (of them).' [WITCH2]

(23c)	Mûep	**two**	t'ong	**tar**	**kwan**.
	3Pl	**kill(pl)**	IRR	**tear(pl)**	**throw_away(pl)**

'They killed (them), (and) would tear (them) apart (and) throw (them) away.' [LIIT]

This is a very typical pattern in Chadic languages, for which Newman (1990) coined the term 'pluractionals'. Different from other Chadic languages, though, number marking is not used for encoding a plural action (e.g., iterative, frequentative).

3.1.3 *Nominalization*

While number agreement reliably distinguishes between transitive and intransitive verbs, this criterion can only be applied to those verbs that mark number. It is not available for the vast majority of verbs, though. This is especially problematic since the direct object can be omitted.[9] The general condition for any omission is that the argument is recoverable from context and that the verb action is emphasized (24a). Note that semantic recoverability is not enough to warrant the omission of an argument. E.g., in the case of unspecified direct objects or generic actions, the object has to occur in the form of a cognate object (24b).

(24a)	Ya	**ndûûsnaan** /	ya	at	de	goe	tu	yi.
	catch(sg)	**insect**	catch(sg)	bite(sg)	COMP	OBL	kill(sg)	SUB

'He caught the **insect**, caught (**it**) (and) bit (**it**) so that he would kill (**it**).' [ANIMAL5]

(24b)	Mûep	d'e	t'ong	*s'oe*	**s'oe**	yi.
	3Pl	exist	PROGR	*eat*	**eating**	PROGR

'They are *eating* **food**.' [FUAN2]

[9] Some subject arguments can be omitted, too. Generally, the 3rd singular subject pronoun *ni* is omitted if it is recoverable from context. If it is realized, it invites the pragmatic implicature of non-co-reference with an accessible antecedent (an implicature that could be cancelled, though).

(i) Liit	mûaan	de	**ni**	goe	tal	ni	yi.
lion	go(sg)	COMP	**3Sg**	OBL	greet	3Sg	SUB

'The lion went so that **he** (preferred interpretation: not the lion) should greet him.' (LL, 15/2/00)

The 3rd plural subject pronoun *mûep* can optionally be omitted if the subject slot is already filled by a noun.

While a direct object can thus be omitted in a verbal clause, it cannot be omitted if this clause is nominalized (25a). There, it has to occur either as the head noun, whereby the subject is then encoded as a possessive modifier (25b), or as the direct object within the nominalized clause (25c).

(25a)	* mat	goe-tu
	woman(sg)	NOMZ-kill(sg)

* 'the woman who killed/was killed' [LL, 16/2/00]

(25b)	mat	goe-tu	**muk**
	woman(sg)	NOMZ-kill(sg)	**3Sg.Poss**

'the woman whom he killed' [LL, 16/2/00]

(25c)	mat	goe-tu	**ni**
	woman(sg)	NOMZ-kill(sg)	**3Sg**

'the woman who killed him' [LL, 16/2/00]

It is only possible to omit the direct object of a nominalized transitive clause under the condition that the verb is adverbialized first (cf. 4.1), e.g.:

(26)	Twen	hok	a	**goe-n-fum**.
	cloth	DEF	FOC	**NOMZ-ADVZ-fold**

'The cloth is a folded (one).' [DIS_AS/LL_13.3]

Intransitive verbs could not occur in the above example. Nominalization thus helps to determine the basic valence of a verb: the direct object of transitive verbs obligatorily occurs in the nominalized form—unless adverbialization has taken place first.

Applying these criteria (syntactic position, number marking, nominalization), all verbs can be divided into one of three classes: intransitive verbs, transitive verbs, and labile verbs.[10] The latter occur both in transitive and in intransitive constructions, whereby the less active participant fills the subject slot of the intransitive (27a) and the direct object slot of the transitive construction (27b). The number agree-

[10] Many of the labile verbs in Goemai correspond to verbs that undergo the causative alternation in English. These are often assumed to be basically intransitive verbs, describing an internally controlled action, which under certain circumstances can be externally controlled (cf. e.g. Levin 1993). In the case of Goemai, however, I do not have any language-internal evidence that would suggest that labile verbs are either basically transitive or basically intransitive.

ment is always with the less active participant, and clausal nominalization shows both the transitive and the intransitive pattern.

(27a)	D'a	goe-leng	n-s'a	gurum	(...)	**p'yaram**.
	calabash	NOMZ-hang/move(pl)	LOC-hand	person		**break(pl)**

'The calabashes that hung/were in the hand of the person (...) **broke**.' [STAGE_AS_65]

(27b)	Goelong	t'ong	**p'yaram**	wang	(...)	dip.
	Goelong	IRR	**break(pl)**	pot		all

'Goelong would **break** the pots (...), all (of them).' [GOELONG]

Subdivisions among these three transitivity classes are possible on the basis of their participation in constructional alternations. Their discussion goes beyond the scope of this sketch grammar, but cf. Hellwig (in prep. a) for further details.

3.1.4 *Adding and removing arguments*

Goemai has no derivational morphology available that would increase or decrease the number of arguments in a clause. Many Chadic languages, by contrast, use verbal extensions for this purpose (Frajzyngier 1985c, Newman 1977b).[11] This phenomenon is probably responsible for the large number of suppletive intransitive and transitive verb stems, which bear no morphological relationship to each other, e.g.:

Intransitive	*Transitive*
t'ong (sg), *t'wot* (pl) 'sit'	*d'u* (sg), *d'war* (pl) 'cause sitting'
paap (sg), *pap* (pl) 'hide'	*s'ok* (sg), *s'wak* (pl) 'hide'
yool (sg), *yûûl* (pl) 'rise'	*eep* (sg), *aap* (pl) 'raise'
muut (sg), *mûarap* (pl) 'die'	*tu* (sg), *two* (pl) 'kill'
fyal 'boil'	*d'an* 'boil'

There are, however, syntactic possibilities for increasing the number of arguments in a clause: an applicative construction adds an applied object, and a ditransitive construction adds a second object. Both

[11] Goemai shows only remnants of a morpheme *n-*, which might have been used to form transitive caused motion verbs from intransitive motion verbs:

intransitive	transitive
ru (sg), *rwo* (pl) 'enter'	*ruun* (sg), *rwan* (pl) 'insert'
p'et (sg), *p'ûat* (pl) 'exit'	*p'en* (sg), *p'ûan* (pl) 'remove'

constructions add a core argument, which has the syntactic status of a direct object. As such, it occurs preceding boundary morpheme such as *yi* (cf. 3.1.1). Example (28a) below illustrates the applicative construction, and example (28b) the ditransitive construction.

(28a) de hen *f'yer* **ni** yi.
COMP 1Sg *become_big(sg)* **3Sg** SUB

'so that I have grown big **in relation to him**.' (i.e., I am bigger than he is) [LL, 14/11/00, YOUTH]

(28b) S'oot (. . .) d'e t'ong *poe* **men** **wala** yi.
witchcraft exist PROGR *give* **1Pl** **trouble** PROGR

'Witchcraft (. . .) is giving **us trouble**.' [WITCH1]

There is no derivational morphology that would overtly mark the applicative or the ditransitive on the verb. It is the construction alone that licenses the addition of an applied direct object or of a second object.[12] Note that the basic valence of the verb does not change when it occurs in one of these constructions. This point can be illustrated with respect to number agreement and nominalization. Verbs that enter the applicative construction are intransitive—and number marking on the verb agrees with the subject as in example (28c) below (compare this to the number marking of transitive verbs such as in example 23b above). And verbs that enter the ditransitive construction are transitive—in cases of nominalization, only the beneficiary is obligatory, but not necessarily the theme (28d).

(28c) **Hen** *f'yer* mûep toe.
1Sg *become_big(sg)* 3Pl EMPH

'**I** have grown big in relation to them.' [YOUTH]

(28d) t'ong d'u kat gurum goe-*poe* **d'wen/*shita**.
IRR Pl.LogA find person NOMZ-*give* **Pl.LogA/*pepper**

'(They$_1$ said) they$_1$ would find a person who gives **to them$_1$** (beneficiary)/***pepper** (theme).' [LL, 14/11/00, LIGYA]

In the cases above, the syntactic criterion thus conflicts with the number marking and the nominalization pattern: the added argu-

[12] I follow the construction grammar approach laid out, among others, in Goldberg (1995). It assumes that, under specific conditions, constructions can map their argument structure and semantic properties onto elements that enter them.

ment has the syntactic status of a direct object, but the verbs remain basically intransitive and transitive respectively. This conflict only arises through a derivational process, in which a construction (applicative, ditransitive) adds an additional syntactic core argument, but which does not change the valence of the verb.

There are other possibilities to express additional participants: serialization and prepositions. However, these do not add syntactic arguments. Goemai is a serializing language, and this mechanism can be employed to introduce a recipient, which is expressed as the object of the verb *poe* 'give' (29a). By contrast, the benefactive argument is marked by the preposition *N-* (29b).

(29a)	Ni	s'eet	shim	**poe**	hen.
	3Sg	trade(sg)	yam	**give**	1Sg

'He bought yam for me.' (and gave it to me) [LL, 17/2/00]

(29b)	Ni	s'eet	shim	**n**-hen.
	3Sg	trade(sg)	yam	**BEN**-1Sg

'He bought yam for me.' (for my benefit, e.g., because I asked him to) [LL, 17/2/00]

This type of serialization differs from other types found in the language in that the verbs form a tighter unit. This can be shown with respect to negation, where the negation morpheme negates the whole event. In addition, the verb *poe* 'give' and the recipient-morpheme *poe* can co-occur, which points to them having different functions. Moreover, *poe* can mark the 'recipient', i.e., the addressee, of speech act verbs. There is thus evidence for semantic bleaching and some grammaticalization of this construction.

Prepositions not only mark the benefactive, but also several other roles. These go back to the two locative prepositions, *goe* 'SPACE' and *N-* 'LOC' (cf. Hellwig, in prep. b). They have comitative and instrumental uses, whereby *N-* introduces a pronoun, and *goe-* a noun or an animate companion, e.g.:

(30)	reep	nnoe (. . .)	ba	**goe**	s'a	muk /
	girl(sg)	LOC.ANAPH	return(sg)	**COM**	hand	3Sg.Poss
	het	yit	noe	**n**-ni.		
	hit	face	1Sg.Poss	**COM**-3Sg		

'this girl (. . .) moved **with** her hand, (and) hit my face **with** it.' [WITCH1]

The benefactive preposition (cf. example 29b above) does not show the same alternation between *N*- and *goe*, but invariably assumes the form *N*-, suggesting a different grammaticalization path. The same alternation is found again in the marking of the theme role, though. A sub-set of transitive verbs (e.g., *s'eet* 'trade', *shye* 'teach/learn' or *nin* 'point/show') can either encode the theme role as a direct object or the benefactive role as an applied direct object. In the first case, the verb action is interpreted as being directed towards the theme (with the interpretation 'buy', 'learn', or 'point'), and in the second case, as towards the beneficiary ('sell', 'teach', or 'show'). In the later case, the theme role is encoded with the prepositions *goe* (plus noun) or *N*- (plus pronoun), e.g.:

(31)	Ni	s'eet	men	**goe**	*shim*	*hok.*
	3Sg	trade(sg)	1Pl**TH**	*yam*	*DEF*	

'He sold us the yam.' (lit. 'he traded in relation to us with the yam') [LL, 15/12/99]

Finally, an associative reading is conveyed with the help of the conjunction *ndoe* 'and', which occurs in the same slot as the prepositions. It differs semantically from the comitative preposition, though, in that the participant is more involved in the action, taking an active part in it, e.g.:

(32)	K'ur	yool	**ndoe**	mûep.
	tortoise	rise(sg)	**CONJ**	3Pl

'The tortoise rose together with them.' [KUR]

The same morpheme is used with the verb *k'wal* 'talk' to introduce the addressee of the speech act. In fact, the addressee can occur in the syntactic direct object position, conveying the sense of 'tell/ instruct s.o.' (33a). In the sense of 'talk to s.o.' it occurs in the adjunct position (33b).

(33a)	A	bi	mmoe	weel	nwa	toe	poenoe?
	FOC	thing	what	disturb	Pl.LogB	EMPH	thus
	Nwa	k'wal	k'wal	**ndoe**	**ni**	*yi.*	
	Pl.LogB	talk	talking	**CONJ**	**3Sg**	*SUB*	

'What is it that worries them like this? They should tell him.' [LIIT]

(33b) Mûep d'e t'ong k'wal k'wal *yi* **ndoe sh'ak**.
3Pl exist PROGR talk talking *PROGR* **CONJ each_other**

'They are talking to each other.' [STAGE_AS_22]

This conjunction thus seems to be on its way to grammaticalize into a verbal extension, assigning syntactic direct object status to the element following it.

Goemai does not have corresponding mechanisms dedicated to decreasing the number of arguments. Recall, however, that nominalization and adverbialization convey a passive-like reading to transitive verbs (cf. 3.1.3, 4.1). In addition, there is an impersonal passive construction, which transitive verbs can enter:

(34a) Mûep leng yim sek t'eng.
3Pl hang/move(pl) leaf BODY tree

'They hung the leaves on the tree/The leaves were hung on the tree.' [TRPS_VL_41]

This construction is formally identical to a transitive construction containing the 3rd person plural pronoun *mûep*. Semantically, the clause is interpreted as agentless (e.g., in the example above, it is unlikely that the speaker had an agent in mind who put the leaves onto the tree). This has a formal correlate in that an impersonal construction cannot contain logophoric marking. Recall that logophoric possessive pronouns are used to indicate co-reference with an antecedent (cf. 2.4). An impersonal passive construction can only contain the non-logophoric form, suggesting that the pronoun *mûep* is interpreted as an impersonal pronoun.

(34b) **Mûep** leng le n-k'ek **mûep/*d'wen**
3Pl hang/move(pl) load LOC-heads(pl) **3Pl.Poss/*Pl.LogA.Poss**

'**They$_1$** hung the loads on **their$_2$/*their$_1$** heads.' [LL, 17/2/00]

3.2 *Tense, aspect, modality*

In the domain of tense, aspect and modality (TAM), Goemai differs considerably from other Chadic languages, both formally and semantically (cf., e.g., Jungraithmayr 1979, Newman 1977c, Schuh 1976, E. Wolff 1979). Formally, the categories are not marked through either ablaut, suffixes or tonal changes on the verb, nor through specific TAM pronouns, but rather through free particles and periphrastic constructions whose diachronic origin is still transparent. Semantically, Goemai does not exhibit the perfective/imperfective dichotomy that is said to be typical for Chadic languages. However, there are some semantic and formal similarities with the closely related language Mupun (Frajzyngier 1993).

The following table gives an overview of the TAM forms, their semantics and their diachronic origin.

Table (6): The TAM morphemes of Goemai

Form	Semantics	Diachronic origin
unmarked verb	aorist	–
dok, d'yen, d'in, d'a	absolute tenses	?first verb in a serial construction
t'ong	irrealis, future	first verb in a serial construction
locative verb + *t'ong . . . yi*	progressive	locative verb and subordinate clause marked for irrealis
la . . . t'ong	habitual	conditional clause plus irrealis morpheme
goe, N-	irrealis, future	locative prepositions
. . . kam, . . . lat	resultative, anterior	second verb in a serial construction

Those TAM particles that derive from verbs in a serial construction retain some of their verb properties. In serial constructions, pronouns of set 2 follow the first verb, while those of set 1 precede it (cf. examples 16a to 16c above). And the same behavior is found with respect to such TAM particles: pronouns of set 1 precede them (35a), while those of set 2 follow them (35b). Similarly, the resultative and the anterior particles are treated as the second verb in a serial construction. Pronouns of set 2 thus appear between the main verb and the TAM particle (35c). TAM particles that originated in prepositions, by contrast, do not show this behavior: pronouns of both sets precede the particle (35d).

(35a)	**Hen**	*t'ong*	kut	ndoe	kut.
	1Pl	*IRR*	speak	some	speech

'I will say something.' (lit. 'speak some speech') [FUANUU]

(35b)	*T'ong*	**moe**	kut	a	mmoe?
	IRR	**1Pl**	speak	FOC	what

'What will we speak (about)?' [GOESEM]

(35c)	Goepe	wa	**yi**	*kam* (. . .).
	COMP	return(sg)	**2Sgf**	*RESULT*

'After you came back (. . .).' [TIME_SM]

(35d)	**moe**	*goe*	rwo	n-s'et.
	1Pl	*OBL*	enter(pl)	LOC-bush

'we should enter into the bush.' [SPEAKING]

Even though the TAM morphemes retain some of their original verbal or prepositional properties, they also show formal differences. For example, the 'prepositional' particles follow a subject pronoun—the occurrence of which is restricted to the slot preceding verbs and TAM particles. And the deverbal particles do not behave like verbs when they occur in a nominalized clause. When serial verb constructions are nominalized, only the first verb precedes the clausal subject, while all others follow (36a). In the case of the TAM particles, however, both the particle and the verb precede the subject (36b).

(36a)	Goe-**su**	*muk*	**wa** /	sai (. . .).
	NOMZ-**run(sg)**	*3Sg.Poss*	**return(sg)**	then

'After he had run back home, then (. . .).' [WITCH1]

(36b)	La	hok	man	bi	goe-**t'ong**	**shin**	*muk*	ba.
	child(sg)	DEF	known	thing	NOMZ-**IRR**	**do**	*3Sg.Poss*	NEG

'The boy did not know what he should do.' [FROG_LL]

Finally, the absolute tenses and the habitual can occur both in verbal and in verbless clauses, suggesting that they are a property of the clause, and not of the verb phrase. However, for the sake of presentation, all TAM morphemes are discussed in the present section.

3.2.1 *The unmarked verb: aorist*

Goemai has a verb form unmarked for TAM (aorist), in which the unmarked verb stem directly follows the subject pronoun. It is used in cases of tense neutralization, i.e., it is the default choice once temporal reference is established, e.g.:

(37a)

Fûan	**dok**	**shin**	bi	goe-dam	t'yak	noe (. . .).
rabbit	**PAST.REM**	**do**	thing	NOMZ-spoil	heart	1Sg.Poss

'The rabbit did something that made me angry (. . .).

Moe	**tang**	ni	yi	de-goe	doe	tu.
1Pl	**seek**	3Sg	SUB	PUR	come	kill(sg)

So we looked for him to kill (him) here.

See	**mang**	s'a	muk	**nin**	n-yit	noe.
then	**take**	hand	3Sg.Poss	**show/point**	LOC-face	1Sg.Poss

Then he took/raised his hand (and) pointed (it) at my face.' [LIIT]

During narratives, this form is thus generally used to tell the main story-line. Other TAM morphemes are introduced when the temporal sequence is interrupted (37b), or in quoted speech (37c).

(37b)

Mûep	**t'wot**	shin	nye-d'ûe	nnoe, (. . .).
3Pl	**sit(pl)**	do	word-voice	LOC.ANAPH

'They sat having this discussion, (. . .).

Mûep	**yûûl**	**p'ûat**	de-goe	mûen.
3Pl	**rise(pl)**	**exit(pl)**	PUR	go(pl)

They rose (and) went out to go.

Fûan	**d'in**	**t'ong**	d'i	goe-t'oor (. . .).
rabbit	**PAST.CL**	**sit(sg)**	LOC.ANAPH	SPACE-flank

The rabbit had sat there at the side (. . .).' [LIIT]

(37c)

Liit	**ter**	**d'yem**	goe-t'oor.
lion	**branch_off**	**stand(sg)**	SPACE-flank

'The lion branched off (and) stood at the side.

See	bi	hok	**tal**	kûût.
then	thing	DEF	**greet**	just

Then the thing just greeted him.

Yin	gwa	**t'ong**	**mûaan**	a	nnang-hoe	a?
SAY	Sgm.LogB	**IRR**	**go(sg)**	FOC	where-exactly	INTERR

Saying, where exactly would you go to?' [LIIT]

Finally, the aorist is used to convey a generic reading, which may substitute for the habitual, especially when talking about personal habits, e.g.:

(37d)	Hen	**yool**	yitsaam	m-pûûs	poemo	m-b'itlung.
	1Sg	**rise(sg)**	sleep	LOC-sun/time	six	LOC-morning

'I always rise from sleep at six in the morning.' [TQ_LL_71]

There is some controversy as to whether forms unmarked for TAM have a semantic content of their own, or whether they derive a default meaning from being in pragmatic opposition to other TAM markers in the system (e.g., Bybee 1994, cf. also Levinson 2000 for a pragmatic framework to handle such default meanings). In Goemai, there are indications that the unmarked form can replace all other TAM morphemes under certain conditions, which would argue in favor of an analysis in terms of pragmatic implicatures.

One alternative option would be that the unmarked aorist encodes the perfective, while the forms marked in one way or other with *t'ong* encode the imperfective. Semantically, this would be possible as *t'ong*-marked forms encode notions such as irrealis, progressive or habitual. However, in Goemai, the unmarked form is used in both typically perfective and typically imperfective contexts.[13]

Another possibility would be an interpretation in terms of tense. A verb in the aorist form usually receives a default non-future interpretation (past or present), while the future tense would be marked with the particle *t'ong*. However, *t'ong* actually marks a modality, not a tense (cf. 3.2.4). Moreover, the default non-future interpretation of the aorist can be cancelled, and the unmarked verb can refer to a future event, e.g.:

(38a)	*Goed'aar*	toe	moe	**mûen**	n-Jos.
	tomorrow	EMPH	1Pl	**go(pl)**	LOC-Jos

'It is *tomorrow* that we **go** to Jos.' [FRIENDS]

It is cross-linguistically common that unmarked forms receive a default past/present tense interpretations, whereby the interpretation tends to correlate with the aspectual class of the verb (Bybee 1994, Comrie 1985, Dahl 1985): in Goemai, stative verbs receive a default 'present tense' and non-stative (including inchoative) verbs a default 'past tense' interpretation.

[13] This was established with the help of the Tense/Aspect questionnaire developed by Dahl (1985). It attempts to control for cross-linguistic variation found in the encoding of different tense/aspect categories. In Goemai, no correlation emerged between the unmarked aorist and either the perfective or the imperfective category.

Finally, the third option would be to interpret the system as having a basic realis (unmarked aorist) vs. irrealis (*t'ong*) distinction. However, the unmarked aorist does not necessarily convey a realis reading, as it is used in future contexts (38a), or in the expression of epistemic modality (38b).

(38b)	Hen	rang	goepe	mûep	**poe**	n-daas	ba.
	1Sg	think	COMP	3Pl	**give**	BEN-men(pl)	NEG

'I think that they do not give (it) to the elders.' [HAND_AS/LL]

All interpretations of the aorist (perfective, non-future, realis) are default interpretations. They arise because of the existence of other TAM particles that semantically encode aspectual and modal categories. The unmarked form then pragmatically picks up the interpretations not encoded in these particles. They are not part of its meaning, though, and can thus be cancelled.

3.2.2 *Tense*

Goemai has four absolute tenses, three past tenses and one future tense: *dok* (remote past), *d'yen* (yesterday), *d'in* (earlier today) and *d'a* (tomorrow). These locate an event in time, usually with respect to the time of speech, i.e. the present moment is taken as the point of reference. They are only rarely used as relative tenses, i.e. relative to some other reference point that is established by the context. This behavior is cross-linguistically quite common (Comrie 1985, Dahl 1985).

Formally, these particles occur preceding the verb, e.g.:

(39a)	Mûep	**dok**	*maar*	maar	nt'it	ba.
	3Pl	**PAST.REM**	*farm*	farming	thoroughly	NEG

'They did not farm properly in the past.' [TARIHI]

(39b)	B'it	la	**d'a**	*lin* / (. . .).
	day	COND	**FUT.CL**	*dawn*

'When the day dawns tomorrow, (. . .).' [PEOPLE]

In addition, they behave like the first verb in a serial construction, i.e. pronouns of set 2 follow these particles.

The tenses can combine with modal and aspectual particles, whereby the past tenses can occur with the progressive and the habitual, and all four tenses can occur with the irrealis. In the latter case they assume different syntactic positions: the past tense markers occur before the irrealis morpheme *t'ong* (40a), and the future tense follows it (40b).

(40a)	**Dok**	*t'ong*	goe	ru	taxi	dakd'ûe	lu (. . .).
	PAST.REM	*IRR*	2Sgm	enter(sg)	taxi	MIDDLE	town/house

'In the past you would enter a taxi into town (. . .).' [JOS]

(40b)	*t'ong*	**d'a**	moe	rwo.
	IRR	**FUT.CL**	1Pl	enter(pl)

'we would enter/arrive tomorrow.' [ARAM]

This different distribution may either reflect principles of iconicity (Haiman 1985), or it may reflect different grammaticalization patterns. The diachronic origin of the tenses is not transparent, though. Three of them have corresponding temporal adverbs: *dokndok* (day before yesterday), *d'yend'yen* ~ *nd'yen* (yesterday) and *goed'aar* ~ *toed'aar* (tomorrow). These are clearly formally related. Cross-linguistically it is well attested that absolute tenses grammaticalize from temporal adverbs (Dahl 1985, cf. also Frajzyngier 1993 for a related analysis for Mupun). In Goemai, however, the temporal adverbs are clearly derived forms, whereby at least some of the derivational morphology is still a productive means in the language to derive adverbs from nouns and verbs (partial reduplication, prefix *N*-, prefix *goe*-). In addition, the tense morphemes occur in the syntactic slot that is reserved for verbs in a serial construction, not for adverbs. This makes it unlikely that these particles derive from adverbs. For the time being, I would thus rather assume a verbal origin.[14]

The grammatical category tense is periphrastically expressed. And it is not obligatory. In a narration, the tense particles usually occur only once to anchor an event in time, and all subsequent reference to that event is done by the unmarked aorist (cf. example 37a above). In addition, tenses usually do not occur when the corresponding temporal adverbs are used to introduce the temporal setting.

[14] Another option would, of course, be that the temporal adverbs derive from the tenses. Such an analysis is conceivable, although it would not be compatible with the principle of unidirectional change in grammaticalization theory (e.g., Heine, Claudi and Hünnemeyer 1991). However, I do not adopt this analysis because of the syntactic position of these morphemes, and because of the adverbialization morphology found in the corresponding adverbs.

3.2.3 *Aspect*

There are four aspectual categories encoded in Goemai: the progressive, the habitual, the resultative and the anterior.

The progressive is a periphrastic construction, which contains an obligatory locative verb and the morphemes *t'ong* and *yi*. Pronouns of set 1 precede the locative verb (41a), while pronouns of set 2 follow the particle *t'ong* (41b)

(41a)	*Mûep*	**t'wot**	**t'ong**	shin	shit	**yi**	b'ak.
	3Pl	**sit(pl)**	**PROGR**	do	work	**PROGR**	here

'They sit doing work here.' [MIL_LL]

(41b)	**D'e**	**t'ong**	*moe*	shin	shit	**yi**	n-ni.
	exist	**PROGR**	*1Pl*	do	work	**PROGR**	COM-3Sg

'We are doing work with it.' [HAND_SM]

The locative verb is taken from a minor form class that contains five verbs, all of which are used to locate objects with respect to another reference object. The same set also occurs as classifiers in the demonstrative word (cf. table 4 above). Cross-linguistically, such verbs are often grammaticalized to become deictic classifiers (Aikhenvald 2000) or progressive morphemes (Kuteva 1999) (cf. Hellwig, in prep. a, submitted). In the progressive, the locative verb has the status of a full verb, not of a TAM particle. This can be shown with respect to their behavior under nominalization (cf. examples 36a and 36b above): when the progressive is nominalized, only the locative verb occurs preceding the clausal subject, e.g.:

(41c)	goe	man	bi	goe-**d'e**	*noe*	**t'ong**	shin	**yi**
	2Sgm	know	thing	NOMZ-**exist**	*1Sg.Poss*	**PROGR**	do	**PROGR**

'you know the thing that I am doing' [ARAM]

The locative verbs encode the position of the agent while he is performing an action. The other two morphemes, *t'ong* and *yi*, go back to the irrealis morpheme *t'ong* (cf. 3.2.4) and to the morpheme *yi*, which marks any subordinate irrealis clause, e.g.:

(42)	*de*	ni	*goe*	shin	ûen	**yi**	n-doe.
	COMP	3Sg	*OBL*	do	medicine	**SUB**	BEN-Sgf.LogA

'so that he should do magic for her.' [MATWO]

This makes it likely that the progressive grammaticalized from a main locative verb plus a subordinate irrealis clause.

Semantically, it refers to an action that is viewed as on-going at reference time. In addition, stative verbs can occur in the progressive construction, in which case they receive a habitual interpretation.

Like the progressive, the habitual is a periphrastic construction, which contains the morphemes *la* ~ *d'a* and *t'ong*. Again, pronouns of set 1 precede the morpheme *la* (43a), while those of set 2 follow (43b).

(43a)	*Mûep*	**la**	yil	goe-nnoe	**t'ong**
	3Pl	**HAB**	write	NOMZ(sg)-LOC.ANAPH	**HAB**

'They used to decorate this one' [HAND_AS/LL]

(43b)	**La**	*moe*	yong	ni	**t'ong**
	HAB	*1Pl*	call	3Sg	**HAB**

'We used to say it' [TARIHI]

The habitual is used in reference to any event that is characteristic for an extended period of time (taking place habitually or repeatedly). Formally, it was grammaticalized from a conditional clause. The first element *la* ~ *d'a* is identical with the conditional morpheme (in form and in syntactic position), and the second with the irrealis morpheme *t'ong*. Both usually occur in a conditional clause, e.g.:

(43c)	Neen	**la**	tu	ni /	**t'ong**	at	goe.
	hunger	**COND**	kill(sg)	3Sg	**IRR**	bite(sg)	2Sgm

'When(ever) it becomes hungry, it would bite you.' [ANIMAL1]

In the development from the conditional to the habitual, a reanalysis of the clause boundaries must have taken place, so that *la* and *t'ong* occur now within the same clause.

Finally, Goemai has two phasal verbs, *lat* 'anterior' and *kam* 'resultative', which originated in the intransitive verbs *lat* 'finish' and *kam* 'stay' respectively.

Lat 'anterior' is used to describe an event prior and relevant to the situation at reference time. It thus very often occurs in complex sentences during narratives, conveying a temporal order:

(44)	La	*fi*	**lat**, (. . .)	goe	wus	nd'ûûn	sher.
	COND	*become_dry(sg)*	**ANT**	2Sgm	roast	INSIDE	pot

'After it has become dry (= finished to become dry), (. . .) roast it nside a pot.' [CROPS]

The anterior morpheme occurs with any verb (including stative verbs), indicating that the event has ended. *Kam* 'resultative', by contrast, is more restricted in its occurrence. Generally, it occurs with verbs of motion and caused motion, but it is marginally acceptable with any verb that can be construed as involving an element of (metaphorical) motion, i.e. with inchoative verbs ('getting into a state'). With caused motion and with inchoative verbs, it focuses on a state existing as the result of an action, e.g.:

(45a) *Ruun* gong muk **kam** n-t'uun.
insert(sg) nose 3Sg.Poss **RESULT** LOC-hole

'He inserted his nose into a hole.' (i.e., the nose still is in the hole) [FROG_LL, 11/2/00]

(45b) Neng hok *f'u* **kam** b'e.
cow DEF *become_scattered* **RESULT** EMPH

'The cows have scattered.' (i.e., they are scattered now) [LL, 11/2/00]

In the case of goal-encoding motion verbs, two interpretations are possible. When the goal is overtly encoded, *kam* 'resultative' stresses that the goal has been reached (46a), when it is not encoded, it stresses that the motion itself continues (46b). With manner of motion verbs, only the latter reading is possible (46c).

(46a) P'aar *t'a* **kam** n-hangoed'e.
jump *fall(sg)* **RESULT** LOC-water

'He jumped (and) fell in the water.' (i.e., the falling event is over) [FROG_LL, 11/2/00]

(46b) T'eng *t'a* **kam**! T'eng *t'a* **kam**!
tree *fall(sg)* **RESULT** tree *fall(sg)* **RESULT**

'The tree is falling! The tree is falling!' (i.e., the falling event is taking place now) [LL, 11/2/00]

(46c) Ball *b'iring* **kam** nd'ûûn goegyat.
ball *roll* **RESULT** INSIDE net

'The ball is rolling in the net.' (i.e., the rolling event is taking place now) [LL, 11/2/00]

In addition to these four categories, younger speakers increasingly use Hausa words to convey aspectual notions. The following are attested in my database: *tab'a* 'have previously done', *k'ara* 'repeat an action', *riga(ya)* 'have already done', *rik'a* 'keep on doing', and *gama* 'stop doing'. Formally, these are used like the first verb in a serial construction, e.g.:

(47)	**k'ara**	ji	tang	pe	goe-d'e	fûan	zak-yit	mou.
	repeat	Sgm.LogA	seek	place	NOMZ-exist	rabbit	again	NEG

'(He$_1$ said) he$_1$ would never again look for the place where the rabbit is.' [LIIT]

Their text frequency is very low, and older speakers reject these as foreign words and hardly use them. For the time being, these cannot be considered as integrated loans into Goemai, rather they are used when bilinguals mix or switch codes.

3.2.4 *Modality*

Goemai has three morphemes, *t'ong*, *goe*, and *N-*, which are used to express both irrealis (modality) and future (tense). Cross-linguistically, these two categories show much overlap: they are either encoded in the same form, or the irrealis marker is in the same formal system as the past/present tense. In addition, grammaticalization chains are attested from the irrealis modality to the future tense (Bybee, Perkins and Pagliuca 1994, Comrie 1985, Dahl 1985, Palmer 1986). This overlap is not surprising because, as Dahl puts it, "[n]ormally, when we talk about the future, we are either talking about someone's plans, intentions or obligations, or we are making a prediction or extrapolation from the present state of the world." (Dahl 1985: 103).

The particle *t'ong* 'future' derives from the verb *t'ong* 'sit (sg)'. It is obligatorily present in reference to both the intention-based (48a) and the prediction-based future (48b).

(48a)	Goe-vel /	hen	**t'ong**	poe	a	n-la	noe
	ORD-two	1Sg	**IRR**	give	FOC	BEN-child(sg)	1Sg.Poss

'The second one, I will give (it) to my child' [GOESHANW]

(48b)	La (...)	goe	p'et	nkwa	**t'ong**	goe	muut.
	COND	2Sgm	exit(sg)	away	**IRR**	2Sgm	die

'If (...) you go away, you will die.' [GWAKTAK]

Following Comrie (1985), it thus has properties of a future tense category: it is near-obligatory (but cf. example 38a above and the discussion surrounding it), and it occurs in prediction-based contexts. However, in addition to its uses in the future context, it is also used in the irrealis context. This includes the encoding of epistemic modality (49a), of intention (49b), and of counterfactual (49c).

(49a)	**T'ong**	d'e	n-Jos	nd'as'oenoe.
	IRR	exist	LOC-Jos	now

'(I think) he should be in Jos now.' [LL, 16/2/00]

(49b)	**t'ong**	d'u	k'wal	a	k'a	goepe (. . .).
	IRR	Pl.LogA	talk	FOC	HEAD	COMP

'(They$_1$ said) they$_1$ should talk about (the fact) that (. . .).' [LIIT]

(49c)	D'in	la	goe	zem	d'ûe	noe,
	PAST.CL	COND	2Sgm	like	voice	1Sg.Poss
	d'in	**t'ong**	goe	bi	fûan	ba.
	PAST.CL	**IRR**	2Sgm	follow	rabbit	NEG

'If you had listened to my voice, you would not have followed the rabbit.' [LIIT]

The particle *t'ong* thus encodes basically a modality, and only secondarily a future tense: the morpheme can occur in non-future contexts, future can be expressed with the help of the unmarked aorist, and *t'ong* is not part of the same formal system of oppositions as the absolute tenses (with which it can co-occur). In labeling it a modality category, I follow Comrie's methodological caution, when he says that in order to establish whether a language has a category of future tense, one has to ascertain first that its use "cannot be treated as a special use of a grammatical category with basically non-tense meaning." (Comrie 1985:46).

A similar argumentation holds for the two other morphemes, *goe* 'obligative' and *N-* 'permissive'. The form *goe* derives from the locative preposition *goe* 'SPACE' (cf. 4.2). It encodes both the obligative (50a) and the definite future, focussing on the fact that an event will definitely take place (50b). In the latter case, it usually combines with *t'ong* 'irrealis'.

(50a)	pa	**goe**	nyap	hura.
	Sgf.LogB	**OBL**	prepare	gruel

'(He$_1$ said) she$_2$ should prepare gruel.' [REEP]

(50b)	Hen	t'ong	**goe**	yil	longvilip.
	1Sg	IRR	**OBL**	write	letter

'I definitely plan to write a letter.' [TQ_LL_22]

The form *N-* derives from the locative preposition *N-* 'LOC' (cf. 4.2). It encodes the permissive (51a) and the immediate future (51b). In the latter case, it usually combines with *t'ong* 'irrealis'.

(51a)	Hen	**m**-mang.
	1Sg	**PERM**-take

'Let me take it.' [TL_99]

(51b)	Mûep	t'ong	**n**-yûûl.
	3Pl	IRR	**PERM**-rise(pl)

'They are about to rise.' [LL, 29/12/00]

Note that both *goe* and *N-* fill a syntactic slot that is different from that of the future tense *d'a* (cf. 3.2.2): pronouns of set 2 follow the tense, but they precede the two modalities. Note also that none of them can be assigned to an objective time measure. They are not part of Goemai's tense system.

4 *Minor word classes*

4.1 *Adverbs*

Adverbs generally follow the verb phrase they modify. They are defined as a form class by their syntactic position following boundary morphemes such as progressive *yi* (52a) (cf. 3.1.1). This is the syntactic positions for all adjuncts, including prepositional phrases (52b). Adverbs differ in that they occur in this slot without any prepositional marking.

(52a)	Mûep	t'wot	t'ong	shin	shit	*yi*	**b'ak**.
	3Pl	sit(pl)	PROGR	do	work	*PROGR*	**here**

'They sit doing work here.' [MIL_LL]

(52b)	Hangoed'e	t'o (. . .)	t'ong	su	*yi*	**n-yil**.
	water	lie(sg)	PROGR	run(sg)	*PROGR*	**LOC-ground**

'The water lies running on the ground.' [MIL_LL]

It is a heterogeneous class, containing a small core of non-derived forms. In addition, reduplication and prefixation are productive processes to derive adverbs from verbs.

Non-derived forms comprise locational and deictic adverbs, temporal adverbs, and quantifying adverbs. A large number of these contain an initial element *N-* or *goe-*, both of which are also locative prepositions that attach to nouns (cf. 4.2). In addition, a prefix *N-* derives adverbs from verbs (cf. below). It is thus likely that these adverbs originally derive from nouns and verbs, e.g.:

goe-sam-pe	'outside'	*n-date*	'straight'
goe-t'eng	'upward'	*n-duni*	'much'
goe-tûûn	'beyond'	*n-d'yen*	'yesterday'
goe-d'aar	'tomorrow'	*n-gong*	'night time'

Another set occurs in partially or completely reduplicated form. And again, partial reduplication is a productive process for forming adverbs from verbs.

toe-t'ei	'all'	*d'yen-d'yen*	'yesterday'
toe-d'aar	'tomorrow'	*mpûe-mpûe*	'always'

There is only a very small core of non-derived adverbs: *b'ak* 'here', *d'i* 'locative anaphor', *jar* 'straight' and *dip* 'all'. But even here, some occur in alternating forms (*d'i* ~ *goe-d'i*, *dip* ~ *n-dip*). Although most adverbs thus seem to be derived forms, the original nouns or verbs do not exist anymore in the language. For this reason, I consider them to be synchronically non-derived.

Additionally, Goemai has two productive processes to derive adverbs. First, a prefix *N-* can attach to any verb to form an adverb. These then occur in the same syntactic slot as other adverbs (e.g., following a direct object as in example 53a), and they can even co-occur with the original verb (example 53b).

(53a)	goe	tarap	sonkwa	**m-b'arak**.
	2Sgm	snap(pl)	maize	**ADVZ-become_fresh/wet**

'break the maize **freshly/in a fresh condition**.' [CROPS]

(53b)	Gu	*t'wot*	**n-t'wot**.
	2Pl	*sit(pl)*	**ADVZ-sit(pl)**

'You *sit* **sittingly**.' [QUEST]

Secondly, partial reduplication to the right derives adverbs from a sub-set of verbs. Formally, the first consonant is reduplicated (whereby implosives and voiceless non-aspirated obstruents become voiceless aspirated obstruents), and a schwa is inserted between the reduplicated consonant and the stem. This process is largely restricted to the sub-class of property verbs (54a). However, some transitive verbs can undergo the same process (54b). The latter can then occur as stative predicates (54c).

(54a)	Vûang	a	riga	muk	**poe-pya**.
	wash	FOC	shirt	3Sg.Poss	**RED-become_white**

'(It is) his shirt (that) he washed white.' [LL, 1/2/00]

(54b)	Man	goe	mang	**loe-la**	ba.
	PROH	2Sgm	take	**RED-pain**	NEG

'Do not take it too **seriously/painfully**.' [LL, 2/2/00]

(54c)	Tamtis	noe	**toe-t'at**.
	folktale	1Sg.Poss	**RED-shoot/tell_folktale**(**sg**)

'My folktale is being told.' [KUR]

Adverbialization foregrounds a state, and backgrounds an agent role (if there is one). This results in a stative-like reading in the case of inchoative verbs (example 54a above), and in a passive-like reading in the case of causative verbs (54c). Nominalization has a similar effect in that it allows the inchoative property verbs to occur statively (cf. 2.5). And, in fact, nominalization and adverbialization combine to form a nominalized 'passive' of transitive verbs (cf. 3.1.3). Goemai has only very few lexical stative verbs. Many concepts that are encoded as statives in other languages, are inchoative verbs in Goemai (e.g., property concepts, but also verbs such as *man* 'know' or *zem* 'like'). Nominalization and adverbialization provide one possibility for such verbs to occur statively.

4.2 *Prepositions*

Goemai has two sets of prepositions: prepositions proper, and spatial relators.

Table (7): Prepositions and spatial relators

Prepositions:	
goe	location in space, comitative/instrumental, theme
N-	location at object, comitative/instrumental, theme, benefactive
Spatial relators:	
sek	location at the 'body' of an object
k'a ~ n-k'a	location at the 'head' of an object
goede ~ n-goede	location at the 'bottom' of an object
pûe ~ n-pûe ~ goe-pûe	location at the 'mouth' of an object
nd'ûûn	location inside an object
dakd'ûe	location in the middle of an object
nk'ong	location at the 'back' of an object
ntyem	location at the 'front' of an object
n-t'oor ~ goe-t'oor	location at the 'side' of an object

Both are defined syntactically as being able to head a prepositional phrase. This prepositional phrase has the status of an adjunct, and thus occurs following boundary morphemes such as the subordinating morpheme *yi* (cf. 3.1.1), e.g.:

(55a)	Wang	hok	t'ong	*yi*	**k'a**	pepe.
	pot	DEF	sit(sg)	*SUB*	**HEAD**	cover

'So that the pot sits on the woven cover.' [DIS_AS/LL_2.6]

The two sets differ in that the spatial relators have a nominal origin. This nominal origin shows formally in their co-occurrence with the possessive pronouns (55b) and in their ability to occur without a reference object (55c).

(55b)	Ndoe	shel-n-shye	t'o	**k'a**	*muk.*
	Some	game-LOC-foot	lie(sg)	**HEAD**	*3Sg.Poss*

'Some ball lies on it.' [COMP_NK/SM_12]

(55c)	Moto	n-d'e-nang	d'yem	**k'a**.
	car	ADVZ-Cl:exist-DEM.DIST	stand(sg)	**HEAD**

'That existing car stands on top (of it).' [COLOR_SM]

Prepositions proper would be followed by the independent pronoun (cf. example 41b above), and they cannot occur without an accompanying nominal. Prepositions and spatial relators can co-occur to indicate non-contiguity between the Figure and the Ground, or to indicate a shift from an intrinsic frame of reference to a relative frame of reference, in which case the preposition precedes the spatial relator (Hellwig, in prep a.).

Bibliography

Aikhenvald (Alexandra Y.): 2000 Classifiers: A typology of noun categorization devices, Oxford University Press, Oxford.

Blažek (Václav): 1995 "The microsystem of personal pronouns in Chadic, compared with Afroasiatic", Studia Chadica et Hamitosemitica, ed. by Dymitr Ibriszimow and Rudolf Leger, pp. 36–57, Rüdiger Köppe, Köln.

Burquest (Donald A.): 1973 A Grammar of Angas, University of California Press, Los Angeles.

Bybee (Joan L.): 1994 "The grammaticalization of zero: Asymmetries in tense and aspect", Perspectives on grammaticalization, ed. by William Pagliuca, pp. 235–254, John Benjamins, Amsterdam and Philadelphia.

——, Perkins (Revere) and Pagliuca (William): 1994 The evolution of grammar. Tense, aspect, and modality in the languages of the world, University of Chicago Press Chicago and London.

Claudi (Ulrike): 1985 Zur Entstehung von Genussystemen: Überlegungen zu einigen theoretischen Aspekten, verbunden mit einer Fallstudie des Zande, Helmut Buske, Hamburg.

Comrie (Bernard): 1985 Tense, Cambridge University Press, Cambridge.

Dahl (Östen): 1985 Tense and aspect systems, Basil Blackwell, Oxford.

Diessel (Holger): 1999 Demonstratives: Form, function, and grammaticalization. John Benjamins, Amsterdam and Philadelphia.

Dixon (R.M.W.): 1982 "Where have all the adjectives gone?", Where have all the adjectives gone? And other essays in Semantics and Syntax, pp. 1–62, Mouton, Berlin, New York and Amsterdam.

Dolgopolsky (Aron B.): 1988 "On etymology of pronouns and classification of the Chadic languages", Fucus: A Semitic/Afrasian Gathering in Remembrance of Albert Ehrman, ed. by Yoël L. Arbeitman, pp. 201–220, John Benjamins, Amsterdam and Philadelphia.

Foulkes (H.D.): 1915 Angass Manual: Grammar and Vocabulary, Kegan Paul, Trench, Trübner & Co. Ltd., London.

Frajzyngier (Zygmunt): 1977 "The plural in Chadic", Papers in Chadic Linguistics, ed. by Paul Newman and Roxana Ma Newman, pp. 37–56, Afrika-Studiecentrum, Leiden.

——: 1985a "Borrowed logophoricity?", Studies in African Linguistics, Supplement 9, 114–118.

——: 1985b "Logophoric systems in Chadic", Journal of African Languages and Linguistics 7, 23–37.

——: 1985c "'Causative' and 'benefactive' in Chadic", Afrika und Übersee 68, 23–47.

——: 1993 A Grammar of Mupun. Dietrich Reimer, Berlin.

—— and Koops (Robert): 1989 "Double epenthesis and N-class in Chadic", Current Progress in Chadic Linguistics, ed. by Zygmunt Frajzyngier, pp. 233–250, John Benjamins, Amsterdam and Philadelphia.

Gerhardt (Ludwig): 1983 "Lexical interferences in the Chadic/Benue-Congo border-area", Studies in Chadic and Afroasiatic Linguistics, ed. by Ekkehard Wolff and Hilke Meyer-Bahlburg, pp. 301–310, Helmut Buske, Hamburg.

——: 1987 "Some remarks on the numerical systems of Plateau Languages", Afrika und Übersee 70, 19–29.
—— and Wolff (Ekkehard): 1977 "Interferenzen zwischen Benue-Kongo- und Tschad-Sprachen", Zeitschrift der Deutschen Morgenländischen Gesellschaft, Supplement II, 2, 1518–1543.
Goldberg (Adele E.): 1995 Constructions: A construction grammar approach to argument structure, The University of Chicago Press, Chicago and London.
Haiman (John), ed.: 1985. Iconicity in Syntax, John Benjamins, Amsterdam and Philadelphia.
Heine (Bernd), Claudi (Ulrike) and Hünnemeyer (Friederike): 1991 Grammaticalization, University of Chicago Press, Chicago and London.
Hellwig (Birgit): submitted 'To sit face down': location and position in Goemai.
——: in prep. a Locative verbs, deictic classifiers and nominal classification in Goemai.
——: in prep. b The 'goe' in Goemai.
Hoffmann (Carl): 1970 "Ancient Benue-Congo loans in Chadic?", Africana Marburgensia 3(2), 3–23.
——: 1975 Towards a Comparative Phonology of the Languages of the Angas-Goemai Group. Ibadan, unpublished manuscript.
Ibriszimow (Dymitr): 1988 "Some remarks on Chadic numerals", Afrikanistische Arbeitspapiere, Sondernummer, 67–74.
Jungraithmayr (Herrmann): 1963a "Die Sprache der Sura (Mwaghavul) in Nordnigerien", Afrika und Übersee 47, 8–89, 204–220.
——: 1963b "On the ambiguous position of Angas (N. Nigeria)", Journal of African Languages 2(3), 272–278.
——: 1964a "Materialien zur Kenntnis des Chip, Montol, Gerka und Burrum (Südplateau, Nordnigerien)", Afrika und Übersee 48(3), 161–182.
——: 1964b "Texte und Sprichwörter im Angas von Kabwir (Nordnigerien), mit einer grammatischen Skizze", Afrika und Übersee 48(1), 17–35, 114–127.
——: 1979 "Apophony and tone in the Afro-Asiatic/Niger-Congo frontier area", Études Linguistiques 1(1), 130–140.
Kraft (Charles H.): 1974 "Reconstructions of Chadic pronouns I: possessive, object, and independent sets—an interim report", Third Annual Conference on African Linguistics, ed. by Erhard Voeltz, pp. 69–94, Indiana University, Bloomington.
——: 1981 Chadic Wordlists, Dietrich Reimer, Berlin.
Kuteva (Tania A.): 1999 "On 'sit'/'stand'/'lie' auxiliation" Linguistics 37(2), 191–213.
Levin (Beth): 1993 English verb classes and alternations: A preliminary investigation, University of Chicago Press, Chicago and London.
Levinson, (Stephen C.): 2000 Presumptive meanings: The Theory of Generalized Conversational Implicature, MIT Press, Cambridge, MA, and London.
Lyons (John A.): 1977 Semantics, vol. 2, Cambridge University Press, Cambridge.
Newman (Paul): 1977a "Chadic classification and reconstructions", Afroasiatic Linguistics 5(1), 1–42.
——: 1977b "Chadic extensions and pre-dative verb forms in Hausa", Studies in African Linguistics 8(3), 275–297.
——: 1977c "The formation of the imperfective verb stem in Chadic", Afrika und Übersee 60, 178–192.
——: 1990 Nominal and Verbal Plurality in Chadic, Foris Publications, Dordrecht and Providence.
Palmer (Frank R.): 1986 Mood and Modality, Cambridge University Press, Cambridge
Schuh (Russell G.): 1976 "The Chadic verbal system and its Afroasiatic nature", Afroasiatic Linguistics 3(1), 1–14.
——: 1990 "Re-employment of grammatical morphemes in Chadic: implications for language history", Linguistic Change and Reconstruction Methodology, ed. by Philip Baldi, pp. 599–618, Mouton de Gruyter, Berlin and New York.

Sirlinger (Eugene): 1937 Dictionary of the Goemai language, unpublished manuscript.
——: 1942 A grammar of the Goemai language, unpublished manuscript.
——: 1946 An English-Goemai dictionary, unpublished manuscript.
Wolff (Ekkehard): 1979 "Grammatical categories of verb stems and the marking of mood, aktionsart, and aspect in Chadic", Afroasiatic Linguistics 6(5), 161–208.
Wolff (Hans): 1959 "Subsystem typologies and area linguistics", Anthropological Linguistics 1(7), 1–88.

DAS BIRGIT, EINE OSTTSCHADISCHE SPRACHE—VOKABULAR UND GRAMMATISCHE NOTIZEN

Herrmann Jungraithmayr
(University of Frankfurt)

Einleitung

Anfang der siebziger Jahre[1] hatte ich im Rahmen meines von der Deutschen Forschungsgemeinschaft geförderten Tschad-Projektes Gelegenheit, die im folgenden gebotene Wortliste aufzunehmen. Da meines Wissens bis heute über diese Sprache keine nennenswerte Dokumentation vorliegt, hielt ich es für richtig und notwendig, diese kleine Sprachprobe, wenn auch in einer noch keineswegs endgültigen Gestalt, zugänglich zu machen. Die langgehegte Absicht, das vorliegende Material erst noch einmal im Felde zu überprüfen und gegebenenfalls zu erweitern, halte ich heute, angesichts meiner fortgeschrittenen Lebensjahre, nicht mehr für realistisch.

Der Artikel ist dem Andenken an Werner Vycichl gewidmet, einen hochverehrten Kollegen und Freund, dessen Lebenswerk uns in der hamitosemitischen Sprachforschung viele neue Wege und Perspektiven eröffnet hat.

Die Wortliste wird unverändert auf Französisch—d.h. Birgit-Français und Français-Birgit—präsentiert, so wie sie ursprünglich aufgenommen worden ist.

---

[1] Die Aufnahmesitzungen fanden zwischen dem 9. und dem 19.4.1973 im Hause der Missionarsfamilie Houriet in Mongo statt. Mein herzlicher Dank geht an Herrn und Frau Houriet für ihre großzügige Gastfreundschaft. Sodann gilt mein Dank der Deutschen Forschungsgemeinschaft für die stets große und uneingeschränkte Unterstützung bei meinen wissenschaftlichen Arbeiten. Ein besonderer Dank ist an die beiden Birgit-Gewährsleute gerichtet, ohne deren tatkräftige, interessierte und geduldige Mitarbeit diese kleine Studie nicht möglich gewesen wäre. Herrn Dr. Gábor Takács schulde ich großen Dank für seine freundliche Bereitschaft, meine Vorlage in eine computergerechte Fassung zu verwandeln, vor allem aber auch dafür, daß er mich mit viel Geduld und Nachdruck zur Veröffentlichung dieser Materialien gedrängt hat.

1. *Das Birgit—Verbreitung und Klassifikation*

Das Birgit (Bìrgìtáyò) wird in etwa 20 Ortschaften unmittelbar im Osten der Abu Telfan-Berge, Präfektur des Guéra, Republik Tschad, von ca. 5.000 Menschen gesprochen. Als Hauptort gilt Abge (àbgé). In der gängigen Klassifikation wird Birgit als ein Mitglied der osttschadischen Mubi-Sprachgruppe geführt.

2. *Zur Struktur der Sprache*

2.1. *Kurzer Abriß der Phonologie*

Birgit ist, wie die meisten seiner osttschadischen Verwandten, eine Fünfvokalsprache (a, e, i, o, u). Vokallänge ist phonemisch, z.B. in *'àamí* „pflücken" und *ḍòoyí* „hören".

Das Konsonanteninventar enthält folgende Vertretungen:

p	t	c	k	'
b	d	j	g	
ḅ[2]	ḍ[2]	'j		
	s		x	h
m	n	ny	ŋ	
	l			
	r			
w		y		

Die Konsonantenphoneme treten einfach und geminiert auf, z.B. *gàr-ráadó* „Ring", *jòffí* „sich niederhocken", *sìkkí* „abschneiden", *mìkkà* „sechs". Die meisten arabischen Lehnwörter erscheinen im D-Stamm, d.h. mit geminiertem 2. Radikal, z.B. *'àllàmí* „lernen", *xàbbàní* „sich ärgern", *shàddàgí* „schlagen", *gàrrà'í* „lesen".

---

[2] Für die konventionellen ɓ bzw. ɗ werden in diesem Aufsatz, aus technischen Gründen, ḅ bzw. ḍ verwendet (Anm. von Gábor Takács).

Zum Vokal- und Konsonantinventar treten zwei Toneme: *á* hoch und *à* tief, z.B.:

bàrà	„Blut"	bàrá	„Schakal"
gàarí (pf.)	„sprechen"	gàarì	„Sprache"
càarí	„tanzen"	càarì	„Wurzeln, Adern"
dáatì	„Frau"	dàatì	„Frauen"
dàmbì	„Stein"	dámbì	„Steine"

Das Birgit kennt folgende Silbenstrukturen: CV, CVV und CVC. Beispiele:

cìfì	„spucken"	cènní	„kochen"
díwó	„Fliege"	'íbìn	„Durst"
dèkkí	„niederknien"	màrtí	„grüßen"

An Wortstrukturen herrschen vor: CVCV, CVVCV, CVCCV.

2.2. *Zur Morphologie*

2.2.1. *Das Nomen*

Genus (m./f.) und Numerus (Sg./Pl.) werden generell durch Suffixvokale markiert.

2.2.1.1. Genus

Bei der Markierung des grammatischen Geschlechts läßt sich keine eindeutige Zuordnung vornehmen, da fast alle Vokale sowohl für maskulin als auch für feminin vorkommen. Es besteht aber eine gewisse Präferenz für *-o* und *-a* als maskulin bzw. *-e* / *-i* als feminin, z.B.:

màmèrŋà	„Dieb"	màmérŋè	„Diebin"
màlàamà	„Hexer"	màláamì	„Hexe"
gòwàaró	„Geier" (m.)	gòwàaréy	„Geier" (f.)
màadó	„Stier"	màadì	„Kuh"

Beispiele für Maskulina auf *-ó* (auch *-ò*): *dàgáayó* „Wolke", *bàŋgó* „Loch", *'ókóló* „Leber", *mìdìwó* „Mensch", *'òrnó* „Schatten", *lòkòmó* „Kamel", *kùmó* „Ratte", *káyfò* „Hase", *kílmó* „Kohle", *kírdó* „Hagel". Daß *-ó* stark maskulin besetzt ist, zeigt *mátáró* „Regen" (von arab. *maṭar-* abgeleitet).

Beispiele für Feminina auf *-ì* / *-è*: *lóodì* „Sache", *jìrgì* „Bohne", *jíilì* „Penis", *'ábì* „Holz", *gùlàalì* „Hoden", *mùutì* „Tod", *léelè* „Tag", *mì* „Rauch", *'ìtàatì* „Floh".

Vgl. aber auch die Maskulina auf *-ì*: *bì* „Mund", *fáadì* „Schenkel", *gífì* „Knie". Auch *tèrè* „Mond" ist maskulin!

2.2.1.2. Numerus

Die Mehrheit der Nomina bildet ihre Pluralformen mit Hilfe eines Suffixvokals bzw. -morphems. Dabei herrschen eindeutig die Vordervokale *-i* und *-e* (inklusive *-éy* und *-ây*) sowie der tiefe Vokal *-a* vor; zum Beispiel:

- Plurale auf *-ì*:

Sg.	Pl.	Bedeutung
gàyímó (m.)	gàyímì	„Wildkatze"
gòcòm (m.)	gòcómì	„Kinn"
jùgùnéy (f.)	jùgúnì	„große Kalebasse"
sàŋó (m.)	sáŋì	„Zahn"
cáaró (m.)	càarì	„Wurzel"
'ásó (m.)	'ásì	„Knochen"
gàrtéy (f.)	gártì	„Lanze"
'àynéy (f.)	'àynì	„Ziege"

- Plurale auf *-éy*:

kùlló (m.)	kùlléy	„Strauß"
'ósòm (m.)	'òsòméy	„Name"
ḍúrkùl (m.)	ḍúrkùléy	„Esel"
gìirì (m.)	gìiréy	„Gehöft"
càkwó (m.)	càkwéy	„Perlhuhn"

- Plurale auf *-ây* (selten *-áy*):

kàbànó (m.)	kàbànây	„Büffel"
kùmbá (m.)	kùmbây	„Hütte"
sáukà (m.)	sàukáy	„Pferd"
náŋgàréy (f.)	náŋgàrây	„Messer"
'àndàŋè (m.)	'àndàŋây	„Nacht"
fìdì (m.)	fìdây	„Regenzeit"

- Plurale auf *-à* (selten *-â*):

'étèŋ (m.)	'ètéŋà	„Nase"
'ísìŋ (m.)	'ìsíŋà	„Bein"
'údúŋgì (f.)	'údúŋgà	„Ohr"
kìḍó (m.)	kìḍà	„Erde"

- Plurale auf *-ànàŋ* / *-ànàn* / *-nànàŋ* / *-áawànàn* / *-ànà*:

bàŋgó (m.)	báŋgànàŋ	„Loch"
dúyó (m.)	dúyànàŋ	„Hyäne"
fiifó (m.)	fiifànàn	„Brust"
lìisì (m.)	lìisánàn	„Zunge"
géefó (m.)	géefànàŋ	„Horn"
fáadì (m.)	fáadànàn	„Hüfte"
dòkkò (f.)	dòkkánàn	„Brustkorb"
'árà (m.)	'árnànàŋ	„Rücken"
bùtùrì (m.)	bùtùráawànàn	„Bauch"
kàmáaḍéy (f.)	kàmáaḍànà	„Topf"

- Rein tonal differenzierte Singular-/Pluralpaare kommen nur in beschränkter Zahl vor:

dáatì (f.)	dàatì	„Frau“
dàmbì (m.)	dámbì	„Stein“
'èlì (m.)	'élì	„Schlange“
tóntòró (m.)	tóntórò	„Ameise“

- Interne, gebrochene Plurale sind ebenfalls selten:

mòrfì (m.)	mòróofáy	„Weg“
tùrkó (m.)	tùráakáy	„Zaun (fr. secko)“
'údì (f.)	'ódò	„Auge“
ròn- (m.)	ríŋ-	„Sohn“
rúŋ- (f.)	ríŋ-	„Tochter“
jùgó (m.)	jígì	„Arm, Hand“
kùlmó (m.)	kùlúmè	„Tamarinde“

- Zu den inneren Pluralen können auch die folgenden unregelmäßigen Formen gezählt werden:

a)

'á'jántà	'áa'jántà	„leer, trocken“
zírkántà	zíráakántà	„schlank“
dàgàmá	dàgàamá	„kurz“
sìrká	sìràaká	„hoch“
níiránta	níyáarántà	„korpulent“

b)

bà'jà (f.)	bán'jàw	„Anus“
ká'jà (f.)	kàn'jâw	„Kopf“

Suppletivplurale sind selten:

'jílínkè (m.)	'àláakâw	„Jahr"
'ùrúmbùléy (m.)	'áayì	„Nabel"
léelè (f.)	'úléy	„Tag"
'àbì (f.)	'àtây	„Baum"

2.2.2. *Das Verb*

2.2.2.1. Zur Silbenstruktur der Verbalbasen
Die uns bisher bekannt gewordenen Verbalstämme entfallen in ihrer Mehrheit auf die Silbenstrukturen C_1VC_2-, C_1VVC_2-, $C_1VC_2C_2$-, $C_1VC_2C_3$-, $C_1VC_2VC_3$-, $C_1VC_2VVC_3$-, $C_1VC_2C_3VC_4$-. Ob es sich bei den partiell monoradikaligen Verbalstämmen—z.B. *náyà* (*ná, nò*) „reifen"—nicht doch um den Typus C_1VC_2- (wobei C_2 infirm wäre) handelt, müssen weitere Analysen in Zukunft klären. Ein gutes Drittel der Verbalstämme besitzt drei Radikale ($C_1VC_2C_2$-, $C_1VC_2C_3$- und $C_1VC_2VC_3$-). Nimmt man die im Corpus stark vertretenen Verben mit C_1VVC_2-Struktur im Sinne von *mediae infirmae*-Verben hinzu, kann festgestellt werden, daß die überwiegende Mehrheit der Birgit-Verben als dreiradikalig gelten darf; ein Befund, der ja allgemein für das Osttschadische nachgewiesen worden ist. Hinzu kommen die etwa zwanzig arabischen Lehnverben, die meist im zweiten Stamm (D-Stamm) auftreten.

2.2.2.2. Die Grundform der Verbalstämme
In der Wortliste wurden die Verben in ihren drei Grundformen präsentiert: Perfektstamm (Präsensstamm, Subjunktivstamm), z.B.: „zahlen" 'àfàlí ('àfálà, 'àfálò). Das binäre Aspektsystem basiert auf dem klassischen Suffixvokalgegensatz *-i* (Perfektiv) / *-a* (Imperfektiv); dazu kommt der ebenfalls charakteristische Modalstammvokal *-o*. Stamminterner Vokalablaut ist nur (noch) in schwachen Resten erhalten, so z.B., wenn im Präsensstamm neben *'éeḍà* „pétrir" auch die Variante *'íiḍà* und neben *'éenyà* „gießen" auch *'íinyà* gelten.

Diese Triade gilt ausnahmlos für alle aufgezeichneten Verben des Birgit, einschließlich der aus dem Arabischen entlehnten Verbalstämme, z.B. „lernen" *'àllàmí* (*'àllámà, 'àllámò*). Künftige Untersuchungen werden die Frage nach der tonalen Struktur der drei Verbalstämme klären müssen. Während der Perfektstamm das einheitliche Tonmuster TH bzw. (T)TH aufweist, verteilen sich Präsens- und Modalstamm auf folgende Musterpaare:

Tonmuster	Präsensstamm	Subj.-Stamm	Bedeutung
(T)HT : (T)HT	fáanà	fáanò	„weben"
(T)HT : (T)HT	'èfénà	'èfénò	„nehmen"
(T)TH : (T)HT	ḍòsá	ḍósò	„keimen"
(T)TH : (T)HT	bìrá	bírò	„geben"
(T)TH : (T)TH	'èddá	'èddó	„zählen"

Es fällt auf, daß CVC-Verbbasen im allgemeinen zur kontrastiven Paarbildung TH : HT neigen, während die dreiradikaligen Basen (inkl. CVVC) eine gleiche Tonstruktur im Präsens- und Modalstamm zeigen. Die einsilbigen Verben bilden einheitlich ein H : T-Tonkontrastpaar:

Präs.-Stamm	Subj.-Stamm	Bedeutung
ḍá	ḍò	„fühlen"
lá	lò	„machen"
ná	nò	„reifen"
rá	rò	„singen"
sá	sò	„trinken"
tá	tò	„essen"
wá	wò	„gebären"

2.2.2.3. Pluralische Verbalbasis

In einigen Fällen ist eine pluralische Verbalbasis belegt, bei der ein langes *-aa-* nach dem zweiten Radikal in die Verbalbasis eingeschoben wird; vgl. die folgenden Perfektivstämme:

Sg.	Pl.	Bedeutung
gìmìlí	gìmàalí	„verstecken“
sàwtí	sàwàatí	„(sich) lösen“
’ùulí	’ùwàalí	„tätowieren“
dòrí	dòròowí	„stechen“
kìbí	kìbàawí	„werfen“
’ùnàayí	’ùnàawí	„anbinden“

3. *Birgit-Français*

’a

’áalàŋ m. „centre“
’áarìt (ar.) „diable“
’ààmí (’áamà, ’áamò) „arracher“
’àawàní (’àawánà, ’àawánò) (ar.) „aider“
’àbí dáatì (’ábà dáatì, ’ábò dáatì) „se marier“
’áayó m., pl. ’áayànàŋ „queue“
’ábì f., pl. ’àtây „arbre, fagot“
’àcí (’àcá, ’ácò/’àccó) „laver (chose et corps)“
’àddàlí (’àddálà, ’àddálò) „prêter, emprunter“
’àḍḍí (’áḍḍà, ’áḍḍó) „manger (dur)“
’àfàlí (’àfálà, ’àfálò) „payer“
’áfàtù „mon oncle (paternelle)“
’àjàrá „laid“
’á’jántà, pl. ’áa’jántà „vide, sec“
’àkkí dò (’ákkà dò, dò ’ákkò) „bouillir (trans.)“
’àkù f. „feu“
’álíf (ar.) „mille“
’àllàmí (’àllámà, ’àllámò) (ar.) „apprendre“
’àllàmí dò (’àllámà dò, dò ’àllámò) „enseigner“
’àm ’àbât (ar.) „maïs“
’àmárnó m., pl. ’àmárnây „panier“
’àmì pl. „eau“
’àmì jòomá („eau beaucoup“) „orage“
’àmí (dò) (’áamà [dò], ’áamò) „dormir“
’àndàŋè m., pl. ’àndàŋây „nuit“
’ànḍì m. „boule“
’ànyí (’ànyá, ’ányò) „nager“
’àŋgìcíicì m./f. „rayé“
’àŋgúkùrúnà f., pl. gúkùrù „grenouille“
’árà m., pl. ’árnànàŋ „dos“, ’ártù „mon dos“
’àrḍà m., pl. ’árḍì „bracelet“
’àrḍí (’árḍà, ’árḍò) „courber“

'àrí ('àrá, 'árò) „laisser"
'àsà'í ('àsá'à, 'àsó'ò) (ar.) „élargir"
'àsí ('ásà, 'ásò) „venir", 'àsí dò „amener"
'ásó m., pl. 'ásì „os"
'àtàkí ('àtákà, 'àtákò) „chasser"
'àwḍí ('àwḍà, 'áwḍò) „preparer la boule"
'àwí ('áwà, 'áwò) „goûter"
'àwlí ('áwlà, 'áwlò) „remuer"
'àygí ('áygà, 'áygò) „moudre"
'àynéy f., pl. 'àynì „chèvre"
'àyyàbí ('àyyábà, 'àyyábò) (ar.) „honteux"

b

bàabá „dieu"
bàadàlí (bàadálà, bàadálò) „se dépêcher"
bàamí (báamà, báamò) „attraper, tenir"
bàdí (bàdá, bádò) „commencer"
bàgáy f., pl. bàgì „sauterelle"
bà'jà f., pl. bán'jàw „anus"
bà'jìitù „mon beau-père"
bàŋgó m., pl. báŋgànàŋ „trou"
bàrá m.f., pl. bàrây „chacal"
bàrà pl. „sang"
báaràkáydò „neuf (9)"
bàsíirì „sept"
bàyyó f. „gombo"
bèe'jà „cinq"
bèlnyá „bleu"
bèrí (bèrá, bérò) „voler"
bì m., pl. bìŋgànán „bouche", bìitù „ma bouche"
bíḍḍèŋ m., bíyáḍḍèŋ, pl. níyáḍḍèŋ „petit"
bìitá m., pl. bìitíniŋgè „porte"
bìlèesó pl. „sel"
Bìrgìtáyò „Birgit"
birí (bìrá, bírò) „donner"
bísìyó m., pl. bísìyà „moustique"
bìsó m., pl. bìsì „poisson"
bògòró m., pl. bògòréy f., pl. bògòréy „Cephalophe de Grimm"
bòobà m., pl. bóobì „aveugle"
bòocì pl. „fleur"
bóròm m.f., bòrómì „lion"
bòwà m., pl. bòwàwíŋgè „champs"
bùgùr m., búgúréy f., pl. búgúréy „varan"
bùrúndùllè „poussière"
bùtà pl. „farine"
bùtì f. „cendre"
bùtùrì m., pl. bùtùráawànàn „ventre"
bùurùny „vert (pas mûr)"
bùwà pl. „lait"

ḅ

ḅàají (ḅàajá, ḅàajò) „foquer"
ḅèrnà m., pl. ḅèrnéy „esclave"

c

càací (cáacà, cáacò) „crier à tue-tête“
càalí (cáalà, cáalò) „se lever“
càarí (cáarà, cáarò) „danser, jouer“
cáaró m., pl. càarì „racine, veine“
càbàlá „léger“
càkwó m., pl. càkwéy „perdrix“
cálkùwéy f. (≈ waidalo) „poule de rocher“
cènní (cènná, cènnó) „cueillir“
cìfí (cìfá, cífò) „cracher“
ciilí (cíilà, cíilò) „construire“
còorí (cóorà, cóorò) „shier“

d

dáatì f., pl. dàatì „femme“
dàawí (dàawá, dàawó) „casser (calebasse)“
dáayà (dá, dò) „tuer“
dàgáayó m., pl. dàgáayì „nuage“
dàgàmá (ŋ), pl. dàgàamá „court (peu profond)“
dàmbáy f., pl. dámbì „meule“
dàmbì m., pl. dámbì „pierre“
dàná „bon (chose)“; dàná ḍà „pas bon“
dèkèlkè'jí (dèkèlké'jà, dèkèlké'jò) „chatouiller“
dèkkí (dékkà, dékkò) „s'agenouiller“
déttá róntù „ma belle-fille“
dìḅàakí (diḅáakà, diḅáakò) „ramper“
díirì m., pl. díirànàŋ „ver“
dìkkí (díkkà, díkkò) „porter“
díwó m., pl. dìwì „mouche“
dògòrà m., pl. dógórì f., pl. dógóréy „sourd“
dòkí (dòká, dókò) „taper“
dòkkò f., pl. dòkkánàn „poitrine“
dòrgà m., pl. dòrgínìŋgè „case en paille“
dòrí (dòrá, dórò), pl. dòròowí „percer“
dùwí (dùwá, dúwò) „mettre“
dúyó m., dúyéy f., pl. dúyànàŋ „hyène“

ḍ

ḍáyà (ḍá, ḍò) „sentir“
ḍèelá „fort“
ḍíiḍó m., ḍíiḍìyà f., pl. ḍíiḍì „oiseau“
ḍòoyí (ḍóoyà, ḍóoyò) „entendre“
ḍòsí (ḍòsá, ḍósò) „germer“
ḍòyyí (ḍòyyá, ḍòyyó) „acheter“
ḍúrkùl m., ḍúrkùléy f., pl. ḍúrkùléy „âne“

'e

'èccí ('èccá, 'èccô) „tousser“, 'éccì m. „toux“
'èddí ('èddá, 'èddó) „compter“ (ar.)
'èeḍí ('éeḍà/'iiḍà, 'éeḍò) „pétrir“

'èenyí ('éenyà/'íinyà, 'éenyò/ar'éenyà) „verser dedans"
'èfènì ('èfénà, 'èfénò) „ramasser (p.ex. fruits, mil)"
'èlì m., pl. 'élì „serpent"
'èŋkí ('éŋkà, 'éŋkò) „gratter"
'èrŋí ('èrŋá, 'èrŋó) „quereller"; 'èrŋá/'írŋà nàymá „l'action de quereller est bon"
'étèŋ m., pl. 'ètéŋà „nez"

f

fáadì m., pl. fáadànàn „cuisse"
fàaní (fáanà, fáanò) „tisser"
fàanó m., pl. fàanây „hache"
fàkkàrí (fàkkárà, fàkkárò) (ar.) „penser"
fàrní (fàrná, fárnò) „choisir"
fàrŋáatì „chasseur"
fàttàshí (fàttáshà/fàttàshá, fàttáshò) (ar.) „chercher"
fèrfèr m., pl. fèrférà „épaule"
ficìrí (ficírà, ficírò) „fendre"
fidì m., pl. fidáyì „saison de pluie"
fiifó m., pl. fiifànàn „sein"
fi'jàyí (fi'jàá, fi'jàwó) „uriner"
fi'jì „urine"
filí (filá, filò) „écorcher"
firáayà m. „maladie, fièvre"
fòocí (fóocà, fóocò) „refuser"
fòoḍì „quatre"
fòotó m., pl. fòotây „soleil, journée"; fòotó gàalí „le soleil s'est couché"
fóróorà „blanc"

g

gàalí (gàalá, gàaló) „tomber"
gàarí (gàará, gàaró/gáarò) „parler, répondre"
gàarì f. (?) „langue"
gàḍáyó m., pl. gàḍáyì „joue"
gàliŋ m., pl. gàliŋáy „corde"
gá màatí, pl. gú màatí „cadavre" (v. maati)
gàrá „rouge"
gár'jì m.f., pl. gàr'jây „éléphant"
gàrráadó m., pl. gàrráadây „bague"
gàrrà'í (gàrrá'à, gàrró'ò) (ar.) „lire"
gàrtéy f., pl. gártì „lance"
gàttí (gáttà, gáttò) „becher"
gàwní (gáwnà, gáwnò) „cultiver, sarcler"
gàyímó m., pl. gàyímì „chat sauvage (grand)"
gèdìgèrì f., pl. gèdègérà „aile"
géefó m., pl. géefànàŋ „corne"
gèewí (géewà, géewò) „pétrir"
gèmsí (gémsà, gémsò) „rire"
gèrgèrí (gèrgérà, gèrgérò) „se retourner"
gérwà m., gèrwéy f., pl. gérwì „phacochère"
gífi m., pl. gìfáayì „genou"
gìirì m., pl. gìiréy „concession"
gìllí (gìllá, gìlló) (ar.) „soulever"

gìmìlí (gìmílà, gìmílò), pl. gìmàalí (gìmàalá, gìmàaló) „cacher"
gòcòm m., pl. gòcómì „menton"
gòmḍí (gómḍà, gómḍò) „se cacher"
gòoyí (góoyà, góoyò) „frire"
gòrḍòm pl. „bouillie"
gòotòwéy f., gòotùwì „houe"
gòlóo'jó m. „héron"
gòokínàyà f., pl. gòokínèy „milles-pates"
góoró m., pl. góorây „gorge"
gòwàaró m., gòwàaréy f., pl. gòwàaréy „vautour"
gùḍí (gùḍá, gúḍò) „courir"
gùlàalì f., pl. gùláalà „testicule"
gúrgùró m., pl. gúrgùrì „scarabée"
gùrùggùrùc „doux"
gùrùm m., pl. gùrúmì „vagina"

h

hàgíiyà (ar.) „verité"
hàhí (hàhá, hàhó) (ar.) „s'eventer"
hàllàfí (hàlláfà, hàlláfò) (ar.) „jurer"
hèelí (héelà, héelò) „voir"
hèsí (hèsá, hèsò/hésò) „se reveiller"

x

xàbbàní (xàbbàná, xàbbànó) (ar.) „se facher"
xàddàrí (xàddárà, xàddárò) (ar.) „voyager"
xàddàsí (xàddásà, xàddásò) (ar.) „plonger"

'i

'ìbbí ('íbbà, 'íbbò) „allumer du feu"
'íbìn m. „soif"
'ìbìní ('ìbínà, 'ìbínò) „connaître, savoir"
'ìcí ('ìcá, 'ícò) „prendre"
'ídínó m., pl. 'ídínây „mortier"
'íiḍà v. 'èeḍí
'íinyà v. 'èenyí
'íisìyà f., pl. 'íisànàŋ „oeuf"
'ìmìyó m., pl. 'ìmì „abeille"
'ìnjámó m., pl. 'ìnjàm „épine"
'ìrìndídìyà f., pl. 'ìrìndíidèy „scorpion"
'ìsèy pl. „déchets"
'ísìŋ m., pl. 'ìsíŋà „jambe"
'ìssí ('íssà, 'íssò) „brûler"
'ìtàatì f., pl. 'ìtáatà „pou"

j

jà m., pl. gáy „homme, personne"
jàawí (jáawà, jáawò) „se promener"
jèenó m., pl. jèenây (ar.) „petite calebasse"
jíilì m., pl. jìiléy „pénis"

jìrgì f. „haricots"
jòffì (jóffà, jóffò) „s'acroupir"
jòltó m., pl. jòltì „crapaud"
jòmí (jòmá, jómò) „trouver"
jóŋgòló m., pl. jóŋgòlây „rocher"
jówáawó m., pl. jòwà „jujubier"
jówáy f., pl. jòomá „couteau de jet"
jùgó m., pl. jígì „main, bras", jìgíitù „ma main"
jùgùnéy f., pl. jùgúnì „grande calebasse"
júrùf (ar.) „bord"
jùwí (jùwá, jùwó/júwò) „vomir"

'j

'jèemá „amer"
'jílínkè m., pl. 'àláakâw „année"
'jòomí ('jóomà, 'jóomò) „aimer"

k

kàalì f., pl. káalànàŋ „étoile"
kàatí (káatà, káatò) „aller, sortir"
kàawí (káawà, káawò) „pleurer"
kàbàlí (kàbálà, kàbálò) „preparer la souce"
kàbànó m., kàbànéy f., pl. kàbànây „buffle"
kàddàbí (kàddábò, kàddábò) „mentir"
kàffàní (kàffánà, kàffánò) (ar.) „envelopper (des mortes)"
kájàŋ m., kàjàŋáy f., pl. kàjíŋì „chien"
ká'jà f., pl. kàn'jâw „tête"
kàlsó m., pl. kàlsây „petite case"
kàmáaḍéy f., pl. kàmáaḍànà „marmite"
kámòokòmòokò m. „soir"
kànyí (kányà, kányò) „tirer"
káydò m., káadò f. „un"
káyfò m., pl. káyfànàŋ „lapin"
kèttèbí (kèttébà, kèttébò) (ar.) „écrire"
kìbí (kìbá, kíbò), pl. kìbàawí (kìbàawá, kìbàawó) „jeter"
kíḍísò m., pl. kíḍísây „pilon"
kìḍó m., pl. kìḍà „terre"
kì'êeb m., pl. kì'èebât (ar.) „faucille"
kìití (kíità, kíitò) „déshabiller"
kílmó m., kìlmà „charbon"
kírdó m., pl. kìrdì „grêle"
kòkòréy f., pl. kòkórì „poule"
kòlí (kòlá, kólò) „appeler"
kòomí (kóomà, kóomò) „sauter"
kòorí (kòorá, kóorò) „déchirer"
kóotù „ma grand-mère"
kór'jò f. „sorgho"
kórkò'jó m., pl. kórkò'jì „caillou"
kórkó'jò m., pl. kòrkó'jèy „coude"
kòrnì f., pl. kórnànàŋ „doigt"
kòróocùmó m., pl. kòróocùmây „calebasse"
kòsòkí (kòsòká, kòsòkó) „bailler"

kòssò pl. „sueur“
kòyí (kòyá, kóyò) „finir“
kùbús-kúbùs m. „poumon“
kùdúŋgó m., pl. kùdúŋgáy „jarre“
kùlló m., pl. kùlléy „autruche“
kùlmó m., pl. kùlúmè „tamarinier“
kùmbá m., pl. kùmbây „case“
kùmó m., kùmáy f., pl. kúmì „rat“
kùràa'jì f., pl. kùráa'jà „fesses“
kùrùkùrùkí (kùrùkùrùká, kùrùkùrúkò) „préparer le bouillon, mélanger mil et eau“

l

làamí (làamá, làamó) „ensorceler“
láasántà „mou“
láŋgànyóotù „mon ami“
làw'jí (láw'jà, láw'jò) „rouler“
làw'jí (láw'jà, láw'jò) „tordre“
léelè f., pl. 'úléy „jour“
lèmmí (lèmmá, lèmmó/'árlímmà) „joindre“
lí (lá, lò) „faire“
lìisì m., pl. lìisánàn „langue (anat.)“, lìisì-tù „ma langue“
límmà v. lèmmí
lìssí (líssà, líssò) „mélanger (mil et arachide)“
lòkòmó m., pl. lòkòmáy „chameau“
lóodì f., pl. lí „chose“
lùwí (lùwá, lúwò) „semer“

m

màaḍí (máaḍà, máaḍò) „demander“
màadó m., màadì f., pl. màadà „taureau“
máagìrtù „mon oncle (paternelle)“
màa'jèŋ „bon (pers.)“, máa'jéŋ ḍà „pas bon“
màatí (máatà, máatò) „mourir“
màbà f., pl. màbáyì „serpent („boa“)“
mágáráy f., pl. mágárây „marmite à bierre“
màgàyí (màgàwá, màgàwó) „échanger“
màgàrfà m., pl. màgárféy „forgeron“
màgí (màgá, mágò) „changer“
màlàamà m., màláamì f., pl. màláaméy „sorcier (mange de gens morts)“
màmèrŋà m., màmérŋè f., pl. màmérŋéy „voleur“
màránjàlló m., pl. màránjàllè „tanier“
márínyáy f. „mil rouge“
márí'jó m., pl. márí'jèy/rúmàyé f., pl. rúmà (q.v.) „jeune“
màrìyùŋtà „neuf“
máarták „huit“
màrmàakí (màrmàaká, màrmàakó) (ar.) „se rouler“
màrtí (màrtá, màrtó) „saluer“
mátáró (ar.) „pluie“
máawà m. „saison sèche“
màyà f. „faim“
mèe'jí (mée'jà/míi'jà, mée'jò/'ármíi'jò) „essorer“
mèŋkèḍèeḍùwà m. „arc-en-ciel“

mì f. „fumée"
mìdìwó m., pl. mìdì „homme"
míi'jà v. mèe'jí
mì'jì' m.f., pl. mì'jây „porc-épic"
mìkkà „six"
míyà (ar.), míyà káadò „cent"
mòkòotù „mon grand-père"
mòlgìyó m., pl. mòlgáy „arbre sp."
mòodí (móodà, móodò) „croître"
mòotá „près, proche"
mòrfì m., pl. mòróofáy „route"
mùrḍí (mùrḍà, múrḍò) „engendrer"
mùsìyó f., pl. mùsséy „tombe"
múuséy f., pl. mùusì „biche"
mùutì f. „mort"

n

náanì pl. „salive"
nàayá „loin"
náayà „mûr"
náŋgàréy f., pl. náŋgàrây „couteau"
náyà (ná, nò) „mûrir"
nàykì m., nàykéy f. „orphelin"
nàymá „chaud"
nèemí (néemà/níimà, néemò/'ár níimà) „casser (bâton)"
nèsí (nèsá, nésò) „se réposer"
níimà v. nèemí
níirántà, pl. níyáarántà „gros"
nírya pl. „cotton"

ny

nyàaló f. „paille"
nyàamí (nyáamà, nyáamò) „tresser (cheveux)"
nyàamí dò (nyáamà dò, dò nyáamò) „envoyer"
nyàŋgí (nyàŋgá, nyàŋgò) „essuyer"
nyògòló „gauche"

ŋ

ŋàamí (ŋáamà, ŋáamò) „rencontrer"
ŋàrŋàrí (nàrŋárà, ŋàrŋárò) „trembler"
ŋòrḍòkí (ŋòrḍókà, ŋòrḍókò) „ronfler"

'o

'òggí ('óggà, 'óggò) „tourner"
'ògòŋ m. „lieu"
'òjòolí ('òjóolà, 'ò'jóolò) „avoir peur"
'ójóolà m. „peur"
'ókóló m. „foie"
'ònyí ('ònyá, 'ónyò) „entrer"
'óo'jà pl. „sommeil"

'òo'jí ('óo'jà, 'óo'jò) „se coucher"
'óolà „froid"
'òoyá „beau"
'òrbí ('órbà, 'órbò) „coudre"
'òrnó m., pl. 'òrnínìŋgè „ombre"
'òrók „dix", 'òrók kà káydò „onze"
'òròy bèe'jà „cinquantre"
'ósòm, pl. 'òsòméy „nom"
'òtòrôn pl. „natron"
'òttí ('òttá, 'óttò) „toucher"

r

ràabó m. „argile"
ráayà (rá, rò) „chanter"
ràdí dò (ràdá dò, dò rádò) (ar.) „accepter"
ráusà „noir"
ràwàalí (ràwàalá, ràwàaló), pl. rùwàalí „perdre"
ràwtí (ráwtà, ráwtò) „oublier"
rèwí (rèwá, réwò) „se fatiguer"
rèwí m. „fatigue"
rìjàawí (rìjàawá, ríjò) (ar.) „attendre"
riyêy pl. „chanson"
ròntù, pl. ríŋtù „mon fils"; voir rúŋtù
róorò f. „araignée"
rúmàyé, pl. rúmà „jeune"
rúŋtù, pl. ríŋtù „ma fille"

s

sáagó m., pl. sáagànàn „jambe (Unterschenkel)"
sàa'jí dò (sàa'já, dò sàa'jó) „verser dehors"
sàllí (sàllá, sàlló) (ar.) „prier"
sámà (ar.) „ciel"
sàŋgí (sàŋgá, sàŋgó) „balayer"
sànyó m. „sable"
sàŋó m., pl. sáŋì „dent", sàŋó-tù „mon dent"
sáukà m., sàukáy f., pl. sàukáy „cheval"
sàw'já „lourd"
sàwtí (sàwtá, sáwtò), pl. sàwàatí (sàwàatá, sàwàató) „(se) détacher"
sáyà (sá, sò) „boire"
sèerí (sèerá, sèeró) „quitter"
sèrḍá „goût de natron"
séréeḍà m., pl. séréeḍì „lézard"
sèrlí (sérlà, sérlò) „se battre", sèrlèy „lutte"
séwèn pl. „huile"
shàddàgí (shàddágà, shàddágò) (ar.) „gifler"
síbîr m., pl. sìbíréy „girafe"
sìḍá „profond"
sìḍí (sìḍá, síḍò) „avaler"
sìikí (síikà, síikò) „raser"
síirì „deux"
sìkì m. „faucon"
sìkkí (síkkà, síkkò) „couper"

sìntù „mon frère"
sìràafì f., pl. sìráafà „côtes"
sìrká, pl. sìràaká „haut"
sírò m. „escargot"
sìyí (sìyá, síyò) „quémander"
sòḍòḍá „acide"
sógónó f., pl. sògónì „foyer"
sògòryó m., pl. sògórì „écureuil"
sòomí (sóomà, sóomò) „ramasser"
sòoní (sóonà, sóonò) „rêver", sóonà „rêve"
sòtù „ma soeur"
sòwàalí (sòwàalá, sòwàaló) „siffler"
súubù „trois"
súḍḍì m. „viande, chair"
súnsúnà f. „conte"
sùumí (sùumá, súumò) (ar.) „vendre"

t

táabùtì m., pl. tàabùtây pl. „petite chauve-souris"
tàaḍí (táaḍà, táaḍò) „monter"
táfó m., pl. tàfì „feuille"
tàŋkó m., tàŋkáy f., pl. táŋkànà(ŋ) „mouton"
tàrḅàlí (tàrḅálà, tàrḅálò) „fondre"
tàtù „mon père"
táyà (tá, tò) „manger"
tèḍèeŋí (tèḍéeŋà, tèḍéeŋò) „partager"
téesó m. „chèvre"
tèŋkí (téŋkà / tíŋkà, téŋkò) „rôtir, griller"
tèrè m., pl. tèréewé „lune"
tìḍḍó m., pl. tíḍḍì „gommier rouge"
tìifí (tíifà, tíifò) „arracher"
tíifiyà f., pl. tíifiyây „aisselle"
tìŋgí (tíŋgà, tíŋgò) „planter"
tíŋkà v. tèŋkí
tìrìnyí (tírínyà, tírínyò) „accompagner"
tìrsí (tírsà, tírsò) „enterrer"
tìwì pl. „sauce"; cf. táyà
tòkòrí (tòkórà, dò tòkórò) „pousser"
tòlkó m., pl. tòlkà „pomme de Sodom"
tóntòró m., pl. tóntórò „fourmi"
tòotó „droite"
tòorì f., pl. tóoràǹàŋ „colombe"
tórlòl m., pl. tòrlóolànàn „fleuve"
tùrgá'à (ar.) „fondre"
tùrkó m., pl. tùráakáy „secko"

'u

'ùbàalì f., pl. 'ùbáalà „braise"
'údì f., pl. 'ódò „oeil"
'údúŋgì f., pl. 'údúŋgà „oreille"
'ùggì m., pl. 'ùggánàn „reins"
'ùlḍí ('úlḍà, 'úlḍò) „lêcher"

'ùmí ('ùmá, 'úmò) „mordre“
'ùnàayí ('ùnàayá, 'ùnàayó), pl. 'ùnàawí „attacher“
'ùní ('ùná, 'únò) „remplir“
'ùntí ('úntà, 'úntò) „s'asseoir“
'úrdó m., pl. 'úrdìŋgè „grenier“
'ùrḍí ('úrḍà, 'úrḍò) „peter“
'úrèy m., pl. 'ùráawànàn „cou“
'ùrúmbùléy m., pl. 'áayì „nombril“
'ùskí ('ùská, 'ùskó) „habiller“
'úsì m. „vent“
'ùstàŋ m. „matin“, 'ùstáŋḍèŋ „aube“
'ùulí ('úulà, 'úulò), pl. 'ùwàalí ('ùwàalá, 'ùwàaló) „tatouer“

w

wàací (wáacà, wáacò) „poignarder“
wàagí (wáagà, wáagò) „piler“
wàa'jí (wáa'jà, wáa'jò) „sucer“
wáayà (wá, wò) „mettre au monde“
wàḍḍàsí (wàḍḍásà, wàḍḍásò) „eternuer“
wáagàréy f. „frontière“
wàjí (wàjá, wájò) „retourner“
wàràayí (wàràawá, wàràawó) „insulter, maudire“
wàsákkó m., pl. wàsákkáy „fil“
wàssàbí (wàssábà, wàssábò) (ar.) „montrer“
wàssí (wàssá, wàssó) „tisser“

y

yàakí (yàaká [dò], [dò] yàakó) „secouer“
yáa-tù „ma mère“, yát-tà mét-tù „mère de mon mari“

'y

'yúrùk m.f., pl. 'yúrúwéy „panthère“

z

zàamà m., pl. záamì „peau“
zàlí (zàlá, zálò) „suspendre“
zàwyó m., pl. zàwyà „chauve-souris“
zì m., pl. zìŋgánàn „corps“
zìigí (zíigà, zíigò) „descendre“
zìigí dò (zíigà dò, dò zíigò) „déposer“
zírkántà m.f., pl. zíráakántà „mince“
zòbòló m. „pintade“
zòoḍí m.f.pl. „vieux“
zúgúlì m., pl. zúgúléy „singe“

4. *Français-Birgit*

a

abeille 'ìmìyó
accepter ràdí dò (ar.)
accompagner tìrìnyí
s'accroupir jòffí
acheter ḍòyyí
acide sòḍòḍá
s'agenouiller dèkkí
aider 'àawàní
aile gèdìgèrì
aimer 'jòomí
aisselle tíifiyà
aller, sortir kàatí
allumer du feu 'ìbbí
amener 'àsí dò
amer 'jèemá
mon ami láŋgànyóotù
âne ḍúrkùl
année 'jílínkè
anus bà'jà
appeler kòlí
apprendre 'àllàmí (ar.)
araignée róorò
arbre, fagot 'ábì
arbre sp. mòlgìyó
arc-en-ciel mèŋkèḍèeḍùwà
argile ràabó
arracher 'ààmí, tìifí
s'asseoir 'ùntí
attacher 'ùnàayí
attendre rìjàawí (ar.)
attraper, tenir bàamí
aube 'ùstáŋḍèŋ
autruche kùlló
avaler sìḍí
aveugle bòobà

b

bague gàrráadó
bailler kòsòkí
balayer sàŋgí
battre, se sèrlí
beau 'òoyá
beau-père, mon bà'jìitù
becher (ar. haffar) gàttí
belle-fille, ma déttá róntù
biche múuséy
Birgit Bìrgìtáyò
blanc fóróorà

bleu bèlnyá
boa (serpent) màbà
boire sáyà
bon (chose) dàná
bon (pers.) màa'jèŋ
bord júrùf (ar.)
bouche bì
bouillie gòrḍòm
bouillir (trans.) 'àkkí dò
boule 'ànḍì
boule, preparer la 'àwḍí
bracelet 'àrḍà
braise 'ùbàalì
bras, main jùgó
brûler 'ìssí
buffle kàbànó

c

cacher gìmìlí
cacher, se gòmḍí
cadavre gá màatí
caillou kórkò'jó
calebasse kòróocùmó
calebasse, grande jùgùnéy
calebasse, petite jèenó (ar.)
case kùmbá
case en paille dòrgà
case, petite kàlsó
casser (bâton) nèemí
casser (calebasse) dàawí
cendre bùtì
cent míyà ~ míyà káadò (ar.)
centre 'áalàŋ
Cephalophe de Grimm bògòró
chasser 'àtàkí
chacal bàrá
chair, viande súḍḍì
chameau lòkòmó
champs bòwà
changer màgí
chanson rìyêy
chanter ráayà
charbon kílmó
chasseur fàrŋáatì
chat sauvage (grand) gàyímó
chatouiller dèkèlkè'jí
chaud nàymá
chauve-souris zàwyó
chauve-souris, petite táabùtì
chercher fàttàshí
cheval sáukà
chèvre 'àynéy, téesó
chien kájàŋ

choisir fàrní
chose lóodì
ciel sámà (ar.)
cinq bèe'jà
cinquantre 'òròy bèe'jà
colombe tòorì
commencer bàdí
compter 'èddí
connaître, savoir 'ìbìní
concession gìirì
construire cìilí
conte súnsúnà
corde gàlìŋ
corne géefó
corps zì
côtes sìràafì
cotton níryà
cou 'úrèy
coucher, se 'òo'jí
coude kórkó'jò
coudre 'òrbí
couper sìkkí
courber 'àrḍí
courir gùḍí
court (peu profond) dàgàmá
couteau náŋgàréy
couteau de jet jówáy
cracher cìfí
crapaud jòltó
crier à tue-tête càací
croître mòodí
cueillir cènní
cuisse fáadì
cultiver, sarcler gàwní

d

danser, jouer càarí
déchets 'ìsèy
déchirer kòorí
demander màaḍí
dent sàŋó
dépêcher, se bàadàlí
déposer zìigí dò
descendre zìigí
déshabiller kìití
détacher, (se) sàwtí
deux síirì
diable 'áarìt (ar.)
dieu bàabá
dix 'òrók
doigt kòrnì
donner bìrí
dormir 'àmí (dò)

dos 'árà
doux gùrùggùrùc
droite tòotó

e

eau 'àmì
échanger màgàyí
écorcher filí
écrire kèttèbí (ar.)
écureuil sògòryó
élargir 'àsà'í (ar.)
éléphant gár'jì
emprunter, prêter 'àddàlí
engendrer mùrḍí
enseigner 'àllàmí dò (ar.)
ensorceler làamí
entendre ḍòoyí
enterrer tìrsí
entrer 'ònyí
envelopper (des mortes) kàffàní (ar.)
envoyer nyàamí dò
épaule fèrfèr
épine 'ìnjámó
escargot sírò
esclave ḅèrnà
essorer mèe'jí
essuyer nyàŋgí
eternuer wàḍḍàsí
étoile kàalì
s'eventer hàhí

f

facher, se xàbbàní (ar.)
fagot, arbre 'ábì
faire lí
faim màyà
farine bùtà
fatigue rèwí
fatiguer, se rèwí
faucille kì'êeb
faucon sìkì
femme dáatì
fendre fìcìrí
fesses kùràa'jì
feu 'àkù
feuille táfó
fièvre, maladie firáayà
fil wàsákkó
filer wàssí
fille, ma rúŋtù
fils, mon ròntù

finir kòyí
fleur bòocì
fleuve tórlòl
foie 'ókóló
fondre tàrḅàlí, tùrgá'à (ar.)
foquer ḅàají
forgeron màgàrfà
fort ḍèelá
fourmi tóntòró
foyer sógónó
frère, mon sìntù
frire gòoyí
froid 'óolà
frontière wáagàréy
fumée mì

g

gauche nyògòló
genou gífì
germer ḍòsí
gifler shàddàgí (ar.)
girafe síbîr
gombo bàyyó
gommier rouge tìḍḍó
gorge góoró
goût de natron sèrḍá
goûter 'àwí
grande calebasse jùgùnéy
grand-mère, ma kóotù
grand-père, mon mòkòotù
gratter 'èŋkí
grêle kírdó
grenier 'úrdó
grenouille 'àŋgúkùrúnà
griller, rôtir tèŋkí
gros níiràntà

h

habiller 'ùskí
hache fàanó
haricots jìrgì
haut sìrká
héron gòlóo'jó
homme mìdìwó
homme, personne jà
honteux 'àyyàbí (ar.)
houe gòotòwéy
huile séwèn
huit máarták
hyène dúyó

i

insulter, maudire wàràayí

j

jambe 'ísìŋ
jambe sáagó
jarre kùdúŋgó
jeter kìbí
jeune márí'jó, rúmàyé
joindre lèmmí
joue gàḍáyó
jouer, danser càarí
jour léelè
journée, soleil fòotó
jujubier jówáawó
jurer hàllàfí (ar.)

l

laid 'àjàrá
laisser 'àrí
lait bùwà
lance gàrtéy
langue gàarì (ŋ)
langue (anat.) lìisì
lapin káyfò
laver (chose et corps) 'àcí
lêcher 'ùlḍí
léger càbàlá
lever, se càalí
lézard séréeḍà
lieu 'ògòŋ
lion bóròm
lire gàrrà'í (ar.)
loin nàayá
lourd sàw'já
lune tèrè
lutte sèrlèy

m

main, bras jùgó
maïs 'àm 'àbât (ar.)
maladie, fièvre fìráayà
manger táyà
manger (dur) 'àḍḍí
marier, se 'àbí dáatì
marmite kàmáaḍéy
marmite à bierre mágáráy
matin 'ùstàŋ
maudire, insulter wàràayí
mélanger (mil et arachide) lìssí

mélanger (mil et eau) kùrùkùrùkí
mentir kàddàbí
menton gòcòm
mère, ma yáatù
mettre dùwí
mettre au monde wáayà
meule dàmbáy
mil rouge márínyáy
mille 'álíf (ar.)
milles-pates gòokínàyà
mince zírkántà
monter tàaḍí
montrer wàssàbí (ar.)
mordre 'ùmí
mort mùutì
mortier 'ídínó
mou láasántà
mouche díwó
moudre 'àygí
mourir màatí
moustique bísìyó
mouton tàŋkó
mûr náayà
mûrir náyà

n

nager 'ànyí
natron 'òtòrôn
natron, goût de sèrḍá
neuf màrìyùŋtà
neuf (9) báaràkáydò
nez 'étèŋ
noir ráusà
nom 'ósòm
nombril 'ùrúmbùléy
nuage dàgáayó
nuit 'àndàŋè

o

oeil 'údì
oeuf 'íisìyà
oiseau ḍíiḍó
ombre 'òrnó
oncle (paternelle), mon máagìrtù
oncle (paternelle), mon 'áfàtù
onze 'òrók kà káydò
orage (eau beaucoup) 'àmì jòomá
oreille 'údúŋgì
orphelin nàykì
os 'ásó
oublier ràwtí

p

paille nyàaló
panier 'àmárnó
panthère 'yúrùk
parler, répondre gàarí
partager tèḍèeŋí
payer 'àfàlí
peau zàamà
perdre ràwàalí
perdrix càkwó
pénis jíilì
penser fàkkàrí (ar.)
percer dòrí
père, mon tàtù
personne, homme jà
peter 'ùrḍí
petit bíḍḍèŋ
petite calebasse jèenó (ar.)
petite case kàlsó
petite chauve-souris táabùtì
pétrir 'èeḍí, gèewí
peur 'ójóolà
peur, avoir 'òjòolí
phacochère gérwà
pierre dàmbì
piler wàagí
pilon kíḍísò
pintade zòbòló
planter tìŋgí
pleurer kàawí
plonger xàddàsí (ar.)
pluie mátáró (ar.)
pluie, saison de fìdì
poignarder wàací
poisson bìsó
poitrine dòkkò
pomme de Sodom tòlkó
porc-épic mì'jì'
porte bìità
porter dìkkí
pou 'ìtàatì
poule kòkòréy
poule de rocher cálkùwéy
poumon kùbús-kúbùs
pousser tòkòrí
poussière bùrúndùllè
prendre 'ìcí
préparer le bouillon kùrùkùrùkí
préparer la boule 'àwḍí
préparer la souce kàbàlí
près, proche mòotá
prêter, emprunter 'àddàlí
prier sàllí (ar.)

proche, près mòotá
profond sìḍá
promener, se jàawí

q

quatre fòoḍì
quémander sìyí
quereller 'èrŋí
queue 'áayó
quitter sèerí

r

racine, veine cáaró
ramasser sòomí
ramasser (p.ex. fruits, mil) 'èfènì
ramper dìḅàakí
raser sìikí
rat kùmó
rayé 'àŋgìcíicì
refuser fòocí
reins 'ùggì
remplir 'ùní
remuer 'àwlí
rencontrer ŋàamí
répondre, parler gàarí
réposer, se nèsí
retourner wàjí
retourner, se gèrgèrí
rêve sóonà
reveiller, se hèsí
rêver sòoní
rire gèmsí
rocher jóŋgòló
ronfler ŋòrḍòkí
rôtir, griller tèŋkí
rouge gàrá
rouler làw'jí
rouler, se màrmàakí (ar.)
route mòrfì

s

sable sànyó
saison de pluie fìdì
saison sèche máawà
salive náanì
saluer màrtí
sang bàrà
sarcler, cultiver gàwní
sauce tìwì
sauter kòomí
sauterelle bàgáy

savoir, connaître 'ìbìní
scarabée gúrgùró
scorpion 'ìrìndídìyà
sec, vide 'á'jántà
sèche, saison máawà
secko tùrkó
secouer yàakí
sel bìlèesó
sein fiifó
semer lùwí
sentir ḍáyà
sept bàsíirì
serpent 'èlì
serpent („boa") màbà
shier còorí
siffler sòwàalí
singe zúgúlì
six mìkkà
soeur, ma sòtù
soif 'íbìn
soir kámòokòmòokò
soleil, journée fòotó
sommeil 'óo'jà
sorcier (mange de gens morts) màlàamà
sorgho kór'jò
sortir, aller kàatí
souce, preparer la kàbàlí
soulever gìllí (ar.)
sourd dògòrà
sucer wàa'jí
sueur kòssò
suspendre zàlí

t

tamarinier kùlmó
tanier màránjàlló
taper dòkí
tatouer 'ùulí
taureau màadó
tenir, attraper bàamí
terre kìḍó
testicule gùlàalì
tête ká'jà
tirer kànyí
tisser fàaní
tombe mùsìyó
tomber gàalí
tordre làw'jí
toucher 'òttí
tourner 'òggí
tousser 'èccí
toux 'éccì
trembler ŋàrŋàrí

tresser (cheveux) nyàamí
trois súubù
trou bàŋgó
trouver jòmí
tuer dáayà

u

un káydò
urine fí'jì
uriner fì'jàyí

v

vagina gùrùm
varan bùgùr
vautour gòwàaró
veine, racine cáaró
venir 'àsí
vendre sùumí
vent 'úsì
ventre bùtùrì
ver díirì
verité hàgíiyà
verser dedans 'èenyí
verser dehors sàa'jí dò
vert (pas mûr) bùurùny
viande, chair súḍḍì
vide, sec 'á'jántà
vieux zòoḍí
voir hèelí
voler bèrí
voleur màmèrŋà
vomir jùwí
voyager xàddàrí (ar.)

FRÜHE LEXIKALISCHE QUELLEN ZUM WANDALA (MANDARA) UND DAS RÄTSEL DES STAMMAUSLAUTS

H. Ekkehard Wolff und Christfried Naumann
(Institut für Afrikanistik, Universität Leipzig)

1. *Frühe Quellen*

1.1 *Einleitung*

Das *Wandala*, besser bekannt in der *Kanuri*-Version derselben Bezeichnung *Mandara*,[1] gehört zu denjenigen afrikanischen Sprachen, von denen bereits sehr früh zumeist ausschließlich lexikalische Belege nach Europa gelangten und damit die Aufmerksamkeit der ersten philologisch interessierten Kompilatoren von populären Wörtersammlungen erweckt hatten, d. h. zumindest seit dem Jahre 1826 (Denham, Claproth). Dies ist im wesentlichen der geographischen Nähe zu verdanken und den vielfältigen historischen Beziehungen des Wandala, der Sprache eines kleinen Sultanats und Königreiches im westlichen bzw. zentralen Sudan, zum viel bedeutenderen Kanem-Bornu Reich mit seiner Staatsprache *Kanuri-Kanembu*, das wiederum von zentralem soziopolitischen Interesse für die frühen europäischen Reisenden und Forscher war.

Auch unter den tschadischen Sprachen, der zahlenmäßig bedeutendsten Sprachfamilie des afroasiatischen Sprachstammes, nimmt das Wandala aufgrund seiner frühen Beleggeschichte[2] eine besondere Stellung ein: Aufzeichnungen zum fast benachbarten zentraltschadischen *Kotoko* von *Affade* datieren schon etwa 10 Jahre früher (Seetzen 1807–09,

---

[1] Die Verwendung der Kanuri-Bezeichnung scheint ursprünglich auf Denham zurückzugehen, der aus zunächst soziopolitisch gebrauchtem *Mandara* (vgl. „*Mora—The capital of Mandara*“) den Terminus *Mandara language* ableitet (Denham [1826:110ff]).

Man beachte die beiden auch innerhalb der sog. Wandala-Lamang-Gruppe des Zentraltschadischen selbst belegten Lautentsprechungen *w* <> *m* und *l* <> *r*, die vermuten lassen, das die Kanuribezeichnung *Mandara* nicht im direkten Kontakt, sondern durch Vermittlung einer anderen tschadischen Sprache übernommen wurde.

[2] Für freundschaftliche Hilfe bei der Beschaffung von Kopien der frühesten Quellen danken wir ausdrücklich den Kollegen Bernard Caron (Paris), Norbert Cyffer (Wien), Dymitr Ibriszimow (Bayreuth), Philip Jaggar (London).

aufgenommen in Kairo; vgl. Seetzen 1810) und wurden posthum von J.S. Vater 1816 herausgegeben, doch sind diese—ganz anders als das Wandala—erst mit großer Verzögerung in das allgemeine Bewusstsein der Afrikalinguistik geraten (Sölken 1957, 1967), wiewohl etwa bereits Latham (1862:578) explizit auf Informationen von Seetzen verweist. Noch älter sind, wie zu erwarten, die ersten Belege aus dem westtschadischen *Hausa*, die unter wiederum einer Kanuri-Bezeichnung („Afnu" = *àfùnó*)[3] Aufnahme in den Mithridates von 1812 gefunden hatten und auf noch ältere Quellen (Niebuhr 1790–91, Lucas 1790) zurückgehen. Damit ist, nach Hausa und Kotoko, das Wandala die überhaupt erst dritte tschadische Sprache, über die neuzeitliche Kenntnis nach Europa gelangt ist und die erste überhaupt aus dem Kreise der später von Johannes Lukas (1934, 1952) zunächst als „Mandara Gruppe" [sic!] bezeichneten, dann als „tschadische [Chadic]" von den sog. „tschadohamitischen [Chadohamitic]" (im wesentlichen mit Westermanns früherer „Hausa-Kotoko Gruppe" [sic!] identischen) getrennten Sprachen.[4]

[3] Neben einer auf den Ortsnamen Katsina zurückgehenden Bezeichnung „Kaschna/Kaschne" bei Simon Lucas (1790). Zur frühen Kontaktgeschichte zum Hausa s. Hair (1967).

[4] Umso mehr erstaunt, dass diese wissenschaftshistorisch bedeutsame Information nicht im *Lexikon der Afrikanistik* (hg. von H. Jungraithmayr und W.J.G. Möhlig, Berlin 1983) auftaucht, das weder einen Verweis auf das Kotoko, noch einen auf das Wandala/Mandara enthält. (Weniger überraschend gilt dies auch für das jüngst erschienene *Afrika Lexikon*, hg. von J.E. Mabe, Wuppertal/Weimar 2001).

Ob und wann Wissen über das Wandala aufgrund der eigenen islamischen Tradition des Sultanats (als offizielles Datum der Islamisierung gilt das Jahr 1723; vgl. Löhr 2002:29) bzw. als südliches Nachbarreich von Kanem-Bornu ggf. früher in die arabisch-islamische gelehrte Welt gelangt ist und eventuell auf diesem Umweg auch schon Europa erreicht hatte, ist eine Frage, der wir bei der Vorbereitung dieses Beitrags nicht nachgehen konnten. Zur weitgehend oral tradierten Geschichte und Bibliographie des Wandala-Reiches sei hier auf Mohammadou (1982) verwiesen, nach dem die Wandala-Geschichte einsetzt als Teil der ursprünglichen und nach ihrem ersten Ahnen so genannten *Malgwa* (Kanuri: *Gamergu*) Bevölkerung im heutigen Bornu vor Einwanderung und Verdrängung durch die Kanuri. Die Geschichte beginnt daher gegen Ende der ersten Jahrtausends unserer Zeitrechnung zwischen den westlichen Zuläufen des Tschadsees, Komadugu Yobe und Yedzeram, als Teil des Bevölkerungskomplexes der legendären *Saw(a)* oder *So*. Das heutige Wandala wäre demnach die Sprache der am weitesten nach Süden und Südosten abgedrängte ursprüngliche Malgwa-Bevölkerungsgruppe, die unter eigenem Namen *Wandala* (< *Wa-Indala* „Abkömmlinge des *Indala*") zu Glanzzeiten ihres Königreiches im 18. und 19. Jahrhundert, das sich vermutlich im 13. oder 14. Jahrhundert heauszubilden begonnen hatte, einen Raum von beachtlicher Größe dominierten, der Gebiete der heutigen Staaten Nigeria, Kamerun und Tschad umfasste und wie folgt grob begrenzt werden kann:
(1) östlich einer Linie, die in Nigeria Dikwa—Bama—Madagali verbindet,

Zugleich ist das Wandala eine derjenigen tschadischen Sprachen, die—neben dem Hausa—eine bemerkenswerte, wenn auch diskontinuierliche wissenschaftliche Beschäftigung erfahren haben, die von den Anfängen bis in unsere Tage andauert. Das Wandala ist hinsichtlich der Zahl der dieser Sprache gewidmeten wissenschaftlichen Beiträge und der Vielzahl der Autoren, die sich zentral oder angelegentlich mit ihr in Publikationen zur Lexik, Grammatik oder Orthographie beschäftigt haben,[5] wohl als die zentraltschadische Belegsprache *par excellence* anzusprechen, auch wenn bis heute eine monographische Grammatikbeschreibung fehlte[6] und andere zentraltschadische Sprachen, aufgrund des Vorliegens bzw. der leichten Zugänglichkeit entsprechender Monographien, eine höhere Zitierfrequenz aufweisen mögen. Die wissenschaftsgeschichtliche Bedeutung des Wandala spiegelt sich auch in der Tatsache, dass J. Lukas 1934 bewusst die Bezeichnung „Mandara-Gruppe" für die Sprachen des später in der Folge der Subklassifikationen von P. Newman (z. B. in Newman 1990) „Zentraltschadisch A" genannten Unterzweiges der Tschadischen Sprachen gewählt hatte.

Aufgrund der für eine ungeschriebene afrikanische Sprache relativ guten historischen Tiefe der Dokumentation—Denhams Aufzeichnungen sind inzwischen 180 Jahre alt !—wird das Wandala weiterhin namengebend als Teil einer enger verwandten Gruppe von zwischen

(2) westlich einer Nord-Süd-Linie, die westlich unweit von Yagoua (Tschad) verläuft,
(3) nordöstlich einer Linie, die Madagali (Nigeria) mit Gidar (Kamerun) und Lere (Tschad) verbindet,
(4) südwestlich einer Linie, die Dikwa (Nigeria) mit Waza (Kamerun) und Yagoua (Tschad) verbindet.

Dieser Raum ist heute, abgesehen von versprengten Kanuri-Ansiedlungen an der nordöstlichen Peripherie und rezentem verstärkten Vordringen des Fulfulde von Süden her, fast ausschließlich von Sprechern verschiedener zentraltschadischer Sprachen bewohnt. Eine Zusammenfassung der teilweise sehr widersprüchlichen Annahmen und Aussagen über die Geschichte der Wandala/Malgwa findet sich bei Löhr (2002:23–37).

[5] Die uns vorliegenden Publikationen und Arbeitspapiere, die sich mit dem Wandala zentral oder angelegentlich beschäftigen und sprachliche Daten enthalten, ohne spezielle Arbeiten zum Malgwa und ohne Alphabetisations- und Postalphabetisationsmaterial, umfasst z. Zt. 27 Einheiten aus der Hand von insgesamt fast genau so vielen Autoren/Kompilatoren (vgl. auch Newmans Bibliographie [1996], die mindestens um folgende uns bekannte Angabe zu ergänzen wäre: Perrin, Mona. 1984. *Les noms verbaux en gude et en mandara*. MESRS/ISH und SIL, Yaoundé. [Unveröff.])

[6] Abhilfe schafft hier, zumindest ersatzweise, die Monographie von Doris Löhr zum *Malgwa* (auch bekannt als *Gamergu*, so bei Barth/Benton [1912]), aus der für uns klar hervorgeht, dass es sich dabei um einen Dialekt derselben Sprache, des Wandala, handelt.

sieben und neun separaten Sprachen[7] angesehen. So spricht Newman in seinen Subklassifikationen des Tschadischen (z. B. 1990, im folgenden modifiziert zitiert) wiederum von einer „Mandara Gruppe“:[8]

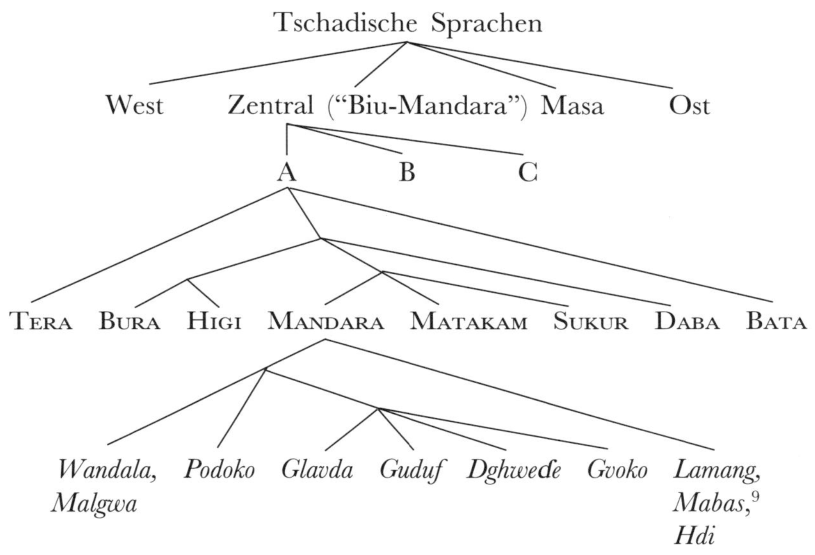

[7] Es besteht für uns wenig Zweifel an der sprachlichen Eigenständigkeit der unter folgenden Bezeichnungen geführten Sprachen: *Dghweɗe, Glavda, Guduf, Gvoko, Lamang, Podoko, Wandala.* Aus Frajzyngier/Shay (im Druck; diese Arbeit lag uns leider noch nicht vor) sollte demnächst ebenso zweifelsfrei hervorgehen, ob wir berechtigt sind, die unter den Bezeichnungen *Mabas* und *Hdi* bekannten Sprachen als eigenständig zu betrachten oder eher als regionale Varietäten des *Lamang*. Zusätzlich finden wir zumindest Spuren weiterer Sprachen, die vermutlich einmal zu dieser Gruppe gehört haben und aufgrund der Ergebnisse von ethnohistorischen und soziolinguistischen Prozessen heute eher als Varietäten der sie umgebenden dominanten Sprachen angesehen werden (müssen), wie es in den Fällen des *Cena~Cinine* (dominante umgebende Sprache: *Glavda*) und des *Gwara* (dominante umgebende Sprachen: *Margi* aus der benachbarten Bura-Margi Gruppe des Zentraltschadischen) anzunehmen ist (Wolff 1974/75, 1979). Inwieweit die als Wandala-Lamang Gruppe zusammengefassten Sprachen in der Tat eine eigenständige und sich von anderen benachbarten zentraltschadischen Sprachen durch wohl definierte Isoglossen und gemeinsame Innovationen abhebende linguistisch-klassifikatorische Einheit darstellt, muss intensiven komparativen Untersuchungen vorbehalten bleiben, wie sie derzeit am Institut für Afrikanistik der Universität Leipzig durchgeführt werden.

[8] Dies allerdings mit gänzlich anderem Inhalt als etwa Lukas (1934). Wir halten im folgenden an zwei von Newmans Terminologie abweichenden Bezeichnungen fest: *Zentraltschadisch* (statt „*Biu-Mandara*“ bei Newman), und—nach ihren vermuteten genealogisch peripheren Hauptrepräsentanten—*Wandala-Lamang Gruppe* (statt „Mandara-Gruppe“ bei Newman). Die hier gewählte Anordnung der Sprachen im Stammbaum spiegeln in etwa die jeweilige räumliche Nachbarschaft wider.

[9] Hinter der Bezeichnung *Mabas* (auch: Vemgo) verbirgt sich ein Orts- bzw.

Für diese Sprachgruppe hat sich in jüngerer Zeit eine große Dichte an monographischen Beschreibungen entwickelt, man vergleiche die (jüngst) publizierten oder in Vorbereitung befindlichen umfassenden Beschreibungen der Sprachen *Lamang* (Wolff 1983), *Podoko* (Jarvis 1989), *Hdi* (Frajzyngier/Shay [im Druck]), *Malgwa* (Löhr 2002), *Guduf* (Kim [in Vorb.]).

Im folgenden beschränken wir uns auf die frühesten uns zugänglichen und damit vorkolonialen Quellen zum Wandala aus dem 19. Jahrhundert, d. h. solche, die zwischen 1829 und 1884 in Europa publiziert wurden.[10]

1.2 *Die erste Quelle: D. Denham und N.J. Claproth (1826)*

Die beiden uns bekannten frühesten Quellen zum Wandala, die eine in englischer, die andere in französischer Sprache mit den entsprechenden Übersetzungen im Glossar, beziehen sich offenkundig auf dieselbe ursprüngliche Wortliste, die, wie beide Quellen vermerken, „aus dem Munde [bzw. auf Diktat] des *Achmet Mandara* [*Akhmet Mandaran* bei Claproth], einem Sklaven des Scheichs von Bornu", aufgezeichnet wurde. Die Originalliste ist mit hoher Wahrscheinlichkeit von Denham selbst verfasst worden,[11] der sich zusammen mit Clapperton und weiteren Begleitern von 1823 bis 1824 im Dunstkreis des Reiches Kanem-Bornu aufhielt, während Claproth offensichtlich nur eine auf den französischen Leserkreis abzielende Überarbeitung vorgenommen und dabei selbst, etwa durch Abtrennung von Possessivpronomina, Grundformen eruiert sowie teilweise falsch „korrigierte" Formen[12] eingebracht hat. Auch sind wenigstens zwei Kopierfehler festzustellen:

Flurname, ähnlich wie hinter dem Namen Tur(u) ~ Tourou, unter dem wiederum das *Hdi (Hide~Hedi)* in früheren Quellen auch bekannt war. Zusammen mit den Sprachen der Bevölkerungen der Ortschaften Woga, Vemgo (Mabas), Vizik und Tur(u) wurden diese später unter dem Namen *Lamang* zusammengefasst (Wolff 1971, nach dessen verfügbaren Informationen es sich hierbei um ein—als solches noch nicht untersuchtes—Dialektkontinuum handelt könnte).

[10] Dabei verzichten wir bewusst auf Barths Gamergu (*Malgwa*) Vokabular von 1852, das—zunächst verschollen—von Benton (1912) veröffentlicht wurde. Das exakte Verhältnis der Varietäten Wandala und Malgwa zueinander wäre unter Zugrundelegung der Monographie von Löhr (2002) zu bestimmen; diese lag uns jedoch erst kurz vor Fertigstellung dieses Beitrags vor und konnte daher nur sporadisch eingearbeitet werden. Insofern steht eine abschließende Bewertung des Malgwa für eine sprachhistorische Bearbeitung des Wandala noch aus.

[11] Achmet Mandara wird bei Denham allerdings nicht im eigentlichen Reisebericht, sondern lediglich im Titel der im Anhang befindlichen Wortliste erwähnt. Von Claproth lag uns ausschließlich eine Kopie des Vokabulars vor.

[12] Beispielsweise notiert Claproth *Auvrè* „montagne", offenbar eigenständig eruiert

Claproth		Denham	
Mauvais chemin.	*Aungala mangara.*[13]	*Oungala mangoua*	Bad road,
Viens ici.	*Sauak*[14] *sokena.*	*Souah sokena.*	Come here,

Die beiden Wortlisten umfassen Numeralia, mehrheitlich Nomina sowie ein Verbum in Isolation, einige Nominalgruppen (Nomen + Modifikator/Nomen) sowie wenige Beispiele für Nomina + Possessivpronomen der 1. bzw. 2. pers. sg., ergänzt durch einige kurze Prädikationsausdrücke. Die Anordnung der Belege ist in beiden Quellen unterschiedlich, dabei scheint auf ersten Blick Denham im Vergleich zu Claproth formal unvollständig zu sein, was jedoch auf die von uns vermutete eigenhändige „Bearbeitung" der ursprünglichen Liste durch Claproth zurückzuführen ist. Ebenso werden an der jeweiligen europäischen Glossarsprache orientierte unterschiedliche Wiedergabekonventionen verwendet, wie z. B. frz. „*ch*" ~ eng. „*sh*", frz. „*ou*" ~ eng. „*oo*", frz. „*au*" ~ eng. „*ou*". Diese Orientierung an der Orthographie des Französischen bzw. Englischen gilt jedoch nicht ohne Einschränkungen, wie gleich das erste Beispiel „homme~man" zeigt: Claproths „*ghî*. . ." Sequenz in *ghîla* und Denhams „*gee.*" in *geela* dienen beide der Transkription von IPA [ʒiː], wie modernere Transkriptionen, so z. B. *zhílé*[15] in Mirts Feldaufzeichnungen von 1969/70[16] vermuten lassen.

---

aus *Auvrè yeakay* „grande montagne". Die Formen *Ouvra* (!) und *Ouvre yeakay* bei Denham sind wahrscheinlicher, da in *Ouvre yeakay* offenkundig eine auch für das moderne Wandala belegte Assimilation /a‿y/ > [ɛ(y)] vorliegt. Vergleiche auch die Possessivformen, die Denham einmal richtig (*Uksarwa* „My country", *Uksangra* „Your country"), jedoch zweimal aufgrund personaldeiktischer Verwechslung falsch angibt, während Claproth die unkorrekte Bedeutungsangabe von *-rwa* bzw. *-nga* verallgemeinert (daher fälschlicherweise *Uksa-rwa* „Ton pays").

[13] Vgl. auch in derselben Liste (Claproth) die Schreibung *mangaua.*

[14] Vermutlich ein Kopierfehler: Der affirmative Imperativ im Wandala sollte kein suffigiertes Element **-k(a)* enthalten (infrage käme der Negativmarker *ka*, nicht infrage käme das Pronomen der 2. pers. sg. *-ka* in dieser Position); vgl. auch Barth *sāwa* 'komm!'.

[15] Der Digraph *zh* bei Mirt ist als IPA [ʒ] zu lesen. Die Quellen scheinen zudem eine Prominenz der ersten Silbe zu kodieren, nämlich *ee* bei Denham, *î* bei Claproth. Dem entspricht der Hochton in Mirts Aufzeichnungen, verbunden vermutlich mit einem hörbaren, jedoch nicht distinktiven pänultimativen Akzent. Das Beispiel ist zugleich geeignet, den an Diachronie interessierten Tschadisten zu elektrisieren, was die Repräsentation des auslautenden Vokals betrifft: *a* in den frühen Quellen, *e* in modernen Transkriptionen; diesem Thema widmet sich der zweite Teil unseres Beitrags.

[16] H. Ekkehard Wolff dankt an dieser Stelle Frau Dr. Heide Reboul (geborene Mirt) noch einmal ausdrücklich für die freundschaftlich-kollegiale Überlassung von Kopien ihrer (auch unpublizierten) Feldaufzeichnungen vor vielen Jahren, die an dieser Stelle, wenn auch nur in kleinen Auszügen, zum ersten Male publiziert werden.

Trotz vieler Übereinstimmungen zwischen den Aufzeichnungen nach Achmet Mandara und rezenten Belegen zu Wandala-Wortformen im allgemeinen fällt doch auf, dass sich zahlreiche Abweichungen im Detail nicht durch eine möglicherweise mangelhafte Originaltranskription durch Denham erklären lassen. Während einige Erscheinungen sich einer plausiblen Erklärung erschließen,[17] stellt sich besonders bei dem oft zu beobachtenden Wechsel zwischen auslautendem *a(h)* (Denham, Claproth) und *e* bzw. *i* (übrige Quellen)[18] die Frage, ob es sich dabei um dialektal bedingte Unterschiede, diachrone Sprachveränderung oder nicht gar fehlende Sprachkompetenz des Informanten handelt. Unserer Meinung nach ist letzteres generell und besonders aus drei Gründen nicht auszuschließen: (a) selbst im Malgwa/Gamergu[19] gleichen die Numeralia den später belegten Formen auf *-e* im Wandala und nicht denen von Denham und Claproth, (b) ein derart rascher Sprachwandel, wie er bis zur Datensammlung durch Koenig (1839) erfolgt sein müsste, erscheint unwahrscheinlich, und (c) waren die Wandala seit 1723 islamisiert und sollten damit nicht (mehr) als Sklaven verkauft worden sein,[20] wohingegen zahlreiche Angehörige von in Nachbarschaft zu den Wandala lebenden Sprachgruppen, besonders den Musgu, zu Denhams und Barths Zeiten weiterhin versklavt und u.a. an das mit Mandara alliierte Reich Kanem-Bornu verkauft wurden (vgl. Denham 1826:111–119). Wie wir es im Fall von Koelles (1854) Informant vermuten, erscheint es uns nicht abwegig davon auszugehen, dass auch Achmet Mandara sich zwar über einen längeren Zeitraum bei den Wandala aufgehalten hat, dass eine Erstsprachkompetenz aber möglicherweise nicht vorliegt.[21]

---

[17] So stellte Christfried Naumann bei phonetischen Untersuchungen an den uns freundlicherweise von unserem Kollegen Kim Hak-Soo (Doktorand an der Universität Leipzig und Stipendiat des Max Planck-Instituts für Evolutionäre Anthropologie, Leipzig) zur Verfügung gestellten Mandara-Audioaufnahmen tatsächlich eine häufig auftretende, allerdings nicht-phonologische, aspirierte Realisierung von auslautendem /a/ als [aʰ] fest, die die Transkriptionen bei Denham zu unterstützen geeignet ist und Licht auch auf Barths Transkriptionen wirft, der—allerdings nicht regelmäßig—an diesen Stellen eine diakritische Markierung für Auslautlänge (?) verzeichnet, vgl. für „Pferd" *bilsah* (Denham, Claproth) mit *bélissā* (Barth)—*bə̀lsá* bei Mirt.

[18] Z. B. *teesah/tîsah* (Denham/Claproth) „nine/neuf" mit *tī́si, tī́se, tíisè* (Koenig, Barth, Mirt).

[19] Nach Barth (1852), publiziert in Benton (1912).

[20] Andererseits berichtet Barth [1862/1971:XII], sein Informant sei „Sklave" der Wándalā-„Nation" gewesen.

[21] Mit den von späteren Quellen abweichenden Lexemen *Okay* „Mund" (Wandala *wé*) und *Sardah* „zwei" (Wandala *bùwà*) liegen Lexeme vor, die wir nicht eindeutig zuweisen können und die auch nicht auf das Musgu hinweisen. Zu „Mund" vgl.

Eine Gegenüberstellung der Einträge Denhams mit auslautendem *-a(h)* bzw. *-ay/-ey* mit Formen auf *-a* bzw. *-e* in jüngeren Quellen lässt keine Rückschlüsse auf systematische Zusammenhänge im Sinne von regelmäßigen Lautentsprechungen zu.[22] Denhams Formen auf *–a(h)* sind offenbar auch keine historisch älteren Formen als die später aufgezeichneten Wörter auf *-e*, denn ist es nicht möglich, aus den Quellen allgemeine phonologische Bedingungen für eine derartige Auslautverschiebung *-a(h)* > *-e* zu finden. So bliebe offen, warum der Auslaut in *Veggea* > *vàɠíyá* (Mirt) „Nacht" erhalten geblieben wäre, aber in *Kighah* > *kíɠyé* ~ *kə́ɠyé* „drei" und *Vouyah* > *vúuyè* „sieben" einer Veränderung unterlaufen sei.[23] Andererseits ergibt sich ein ebenso wenig schlüssiges Bild, wenn man annimmt, Achmet Mandara habe das synchron für das heutige Wandala und hier allein für den Stammauslaut postulierbare Phonem /e/ (s. weiter unten) allophonisch als [*-a(h)*] realisiert. Vgl. die folgenden Quasi-Minimalpaare, die Denham mit jeweils unterschiedlichem Auslaut notiert hat.

	Mirt: *-e*	Denham: *-ay, -ah, -a*
Schaf	*kyáwé*	*Keoay*
groß/(großer) Bruder	*málé*	*Malay*
Wasser	*yéwé* (= *yáwé*)	*Yowah*
junges Mädchen	*gyáalé*	*Gala*

Glavda *ghày*, Buduma *gay*; zu „zwei" Margi *sə̀dàŋ*, aber auch Osttschadisch Dangla *sɛ̀ɛ̀r*, Migama *sê:rà*. In *Okay* könnte allerdings eine sprachhistorisch interessante, möglicherweise ältere Form für heute lautlich reduziertes *wé* zu erkennen sein: *wé* < ? *Okay* ? < *[*ɔkkʷe*] < */*kkʷa-y*/. (Eine Reduktion von anlautender Doppelkonsonanz mit obligatorischem, assimilierten prothetischen Anlautvokal zu einem „einfachen" Anlautkonsonanten ist aus zumindest einem weiteren Beispiel in Mirts Wandala-Wortliste belegt: *tlá* ~ *ə́ttlá* „Rind, Kuh".)—Eine eindeutige Identifikation des erstsprachlichen Hintergrundes von Ahmet Mandara ist uns bislang nicht möglich.

[22] Bei Denham entsprechen auslautendes *-ah* und *-a* beiden Auslautqualitäten bei Mirt (1969/70): *-a* und *-e*, vgl.

bilsah	:	*bə́lsá*	Pferd
quatana	:	*kwátə̀ná*	Sklavin
vouyah	:	*vúuyè*	sieben
drimka	:	*d(ə̀)rə̀mkè*	hundert

Auch ein Zusammenhang zwischen Denhams *-ah/-a* und Tonalität (oder generell prosodischer Prominenz) bei Mirt lässt sich nicht herstellen, vgl.

kighah	:	*kíɠyé* ~ *kə́ɠyé*	drei (finaler Hochton)
vouyah	:	*vúuyè*	sieben (finaler Tiefton)

[23] Gleiches gilt für *Souah* „Brunnen" > *sùwà* im Gegensatz zu *Yowah* „Wasser" > *yéwé* (< *yáwé*).

In jedem Fall ist vor eilig gezogenen Rückschlüssen auf diachrone Entwicklungen im Wandala durch einen Vergleich moderner Quellen mit Denham bzw. Claproth zu warnen.

1.3 *Die zweite Quelle: E. Koenig (1839)*

Zehn Jahre nach Denham bzw. Claproth erscheint eine beträchtliche Ergänzung zu den inzwischen bekannten lexikalischen Belegen aus dem Wandala bei Koenig (1839:190–197) in einem alphabetischen Wörterverzeichnis Français-Mandaraoui-Baghermaoui. Diese Quelle ist augenfällig eigenständig und besticht durch eine beträchtliche Präzision bei der Transkription, wobei auch für das an europäischen klassischen und modernen Sprachen geschulte Ohr ungewöhnliche Laute, wie die lateralen Frikative [ɬ] bzw. [ɬ^{y}] der zentraltschadischen Sprachen, einheitlich notiert werden (< s > bzw. < ch >). Vereinzelt treten Kopierfehler auf (bes. zwischen handschriftlich leicht verwechselbarem „u" und „n"), vgl. *sona* „puits" gegenüber *souah, sūwa, sùwà* in anderen Quellen. Wegen der beträchtlichen Übereinstimmungen von Koenigs Aufzeichnungen mit Barth und modernen Quellen, abgesehen von der jeweils unterschiedlichen Transkription, schätzen wir beide, Koenig wie Barth, als recht zuverlässige Quellen ein. Umso bemerkenswerter erscheint daher ein systematisch auftretender Unterschied der Formen bei Koenig und den anderen Autoren des 19. Jahrhunderts im Gegensatz zu jüngsten Belegen aus dem Wandala: Zahlreiche Beispiele für anlautendes *a* in den alten Quellen, so in *afâ* „arbre", *aoué* „chèvre", *avé* „esclave", aber auch *aktaré* „nez" bei Koenig, wurden anscheinend seither entweder lautlich ausgebaut oder reduziert, vgl. *(n)áfá, náwè, návè, əktàrè* bei Mirt. Möglicherweise vollzieht sich hier seit gewisser Zeit ein auffälliger Prozess zur Vermeidung von anlautendem *a(a)*.[24]

[24] Eine solche Entwicklung könnte erklären, warum Mirt [1969:1097], die zunächst mit von Johannes Lukas im Jahre 1933 und Heinrich Barth noch 80 Jahre früher gesammeltem Sprachmaterial arbeitete, noch drei Belege für *aa* im Anlaut findet, während Fluckiger/Whaley [1981:15] dies nicht (mehr?) angeben. Hinweise auf einen ablaufenden Prozess sehen wir darin, dass Mirts Wortliste anlautendes *a* vermeidendes prothetisches *n* in einigen Belegfällen in Parenthese setzt und damit offenbar die Existenz von Doppelformen andeutet, z. B. *(n)áx̱ápáx̱ápé* „Schulter", *(n)èylè* (< /*(n)àylə̀*/ nach Mirt 1969) „Dieb", *(n)áfá* „Baum", *(n)ázòw másá* „Sichel", *(n)ápálápálá* „Fledermaus", *(n)àvíiré* „Hase", *(n)àlbásáré* „Zwiebel", *(n)ànə́m* „Süden"; vgl. auch *(n)àaɗàfà* „rechts" vs. *nàadlàɓà* „links". Andere anlautende *na* . . . Sequenzen sind offenbar stabil, wiewohl der Vergleich mit benachbarten Sprachen der Gruppe in diesen keinen anlautenden Nasal aufweist, wie z. B. *nàmà* < > *omo* (Lamang) „Honig", *náwè* < > *ogo* (Lamang) „Ziege" etc. (Dieses prothetische [*n*-] hat eine

1.4 *Die dritte Quelle: S. Koelle (1854)*

Die bekannteste frühe Quelle für westafrikanische Sprachen generell dürfte Koelles *Polyglotta Africana* (1854; Nachdruck 1963) sein, die auch Daten zum Wandala enthält. Pikanterweise bleibt gerade diese Sprache in Koelles Einleitung unerwähnt, d. h. wir erfahren nichts über den (oder die) Informanten. Das Wandala taucht daher eher unvermutet im Vergleichsvokabular auf unter der Bezeichnung „Mándara", und zwar in Gruppe XII („Unclassified and Isolated Languages"), Abteilung C („Unclassified Central-African Languages") und ist in der begleitenden Karte geographisch korrekt eingezeichnet. Auch ist die Belegsituation für das Wandala für die *Polyglotta* untypisch lückenhaft. Dort, wo Belege vorliegen, weichen diese mitunter beträchtlich von den uns bekannten Lexemen aus anderen Quellen ab und es entsteht der Eindruck, als sei hier entweder die erstsprachliche Kompetenz des Informanten, eines ehemaligen Sklaven, aus biographischen Gründen früh und dramatisch verloren gegangen, oder es handele sich gar nicht um Erstsprachkompetenz. Für letztere Hypothese spricht einerseits das bereits angesprochene außerlinguistische Faktum der Islamisierung im frühen 18. Jh., das die Wandala in der Mitte des 19. Jh. nicht nur vor Versklavung hätte schützen müssen, sondern diese sogar selbst zu Sklavenjägern unter ihren nicht-muslimischen Nachbarn machte. Andererseits lassen sich mehrere stark abweichende angebliche Wandala-Wörter und komplexe Wortformen linguistisch einfach und plausibel durch Herkunft bzw. Einfluss z. B. aus dem Musgu erklären. Vgl.

	Koelle	Barth / Benton	andere Quellen
	"Mandara"	Musgu	Wandala ~ Mandara
slave	*báke*	*bĕgē*	*affee, avé, ēve, náve*
fire	*áfu*	*ăfū*	*kara, kárā, kárá*
sun	*fúti*	*fĕti* (Lukas *fúti*)	*vechea, vatchia, wátšia, vàcíyá*
ears	*şíme*	*shímme*	*shimmah, chema, šema, x̧əmà*
mouth	*mę́me*	*ma* ~ *mā* (Lukas)	*okay, oué, wuē, wé*

Entsprechung im epenthetischen [-*n*-] in Nominalassoziationen N_1+N_2, in denen N_2 mit Vokal anlautet—vgl. weiter unten.)—Man beachte, dass der Fall *aktaré* „Nase" anders liegt insofern, als im Anlaut nach unserer Analyse ein nicht-phonemischer prothetischer (unterspezifizierter) Vokal vorliegt, der durch die anlautenden unterliegende Doppelkonsonanz regelhaft bedingt ist: */ktara-y/ > [əktare ~ aktare]. Im Gegensatz dazu ist anlautendes /a/ in den anderen Beispielen als phonemisch und wurzelhaft anzusehen.

Bei den flektierten Verbalformen finden sich sogar auffällige hybride Bildungen, an denen offenbar Elemente des Musgu, Mandara sowie, in einem Falle, sogar des Hausa, beteiligt sind: Reduplizierte und das postverbale Subjektspronomen der 1. pers. sg. {*-an-*} sowie ein Erweiterungsmorphem {*-[V]m-*} enthaltende Formen wie *s-án-um-sa* „I come" oder *dz-án-um-dza* „I sit down" entsprechen vollständig den Formen bei Mirt (1979/71:38) für die 1. pers. sg. mit der entsprechenden Verbalerweiterung, vgl. *s-àn-ə́m-sá* „ich bin gekommen" (Mirt 1970/71:23). Hingegen sind Formen mit Personalpronomen *mu-*, wie *mú-madá-lei* „I speak", durch die Bildung der 1. pers. sg. im Musgu beeinflusst worden; vgl. Lukas (1941:33) für das Subjektspräfix *mu-~ma-~m-* im Musgu. Zugleich handelt es sich bei *mú-madá-lei* und *yá-ḥad-án-lei* „I break" auch um Verben aus dem Musgu: *mé̱da* ~ *me̱daŋ* ~ *múda* „sprechen, sagen", *hada* „brechen". Im Falle von *yá-ḥad-án-lei* handelt es sich um eine hybride Kombination eines Musgu Verbums mit dem Personalpronomen *ya-* der 1. pers. sg. für nicht-reduplizierte Verbformen aus dem Wandala plus Erweiterungssuffix *-an-* ebenfalls aus dem Wandala. Man beachte auch das typische Musgu-Suffix *-li~-lai* „Perfekt" (vgl. Lukas 1941:33, 66, 37) in Formen wie *yá-ḥad-án-lei* und *mú-madá-lei*. Im Beispiel *inā-dṣu-ā́n-dṣūa* vermuten wir Interferenz des Hausa—vgl. *ínàa* "1. pers. sg. Progressiv"—in Verbindung mit einem reduplizierten und erweiterten Wandala Verbum *cəw-a* „weinen" (Mirt 1970/71:75). Es handelt sich hier nach unserer Auffassung um eindeutig hybride Formen, wie sie für gewisse Strategien des *code-switching* bei bilingualen Sprechern in Afrika auch in heutigen Zeiten charakteristisch sind.

1.5 *R.G. Latham (1862)*

Latham stellt, unter der von Denham eingeführten Bezeichnung Mandara, das Wandala als eine Sprache aus dem „Inneren" Afrikas[25] (an anderer Stelle: des „heidnischen" [sic!] Afrika) vor und belegt diese durch eine knappe Auswahl aus der Wortliste, die wir bereits von Denham kennen. Dabei fallen Auswahl und eine erschreckend hohe Zahl von Kopierfehlern (?) auf. Vgl.

[25] „The Mandara is the nearest approach we have to a language of the interior of Africa, being the only one spoken south of the tenth degree of latitude in any part of the continent equally central . . . towards the eastern and western extremities of the zone thus described, Burton, Livingston, and others have explored; but for the interior Denham and Barth are our only authorities." (S. 577)

Denham	Latham	
Geela	*geela*	Man,
Mug'sa	*mugsa* [sic]	Woman,
Gala	*gala*	girl,
Erey	*erey*	Head,
Echey	*echey*	Eyes,
Ukteray	*ukteray*	Nose,
Okay	*okay*	Mouth,
Yowah	*yowah*	Water,
Mtaque	*mtague* [sic]	One,
Sardah	*sandah* [sic]	Two,
Kighah	*kighah*	Three,
Fuddah	*fuddah*	Four,
Elibah	*elibah*	Five,
N'quaha	*n'quaha*	Six,
Vouyah	*vouhay* [sic]	Seven,
Teesah	*teesa* [sic]	Eight,
Musselman	*musselman*	Nine,
Klaou	*klaon* [sic]	Ten,

Als originäre sprachliche Quelle zum Wandala entfällt Latham daher.

1.6 *Die vierte Quelle: H. Barth (1862/66)*

Barths zentralafrikanische Vokabularien (in 2. Auflage 1971 in 2 Bänden noch einmal erschienen) enthalten in Bd. 1 zugleich Barths eigene bemerkenswerte linguistische Analyse seiner Sprachdaten zum *Wándalā*,[26] einschließlich erster komparatistischer Ansätze. Ebenso enthält das eigentliche Wörter- und Satzverzeichnis in Bd. 2 Barths Anmerkungen zum vermuteten morphologischen Aufbau von Formen; die meisten seiner spekulativen Annahmen können wir heute allerdings nicht akzeptieren. Es handelt sich um die umfangreichste der frühen Quellen zum Wandala.

Barth seinerseits kannte die Wortlisten von Denham sowie Koelle und kommentiert Abweichungen zu seinen eigenen Aufzeichungen. Er bezieht sich nach eigenen Angaben auf durch das Kanuri vermittelte

[26] Charakteristisch für Barth, benutzt er die Eigenbezeichnung und nicht die Kanuri Fremdbezeichnung *Mandara*, unter der ihm die Sprache bereits in der wissenschaftlichen Vorbereitung seiner Forschungsreise bekannt geworden war. Barths Aufzeichungen zum von ihm nach der Kanuri-Bezeichnung so genannten *Gamergu* (Eigenbezeichnung: *Malgwa*) gingen zunächst verschollen und sind daher nicht in seinen Vokabularien (1862) enthalten; sie wurden erst 50 Jahre später von Benton (1912) veröffentlicht und werden hier nicht berücksichtigt.

Informationen eines Sklaven der Wandala, die später durch weitere Sprecher kontrolliert und bestätigt worden seien.

1.7 *F. Müller (1877)*

Diese Quelle zur „Wandalā- (Mandara-) Sprache" bezieht sich im Einzelfall explizit auf Barths Vokabularien (1862–66) und enthält Müllers Versuch einer quasi Re-Analyse bereits bekannter Daten. Gelegentlich fließen Verweise hinsichtlich ihm geläufiger struktureller und lexikalischer Ähnlichkeiten mit Nachbar- und anderen westafrikanischen Sprachen ein (z. B., in Müllers Schreibung, *Logonē, Kanuri, Son̊rhay, Hausa, Banyun, Maba, Fulah, Wolof*). Eine tatsächliche Erweiterung unserer Kenntnisse über das Wandala liefert diese Quelle nicht.

1.8 *G.A. Krause (1884)*

Diese Quelle braucht hier ebenfalls nur der Vollständigkeit halber angeführt zu werden. Sie enthält keine neuen Daten zum Wandala, sondern nur Krauses etymologische Hypothesen zur „Wurzel *za*" („gehen") und zur „Form für Fuss" im sog. „haussa-musukanischen Sprachstamm", die er, unter Berufung auf Barths Vokabularien (1862), zu Vergleichszwecken heranzieht (1884:68f.).

1.9 *Vergleichsliste*

Es ist überraschend, wie stark—neben und unabhängig von unterschiedlichen Schreibkonventionen—die wichtigsten frühen Quellen materiell divergieren. Hier liegt ein interessanter Ausgangspunkt für detaillierte sprachhistorische, entdeckungsgeschichtliche und biographische Forschungen, die uns Aufschluss geben könnten über einige Aspekte der soziolinguistischen Situation im ausgehenden 18. und der ersten Hälfte des 19. Jahrhunderts im Tschadseeraum. Bei der relativ geringen Ausdehnung des Kerngebiets der muttersprachlichen Wandala damals wie heute, das in keiner Weise mit der oben erwähnten beachtlichen räumlichen Ausdehnung ihres gleichnamigen Reiches im 18. und 19. Jahrhundert gleichzusetzen ist,[27] können wir annehmen,

[27] Innerhalb der maximalen Ausdehnung des Wandala-Reiches dürften, neben Kanuri im Norden und dem von Süden eindringenden Fulfulde, in der Größenordnung von 30 oder mehr zumeist zentraltschadische Sprachen anzutreffen gewesen sein.

dass die beobachteten Divergenzen weitgehend auf Sprachkontakt und Interferenzerscheinungen zurückzuführen sind. In diesen bilden sich vermutlich die Biographien der Informanten ab, die ja alle in bemerkenswerter Weise mehrsprachig gewesen sein müssen, um überhaupt als Informanten für die frühen europäischen Reisenden und Forscher infrage gekommen zu sein.[28]

Wir stellen im folgenden die originären frühen Quellen Denham, Koenig, Koelle und Barth sowie eine moderne Quelle, nämlich Mirts unveröffentlichtes Wandala-Vokabular (unveröff. Feldaufzeichnungen von 1969/70) zum Vergleich nebeneinander. Dabei berücksichtigen wir nur solche Belege, die—neben Barth und Koelle—in wenigstens einer der noch früheren Quellen enthalten sind.

Glossar	**Denham**	**Koenig**	**Koelle**	**Barth**	**Mirt**
Un	 *Mtaque*		*pále*	*palle*	*pállé,* *m̀tə̀kwè*
Deux	*Sardah*		*bū́a*	*búā*	*bùwà*
Trois	*Kighah*		*kádṣi*	*keyē*	*kíɗyé~kə́ɗyé*
Quatre	*Fuddah*		*úfade*	*úfadē*	*úufáɗé*
Cinq	*Elibah*		*ī́live*	*íldebē*	*íidlə̀ɓè*
Six	*N'quaha*		*ń'kōhe*	*ún̊kohē*	*úŋkwáhé*
Sept	*Vouyah*		*vū́i ~ vū́yi*	*wūye*	*vúuyè*
Huit	*Teesah*		*tī́si*	*tīse*	*tíisè*
Neuf	*Musselman*		*múselemani*	*masilmánne*	*másə́lmànè*
Dix	*Klaou*		*kalā́wa*	*kelaua*	*kə̀làwà*
Vingt	*Kulboa,* *kulla boa*		*kúlbūa,* *kúlu bū́a*	*kul-búā*	*kùl bùwà*
Trente	*Kullo kegah*			*kul-keyē*	*kùl kə́ɗyé*
Quarante	*Kullo* *fuddah*			*kul-úfadē*	*kùl ùufáɗé*
Cinquante	*Kullo elibah*			*kul-íldebē*	*kùl íidlə̀ɓè*
Soixante	*Kullo N'quaha*			*kul-ún̊kohē* *kul-ún̊kō ī*	*kùl ùŋkwáhé*
Soixante-dix	*Kullo Vouga*			*kul-wūye*	*kùl vúuyè*
Quatre-vingt	*Kullo Teesa*			*kul-tīse*	*kùl tíisè*
Quatre-vingt-dix	*Kullo Musselman*			*kul-masilmánne*	*kùl másə́lmànè*
Cent	*Drimka*			*dermke*	*d(ə)rə̀mkè*

[28] So hat Ekkehard Wolff bei eigenen Feldforschungen an der westlichen Peripherie des ehemaligen Wandala-Reiches in den 1970er und 1980er Jahren immer wieder Menschen getroffen, die bis zu 7 Sprachen, mit allerdings unterschiedlicher Kompetenz, aktiv beherrschten. Neben den damals wie heute wichtigsten überregionalen Verkehrssprachen (Hausa, Fulfulde) bzw. Amtssprachen (Englisch in Nigeria, Französisch in Kamerun) waren dies auch die ehemalige lingua francae mit heute deutlich abnehmender Bedeutung, Kanuri, sowie mehrere der lokalen Sprachen. Wandala selbst war vor 20–30 Jahren als lingua franca in diesem Teil Nigerias nicht mehr virulent, sondern spielte nur noch als Lokalsprache eine Rolle.

Table (*cont.*)

Glossar	**Denham**	**Koenig**	**Koelle**	**Barth**	**Mirt**
Deux cents	*Dibboo*[29]			*dermke búā*	
aller	*Amindala* I must go	*ellala* marcher	*lándala* I go	*dalā* Marsch *yé-delā, y(e)-éldalā*	*dlálá*
ami	*Tukkatarwa* I am your friend		*ṣlagate*	*θíggete, tsákkatē*	*tlákáté*
Ane	*Anzouwah*	*ezgô*		*ésuṅgā*	*ə́zzùŋwà*
Arbre		*afâ*	*hā́lda*	*afā*	*(n)áfá*
Barbe		*ouma*		*wūma*	*ùumà*
Beurre	*Wyay*	*ouèyé*			*wéyé*
Blanc		*dzéyé*	*fáde*		*dzèyè*
Boire		*chouchè*	*sánumsa* I drink	*ye-šenne*	*shá*
Bouche	*Okay*	*oué*	*mẹ́me*	*wuē*	*wé*
Bras		*ouroura*	*dán·gala* *árūfa*	*úrurā,* *bettaua*	*ə́rvà*
Buffle		*sákilé*		*tsá-kilē*	*ə́ttlá káambà*
Chemin	—				*úŋŋùlè*
Chat		*pâtô*	*pā́tu*	*pātu*	*pàatú*
Cheval	*Bilsah*	*béléssa*	*búlēsa*	*bélissā*	*bə́lsá*
Cheveux		*onkdjé*[30]	*ágūdṣi*	*ugdž-yīre*	*úgjè*
Chèvre		*aoué*	1. *dṣẹ̄́woi* 2. *áwui* ewe	*auē*	*náwè* *kyáwè* ewe
Chien		*kré*	*hargẹ̄́ge*	*krē*	*kré*
Ciel		*amjigla*	*aldṣéna*	*dádedem* *émdž̄iglā*	*sàmá ~* *sàmàyà*
Cœur		*erfangoulé*		*erváṅgde*	*ə́rvóŋɗè*
Cou		*yé*	*ū́le* throat	*yé,* *bokúlalā (?)*	*yé* neck *kwárá* throat
Crocodile		*bibizougra*[31]		*kirwē*	*kírwè*
Cuisses		*eddagnala*	*dán·gala*	*eg-dágnala*	*ə́gdàŋàdlà*
Danser		*échchigla*		*ye-šikle*	*shíkə̀là*
Demain		*makouralla*	*dáwei*	*makurálla*	*mákúrállà*
Dents		*saré*	*ṣláre*	*sarē*	*tláré*
Diable		*azengné*	*sátẹn*	*dž̄inni*	
Dieu		*allah*	*álla*	*dadá-mia,* *dáme*	*dàdáamìyà,* *állà*
Doigt		*golanda*	*árūfa* finger *gúlāndo* toe	*golónd(o)* *erwā*	*gùlàndà*
dormir	*Wenwyah* *yeksentia sah* je veux dormir	*lelleva*		*yē pāharē* ich schlafe	*pá háaré ~* *páaré*
Dos		*îga*		*yīga*	*íigà*

[29] Die Bedeutung ist „tausend", vgl. auch bei Barth *debū*.

[30] Wahrscheinlich Druckfehler, eigentlich *oukdjé*?

[31] Wahrscheinlich Verwechslung; vgl. *bíbízuguru* „hippopotamus" (Fluckiger/Whaley [1981:5]).

Table (*cont.*)

Glossar	**Denham**	**Koenig**	**Koelle**	**Barth**	**Mirt**
Eau	*Yowah*	*yôé*	*yọ́uẹ*	*yō ë*	*yéwé*[32]
Eléphant		*goué*		*guvē*	*gúwé*
Entrailles		*enjè*		*andžē*	*nànjè*
Epaule		*ach̄iapach̄iapè*	*gába*	*áχepē χapē*	*(á)x̰ápáx̰ápé*
Esclave	*Affee*[33]	*avé*	*báke* (male)	*ēve, ēwe*	*návè*
			áfi (female)		
Esclave femelle	*Quatana*			*kóttena (?)*	*kwátə̀ná*
Est		*tejigla*		*até-džiglā*	*gə̀ɗí*
Etoile		*trioko*		*trē yókua*	*tŕ ɣ̰àkwá*[34]
Femme	*Mug'sa*	*moksé*	*múske*	*moksa*	*m̃úksé*
Fer		*îré*			*íiré*
Feu		*kara*	*áfu*	*kárā*	*kárá*
Fille		*edzirikzâkouá*	*áktse dṣā́le*	*yāle*	*ə́gdzà gyáalé*
Fille jolie	*Shugra*				vgl. *shágr̀kà*[35]
Jeune fille	*Gala*		*áktsedṣā́le*	*édzirík, yāle*	*gyáalé*
Flèche		*gourmé*	*1. dṣọ́ulo*		*gúrmè*
			2. gúrumi bow		
Fleur		*oukbené*		*úbenē n afā*	*úgbə̀nè*
Forgeron		*eglda*		*θe-égda*	*já gdlà*
					to forge
Frère	*Malay*[36]	*edzammouroua*	*áktsam*		*ə́gdzà màmà zhílé*
			(áktsamrūa)		
Froid		*akchyé*	*ágḥli*		*lèlèɗè, kìɗə̀mmè*
Front		*ouâfké*	*dún·ura*	*wofke*	*ə́fkè* face
			forehead		
Gazelle		*zârakamba*		*zāra kamba*	*zárá káambà*
Grand	*Yeakay*	*guiakké*	*yẹ́ke*		*málé, kyàkkè*
Gros		*annaça*			*án ŋàtlà*
Herbe	*Massah*			*masā*	*másá*
Hier		*aoaya*	*wū́tsa*	*áwayā*	*áwàyà*
Hiver		*slaslakè*		*ikθe, ékχie*	*tláktláké*
				kalte Jahreszeit	dry season
Homme	*Geela*	*gilè*	*ṣíle*	*džil(-na)*	*zhílé*
Hyène		*indèlè*		*índ-alē*	*íindàlè*
Insectes		*ouchigué*		*úgdžindžā*	*úgjànjà*
Jambe		*sera*	*gába*	*serā*	*sə́rá*
Jardin		*fé*		*fē*	*fé*

32 Andere moderne Quellen, z. B. Kordass (1979: 7), geben *yáwé* an.

33 Da hier [i(:)] im Auslaut sowohl von Denham als auch von Koelle (*áfi*) notiert wird—entgegen [*e*] in späteren Quellen—, könnte dies durchaus einen ersten Hinweis auf eine partielle Assimilation und spätere Umlautung *-aKi > -aKe darstellen (K = Konsonant), und damit eine zweite mögliche sprachhistorische Quelle für auslautendes [e] im modernen Wandala (zusätzlich zu der von uns favorisierten Entstehungstheorie von auslautendem [e]; s. weiter unten).

34 Nicht näher identifizierte Transkription eines stimmhaften vierten lateralen Frikativs bei Mirt: ɣ̰ (mit untergesetzter Tilde), neben x̰ und tl, dl—in Anlehnung an Lukas (1937:115; x̰ und ɣ̰ dort als „velare Laterale mit Reibung").

35 Ugly = not beautiful.

36 Eigentlich „groß" (vgl. Beleg „Grand" bei Mirt).

Table (*cont.*)

Glossar	**Denham**	**Koenig**	**Koelle**	**Barth**	**Mirt**
Jaune		*sirkè*			*tlə̀rkè* green
Jeune		*tchikô*	*ọ́gvi*		*dàwàlè* youth
Joue		*gaïda*		*ingaida* Wangenknochen	*dəŋəlá*
Jour	*Vechea*	*vatchia*	*1. savā́rīe* *2. fúti* sun	*1. har,* *2. wátšia* Sonne	*1. = 2.* *vàcíyá*
Lait		*ouba*			*úuɓá*
Lance		*ompa*			*úupá*
Langage		*arakha, elva*			*ə́lvà*
Langue		*erakha*	*alási*	*āra*	*nàrà*
Lèvres		*zadaoué*		*zádawe*	*gàjè*
Lièvre		*aguigré*		*awīra*	*(n)àvíiré*[37]
Lion		*errefarè*		*érvalē, érverē*	*ə́rvàrè*
Lune		*tré*	*wóye* full moon?	*trē*	*tré*
Maigre		*anounba*			*shàrrè*
Main		*errfa*		*erwā*	*ə́rvà*
Maïs		*gossa*		*hīa massaré*	*híyá másáré*
Maison		*bré*	*búre*		*brè*
Malade		*aouanofoua*		*kuzā annówuā*	*lápìikíiré*
Mamelle		*oubè*	*úba*	*wūbe*	*ùuɓè*
Manger	*Zuzie*	*zouzé*	*tsanū́si* I eat	*ye-zā* ich esse	*zá*
Mauvais	—		*ṣḗgrā*		*shágr̀kà*
Menton		*kouma*		*kumma*	*kúmà*
Mère	*Mama*	*omma*	*mo*	*ūma*	*m̀mà*
Midi		*vatchiétiré*		*wátši(a) átirē*	*(n)ànəm*
Miel	*Ammah*	*ama*			*nàmà*
Millet		*koujiaré*		*medž-ébuē*	*màsàkwà*
Montagne	*Ouvra*	*ouà* stone	*wū́a*	*wūa*	*wà*
Mort (la)		*amtza*		*amtsa*	*ḿtsá* to die
Mou		*ferferè*		*ufodžókia* Lunge	*ə́ffíɗyówkà*
Mouche		*djuñḡa*		*ndžaňga*	*njúŋwá*
Mourir		*amtsamsta*	*mudṣánmutsá* I die	*ye-mtsa* ich sterbe	*ḿtsá* to die
Mouton	*Keoay*	*gilkiaoué*	*1. áwui* *2. dṣẹ̄́woi* goat	*ki-auē*	*kyáwè*
Nez	*Ukteray*	*aktaré*	*áktare*	*é-tarē*	*ə̀ktàrè*
Noir		*amagafrendiré* *dongué* bleu	*dón·e*		*dòŋwè*
Nord		*âmyela*		*kadím-yaglā*	*yàlá*
Nuit	*Véggea*	*vatnè*	*gulā́gu*	*wégia*	*vàɗíyá*
Œuf		*saya*	*ṣláke*	*θáya (?)*	*tláyá*
Oiseau		*etzaguié*		*gīye, gáye*	*ɗyíyé*
Ombre		*chidoukoué*		*tšilkō*	*shíɗúkwé*
Ongle		*serba*	*fálidṣe* *(fálidṣā́rūa)*	—	*tlə́rbà*

[37] „Erdhörnchen" bei Lukas 1937.

Table (*cont.*)

Glossar	**Denham**	**Koenig**	**Koelle**	**Barth**	**Mirt**
Or		*dindar*	*díndar*		*díindàr*
Oreilles	*Shimmah*	*chema*	*ṣíme*	*šema*	*x̰ə́mà*
Ossemens		*c̄h̄iac̄h̄ié*		*šešē*	*x̰éx̰é*
ouest		*atirzala*		*atír-zalā,futē*	*pùutá*
Pays	—	*axé*			*háhá* ground *ə́ksè* village
Peau	—	*bogua*	*káti*	*gogó*	*gògwà*[38]
Père	*Dada*	*edderoua*	*adé* (*adúrūa*)	*edda*	*əddà*
Petit	*Chequah*	*tchukó*	*dṣúgān·gudé*		*cúkwà*
Pierre		*tzanakoa*		*wūa*[39]	*nákwá*
Pied		*pléasra*		*pilla yá-serā*	*pə́làyáa sə́rá*
Poisson		*kilfé*		*kilfē*	*kə̀lfè*
Poitrine		*atoar, foudlé*	*gúlidṣi*	*áksuē*	*úksùwè*
Porte		*ongoulé*	*tágala*		*wáa wúubrè*
Pudenda mulieris		*aktchia*		*éktšia*	—
Pudenda viri		*byé*		*kudā*	*kúɗá*
Puits	*Souah*	*sona*	*vū́a*	*sūwa, gōa*	*sùwà*
Repas (en général)	*Dafah*				*ɗáfá*
Rivière	*Gouah*	*hayé*			*gúwá*
Riz	*Acheiah*	*koujeretré*	*ṣin· kāba*	*kúdžer(e) áktre*	
Sable		*khakha*		*šigga*	*shílí*
Sang		*oujé*		*wūže*	*úuzhè*
Sec		*oulèsoulè*	*gadán·*		*án ùulà*
Sel		*iji*	*ī́si*		*íizhè*
Serpent		*kavalé*	*mén·e*	*zāhe*	*zàhè*
Singe		*bechouclé*		*bašú-alē*	
Sœur	*Koudray*	*etsamroutsâko*	*yāwá* (*yuā́rūa*)		*ə́gdzà màmà múksé*
Source	*Pooshay*			*yetšua yōë*	*gòmbàzhè*
Sultan.	*Tsuksa*		*ṣlókse*	*tuksē*	*tlə́ksé*
Taureau		*ltha*[40] *exeltha* veau	*gā́ri*	*dālo* Kalb	*dàalúu* bull
Tête	*Erey*	*îré*	*ī́re*	*yīre*	*ìirè*
Vache	*Tsah* ox	*sa*	*ṣlā́geī*	θā	*tlá* ~ *ə́ttlá*
venir		*saoua*	*sánumsa* I come	*sāwa* *ye-sō bā-ya* ich komme	*sàwà* to come
Ventre		*houdé*	*húde*	*hodē*	*hùɗè*
Vert		*srekké*			*tlə̀rkè*
Viande	*Souah* meat	*c̄h̄ioua*			*x̰ùwà*
Vieux		*oumdjougô mokse*	*bādṣíbātsi*	*úmdžugē*	*ḿgyùgwà*
Yeux.	*Echey*	*îché*	*ī́tsi* (*ītsā́rūa, ītsā́n·a*)	*ítše*	*ìicè*

[38] Lukas 1937.
[39] Vgl. Berg.
[40] Vgl. Kuh, Rind.

2. *Das Enigma des lexikalischen Auslauts im Wandala*

2.1 *Konkurrierende synchrone Analysen*

Nach Mirt (1969)[41] verfügt das Wandala über zwei kurze vokalische Phoneme,[42] repräsentiert durch /a/ und /ə/, in denen sich ein einziger grundlegender phonologischer Kontrast (tief vs. nicht-tief) spiegelt, wie er auch für benachbarte zentraltschadische Sprachen von Bedeutung ist (vgl. z. B. bei Wolff 1983a, Wolff et al. 1981). Charakteristisch ist für derlei Vokalsysteme eine überraschend komplexe komplementäre Distribution von Allophonen dieser Phoneme, die allein und in Kombination mit den Approximanten /y/ und /w/ bis zu 12 phonetische Realisierungen für eine engere phonetische Transkription bereit halten können. Dabei sind unterschiedliche Inventare in den relevanten Positionen des phonologischen Wortes, d. h. initial, medial, und final, zu verzeichnen. Wir geben im folgenden unser kritisches Verständnis der Analysen zunächst von Mirt (1969) und anschließend von Fluckiger/Whaley (1981) wieder (die eingerahmten Realisierungen stellen Allophone desselben Phonems dar):

nach Mirt (1969)

Initialposition

	phonetisch nicht-lang[43]		phonetisch lang	
	[ə] /ə/	**[u]** *in velarer Umgebung*	**[i:]** /ə+y/	**[u:]** /ə+w/
[e] *in palataler Umgebung*	**[a]** /a/	**[o]** *in velarer Umgebung*	**[a:]** (*selten*) /aa/	

[41] Heide Mirts bahnbrechende Analyse beruht auf Daten von Lukas unter Einbeziehung der Barthschen Materialien; ihre eigenen Feldforschungen sollten erst nach Erscheinen jener Untersuchung in Angriff genommen werden und sind leider unveröffentlicht geblieben.

[42] Der unklare Status von /aa/ als drittes synchrones Vokalphonem kann hier zunächst außer acht gelassen werden.

[43] Auf eine nähere Bestimmung der phonetisch nicht-langen Vokale, hinter denen sich ein phonologischer Unterschied zwischen „kurzen" phonologischen Vokalen und extrem kurzen (nicht-phonologischen) pro- und epenthetischen Vokalen verbirgt, kommen wir weiter unten zurück.

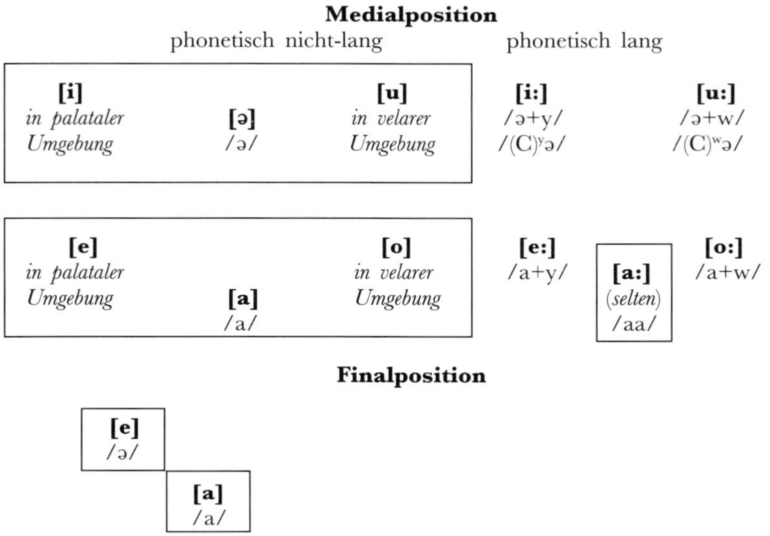

Spätere und intensivere Untersuchungen aufgrund ausgedehnter Feldforschung im Wandala-Sprachgebiet (Fluckiger/Whaley 1981), allerdings eher konservativ und an praktischen Belangen der Alphabetisation und Postalphabetisation orientiert, ergeben folgendes synchrones Gesamtbild für das Wandala Vokalsystem, basierend auf 5 angenommenen Vokalphonemen, das deutlich von Mirts mutig abstrakter Analyse, die komparativ und intuitiv viel für sich hat (s. u.), abweicht:

nach Fluckiger/Whaley (1981)

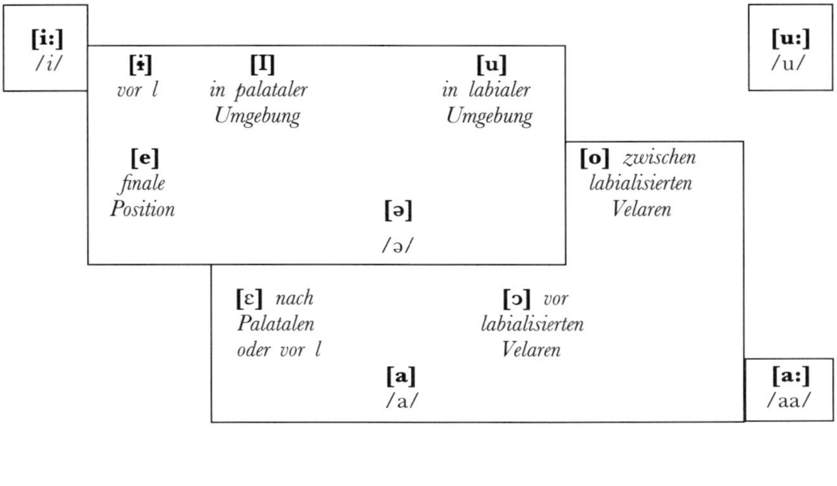

Es bleibt als Fazit die unbefriedigende Situation, dass zwei zuverlässige moderne Quellen hinsichtlich der phonologischen Analyse des synchronen Vokalsystems erheblich differieren:

Autor	Inventar	kurz	lang
Mirt	3 Vokalphoneme	/a/, /ə/	/aa/
Fluckiger/Whaley	5 Vokalphoneme	/a/, /ə/, /i/, /u/	/aa/
	2 Fremdphoneme[44]		/ai/, /au/

Wir beginnen die Suche nach möglichen Erklärungen für diesen widerstreitenden Befund zunächst mit den Beobachtungen verschiedener Forscher zu systematischen Qualitätsveränderungen von Vokalen im Auslaut des Wandala.

2.2 *Grammatisch bedingte Veränderungen des Auslautvokals*

(1) Auslaut des Nomens

Barth (1862: CCXLII) erkennt bereits 3 Strategien der nominalen Komposition und Syntax, von denen eine mit einer Veränderung des Auslautvokals eines voranstehenden Nomens verbunden ist:

> α) . . . indem man einfach die Ausdrücke neben einänderstellt, wie z. B. . . . *ugž-yīre*, ‚Haar des Kopfes', ‚Kopfhaar'; . . .
>
> α, α) Auch zusammengezogene Formen wie *χaχúndalā* für *χaχa Wándalā*, ‚Land der Wandala', gehören hierher, sowie solche Zusammensetzungen, wo ein Vokal eines der beiden Wörter eine leichte Veränderung erleidet, wie z. B. *edze **a**kse*, ‚Kind der Stadt' (*ekse*), d. h. ‚Landsmann'; *eks**á** teksē*, ‚Stadt (*ekse*) des Häuptlings', d. h. ‚Residenz, Hauptstadt'.
>
> β) Indem man ein *n* oder *na* . . . einschiebt, wie z. B. *edza-**n**-afā*, ‚Kind vom Baum', d. h. ‚Frucht', . . . *kurgún **na** hodē*, ‚Arznei vom Leib', d. h. ‚Abführmittel'."[45]

---

[44] Nur im Auslaut von Fremdwörtern, z. B. aus dem Kanuri und Arabischen.

[45] Vgl auch Barths Verweis (1862: CCXLIV) auf parallele Konstruktionen, in denen er „Eigenschaftswörter, die einen Besitz anzeigen" sieht und entsprechend analysiert:

á-hodē	mit einem Leibe, d. h. schwanger
á-n-θarē	mit einer Schneide, d. h. scharf
á-n-takaī	mit Süssigkeit, d. h. süss
á-n-ūra	mit einem Mann, d. h. verheirathet, von der Frau.

Vgl. dazu allerdings die synchrone Beschreibung einer Präposition *an* „mit" bei Fluckiger/Whaley (1981a) als der semantisch allgemeinsten von drei Präpositionen, die der Einführung eines sog. „point of reference" dienen: *an* „with", *atə* „on", *am* „in".

Man ist daher nicht wenig verwundert, wenn Lukas (1937:116) in Kenntnis der Barthschen Analyse auf der Basis seiner eigenen Feldforschungen des Jahres 1933 für das Wandala dennoch apodiktisch feststellt: „Der Genitiv wird ohne verbindende Partikel nachgestellt . . .“[46]

Auch Eguchi (1969: 139) findet bei $N_1 + N_2$ Konstruktionen einen Fall von Auslautwechsel einer Fußnote wert. Als Beispiel einer N+Adj Konstruktion findet er zunächst

/brɛ̄ cūkwa̱/[47]	small house

und notiert dann:

> Example of the case when noun is modified by noun, is shown below, viz. */brā trɛ̄ /* ‘moon house’. In this case, the final vowel changes into /-a/.

Man ist auf Basis der Informationen von Barth (und Eguchi) geneigt, im Wandala einen Unterschied zwischen Juxtaposition (Nominalkomposition) auf der einen, und markierter Nominalassoziation („Genitiv“) auf der anderen Seite zu vermuten, wobei letztere mit einer overten, ggf. allomorphische Variation zulassenden, Markierung durch *-a(n)* oder *-á(a)* in Verbindung zu bringen wäre. Auszüge aus Mirts unveröffentlichter Wortliste (1969/70) lassen vermuten, dass zumindest die Kategorie des „unveräußerlichen Besitzes“ durch das Morphem *-áa* markiert wird, das den lexikalischen Auslaut ersetzt:

gùlàndáa sə́rá	Zehe (vgl. „Finger“) des Beines
pə́làyáa sə́rá	Fuß des Beines
háa kúré	Blase (vgl. „Gehöft“) des Urins
ə́lpáa kárá	Asche des Feuers
x̱ìmáa náfá	Blatt (vgl. „Ohr“) des Baumes
tlálwáa náfá	Wurzel des Baumes
ə́rváa náfá	Ast (vgl. „Arm“) des Baumes
úksùwáa náfá	Stamm des Baumes
ə́gdz̨áa náfá	Frucht vgl. („Kind“) des Baumes
wáa wúubrè	Tür (vgl. „Mund“) des Hauses
ìiráa brè	Dach (vgl. „Kopf“) des Hauses
bráa gúrmè	Köcher (vgl. „Haus“) des Pfeiles

[46] Lukas’ Beispiele sind allerdings nun jedoch gerade solche, in denen das voranstehende Nomen lexikalisch ohnehin auf *a* auslautet, so dass eine Genitivmarkierung mittels **-a*, wenn sie ohne die Prominenz der Silbe verstärkende begleitende Prosodie (Dauer, Intensität, ggf. Hochton) daherkäme, praktisch nicht erkennbar wäre!

[47] Diakritika bei Eguchi beziehen sich auf die Tonhöhennotierung.

Weitere Bestätigung für eine overte Markierung des „Genitivs" bringen Fluckiger/Whaley, die in einem unveröffentlichen Arbeitspapier zu Orthographievorschlägen für das Wandala folgende Aussage machen (1981:3.1 Noun Phrase—Grammatical markers):

> The genitival marker in Mandara is *aa* linking the nouns, or the verb and noun. An adjectival construction is often marked by *a*.

Man beachte, dass die Autorinnen zwischen zwei verschiedenen Konstruktionen der Nominalassoziation differenzieren, die sich auch durch die Form der jeweiligen Markierung am voranstehenden Nomen (*-aa* vs. *-a*) unterscheiden.

(2) Auslaut des Verbums
Der Vollständigkeit halber sei angemerkt, dass wir hinsichtlich des Verhaltens von [*a*] und [*e*] im Auslaut von Verben im wesentlichen auf Mirt (1970/71) angewiesen sind. Bevor eine abschließende Analyse der Verbalmorphologie des Wandala vorliegt, bleibt es bei Mirts unbefriedigender Feststellung (1970/71:8, 10), die jedoch auf das engste mit ihrer eigenen Analyse des Vokalsystems (Mirt 1969) verbunden ist, und die von als „primär" und „sekundär" unterschiedenen Verbalstämme ausgeht:

> Als Stammvokale fungieren [-a] und [-e], Pausalrealisierungen der beiden vokalischen Phoneme /a/ und /ə/. Die Funktionen des primären Stammvokals können /-a/ [-a] oder /ə/ [-e] übernehmen—wobei /-a/ [-a] bei weitem überwiegt—, die des sekundären nur /ə/ [-e]. Somit sind bei einem Teil der Verbalstämme primärer und sekundärer Verbalstamm identisch . . .
>
> Die Frage, warum ein Teil der primären Verbalstämme auf /-a/ [-a] und ein anderer auf /ə/ [-e] auslautet, lässt sich vorderhand nicht beantworten. Dasselbe gilt für die Frage, warum einige der Verbalerweiterungen in Verbalkomplexen mit reduplizierter Verbalwurzel einen Verbalstamm auf /ə/ [-e] verlangen.

Während der Primärstamm als eigenständiges Wort gebraucht werden kann, z. B. als einfaches Verbalnomen oder im Imperativ Sg., ist der Sekundärstamm auf das Vorkommen in reduplizierten Verbalstämmen mit bestimmten Verbalerweiterungen beschränkt. Mirt illustriert die Existenz von zwei Verbalstämmen mit folgenden Beispielen:

	Primärstamm		Sekundärstamm
(eines) hinstellen	*[f-a]*		*[f-e]*
(mehreres) hinlegen	*[puw-a]*		*[puw-e]*
stochern	*[habaz-a]*		*[habaz-e]*
stehen		*[ts-e]*	
verbergen		*[shiɓ-e]*	
sich Kummer machen		*[shuŋgul-e]*	

Es bleibt festzustellen, dass es bislang keine publizierte und uns zugängliche grammatische Erklärung dafür gibt, dass und warum einige morphologische Bildungen im Verbalsystem, offenbar ohne funktionalen Kontrast, sondern allein lexikalisch oder als komplementäres Allomorph, sich in der Auslautqualität des Verbalstammes unterscheiden: [*a*] vs. [*e*].—Wir werden daher die Verhältnisse im Verbalsystem des Wandala im weiteren Verfolg unserer Untersuchung außer acht lassen müssen.

2.3 *Weitere Fälle von Auslautveränderung bei Nomina*

J. Lukas (1937:116) stellt systematische Veränderungen des lexikalischen Auslauts im Wandala fest, ohne dass er sich zu einer besonderen Erklärung genötigt sähe, etwa bei der nominalen Pluralbildung:

> Der Plural des Nomens wird durch das Suffix *-hà* gebildet; auslautendes *e* oder *e̱* [entspricht IPA *ɛ*- Anm. d. Autoren] verwandelt sich vor dem Suffix zu *a*. . . . In *ı̄́rè* Kopf verwandelt sich im pl. *e* in *e̤* [entspricht IPA *ə*—Anm. d. Autoren] . . .

In anderem Zusammenhang findet er das folgende Beispiel einer entsprechenden Fußnote wert („Der Wechsel von *e* und *i* ist auffällig.“; 1937:116):

é̤gjè	Großvater
há gjìrùwà	das Haus meines Großvaters

Daneben finden wir bei Mirt (1969/70) die folgenden Belege, die auf systematische (?) Apokope und Ersatz durch *-à* bei der Nominalkomposition im Singular deuten:

ə́gdzə̀r ~ ə́gdzà pl. *ə́gdzàrà*	Kind, Abkömmling[48]
ḿgyùgwè ~ ḿgyùgwa pl. *ḿgyùgwàrà*	alt, Alte(r)

markiert: Apokope	unmarkiert	
	ə́gdzə̀r zhílé pl. *ə́gdzàrà zálà*	son, boy
	ə́gdzə̀r múksé pl. *ə́gdzàrà ŋwáshà*	daughter
	ə́gdzə̀rcúkwà pl. *ə́gdzàrà cúcúkwà*	baby
ə́gdzà màmà zhílé brother	pl. *ə́gdzàrà mama(hà) zálà*	
ə́gdzà màmà múksé sister	pl. *ə́gdzàrà mama(hà) (ŋwáshà)*	
ə́gdzà màmà zhílé brother	pl. *ə́gdzàrà mama(hà) zálà*	
ḿgyùgwè zhílé old man	pl. *ḿgyùgwàrà zálà*	
ḿgyùgwà múksé old woman	pl. *ḿgyùgwàrà ŋwáshà*	

Dabei fällt im letzten Beispiel besonders das Spiel mit der Vokalqualität des Auslaut auf: *ḿgyùgwè* (mask.) versus *ḿgyùgwà* (femin.)!

Fluckiger/Whaley (1981:2.2 Phonological changes—vowels) liefern erste Hinweise zur Sytematik des auffälligen morphophonologischen Verhaltens—„in breath group medial position"—von Auslautvokalen; nach ihren Beobachtungen lassen sich zwei Gruppen erkennen:

a *e*	unterliegen der Reduktion, entweder zur Reduktionsstufe [ə] oder gar zur Schwundstufe (z. B. stets nach /l, w, y/ und oftmals nach /n, m/, also Sonoranten) vor anlautendem Konsonanten des nachfolgenden Wortes; beginnt das nachfolgende Wort mit einem Vokal, tritt stets die Schwundstufe ein.
i,u *aa* *ai, au*	unterliegen keiner Reduktion; es handelt sich hierbei, abgesehen vom Auslaut /*aa*/, in der Regel um Fremdwörter aus dem Kanuri und/oder Arabischen.

[48] Nach Forkl (1986:75) bezeichnet die von uns als apokopiert bezeichnete Form „Kind" in einem engeren Sinn („child") und die nicht-apokopierte Form einen entfernteren Verwandten der 1. absteigenden Generation („a more distantly related child; descendant"); offenbar wird diese Differenzierung in der gemeinsamen nicht-apokopierte Pluralform nicht aufrecht erhalten. Diese zunächst Skepsis erzeugende ethnosoziologische Differenzierung durch Manipulation der morphologischen Repräsentation desselben Lexems (*kinship term*) erfährt jedoch Verstärkung durch weitere Beobachtungen, wie wir sie weiter unten vorstellen.

Auf der Basis eigener ethnologischer Feldforschungen im Wandala-Sprachgebiet setzt sich Forkl (1986) mit Fluckiger/Whaleys Orthographie-Vorschlägen kritisch auseinander:

- In impliziter Übereinstimmung mit diachron motivierten radikaleren phonologischen Analysen von Nachbarsprachen (s. u.) stellt er den phonemischen Status von *ə* (schwa) generell in Frage.
- Seine Scheidung von „restriktiven" (Marker *-aha*) und „kollektiven" (Marker *-a*) Pluralen erklärt das Auftreten auslautender Vokalveränderungen in einigen besonderen Fällen von Ethnonymen:[49]

	Singular	**Kollektiv**: „alle. . . ."	**Restriktiv**: „einige. . . ."
Wandala	*ura Wandala*	*Wandalá*	*Wandalaha*
Kotoko	*ura Lagane*	*Lagana*	*Laganaha*
Kanuri	*Mufake*	*Mufaka*	*Mufakaha*
mit gelegentlichen Fällen von formaler Neutralisation:			
Muzgu	*Muzgwa*	*Muzgwa*	*Muzgwaha*
Tupuri	*Tupəri*	*Tupəri*	*Tupəriha*

- Forkl bestätigt die Existenz der oben genannten Scheidung von zwei Vokaltypen hinsichtlich des Reduktionsverhaltens anhand von weiteren Pluralbildungen, indem auch in seinen Daten finales *a* und *e* gleichermaßen vor dem Suffix auszufallen scheinen, während *i* und *u* als Gleitlaute bei der Suffigierung erhalten bleiben:

-a	*gabaga* > *gabag-aha*	cotton strip
-e	*zane* > *zan-aha*	gown
-i	*haatimi* > *haatimy-aha*	magic book
-u	*duku* > *dukw-aha*	musician

- Forkl vermutet Unterschiede des Sprechtempos hinter den Transkriptionen von Genitivkonstruktionen bei Fluckiger/Whaley:

> . . . I could perceive neither a long *aa* nor a high tone between nominative and genitive in genitive constructions and I would like to think that *áa* was only pronounced by *Wandalaha* if asked by the fieldworker to repeat a word again and again, but not if speaking more fluently. (1986:73)

Hier wird ein Problem angesprochen, das auch im benachbarten Lamang zu komplexen Annahmen für die Analyse führt (vgl. Wolff [1983:87f., 191ff.]). Dort wird angenommen, dass ein Nomen, bevor

[49] Forkls wenige Angaben zur Tonalität sind hier leider nicht aussagekräftig.

es eines von mehreren möglichen Assoziativ-/Genitivmorphemen (bzw. auch andere Markierungen) annehmen kann, zunächst in den sog. „Modifizierten Nominalstamm" verwandelt wird, der für alle Nomina, unabhängig vom lexikalischen Auslaut, auf *-á* enden muss! Die Situation im Wandala scheint ähnlich zu sein, zumal auch im Wandala mehrere Assoziativ-/Genitivmorpheme zur Verfügung stehen (s.o. bereits bei Barth 1862: CCXLII); Forkl verweist in diesem Zusammenhang explizit auf Mouchet (1950:67), der die Genitivkon-struktion wie folgt schematisiert:

nominatif + copule N, AN ou zéro + génetif

Analog zum Lamang wäre für das Wandala, in Erweiterung der Mouchet'schen Formel, das folgende Schema denkbar:

N_1 modifiziert	**Markierung**	**N_2**	
N_1-*a*	ZERO	N_2	vgl. „Adjektiv-Konstruktion" bei Fluckiger/Whaley
N_1-*a*	*-á*	N_2	Genitivkonstruktion, N_2 ist konsonantisch anlautend
N_1-*a*	*-n*	N_2	Genitivkonstruktion, N_2 ist vokalisch anlautend (Epenthese)

Dabei scheint Forkls zusätzliche Annahme plausibel, in bestimmten Fällen von Kombinationen lexikalischen Auslauts mit der („stamm-modifizierenden") Endung *-a* auch von Vokalkoaleszenz und anschließender Monophthongisierung (*i*+*a* > [*e*]) auszugehen, vgl. folgende Beispiele bei Forkl (Morphemtrennung von uns eingefügt):

1. Nomina auf *-a*

mala	*mal-a slala*	chief of a quarter
haja	*haj-an Aysəta*	the (female) pilgrim Aysəta

2. Nomina auf *-e*

mukse	*muks-a əgdzamruwa*	the wife of my brother
nawe	*naw-a Mbarara*	Bororo sheep

3. Nomina auf *-i*

muŋri	**muŋri-a > muŋre ndra*	feast of hunger (end of Ramadhan)

4. Nomina auf *-C*

lawan	*lawan-a Kassa*	the chief of Kossa
Bukar	*Bukar-a Gyama*	Bukar, son of Gyama
	Bukar-an Arɓaana	Bukar, son of Arɓaana

Zwei Erkenntnisse[50] hinsichtlich des lexikalischen Auslauts von Nomina bieten sich als Fazit an, nämlich dass

1. [*a*] und [*e*] gemeinsamen phonologischen Status haben, der sich generell in ihrem identischen morphophonologischen Verhalten äußert, insbesondere auch als
2. [*a*] und [*e*] anscheinend spurlos durch „stamm-modifizierendes" *-a* ersetzt werden.

2.4 *Eine diachrone Hypothese: Die Wirkung von „Y-Prosodie" im nominalen Auslaut*

Umfang und Zielsetzung unseres Beitrages erlauben nicht, an dieser Stelle eine umfassende Reanalyse des Wandala Vokalsystems vorzunehmen. Wir beschränken uns daher auf das auffälligste Subsystem, nämlich das der Stammauslaut-Position. Hier sind sich beide synchronen Analysen (Mirt 1969, Fluckiger/Whaley 1981) einig: Der lexikalische Auslaut des Wandala lässt offenbar nur zwei Vokale zu, nämlich [*e*] und [*a*], hinter denen sich—dies wäre die einfachste Erklärung, die dann auch beide Untersuchungen in Anspruch nehmen—der phonologische Kontrast der Phoneme /*ə*/ und /*a*/ verbergen müsste. Es ergeben sich allerdings folgende Beobachtungen und Fragen, die Zweifel an der Berechtigung dieser Analyse nähren:

– [*e*] bei Mirt[51] ([ɛ] bei Fluckiger/Whaley) in medialer und initialer Position ist ein durch die Lautumgebung plausibel vorhersagbares

[50] Irritierend bleibt der bislang einzige uns bekannte Fall des Kontrastes von *ḿgyùgwè* (mask.) vs. *ḿgyùgwà* (femin.) „Alter" vs. „Alte".

[51] Vgl. Mirt (1969: 1097, Fn. 6) zu den Vokaltranskriptionen bei Lukas: „[ɛ] und [e] bzw. [ɔ] und [o] wechseln zunächst in der Schreibung des Feldmaterials sehr häufig. Da J. Lukas aber keine Opposition der beiden Phone feststellen konnte, unterschied er sie in seinen weiteren Aufzeichnungen nicht weiter." Erst späteren Analysen in benachbarten Sprachen (z. B. Wolff 1983) blieb es vorbehalten zu erkennen, dass sich hinter diesen Vokalqualitäten Allophone unterschiedlicher Vokalphoneme verbergen: [ɛ] und [e] bzw. [ɔ] und [o] sind in der Regel und sprachhistorisch gesehen in den untersuchten Sprachen keine Allophone von /e/ bzw. /o/: [ɛ] und [ɔ] sind eher Allophone von /a/ in palataler bzw. labial(isiert)er Umgebung, wohingegen [e] und [o] ganz anderer Erklärungen bedürfen: Es kann sich bei ihnen um distributionelle Allophone von /i/ und /u/ handeln (durch assimilatorisch bedingte Vokalabsenkung), aber auch um Monophthongisierungen von Sequenzen, an denen wiederum /a/ sowie die Approximanten /y/ und /w/ bzw. palatalisierte oder labialisierte Konsonanten (/K^y/, K^w/) beteiligt sind: /a + (K)y ~ (K)y + a/ bzw. /a + (K)w ~ (K)w + a/.

Allophon von /*a*/—dies gilt jedoch nicht für die Auslautposition; hier ist [*e*] eher unvermutet die einzig mögliche („präpausale") Realisierung von /*ə*/—eine phonetisch plausible Erklärung bietet keine der Autorinnen an.

- Wenn [*e*] in finaler Position, analog zu den anderen Positionen im Wort, kein Allophon von /*ə*/ ist und dennoch mit [*a*] kontrastiert, welches ist dann die Erklärung für diesen Kontrast? Liegt hier ein unidentifiziertes drittes Vokalphonem (/e/?) mit höchst restriktiver Distribution vor, welches nur im Wortauslaut auftritt?
- Verhalten sich [*a*] und [*e*] phonetisch überhaupt gleich, z. B. hinsichtlich ihrer phonetischen Dauer?
- Ist /ə/ überhaupt ein Phonem in der Sprache, oder lassen sich alle Vorkommen als pro- oder epenthetisch vorhersagen?
- Spielt Sprachwandel eine Rolle etwa im Sinne einer diachronen Lautverschiebung von [*a*] zu [*e*] oder umgekehrt, und geben die frühen Quellen zum Wandala hierüber eventuell Auskunft?

Im Rahmen unserer längerfristigen Beschäftigung mit der Rekonstruktion zentraltschadischer Vokalsysteme wurde—in Übereinstimmung mit ursprünglich von Carl Hoffmann (1965) für die synchrone Beschreibung zentraltschadischer Sprachen zur Diskussion gestellten, später von anderen Tschadisten (Mohrlang 1971 und 1972, Ma Newman 1977, Wolff et alii 1981, Wolff 1983a, Barreteau 1983) weiterentwickelten Ansätzen—eine spezifische diachrone „Prosodie"-Theorie für zentraltschadische Sprachen entworfen, die geeignet ist, zumindest die Auslautdistribution von solchen Vokalen historisch zu erklären, die sich der Identifikation von plausiblen Lautentsprechungsreihen nach den etablierten Prinzipien der Komparatistik entziehen (vgl. Wolff 1983a). Diese in komparativer Absicht entwickelten historischen Annahmen sollen hier für eine Erklärung der synchronen Verhältnisse im Wandala herangezogen werden, d. h. wir unternehmen hier erstmalig den Versuch einer internen Rekonstruktion des Wandala Vokalsystems.

Entscheidende theoretische Konstrukte unserer diachronen Theorie sind „Vokalisationsmuster" und „Prosodie(n)". Die postulierten sog. Vokalisationsmuster („Null-" vs. „a-Vokalisation") erinnern nicht von ungefähr an das aus anderen afroasiatischen Sprachen, besonders dem Semitischen, bekannte „root and pattern" System; bei den Prosodien können wir uns im Wandala auf die „Palatalisierungsprosodie" (Y-Prosodie) beschränken. Die sprachhistorische(n) Quelle(n) dieser Y-Prosodie ist bzw. sind in einer früheren morphologischen Markierung zu suchen, die wir hoffen, im Verlaufe unserer laufenden Forschungen zur historischen Grammatik der Wandala-Lamang Sprachen abschließend identifizieren zu können—insofern ist die hier vorgestellte Analyse vorläufig.[52]

Vokalisationsmuster

Prosodien	medial		final			
[-Y Prosodie]	—	**ø**	**ø**	*[ə́gdzə̀r]*	< */g dz r/*	Kind, Sohn
	ø	**a**	**ø**	*[díindàr]*	< */d y nd a r /*	Gold
	—	**ø**	**ø**	*[shílí]*	< */ sh l y /*[53]	Sand
	—	**ø**	**ø**	*[kə́ní]*	< */ k n y /*	auch
[+Y Prosodie]						

Vokalisationsmuster

Prosodien	medial		final	Beispiele		
[-Y Prosodie]	—	**a**	**a**	*[nàmà]*	< */n a m a/*	Honig
	ø	**a**	**a**	*[ə́gdzàrà]*	< */g dz -a-r-a/*	Kinder
	a	**a**	**a**	*[mòkfòkfà]*	< */m a* k^w *f a* k^w *f a/*	Leber
	—	**ø**	**a**	*[íigà]*	< */ y g a /*	Rücken
	ø	**ø**	**a**	*[líipəlà]*	< */ l y p l a/*	Silber
	ø	**a**	**a**	*[gùlàndà]*	< */*g^w *l a nd a/*	Finger
[+Y Prosodie]	—	**ø**	**a**	*[hùɗè]*	< */*h^w *ɗ a/*	Bauch
	ø	**ø**	**a**	*[d(ə)rə̀mkè]*	< */d r m k a/*	Hundert
	ø	**ø**	**a**	*[kírwè]*	< */k r w a/*	Krokodil
	—	**a**	**a**	*[gàjè]*	< */g a dz a/*	Lippe
	a	**a**	**a**	*[gòmbàzhè]*	< */*g^w *a mb a z a/*	Quelle
	ø	**a**	**a**	*[ə́rvóŋɗè]*	< */r v a* $ŋ^w$ *ɗ a/*	Herz

Die Konsequenz für unsere synchrone Analyse des Wandala Vokalsystems, basierend auf und in Übereinstimmung mit dieser diachronen Erklärung, wäre die interne Rekonstruktion eines auslautenden unterliegenden Diphthongs */-AY/* mit phonetischer Monophthongisierung zu *[e]*.[54] Dies würde bedeuten, dass im lexikalischen Auslaut des Wandala, zumindest bei den Nomina, nur ein einziger echter phonologischer Vokal stehen kann, wenn überhaupt, nämlich */a/*. Die

[52] Eine der infrage kommenden Quellen dürfte in einem Morphem *-Y/I des proto-tschadischen Deixis- bzw. Genussystems (vgl. Schuh 1983) zu suchen sein.

[53] Vgl. Plural *shílíyáhà* < */sh l y -a-ha/*.

[54] Aus diesem Grund sollte es nicht überraschen, dass dieses auslautende [e] (eigentlich [e:]) eine den „langen" Vokalen [i:] und [u:] vergleichbare Dauer hat, s.u.

Entstehung des postulierten unterliegenden Diph-thongs werden wir weiter unten mit der Annahme einer morphologischen Markierung des Nominalstammes durch ein rekonstruierbares Suffix *{*-y*} begründen.

2.4.1 *Evidenz aus den frühen Quellen?*

Können die frühen Quellen in irgendeiner Weise dazu beitragen, die Frage nach den Auslautvokalen im Wandala zu beantworten bzw. eine der vorgeschlagenen Lösungen zu unterstützen? Dies wäre z. B. der Fall, wenn die von uns vermutete Monophthongisierung des finalen */*ay*/ < */*a*/ + {*-y*} in den alten Quellen noch nicht eingetreten oder gar Formen belegt wären, in denen statt des von uns postulierten Diphthongs noch (?) eine Form, die schlicht auf /a/ auslautet, belegt wäre.

Denham (1826) ist in dieser Hinsicht besonders aufschlussreich, als er in etlichen Beispielen eine auslautende Sequenz *ah* transkribiert, die einen Hinweis bieten könnte auf die von uns bei der phonetischen Untersuchung identifizierte Behauchung von Auslautvokalen; bezeichnenderweise notiert Delham diese „Aushauchung" nur bei auslautendem /*a*/,[55] vgl.

Denham		Mirt / Lukas (L)
Shimmah	Ears,	*x̱ə̀mà*
Oobellah	Tiger-cat,	*ùbè̤là* 'Leopard' (L)
Bilsah	Horse,	*bə̀lsá*
Anzouwah	Ass,	*ə̀zzùŋwà*
Tsah	Ox,	*tlá* ~ *ə̀ttlá* 'Rind, Kuh'
Gouah	River,	*gúwá*
Souah	Well,	*sùwà*
Yowah	Water,[56]	*yéwé*
Massah	Grass,	*másá*
Dafah	Meal, breakfast, or supper,	*ɗáfá*
Souah	Meat,	*x̱ùwà*
Ammah	Honey,	*nàmà*
Chequah	Little,	*cúkwà*

[55] Wir sehen hierin einen Hinweis darauf, dass der Vokal in der Tat in absoluter wortfinaler Position steht.

[56] Nota bene: Im Beispiel „Wasser" stimmt die Qualität des Auslautsvokals nicht überein: *-ah* bei Denham, *-e* bei Mirt, dazu weiter unten.

Auffällig viele Nomina lauten bei Denham mit einem transkribierten Diphthong aus: *ay*, *ey*; dem entspricht bei Mirt in der Regel tatsächlich der Monophthong [*e*],[57] vgl.

Erey	Head,	*ìirè*
Echey	Eyes,	*ìicè*
Ukteray	Nose,	*əktàrè*
Okay	Mouth,	*wé*
Keoay	Sheep,	*kyáwè*
Wyay	Butter,	*wéyé*
Yeakay	Great,	*kyàkkè*

Weiter fällt auf, dass die Vokalqualität des Auslauts in der Tat zwischen älteren Quellen wie Denham und modernen Quellen wie Mirt differiert, und zwar entspricht in vielen Fällen einem /*a*/ (transkribiert meist als *ah* bei Denham) ein [*e*] in späteren Quellen, dies gilt sowohl für Koelle, Barth und Mirt, vgl. z. B. die Zahlen 3 bis 8, aber auch „Wasser“: Denham *Yowah*, Mirt *yéwé*:

	Denham: *-ah*	Koelle: *-i* ~ *-e*	Barth: -è ~ *-e*	Mirt: *-e*
3	*Kighah*	*kádṣi*	*keyē*	*kíɠyé* ~ *kəɠyé*
4	*Fuddah*	*úfade*	*úfadē*	*úufáɗé*
5	*Elibah*	*ī́live*	*íldebē*	*íidlə ɓè*
6	*N'quaha*	*ń·kōhe*	*úńkohē*	*úŋkwáhé*
7	*Vouyah*	*vū́i & vū́yi*	*wūye*	*vúuyè*
8	*Teesah*	*tī́si*	*tīse*	*tíisè*

Wir vermuten in derlei Fällen, dass die moderneren Formen ein zusätzliches phonologisches Element (im Sinne einer synchron defunkten, petrifizierten morphologischen Markierung) enthalten, das für die Qualitäts-und Quantitätsunterschiede (s.u.) des Auslautvokals verantwortlich ist.

2.4.2 Interne Rekonstruktion eines determinierenden Morphems *{*-y*}

Wie bereits aus verschiedenen älteren und jüngeren Quellen belegt, sind Nomina, die synchron auf /*i~y*/, /*u~w*/ oder /*aa*/ auslauten, in Bezug auf diese Vokalqualitäten stabil. Hingegen kann man bei auf /*a*/ auslautenden Nomina eine Reduktion zu [*ə*] oder *Ø* vor Enklitika,

[57] Wir werden weiter unten ausführen, dass dieser Vokal sich phonetisch und in seiner auffällig längeren Dauer anders verhält als auslautendes /a/, auch hieraus schließen wir, dass auslautendes [e:] unterliegend eine Sequenz */a+y/ repräsentiert; s.u.

Pluralsuffixen und anderen Erweiterungen beobachten, und zwar sowohl bei Wandala- als auch bei Fremdwörtern. Wir führen im folgenden zur Illustration auch Beispiele aus der jüngst erschienenen Malgwa-Monographie (Löhr 2002) an, da eine explizite Beschreibung eines anderen Wandaladialektes nicht zur Verfügung steht und wir Grund zu der Annahme haben, dass sich die bei Löhr beschriebenen Verhältnisse auf das Wandala insgesamt übertragen lassen.

Auslaut /*i~y*/ (Fluckiger/Whaley 1981:19, Löhr 2002:98)

maʃídi [maʃí:di]	Moschee
> *mashídi na* [maʃí:dina]	diese Moschee
vgl. Malgwa *nákwati*	Schachtel
> *nákwatiyáha*	Schachteln

Auslaut /*a*/, ererbtes und entlehntes Wortgut (Fluckiger/Whaley 1981:19, Löhr 2002:227, 302)

duksá [dʊksá]	Ding
> *duksá na* [dʊksə́na]	dieses Ding
larúsa [laruːsa]	Hochzeit
> *larúsa na* [laruːsəna]	diese Hochzeit
vgl. Malgwa *mótowa*	Auto
> *mótowárúwa*	mein Auto

Auf [*e(:)*] auslautende Nomina hingegen verhalten sich unterschiedlich. Der Auslaut ererbter Wandala-Formen wird, genauso wie bei Nomina auf /*a*/, bei Erweiterung zu [*ə*] oder *Ø* reduziert, finales [*e(:)*] in Fremdwörtern bleibt jedoch unverändert.

Auslaut [*e(:)*] der Zitierform, ererbtes Wortgut (Fluckiger/Whaley 1981:19f.)

əkse [əkse(ː)]	Dorf
> *ekse na* [əksəna]	dieses Dorf
dawale [dawale(ː)]	jg. Mann
> *dawale na* [dawalna]	dieser junge Mann

Auslaut [e(ː)] der Zitierform, Fremdwörter (Fluckiger/Whaley 1981:20, Löhr 2002:251)

táihái [té(ː)hé(ː)]	Waise
> *táihái na*" [té(ː)hé(ː)na]	dieser Waise
vgl. Malgwa *dóole*	Notwendigkeit
> *dóoleyárúwa*	es ist ein Muss für mich

Fluckiger/Whaley (1981) schließen aus dem divergierenden Verhalten von auslautendem [*e(ː)*] auf zwei unterschiedliche zugrunde liegende Phoneme bzw. Phonemfolgen, nämlich reduzierbares /*e*/ in Wandala Erbwörtern sowie stabiles /*a*/ + /*i~y*/ in Fremdwörtern. Unser alternativer Erklärungsansatz für dieses Phänomen besteht jedoch darin, [*e(ː)*] im Auslaut von Nomina genauso wie im Wortinnern phonologisch in jedem Falle auf /*a+y*/ zurückzuführen und lediglich die gelegentliche Abwesenheit des Phonems /*i~y*/ vor morphologischen Ergänzungen des Nomens (d. h. die Rekonstitution von lexikalischem Auslaut /a/ bzw. dessen Schwund- oder Reduktionsstufen [ə] bzw. Ø) zu begründen. Ausgehend von dieser Hypothese müsste finales /*ay* ~ *ai*/ in Fremdwörtern zum Wortstamm gehören. Im ererbten Wortgut sollte /*-i* ~ *-y*/, mit vorangehendem stammauslautendem /*a*/ zu [*e(:)*] verschmolzen und monophthongisiert, nur bei nichtmodifizierten Nomina (vorwiegend im Singular) auftreten. Daraus ergäbe sich dann die Frage, ob für das angenommene Element *{*-y*} mittels interner Rekonstruktion (und/oder über den Sprachvergleich) eine morphosyntaktische Bedingung oder gar Funktion erschlossen werden kann.

Für Wandala-Nomina mit auslautendem [*e(ː)*] in der Zitierform treten reduzierte Formen mit /*a*/, [*ə*] oder *Ø* in folgenden Konstruktionen auf:

1. mit Genitiv markierendem /*á*/,
   vgl. Malgwa *búce* "Matte" > *búc-á Manye* "Manyes Matte" (Löhr 2002:101);
2. in Nominalkomposita,
   vgl. Malgwa *múkse* "Frau" + *bə̀lsa* "Pferd" > *múks-a bə̀lsa* "Stute" (Löhr 2002:92);
3. vor demonstrativen oder Definitheit markierenden Enklitika, s.o.;
4. im Plural,
   vgl. *Mufake* "Kanuri" > *Mufak-a* "die Kanuri", *Mufak-a-ha* "Kanuris" (vgl. Forkl 1986:72);
5. der Prädikationsbasis vorangestellte prädikativ gebrauchte Nomina qualitatis und teilweise attributive Pluralformen von diesen,
   vgl. Malgwa *dóŋwe* "schwarz" > *dóŋw-á Bukare* "Bukar ist schwarz"; *páçe* "kurz" > *páç-páça* "kurz (Plural)" (Löhr 2002:105).

Da das vermutete Element *{*-y*} im Singular in paradigmatischer Beziehung zu determinierenden Markierungen in determinierenden Konstruktionen (vgl. 1., 2.) bzw. generell zu Determinatoren (vgl. 3.)

steht, soll es hier tentativ als gleichermaßen inhärent "determinierend" definiert werden. Freilich ist *{*-y*} synchron nicht mehr produktiv wirksam, sondern ist nur petrifiziert in einem den semitischen Sprachen ähnlichen "Status absolutus" erhalten geblieben. Für eine ursprüngliche determinierende Funktion von *{*-y*} sprechen drei weitere Gesichtspunkte:

– Die meisten Nomina qualitatis lauten in ihrer Zitierform auf [*e(ː)*] aus und nur wenige auf /*a*/, vgl. Malgwa *dóŋwe* "schwarz", aber *kwákkya* "viel". Attributiv gebraucht folgen sie dem näher zu bestimmenden Nomen, so z. B. *kábowə kwákkya* "viel Geld" (Löhr 2002:104f.). Werden sie jedoch prädikativ eingesetzt, stehen sie (meist?) vor dem Nomen und enden auf ein hochtoniges *-á*, das Löhr (2002:105) als „Genitivmorphem" analysiert, vgl.

  dóŋw-á Bukare Bukar ist schwarz.

  Eine genitivische Konstruktion für Nominalprädikationen muss jedoch zumindest als höchst untypisch gelten, da der Genitiv universal vor allem bei Nominalattributionen (vgl. Bußmann 1990: 273), wo er in Bezug auf Nomina qualitatis im Malgwa gerade nicht in Erscheinung tritt, benutzt wird und für Prädikationsbasen eher neutrale Formen zu erwarten wären. Das „Genitivmorphem" spielt außerdem bei anderen Nominalprädikationen im Malgwa keine Rolle (Löhr 2002:242–245). Des weiteren führt Löhr selbst (2002:105) das nicht kommentierte Beispiel einer auf /*a*/ auslautenden attributiven Verwendung von *mândale̱* "groß" an: *ŋávale mândala̱* . . . "eine große Kobra . . ." (vgl. *mândal-á̱ ŋávale* "eine Kobra ist groß"). Deswegen ist zu vermuten, dass die historischen, evtl. sogar die synchron indefiniten Grundformen von Nomina qualitatis auf /a/ auslauten und so prädikativ (mit „kopulativem" Hochton?) verwendet werden, hingegen die heutigen Zitierformen das Element *{*-y*} wegen des häufigen determinierenden Gebrauchs enthalten. *{*-y*} bei anderen Nomina hat allerdings synchron keine Definitheit markierende Funktion mehr, vgl. "*ŋávale̱ mândala* . . ." "eine große Kobra . . .".

– Ein weiteres Argument für ein petrifiziertes, ehemals vermutlich determinierend gebrauchtes Element *{*-y*} liegt in der Distribution von auslautendem [*e(ː)*] bei Nomina des semantischen Merkmals [+Mensch], bei denen universal von einer hohen Diskursreferenzialität auszugehen ist. Während Nomina, die engste Verwandtschaftsverhältnisse bezeichnen und daher oft inhärent definit sind, /*a*/ im Auslaut aufweisen, vgl. Malgwa *dá, ada, dáda* "Vater", *ma, mama, ə́mma* "Mutter", *máala* "Vorfahr, Ältester", *kwáta* "Tochter", *hágwala* "Junge, der als sechstes Kind geboren wird" oder *ə́ggya* "Großeltern, Enkel", lauten sehr viele Bezeichnungen für weniger enge, nicht inhärent definite Verwandtschaftsverhältnisse, Menschen allgemein und tierische Protagonisten von Fabeln auf [*e(ː)*] aus: Malgwa *kúdəre* "jüngere Geschwister (sg.)", *hə́me* "Schwager, Schwägerin", *shówóle* "Schwiegerleute"; *múkse* "Frau", *ʒíile* "Mann", *gyáale* "Mädchen", *ɬə́kse* "König"; *ə́rvare* "Löwe", *navíre* "Hase", *vəré* "Affe", *guwé* "Elefant", *íindale* "Hyäne".[58]

– Schließlich erwähnt Löhr (2002:88ff.) ein zur Bildung von Komposita herangezogenes finales Element "-*e*", dessen Funktion sie als "nominalisierend" beschreibt, wobei diese Funktion kaum für alle drei folgenden Beispiele gelten kann. Unserer Meinung nach verbirgt sich hinter dem „-*e*" wiederum das ehemals determinierende Element *{-*y*} in Verbindung mit stammauslautendem /*a*/:

nánjé	Darm
< *ná-* + *nja* 'Sitzen' + *-e* NOMIN (Löhr 2002:88)	
kwátsape	Grasart
< *kwáta* 'Tochter' + *sápa* 'Worfeln' + *-e* NOMIN	(S. 92)
kwátambé	Ortsname
< *kwáta* 'Tochter' + *ʔámba* 'Haus' + *-e* NOMIN	(S. 92).

Uns erscheint die bisher vertretene Meinung, die von einem Phonem /*e*/ mit auffällig restringierter Distribution (nur im Stammauslaut!) ausgeht bzw. von einem Phonem schwa, das wiederum nur für die Stammauslautposition als eigenständiges Phonem gebraucht würde und überall sonst problemlos als pro- und epenthetischer, extrem flüchtiger (s. unten) und unterspezifizierter Vokal vorhergesagt werden kann, wenig plausibel. Die hier vorgestellte alternative Hypothese eines petrifizierten, historischen determinierenden Elementes *{-*y*} kann

– Auslautveränderungen erklären, ohne auf unsystematisch wirkende Vokalelisionen bzw. -koaleszenzen zurückgreifen zu müssen,

[58] Man vgl. in diesem Zusammenhang auch die von Forkl [1986:75] beschriebene Differenzierung zwischen *ə́gdza* „child" und *ə́gdzəre* „a more distantly related child; descendant".

– unterschiedliche Formen bei Nomina qualitatis sowie Nominalkompositionen einfach begründen, und
– [*e(ː)*] einheitlich als zugrunde liegende Phonemfolge von /*a*/ + /*i~y*/ im In- und Auslaut analysieren.

Die hier vorgestellte diachron begründete Analyse des Nominalauslauts im Wandala geht zugleich von einem fortschreitenden Petrifizierungsprozess aus, der wiederum geeignet ist, einen Deutungsansatz zu liefern für das Fehlen von systematischen Auslautentsprechungen zwischen Denhams Wortliste und jüngeren Quellen einerseits, und relativ eng verwandten Sprachen der Wandala-Lamang Gruppe insgesamt andererseits (Wolff 1983a).

2.4.3 Synchrone Evidenz: Phonetische Dauer der Vokale
Es wäre nun zu prüfen, ob wir synchrone Evidenz für unsere historische Analyse finden können, die sowohl auf der oben ausgeführten internen Rekonstruktion als auch auf hier nicht weiter begründeter komparativer Evidenz (vgl. Wolff 1983a) beruht.

Eine 25 Wörter umfassende phonetische Untersuchung von rezenten Wandala-Daten[59] ergibt hinsichtlich der Qualität und Dauer der in Frage stehenden Vokale folgende Ergebnisse.

1. Zunächst lassen sich in einer engen Transkription die Vokale genauer bestimmen: [ə] steht für IPA [ɘ], und [a] entspricht IPA [ɐ], während [iː] recht offen realisiert wird: IPA [i̞ː] oder [e̝ː]. Die Allophone von Fluckiger/Whaleys /ə/ entsprechen in der Tat IPA [ɪ], [ɘ] und [ʊ].
2. Die komplementäre Distribution von [e] and [ɛ] kann bestätigt werden.
3. Phonetisch sind drei Längenstufen zu unterscheiden:
   Die Allophone von Fluckiger/Whaleys /ə/ in initialer und medialer Position sind sehr kurz (0.03 s bis 0.04 s);

   /u/ [uː], /i/ [iː] und praktisch alle Fälle von finalem [e] (= [eː] !) werden sehr lang realisiert, d. h. zwischen 0.14 s und 0.18 s;

[59] Kim Hak-Soo führte im Rahmen von Feldforschungen zum Guduf u. a. auch Erhebungen zu benachbarten Sprachen der Wandala-Lamang Gruppe durch, darunter das Wandala selbst. Wir danken ihm für die freundliche Überlassung seiner Wandala Audiodaten, die Christfried Naumann dann einer engeren phonetischen Untersuchung unterzog.

die Dauer der Allophone [a] und [ɛ] des Phonems /a/ rangieren zwischen 0.06s und 0.12s,[60] d. h. deutlich länger als die Allophone von Fluckiger/Whaleys /ə/ in initialer und medialer Position, und deutlich kürzer als die Allophone von /i/und/u/.

Wir schließen daraus, dass unsere diachron motivierte Analyse des Wandala zutrifft, nämlich dass

1. schwa mit seinen umgebungsbedingten Varianten [ɪ], [ɘ] und [ʊ] kein Phonem repräsentiert, sondern stets nur als pro- oder epenthetischer Vokal auftritt; Merkmale seines nicht-phonemischen Status wären die extrem kurze Dauer und die charakteristische Unterspezifizierung hinsichtlich der Qualität;
2. /a/, und nicht nur im Auslaut, das einzige echte „kurze" Vokalphonem darstellt;
3. /i/ und /u/ vermutlich nichts anderes sind als silbische Realisierung der schwachen Radikale /y/ und /w/, ggf. unter Mitwirkung pro- und epenthetischer Vokale bei Doppelkonsonanz (vgl. bereits Mirts Analyse für [i:] und [u:] als *ə+y und *ə+w);
4. [e:] auch im Auslaut tatsächlich, nicht zuletzt aufgrund seiner phonetischen Dauer, einen monophthongisierten Diphthong */-ay/ darstellt; damit wären (a) sowohl innerhalb des Systems das Auftreten von [e:] einheitlich erklärt, als auch (b) die Annahme bestätigt, dass sich hinter auslautendem [e:] eine morphologisch komplexe Stamm-„Endung" verbirgt, an der ein rekonstruierbares Affix *{*-y*} beteiligt ist.

2.5 *Schluß und Ausblick*

Wir sind abschließend geneigt, folgende vorläufige Analyse des Systems von Vokoiden im Wandala zusammenfassend zur Diskussion zu stellen.[61] Die gerahmten Felder stellen die vokoiden Phoneme des Wandala dar—sowohl diachron als auch synchron. Alle anderen

---

[60] Die Messungen der Auslautvokale erwiesen sich allerdings als schwierig, weil der lange Intensitätsabfall, verbunden mit Aspiration (?; s.o.), den finalen Punkt nicht leicht bestimmbar macht.

[61] Unsere Analyse legt es nahe, in Sprachen wie dem Wandala nicht weiter von „Vokalen" und „Vokalsystemen" im herkömmlichen Sinne zu sprechen, sondern in einem abstrakteren Sinne von „Vokoiden", zu denen wir Vokale im engeren Sinn und die traditionell sogenannten „Semivokale" (und ggf. weitere Einheiten des phonologischen Inventars) zählen; damit wird die Dichotomie Vokal: Konsonant aus typologischen Gründen bewusst aufgehoben.

auftretenden phonetischen Vokale sind vorhersagbar in ihrer pro- und epenthetischen Funktion und Distribution und stellen keine Vokalphoneme dar:[62]

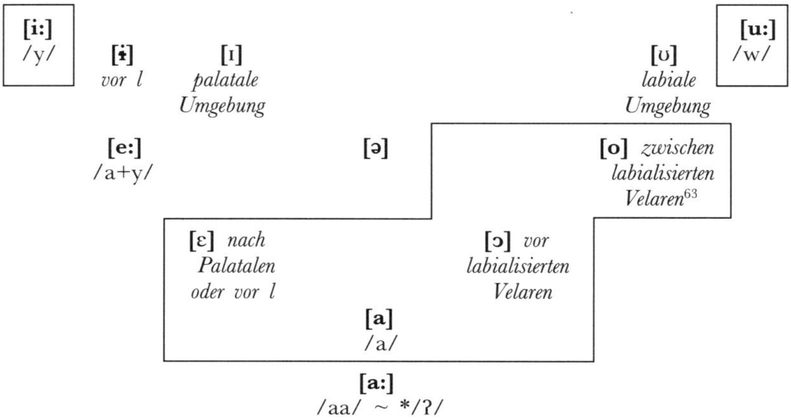

Damit wird Mirts bahnbrechende Analyse (1969) einerseits bestätigt, andererseits zugleich konsequent weitergeführt. Statt der bei Mirt postulierten Opposition von zwei kurzen Vokalphonemen */a/* und */ə/* und der Annahme eines eher marginalen Vokalphonems */aa/* glauben wir davon ausgehen zu sollen, dass die grundlegende „vokoide" Opposition im Wandala ursprünglich, wenn überhaupt, allenfalls die zwischen */a/* und */aa/* ist.[64] Die alleinige Opposition von */a/* und */aa/* lässt kaum noch zu, im Falle des Wandala von der Existenz eines klassischen „Vokalsystems" mit mehreren Opposition zu sprechen—auf abstrakter Ebene opponieren allenfalls „Anwesenheit" und „Abwesenheit" von /a/ in Positionen, die als potenzielle Silbennuclei in Frage kommen.

Gleichzeitig scheint das Wandala einen sprachhistorischen Prozess zu durchlaufen, dessen Ergebnis die Etablierung eines Vokalsystems

[62] Als marginale Einheiten kämen zum synchronen System hinzu Mono- und Diphthonge wie [e ~ ai] und [o ~ au] in Fremdwörtern.

[63] Sowie, analog zu [e:] < /a/ +/(K)y/, [o] als Assimilationsprodukt aus /a/ + /(K)w/.

[64] Wir sind geneigt, zu einem späteren Zeitpunkt die Analyse von /aa/ als Phonem im Wandala und verwandten Sprachen ebenso in Frage zu stellen und, analog zu /y~i/ und /w~u/, synchron-phonologisches phonetisches [a:] auf die silbische Repräsentation eines unterliegenden Vokoiden */ʔ/ zurückzuführen. Damit wäre das Wandala, zumindest in diachroner Perspektive, als Sprache ohne echtes „Vokalsystem" zu beschreiben.

mit 5 (oder 6 inklusive schwa) Qualitäten wäre, ggf. ergänzt durch die Phonologisierung von Vokallänge, d. h. durch systematische Phonologisierung der vorhandenen phonetischen Kontraste, die die Sprache jetzt und bereits seit langem an der phonetischen Oberfläche ihres phonologischen Systems erlaubt.

Interessanterweise erlauben also tschadische Sprachen nicht nur die Beobachtung von „Tonogenese" (vgl. Wolff 1983b, 1987), d. h. des typologischen Übergangs von nicht-tonalen Prosodien zur Tonalität, sondern zugleich, zunächst jedenfalls das Wandala und seine nächsten Verwandten in der Wandala-Lamang Gruppe, auch die Beobachtung von „Vokalgenese", d. h. des typologischen Übergangs von phonologischen Systemen auf der Basis von abstrakten „Vokoiden" (d. h. ohne echte Vokale) zu Systemen mit echten Vokalen. Hierin liegt die weitere herausragende typologische Besonderheit des Wandala—neben der in der Einleitung hervorgehobenen Tatsache, dass es sich zugleich um eine wissenschaftshistorisch besonders bedeutende (zentral-) tschadische Sprache handelt.

Literaturverzeichnis

Barreteau, D. 1983. Phonémique et prosodie en higi. In Studies in Chadic and Afroasiatic Linguistics, hg. von E. Wolff und H. Meyer-Bahlburg, 249–276. Hamburg: Helmut Buske.

Barth, H. 1862. Sammlung und Bearbeitung Central-Afrikanischer Vokabularien. 2 Bde. Gotha: Justus Perthes. (2nd edition: London 1971.)

Benton, P.A. 1912. Notes on Some Languages of the Western Sudan, including 24 unpublished vocabularies of Barth, extracts from correspondence regarding Richardson's and Barth's expeditions, and a few Hausa riddles and proverbs. London: OUP.

Bußmann, H. 1990. Lexikon der Sprachwissenschaft. Stuttgart: Kröner.

Claproth, N.J. 1826. Essai sur la langue du Bornou, suivi de vocabulaires du Begharmi, du Mandara et de Timbouctou. Paris.

Denham, D. [H. Clapperton, W. Oudney.] 1826. Narrative of Travels and Discoveries in Northern and Central Africa, in the Years 1822, 1823, and 1824, by Major Denham, Captain Clapperton, and Doctor Oudney . . . London.

Eguchi, P.K. 1969. Notes on the Mandara Language of Mora. Kyoto University African Studies 3: 133–141.

Fluckiger, Ch. and A. Whaley. 1981. A proposed writing system for the Mandara language. SIL. (Unveröff.)

——. 1981a. The uses of three prepositions in Mandara. In Chadic language studies in Northern Cameroon, hg. von U. Wiesemann. Africana Marburgensia, Special Issue 5, 4–16.

Forkl, H. 1986. Some suggestions for improving Fluckiger/Whaley's writing system for the Wandala language. African Marburgensia 19/2: 67–78.

Frajzyngier, Z. und E. Shay. [Im Druck]. A Grammar of Hdi. The Hague: Mouton de Gruyter.

Hair, P.E.H. 1967. The Early Study of Nigerian Languages: Essays and Bibliographies. Cambridge: CUP.
Hoffmann, C. 1965. A tentative analysis of the phonology of Higi. (Mimeogr.)
Kim, H.-S. [in Vorber.] Grammatik des Guduf. (Dissertation an der Universität Leipzig.)
Koelle, S.W. 1854. Polyglotta Africana. London. (Nachdruck: Graz 1963).
Koenig, E. 1839. Vocabulaires appartenant à diverses contrées ou tribus de l'Afrique. Vocabulaires des mots des idiomes de Dar-Four, de Barnou, de Mandara et de Baghermi. In: Recueil de voyages et de mémoires publié par la Societé de Géographie. Tome Quatrième, 181–197. Paris.
Krause, G.A. 1884. Proben der Sprache von Ghat in der Sahara. Leipzig: F.A. Brockhaus.
Latham, R.G. 1862. Elements of Comparative Philology. London: Walton and Maberly.
Lukas, J. 1934. Die Gliederung der Sprachenwelt des Tschadsee-Gebiets in Zentralafrika. Forschung und Fortschritt 10.29: 356–357.
——. 1937. Zentralsudanische Studien. Hamburg.
——. 1952. „Chadic", „Chadohamitic". In Handbook of African Languages, Part II: The Languages of West Africa, hg. von D. Westermann und M.A. Bryan. London: OUP.
Löhr, D. 2002. Die Sprache der Malgwa—Nárá Málgwa. (Studien zur Afrikanistik 6.) Frankfurt: Peter Lang.
Mirt, H. 1969. Einige Bemerkungen zum Vokalsystem des Mandara. ZDMG Suppl. I., 1096–1103.
——. 1969/70. Word List (547 lexical items) collected from Namada Brayim from Mora, Cameroon. (Unveröff.)
——. 1970/71. Zur Morphologie des Verbalkomplexes im Mandara. Afrika und Übersee 54/1–2: 1–76.
Mohammadou, E. 1982. Le Royaume du Wandala ou Mandara au XIXe Siècle. (African Languages and Ethnography XIV). Tokio: ILCAA.
Mohrlang, R. 1971. Vectors, prosodies, and Higi vowels. Journal of African Languages 10/1: 75–86. Special Issue, hg. von P. Newman.
——. 1972. Higi Phonology. Studies in Nigerian Languages 2. Zaria, Kano.
Mouchet, J.-J. 1950. Vocabulaires comparatifs de quinze parlers du Nord-Cameroun. Etudes Camerounaises 29/30: 5–74.
Müller, F. 1877. Grundriss der Sprachwissenschaft. (Bd. I, Abt. II. Die Sprachen der wollhaarigen Rassen.) Wien: Alfred Hölder.
Newman, P. 1990. Nominal and Verbal Plurality in Chadic. Dordrecht: Foris.
——. 1996. Hausa and the Chadic Language Family: A Bibliography. Köln: R. Köppe.
Schuh, R.G. 1983. The evolution of Chadic determiners. In Studies in Chadic and Afroasiatic Linguistics, hg. von E. Wolff und H. Meyer-Bahlburg, 157–210. Hamburg: Helmut Buske.
Seetzen, U.J. 1810. Über das große afrikanische Reich Burnu und dessen Nebenländer, und über die Sprache von Áffadéh. Monatliche Correspondenz zur Beförderung der Erd- und Himmelskunde 22: 269–341.
Sölken, H. 1957. Seetzens Áffadéh—Einführung in die Bearbeitung eines älteren Kotokovokabulars. Anthropos 52: 199–238.
——. 1967. Seetzens Áffadéh in kritischer Sicht—ein Beitrag zur Kotokosprachdokumentation. Berlin.
Wolff, [H.]E. 1971. Die sprachliche Situation im Gwoza-Distrikt, Nordostnigeria. Journal of African Languages 10/1: 61–75. Special Issue, hg. von P. Newman.
——. 1974/75. Sprachwandel und Sprachwechsel in Nordostnigeria. Afrika und Übersee 58: 187–212.

——. 1979. Spachkontakt und Ethnizität: Sprachsoziologische Anmerkungen zum Problem der historischen Interpretierbarkeit genetischer Sprachbeziehungen. SUGIA 1: 143–173.
——. 1981. Vocalization Patterns, Prosodies, and Chadic Reconstructions. *Studies in African Linguistics* Suppl. 8: 144–148.
——. 1983. A Grammar of the Lamang Language (*Gwàɗ Làmàŋ*). Glückstadt: J.J. Augustin.
——. 1983a. Reconstructing Vowels in Central Chadic. *Studies in Chadic and Afroasiatic Linguistics*, hg. von E. Wolff and H. Meyer-Bahlburg, 211–232. Hamburg: H. Buske.
——. 1983b. Tonogenese in tschadischen Sprachen. *Afrika und Übersee* 66: 203–220.
——. 1987. Consonant-Tone Interference in Chadic and ist Implications for a Theory of Tonogenesis in Afroasiatic. In *Langues et Cultures dans le Bassin du Lac Tchad*, ed. by D. Barreteau, 193–216. Editions de ORSTOM.
——, A. Hauenschild und Th. Labahn. 1981. Biu-Mandara Vowel Systems. *Berliner Afrikanistische Vorträge*, hg. von H. Jungraithmayr und G. Miehe, 259–276. Berlin: D. Reimer.

SECTION FIVE

COMPARATIVE SEMITO-HAMITIC (AFRO-ASIATIC) LINGUISTICS

ETYMOLOGY OF SOME HAMITO-SEMITIC (AFROASIATIC) ANIMAL NAMES

Aharon B. Dolgopolsky
(University of Haifa)

The etymology of the Hamito-Semitic lexems is being investigated in the framework of the Nostratic theory that claims genetic relationship between HS (Hamito-Semitic), IE (Indo-European), Kartvelian, Uralic, Altaic, and Dravidian.

1. **Ham.-Sem.**: Central Sem. *ʔarᒥyᒣay- 'lion' or sim. > Hebrew אַרְיֵה ʔar[1]yē, אֲרִי ʔ^{a}rī 'lion', Phoen. ʔrw, Ugar. ʔ$_{a}$rw, Bibl. Aram. אַרְיֵה ʔar'yē, pl. ʔarˌyāwā'tā, Jewish Aram. אַרְיָה ʔar'yā, West Syriac ʔar'yo 'lion', as well as Geʿez ʔarwē 'wild beast'; ? Canaanite > New Egyptian ỉr 'lion' || Egyptian (from Pyramide texts), Demotic Eg. rw 'lion' || Chadic: East Ch.: Mubi {Jungraithmayr} ʔórúwà, Migama {Jungr.} ʔā́rúm 'lion', Tumak {Caprile} ɜ̍rɜ̍w 'leopard' ┆┆ ?? Central Ch.: Musgum-Pus {Tourneux} àhìráw, {Mouchet} ahraw id. ┆ Lamang {Lukas} ərvárè 'lion' ┆ Mandara {ChL} ʔʊrʊv^{w}ɜ̀rì, {Mouchet} ərvạrẹ, Glavda {Rapp} árɜ̀vara, {ChL} árvàrà, Gava {ChL} ʔúrvárà, Dghwede {Frick} rvírè, {ChL} àrvírè id. ┆ Logone {Lukas} rə́vəni id. || **Dravidian** {tr., GS} *uṙuv- 'tiger' > Tamil uṟuvai̯, Telugu duvvu, Kolami duv, ḑū, Gondi ḑū, ḑūal 'tiger', ḑuwāl, ḑuwwal 'panther' ◇ The Nostratic reconstruction is *ʔᒥUᒣŕ∇w∇ 'large feline'.

2. **HS**: Sem. *ʔarway- > Amorite {Gelb} ʔarwiyum 'gazelle', Akkadian arwium ~ arwûm 'gazelle (male)', Arabic أُرْوِيَّة ʔurwiyyat- (pl. أَرْوَى ʔarwā) 'mountain goat' ({Freytag} 'capra montana, rupicapra'), Geʿez አርዌ ʔarwē 'beast, animal' || Cushitic: ?? Beja {Reinisch} ra '∈ antelope' ┆┆ Dahalo ʔā́rōle 'eland' ┆┆ ¿¿ South Cushitic: Ehret ties in Kwadza ʔaʒa dilingoyi 'bushbuck' || **Alt.**: Mongolian: Class. Mong. orungu, Halha, Buryat orongo '∈ small dark antelope with long flat horns', ⇸ Manchu orongo 'wild goat, wild mountain ram', {Hauer} 'schwarze Hirschziegenantilope', {Zaxarov} 'wild dark-coloured ram, resemblin a chamois' || Tungusian *oron 'reindeer' > Ewenki oron, Lamut orъn, Negidal oyon, Orochi oro, Ude oro~olo, Ulcha oro(n-), Nanay orõ 'domestic reindeer', Manchu oron buxu id. || **Drav.** *Uṙʟ-ay-ɹ 'deer' > Tamil uṟay, Tulu

uræ, ule, dial. uḻe 'deer', Parji uṙup 'spotted deer' ◇ The Nostratic reconstruction is *ʔoŕ⌜u⌝ '(male) antelope, deer'.

3. **Ham.-Sem.**: Sem.: Arabic ʔaym- 'serpens, viperae mas', ʔīm- 'serpens albua, tenuis' | | Chadic: West Ch.: proto-Angas-Goemay {Stolbova} *ŋgwo 'snake' > Sura {Jungr.} ŋ̀wɔ̄, Angas ^{ŋ}g^{w}ɔ̀ŋ, Chip nwò ¦ ? Hausa (Sokoto, Zaria) ganwo 'a coiled snake, coil of rope' ¦¦ ?? Central Ch.: Masa {Mouchet} gwī, {Jungr.} gúydá ¦¦ East Ch.: ? Kera hə̀nǯí 'snake' | | **IE**: Narrow IE {Pokorny} *ang^{wh}i- ~ *ang^{w}i-, {Devoto} *e(n)g^{wh}- 'snake, worm' > Latin anguis 'snake' ¦¦ Lithuanian angìs id., Latvian ùodze 'adder, viper' ¦ proto-Slavic *ǫžь > Russian уж 'grass-snake', Polish wąż 'snake' ¦¦ Armenian օձ ôʒ (< *au̯ʒ) 'snake' ¦¦ Middle Irish esc-ung 'eel' ("water snake": esc 'water', ung < *ang^{w}hō), Welsh llys-yw-en 'eel' ¦¦ OHG (= Old High German) unc 'snake, adder' | | **? Kartvelian**: Early New Georgian ankara '∈ small snake', New Georgian anḳara 'grass-snake (ужъ)', {Chxenkeli} 'blind worm (Blindschleiche, Anguis fragilis)' (a loanword?) ¶ The consonant ḳ and the final element -ara remain puzzling ◇ The Nostratic reconstruction is *ʔEŋU '∈ snake'.

4. **HS**: West Sem *'ʕayr- ~ *ʕīr- 'male wild ass, ass foal' > Bibl. Heb. עַיִר 'ʕayir, with possessive suffixes: ʕīr-: עִירוֹ ʕī'r-ō 'his male ass' (the pl. form of the Masoretic tradition עֲיָרִים, עֲיָרִם ʕ^{a}yā'rīm is on the analogy of *'1a2a3- nouns, cp. the Samaritan Hebrew cognate form עירם 'īrəm), Ugar. ʕr {Aistleitner} 'ass foal', {Olmo Lete & Sanmartín} 'ass', Jewish Aram. [Targum] pl. עַיְרִין ʕay'r-īn id., Arabic ʕayr- 'wild ass, domestic ass', West Sem. ↛ Mari Akkadian xāru ~ xaʔaru ~ ayaru 'ass foal' | | Egyptian (from Old Kingdom) ʕꜣ 'ass' > Demotic Eg. ʕꜣ > Coptic: Sahidic ⲉⲓⲱ eiō, Bohairic ⲓⲱ iō | | ?σ Cushitic: Dahalo hẽ̄ri 'goat, sheep' ¦¦ South Cush.: Iraqw, Gorowa, Alagwa, Burunge ara 'goats' | | ?σ Chadic: West Ch.: Montol, Yiwom ur 'he-goat' ¦¦ East Ch.: Lele ōrē 'goats' | | **Kartv.** *°ir- > Old and New Georgian irem- 'deer' | | **IE** *⌜ĥ⌝er(i)- > Narrow IE *er-, *eri- '∈ horned artiodactyl' > Latin ariēs (gen. ariētis) 'ram', Umbrian erietu 'arietem' ¦¦ Balto-Slavic: Prussian eristian, Lith. (j)ḗras, Latvian jêrs 'lamb' ¦ Slavic *jarьka 'female lamb' > Old Russian ꙗрька jarъka, Russian 'ярка, 'ярочка 'lamb (female)', Ukrainian ярка, Slovak jarka 'year-old sheep', Polish jarka 'heifer, a lamb of this year' ¦¦ ? Armenian որոջ oṙoǯ 'lamb' initial o- from *e- by assimilation, acc. to Pokorny) ¦¦ Tocharian yriye, yari 'lamb' ⌉ Narrow IE *er(i)-b^{h}- (with the suffix *-b^{h}(o)- of animal names) '∈ horned

artiodactyl' > Greek ἔριφο-ς 'kid' ¦¦ Celtic: Old Irish heirp (*erb^h-ī-) 'dama, capra', erb(b) (*erb^h-ā-) 'cow', Irish earb 'goat', Scottish Gaelic earb 'roe (deer)' | | **Drav.** *ir- '(∈) deer, stag' > Tamil iralai̯ 'stag', '∈ deer', Kannada eraḷe ~ erale '∈ antelope, deer', Tulu eraḷe 'antelope, deer', Epigraphic Telugu iri (pl. irilu) 'stag', iṟṟi 'antelope', Malto ilaru 'mouse deer' ◇ The Nostr. reconstruction is *ʕir⌜i⌝ '(male, young) ungulate'.

5. **HS:** Sem. *baḳḳ- > Akk. baḳḳum '(small) gnat', Arabic baqq- 'punaise', Jewish Aram. בַּקָּא baḳ'ḳ-ā 'gnat', West Syriac ܒܩܐ bo'ḳ-o 'culex' | | East Cush.: Oromo bōkē 'gnat, moskito' | | **Kartv.:** Pshauri Georgian buḳuḳa 'gnat' | | **IE:** Narrow IE *b^{h}oṷk-/*b^{h}uk- 'bee' > Latin fūcus 'drone bee' (< *b^{h}oṷkos) ¦¦ Celtic: Gaulish {Meyer-Lübke} *bekos 'bee' [↦ Miranda Portuguese, Modena Italian bega, Limousin Provençal (dial. of de Creuse) beko, bi͡eko 'bee'], Old Irish bech 'bee', Welsh begegyr 'frelon' ¦¦ Slavic *°bučьnь > R (dial.) 'бучень 'wild bee; (∈) a green fly with a sting' 'бучень, 'бучинь 'bumble-bee'; Slavic *bъčela (< *b^{h}ukelā) ~ *bьčela 'bee' > OCS (= Old Church Slavonic) **БЪЧЕЛА** бъчела ~ **БЬЧЕЛА** бьчела, Russian, Bulgarian пче'ла, Ukrainian бджо'ла, Serbo-Croatian čèla, pčèla, Slovene bčȇla ~ bečȇla, Czech, Slovak včela, Polish pszczoła | | Altaic *bö|ük'e ≈ 'botfly, gadfly, mosquito' ({A. Dybo} *bük'∇ 'fly') > Turkic *bü|öke-lik {ADb.} 'blue fly, botfly' > Türkmen bökelek, Turkish (dial.) bökelek, bükelek 'botfly, gadfly', Azeri büyäläk, dial. bögäläx, Uzbek (dial.) bωkalak, Volga Tatat bь̊gelik̆, Bashkir bь̊gäläk, Yakut bügülex 'botfly', Qazaq бүгелек, {Radloff} bügölük 'Pferdebremse, овод, botfly'; with other sxs.: Qazaq bügöžök, Volga Tatar {Radloff} bь̊gы̊lčω̈k, bь̊gäčän, Noghay büklesin id.; ?? Turkish (dial.) büven, Chuvash pъvan 'gadfly' | | Mongolian *böküɣene 'horse-fly, gadfly' > Middle Mongolian [Hua-yi yi-yü] bökö'üne 'cousin, moustique', Class. Mong. böküne, bükügenë, Halha бөхнө id., Literary Oyrat böküüne 'mosquito', Kalmuck бөкүн bökṻnə 'gnat', Ordos b_ö^{h}k͡χöŋ 'cousin, moucheron, ∈ petites mouches qu'on voit sur le bétail', Naringol Monguor p'ug_unog_ 'taon' ◇ The Nostr. reconstruction is *buḳE (or *büḳE) '∈ a stinging insect ('gadfly', 'gnat' or sim.)'.

6. **HS:** Sem. *ba'ḳar- 'cattle' > Bibl. Heb. בָּקָר bā'ḳār 'cattle, herd', Phoen. bḳr 'cattle', Ugar. bḳr 'herd (of cattle, sheep)', Jewish Aram. בַּקְרָא baḳ'r-ā, West Syr. ܒܩܪܐ baḳ'r-o 'cattle', Arab. baqar- '(wild\domesticated) bovines, ox\bull\cow', Sabaic bḳr 'bovines, head of cattle', Eblaitic {Krebernik} baḳarum 'cattle'; Sem. derivative *buḳār-

> Arab. buqār- 'head of (large) cattle', Akkad. buḳār- 'cattle' | | Chadic: East Ch.: Birgit {Jungr.} bògòrò 'male antelope', bògòréy 'female antelope', East Dangaleat {Fédry} bógór 'antelope', ? Mokolko {Jungr.} ḅòrgú 'horse antelope (kudu), ? Migama {Jungr., Abakar Adams} ḅâɍgú 'oryx antelope'; Ndam Dik {Jungr.} pàgɜ̀r 'antilope' (p- due to the influence of the reflex of Nostr. *p̣oḲü 'pack, herds of ruminant animals'?) | | **IE:** Narrow IE ≈*bu(:)k-/bou̯k- 'bull' > Slavic *bɨ́kъ / gen. *bɨ'ka (< *būko-) 'bull' > Bulgarian бик, Serbo-Croat. bîk, Slovene bìk, Czech, Slovak býk 'bull', Polish byk 'sire bull', Old Russian bɨkъ, Russian бык ъ 'bull'; Slavic *bъkъ (< *buk-) > Serbo-Croat. bȁk 'bull' ¦¦ Celtic f. *bukk-ō (= {Stokes & Bezzenberger} *bowkk-ā) 'cow' > Old Welsh buch 'iuvenca', Welsh buch, Cornish bugh, Middle Breton buch, Breton buoc'h~ buc'h 'cow' ¶ IE *b- < *b^h- due to the IE law of incompatibility of voiced aspirates and voiceless cnss. in the same root | | **Alt.:** Turkic *buka 'bull, sire bull' > Old Turkic بوقا buqa ({Clauson}: buqā), Chaghatay buɣa, Turkish boğa, Türkmen, Volga Tatar buga, Qazaq, Uzbek, East Turkic, Tobol buqa, Azeri, Crimea Tatar, Karaite, Qumuq, Noghay, Qaraqalpaq, Bashkir, Yakut buɣa, Khakas puɣa, Tuva pūɣa, Tofalar pūfia 'bull' | | Mong. (↚ Turkic?) *buqa 'bull' > Middle Mong. buqa '{Haenisch} 'Rind, starkes Rind (Stier)', Class. Mong. buqa 'bull', Halha бух, Buryat бyxa, Kalmuck бух buχu 'sire-bull', Middle Moghol buqa, Moghol buqa, Ordos b_uxa 'bull' | | ? Tungus. *buka > Ewenki buka, Solon buxa 'bull, male reindeer', Manchu buqa 'ram, male goat' ◇ The Nostr. reconstruction is *buḲa 'bovines'.

7. **HS:** Sem.: [1] Central Sem. *c̣ippur- '(little) bird, sparrow' > Bib. Heb. צִפֹּר ~ צִפּוֹר c̣ip'pōr (pl. צִפֳּרִים c̣ippŏ'rīm) 'bird(s)', Punic ṣpr, Jewish Aram. צִפּוֹר c̣ip'por (st. emph.) צִפְּרָא c̣ippə'r-ā 'fowl, bird', Deir-Alla ṣpr, Official Aram. ṣnpr '∈ bird, sparrow', Palmyrene ṣprʔ, West Syr. ܨܶܦܪܳܐ ṣɛppə'r-o 'bird', Arab. ʕuṣfūr- 'sparrow, small bird'; the innovative variant *c̣ippar- is represented in Aram. only: Jewish Aram. צִפַּר c̣ip'par, West Syr. ܨܶܦܰܪ ṣɛp'par 'bird'; [2] Akkad. ṣibāru '∈ bird' (probably 'sparrow') | | ??φ,σ Chadic: West Ch.: Hausa zȁbṓ, Gwandara ǯàbùwà 'guinea fowl' ¦ Mburku 'čápùr, Jimbin ǯáḃʉr, Warji zábríyái̯, Tsagu sáḃún, Kariya zábúr, Miya {Skinner} zábùrkʉ, {ChL} ʒàbɨ̀ràkú, Pa'a ǯàvʉna, ? Siryanchi {Gowers} zuhunchi, Diri ʒāvúná id. ¦ Boghom šàp, Kir šấpm̩̀, Tala {Gowers} zubben, Polchi ẑìbın id., Zar ẑʋbm̀, Zar of Kal ẑèpm id. ¦ Ngizim zấbànú, Bade sấvàńín id. ¦¦ Central Ch.: Tera čívàn ¦ Bura čɨ̀vʋr, Margi čɨvʋ̀r,

Kilba čivɨ̀r ¦ Higi Futu zɨ̀vɨnu, Higi Ghye sʊ̀vʊ̀ne ¦ Gude zòvɨna id. ¦ Lamang {Lukas} zɜvɜ̀nā̀ká id. ¦ Glavda žɐ́bɜ̀rá, Gava žaburà, Dghwede {ChL} zàvɨ̀ra, {Frick} zàvərá id. ¦ Matakam zàpân, proto-Mafa-Mada {Rossing} *ʒavan > Giziga {Lukas} čivoŋ ≗ cuvoŋ, (Rossing} čùvún, Muktile zàvúr, Mada zàvár, Muyang, Mofu ʒàvár, Hurza sávnà ¦ Daba zàvín ¦ Gidar {Mouchet} zavuna ¦ Logone {Bouny} sàfàŋ id. ¦¦ East Ch.: Sumray {Jungr.} šíbɜ̀rɨ, East Dangaleat zòpùlò, Migama zóbíló, Mokilko sùbìló, Jegu zóbóló, Birgit zòbòló id. | | **IE:** Narrow IE *sper-, *sparw-, ? *sperg- 'sparrow, little bird' > Gothic sparwa, Anglo-Saxon spearwa, OHG sparo, Old Norse spǫrr 'sparrow'; Old Saxon sprā, Dutch spreew, Middle Low German sprēn, New Low German sprehe 'starling' ¦¦ ? Celtic: Cornish fraw 'crow', Breton frav 'crow, raven' (< *sprawa) ¦¦ Tocharian: A ṣpār (nom. pl. ṣpārāń), B ṣparā- '∈ bird' (< IE *spōr-) ¦¦ Greek [Hesychius] (σ)πέργουλος · ὀρνιθάριον ἄγριον 'a little bird living in fields', σπαράσιον · ὄρνεον ἐμφερὲς στρουθῷ 'a bird resembling the sparrow' ¦¦ Prussian spurglis 'sparrow' | | **Alt.:** Tungusian *Ci̱pi̱- 'little bird' > Ewenki Civkān, Cipkān 'little bird, sparrow' (-kān is a diminutive sx.), CipiCā 'little bird, tit', Lamut Cīprı 'nestling (not fully fledged), Cıptaka 'young of partridge', Lamut Ci̱wka-Cān ≗ Cu̱qa-Can, Negidal Ci̱wi̱t-kān, Ciw(kā)-kān 'little bird', Ude ćiwyau 'sparrow', Naykin Nanay či̱pi̱aqo ~ -u, Kur-Urmi Nanay čīf́aqo, Bikin Nanay či̱fqo 'swallow', Manchu cibin id. | | proto-Korean {Starostin} či̯ɜ̄pì > Middle Korean ci̯ɜ̄pì, Phyongyang Korean čebi 'swallow' | | ? Turkic *Cibi 'young of a bird' > Qïrgïz čibi(y) id.; (reduplication) Turkic *CibCik ~ *CimCik 'little bird, sparrow' > Chaghatay čipčik ~ čimčik, Turkish çimçek / -ği '∈ small sparrow', Karaite cipcik ≗ cıpcık 'little bird, sparrow', čıpčıx 'bird', Trakai Karaite {Radlow} čıpčıx, East Turkic čipčik, Qazaq šımšıq 'sparrow', Noghay šımšıq 'any little bird', Volga Tatar чыпчык śipśiq, Qumanda čibilčik '∈ bird' | | **Drav.** *cīpp- (~ *cīv-), *°cīpp∇r̀- 'young of birds' > Kannada sīpr̀i, sīpi 'chicken', Gondi cīva ≗ cīwā(l) ≗ civnā̃ ≗ civā, Kui sīpa, Kuwi hippa ≗ hipā ≗ hīpa id. 'chick' ◇ The Nostr. reconstruction is *ç̑ipu(-ŕ∇) 'little bird'. The onomatopoeic element in this word is not sufficient to account for the striking resemblance between Heb. ç̣ip'por, Tocharian ṣpār and Kannada sīpr̀i. But some phonetically deviant short words (especially in Chadic) may be due to a parallel onomatopoea.

8. **HS** *dʳuˀr- 'ram, sheep' > Omotic {Blažek} *dur- 'sheep, ram' > North Omotic: Wolaytta {Beke} dŭrsa, Wolaytta/Zala/Gofa/Chara

{Cerulli} dorsā, Koyra {Cerulli} dorō, Oyda {Fleming} duro, dorsa, Zaysse {Feming} doro, Basketo {Fleming} dōri 'sheep', She {Cerulli} dor 'ram' ¦¦ South Omotic: Ari {Bender} dertí 'sheep', Dime {Bender} d̲e̲r 'goat' | | ? Cush.: Beja {Reinisch} ˈdirfin 'lamb' ↛ | ↚ Tgr ድርፍን dɜrfɜn 'lamb, ram' | | Chadic: West Ch. {Stolbova} *d∇r-, *d∇r-gaŝi 'ram' > Ron {Jungr.}: Daffo-Butura d̰ȗ:r, Bokkos ʔad̰ûr (pl. d̰uráy), Sha dur 'ram' ¦ North Bauchi: Mburku darnǵáẑì, Jimbin tirǯȇẑi 'ram' ¦¦ Central Ch.: ? Matakam {Schubert} drɔ̀k, {ChL} ḍrɔk id. | | S: ? Ugar. drx 'mountain goat' | | **Kartv.:** Georgian duraq- ~ duraɣ- 'yearly capricorn', {D. Chubinov} duraɣ-i 'junger Steinbocḳ | | **? Drav.** {GS} *dū⌜ṙ⌝ a > Telugu dūḍa 'calf', Kannada dūṙa id. (↚ Telugu?), Gondi ḍuḍḍe 'female young of buffalo' ◇ The Nostr. reconstruction is *duŕ∇˪9|q∇˩ 'lamb, kid (of a wild ram, etc.)' 'lamb, kid (of a wild ram, etc.)'.

9. **HS:** Sem.: Arabic zalħab- 'wolf' | | East Cush.: Afar {Parker & Hayward} dálħu (pl. dalāħá) 'striped hyena', Saho {Reinisch} dālehō (pl. dalāh) "der Wolf" (= 'lycaon pictus'?) ¶¶ In HS there is metathesis and an obscure devoicing: *-ɣL- > *-lħ- | | **Kartv.** *ǯaɣ]̥- 'dog' > Old & New Georgian ʒaɣl-, Megrelian ǯoɣor-, Laz ǯoɣo(r)-, Svan žeɣ (dat. žaɣw) | | **Drav.** *cāki]-, {GS} *ǯ|ʒāɣi]- '∈ dog' > Kannada jāyila 'dog', Tulu jāvaḷa nayi 'wolf-dog', Telugu jāgilamu 'hound, hunting dog' ◇ The Nostr. reconstruction is *ʒaɣiĺ|]∇ 'wolf, dog'.

10. **HS:** Sem. *'δiʔib- 'wolf' > Bib. Heb. זְאֵב zəˈʔēḇ, pl. זְאֵבִים zəʔēˈbīm, Official Aram. דאב dʔb, Jewish Aram. דֵּב dēḇ, st. emph. דִּיבָא dīḇā, Samaritan Aram. דיב dyb, West Syriac (spelled Syr. ܕܐܒܐ ḏēʔḇā), Arabic ذِئْب δiʔb- (↛ Beja {Reinisch} dīb), Akkad. zīb-'wolf', Geʿez ዝእብ zəʔb 'hyena' (the posttonic vowel is evidenced by Hebrew, where pSem. *-ˈiʔi- yields -əˈʔē-) | | Eg. (from Pyramide texts) zɜb 'jackal' (either a cognate of or a loan from Sem.) ¦¦ ?? New Eg. ỉshb (= [*ʔ∇sh∇b-]) '∈ wolf or dog' (acc. to Erman and Grapow, a foreign word) [with a prostetic ʔ∇- and with assimilation *(-δʔ- >) *-sʔ- > sh] | | Cush.: East Cush. *z∇Hb-: Highland East Cush. *zōbb- 'lion' > Sidamo dōbb-iččo, pl. dōbb-a, Alaba zobe-ččo, Kambatta zōbbe-čču, Tembaro zobˈbe-ččo, Qabenna zōbbō 'lion' ¦¦ ? South Cush.: Iraqw duʔuma 'leopard' | | Chadic: West Ch. ? *ǯi˪ʔ∇˩b- ({Stolbova} *ǯiʔ∇b-) > Ngizim ǯíb-dà 'civet cat (Viverra civetta)' ¦¦ East Ch. *ǯabiy- 'hyena' > Bidiya ǯebay-gi 'striped hyena', Migama ǯábiyá 'bown hyena' | | **Kartv.:** Georgian čiba 'young dog' (K *č- < **ǯH-?), ? ciba 'small dog', a call-word for dogs, Kaziquri Georgian

ciba ‘Hündchen’ (c- is still obscure) ◇ The Nostr. reconstruction is *ǯiʔ∇b∇ ‘(young?) wolf’.

11. **HS:** Sem. *'gadiy- ‘kid’ (→‘lamb’) > Bib. Heb. גְּדִי gə'd̲ī ‘kid of goats and sheep’ (pl. גְּדָיִים gədā'yīm with -ā- possibly due to the generalized model of pl. of the segolat nouns), Epigr. Old Heb. גדי gdy, Punic gdʔ, [Plautus] GADE, Ugar. gd(y) ‘kid (cabrito)’, pl. gdym, Old Aram. gdʔ ‘goat’, Jewish Aram. [Targumim] גַּדְיָא gad̲'y-ā ‘kid\lamb’, West Syriac ܓܰܕܝܳܐ gad̲'y-o ‘kid’, Mandaic gadia ‘kid, young goat’, Arab. ǧady- ‘kid (chevreau)’, North Yemenite Arabic ǯadi ≗ ǯidi, New Babylonian Akkadian gadû ‘male kid’ (⇷ West Sem.) || Berber *ɣ̮ai̯d ‘kid, (young) goat’ > Ahaggar {Foucauld} e-ɣ̮əi̯d (pl. i-ɣ̮əi̯d-ən), Tayert, East Tawellemmet e-ɣ̮ъyd (pl. i-ɣ̮ъyd-ъn, Tayert i-ɣ̮əyd-ъn) ‘chevreau’, Ghat {Nehlil} i-ɣ̮id (pl. i-ɣ̮id-ən), Ghadamsi {Lanfry} a-ʕīd (pl. ʕid-ān) id., Aït-Izdeg {Mercier} i-ɣ̮əyd (pl. i-ɣ̮əyd-ən) ‘young billy-goat (jeune bouc, chevreau)’, Tazerwalt Tashelhit a-ɣ̮åd̮ ‘billy-goat’; fem. *t∇-ɣ̮ai̯d∇-t ‘she-goat, female kid’ > Tayert, East Tawellemmet te-ɣ̮ъydət ‘chevrette’ (pl. Tayert tiɣ̮əydad, East Taw. šiɣ̮idad), Ghadamsi taʕid̮ɛt (pl. təʕid̮ād̮) id., Ghadamsi tē-ʕat̮ ~ tē-ʕɛt, Kabyle t̲ə-ɣ̮at̮ (pl. t̮i-ɣ̮ət̮t̮in), Tazerwalt Tashelhit ta-ɣ̮åt̮t̮ (pl. ti-ɣ̮īd̮-ın), Aït-Izdeg ta-ɣ̮at̮t̮ (pl. ti-ɣ̮ıt̮t̮ən), Siwa tɣāt̮ (pl. tɣāt̮in), Srair Senhazha t̲aɣ̮at ‘she-goat’ ¶ The emphatic *ɣ̮ (for the expected *g) is puzzling || East Cush.: Oromo {Borello, da Thiene} gadamsa ‘kudu antelope’, Borana Oromo B {Venturino} gadamsa Burji {Sasse} ga'dama ‘greater kudu antelope’, Gedeo gadansa ‘antelope, buffalo’ (⇷ Oromo?) || Chadic: West Ch. {Stolbova} *gada ‘∈ antelope’ > Hausa gàdā́ ‘crested duiker (antelope) Cephalophus Grimmi (= Sylvicopra grimmia)’, gàdár kúrmì ‘duiker Cephalophis rufilatus’¦ Bole-Tangale: Gera gadere ‘bushbuck’ ¦ North Bauchi: Pa’a gàtará ‘buck̦’ ¦ ? South Bauchi: Jimi {Gowers} kito, Geji {ChL} kiti, Buli {Gowers} kīt, Zar {Gowers} kiddi, Zakshi Saya {Gowers} kidu ‘antelope’, Dwat {ChL} kidi ‘duiker’ ¦ Ngizim gádùwà ‘crester duiker’ ¦¦ Central Ch.: Zime-Batna {Jungr.} gódaỳ, {Sachnine} gútay ‘buck, Dghwede {Frick} ɤə́də́ gírè ‘antelope’ || **IE: Narrow** IE *g^{h}|ĝ^{h}ai̯do- ‘(young) buck, goat’ > Latin haedus ‘kid, young goat’ ¦¦ Gothic gaits, OHG geiʒ, Anglo-Saxon ʒāt ‘goat’ > English goat ¶ The *media* *-d- (for the expected *-d^{h}-) is obscure. It may be explained if the IE word is a lown from HS or one of its branches ||**D** *kaţ-, {GS} *kyaḓ- ‘young male of horned domestic animal’ > Tamil kaṭā, kaṭavu, kaṭay ‘male of sheep\goat\buffalo’, kaṭāri, kiṭāri ‘heifer, young cow’,

? kiṭā ‘buffalo, bull, ram’ (why -i-?), Malayalam kaṭā, kiṭā, kiṭāvu ‘young male of cattle’, Kota kar̂c nag ‘buffalo calf between 2 and 3 years’, kar̂c kurl ‘cow calf between 2 and 3 years’, Kannada kaḍasu, Kodagu kaḍɨci, Tulu gaḍasə ‘young cow\buffalo’, Gondi kār̂ā ‘young buffalo’, Konda gr̂ālu, Kui grāḍu ‘calf’, kr̂ai̯ ‘young female buffalo\goat’, Kurukh kar̂ī id., kar̂ā ‘young male buffalo’, Brahui xar̂ ‘ram’, xarās ‘bull, bullock; Drav. ⇸ proto-Indo-Aryan {Turner} *kaṭṭa- and *kaḍḍa- ‘young male [horned domestic] animal’ (*kaṭṭa- > Kashmiri kaṭ^{h} ‘ram, sheep in general’, Lahnda kaṭṭa ‘buffalo calf’, Hindi kaṭiyā ‘buffalo heifer’; *kaḍḍa- > Oriya kar̂ā ‘castrated male buffalo’, kar̂āi̯ ‘young buffalo cow’, Brahui kār̂ā ‘male buffalo calf’) and Sanskrit kaṭahā- ‘young female buffalo’ ◇ The preconsonantic (rather than expected postconsonantic) position of *i̯, *y in Berber and IE is due to metathesis (possibly favoured by root structure patterns in both languages.). Illich-Svitych assumed that IE *g^{h}aydo- is a loan from Sem., because the root-internal vowel *a is not typical in IE. But I do not find it a sufficient argument for a loan hypothesis since there are still other IE nominal roots with an internal *a ◇ The Nostr. reconstruction is *gadi (or *gati?) ‘kid, young goat’, ? ‘(∈) antelope’.

12. **HS:** Central Sem. *gall- ⌞‘tortoise’⌝ > Middle Heb. גַּל gal (pl. גַּלִּים gal'līm) id., West Syr. ܓܠܐ ~ ܓܠܠܐ gal'lo id. | | West Chadic: Dera gùldúkú ‘small tortoise’ | | **IE:** Narrow IE *g^{h}elū ~ *g^{h}(e)lōu̯ ‘tortoise’ > Greek χέλῦς, χελύνη id. ¦¦ Slavic *želɨ / *želъv- > Church Slavonic **ЖЄЛЪІ** želɨ, gen. **ЖЄЛЪВЄ** želъv-e, Serbo-Croatian (dial.?) žȅlva, Slovene žȇlva, Old Czech želva, Polish żółw, gen. żółwi, Russian dial. жолвь ‘tortoise’ | | ?φ **Alt.:** Tungusian: Manchu ǵaltu (spelled giyaltu) ‘∈ cattlefish’ ¶ The palatality of the initial stop is puzzling | | ??φ **Drav.:** [1] Drav. {GS} *gull- ‘∈ mollusk, shell’ > Tulu gulla ‘∈ small mollusc’, Telugu gulla ‘a shell, a white pustule’, Parji gula ‘snail’, gulli ‘shell, cowrie’, Kui gola, goli ‘shell’ (reborrowing from Oriya?) ⫴ [2] proto-Tamil *kiḻiñcil > Tamil kiḻiñcil ‘bivalve, mussel, oyster-shell’, Malayalam kiḻiñci ‘a shellfish’, kiḻiññil ‘oyster shell’ ◇ The Nostr. reconstruction is *gaLu ‘tortoise’, but the odd elements in the Manchu and Drav. cognates (palatal ǵ- in Mc, *-u- and *-i- in D) suggest that the original word had some additional internal phonemes, so that the etymon may be something like *gayu|üĺu.

13. **HS:** Sem.*√ʕry or *°√ħry Akkadian (from Old Babylonian) erû (~ arû) ‘eagle’, Late Bab. Akk. arâniš ‘like an eagle’; Old Aramaic

(?) ʕr 'bearded vulture', Jewish Aramaic [Targumim] עַר ʕar, st. emph. עַרְיָא ʕar'y-ā {Jastrow} '∈ bird of prey' (prob. 'Lammergeyer'), {Levy} '∈ eine Adlerart, Aar' (but {Dalman} עָר ʔār, em. עָרָא ʕā'r-ā '∈ bird of prey') | | Egyptian (18th dyn.) ħȝy.w '∈ bird of prey', {Fk.} 'carrion-birds'; ? New Eg ħȝy.t '∈ edible bird' | | Cush.: Beja {Reinisch} 'ērʔe 'white-tailed sea-eagle' | | **IE** *x̑er- 'eagle, large bird' > Narrow IE *er-/*or- > Old Irish irar, Welsh eryr, Middle Beton erer, Breton, Cornish er 'eagle' ¦¦ Germanic {Pokorny} *aran- > Gothic ara, Old Norse ari, ǫrn (< Germanic *arnuz) 'eagle', Anglo-Saxon earn, OHG aro, aru 'large bird of prey, eagle', New High German Aar 'large bird of prey'; Middle High German adel-ar (lit. 'noble bird of prey') 'eagle' > New High German Adler 'eagle' ¦¦ Balto-Slavic (derived word): Lith. erẽlis, dial. arẽlis, Prussian arelie (copyist error for arelis), Latvian ȅrglis (< *ȅrdlis) 'eagle' ¦ Slavic *o'rь̀lъ (G *orь'la) 'eagle' > OCS **орьлъ** orьlъ, Bulgarian o'рел, Serbo-Croatian òrao (G órla), Slovak órel (G órla), Czech orel, Slovak orol, Polish orzeł, Russian o'рёл (gen. ор'ла), Ukrainian o'рел ¦¦ Greek ὄρνῑ̆ς (G ὄρνῑθος), Doric Greek ὄρνις (G ὄρνῑχος) 'bird; cock, hen', Greek ὄρνεον 'bird' ¦¦ Armenian **որոր** oṙoṙ 'sea-mew, sea-gull, cob', **ուրուր** uṙuṙ 'buzzard' | | Hittite haras, haran-, Palaic haras(-) (gen. ˪ha˩ranas) 'eagle' | | **Drav.** (attested in Macro-Tamil) *°eruvay > Tamil eruvai̯ '∈ kite', Malayalam eruva 'eagle, kite' ◇ The Nostr. reconstruction is *ɣer∇ or *xer∇ 'eagle'. Aramaic ʕ- does not correspond to Egyptian ħ-, hence either Aramaic √ʕr˪y˩ belongs here, the rec. must be *ɣer∇, otherwise (if the Eg. cognate is accepted), it must be *xer∇.

14. **HS:** East Cush: Afar kúllum, Somali kallūn, Northern Somali kállȗn 'fish', kallūm- 'to catch fish' | | Chadic: West Ch.: Hausa kúlmā́ '∈ large fish' ¦¦ Central Ch. *k∇l∇p- 'fish' > Bura-Margi *k∇lf∇ > Kilba kàlfi, Bura kɨlfà, Margi xilif, West Margi kúlfà ~ kûlfà, Ngwakhi kulfu, Hildi kalfī, Wamdiu kálfi ¦Macro-Higi: Higi Nkafa kɨ̀lɨ̀pɛ́, Higi Baza kɨ̀lɨ̀pó, Kapsiki kùlùpʷɛ́, Higi Ghye kùlùbí, Higi Futu kùlùpu ¦ Macro-Mandara: Mandara kúlfè, Glavda kílfà, Dghwede kúlfè, Gava kilifa, Nakatsa kə̀lə̀té ¦ Matakam klef, proto-Mafa-Mada {Rossing} *kilif > Mada, Zulgo kléf, Muyang, Giziga, Mofu kìlíf, Muktile klífi, Moloko kìléf ¦ Daba kìlíf, Kola kilíf ¦ Masa kuluf-fa, {Kraft} kulufna, Banana kúlùvá ¶ It is not clear if the West Ch. word *keruf- 'fish' (> Hausa kīfī, proto-Angas-Goemay *kirap-, proto-Bole-Tangale *kɛrapo, etc.) belongs here | | ? Southeast Sem.: Jibbali {B. Thomas} kāl, Mehri {Thomas} kell 'whale' ¦¦ ?? Akkadian

kulīl- ~ kulull- 'a fabulous creature, part man and part fish' (a reborrowing from Sumeric or borrowing of a Sumeric cognate of the Nostr. word?) | | **IE:** Narrow IE *k^{w}o|al- '∈ large fish' > Khotan Saka, Young Avestan kara, Sogdian krw kpy '∈ monster fish' ¦¦ Germanic *x^{w}alaz ~ *x^{w}aliz 'whale' > Old Norse hvalr, Anglo-Saxon hwæl, English whale, OHG wal, German Wal-fisch; OHG *h^{w}alis > Middle High German wẹls > German Wels 'sheat-fish, Silurus'; Germanic *x^{w}alirōn id. > OHG hwelira ¦¦ Prussian kalis 'sheat-fish, Slurus glanis' | | **Uralic** *kala 'fish' > Finno-Ugrian *kala > Finnish, Estonian kala ¦ proto-Lapp {Lehtiranta} *kōlē > South Lapp güollie, Lule Lapp kuollē, North Lapp guolle, Kildin Lapp kūll' ¦ Erzya & Moksha kal ¦ Chreremis kol ¦¦ Ob-Ugrian *kūl > proto-Vogul *kūl > Vogul kōl ≗ xūl ≗ kūl ≗ kul; proto-Ostyak *kul > Ostyak qul ≗ quɬ ≗ χuť ≗ χŭt ≗ χŭɬ ≗ χul ¦ Hungarian hal | | Samoyedic {Janhunen} *kålä, {Helimski} *kale 'fish' > Tundra Nenets халя, {Lehtisalo} χāĺ·e, Forest Nenets kāɬ́ɬ́ə͡ä, Nganasan kolɨ, Enets {Castrén} kaɦe ~ kare, Taz Selqup qɜ̄lɨ, Kamassian k'ōłă, Koyal {Spassky} кола, Motor {Helimsky} *kälä | | ?? proto-Yukagir {Nikolayeva} *qal- 'fish (??)' > compounds: Tundra Yuk. qaldawa {Nik.} 'scales, hide', {Kurilov} 'scales, bark' (qal- 'fish [?]' + sawa 'hide, skin') | | **A**: [1] Alt. *k'ol∇ 'fish' > Mong. *^{o}qoli-sun 'fish-skin' > Class. Mong. qolisun, Halha холис(он) | | Tungusian *xol-sa 'fish' > Ewenki ollo, Lamut olrъ, Negidal olo, Orochi okto, Ude oloho, Ulcha xolto(n-), Nanay xolto | | Middle Korean {Vovin} kwòlày 'whale' ⅂⅂ [2] (a loanword?) Mong. *qalimu 'whale' > Cl. Mong. qalimu, Halha, Buryat халим id.; Mong. ↛ (possibly) Tungusian *kalima 'whale' > Ewenki kalim, Lamut qalım, Negidal kalım, Orochi kalima ~ kālma, Ude kalima, Ulcha qalma, Orok, Nanay qalıma, Manchu qalimu 'whale' | | **Drav.** *koll- ({GS} *k-) '∈ fish' > Malayalam kolli, Tulu koleji 'a kind of fish'; ? Gondi kīl 'fish' ◇ The Nostr. reconstruction is ***Ḳol∇** '(big) fish'.

15. **HS**: S: [1] S *'kal˛a˛b- 'dog' > Bibl. Heb. כֶּלֶב 'kɛlɛḇ, Phoen., Ugar., Official Aram., Sabaic klb, Amorite {Gelb} kalbum, Jewish Aram. כַּלְבָּא kal'b-ā, West Syr. kal'b-o (abs., cs. kə'leḇ with e due to a late Aram distribution law: the second vowel in nomina segolata is always e unless preceding a laryngeal or r), Mandaic kalba, Arab. kalb-, Ge'ez kalb, Tigre kälb, Tigray kälbi, Akkadian kalbu(m) 'dog', Soqotri {Leslau} kalb 'dog, wolf', Mehri kawb (pl. kɜlōb), Harsusi kawb ~ kōb (pl. kɜlōb), Eastern & Central Jibbali kɔb (pl. 'kɔ'lɔb)

'wolf, dog' ¶ The Southeast Sem. cognates (Mh kawb etc.) point to Sem. *'kalb- rather than *'kalab-, because the reg. Mehri reflex of *'kalab- would have been ⁂kəlēb ⌉ [2] a variant without deglottalization: Sem. *°√ḳlb in Old Yemenite ḳlwb ({Selwi} qillawb-) 'Schakalwolf' | | Berber: Tayert {Foucauld} ăkūlən 'wolf, lycaon' | | Central Chadic 'dog': Bura-Margi: Bura Pele kıla, Bura kilà, Chibak {ChL} kıyà, West Margi kıya, kìyà ¦ Kotoko: Buduma {Cyffer} kə̀lé, Logone {Lukas} kə̀lè, {Bouny} gə̀léw, Gulfei {Lukas} gɜleu̯ (pl. gɜllē) | | **IE**: Narrow IE *°kʷol-/*°kul-, *kʷelb-/*kʷolb- '(young?) dog' > Lith. kalė̃, kãlė 'bitch' ¦¦ Germanic *xʷelpo-z, *xʷalpo-z 'whelp, young dog' > Old Norse hvelpr, Danish hvalp, Swedish valp, Anglo-Saxon, Old Saxon hwelp, English whelp, Middle Dutch welp, wulp, wolp, OHG hwelf, German Welf id. ¦¦ ? Elian Greek [Hs.] κύλλα · σκύλαξ ('young dog' or 'young animal') ◇ The Nostr. reconstruction is ***ḲUL∇ (b∇)** 'dog\wolf, whelp'. The element *b∇ is a Nostr. marker (> suffix) of animal names. The identification of the rounded vowel in proto-Nostratic is still a problem. The Elean Greek and Tayert Twareg cognates suggest *u.

16. **HS**: Sem. *√klm ~ West Sem. *√ḳlm ~ West Sem. *√ḳml: [1] √klm > Akk. kalmatu 'parasite, louse (on animals, plants and human beings)', Jewish Aram. כַּלְמָא kal'mā, כַּלְמְתָא kalmə'ṯā 'vermin' (assimilation *-lm- > -nm-): Mehri kɜnɜmūt (pl. kɜ'nawm), Bathari kɜnɜmīt, East Jibbali 'šinit, Central Jibbali 'š̓init, Soqotri {Leslau} 'konəm 'louse', Bibl. Heb. כִּנָּם kin'nām 'gnats', Middle Heb. כְּנִימָּה kə'nim'mā 'worm'; [2] *√ḳml ~ *ḳlm > Old Aram. ḳml 'louse', Jewish Aram. קַלְמְתָא ḳalmə'ṯā 'vermin', West Syr. ܩܰܠܡܳܐ ḳal'm-o 'louse', Arab. qaml-at- 'louse', nomen genericum qaml- 'lice, louse', Sabaic ḳmlt, ḳlm, ḳlmt 'insect pests, (?) locusts', Geʿez ḳʷəmāl ~ kəmāl 'louse' | | ? Egyptian kmy '∈ snake' | | Cush.: East Cush. {Sasse} *kilm- 'tick (insect)' > Afar kilim, -i 'ticks', Saho {Reinisch} kilin, Burji 'šilm-ā, Oromo 'silm-iʔ ⫡ šilm-a/šilm-ī id., South Oromo šilmī 'small tick (on cows)', proto-Sam {Heine} *čilim > North Somali šílín (pl. šílmó), Rendille čilím, Boni šílm-í 'tick' | | Chadic: Central Ch.: Buduma komāli 'black ant' ¦¦ West Ch.: Hausa ḳùmā́ 'flea (of rats, dogs)', Gwandara kuma 'flea of dogs' ¶¶ In Sem. and West Ch. there is secondary glottalization (*ḳ- for the expected *k-) of tabuistic and "expressive" origin and\or due to contamination with other roots | | **Uralic**: Finno-Ugrian *°kum∇ʅ∇ ~ *°kam∇ʅ∇ > Ob-Ugrian *kŏm∇ʅ∇k ~ *kāməʅək 'beetle' > proto-Vogul {Honti} *kŏmlāk >

Vogul komləx ᵈ~ xomləx ~ xω̆mləx ᵈ~ komlā̆k ᵈ~ komlāk ᵈ~ komläk ᵈ~ kamlāk ᵈ~ xomlax id.; proto-Ostyak {Honti} *kamə]kay > Ostyak qamə]qɨ ᵈ~ qåmə]qɨ ᵈ~ qåməlqɨ ᵈ~ xŏməlxay ᵈ~ xăməlxay ᵈ~ xŏməlxȧy ᵈ~ xŏməlxa ᵈ~ xŏmə]xa 'small insect, beetle' | | **Alt.**: Tungusian *kụmi˪r˩, *kumi-kēn > Ewenki kumikз̄n, Barguzin Ewenki kumir, kumirkз̄n '(small) insect', Solon xumīxз 'ant'; Tung. *kum∇ (-ke) 'louse' > Orochi kumз, Ewenki, Lamut, Negidal kumkз, Solon xuŋkз, Nanay kuŋkз, Ude kumugз ᵈ~ kumuз 'louse' | | proto-Korean {S. Starostin} *kз̀m+i 'spider' > Middle Korean kз̀m+i, Phyongyang Korean kзmi ◇ The Nostr. reconstruction is ***k⌈u⌉m**∇(]∇) '(stinging) insect'.

17. **HS**: South Cush.: Iraqw {Whiteley} qaínâʔi/a, {Ehret} qaynaʔi 'civet cat'; ?? South Cush. ⇸ Mbugu kendá 'zorilla' | | ? Chadic: West Ch.: Hausa kʸâŋwà, Pero kā́ndà 'cat', Bole šзnwa 'wild cat' ⁞⁞ East Ch.: Somray {Nachtigal} kójna 'cat' | | ? Sem. *ᵒḳ∇nd∇r- (< **ḳ∇nr-?) > Arabic قندر qndr (with unknown vowels) 'beaver' | | **Kartv.** *ḳwenr- 'marten' > Old Georg. ḳuerna-, Georg. ḳverna-, Megrelian ḳvinor-i, Laz ḳvenur-i id.; Svan: Upper Bal ḳwen, Lakhsh ḳen, Lentekh ḳwen ~ rḳwen id. | | **IE**: Narrow IE *ᵒkeu̯n-/*ᵒkou̯n- 'marten' > Lithuanian kiáunė, kiaunẽ, Latvian caûna, -e, Prussian caune id. ⁞ Slavic *kuna 'marten' > Church Slavonic коуна kuna 'αἴλουρος, felis', Bulgarian 'куна, Serbo-Croatian, Slovene kúna, Czech, Slovak, Polish kuna, R dial. 'куна ~ ку'на, Ukrainian ку'на 'marten'; Slavic (< diminutive) *kunica 'marten' > Church Slavonic коуница kunica 'αἴλουρος, felis', Bulg. dial. 'куница 'Mustela foina', Serbo-Croatian kùnica, Slovene kúnica, Polish kunica, R ку'ница, Uk ку'ниця 'marten' | | **Alt.** *Küŕänä (metathesis < **Künäŕä) 'marten, polecat' > Turkic *Küŕä|en > Old Turkic küzän id., Cuman kara küzen 'polecat', Türkmen göбen, Uzbek сассиқ кўзан sassiq kωzan, Qazaq, Altay, Khakas küzen, Volga Tatar көзән kь̊zän, Bashkir kь̊бän 'polecat', Tuva küzen 'marten' ⁞ Bulghar Turkic *kü|ören ⇸ Hungarian görény 'polecat' | | Mong. *kürene > Cl. Mong. kürene, Halha хүрнз 'skunk, polecat, weasel', Kalmuck күрн kürnə, kürn̥ 'polecat', {Ramstedt} kürn̥ 'iltis', Oros {Mostaert} k'ürene ~ k'ürine 'espèce de putois' ({Potanin} 'Mustela putorius') ◇ The word may have denoted some small carnivore (marten, polecat, wild cat, or ichneumon; all of them live in different parts of Southwestern Asia; in modern Israel the marten is known as נְמִיָּה nemi'ya) ◇ The Nostr. reconstruction is ***ḳun**|ɦ∇(**ŕ**∇) 'small carnivore (marten, polecat, wild cat, or sim.)'.

18. *q̧oR∇ 'frog, toad' (→ 'tortoise') > **HS**: New Egyptian ḳrr 'frog' (> proper name [in Akkad. script] Paḳruru), Demotic Eg. ḳrr, Coptic: Sahidic κρογρ krur, Bohairic χρογρ k^{h}rur id. | | Sem. *^{o}ḳ⌈u⌉rr- > Arabic qurr-, qurr-at- ~ qirr-at- 'frog' | | Berber (with onomatopoeic associations): Iznacen qarqriw, Rif aqarqur, Matmata umg^{w}ərg^{w}ər 'toad', Srair Senhazha aqarqur, Beni-Menacer amqərqūr 'frog' | | Chadic: West Ch. {Stolbova} *kur∇ 'tortoise' > proto-Angas-Goemay {Hoffmann} *ḳur id. > Goemay ḳur, Kofyar (da)kur, Sura {Jungr.} (dā́)kúr, Angas (ka)kur id., Mupun dàkúr 'turtle' ¦ Zar of Lusa, Polchi, Buli, Wangday kúrbì, Zar kúrvì id., Zar of Kal kù-kurbi 'tortoise', ? Warji kúrsì 'frog' ¦ Bade {Mouchet} karenakau 'frog' ¦¦ Central Ch.: Bachama k͡póròwé 'tortoise' ¦ Kilba k^{w}à-kúrùm, Hildi k^{w}à-kúrúmú, Fali of Kiria k^{w}ɔ̀-kúrúm, Bura k^{w}ù-kùrmú 'turtle' ¦ ? Gava kírè, Dghwede kr̥̀ŋdá 'frog' ¦ Daba {Lienhard} kırın, {ChL} kɨ̀rríŋ id. ¦¦ East Ch.: Sokoro {Nachtigal} kóriŋgē, Mubi {Jungraithmayr} kírḗnì (pl. kèrèn) 'frog' | | **Kartv.**: Old Georgian, Early New Georg. mq̣uar-i 'βάτραχος, frog', New Georgian mq̣vari 'toad' | | **IE**: Narrow IE *^{o}g^{w}red^{h}- 'frog, toad' > Middle Low German krēde, krode, OHG krëta, krota 'toad', German Kröte id., Schildkröte 'tortoise, turtle' ¦¦ Greek βάτραχος, Ionian Greek βρόταχος, βαδρακος 'frog' ¦¦ ? Vulgar Latin {Meyer-Lübke} *brūskus 'toad' ({Ernout}: ↚ Oscan-Umbrian < IE *g^{w}rot-skos) > Medieval Latin [glossa] bruscus '∈ frog (ranae genus)', Rumanian broască 'toad', Macedo-Rumanian broască, Old Milanese brosca 'tortoise', ↛ Albanian breshkë 'little turtle' ¶ *g^{w}red^{h}- for **k^{w}red^{h}- according to the IE incompatibility law ruling out roots with a voiced aspirate and a voiceless consonant | | **Alt.**: Tungusian *xere 'frog' > Nanay, Orok xɜrɜ, Ulcha xɜrɜ; deriv. *xere-kī > Orochi (↚ Nanay) xɜrɜkī, Ude ɜ̄xī, Orochi ēki, Negidal ɜyɜxī, Lamut ɜrikī, Ewenki ɜrɜkī id. | | ???σ Turkic *kʟ'ᴊur-bāKa '∈ frog\toad' (*kur- '?' + *baka 'frog') > Old Turkic qurbaqa id., Old Qïpchaq qurbaɣa id., Turkish kurbağa 'frog, toad', Türkmen qurbāɣa, Azeri gurbaɣa, Qazaq qūrbaqa, Qaraqalpaq, Uzbek qurbaqa 'frog', Qumïq, Noghay qırbaqa, Qïrgïz qurbaqa 'toad', Volga Tatar qır baqası 'grass frog' ◇ The Nostr. reconstruction is ***q̧oR∇** 'frog, toad' (→ 'tortoise'). But if Turkic *kʟ'ᴊur-baKa belongs here, the N etymon is to be reconstructed as ***q̧Ur∇**.

19. **HS**: S *karr- 'lamb' > Bibl. Heb. כַּר kar 'young ram', Ugar. kr 'lamb', Old Akkadian kerru 'ram', Mari Akkkadian karru 'ram', Akkad. kirru '(∈ a breed of) sheep' | | Berber *-k∇̆rar- > Ahaggar ē-krər, Tayert e-ḵrɐr 'ram', Nefusi a-krar 'billy-goat'; Berber *karr-, *karrī

> East Tawellemmet ъ-ƙъrr, Iznacen i-ẍərri (pl. aẍrarən), Rif i-k̲arri ≗ išarri, Senhazha Srair i-k̲arri (pl. ak̲rarən), Kabyle, Matmata i-śərri, Beni-Snus i-šərri 'ram', Tashelhit t̲i-k̲ərr-ət̲ 'ewe'; Berber *k∇rw- 'lamb' > Ahaggar, Ghat a-kərwāt, pl. ikərwātən, Tayert, East Tawellemmet ъ-kərw-ъ 'lamb', Tashelhit i-kru 'young ram' | | East Cush.: Arbore kāriy-té (coll. kāríy) 'heifer goat' | | Chadic: West Ch.: Angas {Foulkes} kīr 'fattening ram', Wangday, Saya kɜ́rò 'ram', Zar of Kal kárò 'sheep', Tangale kā́rwa 'cattle' | | **Kartv.** *ḳraw-/*ḳrw- 'lamb' > Old Georg. ḳraw-, Georgian ḳrav-, Megrelian ḳɜrib- ~ ḳirib- | | **A**: T *Kori (or *Kurı?) 'lamb' > Narrow Turkic *Ko|uzı > Old Turkic qozı, {Cl.} quzı, Chaghatay, Qazaq, Altay qozı, Turkish kuzu, Türkmen guϬı, Azeri guzu, Uzbek qωzi, Qïrgïz qozu, East Turkic qoza 'sucking lamb', Tuva qozaɣa 'kid (of a wild goat)' | | Mong. *quri- ⇸ [1] *quri-gan 'lamb' > Middle Mong. quriqan, quriɣan, quraɣan, Cl. Mong. qurigan ~ quragan, Halha xypra, Kalmuck xurɣŋ̊, Monguor xorg_a ≗ xurga, Moghol {Ramstedt} qurɤana [sic], Dongxiang qugan, Bao'an xurɣaŋ 'lamb', Middle Moghol qurɣan 'lamb, kid'; [2] *quri-sqa(n) 'skin of a newborn lamb' > Cl. Mong. qurisqan, Ölöt Kalmuck xursxъ, Dörböt Kalmuck xüŕsxъ id. | | **Drav.** *kor̲i, {GS} *kor̤-i 'sheep' > Tamil kor̲i, Toda kur̤y, Kodagu kori, Tulu kuri, Old Telugu gor̲iya, Telugu gor̲e, gor̲r̲e, gor̲r̲iya, Kolami, Naikri, Naiki gorre id., Kota kory a·ṙ id. (a·ṙ 'goat'), Kuwi gōri ~ gorri ~ gōre, Gondi gorre ≗ gore id., 'goat', Malayalam kor̲i '∈ a small kind of sheep', Kannada kur̲i, kor̲i 'sheep, ram', Konda gor̤e 'goat' ¶¶ The Kartv. and Turkic reflexes suggest an emphatic Nostr. *ḳ-, that lost its emphaticity (was deglottalized?) in HS due to a reg. change (*ḳ- > *k-) in some (prosodic?) conditions ◇ The Nostr. reconstruction is ***ḳor⌈üy⌉∇** (or ***ḳoŕi**) 'lamb'.

20. **HS**: Central Sem. *ḳāriʔ- (or *ḳawriʔ-?) 'partridge' (secondary association with the verb √ḳrʔ 'to cry, exclaim') > Bib. Heb. קֹרֵא ḳō'rē 'partridge', Arabic qāriyat- 'partridge (Ammoperdix heyi)', 'Merops apiaster' | | Chadic: West Ch.: South Bauchi {Stolbova} *kʷ˪a˩r / *k∇w∇r 'hen' (or 'chicken = hen\cock') > Zar kʷə̄̀r id., Geji kowùl, Buli kor, Polchi koro 'hen' ¦ Tangale {Jungraithmayr} kʷartɛ ~ kʷatrɛ 'guiney-fowl' ¦¦ Centr. Ch.: Muktile kʷátà-kùrúk 'francolin', Gude kúrɜ́kìnɜ 'chicken house', ? Gude kúrɜ́kútà, Gudu kúrkútò 'dove' ¦ ? Lame kòrókú, Lame-Peve kuruk 'dove' | | ??φ East Cush.: Burji go'r(r)-itte (pl. go'r-ṓna) 'hen' | | **IE**: Narrow IE *k˪ʷ˩ou̯r(o)- id. > Old Indian 'cakoraḥ 'Perdix rufa' (< reduplicated *k˪ʷ˩ek˪ʷ˩ouro-)

¦¦ Slavic *kurъ 'cock' > OCS, Old Russian коуръ kurъ, Bulgarian, Ukrainian, Russian dial. кур, Serbo-Croatian dial. kȕr, Slovak kùr, Polish kur id.; ↔ Sl *kur-a 'hen' > Slovene kúra, Old Czech kura, kúra, Polish kura, Old Russian коура kura, R pl. 'куры, R (derived) 'курица, Ukrainian 'кура 'hen'; compound Slavic *kuro-pъtɨ (gen. *kuro-pъtъve) [with *pъtɨ 'bird'] 'partridge' > Serbo-Croatoan, Slovak, Czech dial. kuroptva, Old Czech kurotva, Czech kuroptev (gen. kuroptve), Polish kuropatwa, Ukrainian куро'патва, R куро'патка id., Slovene kuroprat 'Scolopax rusticola' | | **Alt.**: Mong. *qoru > Cl. Mong. qoru, {Ramstedt} qora 'hazel grouse, grey hen', {Ramstedt} 'capercailye', Literary Oirat xoru, Kalmuck хор xor_o 'capercailye' | | Turkic *Kür-tük 'black grouse' > Altay, Shor kürtük, Khakas kürkü ~ kürtü, Chulïm kürtü, Küerik kürtä, Tuva kürtü, Tofalar hu̇rt·u̇, Yakut kurtuyax id. | | **Drav.** *kōr̂i, {GS} *kōr̂- 'gallinaceous fowl' > Tamil kōṟi id., Malayalam kōṟi, Kota ko·y, Toda kwɨ·ḍy, kwɨ·y, Kodagu ko·ḷi, Tulu kōri, kōḷi, Telugu kōḍi, Gondi gōgōr̂i ≗ gugor̂i ≗ g^hogr̂i ≗ gogr̂ 'fowl', Kannada kōṟi 'cock, hen', 'fowl' (generic) ◇ The Nostr. reconstruction is ***ḲoʟwɹŕE** or ***ḲuŕE** '∈ a gallinacean'.

21. **HS**: Sem.: [1] West Sem. *'ḳ⌈u⌉rʟaɹd- 'tick' > Arabic qurd-, qurād-, Tigre ቀረድ ḳärad id.; [2] Sem. *°√ḳrdʕ ~ *°√ḳrṭʕ > Arab. qirdaʕ-, qirdiʕ- '∈ louse (living on camels and hen)', qarṯaʕ-, qirṯiʕ- '∈ louse (living on camels), qurdūʕ- 'small ant' | | Cush.: Agaw: Bilin {Reinisch} q^wər$^?$ad-ā (pl. $ḳ^w$ər$^?$ad) 'tick'; Agaw ↦ Tigre {Reinisch} $ḳ^w$ɜrʔɜday, Tigray {Reinisch} $ḳ^w$ɜrʔɜdɜt id. | | **Kartv.**: Georgian ḳvirṭ-i, ḳruṭ-i 'wasp' | | **Drav.** *kur∇ṭ... ({GS} *k-) 'leech' > Parji kurṭubi, Gadba kurṭum id. ◇ The Nostr. reconstruction is ***ḳ⌈u⌉R⌈ʕ∇⌉d∇** or ***ḳuRṭ∇ʕ∇** 'stinging insect'.

22. **HS**: WS *√ḳŝʕ(m) 'hyena' > Central Jibbali 'ḳe'ŝɛt (pl. 'ḳe'ŝɔŝ) 'wolf', Arabic qašʕ- 'male hyena', qušāʕ- 'cri de l'hyène', qašʕam- 'hyena', ? 'lion' (unless the latter is from qašʕam- 'old'), Old Yemenite قشة qšḫ ({Selwi} qišša) 'beast of prey', Yemenite Arabic qiša (pl. qišāt) id. | | Berber *qq∇zīn ~*qq∇zzūn 'young dog, dog' > Aït-Izdeg a-ḵzin (pl. i-ḵzin) 'chien, chiot', Iznacen {Rn.}, Waryaghel/Tuzin Rif aqzin (pl. iqzinən), Rf Boqoyya/Beni-Amret Rif aqəzzun (pl. iqzinən), Beni-Snus a-qzīn, Tamazight ikzin (pl. ikzinn), Ait-Seghrushen iqzin ~ aqzin (pl. iqzinn), Beni-Menacer aqžun (pl. iqzan), Gurara aqzin (pl. iqzinan), Jerba aɣzim, Zwawa aqžun, Shawiya {R. Basset} اقزن aqzin, {Huyghe} agzim (pl. igzemen) 'petit chien', Senhazha-Srair ṯa-qzin-t 'chienne', Kabyle aqžun (pl. iq^wžan) 'dog' | | South Omotic {Blažek} *aksi 'dog' > Ari {Bender} (ʔ)aksi 'dog', Bako Ari

{Fleming} aks, aksi (pl. aksɜn), Ubamer {Fleming} aksi, Galila {Bender} akši, Hamer {Fleming, Lydall} ḳaski ≗ kaski | | **Uralic**: Finno-Ugr. *°kaćʟć⅃∇ (or *°kUćʟć⅃∇) > Permian {Lïtkin & Gulyayev} *ku|ùć∇ 'young dog' > Ziryene кычи k+ći, кычан k+ćan, Votyak кучапи kućapi id. | | ?? **Kartv.**: one may take into account Svan {Nizharadze} ḳoc̣ol 'young dog' (unless a semantic derivative from ḳoc̣ol ~ ḳoč̣ol 'little') ◇ The Nostr. reconstruction is ***Ḳaĉɛ∇** 'young dog\wolf'.

23. **HS**: [1] Sem. *'namʟa⅃l- 'ant', n. coll. *namāl- (metathesis from *√nlm?) > Arabic naml- ~ numl- 'ant(s)', n. unit. naml-at-, Bib. Heb. נְמָלָה nəmā'l-ā 'ant', pl. Middle Heb. נְמָלִים nəmā'l-īm 'ants', West Syr, ܢܡܠܐ nəmo'l-o 'ant nest', Mehri nōmīl (pl. nōmōl), Harsusi lōmēl (pl. lōmōl), Soqotri {Johnstone} 'nɜmhɛl, Akkad. namālu, namlu, lamattu (< *la'manatum < *na'malatum) 'ant' ˥ [2] Sem. *°nimm- > Arabic nimm-at- 'ant, louse' ¶ The change *n...lm- > *n...mm- is due to the S incompatibility law that rules out a sequence of two dental sonorants in the same root | | Chadic: ? West Ch.: Sura ŋ̀gum, Angas ŋgum 'insect' ¦¦ East Ch.: Jegu lólmó 'ant' | | **A**: Tg *ŋalma- 'gnat' > Orok ŋalma-qta ~ nalma-qta ~ nalpa-qta ~ namma-qta, Ude ŋama-kta, Orochi gama-kta, Ulcha galma-qta ~ garma-qta, Nanay galma-qta ~ garma-xta ~ garma-qta, Ewenki, Negidal ŋanma-kta, Solon nama-kta ~ namma-kta ~ namma-tta, Class. Manchu galma-n, Sibä Manchu (galəmən) [gaɬmən] id. | | **Drav.**: [1] *°nuḷamp- 'mosquito, gnat' > Tamil nuḷampu 'gnat, eye-fly, mosquito', Malayalam nuṟampu 'gnat, eye-fly' ˥˥?? [2] D *umm∇ḷ- '∈ stinging insect' > Kannada ummuṇi '∈ insect', Tulu umil° ~ umbḷi 'mosquito, gnat', Naikri ummel 'mosquito' | | In addition, a root in Uralic deserves attention: **Uralic**: Finno-Permian *n|ǹo|ume 'small fly or mosquito' > proto-Cheremis *lum- > Highland Ceremis lъme, East Cher. lŭmey ≗ lumiy ≗ lume 'a very small fly' ¦ Permian *nomi 'mosquito' > Ziryene nom / nomy- 'mosquito, gnat', Yazva num 'mosquito', Votyak n+m+ 'gnat', Central Votyak n+m+ 'mosquito' ◇ The Nostr. reconstruction is ***ŋ∇ĺ∇ ⌜h⌝∇mP⌜i⌝** 'gnat, mosquito' (= ***ń∇ĺ∇** 'insect' + **⌜h⌝∇mP⌜i⌝**? 'stinging insect'; both are reconstructed independently, see my forthcoming *Nostratic Dictionary*).

24. HS: S *parr- 'bull, young ruminant' > Bibl. Heb. פַּר par 'bull, steer', Middle Heb. פַּר par 'two- to five-year-old bull', Ugar. pr 'Stier, junges Rind', {Olmo Lete & Sanmartín} 'young bull', ˀalp pr 'calf', West Syriac pa'r-o, Mandaic para 'lamb', Arabic [Zuhayr in Ahlwardt's

Diwans] farr- 'calf', Akkadian parru 'lamb'; Sem. *parr-at- 'female young ruminant' > Bibl. Heb. פָּרָה pā'rā, Ugar. prt 'cow', Jewish Aram. פַּרְתָּא parətā id., West Syr. parə'ṯ-o, Mandaic parta, Akkad. parratu 'ewe lamb'; other derivatives: Arabic furār- 'young of sheep, goats, wild cows', farīr- 'a young of wild animals (gazelle, etc.)' | | ?? Egyptian pry 'Kampfstier (?)' ({Erman & Grapow} pry als Bezeichnung des Kampfstiers), {Faulkner} 'ferocious bull' | | Berber *°√ɸrw ({Pr.} *√$h_2$rw) 'goats and sheep' > Ahaggar e-here (pl. i-hərawən) 'goats and sheep', East Tawellemmet, Tayert e-ħʙre (pl. iħərwan) 'bétail', Semlal Tashelhit hruy 'moutons', tahruyt (pl. tihray) 'a sheep', *√ɸry 'calf' > East Tawellemmet, Tayert e-heri (pl. i-həran) 'jeune bœuf de 2 à 3 ans' | | East Cush.: Somali farow, North Somali fáraw 'zebra' | | Chadic: Central Ch.: Margi {Hoffmann} fúr 'buffalo', Bura Pele {Meek}, Kilba {Meek} fur, Margi Putai {Meek} fir id. ¦¦ ? West Ch.: Angas {Foulkes} fīr 'roan antelope' | | **Kartv.** *pur- 'female bovine' > Georgian puri 'female bovine (buffalo, deer, cow, etc.)', Megrelian puǯi 'female domestic bovine (cow, etc.)', Laz puǯ-i 'cow', Svan pür ≗ pirw ≗ pwir ≗ pur 'cow' | | **Drav.**: [**1**] *po(:)ri '(young) bull, buffalo' > Tamil pori 'calf of buffalo', Kota po·ry 'young bullock', Kannada hōri 'bull calf, bullock', Kodagu po·ri 'male buffalo', Tulu bōri 'bull, ox'][[**2**] D *pār∇ɭ ({GS} *p-) 'a young (female?) buffalo' > Tulu pāroḷu 'a young she-buffalo', Toda po·ɬ̣ 'female buffalo calf between 1 and 2 years old', Konda pa·ɭ 'buffalo calf between one and two years old' (*-ɭ- is a suffix for female be) ◇ The original rounded vowel have been preserved in Kartv. *pur-, proto-Margi *fur- and in Drav. *po(:)ri, while the vowel *a in Sem. *parr- 'bovine, young ungulate' and in Drav. *pār∇ɭ 'young (female) buffalo' is due to contamination with N *p|p̣Ar∇ 'to bring forth, young of animal' ◇ The Nostr. reconstruction is ***⌈p̣⌉or⌊w⌋∇** '(female, young?) ungulate (esp. bovine)'.

25. **HS**: S *θu'ʕal- 'fox' > Heb. שׁוּעָל šuʕāl, Old Aram. šʕl [θ-ʕ-l], Jewish Aram. תַּעֲלָא taʕ^{a}'l-ā, West Syr. taʕ'l-o, Mandaic tala, Arabic θuʕal- ~ θuʕāl- 'fox', Ugar. θʕl (n. pr.)] Sem. *θaʕlab- 'fox' > Arabic θaʕlab-, Akkadian šēlebu(m) id. | | Chadic {Stolbova} *č⌈u⌉lib- 'wolf, jackal' > Central Ch.: Musgu če-čelebe 'jackal' ¦¦ East Ch.: Mokilko {Jungraithmayr} sùllíbè 'wolf' | | **Uralic**: Finno-Permian: North Lapp {Friis} čälp ~ čellup ~ čolp 'wolf', Ter Lapp č̣ạl̄p id. ◇ HS data suggest a N *č-, while Lapp č- seems to point to other sibilants (*c-, *ć- *ç-, *ç̣- or *ś-) ◇ The Nostr. reconstruction is ***⌈č⌉∇ƹL∇**

(-**b∇**) '∈ canine'. The element ***b∇** is a marker (> suffix) of animal names.

26. **HS**: S {AD} *'θawar- 'bull' > BHb שׁוֹר 'šōr, pl. שְׁוָרִים šəwā'rīm, ? Phoen. (Greek transcription) θωρ, Ugar. θr (θōr-), Bibl. Aram. pl. תּוֹרִין tō'rīn, Jewish Aram. תּוֹרָא tō'r-ā, West Syr. ܬܘܪܐ taw'r-o, Arabic ثور θawr-, Old South Arabian θwr, Geʿez, Tigre ሰር sōr, Akkadian šūr-, Eblaic šu-lum (= θō|ūr-um); Sem. ⇸ IE *tawro-s 'bull, aurochs' > Mycenian Greek tawros, Greek ταῦρος id.; proto-Albanian {Orël} *taṷra > Albanian ter 'bull'; Latin taurus, Oscan (accus.) ταυρομ, Umbrian (accus. pl.) turuf, TORU id.; Gaulish TARVOS, Old Irish tarb, Irish tarbh, Welsh tarw, Breton tarv, Cornish tarow id.; Slavic *turъ > OCS **тоуръ** turъ 'aurochs'; Lith. taũras 'aurochs', Old Prussian tauris 'bison'; Baltic ⇸ Finnish tarvas 'reindeer'; Old Norse þjórr, Swedish tjur, Dutch dial. deur 'bull'; ?? Anatolian IE: Hieroglyphic Luwian Tarawas 'god of the weather' || Eg: (Old Kingdom) sꜣ 'young bull' || South Cush. ⇸ Mbugu čurú 'bull' || **IE**: Narrow IE *steṷr-/stoṷr- 'bull' > Avestan staora 'large cattle', Middle Persian stōr 'draught-animal', New Persian ستور sotūr ~ استور ostūr 'beast of burden (horse, mule)' ¦¦ Gothic stiur 'male calf, bull', Old Norse stiórr, OHG stior, German Stier, Anglo-Saxon stēor 'bullock, steer', English steer || ? **Alt.**: Tungusian *°c̣ur- (~ *c̣i̱r-?) > Ewenki c̣urup 'wild deer (two- to three- years old)' and possibly Urmi Ewenki c̣irak, Maya Ewenki c̣irāp 'elk (4 years old)', Negidal c̣ırap 'male elk (3–4 years old)' ¶ Possibly Altay, Teleut, Quu-Kizhi ćar 'ox, bullock (Ochs, Arbeitsochs)', Baraba, Küerik čar 'ox' ⇸ Cl. Mong. {Ramstedt} car, Kalmuck car, Halha шар 'castrated ox' (in this case N *awR > Alt. *aR) || **D**: [1] Drav. {tr.} *cař- > Gadba sařit 'bullock', Pulgura Konda sařa 'bull', Kuwi sřahnu kōḍi 'bullock' (kōḍi 'cow, ox') | [2] ?? Drav. {tr.} *cir, {GS} *cir 'buffalo' > Kolami sir, Naikri śir 'female buffalo', Naiki sir id., 'buffalo', Parji cir, Gadba sir ≗ cirru 'buffalo'; Drav. ⇸ Old Indian saịribha id. ◇ The Nostr. reconstruction is ***čʳaˀwʳuˀŕ∇** (or ***čaw∇yr∇**, ***čawir∇**, ***čuR∇** ??) 'bull, calf'.

For lack of space I cannot indivate here the references. For the references and further details see my forthcoming *Nostratic Dictionary*.

Symbols: ←b– = "borrowed from"

–b→ = "source of borrowing" (A –b→ B = "B is a loan from A")

←b– = "borrowed from"

–d→ = "source of derivation" (A –d→ B = "B is derived from A")

÷ = "akin to"

~ = "variant"

$\overset{d}{\sim}$ between forms denotes dialectal variants

*ᵒ means that the reconstructed forms is represented in one daughter language or one branch only

∈ = "a kind of"

| = "or" (ä|e = "ä or ĕ")

⌈ ⌉ = "or similar", symbol of dubious identification (*⌈b⌉ = "probably *b")

⌊ ⌋ = "or zero" (Sem. *'šem⌊a⌋n- = *'šaman- or *'šamn-)

?σ = doubtful for semantic reasons

?φ = doubtful for phonetic reasons

Capital letters in reconstructions denote unspecified phonemes of a certain class (P = unspecified bilabial stop, U = unspec. rounded vowel, Ḳ = ḳ or q̣). ∇ denotes an unspecified vowel.

Abbreviations: ChC = *Chadic Word Catalogue*, compiled by H. Jungraithmayr a. o. Ms. files. Marburg / Frankfurt.

ChL = *Chadic Wordlists*. Collected and ed. by Ch.H. Kraft. I–III. Berlin, D. Reimer, 1981.

{tr.} = taditional reconstruction (in Dravidian)

{GS} = reconstruction according to G. Starostin's theory

{Pr.} = reconstruction according to K. Prasse's theory

st. emph. = status emphaticus

We distinguish between *transcription script* (a, b, c, d) [used in transcription and reconstruction) and *transliteration script* (a, b, c, d) [used both in transliteration and in literal quitation of the original Latin script, as well in quoting phonetically unreliable data from old scholars or unprofessional authors], as well as a special *Roman quotation script* (A, B, C, D) used for quoting the original Latin script of Oscan, Umbrian, Gaulish and Punic. ( ) - brackets for morphopfonemic transcription.

Special transcription signs: ɣ = fricative velar voiced cons. (Spanish g in Malaga, Modern Greek γ); ɤ = fricative uvular voiced cons.

(Arabic غ; ħ = Orientalistic ḥ; x = Orientalistic ḫ (uvular fricative); ϰ = voiceless fricative velar (Russian x); c = IPA ʦ (German z); ʒ = IPA ʣ (Ital. z in mezzo); ǯ = English j; underdot (ṭ, ç, p̣, q̣, ḅ, ḍ) is for glottalization (both ejective and injective); ɡ = uvular voiced stop; q = uvular voiceless stop; ŝ is a domal infradental infralabialized sibilant (Johstone's s̃); ṛ = alveolar trill (in contrast with postdental r in Drav.); ɽ (Castrén's notation) = intermediate between r and l; δ = English th in this; C - voiceless sibilant consonant (without phonemic distinction between different affricates and different s-sounds); ɕ = voiceless palatal stop; J = voiced palatal stop (Hungarian gy); з = central vowel (British English ir in bird); ə = reduced (ultra-brief) vowel; ъ = reduced low vowel; I = high back vowel (Turkish I); ɨ = high middle vowel (Russian ы); ̮ (ṯ, s̮, etc.) denotes uvularization (as in the Arabic emphatic consonants: ṯ = Arabic ط); ̢ (ʈ, ɖ, ɭ) and a gravis over a cons. letter (ǹ) denote postalveolar (retroflex, etc.) pronunciation; acute over a cons. letter (ń, ĺ, ś) symnolizes palatal consonants (ń = Spanish ñ, ĺ = Ital. gli); upper dot to the right of the letter (l˙) - slight palatalization; ̠ (to the right of the letter: b̠ d̠) denotes (partial or complete) devoicing; ˉ (to the right of the letter: kˉ, pˉ) symbolizes lenis (lax consonants); - (under a vowel letter) denotes the low series of vowel harmony (in Tungusian); ₌ (a̳, e̳, etc.) - breathy vowels; ˜ (before or under consonant letters) denotes prenasalized consonants (˜d = ⁿd).

THE TWO NEGATIVES {n} AND {m} IN EGYPTIAN AND THEIR COUNTERPARTS IN DISTANTLY RELATED LANGUAGES

Saul Levin
(State University of New York at Binghamton)

Joining in the tribute to the esteemed Werner Vycichl, although only to a small extent does my research overlap his, I offer a paper based partly upon a section from the chapter on syntax, in the sequel that I am writing to *Semitic and Indo-European: The principal etymologies, with observations on Afro-Asiatic* (Amsterdam: John Benjamins, 1995).

The difference between the two kinds of negation in Egyptian is illustrated by {n rḫf} 'he does/did not know' (Gardiner 1957:
{m snḏ} 'do not fear' 260, 376).

The most exact parallel to the Egyptian distinction is found in Indo-Iranian: [(Rigveda 1.7.7)
Sanskrit {ná vind^{h}ē asya suṣṭutím} 'I don't stint his praise'
{mā́ tát kar indra} 'don't do that, Indra' (8.45.31).
Avestan makes the same distinction between {na} and {mā}.

{ná} has cognates too in various IE languages, and so has {mā́} but not in the same ones (Pokorny 1959:703, 756–757); e.g.
Latin *nescit* 'he/she doesn't know' (Plautus, *Bacchides* 334, etc.)
but *nōlī īrāscier* 'don't get angry' (*Captiui* 840),
Goth. {þarei þiubos ni ufgraband} 'where thieves don't dig up'
but also {ni huzdjaiþ} 'don't hoard' (Matt. 6:19–20).
Greek τόδ' οὐ κόμπωι λέγω 'this I don't say with a boast'
but μὴ τοῦτο λέξηις 'don't say that'.[1]

The Arabic negative {mā}, unlike either the Egyptian {m} and the Sanskrit {mā́} = Greek μὴ, is restricted to certain INDICATIVE constructions:

---

[1] Euripides, *Helen* 393, *Iph. Aul.* 361. Like the Latin *ne-* as a prefix of adjectives (*nescius* 'unknowing', etc.), **ne-*, as a prefix, occurs vestigially in Greek adjectives: νήκεστον 'incurable' (< *νε- + ἀκεστόν 'curable'; cf. the imperative verb ἄκεσ|σαι 'cure, heal'), νηλεές 'pitiless' (but cf. οὔ σ' ἐλεήσει 'he will not pity you', *Iliad* 24.207).

{mā yuzakkā(ʸ) (ˀ)lˀinsānu} 'the man is not [= no man is] declared righteous' (Caspari – Wright 1898:20);
{wa | mā kafara sulaymānu} 'and Solomon did not disbelieve' (Qur'ān 2.102). If the Qur'ān were translated into Sanskrit, the negative would be {ná}, not {mā́}.[2]

The close correspondence here between Egyptian and certain Indo-European languages is odd, but not unique; cf.

Egyptian {ḫnty}: Latin *ante*, Sanskrit {ánti} 'in front {of}'.[3]

In the Semitic family, Hebrew syntax employs two negatives with nearly the same distinction as in Sanskrit (among IE languages) and in Egyptian:

{lóˀ ˀiʸrɔ́ˀ} 'I shall not fear' (Ps. 56:5,12, etc.)
{ˀal⁻tiʸrɔ́} 'do not fear' (masc. sing., Deut. 1:21, etc.).[4]

Biblical Aramaic likewise distinguishes

{lɔ́ yəhọb̄əd̄úʷn} 'they shall not destroy' (Dan. 2:18) from
{ˀal⁻təhoʷb̄éd̄} 'do not destroy' (2:24).

{loˀ/lɔˀ} is possibly cognate to the Egyptian {n}, since Egyptian seems to have lacked a liquid consonant of this quality. Neither is {l} found in Avestan, and it is rather rare in Sanskrit, although frequent in Latin and nearly throughout IE otherwise. Obviously {loˀ/lɔˀ} is cognate to Akkadian and Arabic {lā}; these Semitic languages, however, use {lā} also where Hebrew and Aramaic have {ˀal}—e.g. the Arabic translation of Deut. 1:21,

{lā taḫaf} 'do not fear', while 'and I do/shall not fear' is
{wa | lā ˀaḫāfu} (Qur'ān 6.81;
{fa | lā ˀaḫāfu} in the Arabic version of Ps. 56:5,12).

With indicative verbs Arabic uses either {lā} or {mā}; the difference between them is fine indeed (Caspari – Wright 1898: 300).[5]

---

[2] Ehret 1995:301, #572, posits cognates of Arabic *ma*, Egyptian *m* in proto-Cushitic "*ma- 'to avoid'" and proto-Chadic "*may-(a) 'hunger' . . ."

[3] Greek ἀντὶ 'instead of'. Hittite {ḫa-an-ti} 'apart' may admit of the meaning 'in front', according to some but not all authorities (Pokorny 1959:49–50, Illich-Svitych 1965:354). Egyptian {šn.t/š.t} 'hundred' resembles these IE forms: Lithuanian *šim̃t | as* (aside from the masculine singular case-ending), Sanskrit {šatám}, Avestan {satəm}, Ch. Slavonic {səto}—more than Latin *centum*, Gr. ἑκατόν, etc. See Levin 1995:382–387, 1998:167–171.

[4] Also {lọˀ⁻ t̄iʸrɔ́ˀ} 'she' or 'you (masc. sing.) shall not fear' (Pr. 31:21, Ps. 91:5, etc.).

[5] A rule of syntax common to Semitic and, in part, to the ancient IE languages is the exclusion of the imperative from negative commands. Indo-Europeanists call the Skt. {kar} in {mā́ kar} injunctive, while the equivalent term of the Semitists

The usual position of the negative before the verb[6] is common to Egyptian, Semitic, and most of Indo-European. The modern Germanic languages have diverged from this; e.g.

> the Old High German *ir ni uuissunt* (John 4:22) was replaced in Luther's version by *ihr wisset nicht* 'ye know not'.[7]

It would be hyper-skeptical to dismiss, as a mere coincidence, the sharing of the two negatives by Egyptian and certain ancient Indo-European languages. Although geographically distant from each other in the age of recorded history, there is nothing improbable about positing a prehistoric time of contact, when the population—on one side, if not on both—was at least partly nomadic.

While valuing this correspondence as far as it goes, I would hardly venture to place the origin of it in a specified epoch of prehistory. I am not committed to the Nostratic theory or a particular version of it, nor to any other theory about the evolution of language groups. Further investigation may bring to light an impressive link between this double feature of basic morphology and some items of vocabulary.

Recently Greenberg (2000:212) remarked:

> Indo-European has two common indicators of negation, **ne* and **mē*. Of these, the first is found in every branch of Indo-European, not only as a sentence negation, but also as a negative prefix before verbs (e.g. Latin *ne-sciō* 'I do not know') and nouns, usually with reduced grade *n̥* (e.g. Greek *án-udros* 'waterless'). In contrast, **mē* occurs primarily as a negation of the imperative in Indic, Greek, Armenian, and Albanian.

---

for the Arabic {taḫaf} (Heb. {tiʸrɔ́}) is jussive. The imperative counterparts are Skt. {kr̥|dʰí} 'do' and Arab. {ḫaf} 'fear' (Heb. {yərɔ́ˀ}). *{mā́ kr̥|dʰi} or *{lā ḫaf}, *{ˀal-yərɔ́ˀ} is out of the question.

Greek shares this rule in regard to the aorist imperative; hence λέξον 'say' but μὴ λέξηις 'don't say'. But the present imperative λέγε is quite compatible with the negative: μὴ λέγε (Aristophanes, *Wasps* 37, etc.). This oddly split rule of Greek surprises us all the more because the difference in meaning between μὴ λέξηις and μὴ λέγε—or between the two imperatives λέξον and λέγε—seems so subtle; it can scarcely be expressed in English.

[6] Or whichever other word is the focus of the negation, as in the Greek examples: μὴ τοῦτο 'not that', οὐ κόμπωι 'not with a boast'.

[7] In recent English versions *you do not know*—which still puts the negative after a verb (< Old English *doþ; know* is from the OE infinitive *cnawan*). The Old High German translated the Latin *nescitis*; Luther went back to the Greek οὐκ οἴδατε, but his placement of *nicht* after the verb is evidently not due to anything in the Greek original but to a diachronic development within his own language. In a subordinate clause, to be sure, *wiss(e)t* or any other verb comes at the end; to that extent the ancient IE pattern has lasted in German down to the present.

From there he goes on to cite parallels in the language families that he groups with Indo-European to comprise the super-family Eurasiatic: Uralic, Altaic, etc. The best of his examples are from Yukaghir (related to Uralic), "*ńe-xaŋide el xonlek* 'don't go anywhere'," and from Turkish (belonging to the Altaic family), "*gel-me-di-m* 'I did not come'." These, however, point in just the opposite direction from the Indo-European *ne-* with the indicative and *mV* with the imperative (or its surrogates).

The plan of Greenberg's book excludes any systematic mention of morphemes shared by Afro-Asiatic and Indo-European languages. His reasons, given briefly in the introductory chapter, leave it unclear to me why he does not call attention to the Egyptian {n} and {m}—if we may presume that he was aware of them from his earlier studies of Afro-Asiatic (among other families of languages in Africa.).

Bibliography

Caspari [Carl]—Wright (W.): 1898. A Grammar of the Arabic Language. 3d ed. Vol. II. Cambridge University Press.

Ehret (Christopher): 1995. Reconstructing Proto-Afroasiatic (Proto-Afrasian): Vowels, Tone, Consonants, and Vocabulary. Berkeley: University of California Press.

Gardiner (Alan): 1957. Egyptian Grammar. 3d ed. London: Oxford University Press.

Greenberg (Joseph H.): 2000. Indo-European and Its Closest Relatives: The Eurasiatic Language Family. Volume 1. Grammar. Stanford University Press.

Illich-Svitych (V.M.): "Материалы к сравительному словарю носратических языков," Этимология 1965, pp. 321–373.

Levin (Saul): 1995. Semitic and Indo-European: The principal etymologies. (Current Issues in Linguistic Theory, vol. 129) Amsterdam: John Benjamins.

——: 1998. "Studies in Comparative Grammar: IV. Egyptian {ḫnty} 'in front of': Hittite {ḫanti}; Latin ANTIQVEI : Hebrew/Aramaic {ʕattiʸqeʸ} 'old'," General Linguistics 36: 167–177.

Pokorny (Julius): 1959. Indogermanisches etymologisches Wörterbuch. Vol. I. Heidelberg: Carl Winter.

SOME NOTES ON THE ETHIO-SEMITIC PARTICLE -S/-Š AND THE EGYPTIAN JS

Adrian Măcelaru
(Center for Arabic Studies, Bucharest University)

1. *Introduction*

The aim of the present article is only to draw the attention once again to some evidence offered by Ethio-Semitic and Egyptian for an isogloss worth being examined. I stress "again" because the parallelism between the same facts has already been drawn by Rundgren (1955). Consequently, I will only try to suggest a possible explanation, if any, for these facts in my view.

2. *Ethio-Semitic enclitic particle* -s/-š

As it is well known, Ethio-Semitic has an enclitic particle construed with a sibilant: Geʿez *-s(s)ä*; Tigrigna *-(ə)s, -si, -sya*; Amharic *-ss(a)*; Argobba *-ss(a)*; Ezha *-š*,[1] *-še*; Ennemor *-š*; Mägär *-š*; Chaha *-š*; Gura *-š*; Gafat *-š*. As to the original form of this enclitic particle, the variant constructed with *s* is deemed to be the original one, the *š* forms being the result of the palatalization of *s*.

Their most common translations are as follows:

1. "Indeed, certainly": Tigrigna *-s*: e.g.: *käydku-s* "certes, je suis allé" (Rundgren 1955:53); Argobba *-ss*; e.g.: *ahaň-əss mäšdul* "now, indeed, it is late" (Leslau 1997:115); *hud su dägg-əss ne kəfu-ss ne?* "this man, is he good or bad?" (lit. "this man good-indeed he-is bad-indeed he-is?") (Leslau 1997:115). Amharic *-ss*; e.g.: *mən bəläw yəhidu? ənnässu-ss ayhedumm* "why should they go? They certainly will not go" (Leslau 1995:890).

[1] Ezha also has an enclitic particle that seems to fulfil the same function as *-š* does, together with which it is sometimes used side-by-side (Hetzron 1977:131). I presume that *-h* might be nothing else but an instance of the same phonetic change that affected the causative morpheme in some Semitic languages, namely *š-/s-* > *h-*.

2. "As for, as to": Tigrigna *-s*; e.g.: *nəssu-s* "quant "lui" (Rundgren 1955:53); Amharic *-ss*; e.g.: *mar səṭäññ, mar-əss yällämm* "give me some honey; as for honey, there isn't any" (or: "well, there is no honey") (Leslau 1995:889); Gunnän-Gurage languages *-š* (Hetzron 1998:549).

3. "Why (indeed)": Amharic *-ss*; e.g.: *lelaw sisära əsswa təčč̣awwätə—ss-alläčč* "when others work, why indeed she is fooling around" (Leslau 1995:889).

4. "What about?": Amharic *-ss(a)*; e.g.: *əne əngliẓəñña astämrallä^{w}h, mistəwo-ss?* "I teach English. What about your wife?" (Leslau 1995:889). Argobba *-ss*; e.g.: *antä-ss* "what about you?" (Hudson 1998:465).

5. "But": Geʿez *-s(s)ä*; e.g.: *qal-(ə)ssä qal-ä Yaʿqob wä-ʾədäw zä-ʿesaw* "as for the voice, it is the voice of Jacob, but the hands are those of Esau" (Gragg 1998:258); Tigrigna *-s*; e.g.: *saʾnas* "uns aber" (Rundgren 1955:53); Amharic *-ss*; e.g.: *təlantənna əzzih wəha alnäbbäräm, zare-ss allä* "yesterday there was no water, but today there is" (Leslau 1995:889); Ennemor *-š*; e.g.: *kətiftä-š-ta aysäβərka* "he will break, but not after having chopped meat" (Hetzron 1977:131).

6. "Rather": Amharic *-ss*; e.g.: *kandu agär wädandu agär əyyäzorhu ənorallä^{w}h ənği wädä hagäre-ss aləmmälläsəmm* "I would rather wander (lit. "I would rather live wandering") from place to place than return to my country." (Leslau 1995:890).

From the examples quoted above we can infer that these enclitic particles do not encode grammatical functions but rather pragmatic ones. This becomes particularly clear when we read the description of Gunnän-Gurage *-š* apud Hetzron (1977:130): "This particle probably has an expressive function. The item marked by it assumes a connotation of novelty, it appears as an element of surprise, sudden realization, contrast (as against what could be expected)". He illustrates this function through examples like: Ezha: *ahä-š yäbahä qar anhärä-we* "Isn't it something *you* said?—with astonishment" (Hetzron 1977:130) (surprise element); Ennemor: *iiya-še* "mine!" ("but not yours!") (Hetzron 1977:130) (contrastive). Finally, in his description of Outer South Ethiopic, the same author assigns to the enclitic Gunnän-Gurage *-š* the value of "interrogative particle 'as for', topicalizer" (Hetzron 1998:549).

The pragmatic function also comes up from Leslau's comment on Amharic *-ss*: "It refers to a preceding statement and is rendered by "as for, as to, why (indeed)" [. . .]. It may also be conceived as expressing a contrast to a preceding or a following statement. (Leslau

1995:889) [. . .] The enclitic *-ss* emphasizes or stresses a statement [. . .] (and) also stresses the meaning of the various conjunctions." (Leslau 1995:890). The values Leslau identifies for the enclitic particle *-ssa* (that is, *-ss-a*) in Amharic are: a) expressing "what about?, how about?, as for, too" (Leslau 1995:891) and b) expressing a finite interrogative or an emphatic statement, when used with the simple gerund (Leslau 1995:892). Argobba *-ss* is described by Leslau (1997:115) as rendering "insistence".

3. *Egyptian* js

Egyptian also possesses a particle quite similar in shape and function to the Ethio-Semitic enclitic discussed above. That is *js*.

Depuydt (1993) summarizes in a very systematic manner the properties characterizing the propositions containing *js*, as well as its relative, *jsk*. These are the following (Depuydt 1993:15–16):

(a) independence
(b) anaphora
(c) subordination
(d) emphasis

Independence means that the proposition construed with *js* or *jsk* expresses an independent thought. Depuydt (1993:16) gives the following example: "*Er fuhr in die Stadt, und das ohne die Erlaubnis seiner Eltern*". "*Er fuhr in die Stadt*" renders a complete idea, while "*und das ohne die Erlaubnis seiner Eltern*" presents another idea, a kind of afterthought. Thus, from the point of view of the logical flow of thoughts, it is an independent clause and not a subordinate adverbial adjunct.

The anaphoric property refers to the role that *js*, respectively *jsk* play. As one can see from the above example, "*das*" points to the previous assertion, so it is an anaphora.

Subordination derives from the anaphoric status of *js/jsk*, due to which an adverbial adjunct can be subordinated to *js/jsk*.

Emphasis renders the fact that the clauses introduced by *js/jsk* aim to emphasize a certain event by adding to it supplementary information conveyed by the adverbial adjunct.

In order to describe the functions *js* has, Loprieno (1995:153–5) also appeals at more than one level of linguistic analysis, namely at semantics, discourse, and syntax. So he states that, "at the semantics level, *js* transforms a "categorial" into a "thetic" sentence" (Loprieno 1995:153), i.e. into a statement that presents an event as a whole in which topic and comment have not to be distinguished as separated parts of the statement. At the discourse level, *js* foregrounds the sentence it marks, conveying a contrastive focus, "i.e. a contextually unexpected argument or state of affairs." (Loprieno 1995:154). Finally, at the syntactic level, *js* is a marker of dependency (Loprieno 1995:154).

Borghouts (1986:66) assumes that *js* expresses "contrastivity" and, therefore, it might be translated "somewhat like "to be precise", "at least", or similar" for it "seems to be used as a pointer put before a word [. . .] which is of specific importance for the predication".

4. *The values of Ethio-Semitic enclitic particle* -s/-š *and Egyptian js*

From the examples and the descriptions above there is no doubt that both the Ethio-Semitic and Egyptian clitics under discussion serve pragmatic functions. In order to establish what these pragmatic functions are, I confronted the Ethio-Semitic and Egyptian data with the taxonomy of pragmatic statuses presented by Payne (1997:268–9). The examples and the descriptions above make me consider that, in the overwhelming majority of the cases, these clitics should be labeled as instances of contrastive focus. According to Payne, a prototypical contrastive focus clause presupposes:

(a) a particular event E (taken loosely to mean any state of affairs) occurred;
(b) there is a group of entities that might have had a role, R, in E;
(c) the addressee "incorrectly" (in the eyes of the speaker) believes that one of the entities did in fact have the role R.

Then, contrastive focus clause asserts:

(a) the "correct" identity of the entity involved, according to the perception of the speaker;
(b) the proposition that the entity the addressee thought have had the role R in fact *did not*. (Payne 1997:269).

The Ethio-Semitic examples under (1) above, where the enclitic particle is rendered by "indeed, certainly", have to be interpreted as cases of truth-value focus, countering the assumed presupposition that the truth value of the entire clause is in question (Payne 1997:268). At the same time, I think that, even here, we cannot entirely exclude a contrastive focus reading without very carefully examining the larger context in which these instances appear. Or, in other words, it might be the case that for instance "Now, indeed, it is late" should be interpreted as "contrary to what the hearer believes, the speaker is convinced that it is late." Moreover, I believe that truth-value focus itself may imply contrast. The emphasis is meant precisely to sweep away from the hearer's mind any possible doubt about the truth of the proposition.

In the Ethio-Semitic examples above, in which we find the enclitic particle translated by "what about?", we clearly deal with focus since interrogation normally entails new information. These again can be equated with contrastive focus. So the Amharic example under (4) could be rendered as: "I teach English. *But* (what about) your wife?". The only instances that do not cope with this interpretation are those translated by "as for, as to". They represent topics and not focuses. The only way out off this dilemma would be if we assumed that even here we were dealing with contrastive focus. Thus, an example as Amharic "give me some honey; as for honey, there isn't any" should be read: "give me some honey; contrary to what you think, there isn't any". In support of a general value of contrastive focus for the enclitic particle we may also bring Hetzron's opinion that in Gunnän-Gurage "[. . .] it combines with imperatives [. . .], possibly to express the fact that orders call for actions that the receiver of the order was not planning to do otherwise" (Hetzron 1977:130).

As far as Egyptian *js* is concerned, I consider that the description provided by Depuydt, Loprieno, and Borghouts point to *js* as having a primarily pragmatic role, that of introducing new information in the discourse. This information, brought into the discourse or narrative by *js*, seems in most cases unnecessary so that the hearer can understand the discourse. That is, if we take Depuydt's German example above, we understand very well and completely what happened in the presented event: "he went to the town". What follows, "and that without his parents' allowance", is meant by the speaker or the narrator for *he* considers this information important. Otherwise, knowing that "he" is a child, we would be rather inclined to believe that he did so after having obtained his parents' permission, or, moreover, we would not have even thought of such an aspect. In this respect, we can hold *js* to be a mark of contrastive focus as described by Payne (1997:268). This would also account for the well-known use of *js* in nominal-predicate constructions that are negated, and where it seems that it signals the negation of the entire following sentence, and not just the negation of the element that follows *js* (Allen 1986:17), since negative clauses are functionally similar to contrastive focus sentences, and, consequently, both types of clauses are often formally similar, too (Payne 1997:282).

5. *The Afroasiatic source of Ethio-Semitic* -s/-š *and Egyptian* js

Due to the remarkable phonetic and functional similarity between the Ethio-Semitic enclitic particles construed with *-s/-š* and Egyptian *js*, one might indeed wonder if there is any genetic relationship between them. I think that the answer to this question is positive (as suggested already by Ember 1914; most recently cf. also Chetverukhin 1993). The common source of both morphemes under discussion might have been a locational construction consisting of a deictic, **yV-* (in many branches of Afroasiatic preserved as a bound form marking in the prefixed verbal forms the third person non-feminine subject), plus a non-core case marker **-s*. The precise value of this latter morpheme has to be established by further studies. However, from the functions of its reflexes attested in different branches of Afroasiatic—dative, locative, allative, instrumental, etc.—it is clear that it was a non-core case marker, maybe even the default one. Thus, I think that Loprieno is absolutely right when he compares Egyptian *js* to Greek *ei*, and Latin *si* "if", which both come from the locative of the Indo-European demonstrative pronoun **so-*, which signifies that the original meaning of "if" was "in case", "in that" (Loprieno 1995:270). Additional support in favour of this hypothesis is offered by Berber. Here, in Chleuh, we find a particle *is* used in interrogative and negative interrogative sentences: *Is iša usrdun?* "Est-ce que le mulet a mangé?" vs. *Is ur iši?* "Est-ce qu'il n'a pas mangé?" (Galand 1988:222). As L. Galand explains, the two clauses are also acceptable without *is*. The same sentences pronounced without rising intonation are not interrogative. The particle *is* with plain or descending intonation serves to introduce an explanation required by somebody to the speaker: *is ta ka ur imyar asklu* "c'est seulement qu'il n'est pas encore habitué *à l'ombre* (Galand 1988:223).

So, it seems to me that the function of *is* in these contexts is only to add more emphasis to the questions, therefore it might be judged a pragmatic device meant to express focus. Galand makes it clear that the particle *is* comes from a deictic element, *i*, to which the particle *s*, denoting concomitance, has been attached. In Ayt Ndhir Tamazight Berber, we also find a particle *is* that introduces verbal "yes/no" questions, e.g.: *is ur nttəddu γər-ssuq asəkka* "Aren't you going to market tomorrow?" (Penchoen 1973:82), as well as sentences used as a strong explicative affirmation, e.g.: *is ax-yušər t̲afunest̲* "It is because he stole our cow!" (Penchoen 1973:83).

This particle is phonetically identical with the "long" form—used only before pronouns—of the preposition "with (instrumental)", *is* (when appearing before parts of speech than other pronouns, this preposition takes a shorter form, namely *s*) (Penchoen 1973:28). Taïfi (1993:217) reports for Tamazight a morpheme *is* having the meaning "if"—presumably describing a variety different from that of Ayt Ndhir, since Penchoen (1973:104) gives as equivalent of English "if" *mš*—as well as a preposition *s* functioning as a marker of instrument, manner, cause, relation, and concomitance (Taïfi 1993:226). Taking into account that in Chleuh, the particle *s* was originally governing a relative subordinate clause, and that in Ayt Ndhir Tamazight the sentence following *is* is subordinated to it and dependency conditions apply (Penchoen 1973:82), here we find another remarkable parallel with Egyptian *js*, that also can govern a subordinate clause.

However, despite all this encouraging evidence, there is something that seems to jeopardize the validity of the hypothesis developed above. That is, the fact that, beside its pragmatic value, an additional meaning "like" is well established for Egyptian *js*. This value is named the archaic use of js (Borghouts 1986:67), because it is, seemingly, the original one. Zeidler (1992:213–4) states that the Egyptian enclitic particle *js* has to be compared to the so-called Semitic terminative-adverbial (or dative-locative) ending **-iš*.

I think that a possible explanation might be formulated as follows. In the Afroasiatic daughter languages (maybe even in Proto-Afroasiatic?), the non-core Proto-Afroasiatic case marker **-s*, when added to a noun ending in consonant, produced a syllable coda consisting of two consonants, a structure which was disallowed by the phonology of those languages. Therefore, an epenthetic vowel was introduced between the last consonant of the noun and the case marker. It seems that this epenthetic vowel was *i*, as attested in Akkadian, e.g. **kalb-š* > *kalb-iš* "like a dog" and, possibly, in Egyptian, and Berber, or *a* as found in Ugaritic and Hebrew. Such an assumption can account for the situation met in Semitic, where some languages seem to suggest an *-*aš* ending for this case (e.g., Ugaritic -*h* [*-*ah*], Hebrew -*ā*) and others (e.g. Akkadian, Eblaite) point to an original *-*iš* (Dolgopolsky 1991:331–2). This hypothesis would similarly explain the *i* vowel found in the preposition *iš*[2] attested in some ancient Semitic languages—for example in Mari Akkadian—as prothetic (maybe also influenced by the analogy with other prepositions beginning with an *i*, such as Akkadian *in(a)*, *itti* or *ištu*?). Then, according to another phonotactic rule, operating in many Afroasiatic languages (maybe in force already in the Proto-Afroasiatic phase), that does not allow syllables lacking onset, a consonantal onset will be added, most probably *ʔ* or *y* (due to the influence of the following i), to the prothetic vowel. Thus, in languages where the reflexes of the Proto-Afroasiatic deictic **yV-* > *i* and an epenthetic *i* vowel was added to the non-core case *-*s*, both Proto-Afroasiatic **yV-s* and *-*s* merged into a phonetically identical morpheme, *(y)is*.

Another possible explanation would be—if not in all the languages that attest reflexes of the Proto-Afroasiatic non-core case marker having a prefixed *i*, at least in some of them—that this morpheme would represent the non-core case marker *-*s* reinforced by a preposition *i*, having a close or even identical meaning (similar situations are documented for Indo-European, e.g. Latin, French, or Quechua). An explanation of this kind might be valid in the case of Berber and might account for the situation met in Ayt Ndhir Tamazight where we find a preposition *i* "to, for"[3] (Penchoen 1973:28) as well as an isomorphic pragmatic device, *i*, used for topicalizing a noun phrase. Its function is given by Penchoen as topicalizing, but note that a contrastive focus reading might as well be possible instead of the

[2] We don't treat in this article the Semitic reflexes of Proto-Afroasiatic non-core case marker *-*s*, which require a more elaborated study. One of the problems awaiting an answer is that of the original position this morpheme occupied in Proto-Semitic; was it an postposition/enclitic or a preposition/proclitic? If we admit that the Proto-Semitic order was VSO, we should consider the former possibility to be the valid one, and, in this case, the suffixed reflexes of Proto-Afroasiatic *-s might be explained as the result of a change in the word order, namely VSO > SOV. However, such an assumption can be regarded as valid only in the case of Akkadian, which presents a SOV word-order—seemingly due to the influence of the Sumerian—but not in the case of Ugaritic or Hebrew, languages having suffixed reflexes of Afroasiatic *-s but VSO word-order. So, before further study is made, it is wiser not to rule out even the possibility that in Proto-Semitic this morpheme was originally proclitic. In this event the vowel preceding it would be protethic in nature and not epenthetic.

[3] A preposition *i* "à" is also found in Chleuh, and in the variety of Berber in Mauritania described by Nicolas (1953:64).

topicalizing one, e.g.: *i-ṯərbaṯin ur ḏa asənṯ ttəkksən azzar γas i-bəṛṛa* "As for the girls, people remove their hair only in the country" (Penchoen 1973:77).

The problem created by the isomorphism displayed by both this preposition and the deictic *i* in different varieties of Berber is evident even from Penchoen's affirmation that "it is not clear whether Berber speakers identify the two as the same element however" (Penchoen 1973:77).

So, one of these two explanations—the phonotactical one, or the morpheme reinforcement—would be held responsible for the presence of a lexical item *js* in Egyptian meaning "like" and signaling contrastive focus, at the same time.

In the lack of a thorough study, it would be extremely hazardous and unwise to take a stand on either of these two possibilities either pro or contra. Therefore, we will not carry on the discussion on this matter here. Anyhow, whatever the source of this prothetic *(y/')i* was, it has no bearing on the final results of our hypothesis.

As far as the possibility is concerned that a construction like the Proto-Afroasiatic **yV-s* "at/to/with–that" evolves into a marker of contrastive focus, a very important indication in this direction is offered, in my opinion, by an observation made by Givón (apud Payne 1997:262), who states that obliques tend to express new information and/or information that is not central to the ongoing development of the discourse, that is exactly the way in which I have interpreted "and that without his parents' allowance" in Depuydt's example. Therefore, an evolution of *js* from oblique adjunct to marker of new information and/or information that is not central to the ongoing development of discourse/narrative is to be conceived. Meanwhile, we also have to keep in mind that clauses introduced in Egyptian by *jsk/sk* (*jsṯ/sṯ*) are also adverbial adjuncts (expressing time: "while"), or otherwise said obliques (Loprieno 1995:100–1). Or, *jsk/sk* (*jsṯ/sṯ*) are considered as compound forms of *js* + *a* deictic element *k(i)* (> *ṯ*). Here we have to make again the analogy Rundgren has already made between these Egyptian items and Ethio-Semitic facts, e.g.: Geʿez, Amharic (')*əskä* "to(wards), till" (Rundgren 1955:28), Geʿez *əskū* "of course", Amharic *sə-* + imperfect, construction that renders concomitance (Rundgren 1955:37).

Another analogy we find in Lamang (Central Chadic) which also developed a focus marker, *-é*, out of an associative marker, *-é*, plus a copula, *yá* (Heine and Reh 1984:157).

Internal support for this suggestion is given by the form *sk* that appears in Old Egyptian (Allen 1986:23). Wilson (1997:112) states that *sk* is preferred to *jsk* when a dependent pronoun follows. This might be explained by the fact that *sk* used to head a clause, just like Chleuh *s* has been doing when governing a relative clause. If we assume that *j* is an anaphoric element, we should expect to encounter *jsk* and not *sk* when followed by a syntactically independent item.

Another value of *js*, and *jsk* is that of coordinator or conjunction, "and" (Wilson 1997:108, 112). The relation between this meaning and the function of focus marker can be accounted for by taking into consideration evidence given by Chadic. As Frajzyngier (1996:32) indicates, Lele (East Chadic) has two types of clause coordination, the former one having a structure in which one clause follows another and the latter one exhibiting a structure clause + sentential conjunction + clause. Frajzyngier proposes that the difference between these two types of structures is a pragmatic one: "[. . .] what appears to be a sentential conjunction is actually a focus marker on the proposition, including an unexpected outcome, a crowning point of an event.". Frajzyngier also establishes grammaticalization paths attested by Chadic evidence. Special interest for our discussion present the following paths:

(a) nominal conjunction > sentential coordinating conjunction > contrastive focus (Frajzyngier 1996:34);
(b) associative marker > nominal conjunction > verbal conjunction > purpose marker (Frajzyngier 1996:61);
(c) locative preposition > coordinating conjunction (Frajzyngier 1996:37);
(d) associative preposition > nominal conjunction > sequential marker/ temporal apodosis (Frajzyngier 1996:32).

Hypothetically, we might suppose the following grammaticalization path for Egyptian *js*: adverbial phrase > nominal conjunction > (sentential conjunction?) > contrastive focus marker.

As far as Semitic is concerned, I think that the locational construction of a deictic **yV* + case marker *s* was inherited from the Pre-Semitic stage. It fulfills the role of an existential predicate which, in some Semitic languages, was extended to cover the function of a copula, too: Hebrew *yēš*, Arabic *laysa* etc. (Akkadian developed for its reflex of this root, namely *išû(m)*, a meaning of "to have"). Afroasiatic **yV-s* might have meant "at/to/with–that". Moreover, it is very plausible that Afroasiatic **yV-s* "at/to/with–that" might also have had an adverbial reading ”there”. The reasons for such a supposition are the following. Firstly, deictic **yV-* might have had an undifferentiated value, functioning both pronominally, “that”, and adverbially, “there”. Secondly, even if we have to reject this supposition (although there seems to be no ground for doing so), the possibility still remains that the adverbs of place were derived in Proto-Afroasiatic from the demonstrative pronouns by adding to them the non-core case marker, as it is still the case in Wolaytta (Omotic): *haga-n(ⁱ)* “here” < *hage* “this” + *n(ⁱ)* “locative case”, *hega-rᵃ* “over there” < *hege* “that one” + *rᵃ* “comitative case” (Lamberti & Sottile 1997:125). The use of locational constructions is a very common means for expressing existence and/or possession in many languages of the world (Payne 1997:122). At this point an interesting observation has to be made. The only Semitic branches that seem to entirely lack the descendants of this word are Sayhadic and Ethio-Semitic. This might be just an alluring appearance, at least, as far as Ethio-Semitic is concerned, because the enclitic particles construed with *s* or with its phonetic outcomes would be in fact nothing but relics of the same Proto-Afroasiatic item grammaticalized as a contrastive topic marker. There are languages which express focus by means of existential particles. Such an example is offered by Bahasa Indonésia, where truth-value focus is rendered by the existential particle *ada* (Payne 1997:268). As regards the presence of a sequence of two *s* in Geʿez, Amharic or Argobba particle under discussion, the former *s* might represent the outcome of a total regressive assimilation, just like the one exposed by Assyrian, *laššu* “there is not”. The *š* occurring in the particle of other Ethio-Semitic languages might be explained as the result of the palatalization induced by an original *y* that afterwards was totally assimilated.

A complication arises when comparing the forms this Afroasiatic **yV-s* takes in Ugaritic (*ʾiṯ*) and Aramaic (Imperial Aramaic *ʾyt*, Nabatean Aramaic, Palmyrean Aramaic *ʾyty*, Biblical Aramaic *ʾīty*, Syriac *ʾīt* “there is, he is”) to that displayed by Arabic (*laysa* “he is not”, *ʾays-* “existence, something existent”). According to the rules of the phonetic correspondences established for Semitic, in words with common Semitic ancestry, Ugaritic *ṯ* corresponds to Aramaic *t* and Arabic *ṯ*. Another intricacy is produced by the forms Modern South Arabian presents: Mehri, Hobyot, Harsusi, Jibbali *śi* “there is” (Simeone-Senelle 1997:419). Soqotri has *śi* only as a component of the negative existential particle *bíśi* “there is not” (Simeone-Senelle

1997:419). Thus, in this group we encounter a form that presupposes a Proto-Semitic *ś as the original sibilant of the root under discussion. A possible solution for these problems I will try to propose in another article (Măcelaru in press). For the time being, I can only tentatively suggest that, seemingly, here we might be dealing with allophonic variance.

Acknowledgements

I would like to express my deep gratitude to the editor of this volume, my good friend Gábor Takács for offering me the opportunity of contributing to this volume dedicated to Werner Vycichl, one of the greatest pioneers in the field of Afroasiatic linguistics, for whose insights we are so much indebted.

I would also like to express my warm thanks to Leo Depuydt for his amiable help he yielded for my work by sending his article cited in this paper.

Bibliography

Allen (James P.): 1986 "Features of nonverbal predicates in Old Egyptian", Crossroad. Chaos or the beginning of a new paradigm. Papers from the Conference on Egyptian Grammar, Helsingør 28–30 May 1986, Edited by Gertie Englund and Paul John Frandsen, pp. 9–44, The Carsten Niebuhr Institute of Ancient Near East Studies, Stougaard Jensen/København.

Borghouts (Joris F.): 1986 "Prominence constructions and pragmatic functions", Crossroad. Chaos or the beginning of a new paradigm. Papers from the Conference on Egyptian Grammar, Helsingør 28–30 May 1986, Edited by Gertie Englund and Paul John Frandsen, pp. 45–70, The Carsten Niebuhr Institute of Ancient Near East Studies, Stougaard Jensen/København.

Chetverukhin (Alexander): 1993 "A Morpheme Meaning 'As, Like' in Old Egyptian and Akkadian", Ancient Egypt and Kush. In Memoriam Mikhail A. Korostovcev, pp. 124–140, Nauka: Moscow.

Cohen (David): 1973 Dictionnaire des racines sémitiques ou attestées dans les langues sémitiques, Fasc. 1, '/H—'TN, Mouton: Paris—La Haye.

Depuydt (Leo): 1993 "Zur Bedeutung der Partikeln jsk und js", Göttinger Miszellen, 136, pp. 11–25.

Dolgopolsky (Aron B.): 1991 "Two problems of Semitic historical linguistics", Semitic studies in honour of Wolf Leslau on the occasion of his 85th birthday, November 14th 1991, vol. 1, Edited by A.S. Kaye, pp. 328–339, Otto Harrassowitz: Wiesbaden.

Ember (Aharon): 1914 "Several Semito-Egyptian Particles", Zeitschrift für Assyriologie 28/2–4, pp. 302–306.

Frajzyngier (Zygmunt): 1996 Grammaticalization of the complex sentence. A case study in Chadic, John Benjamins: Amsterdam/Philadelphia.

Galand (Lionel): 1988 "Le berbère", Les langues dans le monde ancient et moderne, III, Les langues chamito-sémitiques, Edited by J. Perrot et D. Cohen, Editions du Centre National de la Recherche Scientifique: Paris.
Gragg (Gene): 1998 "Geʿez (Ethiopic)", The Semitic languages, Edited by R. Hetzron, pp. 242–262, Routledge: London.
Heine (Bernd) and Reh (Mechthild): 1984 Grammaticalization and reanalysis in African languages, Helmut Buske: Hamburg.
Hetzron (Robert): 1977 The Gunnän-Gurage languages, Istituto Orientale di Napoli.
——: 1998 "Outer South Ethiopic", The Semitic languages, Edited by R. Hetzron, pp. 535–549, Routledge: London.
Hudson (Grover): 1998 "Amharic and Argobba", The Semitic Languages, pp. 457–485, Routledge: London.
Lamberti (Marcello) and Sottile (Roberto): 1997 The Wolaytta Language, Studia Linguarum Africae Orientalis, Rüdiger Köppe: Köln.
Leslau (Wolf): 1995 Reference Grammar of Amharic, Otto Harrassowitz: Wiesbaden.
——: 1997 Ethiopic Documents: Argobba Grammar and Dictionary, Otto Harrassowitz: Wiesbaden.
Loprieno (Antonio): 1995 Ancient Egyptian. A Linguistic Introduction, Cambridge University Press: Cambridge.
Măcelaru (Adrian): in press "Proto-Semitic *yš: Problems and Possible Solutions", Selected Comparative-Historical Afrasian Linguistic Studies in Memory of Igor M. Diakonoff, Edited by M.L. Bender, D.L. Appleyard, and G. Takács, Lincom Europa: München
Nicolas (Francis): 1953 La langue berbère de Mauritanie, IFAN: Dakar.
Payne (Thomas E.): 1997 Describing Morphosyntax, Cambridge University Press: Cambridge.
Penchoen (Thomas G.): 1973 Tamazight of the Ayt Ndhir, Afroasiatic Dialects, Vol. 1, Undena Publications: Los Angeles.
Rundgren (Frithiof): 1955 über Bildungen mit š- und n-t-Demonstrativen im Semitischen, Almqvist & Wiksells Boktryckeri AB: Uppsala.
Simeoe-Senelle (Marie-Claude): 1998 "Modern South Arabian", The Semitic Languages, Edited by R. Hetzron, Routledge: London.
Taifi (Miloud): 1993 "L'expression de l'hypothèse en berbère", A la croisée des études libyco-berbères, Edited by J. Drouin, A. Roth, pp. 215–227, Geuthner: Paris.
Wilson (Penelope): 1997 A Ptolemaic Lexikon, OLA 78, Peeters: Leuven.
Zeidler (Jürgen): 1992 "Altägyptisch und Hamitosemitisch. Bemerkungen zu den vergleichenden Studien von Karel Petráček, pp. 189–222, Lingua Aegyptia, 2.

AN OUTLINE OF COMPARATIVE EGYPTO-SEMITIC MORPHOLOGY

Aaron D. Rubin
(Harvard University, Cambridge)

I. *Introduction*[1]

Even though the genetic relationship of Egyptian and the Semitic is solidly established, the specifics of the relationship are very imperfectly understood, and therefore hotly debated. The problem is especially difficult because the Egyptian language itself is very imperfectly understood, as are also many of the ancient Semitic languages. Ideally we would like to be able to write a comparative grammar of Semitic and Egyptian in the style of Andrew Sihler's *New Comparative Grammar of Greek and Latin* (Oxford University Press, 1995). Sihler does not merely compare Greek and Latin; he traces their developments from their common parent language, the reconstructed Proto-Indo-European. Unfortunately, this is impossible to do for Semitic and Egyptian, as scholars have been unable to discover much about what Proto-Afro-Asiatic, the ancestor of Semitic and Egyptian, may have been like. In fact, it may not even be possible to reconstruct PAA as scholars have reconstructed PIE, for a variety of reasons. The vast majority of AA languages are attested only since the modern era, and many branches of the family are still too poorly known. It is also likely that the AA languages have been diverging far longer than the IE languages, so that much more evidence for the structure of the parent language has been lost.

In analyzing the relationship of Egyptian and Semitic, the standards of the comparative method must be followed. If this standard is not upheld, and we allow ourselves to be satisfied with irregular sound correspondences, we will allow too great a probability for the occur-

[1] An earlier form of this paper was included in Rubin (1999), a work which also included study of comparative Egypto-Semitic phonology. Many thanks to Professor Don Ringe for his immeasurable amount of help with the original work. All mistakes and opinions are naturally mine alone. I would also like to express my gratitude to Gábor Takács for inviting me to include my work in this volume.

rence of chance resemblances; see Hock (1986) and Hoenigswald (1960). For a statistical discussion of the amount of similarity between different languages that can be expected to have arisen by chance, see Nichols (1996) and Ringe (1999).

The starting point for comparison of two languages (or language families) should be in the realm of morphology. Morphological correspondences are also the first place to begin looking for regular phonological correspondences. In addition, the comparison of Egyptian and Semitic morphology is necessarily the launching point for any reconstruction of Afro-Asiatic morphology, as these two branches are the only ones attested in antiquity. It seems that a general outline of Egypto-Semitic comparative morphology is lacking; such a study would be a useful base for further investigation. The present work will attempt to do just that. I will not include AA material outside of Egyptian and Semitic, as that is beyond the scope of this paper. It may not be possible to fully understand all of the facts without looking outside of Semitic and Egyptian, but for the present work we must accept the limitations of analyzing the Egyptian and Semitic data alone.

II. *Morphology*

An exhaustive treatment of the comparative morphology of Egyptian and Semitic is beyond the scope of a paper of this size, as is any attempt to reconstruct Proto-Afro-Asiatic forms. Instead, I will outline the major morphological correspondences between the two language families in order to show that they are indeed related.

A full analysis of all the Egyptian forms would involve an attempt to reconstruct pre-Egyptian forms by internal reconstruction. That, too, is beyond the scope of this paper, and I do not believe it is necessary for the present purposes. The comparison presented here, using attested Egyptian forms, will demonstrate beyond doubt that many parts of the Semitic and Egyptian morphological systems correspond, pointing to an unquestionable genetic relationship. I wish to emphasize that by correspondences in morphological structure, I am referring to correspondences between *actual morphemes*, not typological features. As is well known, only the former can advance proof of a linguistic relationship. The probability that two languages will resemble each other typologically is simply too high.

1. *The Root Morpheme*

Probably the most characteristic morphological feature of the Semitic languages is the system of the consonantal roots, used in conjunction with vocalic templates. These templates, which cause the interlacing of the consonants with vowels and often the addition of prefixes or suffixes, are used to form all words in the language, save the pronouns and various kinds of particles. The roots carry the lexical meanings, while the templates carry the grammatical functions. English does exhibit a similar type of system, for example in ablauting verbs such as *sing, sang, sung*. But in Semitic, this system of templates is the only system used. While in English, vowels can serve to distinguish lexical meaning, as the words *live, love, leave* demonstrate, in Semitic, vowels serve only to express grammatical function.

The majority of Semitic roots consist of three consonants, or radicals, though some roots have two or four radicals. For example, in Hebrew, the root letters **k-t-b** have a meaning associated with writing. Here are some sample Hebrew patterns with their meanings:

CāCaC '3rd masc. sg. perfect' > **kātab** 'he wrote'
CōCēb 'masc. sg. participle' > **kōtēb** 'writer'
niCCaC 'passive pattern; 3rd masc. sg. perfect' > ni**kt**a**b** 'it was written'
miCCāC 'nominal pattern' (see section II.3.D.a below) > mi**kt**ā**b** 'something written (> a letter, edict, etc.)'

These examples are completely typical.

It is clear that Egyptian also makes use of a similar system (see Gardiner 1950, p. 2). Unfortunately, as vowels are not written in Egyptian until the Greek alphabet is adopted in the Coptic period, beginning in the 3rd century C.E., patterns are very difficult to reconstruct. Therefore, this can only be proven to be a typological similarity to Semitic, though it is worth noting that similar systems are found throughout AA and appear to be uncommon among the world's languages. For comparative purposes, most of the better Egyptian evidence comes from the use of affixes, which are treated below in the sections on nominal and verbal systems. The following is an example from Egyptian:

Infinitive: **sḏm** 'to hear'
Past 3rd masc. sg.: **sḏm**-n-f 'he heard'

Loprieno (1995) gives the vocalizations */saḏam/ and */saḏimnaf/ respectively, though these are of course uncertain. Examples of noun and verb pairs with the same root such as <mri> 'to love' and <mrwt> 'love' or <msi> 'to give birth' and <msw> 'children' seem parallel to the Semitic examples above, though the lack of written vowels makes these examples less than ideal. One piece of evidence that Egyptian uses root morphology like Semitic is the fact that Egyptian roots are bi- or tri-consonantal, though occasionally roots of four radicals, and even possibly of one radical, exist. The fact that the number of root consonants is less fixed in Egyptian—the vast majority of Semitic roots contain three consonants—at least reveals that the two systems are not identical.

2. *Pronouns*

The Semitic languages possess multiple sets of pronouns, some independent and some suffixed. It is clear that Proto-Semitic possessed at least one set each of independent and suffixed pronouns. In Egyptian, there is also a set of independent pronouns and suffixed pronouns, along with a third set called "dependent" or "enclitic" pronouns by Egyptologists. I am not concerned with the functions of the sets of pronouns here, simply their forms. It is important to keep in mind, though, that one must be cautious when using pronouns to determine language relationships, as they tend to be short words with a high occurrence of certain consonants, for example /n/. See Meillet (1958) or Nichols (1996), who provides an excellent statistical argument against the use of pronouns as proof of linguistic relationships.

For further theories regarding the Egyptian pronouns, see Loprieno (1995, pp. 63–7). Lipinski (1997, pp. 297–311) gives an extremely detailed account of the Semitic pronominal system. They provide many details which are beyond the scope of this work. The goal of the sections below is to establish that there are cognate morphological forms, which match with expected phonological correspondences.

A. Independent Pronouns

Table 1 lists the independent subject pronouns in Egyptian, Akkadian, Hebrew, and Arabic. There are clear similarities. The first common singular Egyptian <ink> is clearly cognate with the Akkadian and Hebrew (/ʾānōkî/) forms, keeping in mind that Egyptian grapheme

Table 1. Independent Pronouns

	Egyptian	Akkadian	Hebrew	Arabic
1cs	ink	anāku	ʔănî/ʔānōkî	ʔana
2ms	ntk	attā	ʔattā	ʔanta
2fs	ntṯ	attī	ʔat	ʔanti
3ms	ntf	šū	hû	huwa
3fs	nts	šī	hî	hiya
1cd	inn	nīnu	ʔănaḥnû	naḥnu
2mp	ntṯn	attunu	ʔattem	ʔantum
2fp		attina	ʔattēnnā	ʔantunna
3mp	ntsn	šunu	hēm	hum
3fp		šina	hēnnā	hunna

Note that the Akkadian and Hebrew columns include only the standard forms, with no attempt to list archaisms or dialectal forms.

<i> is thought by many to be the glottal stop (Hoch 1997, p. 8). In Semitic, all four second person forms seem to be based on a root /ʔant-/. The /n/ in this root has been regularly assimilated in both Akkadian and Hebrew, though not in Arabic. This root also appears in Egyptian as <nt-> (OE <int->). Egyptian seems to have extended this root to the third person forms as well. In fact, all of the second and third person forms in Egyptian appear to exhibit the <nt-> root followed by the appropriate suffixed pronoun. Such a system most likely resulted from analogical remodeling.

Since most of the Egyptian independent pronouns have apparently been remodeled after the suffixed pronouns, a discussion of the consonant correspondences will be taken up in the section on suffixed pronouns below. One point should be mentioned here, however. The Egyptian second person feminine singular form ends with a consonant written <ṯ>, probably a palatalized /t/, and, in Table 1, seems to correspond with Semitic /t/. Palatalization is common enough to make this correspondence plausible. One might be tempted therefore to equate this to the Amharic 2fs. independent pronoun /anči/, and similar forms in other Ethiopic languages. But then one must find other examples of the palatalization of /t/ in Egyptian, in order to determine if this is a regular sound change. I mention this in order to point out an easy pitfall. The direct comparison of the Egyptian form with the functionally similar forms in some Semitic languages provides a result which is superficially plausible, but cannot be proved or disproved without further investigation in light of the universal principle of the regularity of sound change. To accept this comparison at face value would actually be a mistake; the discussion below will demonstrate that the correct analysis is quite different.

B. Suffixed Pronouns

Table 2 shows the Egyptian suffixed pronouns along with their Semitic counterparts. The Akkadian[2] genitive suffixes are the most helpful for comparative purposes, as they are the most archaic (see Lipinski 1997, pp. 306–311). I have also included the Hebrew suffixes, which are not distinguished for case, as an extra reference. Table 2 shows clearly that the Egyptian suffixed pronouns are very similar to the Semitic ones. The first person pronouns are straightforward, as Egyptian <i> regularly corresponds[3] with Semitic */y/ (see Takács 1999, pp. 78–81). The third person Egyptian forms, except for the masculine singular, correspond very well with the Akkadian suffixes, assuming a regular Egyptian /s/ = Semitic /š/ pattern can be established (Takács 1999, pp. 187–195). The second person forms need to be examined more closely. Egyptian 2fs. <ṯ> suggests that there has been palatalization of an original */k/ by the originally following */i/. If that is correct, then the 2cd. and 2cp. forms also reflect palatalization of */k/ by */i/. This suggests that these Egyptian forms reflect original feminines, since in the singular the palatalizing */i/ is restricted to the feminine. And in fact the <n> of the plural form points to an original feminine form (cf. Heb. 2mp. -kem, 2fp. -ken). The dual form is most likely made on analogy with the plural, since there is no evidence that gender was ever distinguished in the dual, and in Egyptian this is a common analogy (see II.3.B.b below). The question that we must now ask is whether or not this palatalization is a regular sound change of Egyptian. Indeed it is a regular change, also found in the enclitic pronouns (see Table 3a) and elsewhere in Egyptian; see Takács 1999, pp. 234–239.

The reader will notice that the Semitic second person suffixed pronouns all begin with /k/, not the /t/ which appears in the independent pronouns. Given the fact that palatalization of */k/ > <ṯ> before */i/ is a regular sound change of Egyptian, it is clear that the second person suffixed pronouns have been used in Egyptian to

---

[2] All Akkadian forms cited in this paper are of the Old Babylonian dialect, unless otherwise noted.

[3] Any assertion of a regular correspondence in this paper is based evidence presented in Rubin (1999). I now refer the reader to the more easily available work of Takács (1999), a work with which I was unfamiliar at the time of my research, but whose conclusions I most often agree with.

form the independent pronouns. Therefore the similarity of the 2fs. forms in Egyptian and Amharic cited above is merely a coincidence, not a parallel development, since Egyptian <ṯ> reflects an earlier */k/ whereas Amharic /č/ reflects PS */t/.

The one remaining puzzle is the Egyptian 3ms. suffix pronoun <-f>. Loprieno (1995) posits a change of *[su] > *[sw] > *[Φ] > <f>. This is a phonetically reasonable explanation, and it would not be surprising for a clitic form to have been lenited, but without other examples of */s/ > <f>, it remains speculative.

C. Egyptian Enclitic Pronouns

The Egyptian enclitic pronouns, also called dependent pronouns, are listed in Table 3a. The reader will notice that they are quite similar to the suffixed pronouns, in fact identical to the latter in the dual and plural. It is unclear whether this set is inherited, or whether it is an Egyptian innovation. If it is inherited, it remains to be determined whether it corresponds to anything in Semitic. Lipinski (1997, 36.30) believes that it corresponds with the Akkadian independent possessive pronouns, a set which is not found elsewhere in Semitic. The Akkadian forms are given in Table 3b. Lipinski suggests that the Akkadian independent possessives must be inherited precisely because they parallel the Old Egyptian enclitic pronouns. But the parallel is in form only; they certainly do not parallel each other in

Table 2. Suffixed Pronouns

	Egyptian	Akkadian[a]	Hebrew[a]
1cs	-i	-ī/-ya	-î
2ms	-k	-ka	-kā
2fs	-ṯ	-ki	-k
3ms	-f	-šu	-hû
3fs	-s	-ša	-(h)ā
1cd	-ny	(Ugaritic <-ny>)	—
2cd	-ṯny	-kunī	—
3cd	-sny	-šunī	—
1cp	-n	-ni	-nû
2mp	-ṯn	-kunu	-kem
2fp		-kina	-ken
3mp	-sn	-šunu	-hem
3fp		-šina	-hen

a. Genitive suffixed pronouns. Variant forms are ignored here.

Table 3a. *Table 3b.*

	Egyptian Encliti Pronouns	Akkadian Independent Possessive Pronouns
1cs	wi	yûm
2ms	ṯw (OE -kw)	kûm
2fs	ṯn (OE ṯm)	kattum
3ms	sw	šûm
3fs	sy (later st)	šattum
1cd	(*ny)	—
2cd	(OE ṯny)	—
3cd	(OE sny)	—
1cp	n	nûm
2mp	-ṯn	kunûm
2fp		
3mp	-sn	šunûm
3fp		

function, as the Egyptian set normally serves as the direct object of verbs and the object of various particles. Thus there is no conclusive evidence that these two sets are genuinely cognate. If the two sets were more closely parallel in form, or shared a particular unique feature, then a better argument could be made for their relatedness.

D. Interrogative Pronouns

The most common interrogative in Egyptian is <m>, meaning 'who?' or 'what?'. This is cognate with the Semitic interrogatives which Lipinski (1997, p. 328) reconstructs as */man/ 'who?' (Northwest Semitic */miy(a)/) and */ma:/ 'what?' (East Semitic */min/). Each Semitic language exhibits further internal developments of these interrogatives, but they are all very similar. It is unclear whether Pre-Proto-Semitic inherited a single interrogative element */m-/, from which separate interrogatives for animate and inanimate objects were created, or whether Egyptian has reduced its inherited system by eliminating the contrast of animacy. It is also possible that Egyptian <m> had more than one vocalization, reflecting two inherited interrogatives. Coptic is of little assistance; the interrogative pronouns are **ⲛⲓⲙ** /nim/ 'who?' (from Egyptian <in m>) and **ⲟⲩ** /u/ 'what?', which does not reflect the earlier Egyptian <m>. What is clear is that some interrogative element */m-/ is common to both Egyptian and Semitic, as well as to much of Afro-Asiatic (see Lipinski 1997, p. 328; Diakonoff 1988, p. 83).

3. *Nominal System*

A. Gender

Both Semitic and Egyptian possess a masculine and feminine gender. This fact cannot be used as evidence of genetic relationship, as such a system of gender classification is extremely common across the languages of the world. There is however one important piece of comparative evidence: both Egyptian and Semitic form feminine nouns and adjectives with the addition of a productive suffix -(a)t. Examples include the following:

> Akkadian: šarr-u 'king' ~ šarrat-u 'queen', damq-u 'good (m.)' ~ damiqt-u 'good (f.)'
>
> Hebrew: melek (< *malk) 'king' ~ malkā (construct state: malkat) 'queen'
>
> Geʿez: nəguś 'king' ~ nəgəśt 'queen'
> Egyptian: s3 'son' ~ s3t 'daughter', nb 'lord, master' ~ nbt 'lady'

This feminine *-t also appears in the 3fs. form of stative (WS perfect) verbs:

> Akkadian: balṭat 'she is alive' (← balāṭu 'to be alive')
> Geʿez: säkäbät 'she lay down' (← säkäbä 'he lay down')
> Egyptian: rḫ-ti 'she knows' (← rḫ 'to know')

Feminine -t also appears elsewhere in AA (see Lipinski 1997, pp. 229–30; Diakonoff 1988, p. 58). It is also important to note that Egyptian <t> and Semitic */t/ regularly correspond elsewhere (see Takács 1999, pp. 227–231).

B. Number

Both Semitic and Egyptian maintain a distinction between singular, dual, and plural numbers, though in both cases the dual is limited in function. Like the simple gender system, this is a typological feature common enough to be worthless as evidence for genetic relationship. As was the case when examining gender, we must examine the actual morphemes used to mark number. As it turns out, the plural morphemes prove more helpful than the dual ones.

a. Plural

Semitic languages exhibit two types of plural markers, an internal and an external. Internal plurals, also called broken plurals, are marked by internal vowel changes rather than affixes. For example, Arabic /kita:b/ 'book', plural /kutub/, or Geʿez /däbr/ 'mountain', plural /ʔädbar/. The extent of the use of internal plurals in Proto-Semitic is unclear, but it is likely that they were much less common than external plurals (see Moscati 1964, 12.43–44). For external plurals, also called sound plurals, a nominative suffix *-u: and an oblique suffix *-i: can be reconstructed for the masculine noun. These suffixes appear to be lengthened forms of the nominative and genitive singular case endings, *-u and *-i respectively. Feminine nouns have only external plurals in Proto-Semitic, using a suffix -a:t, a lengthened form of the singular suffix -(a)t. There is a third possibility for forming plurals, namely a combination of the internal and external type. This is almost certainly an analogical phenomenon. It occurs most widely in Geʿez, but also in Hebrew, Aramaic, and elsewhere. Other plural morphemes, such as the Akkadian distributive plural suffix -ān and Geʿez -an (< */ān/) are not relevant here, as they are either Semitic innovations or are simply not present in Egyptian.

Akkadian nouns best preserve the original Semitic pattern for external plurals, as there has been significant analogical reworking in Northwest Semitic due to the breakdown of the case system, while the more southerly Semitic languages (Epigraphic South Arabian, Ethiopic, and Arabic) have greatly extended the use of internal plurals. A sample Akkadian declension is:

	masculine	feminine
nom. singular	šarr-u 'king'	šarrat-u 'queen'
nom. plural	šarr-u:	šarrāt-u

Egyptian nouns exhibit a similar system. The masculine plural suffix is written <-w>, while the feminine is simply <-t>, which looks like the feminine singular, though very rarely it is written <-wt>. Plurality is not always indicated in Egyptian writing, however, as the phonetic marking of plural endings is often replaced by plural strokes (three vertical lines), or repetition of the sign, or is simply omitted (see Gardiner 1950, pp. 58–61). The following is a sample declension:

	masculine	feminine
singular	nb 'lord'	nbt 'lady'
plural	nbw	nb(w)t

This appears to be wholly parallel with the Akkadian paradigm, though the Egyptian writing system is not phonetically very telling. An argument for the interpretation of Egyptian <-w> as [u:] is given by Vycichl (1955).

It is also possible, though less likely, that the Egyptian plural morpheme <-w> should be equated with the small class of Geʿez plurals in -aw, such as ʾab ~ ʾabaw 'father(s)' and ʾaf ~ ʾafaw 'mouth(s)'.

The masculine plural marker *-u: also appears in the 3mp. of Semitic stative (WS perfect) verbs and the 3cp. of Egyptian stative verbs:

> Akkadian: balṭu: 'they are alive' (← balāṭu 'to be alive')
> Geʿez: näbäru 'they sat' (← näbärä 'he sat')
> Egyptian: rḫ-w 'they know' (← rḫ 'to know')

Whether Egyptian makes use of internal plurals is much less clear. The evidence is obviously much scantier, as the internal plurals rely solely on vowels, precisely what is lacking from Egyptian writing. Loprieno (1995, pp. 58–9) posits that the internal plural was rarely used alone in Egyptian, but rather was used along with an external morpheme, a fact which he says is common throughout non-Semitic Afro-Asiatic (though also quite common in Ethiopian Semitic). That may be the case, but this suggestion is based heavily on uncertain reconstruction. In Coptic, nouns rarely exhibit a separate plural form, as the plural is marked by the article. However, Loprieno (1995, p. 58; personal communication) argues that some Coptic nouns show reflexes of a stem-vowel alternation in Egyptian. For example:

> **ⲉⲃⲟⲧ** /ebot/ 'month' (Eg. <3bd>), plural **ⲉⲃⲉⲧⲉ** /ebete/ (Eg. <3bd-w>)

Loprieno reconstructs Eg. /3abad/ and /3abu:daw/ respectively, arguing that the Coptic plural form cannot reflect E.g. /3abadaw/. In order for this evidence to be convincing, however, a pattern of sound changes from Egyptian to Coptic must be conclusively demonstrated. Thus it is possible, but not convincingly proven, that internal plurals were formed in earlier stages of Egyptian.

Even though the widespread use of the internal plural may be an innovation in South Semitic and limited in the rest of Semitic, it would still be highly significant for comparative purposes if we could establish that Egyptian clearly exhibited internal plurals. But that remains unclear, and therefore it is *external* plurals which provide all of the evidence.

b. Dual

It is unclear how widespread the dual was in Proto-Semitic. In Hebrew and Aramaic, it is limited to things such as body parts and the number "2", and it has left only a few traces in Geʿez. In Arabic, Old Akkadian, Ugaritic, and Old South Arabian, however, its use is obligatory. Most likely, the dual was regularly used in Proto-Semitic and its use gradually declined in many Semitic languages, rather than the other way around. A similar development is clearly observable in the attested history of Akkadian, Hebrew, Aramaic, and other Semitic languages (see Lipinski 1997, pp. 236–8), as well as the Indo-European languages (see Sihler 1995, pp. 245–6). Proto-Semitic had a nominative dual ending *-a: and an oblique ending *-ay. These endings were used for the masculine as well as for the feminine; in the latter case they were suffixed to the feminine *-t ending.

In Middle Egyptian the use of the dual is not uncommon, though it is mainly limited to natural duals such as the number '2', body parts occurring in pairs, and specific lexemes (see Loprieno 1995, p. 60). The masculine ending is <-wy> and the feminine is <-ty>, though these endings are often omitted in favor of a dual determinative sign (see Gardiner 1950, pp. 58–61). It looks as if an element <-y> has been added to the plural endings. In the case of the feminine, however, it is impossible to tell whether the <-y> is added to the singular or plural ending. This <-y> is very likely related to the Semitic oblique suffix *-ay.

C. Case

Semitic marks three cases: nominative, accusative, and genitive. In the dual and plural, there is only a distinction between a nominative and an oblique case. There have been some attempts to demonstrate that Semitic contains traces of an ergative case system (see Lipinski 1997, pp. 254–7), but that is not relevant here, as Egyptian exhibits no trace of a case system at any stage of development. Akkadian, Arabic, and Ugaritic preserve the Semitic case system very well, while Hebrew, Aramaic, and for the most part Geʿez no longer have a functioning case system.

Hebrew is a convenient example to show how the case system could be lost. The original case endings for the singular were simply short vowels, and at some point in Proto-Hebrew all final short vowels were lost. This affected various morphological categories. In the verb paradigm, for example, 3ms. imperfect */yaktubu/ became /yiktōb/ 'he writes' and 2fs. perfect */katabti/ became /kātabt/ 'you (f.) wrote'. This also meant that case could no longer be distinguished in the singular. Once this happened, it was natural for case to disappear in the dual and plural, which is exactly what happened. In Hebrew, the oblique ending became the normal ending for all forms of the dual and plural.

In Egyptian there are no traces of a case system, and surface syntax is therefore very rigid, as one might expect. Since cases dropped out so early from many Semitic languages, it is reasonable to suppose that this could have happened in Egyptian as well. The loss of final short vowels can also be seen in the paradigm of the suffixed pronouns (see Table 2). Unfortunately, then, case is not going to be relevant for comparative study.

D. Nominal Patterns and Affixes

Semitic possessed a large number of reconstructable nominal patterns. These nominal patterns included the addition of vowel alternations and/or gemination to the root morpheme. Since the Egyptian writing system expresses neither vowels nor geminate consonants, it is nearly impossible to compare Egyptian nominal patterns with Semitic ones. Luckily, some nominal patterns include the use of affixes, and these can be compared successfully.

a. Preformative "Mem"

One of the most common affixes used in Semitic is the prefix *ma-/*mi-/*mu-. This is called the "preformative mem" prefix, and it has a very wide range of meanings. This prefix is used to create nouns of instrument ("thing with which"), location ("place where"), or time, as well as abstract nouns, and the participles of derived verbs. It can be assumed that in Proto-Semitic, or perhaps even in Pre-Proto-Semitic, there was a clear correlation between the prefix vowel and the function of these derivational patterns. Perhaps *mi- formed nouns of instrument, while *ma- formed nouns of place and time, as is the case in Arabic. However, the distributions in the daughter languages are so varied that the original pattern is very difficult to reconstruct with certainty. In Geʿez and Akkadian, the ma- prefix is used (with or without the feminine suffix) to create both nouns of instrument and place. In Geʿez, the prefix mə- (< *mi- or *mu-) can also form nouns of place. In Hebrew the prefixes *ma- and *mi- have fallen together in many environments due to sound change, and have therefore become distributed along phonological rather than semantic criteria. The situation is quite complicated, and there seems to be no satisfying solution. Some typical examples are:

> Arabic: /mifta:ḥ/ 'key'/ (← /fataḥa/ 'he opened'); /maqa:m/ 'place' (← /qa:ma/ 'he stood'), /maktab/ 'office' and /maktaba/ 'library' (← /kataba/ 'he wrote')
>
> Hebrew: /mispār/ 'number' (← /sāpar/ 'he counted'); /miqdāš/ 'holy place, temple' (← /qādaš/ 'it is/was holy'), /milḥāmā/ 'war' (← /lāḥam/ 'he fought')
>
> Akkadian: /maškan-u/ 'location, site' (← /šakānu/ 'to place'), /mušpal/ 'depth' (← /šapālu/ 'to become low, deep')

Egyptian likewise utilizes a prefix <m->, for example:

> mṯwn 'arena, battleground' (← ṯwn 'to gore')
> msḫn 'abode' (← sḫni 'to dwell')
> m3qt 'ladder' (← i3q 'to climb')
> mnḫt 'clothing, fabric' (← wnḫ 'to be clothed')
> mḫtmt 'sealed chest' (← ḫtm 'to seal')
> mrḥt 'fat' (← wrḥ 'to anoint')
> mḫ3t 'balance; scale' (← ḫ3i 'to measure')
> msdmt 'eye make-up' (← sdm 'to paint the eyes')
> mẖnt 'ferry-boat' (← ẖni 'to row, ferry')

The final <-t> of all but the first two forms cited above, which is present in most nouns formed with this prefix, suggests that most nouns with this prefix are feminine. Feminine patterns with this prefix occur commonly in Semitic as well, though not as often as masculine ones (cf. Hebrew /milḥāmā/ and Arabic /maktaba/ above). It may also be the case in Egyptian that the masculine form is used for nouns of place only, though because of the small number of examples this apparent pattern may be accidental.

The Semitic prefix *mu-, which appears on the participles of derived verbal stems, is considered to be the same prefix. Moscati (1964, 16.96–101) believes that some participles also reflect a prefix *ma-, but Lipinski (1997, 42.15) shows that this is a secondary development in various Semitic languages. Egyptian participles are not formed with an m- prefix, though this is not surprising as the Egyptian verbal system does not possess the system of derived stems found in Semitic (see below II.4.B.d).

b. Abstract *-u:t

Another common affix in Semitic is the suffix *-u:t, which is used to form abstract nouns:

> Akkadian: /šarrūt-u/ 'kingship' (← /šarr-u/ 'king'), /mārūt-u/ 'sonship' (← /mār-u/ 'son')
>
> Hebrew: /malkūt/ 'kingship; kingdom' (← /melek/ (construct /malk-/) 'king')
>
> Geʿez: /ḫirut/ 'goodness, excellence' (← /ḫer/ 'good, excellent')

Egyptian utilizes a suffix, <-wt>, which is undoubtedly a cognate morpheme, as the sound correspondences are perfect. Examples are:

> i3wt 'old age' (← i3w 'old man')
> ḫtwt 'furniture' (← ḫt 'wood')
> mswt 'offspring' (← msi 'to bear, give birth')

c. Collective *-t

A suffix *-t, originally identical with the feminine suffix, is also used to mark collectives in both Semitic and Egyptian. The best Semitic examples are probably the masculine numerals (see Table 7 below). Superficially, it looks as if the Semitic masculine numerals greater than 'two' are feminine in form and vice versa, and in fact that is what is alleged by most grammars. But in view of the functions of these forms, that analysis cannot be correct; rather, masculine numerals greater than 'two' exhibit the collective suffix *-t (see Lipinski 1997, pp. 285–6). This analysis is supported not only by the semantics of the forms, but also by their syntax: numerals greater than 'two' were substantives, not adjectives, in PS, and therefore do not have to agree in gender with their nouns, which follow in the genitive plural. At some point in early PS the numerals began to agree in gender, despite the fact that they were still substantives, and the feminine forms of the numerals were created using the bare root morpheme. This created the false impression that the numerals were used in the gender opposite to that of the noun, (see Lipinski 1997, pp. 285–6). This gender polarity of the numerals is reconstructable for PS, and therefore it must be assumed that the lack of gender distinction in numerals was eliminated in a pre-PS period.

The collective *-t seems to have been more productive in Egyptian. Clear examples include the following:

rmṯ 'person', rmṯt 'people, mankind'
sb3 'star', sb3t 'constellation'
inb 'wall', inbt 'fence, stockade'
izr 'tamarisk', izrt 'tamarisk grove'

Egyptian also forms collectives in <-t> with numerals:

diw '5', diwt 'a set of five'

It is reasonable to suppose that the collective *-t and feminine *-t share a common origin. The Proto-Indo-European suffix *-h_2 performs the same dual function, suggesting that such a development is natural (see Sihler 1995, p. 266). Therefore we must realize that the use of feminine *-t to form collectives may be a parallel development of Egyptian and Semitic rather than a shared inheritance. Good evidence of this feature from other branches of Afro-Asiatic would help strengthen the argument for shared inheritance.

E. Adjectives

Morphologically, adjectives are no different from nouns in Semitic and Egyptian, except for the fact that all adjectives have both a masculine and feminine form. One common means of forming adjectives from nouns in Semitic is to use the adjectival or gentilic suffix *-i:y (also *-a:y) which has a general meaning of "belonging to"; a typical example is Hebrew /yəhūdā/ 'Judea', /yəhūdî/ 'Judean, Jewish'. Arabic grammarians called this the *nisba* (literally 'relationship') suffix, and this term has come to be used for all the Semitic languages. Egyptian has an identical, very widely used suffix <-y>, and in fact modern Egyptologists refer to this as the *nisba* suffix; a typical example is <niwt> 'city', <niwty> 'of the city'.

4. *Verbal System*

Because of their complexity, verbal systems are prone to extensive restructuring. The Indo-European language family illustrates this point abundantly; for example, even though Ancient Greek, Latin, and Russian are all IE languages of a conservative type, with closely comparable systems of nominal inflection, their verbal systems are considerably divergent, agreeing in particular points but not in their overall organization. Thus it is not unreasonable to propose that the verbal systems of Egyptian and Semitic could have diverged considerably, even if they are closely related. But though the functions of verbal categories are highly susceptible to radical shifts, their morphology tends to be much more stable. This can clearly be illustrated within the Semitic family. The Akkadian verbal system, especially in regards to the system of tenses, is quite different from Hebrew, and both are different from Arabic or Geʿez. Yet the system of affixes is very easily reconstructable. And in fact, as will be shown below, some of the Semitic verbal affixes can be compared with Egyptian very successfully.

Comparing the complex tense and aspect systems of Egyptian and Semitic is well beyond the scope of this survey. That task would also be especially difficult because even within the field of Semitic philology there is much debate about the verbal system, and the same is even truer for Egyptian. But I will give a brief outline of both systems below, and then discuss what can be compared.

A. Outline of the Semitic Verbal System

There is a considerable difference between the verbal system of East Semitic and that of the West Semitic languages. It seems most prudent here to give a description of the Akkadian verbal system, as it is the most archaic in many ways, most importantly in morphology (see Moscati 1964, pp. 131–34). For a more detailed account of the verbal systems of other Semitic languages, see Lipinski (1997) or Moscati (1964). For a very detailed explanation of the Akkadian system, see von Soden (1995).

a. Tenses and Declension Types

There are two major conjugation types in Akkadian, as in the rest of the Semitic languages, traditionally called the prefix conjugation and the suffix conjugation. In the suffix conjugation, the radicals are placed into the pattern CaCVC—where V is a lexically determined vowel—followed by a person/gender/number-marking suffix. A sample paradigm is given in Table 4. This form is the Akkadian stative tense, also called the permansive in older literature.

The prefix conjugation is more complex, as it is really made up of three tenses with a common set of affixes. Every form has a prefix, though some forms exhibit a suffix as well. There is a "present" tense formed from the pattern CaCCVC (with gemination of the middle radical), a "perfect" tense formed from a pattern CtaCVC (with an infixed -t-), and a "preterite" formed from a pattern CCVC. See Table 4 for a sample paradigm of these tenses.

Table 4. Paradigm of an Akkadian Verb, G-stem (Root /p.r.s./ 'to separate')

	Present	Perfect	Preterite	Stative	Imperative
1cs	aparras	aptaras	aprus	parsāku	
2ms	taparras	taptaras	taprus	parsāta	parus
2fs	taparrasī	taptarsī	taprusī	parsāti	parsī
3ms	iparras	iptaras	iprus	paris	
3fs				parsat	
1cd	niparras	niptaras	niprus	parsānu	
2mp	taparrasā	taptarsā	taprusā	parsātunu	parsā
2fp				parsātina	
3mp	iparrasū	iptarsū	iprusū	parsū	
3fp	iparrasā	iptarsā	iprusā	parsā	

Table 5. Sample of Akkadian Verb Forms

	3ms. pres.	3ms. perf.	3ms. pret.	3ms. stative
G-Stem	iparras	iptaras	iprus	paris
N-stem	ipparras[a]	ittapras[a]	ipparis[a]	napris
D-Stem	uparras	uptarris	uparris	purrus
Š-stem	ušapras	uštapris	ušapris	šuprus

a. The /n/ has been assimilated to the following consonant, but its position appears in boldface.

In addition to the above tenses, there is also an imperative, an infinitive, a participle, and a verbal adjective. The imperative is second person only, and distinguishes gender only in the singular. Each verbal stem (see below) has a unique infinitive, which is treated like any other noun. The participle and verbal adjective are treated like adjectives.

b. Derived Verbal Stems

There are four stem types in Akkadian, each with its own characteristic modifications of the verbal tense patterns given above. The so-called G-stem (for German *Grundstamm*, also called B-stem, basic stem, or simple stem) is the most basic verbal stem. The forms described in the section above are the G-stem forms. An N-stem, so-called because of an n-prefix, uses the same set of affixes as the G-stem. Its meaning is usually a passive of the corresponding G-stem. For example G-stem 3ms. pret. iṣbat 'he seized', N-stem iṣṣabit (< *inṣabit) 'he was seized'.

The D-stem is characterized by a doubling of the middle radical, not just in the present tense, but in all verbal forms. It uses a set of affixes different from those of the G and N-stems, one characterized by a u-vowel in the prefixes rather than /a/ or /i/. Its meaning can be factitive (G-stem 3ms. stative /danin/ 'he is strong', D-stem 3ms. present /udannan/ 'he strengthens'), as well as intensive. The D-stem also includes many denominatives, while other verbs are D-stems for no apparent reason.

The Š-stem is characterized by a prefix š-, and uses the same set of affixes as the D-stem. The primary function of the Š-stem is to form causative verbs. A typical example is G infinitive /maqātu/ 'to fall', Š infinitive /šumqutu/ 'to fell, overthrow'. See Table 5 for sample forms of the four stems just described.

In addition, each of these four verbal stems can undergo two types of stem modifications. The G, D, and Š-stems can take an infix -t- (not to be confused with the perfect marker -t-), to form what are simply called the Gt, Dt, and Št-stems. This infix has a reciprocal, reflexive, separative, or lasting meaning in the Gt, while the Dt and Št forms are simply passives of the D and Š-stems respectively. The existence of an Nt-stem is debated and still uncertain. There is also a -tan- infix, used with all four stems, which imparts a habitual or durative meaning. These are called the Gtn, Ntn, Dtn, and Štn stems.

c. Moods

In addition to the unmarked indicative and the imperative moods, there are also subjunctive and ventive moods in Akkadian. The subjunctive is marked by a suffix -u, and is used when a verb appears in a relative clause. The ventive is marked by the suffixes -am and -nim, the choice depending on whether a consonant or vowel precedes. The ventive suffix adds a meaning of directionality, or motion towards the speaker or addressee. For example the verb 'to jump' means 'to jump into' when used in the ventive.

d. West Semitic Changes

The development of the verbal system in the rest of Semitic is not relevant here, as there are no features common only to West Semitic and Egyptian. But it is worth mentioning a few points, for the benefit of those readers familiar only with West Semitic. One major difference between East and West Semitic is that the inherited suffix conjugation has developed from a stative tense into a perfect or preterite tense in WS. This shift is exactly parallel to one which has occurred repeatedly in Indo-European languages, for example from PIE to Latin and Gothic, and is actually attested in the early history of Greek. The Greek "perfect" is a clearly stative tense in Homer's language, but a real perfect tense in Attic Greek (see Sihler 1995, pp. 564–66). The logic behind the change is as follows. A verb in the stative implies the action leading to the state; for example, 'he is a thief' implies 'he has stolen'. The implication of prior action can become the primary meaning of the tense, which is conventionally called a "perfect", and the perfect can then develop into a preterite ('he has stolen' → 'he stole').

As for the prefixed forms, the West Semitic languages do not retain three separate tenses; they usually collapse them into a single prefix conjugation. For example, Arabic has a single prefixed tense with an imperfect meaning, in contrast to the suffixed tense with a perfect meaning. For details see Moscati (1964) and Lipinski (1997). All West Semitic languages do retain the system of verbal stems and some of the stem modifications, although each language has its own peculiarities and innovations. A very important detail is that the /š/ of the Akkadian Š-stem corresponds to a causative prefix /h/ or /ʔ/ in most of West Semitic. This reflects a sound change which is also found in the third person pronominal suffixes (see Tables 1 and 2) and possibly in other morphological forms. The details of this sound change are debated; see Voigt (1994) for the most current discussion.

B. Outline of the Egyptian Verbal System

Unfortunately, there is less to be said about the Egyptian verbal system. Egyptian was very innovative in creating new synthetic[4] tenses to replace most of the tenses in its presumed inherited system. Moreover, throughout the attested history of Egyptian, beginning with Old Egyptian, there is a gradual replacement of these synthetic tenses with analytic[5] ones. Therefore little of the inherited verb inflection remains. Furthermore, the complex verbal system of Egyptian is not

[4] A synthetic tense is one which marks grammatical meaning by means of affixes. In the case of Egyptian, the innovative tenses can more precisely be called "agglutinating", as each suffix added carries a single grammatical function. This is in contrast to an "inflectional" system, such as that of Latin or Greek, in which a single suffix may convey all grammatical meaning.

[5] In an analytic system, each morpheme is a separate word. In the evolution of the Egyptian verbal system, many verbal constructions involve the use of auxiliaries.

very well understood. Besides actual verbal morphology, which is often not written and must be inferred, the verbal system relied heavily on syntax, rather than inflection, to convey meaning. A brief outline of the basic synthetic tenses will make some of this clear. For a detailed treatment of the Egyptian verb, see Gardiner (1950), Thacker (1954), Polotsky (1968), and Loprieno (1995).

a. Synthetic Tenses

Egyptian has nothing corresponding to the inherited prefix conjugation. Instead there is a new set of uninflected forms using various suffixes. The simplest tense is simply the verbal root plus the suffixed pronoun as its pronominal subject. This is called by Egyptologists the sḏm-f tense, where <sḏm>, meaning 'to hear', is the paradigmatic verb root, and <-f> is the 3ms. suffixed pronoun. To say that this is the 'present' tense would be more than an oversimplification. As Gardiner (1950, p. 42) says, ". . . the sḏm-f form excludes hardly any English tense or mood." Also note that this form does *not* agree with a noun subject, but rather appears simply as <sḏm + noun>. This appears to be a truly synthetic construction, without an inflected verb. There is also a corresponding passive sḏm-tw-f, literally 'one hears him', where <tw> is simply the Egyptian word for 'one' (French *on*, German *man*).

Another very common verb tense is the sḏm-n-f form, which most often functions as a past tense. Again, the verb does not appear to be inflected. The suffix appears only when there is a pronominal subject. There is also a corresponding passive tense, the sḏm(w)-f, though the suffix <-w> is rarely written. These four forms are the most common synthetic tenses in Egyptian. They each can have a very wide range of meanings, usually determined by their position in the sentence and their use in conjunction with various particles. For further information and a description of the other synthetic tenses, see especially Gardiner (1950).

b. Stative

Egyptian does retain the inherited suffix conjugation. In Egyptian philology, this tense is also called the stative (formerly Old Perfective or Pseudo-participle); it employs a set of suffixes unique to it. Unlike the synthetic tenses, the stative *does* agree with a nominal subject. In meaning it is equivalent to the Akkadian stative tense, though syntactically it is slightly different. In Akkadian a stative verb can be a complete sentence, for example, /danin/ 'he is strong'. Egyptian requires an expressed subject; if the subject is pronominal, it is expressed by a pronoun suffixed to a particle, of which there are many. An example is <iw-f ʕḥʕ(w)> 'he is standing', where <iw> is simply a narrative particle used to carry the pronominal suffix, and <ʕḥʕ(w)> is the inflected stative verb. The exception is the first person singular, which can appear without a separately expressed subject. The second and third person forms can also be used alone, though with a specialized exclamatory meaning.

c. Infinitive
Egyptian verbs also have an infinitive form which is treated like any other noun. In most cases the infinitive is indistinguishable from the verbal root, though some classes of weak verbs take a suffix <-t> (see below). The infinitive is also used in various constructions, in conjunction with a variety of prepositions. Typical examples include the following:

r sḏm 'in order to hear'
ḫft sḏm 'upon hearing' or 'upon being heard'
m-ḫt sḏm 'after hearing' or 'after having heard'
ḥr sḏm progressive, 'is hearing', 'was hearing'

d. Imperative and Participle
Finally, Egyptian verbs have imperative and participial forms. The imperative only appears in the second person, and is not distinguished for gender, as far as written evidence shows. There seems to be a very early plural marker <-i>, later <-w>, which is very rarely written; see Gardiner (1950, p. 257). Therefore, when reading, one must rely on syntax and context to distinguish these forms.

The participle is used like its Akkadian equivalent. However, the Egyptian participle appears in two voices, active and passive, and three aspects or tenses, called perfect, imperfect, and prospective. Thus there are six forms of the participle, though in writing no verb will be distinguished in all six forms. The paradigmatic verb <sḏm> will illustrate this:

Imperfect Active: sḏm(y/w)
Imperfect Passive: sḏm(w)
Perfect Active: sḏm(w/y)
Perfect Passive: sḏm(y)
Prospective Active: sḏm(w/y)
Prospective Passive: sḏm(y)

The rules for forming the participles vary for the different classes of verbs and as a whole are unclear as a result of defective writing. For further discussion, see Hoch (1997, pp. 132–7) and Gardiner (1950, pp. 270–80).

C. Comparison of the Two Systems

Direct comparison of the Semitic and Egyptian verbal systems shows that they have little in common. Nothing in Egyptian corresponds to the Semitic prefix conjugation, to which the bulk of the reconstructable PS system belongs. Instead, Egyptian created new synthetic tenses which replaced the inherited system of prefixed tenses. Though it is reasonable to assume that Egyptian verb conjugation, liked Semitic conjugation, relied on patterns of vowel alternations and perhaps gemination, these features are not recoverable in the consonantal Egyptian script. However, see Gardiner (1950, Appendix A) for a discussion of how Coptic evidence can be used to try to recover some of this information. The fact that both systems include imperatives, participles, and infinitives can only be categorized as an unremarkable typological correspondence. Inasmuch as the internal morphology is unknown, these forms are of no use in determining the relationship of Semitic and Egyptian. In regard to inflectional morphology, the only shared categories are the stative (suffix conjugation) and the causative stem, to which I now turn.

a. Stative

The Egyptian stative corresponds point for point with the Semitic suffix conjugation, that is, the Akkadian stative and the West Semitic perfect. Table 6 shows the stative endings for both Egyptian and Akkadian, which best preserves the PS endings, as well as the corresponding Hebrew, Arabic, and Geʿez perfect endings. The 1cs. Egyptian ending <-kwi> (see note to Table 6) matches well with Akkadian /-ku/. It looks as if Egyptian has added the final <-i>, perhaps by analogy with the suffixed pronoun. The 2s. forms have fallen together in Egyptian, but the <t> corresponds to its Semitic equivalent. The 3ms. is curious, as Egyptian occasionally uses a suffix <-w>, while in PS this form was marked with /-a/, or was possibly unmarked. The Egyptian suffix may reflect an analogy with the 3p. forms. The 3fs. forms correspond well, and both exhibit the usual feminine marker -t, discussed in II.3.A above. The 3p. Egyptian forms have fallen together, and correspond with the Semitic 3mp form.

Table 6. Stative Endings (Hebrew, Arabic, and Geʿez Perfect Endings)

	Egyptian	Akkadian	Hebrew	Arabic	Geʿez
1cs	-kwi[b]	-āku	-tî	-tu	-ku
2ms	-t(i)	-āta	-tā	-ta	-kä
2fs	-t(i)	-āti	-t	-ti	-ki
3ms	-w or	—	—	-a	-ä
3fs	-t(i)	-at	-ā	-at	-ät
1cp	-wyn	-ānu	-nū	-na:	-na
2mp	-tiwny	-ātunu	-tem	-tum	-kəmmu
2fp		-ātina	-ten	-tunna	-kən
3mp	-w	-ū	-ū	-u:	-u
3fp		-ā		-na	-a

b. This ending is also written as <k>, <-kw>, and <-ki>

The 1p. and 2p. forms present more of a problem. It appears that there is some correspondence, but the details are unclear. Edel (1955, pp. 272–3) proposes that the Egyptian 1cp. ending <-wyn> may be a particle <wi> plus the suffixed pronoun <-n>. If this is the case, then the Semitic ending is not cognate. But it would be strange for Egyptian to use this innovative construction to make a verb ending for just the first person plural. For the Egyptian 2cp. form, judging from Akkadian /ātunu/, one might expect something like **<twn>. The attested forms <tiwny> and <tiwn> are very similar but cannot be analyzed any further.

b. Causative Stem

The /š/ of the Akkadian Š-stem described above corresponds to the Egyptian causative prefix <s>. This is a regular, well-attested sound correspondence; see the discussion of the 3f. and 3p. suffixed pronouns above (II.2.B). Unfortunately the actual vocalism of this causative stem in Egyptian is not known; it is evident only that Egyptian attaches a prefix <s-> to the verbal root. For example:

smni 'to make firm, establish' (← mn 'to be firm')
sʕnḫ 'to make live, preserve, nourish' (← ʕnḫ 'to live')
smsi 'to make give birth, deliver' (← msi 'to bear')
sḏd 'to relate' (← ḏd 'say')

c. Quadriliteral Verbs

In Egyptian, quadriliteral verbs can be of a reduplicating type (C_1-C_2-C_1-C_2, C_1-C_2-C_3-C_3) or can consist of four different radicals

(C_1-C_2-C_3-C_4). That Semitic quadriliterals are found in these various forms as well is noteworthy, but of no value in determining genetic relationship. More importantly, we find a curious point of correspondence in the morphology of this verbal class.

In Akkadian, the basic quadriliteral verbs are treated not as G-stems, but as N-stems; see von Soden (1995, §§108–110). For example, from the root /b-l-k-t/ there exists an infinitive /nabalkutum/, preterite /ibbalkit/, and present /ibbalakkit/. Gensler (1997) has shown that this N-type quadriliteral is the inherited form in Akkadian. In Geʿez, the N-stem has been lost, but we do find a parallel to the Akkadian quadriliterals in quinqueliteral verbs such as 'an-gargara 'roll' and 'an-sosawa (< *'an-sawsawa) 'walk about'. In Geʿez this type nearly always involves reduplication (N-C_2-C_3-C_2-C_3), while such reduplication is unknown in Akkadian. However, both are formally N + quadriliteral.

In Egyptian, which lacks an N-stem, we also find verbs which can be interpreted as N + quadriliteral, such as <ngsgs> 'overflow' and <nftft> 'leap' (also found as <gsgs> and <ftft>). It seems quite possible that this n-prefix is inherited and should be equated with the /n/ of Akkadian quadriliterals. If so, then the Egyptian situation would exactly parallel that of Geʿez, where the N-stem has been lost, yet a relic is found on certain quadriliterals. It is also possible, however, that this Egyptian verb class is simply a reduplication of a triliteral root; compare the quinqueliteral verb <ḫb3b3>.

d. I-w Verbs

In Egyptian, root initial <w>, as well as <i>, is often lost in nominal derivatives. We find forms such as <ʕbw> 'purification' from <wʕb> 'to be pure'. This is probably to be connected with the same phenomenon in Semitic forms, for example Akkadian /šubtu/ 'dwelling' from /wašabum/ 'to dwell'. Root initial <w> is also lost, in writing at least, in Egyptian mem-preformative nouns such as <mrḥt> 'fat' from <wrḥ>'to anoint'. Semitic parallels to this, such as Geʿez /mulād/ 'birthplace' from /walada/ 'to give birth' and Geʿez /mośar/ 'saw' from /waśara/ 'to saw' are not to be equated with the Egyptian forms. The Geʿez forms cited here derive from */məwlād/ and */mawśar/ respectively. Almost certainly the Egyptian forms can be assumed to derive from a similar treatment of */Vw/ > V(:).

e. Infinitives With Suffixed -t

Egyptian final weak verbs (i.e. those whose final root consonant is <w> or <i>) and causative biliteral verbs exhibit infinitives with a final <-t>; see Gardiner (1950, pp. 223–24). Hoch (1997, p. 64) equates this with the /-t/ which appears on infinitives of third-*he* verbs in Hebrew. This relationship seems difficult to prove, though the correspondence of Egyptian <t> with Semitic /t/ is proven through several other morphological correspondences.

5. *Numerals*

Table 7 shows the Egyptian, Proto-Semitic, Akkadian, Arabic, and Geʿez numerals. The Egyptian column shows marked divergence from the others. Earlier scholars have suggested that some of the Egyptian and Semitic numerals are cognate; see Albright (1927), Loprieno (1995, pp. 71–2), Hoch (1997, p. 78), and Lipinski (1997, pp. 280–290). However, many of their hypotheses must be rejected, because the sound changes posited are supported by no further evidence.

Loprieno (1995, p. 71) suggests that the Egyptian and Semitic words for 'one' are cognate. But among the Semitic languages, only Arabic shows an initial /w/ that could match that of Egyptian. It is far less likely that this consonant has been lost in the other languages than that the Arabic form is an innovation. Almost certainly the Arabic form is a back-formation from derivatives of this numeral, for example /waḥada/ 'to be alone' (cf. Heb. root /y.ḥ.d/ 'be united'); see Lipinski (1997, p. 281). The correspondence of Egyptian <ʕ> and Semitic /ḥ/ is also irregular. Loprieno suggests that Egyptian <ʕ> corresponds with Semitic */d/, arguing that these both reflect PAA */d/, but even if this can be established (see Takács 1999, pp. 346–357), a correspondence of only one of two consonants in this root is a poor argument for cognation. Lipinski (1997, p. 284) is correct in rejecting the proposed relationship of these forms.

The words for 'two' are cognate, as the correspondences of the consonants are regular; see Takács (1999, pp. 124–31; 197–99).[6] The Egyptian form has simply added the dual ending, parallel to the Semitic languages, save Ethiopic.

---

[6] To Takács' examples of Sem /n/ ~ Eg. <n>, I would certainly add the 1cs independent pronoun, all dual and plural suffixed pronouns, and the 1cp and 2p stative endings.

Table 7. Numerals

	Egyptian[a]	Proto-Semitic[b]	Arabic	Akkadian	Geʿez	ESA[c]
1m	wʕ	*ḥad-	wa:ḥid	[ište:n][d]	ʔäḥädu	ʔḥd
1f			wa:ḥida	[ištiat]	ʔäḥätti	ʔḥt
2m	sn(wy)	*θin-	ʔiθna:ni	šina	[kəlʔetu]	θny
2f			ʔiθnata:ni	šitta	[kəlʔeti]	θty
3m	ḫmt(w)	*θlaθ- ~ *ślaθ-	θala:θ	šalāš	śälas	s^{2}lθ
3f			θala:θa	šalāšat	śälästu	s^{2}lθt
4m	fdw	*rbaʕ-	ʔarbaʕ	erba	ʔärbaʕ	ʔrbʕ
4f			ʔarbaʕa	erbet	ʔärbaʕtu	ʔrbʕt
5m	diw	*xamš-	xams	ḫamiš	xäms	xms^{1}
5f			xamsa	ḫamšat	xäməstu	xms^{1}t
6m	sisw < srsw	*šidθ-	sitt	šiš	səssu	s^{1}dθ
6f			sitta	šeššet	sədəstu	s^{1}dθt
7m	sfḫ(w)	*sabʕ-	sabʕ	sebe	säbʕu	s^{1}bʕ
7f			sabʕa	sebet	säbʕätu	s^{1}bʕt
8m	ḫmn(w)	*θma:n-	θama:nin	samane	sämani	θmny
8f			θama:niya	*samānit	sämantu	θmnyt
9m	psḏ(w)	*tišʕ-	tisʕ	tiše	təsʕu	ts^{1}ʕ
9f			tisʕa	tišēt	təsʕätu	ts^{1}ʕt
10m	mḏ(w)	*ʕaśr-	ʕašr	ešer	ʕäśru	ʕs^{2}r
10f			ʕašara	ešeret	ʕäśärtu	ʕs^{2}rt
20	(uncertain)	*ʕaśra: (?)	ʕišru:n	ešrā	ʕəšra	ʕs^{2}ry
100	š(n)t	*miʔt-	miʔat	meʔat	məʔət	mʔt
1000	ḫ3	*liʔm-, *ʔalp-	ʔalf	līm	ʔəlf	ʔlf

a. Questions persist as to the correct transcription of the Egyptian numerals. For discussion see Gardiner (1950, pp. 191–93), Hoch (1997, pp. 78–9), and Loprieno (1995, p. 71). I have adopted the transcription which seems most probable.
b. Reconstructed Proto-Semitic forms are those of Lipinski (1997).
c. There are various dialects of Epigraphic South Arabian, and some exhibit different forms of the numerals. Sabaic forms are given here, as they are the most archaic. The source is Kogan and Korotayev in Hetzron 1997.
d. Forms in brackets do not reflect a PS form.

The words for 'three', 'four', and 'five' are clearly not cognate. Albright (1927) believes that the words for 'three' are cognate, and proposes the following sound changes for Egyptian: */θlθ/ > */θlt/ > */θnt/ > */θmt/ > */fmt/ > */ḫmt/. Even if we except (for the sake of argument) Albright's assumptions that the Proto-Semitic form is also the Proto-Egyptian form, he gives no parallels to support any of these sound changes. With such a method, nearly any pair of forms can be called cognate.

The words for 'six' may be cognate, though it is not obvious how. In Semitic, all languages except for ESA exhibit some phonetic change. Egyptian must have also gone through some phonetic change, though it is impossible to recover the details exactly. The Egyptian sound changes may parallel those Hebrew, where */šidθ/ > */šiθθ/ > /šēš/. Egyptian <s> can correspond with either Semitic /š/ or /θ/, so the consonant correspondences may be regular between Egyptian <sisw> and the Semitic words. Unfortunately, this explanation may be of no value, as Loprieno (personal correspondence) argues that <srsw> is the original Egyptian form. If this is the case, it cannot be argued that the forms are cognate, as Egyptian <r> does not regularly correspond with the Semitic consonants in this word. Edel (1955, p. 169) offers a complex analysis of the Egyptian form, though effectively no good conclusion can be drawn.

It is widely believed that the words for 'seven' are cognate. The initial consonant correspondence is regular, the second consonants are both labials, and the third are both gutturals. But this approximate correspondence is not satisfactory. I can find no other convincing examples of Egyptian <f> corresponding with Semitic */b/, nor <ḫ> with */ʕ/. Egyptian <f> may correspond with Semitic */p/ (see Takács 1999, pp. 114–119), so it is possible that the original form contained a /p/ which was later voiced—for completely unknown reasons— in Semitic. Thus Semitic */šp-/ *may* correspond with Egyptian <sf->. The final consonant still poses a problem. An Original */ʕ/ could in theory have been devoiced in Egyptian, but this would produce /ḥ/, which is similar to /ḫ/, but by no means identical. In short, either we do not understand what has happened to these forms, or they are simply not cognate.

The word for 'eight' is problematic. The second and third consonants correspond perfectly, but the initial consonants do not. The initial consonants show the same correspondence found in the word for 'three'. However, 'three' cannot be considered as another example of a regular correspondence of <ḫ> to */θ/, because in 'three' the remaining consonants do not correspond. Since no regular correspondence of Egyptian <ḫ> and Semitic */θ/ can be established, there are several possibilities. One is that one of the languages has remodeled this form, possibly based on 'three'. Another is that the forms simply are not cognate. Albright (1927) proposes a sequence of sound changes similar to those he proposes for 'three' (see above).

The forms for 'nine' may be cognate, as Albright (1927), Hoch (1997), and many others claim. The second consonant shows a regular correspondence, and the third consonant shows a possible regular correspondence which is not fully understood (see Takács 1999, pp. 261–2). However, the initial consonants are not demonstrably related. This is the same situation that we observe in the case of the numeral 'eight'. The words for 'ten', 'a hundred', and 'a thousand' are not cognate.

It is not known which system Egyptian employed to join the tens with the digits, as they were not written phonetically in hieroglyphs. Even if Egyptian did behave like Semitic, this would merely be a typological correspondence of no value.

Albright (1927) regards the numerals as a stumbling block towards a full understanding of Egypto-Semitic consonant correspondences. His mistake is that he begins with the assumption that forms must be related, and is willing to propose unfounded sound changes to make this work. In reality, a better starting point is the realization that Egyptian and Semitic have been diverging for a long time, so that one or both could have undergone significant changes in the system of numerals, in addition to the regular sound changes.

6. *Prepositions and Particles*

A. Primary Prepositions

Reconstructing the prepositions within Semitic is actually quite complicated. For a traditional, though unfortunately very brief, treatment see Moscati (1964, p. 121). For a much more comprehensive view, though sometimes a rather untraditional one, see Lipinski (1997, pp. 460–4). For comparative purposes it is easiest to start from the Egyptian side. Loprieno (1995, pp. 99–101) and Hoch (1997) propose the following correspondences for the most common Egyptian prepositions:

Egyptian	Semitic
<m> 'in; from; by means of'	*bi
<ir> (later <r>) 'towards; at; more than'	*ʔil
<n> 'to, for; belonging to'	*li
<ḥr> 'on; on account of'	*ʕal

The cognation of Egyptian <m> and Semitic */bi/ is not disputed by most scholars, but this sound correspondence is not regular; see

Takács 1999. It is possible that the proto-form had different allomorphs. Lipinski even believes that Akkadian /ina/ is cognate with *bi, and that one of the PAA allomorphs must have contained /n/. But if we accept /b/, /m/, and /n/ as allomorphs of the same correspondence with no demonstrable conditioning, we have allowed too great an opportunity for chance resemblances.

There is a reasonable likelihood that Semitic *ʔil and *li reflect a single PS lexical item. If that is the case, we must decide whether the Egyptian cognate is <r> or <n>. Lipinski believes that there was an AA form with allomorphs l/r/n, which is the source of both Egyptian prepositions, as well as Akkadian /ana/. This suggestion suffers from the same shortcomings as Lipinski's proposal regarding Egyptian <m> and PS */bi/; there is too much room allowed for chance.

The preposition <ḥr> may be cognate with */ʕal/, though we must determine whether the initial consonant correspondence is regular; this seems not to be the case (see Takács 1999).

Obviously there are many uncertainties regarding these little words, though there do seem to be some correspondences here. One feature which is shared by both Egyptian and Semitic is use of these prepositions with the suffix pronoun. However, this may be typologically unremarkable. Examples include the following:

Akkadian: eli 'on, upon': eliya, elika, eliki, elišu, etc . . .
Arabic: bi 'by means of': bi:, bika, biki, bihi, etc . . .
Egyptian: n 'to': n-i, n-k, n-ṯ, n-f, etc . . .

B. Compound Prepositions

Semitic and Egyptian also form compound prepositions, that is, a combination of two prepositions or a preposition plus a noun to form a single preposition. This is not unusual in itself, but there is at least one good cognate compound. Egyptian <m-q3b> 'in the midst of (<q3b> 'intestine') is exactly parallel with Hebrew /bə-qereb/ (/qereb/ 'interior, intestine'), Moabite <bqrb>, and Akkadian /ina qereb/, all meaning 'in the midst of'. Other such constructions exist as well, such as the following:

Egyptian <ḥr ib> 'in the middle of' (<ib> 'heart'), Akkadian /ina libbi/ (/libb-u/ 'heart')

Egyptian <m-ʕ> 'in the hand of; together with; from' (<ʕ> 'hand'), Hebrew /bə-yād/ 'in(to) the hand of; by (instrumental)' and /miy-yad/ 'from the hand of'

These constructions may be too unremarkable typologically to be considered as cognate formations. The first example is more plausible as a cognate construction, as the use of 'intestines, innards' seems to be less natural than the use of 'hand' or 'heart'.

c. Negative Particles

Egyptian negatives are highly specialized for various syntactic constructions, and many seem to be Egyptian innovations. The most common Semitic negative particles are /*la(:)/ and */ʔal/, which are very likely related. They may be cognate with the Egyptian negative particle <n>, though as we are comparing a single consonant, the probability of chance resemblance is high to begin with. It is therefore impossible to reach any secure conclusions. The less common PS negative particles */ay/ and */in/ do not seem to have any cognates in Egyptian.

Another method of negation in Egyptian is the use of the negative verb <tm>. Loprieno (1995) links this with the Semitic root /tmm/ 'to be complete', as there is also an Egyptian verb <tm> 'to be complete'. If the Egyptian negative particle derives from this verbal root, then obviously the particle would be cognate as well. Lipinski, on the other hand, links Egyptian negative <tm> with the Gafat (South Ethiopic) negative morpheme /tä . . . m/. Either of these may be correct, but neither can be proved. It is highly improbable that both theories are correct, as it would certainly be surprising for a verb to develop into an amphiclitic particle, and the rest of Semitic shows no evidence for this root being used as a negative.

The form <m> is another Egyptian negative, an imperative verb form used to make negative imperatives, translated as 'do not x!'. This has been compared with the Arabic neagative particle /ma:/, but this is almost certainly an Arabic innovation, derived from the interrogative /ma:/. For a discussion of this theory, see Lipinski (1997, 47.15).

IV. *Conclusion*

The regular phonological and semantic correspondences between the morphological systems of Egyptian and Semitic demonstrate clearly that these two languages families are related. These cognate morphological forms also provide some of the best evidence in determining regular phonological correspondences between the two language families. The difficulty in determining a complete system of phonological correspondences and the scarcity of shared lexical items indicate that Egyptian and Semitic had been diverging for a long time before they are first attested. The conclusions of this paper are admittedly unsatisfying, as many questions remain unanswered. However, these reliable conclusions, which are based on rigorous methodology and sound evidence, are much more valuable than satisfying conclusions based on imprecise comparison and speculation.

Bibliography

Albright (W.F.): 1927 "Notes On Egypto-Semitic Etymology". *Journal of the American Oriental Society*, vol. 47, p. 198.

Diakonoff (I.M.): 1988 *Afrasian Languages*. Moscow: Nauka.

Durie (Mark) and Ross (Malcolm), eds.: 1996 *The Comparative Method Reviewed*. Oxford: Oxford University Press.

Gardiner (Sir Alan): 1950 *Egyptian Grammar*. Oxford: Griffith Institute.

Gensler (Orin D.): 1997 "Reconstructing Quadriliteral Verb Inflection: Ethiopic, Akkadian, Proto-Semitic." Journal of Semitic Studies 42: 229–257.

Hetzron (Robert), ed.: 1997 *The Semitic Languages*. London: Routledge.

Hoch (James E.): 1997 *Middle Egyptian Grammar*. Mississauga: Benben Publications.

Hock (Hans Heinrich): 1986 *Principles of Historical Linguistics*. New York: Mouton de Gruyter.

Hoenigswald (Henry M.): 1960 *Language Change and Linguistic Reconstruction*. Chicago: University of Chicago Press.

Lambdin (Thomas O.): 1978 *Introduction to Classical Ethiopic (Geʿez)*. Atlanta: Scholars Press.

Lipinski (Edward): 1997 *Semitic Languages: Outline of a Comparative Grammar*. Leuven: Peeters.

Loprieno (Antonio): 1995 *Ancient Egyptian*. Cambridge: Cambridge University Press.

Meillet (A.): 1958 *Linguistique Historique et Linguistique Générale*. Paris: Société Linguistique de Paris.

Moscati (Sabatino) ed.: 1964 *An Introduction to the Comparative Grammar of the Semitic Languages*. Wiesbaden: Harrassowitz Verlag.

Nichols (Johanna): 1996 "The Comparative Method as Heuristic", in Mark Durie and Malcolm Ross, eds.

Polotsky (H.J.): 1968 "Egyptian Tenses." *Proceedings of the Israel Academy of Sciences and Humanities*. Volume 2. Jerusalem.

Ringe (Donald A., Jr.): 1999 "How Hard Is It To Match CVC-Roots?". *Transactions of the Philological Society of London* 97:2, pp. 213–244.

Rubin (Aaron): 1999 *An Introduction to the Comparative Grammar of Egyptian and Semitic*. M.A. Thesis, University of Pennsylvania.

Sihler (Andrew L.): 1995 *A New Comparative Grammar of Greek and Latin*. Oxford: Oxford University Press.

Takács (Gábor): 1999 *An Etymological Dictionary of Egyptian, Volume I: A Phonological Introduction*. Leiden: Brill.

Thacker (T.): 1954 *The Relationship of the Semitic and Egyptian Verbal Systems*. Oxford: Oxford University Press.

Voigt (Rainer M.): 1994 "Der Lautwendel S^1 > H in wurzellosen Morphemen des Alt- und Neusüdarabischen", in *Semitic and Cushitic Studies*, Gideon Goldenberg and Shlomo Raz eds. Wiesbaden: Harrassowitz Verlag.
Von Soden (Wolfram): 1995 *Grundriss der Akkadischen Grammatik*. Rome: Pontifical Biblical Institute.
Vycichl (Werner): 1955 "Gab es eine Pluralendung -*w* im Ägyptischen? Eine relative Chronologie der ägyptischen Sprache." *ZDMG* 105, pp. 261–70.
——: 1983 *Dictionnaire étymologique de la langue copte*. Leuven: Peeters.

STATUSES AND CASES OF THE AFROASIATIC PERSONAL PRONOUN

Helmut Satzinger
(Kunsthistorisches Museum, Wien)

It is typical of Afroasiatic languages to have three sets of personal pronouns:

A. an absolute pronoun
B. an "object pronoun"
C. a "possessive pronoun" (or suffix pronoun)

We may take examples from Egyptian, as the Afroasiatic language of most ancient attestation, in particular as compared to the Berber, Cushitic and Chadic idioms (we will here and in the following restrict ourselves to the singular forms):

A. Absolute pronoun

i̓nk	*ṯwt* / *i̓ntk*	*ṯmt* / *i̓ntṯ*	*swt* / *i̓ntf*	*stt* / *i̓nts*

B. Dependent pronoun

wj (< *i̓w*)	*kw*, *ṯw*	*ṯm*, *ṯn*	*sw*	*sj*

C. Suffix pronoun

-i̓	*-k*	*-ṯ*	*-f*	*-s*

(*ṯ* < *k* before **i* [and **u*]; f here: < *sw ?)

It is true, some languages have more than three sets; but usually they can be reduced to a reconstruction of three; cf. the indirect object pronoun of Berber which is, by and large, analysable as *a + suffix pronouns, e.g. *a-k*, *a-m*, *a-s*, etc. (Kossmann 1997: 77, with reference to Galand 1966). However, in many presentations and analyses of the Afroasiatic pronoun system, the three pronominal sets are reduced to but two: absolute pronoun, and suffix pronoun. If the individual language or language group has forms for the pronominal object that are distinct from the suffix pronouns they are more or less treated as their variants. This is normal in Semitic (where object pronoun and possessive pronoun are distinguished in the first person singular only); *-nī vs. -ī*; for Afroasiatic in general, cf., e.g., as an example the analysis of Blažek (1995).

We must be strict in keeping apart the level of the forms and the level of the functions. In many languages we can distinguish the three paradigms mentioned, termed absolute, object, and possessive pronoun, or similar. But on closer inspection we will find that each may have additional functions that do not correspond to the respective terms used. The absolute pronoun may also serve for the subject of a nominal sentence. In some languages the object pronoun may express a subject in certain non-verbal sentences. The suffix pronoun will in many languages also be the form of the complement of prepositions (both uses may be summarized as "genitival"), but in some languages—not only Egyptian—it is also used as subject in verbal sentences.

• Absolute pronoun used for the subject of the nominal sentence:
Normal in Semitic; in Egyptian restricted to the first and second persons. Hausa makes use of a demonstrative dummy subject:[1] *nī nē farke* 'I am a merchant', originally: 'it is I, a merchant', or with topicalized subject pronoun, *nī farke nē* 'as for me, I'm a merchant' (very much like Egyptian *ỉnk šwtj pw*), originally: 'as for me, a merchant it is'.

• "Object pronoun" used for the subject:
In Egyptian, it serves as subject of adjectival predicates, as in *nḏm sj* 'she is pleasant'. In Berber, it is used for the subject of certain non-verbal predicates: deictic, or existential predicates, like *ha-t* 'he is here', 'lui voi-ci'; *ulaš-it* 'he is not there'; *ansi-t* wherefrom is he ?'; with deictic (?) *d*: *d ir-it* 'it is bad'; *d elʿali-t* 'it is good'; etc.; cf. Aikhenvald 1995.

• "Possessive pronoun" used as subject of verbs
Normal in Egyptian. Berber: in the Ayt Ziyan dialect, the Kabyle stative conjugation (representative of the Afroasiatic suffix conjugation) is replaced by the stative form of the adjective, with the suffix pronoun as subject expression: Ait Ziyan *zggagg-iyi, zggagg-ik, zggagg-ikm*, etc., 'I am red, etc.', as compared with Great Kabylia *zggwagg-ag, zggwagg-ed*, etc. (Galand 1990: 129; cf. Aikhenvald 1995: 51–52). Semitic: In Geʿez, verbal nouns in the adverbial accusative (as *qatīl-a* 'while/when killing', or the like) may be conjugated by means of the suffix

[1] Egyptian does the same (the demonstrative is *pw*) if the subject is not a personal pronoun: *wḏꜣ.t pw nw* 'This is an intact garment' PyrTexts 740 (the word-order is PREDICATE *pw* SUBJECT).

pronoun: *qatīlō* (< **qatīl-a-hū*) 'when he killed'. A further comparable feature are the circumstantial expressions formed by adjectives that are in concord with their referent: ('you [nominative], or your, or of you [genitive] . . .' *tekūz-e-ka* 'being sad'; 'you [accusative] . . .' *tekūz-a-ka* 'being sad'); cf. Satzinger (1968); Kapeliuk (1998).

It may be assumed that such discrepancies are the result of a long development, from the ancient proto system to the individual branches, groups and languages. In consequence of this we shall not, in the following, use the terms mentioned, but rather the abstract symbols A, B, C. Furthermore, we shall distinguish the A, B, C functions from the A, B, C forms.

A function: isolated use (naming or quotation form), nominal predicates, focalization (further, secondary usages: subject of nominal predicate, topicalization).

A forms: the forms used by the individual languages for the A function.

B function: (direct) object of transitive verbs. NB. In a hypothetical ergative system, as it is assumed for proto Afroasiatic (cf. below), the function corresponding to the B function is the absolutive case of the pronoun, viz. the subject of intransitive verbs, and the patient of transitive verbs. This implies, by the way, that the B pronoun is an unmarked form.

B forms: Mostly the forms used in the individual languages for the B function, unless they are identical with the C forms. In particular, those forms will be regarded as B forms that are obviously derived from the following set of proto Afroasiatic B forms:

1sc. **yV* (**yu* ?) (cf. Egyptian **i̓w* > *wj*; Berber *-iyi*)
2sm. **ku* (?) (cf. Egyptian *kw*, Berber *-k*, *-ik*, Proto Cushitic **ku*, or **kwV*)
2sf. **kim* (and **ki* ?) (cf. Egyptian **km*, Berber *-kim*; comparable forms in some Chadic languages, cf. Blažek 1995)
3sm. **šu* (cf. Egyptian *sw*, also cf. the A forms, Semitic *šūwa*, East Cushitic **usū*)
3sf. **ši* (cf. Egyptian *sj*, also cf. the A forms, Semitic *šīya*, East Cushitic **išī*)

C function: genitival expansion of nouns ("possessive") and prepositions; directly attached to nouns, as in Arabic *baytu-ka*, Egyptian *pr-k*, or indirectly, as in Berber (Nefûsi) *taddārt-enn-ek*, Hausa *gida-n-ka*, or attached to a demonstrative pronoun, as in Egyptian/Coptic *pꜣy-k-pr, pe-k-ēi̯*, all meaning 'your house'; with prepositions, Arabic *ʿinda-ka*, Egyptian *ḫr-k*, Berber *ġer-ek* 'with you, at your place' (but Hausa *garē shī* has the B form, see below).

C forms: those used in C function; in particular, suffixed forms. If there is a discrepancy between possessive and prepositional forms, a decision which is a C form and which not can be made (a) on account of the suffixal character, and (b) any identity with the B forms. Thus, the possessive form in Hausa *gidā-n-a, gida-n-ka, gida-n-ki, gida-n-sa, gida-n-ta* is the C pronoun, whereas the form expanding the preposition *ga, garē-* 'to, for, with, at someone's place' is the C pronoun: *garē ni / ka / ki / shi / ta*; cf. *yaa gan ni / ka / ki / shi / ta* 'he saw me / you, etc.' In the case of the indirect object pronoun, composed of *ma-* (*mi-*) plus pronoun, the decision is not so clear: we find variant forms such as (3sm.) *ma-sa* (like the C pronoun) and *mi-shi* (like the B pronoun).[2]

In the following we will suggest to regard the dichotomy of the Afroasiatic "object pronoun" and "possessive pronoun" not as a secondary feature, restricted to some branches, but rather as a basic feature of the original system.

On the other hand it shall be shown that the forms of the absolute pronoun, as attested in the individual languages and language groups, are of secondary origin: in many cases they are derived from those forms that are regarded as the "object pronoun".

1. *The B and C pronoun form sets are not identical*

	1sc.	2sm.	2sf.	3sm.	3sf.
Egyptian					
B.	*wj* (< *i͗w*)	*kw, ṯw*	*ṯm, ṯn*	*sw*	*sj*
C.	*-i͗*	*-k*	*-ṯ*	*-f*	*-s*
Semitic					
B.	**-nī*	**-ka*	**-ki*	**-šu*	**-ša*
C.	**-ī*	**-ka*	**-ki*	**-šu*	**-ša*

[2] *ma-* may originally have been a verb ('to give'), naturally taking B forms for its complement, and only later have been partly interpreted as a preposition, thus introducing C form complements.

Berber

B. (cf. Kossmann 1997)	*-iyi*	*-k, -ik*	*-kəm, -ikəm*	*-t, -it/*-i*	*-tt, -itt/*-it*
C.	*-i*	*-k*	*-m*	*-s*	*-s*

Chadic: in most idioms, the B and the C set are different in one, two or all three persons. Cf. (reconstructed forms quoted from Blažek 1995):

Hausa,

B forms:				
ni	*ka*	*ki*	*shi*	*ta*
C forms:				
-a, -wa	*-ka*	*-ki*	*-sa*	*-ta*

Ron,

B forms:				
**ʾi/*ni*	**ka*	**ki*	**si*	**ti*
C forms:				
**-ʾin*	**-aka*	**-iki*	**-is*	**-it*

Cushitic

No old B forms in North Cushitic (Bedauye). For East Cushitic, cf.

Somali,

B forms:				
ī	*kū*	./.	*ū*	./.
C forms:				
-ay	*-ā*	./.	*-īs*	*-ē-d*

For South Cushitic, cf. Iraq

B forms:				
i	*-u-*	./.	*g-u-*	*g-a-*
C forms:				
-e	*-ok*	./.	*-os*	./.

Generally speaking, the C forms appear shorter than the B forms. But this is the effect of their suffixal character which implies a phonetic reduction. In the first person, some languages have a B form **nī* (Semitic; Chadic languages, where this form has even intruded into the C set here and there: Jungraithmayer 1999). In the second person, Berber and some Chadic languages and groups (Southern Bauchi, Bade-Ngizim, Kotoko, Musgu, Lai, Mokilko) have a feminine form ending in *-m* in both B and C, whereas Egyptian has it in B only. In the third person, Chadic languages display *-ta* for the feminine forms, both B and C. In Berber, an element *-t-* is found in the third person B forms, whereas the C forms have *-s*, in agreement with the Afroasiatic proto form (cf. Kossmann 1997). Apart from these divergences, both sets have the same stem consonants: first person *y-*, second person *k-*, third person *s-*. Comparing tentative reconstruction forms like,

B.				
**ʾiu : *nī (-V ?)*	**ku*	**kim*	**šu*	**ši*
C.				
**-i; var. -ya*	**-ka*	**-ki(m)*	**-šu*	**-ša*

it appears that the two sets are basically distinguished by vocalic endings which can hardly be anything but case markers.

2. *There is no original set of A pronoun forms*

The forms of the A pronoun, as actually attested in the Afroasiatic languages, are obviously of four types:

1. B pronouns, unmodified (except for not being phoneticaly reduced, due to their bearing full stress in the A function, whereas the B function implies a reduction of stress; perhaps they were marked by a vocalic ending, as in Semitic **šuwa* < **šū-a*, **šiya* < **šī-a*).
2. B pronouns with additions; in the main, a stressbearing ending **-átV*.
3. A base **ʾan-*, to which stative endings or other pronominal elements are attached.
4. Nominal bases with a C pronoun added; this is obviously a late feature.

First person singular *communis*

1. (a) **yV*	Several Cushitic and Chadic languages (Lamberti, Blažek)
(b) **ni*	Several Chadic languages (unless from 3 (b), **an-ī*)
2. **yV(w)-átV*	Akkadian: *yâti* < **yiwâti* (indir. Object in extraposition: *yâšim*; absolute genitive: *yâʾum/ʾim/am*)
3. (a) **ʾan-āku*	Akkadian; Biblical Hebrew; Egyptian; Berber
(b) **an-ī*, **ʾan-ā*	Semitic (except Akkadian), many Cushitic languages; also cf. above, 1 (b), for Chadic

Second person masculine

1. **ku* and varr.	Several Cushitic languages (Lamberti 1999: **kwV*); Berber, Hausa (*kay*) and other Chadic languages
2. **ku-átV*	Akkadian: *kuâti*, *kâti* (for *kâšim*, *yâʾum*/*ʾim*/*am* cf. above); Egyptian (*ṯwt*, perhaps [k'uw'at])
3. *ʾ*an-ta*	Semitic; many Cushitic languages
4. Aliter	North Cushitic (*barū-k*/*batū-k*); most West Cushitic languages; Egyptian, later set (*int-k* [ʔan'tak])

Second person masculine (NB. In Cushitic and in several Chadic languages not distinguished from the masculine)

1. **kimV*	Berber; several Chadic languages
(**kīV* is not attested in A function)	
2. (a) **kim-átV*	Egyptian (*ṯmt*, perhaps [k'im'at])
(b) **kī-átV*	Akkadian: **kiâti*, etc. (cf. above)
3. *ʾ*an-ti*	Semitic
4. *Aliter*	Egyptian, later set (*int-ṯ* [ʔanʿtak'])

Third person masculine

1. *šūV*	Semitic; several Cushitic (including West Cushitic) and Chadic languages
2. *šū-átV*	Semitic (Akkadian *šuâti*, etc. (cf. above); Geʿez *weʾetu* < **huʾat-hu*; cf. also **šuwat* as a variant of **šuwa* (above, 1) in North-West and South Semitic languages); Egyptian (*swt*, perhaps [su'wat])
4. *Aliter*	North Cushitic (*barū-s*/*batū-s*); Egyptian, later set (*int-f* [ʔan'taf]); the Berber form **entā* should perhaps be mentioned here and not under 3, and the same is true of some Chadic forms, like Kotoko **nta-a*, etc.

Third person feminine

1. šīV	Semitic; several Cushitic (including West Cushitic) and Chadic languages
2. (a) šī-átV	Semitic (Akkadian *šiâti*, etc. (cf. above); Geʿez *yeʾeti* < **hiʾat-hi*; cf. also **šiyat* as a variant of

	**šīya* (above, 1) in North-West and South Semitic languages)
(b) šit-átV	Egyptian (*stt*, perhaps [siʾtat])
4. *Aliter*	North Cushitic (*barū-s/batū-s*); Egyptian, later set (int-s [ʔanʾtas]); for the Berber and some Chadic forms cf. above

In formation 3, two layers may be discerned. The form **ʾan-áku* is found in rather ancient Semitic idioms, but also in Egyptian and Berber. It has the same ending as the Akkadian (and Egyptian!) stative, *par(i)s-āku*. It is not, in this respect, in a formational paradigm with *ʾan-ta / ʾan-ti* for these forms (as also the plural and dual forms) have the endings of the Semitic perfect (Arabic *faʿal-ta, faʿal-ti*, etc.). **ʾAn-ī* seems to be formed, not with a conjugational ending, but rather with the C pronoun. The variant form **ʾan-ā* is sometimes thought to display the conjugational prefix of the prefix conjugation, *ʾa-*. (Another possibility is that both *-ī* and *-ā* are most ancient variant forms of the conjugational suffix *-ku*, perhaps not of the stative conjugation proper (*-ā-ku, -ā-ta, -ā-ti*, etc.), but rather of a proto form of the perfect (**-ī/*-ā, -ta, -ti*, etc.). This, however appears rather speculative.) Of the two layers of the **ʾan-* formation, the more ancient has but one representative, viz. **ʾan-áku*. The other forms, viz. **ʾan-ī/-ā, *ʾan-ta, *ʾan-ti*, etc., restricted to Semitic and Cushitic, are seemingly of a later date of origin.

The most ancient feature of the A pronoun forms is the use of B forms in A function (above, no. 1). A further step is their modification by an ending **-átV* (above, no. 2). The two layers of the **ʾan-* formations are probably still later (above, no. 3).

The function of the absolute pronoun covers *grosso modo* those of the absolute state of the noun, as we know it from Akkadian, but also from Berber and Cushitic (see Sasse 1984). Apart from the absolute status, Akkadian has a proper accusative case, in the main for the object of the transitive verb. In Berber and Cushitic, however, the absolute status covers also this latter field: it is also the form of the object. The lack of a proper accusative form in these languages could be accounted for by a somewhat late origin of this category, under the assumption that originally Afroasiatic had not a nominative—accusative morpho-syntactic system (short: accusative system), as it is found in all attested languages, but rather an absolutive—ergative system (short: ergative system); a theory propagated and supported by several, especially in recent research: Berber: Aikhenvald (1995); Akkadic, Hebrew: Andersen (1971); Müller (1985; 1988; 1995); Chadic: Frajzyngier (1984); Egyptian: Loprieno (1995, 83–85); Reintges (1998*a*, 458–461; 1998*b*, 210–211); Roccati (1998; 1999); Zeidler (1992, 210–212).

The main syntactic functions of the noun are:
- Nominal predicate
- Subject of the nominal predicate
- The arguments of the verb, in the ergative system:
  - (a) subject of intransitive verbs, and patient of transitive verbs (absolutive case), and
  - (b) agent of intransitive verbs (ergative case)
- Functions below the sentence level, such as genitival functions and the complement of prepositions, are mentioned for the sake of completeness, though they do not concern us here.

In the following, we want to sketch the system (1.) of ergative and accusative type languages, and (2.) of languages that have the category of the absolute status, and those that do not.

Absolute status, ergative system (assumed for Afroasiatic; of attested languages, cf. Basque, which has, however, not the structure nominal sentence but rather uses an auxiliary verb)

Nominal sentence	*Intransitive verb*	*Transitive verb*
Predicate: *absolute status		
Subject: *absolutive case	Subject: *absolutive case	Patient: *absolutive case Agent: *ergative case

Absolute status, accusative system, no accusative case (Berber, Cushitic)

Nominal sentence	*Intransitive verb*	*Transitive verb*
Predicate: absolute status		
Subject: nominative case	Subject: nominative case	Subject: nominative case Object: *absolute status*

Absolute status, accusative system, accusative case
(Akkadian)

Nominal sentence	Intransitive verb	Transitive verb
Predicate: absolute status		
Subject: nominative case	Subject: nominative case	Subject: nominative case
		Object: *accusative case*

No absolute status, accusative system, accusative case
(other Semitic languages)

Nominal sentence	Intransitive verb	Transitive verb
Predicate: *nominative case*		
Subject: nominative case	Subject: nominative case	Subject: nominative case
		Object: *accusative case*

In most attested Afroasiatic languages the pronominal subject is connotated by the conjugation, it is expressed by the conjugation prefix or suffix. Of the remaining functions, the nominal predicate is expressed by the A pronoun, the object by the B pronoun. The subject of a nominal predicate is partly also covered by the A pronoun but in some constructions by the B pronoun. If we project this situation back to the assumed ergativic state of Afroasiatic we can see in the B pronoun the absolutive case of the pronoun, expressing the patient of transitive verbs and the subject of intransitive verbs, as also the subject of the nominal sentence. The A function—*inter alia* the nominal predicate—could be executed by the same B pronoun, though marked in this role for the absolute case (with the noun, the respective marker is -*a*).

When eventually the language switched to an accusative system the B pronoun was reinterpreted as the object form, and it could now normally not anymore function as a subject, neither in the verbal sentence nor in the nominal sentence. To be exact, the verbal sentence did not need any subject pronoun as its pronominal subject was expressed by the conjugation ending. But the nominal sentence did. It was now the A pronoun—a B pronoun in the absolute status, probably marked by *-a*—that took over, in addition to the A functions, this role. In fact, a pronominal subject is called for much more often than a nominal predicate (except in focalizing constructions: 'It is I who . . .'). Consequently, the need was felt to provide the pronoun of the A function with an additional marker, viz. the morpheme *-tV*.

Ergative system:
B pronoun—for the absolutive case: X; for the A function: X-*a*

Accusative system:
B pronoun—for the object: X; for the subject of the nominal sentence: X-*a*; for the predicate of nominal sentence: X-*a-tV* (e.g., **šū* —**šū-a*—**šū-á-tV*).

The next step was to create entirely new forms. This processus started with the first person, and in many languages it remained at that: creation of the form **ʾanáku* (attested in Egyptian, Berber, and some ancient Semitic languages).

In other languages, it was eventually extended to the second person: **ʾanī/ā*, **ʾanta*, **ʾanti*, etc. (Semitic and Cushitic). In Egyptian, the **ʾanáku* pronoun was supplemented by another formation for the second and third persons: *ỉntk*, *ỉntṯ*, *ỉntf*, *ỉnts*, etc.

In Bedauye, it was the **ʾanī* pronoun that was supplemented by the new formations *barūk/batūk*, *barūs/batūs*, etc.

If these interpretations are right we must see the basic, unmarked pronoun in the ancester of the Afroasiatic B pronouns, i.e., in a series like **ī*, **kū*, **kim*, **sū*, **sī*, etc. They could be raised to the absolute status if syntax asked for an absolute form. On the other hand, they could be marked for dependent function in order to yield the genitival form.

Bibliography

Aikhenvald, Alexandra Yu.: "Split ergativity in Berber languages." *St. Petersburg Journal of African Studies* 4, 39–68.

Andersen, F.I. 1971. "Passive and Ergative in Hebrew." In: H. Goedicke (ed.), *Near Eastern Studies in Honor of W.F. Albright*, Baltimore. 1–15.

Blažek, Václav. 1995. "The microsystem of personal pronouns in Chadic, compared with Afroasiatic." In: Dymitr Ibriszimow & Rudolf Leger (eds.), *Chadica et Hamito-Semitica*. Köln. 36–57.

Frajzyngier, Zygmunt. 1984. "On the Proto-Chadic Syntacitc Pattern." In: James Bynon (ed.), *Current Progress in Afro-Asiatic Linguistics*. Papers of the Third International Hamito-Semitic Congress. John Benjamins Publishing Company Amsterdam/ Philadelphia. 139–159.

Galand, Lionel. 1966. "Les pronoms personnels en berbère." *Bulletin de la Société Linguistique de Paris* 61, 286–298.

Jungraithmayr, Herrmann. 1999. "The 1st person singular pronoun in Chadic." In: *Afroasiatica Tergestina*. Papers from the 9th Italian Meeting of Afro-Asiatic (Hamito-Semitic) Linguistics. Trieste, April 23–24, 1998/Contributi presentati al 9° Incontro di Linguistica Afroasiatica (Camito-Semitica). Trieste, 23–24 Aprile 1998. 335–343.

Kossmann, Maarten. 1997. "Le pronom d'objet direct de la troisième personne en berbère." In: *Afroasiatica Neapolitana. Contributi presentati all' 8° Incontro di Linguistica Afroasiatica (Camito-Semitica)* (*Studi Africanistici*. Serie Etiopica 6). 69–80.

Loprieno, Antonio. 1995. *Ancient Egyptian*. A Linguistic Introduction. Cambridge University Press: 83–85.

Müller, H.-P. 1985. "Ergativelemente im akkadischen und althebräischen Verbalsystem." *Biblica* 66, 385–417.

——. 1988. "Das Bedeutungspotential der Afformativkonjugation." *Zeitschrift für Althebraistik* 1, 74–98, 159–190.

——. 1995. "Ergative constructions in early Semitic languages. *Journal of Near Eeastern Studies* 54, 261–271.

Reintges, C.H. 1998*a*. "Ancient Egyptian in 3D: Synchrony, Diachrony and Typology of a Dead Language." *Orientalia* 67, 447–476.

——. 1998*b*. "Mapping Information Structure to Syntactic Structure: One Syntax for *Jn*." *Revue d'Égyptologie* 49, 195–220.

Roccati, Alessandro. 1997. "Studi tipologici. I. Sull'ergatività dell'egiziano." In: *Afroasiatica Neapolitana. Contributi presentati all' 8° Incontro di Linguistica Afroasiatica (Camito-Semitica)* (*Studi Africanistici*. Serie Etiopica 6). 113–122.

——. 1999. "La funzione del morfema iw in medioegiziano." In: *Afroasiatica Tergestina*. Papers from the 9th Italian Meeting of Afro-Asiatic (Hamito-Semitic) Linguistics. Trieste, April 23–24, 1998/Contributi presentati al 9° Incontro di Linguistica Afroasiatica (Camito-Semitica). Trieste, 23–24 Aprile 1998. 265–268.

Sasse, Hans-Jürgen. 1984. "Case in Cushitic, Semitic and Berber." In: James Bynon (ed.), *Current Progress in Afro-asiatic Linguistics*. Papers of the Third International Hamito-Semitic Congress. John Benjamins Publishing Company Amsterdam/ Philadelphia. 111–126.

Zeidler, Jürgen. 1992. "Altägyptisch und Hamitosemitisch. Bemerkungen zu den *Vergleichenden Studien* von Karel Petráček." *Lingua Aegyptia* 2, 189–222.

TOWARDS RECONSTRUCTING A PROTO-HAMITO-SEMITIC LATERAL SIBILANT *(*Ŝ)*

Olga Stolbova
(Oriental Institute, Moscow)

Within the Hamito-Semitic family only Chadic and Southern Kushitic languages have two non-emphatic laterals (correspondingly: ẑ and ŝ/ ŝ and ĉ). In what follows the first member of each pair will be under consideration.

Reflexes within the SKush group see in (Ehret 208–212). For PChadic a voiceless sibilant[1] (*ŝ) has been reconstructed on the basis of the following correspondence: West: *z-* in Hausa (group 1), *l-* in Sura (2), Bolewa (3), Ron (7), *ẑ-* in Ngizim (6) and in Bauchi (4-Northern, 5-Southern), *ẑ-* in Central Chadic, *l-* in East Chadic, but *s-* in Lai (2).

PCh	PWCh	1	2	3	4	7	6	PCCh	1–12	PECh	1,3,5–7	2
**ŝ-*	**ŝ-*	*z-*	**l-*	**l-*	**ẑ-*	*l-*	*ẑ-*	**ẑ-*	**ẑ-*	**ś-*	**l-*	**s-*

1. *Chadic evidence for *ŝ*

The full list of Proto-Chadic roots with initial *ŝ is given below.

1.1. **ŝi/a'-* 'cut (grass), chop': W 2 Angas (F) *li* 'cut grass', *li-n gwa* 'tribal marks on cheeks', Mupun[2] *lèè* 'cut by taking off slices, harvest', Sura (Jungraithmayr 1963) *láa* 'wound'; 3 Pero *lá* 'cut grass'; C 2 (Kr) **ẑa-* 'chop': Cibak *ẑi-ntà*, Bura *ŝì-mtə*, West Margi *ẑi-ndà*, Kilba *aẑá-ndì*; 4 **ẑa-*: Gude (H) *la* 'cut', (Kr) Fali Mucella *ẑa-bi* 'cut', Fali Jilvu *ẑà-bì* 'chop'; 7 Mafa *ẑa* 'couper (des herbes, de la paille)'.

---

[1] Argumentation against Proto-Chadic **ẑ* see in [Stolbova 1996:49].

[2] We use Bargery 1934 for Hausa data; Barreteau 1988 for Mofu data, 1990—for Mafa, 2000—for Mada; Frajzyngier 1985 for Pero data, 1991—for Mupun; Jungraithmayr 1970 for Ron data, 1989—for Bidiya, 1990—for Mokilko, 1991—for Tangale, 1992—for Migama; Lukas 1936 for Logone data, 1941—for Musgu and 1970—for Gisiga 1970 without any references.

1.2. **ŝaḅ- (< *ŝabVH-)* 'fence': W 3 Tangale *lubo* 'straw hut (on farm)'; C 7 Mofu *ẑəb* 'clôturer (avec des épines)'; 10 Mbara (TSL) *ẑúḅá* 'fence', Musgu *ŝab* 'fence around the house'; E **śaba*: 1 Kera (Eb) *laḅi*; 2 Kabalay (Caprile 1972) *səbǎ*. 3a. **ŝVḅ-* 'plait': W 1 Hausa *zúbì* 'arranging of the warp ready for weaving'; 3 Bolewa (Lukas 1971) *laḅḅ-* 'flechten (Korb, Matte)'; C 12 Zime Batna (S) *ŝə̀ḅá* 'tresser' (irregular reflex).

1.3. **ŝaab-* 'axe', **ŝab-* 'cut wood': W 1 Hausa *záábì* 'an axe with a long point on the opposite side of the shaft' *zààboo* 'kind of sword'; C 7 Mada *áẑàbá* 'hache'. Cp. W 6 Ngizim (Sch) *ẑàbə̀rú* 'split wood'; C 11 Musgu *x̂aba* 'fallow trees'.

1.4. **ŝaḅ- (<*ŝabVH-)* 'praise': W 6 Ngizim (Sch) *gə̀-ẑḅú* 'praise'; C 7 Mafa *ẑə́ba* 'louer, chanter les louanges', Mofu *-ẑáp-*, Mada *áẑbà* 'louer, glorifier'; 12 Zime Batna (S) *ẑàḅ* 'plaire'.

1.5. **ŝVba* kind of flying insect: W 4 Warji (Sk) *ẑəbai* 'butterfly'; C 7 Mafa *ẑəba* 'insecte volant'.

1.6. C Chadic **ŝab-* 'leaf, grass': 7 Mada *ẑbàh* 'feuilles', Mafa *ẑambay* 'feuille de mil'; 10 Logone *ẑébaa* 'green'; 12 Zime Batna (S) *ẑèḅè* 'oseille de Guinée'. See also W 3 Tangale *laba* grass sp.

1.7. **ŝaḅ- (< *ŝabVH-)* 'be wide, stretch': W 2 Bolewa (Lukas 1971) *laḅ-* 'ausbreiten', Tangale *loblob* 'broad and flat'; C 2 (Kr) **ẑaḅ-* 'wideness': Kilba *laḅ-*, Cibak *ẑàbú*, Hildi *ẑàḅu*.

1.8. **ŝamb-/*ŝaḅ-* 'mix, knead' (cp. **ŝamb-* 'beat'): W 3 Bolewa (Lukas 1971) *lomb-* 'vermischen'; 4 **ẑaḅ-* 'knead' (Sk): Warji, Kariya *laḅə-*, Miya *laḅ-*, Siri *ŝàḅa*, (MS) Paa *ẑaaḅàà*; C 12 Zime Batna (S) *ẑàp* (*-p* <*-*b*# is regular) 'mélanger de façon homogéne'; E 1 cp. Kera (Eb) *hálḅé* 'kneten' (< **ha-ŝaḅ-*).

1.9. **ŝaab-* 'hit, strike': W 1 Hausa *záb-čè* 'demolish a wall'; 4 (Sk) **ẑabaḍ-* > Warji, Kariya *ẑabəḍ-* 'beat', Paa (MS) *ẑáábuḍù* 'hit with heavy stick'; C 2 Bura (Kr) *ẑabu* 'beat, kill'; 7 Mada *áẑẑàḅ* 'battre (qqn), frapper'; 11 Musgu *x̂aba* 'beat'; E 3 Tumak (Caprile 1975) *ləb*.

1.10. **ŝamb-* 'slap, flatten': W 4 (Sk) Jimbin *ẑâmb-* 'beat'; C 7 Mafa *ẑə́mbát-* 'taper sur un object dur pour l'applatir'; E 2 Tobanga (Caprile 1978) *sombe* 'gifler'.

1.11. **ŝVḅ-< *ŝVHVb-* 'cover': W 1 Hausa *zóóḅà* 'overlap (eg. edges of a book-cover)'; 3 Bolewa (Lukas 1971) *liḅḅ-* 'bedecken'; C 12 Zime Batna (S) *ẑùḅ* 'recouvrir'.

1.12. **ŝabad-* 'shoulder, armpit': W 4 (Sk) Warji *ẑàbadái*, Kariya *ẑábádə*, Paa *ẑəbədì* 'shoulder'; E 1 Kera (Eb) *alə́bədì* 'armpit'.

1.13. **ŝ[i]Had-* 'push, move aside': W 3 Bolewa (Lukas 1971) *laad-* 'aufschieben'; C 11 Mulwi (T) *ẑidí* 'tirer'; E **ŝVḍ-* (<**ŝiHVd-*): 1 Mobu (Ln) *lede* 'se déplacer'; 2 Tobanga (Caprile 1978) *sì:dé* 'déplacer'; cp. 6 Mokilko *líḍḍè, léḍḍè* '(s')éloigner'.

1.14. **ŝag-* 'pierce, tooth': W 1 Hausa *zágóó* 'harpoon used mainly for killing crocodiles', *zágà* 'canine tooth'; 7 Mafa *ẑagaw* 'croc d'animal', Gisiga *ẑəgə* 'pierce'.

1.15. W **ẑVg-* 'to hang': 3 Tangale *looge* 'to hang up, to suspend'; 6 Ngizim (Sch) *ẑəgú* 'sling over shoulder'.

1.16. **ŝaḳo-* 'desire, love': W 1 Hausa *zàḳu* 'be eager to get something'; 3 Pero *làlák* 'lust'; 7 Ngizim (Sch) *ẑàkwái* 'desire for'; E 5 Migama *ḍyékkó* 'aimer' (< **ĉako-* < **ŝaḳo-*). Cp. C 7 Mada *áẑàkà* 'aider'.

1.17. **ŝVḳ-* 'pull, move': W 4 (MS) Paa *ẑiḳàà* 'pull of'; 5 (Kr) Geji *ŝèki*, Buli *ŝìgu*; C 12 Zime Batna (S) *ẑìk* 'déplacer'; E 2 Tobanga (Caprile 1978) *sogè* 'tirer'.

1.18. Chadic **ẑVʾ-* 'fall, put down': W 2 Sura (Jungraithmayr 1963) *lɛ̂* 'legen, setzen', Mupun *lé* 'put (down)' (pl.); 3 Pero *lú* 'put', Tangale *liye* 'put, place'; C 5 Glavda (R) *ẑa, nẑa* 'fall'.

1.20. W 4 **ẑVḳVf-* 'pierce' (Sk): Warji *ẑəḳəf-*, Kariya *ẑəkəf-*.

1.21. **ŝVnVt-* 'lion': W 4 (Sk) Warji *ẑələtə-na*, Miya *lənte*, Diri *azələtu*; C 12 (Kr) Masa *ŝona*, Banana *ẑonà*, BM *ŝona*.

1.22. **ŝam-* 'be able to do smth': W 2 Bolewa (Lukas 1971) *lom-* 'erreichen (Stelle)'; 6 Ngizim (Sch) *ẑamu* 'do, make, be possible'; C 10 Logone *ẑə̀m* 'genügen'.

1.23. **ŝVm-* 'speak': W 2 Angas (F) *lem*; 5 (Kr) Geji *ẑemi*, Buli *ŝèmi*; C 11 Musgu *ẑəma*, Mbara (TSL) *ŝím* 'call'; E 1 Kwang (dial. Mobu) (Ln) *ləm*.

1.24. **ŝim[am]-* 'to hunt': W cp. 3 Tangale *lilim* 'assembly for special occasion (hunt, drink, etc.)'; C 4 (Kr) **liʾam-* (< CCh **ẑiʾam-*) 'hunting': Mwulyen *lìəm̀ò-tí*, Gudu *lámə́-cú*; 11 Mbara (TSL) *ẑìm*, Mulwi (T) *ẑìmì*; E 6 Mokilko *ʾìlmí* 'poursuivre'.

1.25. **ŝing-* 'house': W 4 (MS) Paa *ẑángá* 'town' (vowel assimilation); C 7 Gisiga *miẑìŋgere* 'Hof'; 11 Musgu *x̂iŋ* 'Haus'.

1.26. **ŝang-ir-* (< **ŝanVg-ir-*) 'cattle (> possessions, wealth)': W 2 Angas (F) *long* 'possessions, wealth', *long ma* (pl.) 'plenty of cattle', Mupun *lóŋ* 'domestic cattle', *loŋ* 'wealth', Sura (Jungraithmayr 1963) *loŋ* 'Besitz; Haustiere'; 4 (Sk) Kariya, Mburku, Miya *ẑangir* 'domestic cattle', Paa (MS) *ẑàngír* 'wealth'; C 7 Gisiga *ẑənge-rek* 'ram'; E 5 Bidiya *lònòy* 'wealth'.

1.27. **ŝap-* 'be flat': W 2 Mupun *làap sár,* Angas (F) *lep sar* 'palm of the hand' (*sár* 'hand'), cp. Mupun *laap* 'place for threshing'; C 7 Mafa *ẑəpa'a* 'large and flat'.

1.28. **ŝVp/b-* 'wear, put on': W 2 Mupun *lèp*; C 12 Peve (Vn) *ẑap* 'wear'.

1.29. **ŝap-* 'like, want': W 3 **lop- < *lo/ap-*: Tangale *lobi* 'agree, accept, like'; C 12 Zime Batna (S) *ẑàp* 'désirer'; E 5 Bidiya *lap* 'avoir des relations sexuelles'

1.30. W **ŝa/y/p* 'pierce, cut': 3 Pero *lépè* 'spear with a wide blade'; 6 Ngizim (Sch) *ẑàpú* 'pierce, stab'; 7 Fyer, Daffo *lef* 'cut'.

1.31. **ẑur-* 'pour; river': W 1 Hausa *zúraàaraa, zúràaree* 'pour water'; 4 Paa (MS) *ẑər* 'pour in, draw water'; C 7 Gisiga *ẑaẑar* 'Bach', Mafa *ẑóẑór* 'ruisseau'.

1.32. **ŝa/it-* 'pull': W 2 cp. Angas (F) *lweet* 'of stretching capacity of rubber'; C 4 (Kr) Gude *lət-ič* 'pull'; 7 Mada *àẑẑát* 'étirer'; 11 Mbara (TSL) *ẑát* 'pull by a strap'; 12 Zime Batna (S) *ẑàt* 'arracher'; E 5 Bidiya *liit* 'etirer, tendre' .

1.33. C Ch **'a-ŝay/w-* 'light' (v., n.): 7 Mafa *ẑáẑáy,* Mada *áwẑá* 'luire, briller'; 8 Daba (Kr) *àẑəw* 'light' (n.)

1.34. C ?? **ŝiy-/*ŝiw-* 'flesh' > 'meat': 1 **ẑiw-* 'flesh': (Kr) Tera *ẑù,* Gaanda *ŝìwa*; 3 (Kr) **ŝti < *ẑi-tV* (devoicing in contact with *-t-*) 'flesh, meat'; 4 (Kr) Fali Mucella *ẑìwu,* Fali Jilvu *ẓ̂iwe,* Mwulyen *lìó* 'flesh' (cp. a derivative *lìó-ŋgó* 'meat'), Gude *lùwa,* 'flesh, meat'; 7 Mafa *ẑe* 'boeuf'.

1.35. **ŝaw/H-* 'receive, take': W 2 Mupun *la* 'receive', Angas (F) *la* 'take'; 3 Pero *làwwò* 'seize'; C 5 Glavda (R) *ẑəγ* 'receive, obtain, take'.

1.36. **(ŝ)VŝV* 'fat, oil': W 4 Paa (MS) *ẑíẑù* 'cooking oil, butter'. C 7 Mada *éẑè* 'être gras, huileux, taché de gras'.

2. *Southern Cushitic *ŝ*

The one-to-one correspondence between Southern Cushitic **hl (*ŝ)* and Chadic **ŝ* proves the Hamito-Semitic origin of the lateral sibilant. See the following examples.

2.1. Chadic 1.1 **ŝi/a'-* 'cut' ~ SKush: Kwadza *hle'o* 'knife' (Ehret 211, N 28), Maa *hla* 'stab, pierce', Burunge *hla'-aniya* 'scar' (Ehret 211, N 22), Iraqw *sloo'i* 'facial tattoos' (Maghway 134).

2.2. Chadic 1.2. **ŝaḇ-* 'fence' (n.) ~ ? S Kush Iraqw, Gorowa *hluma* 'fence' < **hluw-* (Ehret 212, N 36) < **hlub-*. (For S Kush **-b->* Iraqw *-w-* see **tlub-* 'rain' > Iraqw *tluw-*, Burunge *tlub-* 'rain', Alagwa *tlubay* 'rain'(n.) (Ehret 217, N 24).

2.3. Chadic 1.6 **ŝab-* 'leaf' ~ SKush **ŝab-* 'foliage, vegetation': Dahalo *hláv une* 'leaf', *hlávu* 'leaves', Alagwa *hlaba* 'bush, thick undergrowth' (Ehret 208, N2). See also (OS N 2318).

2.4. Chadic 1.22. **ŝam-* 'be able to do smth' ~ SKush: Asa *hlam-* 'allow', Maa *hlama* 'let go, leave off' (Ehret 208, N5). See also (OS N 2327).

2.5. C Chadic 1.34 **ẑiy-/*ẑiw-* 'flesh'> 'meat' ~ SKush **ŝee* 'cow': Iraqw, Burunge, Alagwa *hle*, Kwadza *hleko*, Asa *hleok* (Ehret 211, N 24).

2.6. C Chadic 7 Mafa *ẑáh-* 'égorger', Mada *áẑáhà* égorger, dépecer ~ Maa *-hlaha'-* 'to scarify, to tatoo' (Ehret 211, N 22).

2.7. C Chadic 7 Mada *áẑẑàr* 'vitalité, fécondité (force magique)' ~ SKush **ŝa'ar-*: Burunge *hla'ar-* 'to live', Maa *-hla'ari* 'to help, support, aid' (Ehret 210, N17).

2.8. Chadic 1.20. W Chadic 4 **ẑVḳVf-* 'to pierce' ~ SKush **ŝaḳw-* 'to stab, to pierce': Iraqw *ŝaqw-*, Burunge *ŝakw-* 'to shoot (arrow)' (Ehret 209, N 13).

2.9. Chadic 1.35. **ẑaw/H-* 'receive' ~ S Cush **ŝaw-* 'get': Iraqw, Burunge *hlaw-*, Alagwa *hloom-* 'to get', Maa *-hlaw-* 'accept, receive' (Ehret 211, N23).

2.10. Chadic 1.30. W **ŝa/y/p* 'pierce, cut': cf. S Kush Dahalo *dlappanað* 'to prick' (Ehret, 223, N4).

2.11. Chadic 1.36. **(ŝ)VŝV* 'fat, oil' ~ S Kush **'ahli* 'fat, oil': Kwadza *ahlito*, Dahalo *áhli* (Ehret 285, N31).

2.12. Chadic W 4 (MS) Paa *ẑa* 'open', (Sk) Diri *ẑa* 'open, untie' ~ S Kush Maa *-hlá* 'open' (Ehret 215, N12).

2.13. Chadic **ẑaw/'-* 'burn': W 3 Pero *lààlò*, pl. *lá'úlò* (redipl.); C 5 (Kr) Dxwede *ẑuwayà* ~ S Kush **hlaḥ-* 'to burn smth': Dahalo *hlaḥ-*, Maa *-hlahá* (Ehret 210, N 18).

2.14. Chadic 1.18. **ẑV'-* 'fall, put down' ~ Maa *-hlú* 'fall', *hlúku* 'drop' (Ehret 217, N25).

3. *Proto-Semitic* *ŝ$_x$

As for Proto-Semitic, one more lateral sibilant in addition to *ŝ (yielding *š* in Akkadian, Ugaritic, Arabic, *ś-* in Hebrew, s_2 in Sabaic and a lateral *(ś-)* in MSA languages) was postulated by A. Militarev many years ago. This hypothesis was formulated more accurately in (MK 2001). The new lateral (ŝ$_x$) was reconstructed for PSem on the basis of the following correspondence: Akkadian *š*, Ugaritic *š*, Hebrew *š-*, *-s* (?), Aramaic *š*, *s* (?), Arabic *š*, Sabaic s_2, Geez *s-*, M Eth *s,š*, Mehri, Harsusi *š*, Jibbali (E) *š*, Jibbali (C.) *s̃-*, Soqotri *š* (MK, Introduction, p. C). A number of Proto-Semitic roots with the phoneme under consideration (as well as the commentary) can be found in (MK Introduction C-CV).

However, reflexes in MSA languages quite often violate those given above. See some examples from (MK):

PSem **ḥwŝ*$_x$ 'to care, spare, protect', **ḥaŝ*$_x$ 'far be it', '(God) forfend'. > Soq *ḥáša*, Mhr *ḥaś-e* 'garde toi', C Jib *ḥas̃ɛ́k*, E Jib *ḥáśɛ* 'with all due respect to (you)' (MK CII N4);

PSem. **ŝ*$_x$*rm* 'to have a nose with a cut off tip; have a slit lip' > Mhr *šərēm*, Hrs *meśrīm* 'hare lipped', Jib *s̃érəm* 'to have a hare lip'. (MK N 69).

Judging by these examples, *š* seems to be a secondary reflex of Semitic **ŝ*$_x$ in MSA languages, a (positional?) variant of a lateral *ś*. With the newly introduced reflex in MSA languages, namely—a lateral (*ś*), a number of examples can be presented proving the correspondence: Proto-Semitic *ŝ$_x$ ~ Proto-Chadic *ŝ ~ SKushitic *ŝ (< Proto-Hamito-Semitic *ŝ).

3.1. OS N 2314 Hamito-Semitic **ŝaʾ-/*ŝaw-* 'wish, like': Arabic *šyʾ* 'vouloir' (BK1293) ~ S Kush **ŝa-* 'love, like': Burunge, Alagwa *hlaʾ-*, Kwadza *hlaʾas-*, Asa *hlaʾat*, Dahalo *hlaw-* (Ehret 208, N1), Iraqw *slaʾ* 'want, love' (Maghway 129). Semitic data proving the reconstruction of PS **ŝ*$_x$ are given in (MK CII N3), namely: PS **ŝ*$_x$*ʾ(/h)*: Arabic *šyʾ* 'vouloir', *šwh* 'désirer ardemment', Harsusi *šáwweš* 'to need smth desperately', (?) Soqotri *šišíoh* 'pity', Syraic *šwʾ* (etpe.) 'cupivit', Tigre *säʾa* 'to hope, expect', *təsəwha* 'to desire'. However, Leslau (Leslau 1938:423) compares Arabic *šyʾ* 'vouloir' with Soqotri *śéʾe* 'se soucier' (the latter fits the newly established correspondence).

3.2. MK N 67 Sem * *ŝ*$_x$*g*^{ʕ} 'be rabid, mad': Akkadin *šegû* 'to rage, to be rabid', Hebrew *šg*^{ʕ} (pu., hitp.) 'to behave like a madman', Judaic *šg*^{ʕ} (pa.) 'to become insane', Arabic *šǯ*^{ʕ} 'surpasser quelqu'un en bravoure, en courage, guerrier; avoir l'air menaçant, sévere, austere', *šaǯiʕ-* 'furieux, en fureur (chameau)', *šaǯʕat-* 'faible d'esprit', *mašǯaʕ-* 'tout a fou, achevé' ~ Chadic **ŝVg-* 'to be incited, out of order': W 1 Hausa *zúgà* 'incite a person', *zùuguugù* 'exaggeration'; 2 Mupun *lùk* 'disorganize (things, house)'; 5 Glavda (R) *ẑáágà* 'foolishness'. Cp. S Kush Dahalo *ŝak-* 'be angry, quarrel' (Ehret 209, N11). Note that now we can add MSA data considered as «semantically possible, but phonetically pointing to *ŝ, not to **$ŝ_x$*» in (MK, N 67): Mehri *śəgi-*, Jibbali (E) *śəgāʕ*| 'envious'.

3.3. Okhotin N 245: Sab, Kat *s_2'm* 'buy, purchase (smth from s.o.)', Min *s_2'm*, Had *s_2'm-t* 'achat', Akkadian *ša'āmu* 'to buy', Him *ša'ama* 'kaufen', Harsusi *śōm*, Mehri *śōm (yəŝōm), śɛ̄m* 'to sell', Soqotri *śíom (< *śí'om)* 'vendre'. This root is related to W Chadic **ẑVm-* 'count': 1 Hausa *záámè* 'deduct the sum a person owes from a payment one is making to him'; 5 **ẑim* 'to count' (Cosper): Polci *ẑìím*, Zul *ẑimi*.

3.4. Okhotin N 323: Sabaic *h-ws$_2$ʕ* 'grant favour (s.o.)', Hebrew *šwʕ* (pi) 'um Hilfe rufen', Akkadian *še'û* 'to look for, search, seek out someone' ~ W Chadic 6 Ngizim *ẑàẑìyú* 'beseech, seek blessing' (< Ch **ŝVy-*), S Kush Maa *-hlawi* 'ask, beg for, pray for' (Ehret 214, N1).

3.5. Okhotin N312: Mehri *śff* 'to like so, st', Arabic (Yem) *šaff* 'to sympathize with, to have an affection for'. Cp. also Arabic *šʕf* 'occuper tout entier (passion d'amour)' (BK 1240) ~ Chadic 1.29. **ŝap-* 'like, want'. For a possible cognate see also: Sabaic *$s_2$wf, s_2f* 'look after, protect, defend' (Biella 514), Mehri *məśáwfət* 'protect; protection' (Johnstone 367).

3.6. Sem: Arabic *šwq* 'remplir quelqu'un du désir de quelque chose, exciter quelqu'un (se dit de l'amour)' (BK 1288), Hebrew *təšōqat* (< Sem **$ŝ_x$wq*) 'Drang, Verlangen' (KB 1043), Mehri *ʕāśōḳ* 'to like s.o., st.' (Johnstone 32) ~ Chadic 1.16.**ŝaḳo-* 'want, love'. Note that our data show that PSem **$ŝ_x$* in medial position yields Hebrew *-š-* (not *-s-* as in (MK)). One more example of the kind is: Hebrew *nāḥāš* (KB 690), Ugaritic *nḥš* 'snake' ~ Arabic *ḥanaš-* 'serpent, vipere, etc.' (BK 503)< Sem **nḥ$ŝ_x$/ *ḥn$ŝ_x$* 'snake'.

3.7. Mehri *śśy* 'fat round the kidney' (Johnstone 386) ~ 2.11. Chadic **(ŝ)VŝV* 'fat, oil' ~ S Cush **'ahli* 'fat, oil'.

3.8. Soqotri *śeʕe* 'courir' (Leslau 1938:431) ~ W Chadic 4 (MS) Paa *ẑaẑù* 'run'.

3.9. Soqotri *śe* 'donner', Hebrew *šay* 'cadeau' (Leslau 1938: 420) ~ 2.9. Chadic **ẑaH-* 'receive' ~ S Kush **ŝaw-* 'get'.

3.10. Mehri *śḥḥ* 'sharp' (Johnstone 376) ~ Kwadza *ŝahamo* 'sharp' (Ehret 209, N9).

3.11. Mehri *śar* 'evil' (Johnstone 382), Soqotri *śrˁ* 'laid' (Leslau 1938:434) ~ Chadic W 6 Ngizim *ẑə̀rá* (< Chadic **ŝVr-*) 'being warlike, belligerent'.

3.12. Mhr *nśr* 'to spread out', *náśśər* 'separate' (Johnstone 302, 303), Arabic *nšr* 'dispercer, disséniner' (BK 1258) ~ Chadic **ŝVr-* 'divide, disperce': W 4 (MS) Paa *ẑə̀raa* 'divide', C 11 Munjuk *ẑiri* 'dispercer', Mulwi (T) *ẑirí* 's'éparpiller'.

3.13. Soqotri *šbaḥ, śbaḥ* 'étendre, étendre les pieds' (Leslau 1938: 410), Arabic *šbḥ* 'étendre une peau a l'aide de deux pieux fichés en terre' (BK, 1182) ~ Chadic 1.7. **ŝaḇ- (< *ŝabVH-)* 'be wide, stretch'.

3.14. Mehri *śxk* 'scrape, scratch' (Johnstone 389) ~ W Chadic 6 Ngizim *ẑákwâk* 'rake for clearing farm'.

3.15. Geez *šəˁə'a* 'peel off, scrape, clean', Arabic *šaˁˁa* 'disperce, scatter', Syraic *šaˁ (šˁˁ)* 'smooth' (coming close to 'peel off') > 'plaster', for which cp. Hebrew *šāˁā* (*šˁy*) 'be smeared over' (Leslau 1986:524) ~ S Kush Dahalo *hlaaˁ-* 'to peel' (Ehret 211, N22), Kwadza *hla'-* 'purify, to remove *kisirani*' (Ehret 210, N16).

3.16. Geez *šy', še'a* 'destroy, annihilate', Hebrew *šō'ā* 'desolation' (Leslau 1986:539): ~ S Kush Iraqw *hla'ay* 'no', Maa *-hle* 'to cease' (Ehret 209, N15), cp. W Chadic Hausa *zóózàyee* (< **z-* or **ŝ-*, reduplication) 'damage fence, erode'.

4. *Further types of Psem. *ŝ$_x$*

There are two more PSemitic roots with initial **ŝ$_x$* among those given in (MK) attested both in Hebrew and MSA languages. In both MSA languages show *š* as the reflex of PSemitic **ŝ$_x$*.

4.1. a) **ŝ$_x$bb/*ŝ$_x$bw* 'to burn, heat', b) **ŝ$_x$a/ibV-b-* 'spark' (a derived stem): a) Akkadian *šabābu* 'roast, burn', Arabic *šbb/šbw* 'brûler, allumer le feu', Syraic *šwb* 'aruit, arefactus est', Soqotri *šbb, šwb* 'réchauffer'; b) Akkadian *šibūbu*, Hebrew *šābībā*, Judaic *šəbībā* 'spark', Syraic *šəbibā* 'scintilla', Arabic *šibāb-* 'tout qui sert à allumer le feu' (MK CI-CII). MSA group is represented by Soqotri only, the latter may be an arabism.

4.2. **ŝ$_x$Vm*ŝ$_x$- < *ŝ$_x$Vmŝ$_x$Vm-* 'sun': Akkadian *šamšu*, Judaic *šimšā*, Hebrew *šämäš* (the reflex in Hebrew is of no interest because another one reduplicated root—PSem **ŝrŝ* 'root' yields Hebrew *šoreš*), Arabic *šams-*, Sabaic s_2ms_1, Jibbali (E) *šum*, (C) *s̄um* 'heat of the sun', Soqotri *šam, šhom, šihom* 'soleil, jour' (MK CI). Militarev postulates a reduplicated form with dissimilation of sibilants in Arabic and in Sabaic ($*\hat{s}_x Vm\hat{s}_x Vm$- > **šamšam-* > *šams-*). But the same dissimilation might have yielded *š* in MSA languages (if they ever had a reduplicated stem): $*\hat{s}_x Vm\hat{s}_x Vm$- > **śVms-Vm-* > *śVmšVm->* *šVm-*. Thus, the initial Proto-Semitic $*\hat{s}_x$ in this root is not that evident. On the other hand, a S Kush cognate to this Semitic root definately show an anlaut **ĉ* (corresponding to P Semitic **ŝ*), namely: Alagwa *ĉehemu* 'sun; daylight', Burunge *ĉema* 'sun' (Ehret 360).

Out of the Proto-Semitic roots with $*\hat{s}_x$ yielding MSA *š* given in (MK) there are two still left unexplained: N 271(Arabic *mišfalat-* 'gésier, jabot, estomac', Mehri *hōfəl* 'belly, stomach', Harsusi *hōfel* 'belly', Jibbali *šə́fəl* 'belly', etc.) and N 138 (Arabic *ḫšf* 'être rongeé par la gâle' ~ Jibbali *ḫšfé'* 'pimple', etc.)

5. *Conclusion*

The data presented give more evidence proving that Proto-Semitic sibilant phoneme ($*\hat{s}_x$) introduced in (MK) was really a lateral. It is proved by parallels in Chadic and S Kushitic (all with a lateral sibilant). As for reflexes within Semitic, our data support a *š*-reflex in Hebrew and s_2 in Sabaic but point to a lateral (*ś*) reflex of PSem $*\hat{s}_x$ in MSA languages.

Bibliography

Bargery (George P.): 1934 *A Hausa-English Dictionary*. Oxford University Press, London

Barreteau (Daniel): 1988 *Description du mofu-gudur. 2 vol. (Travaux et documents 206)*. Orstrom, Paris.

——: 1990 *Lexique mafa. (Collection études tchadiques: monographies)*. Geuthner/Orstrom, Paris.

——, and André Brunet: 2000 *Dictionnaire mada. (Sprache und Oralität in Afrika 16.)* REIMER, Berlin.

BK—Biberstein-Kazimirsky A. de: 1860 *Dictionnaire arabe-français*. V. 1–2. Maisonneuve et Cie, éd. Paris.

Caprile (Jean-P.): 1972 Unpub. typescript. *Liste de mots kabalai et lélé.*

——: 1975 *Lexique tumak-français. MSAA 5*. REIMER, Berlin.

——: 1978 «Notes linguistiques sur le tobanga à partir d'un conte en cette langue» In: H. Jungraithmayr and J.Caprile, eds.: *Cinq textes tchadiques: MSAA 12*: 121–75. Reimer, Berlin.

Cosper (Ronald): 1994 *South Bauchi Lexicon*. Halifax. The Author.

Eb—Ebert (Karen): 1976 *Sprache und Tradition der Kera. Teil 2: Lexikon. MSAA 8.* Reimer, Berlin.
Ehret (Christopher): 1980 *The historical Reconstruction of Southern Cushitic.* Reimer, Berlin.
Foulkes H.D.: 1915 *Angass Manual.* Kegan, Trübner and Co. London.
Frajzyngier (Zygmund): 1985 *A Pero-English and English-Pero Vocabulary. MSAA* 38. REIMER, Berlin.
——: 1991 *A Dictionary of Mupun. (Sprache und Oralität in Afrika 11).* REIMER, Berlin.
Hoskison (James T.): 1983 *A Grammar and Dictionary of the Gudu Language.* Ph.D. dissertation, Ohio State University.
Johnstone (Tomas. M.): 1987 *Mehri Lexicon.* University of London.
Jungraithmayr (Herrmann): 1963 «Die Sprache der Sura in Nord-Nigerien». *Afrika und Übersee* 47, pp. 8–89, 204–220.
——: 1970 *Die Ron-Sprachen.* Augustin, Glückstadt.
——: 1990 *Lexique mokilko.* Reimer, Berlin.
——: 1991 *A Dictionary of the Tangale Language.* Reimer, Berlin.
—— and Abakar Adams: 1992 *Lexique migama.* Reimer, Berlin.
—— and Alio Khalil: 1989 *Lexique bidiya.* Frankfurter wissenschaftliche Beiträge/ Kulturwissenschaftliche Reihe, 16. Klostermann. Frankfurt.
Kœhler (Ludwig) and Walter Baumgartner: 1958 *Wörterbuch zum hebräischen Alten Testament.* Brill. Leiden.
Kraft (Charles): 1981 *Chadic Wordlists.* 3 vols. *MSAA* 23–25. Reimer, Berlin.
Leslau (Wolf): 1987 *Comparative Dictionary of Geʿez.* Harrassowitz, Wiesbaden.
——: 1938—Lexique Soqotri. Paris.
Lenssen (Tilman): 1984 «*Studien zum Verb im Kwang*». *Africana Marburgencia*, Special issue 8.
Lukas (Johannes): 1936 *Die Logone-Sprache im zentralen Sudan.* Deutsche Morgenländische Gesellschaft. Leipzig.
——: 1941 Deutsche Quelle zur Sprache der Musgu in Kamerun. Biehefte zur Zeitschrift für Eingeborenen Sprachen.
——: 1970 *Studien zur Sprache der Gisiga.* Augustin. Hamburg.
——: 1971 «Die Personalia ünd das primäre Verb in Bolanci. Mit Beiträge über das Karekare». *Afrika und Übersee* 54, pp. 237–86, 55:114–39.
Maghway J.B.: 1995 Annotated Iraqw Lexicon. African Language Study Series, 2, 1995, Tokio.
Militarev (Alexandr) and Leonid Kogan: 2000 *Semitic Etymological Dictionary.* Vol 1. Anatomy of Man and Animals. Münster.
Okhotin (Nikita): 1999 *Gluhiye neemfaticheskiye soglasnyje araviyskix yazykov.* Ph.D. Dissertation. Moscow.
Orel (Vladimir) and Olga Stolbova: 1995 *Hamito-Semitic Etymological Dictionary. Materials for a Reconstruction.* Brill.
Rapp (Eugen) and Brigitta Benzing: 1968 Dictionary of the Glavda language. Bible Society. Frankfurt.
Sachnine (Michka): 1982 *Le Lamé.* These du doctorat de 3e cycle, Universite de Sorbonne nouvelle. Selaf. Paris.
Schuh (Russel G.): 1981 *A Dictionary of Ngizim.* University of California Press. Berkeley – Los Angeles.
Skinner (Margaret): 1979 *Aspects of Pa'anchi Grammar.* Ph.D. Dissertation. University of Wisconsin. Ann Arbor.
Skinner (Neil): 1977 *North Bauchi Chadic Languages. Afroasiatic Linguistics* 4(1).
Stolbova (Olga): 1996 *Studies in Chadic Comparative Phonology.* Diafragma. Moscow.
Tourneux (Henry): 1980 «Nouvelle approche du radical en mulwi (musgu)». Africana Marburgencia, p. 13(1):70–76.
——, Seignobos (Christian) and Francine Lafarge: 1986 *Les Mbara et leur langue.* Selaf. Paris.

Venberg (Rodney): 1975 Phonemic statements of the Peve language. *Africana Marburgensia* 8(1), pp. 26–43.

Abbreviations

MK	Militarev & Kogan
MSAA	Marburger Studien zur Afrika- und Asienkund

LEXICA AFROASIATICA III

Gábor Takács
(Székesfehérvár & ELTE, Budapest)

Over the past half decade, since the appearence of Marcel Cohen's fundamental "*Essai comparatif sur le vocabulaire et la phonétique du chamito-sémitique*" in 1947, comparative-historical Afro-Asiatic linguistics has undergone a significant development. An enormous quantity of new lexical material has been published (both descriptive and comparative), including a few recent attempts at compiling an Afro-Asiatic compartive dictionary (SISAJa I–III, HCVA 1–5, HSED, Ehret 1995).

During my current work on the "*Etymological Dictionary of Egyptian*" (Leiden, since 1999–, E.J. Brill), I have collected a great number of new comparisons, which—to the best of my knowledge—have not yet been proposed in the literature (I noted wherever I noticed an overlapping with the existing Afro-Asiatic dictionaries). Therefore I started the series "*Lexica Afroasiatica*" in order to contribute to comparative Afro-Asiatic with many new recently observed lexical correspondences.[1]

The present part of this series[2] is a collection of new Afro-Asiatic etymologies with the Proto-Afro-Asiatic initial voiceless labial stop (*p-),[3] which results from my research on comparative Afro-Asiatic (especially Egypto-Chadic) phonology and lexicon at Frankfurt (1999–2000, 2002).[4]

---

[1] The lexical comparisons presented in this paper issue from a long-range project of an Afro-Asiatic comparative dictionary, and henceforth represent the copyright of the author.

[2] The first part of this series (lexical parallels with with PAA *b-) has appeared in *Afrikanistische Arbeitspapiere* (Köln) 67 (2002), 103–151. The second part (additional lexical roots with AA *b-) is published in Kogan, L. (ed.): Studia Semitica (Moscow, 2003, Russian State University for the Humanities, pp. 331–348). The fourth part of "*Lexica Afroasiatica*" (containing new etymologies with AA *f-) is still in press when the present paper has been prepared (forthcoming in *Archív Orientální* in 2003).

[3] The fourth part (forthcoming) of the series is dealing with *ṗ-, *f-, *P-. The latter symbol (*P-) signifies any unknown initial labial, just as, e.g., *T stands for any unknown dental stop (*d, *t or *ṭ) or *K for any unknown velar stop (*g, *k or *ḳ) or *Q for any unknown postvelar/uvulear (*ɡ, *q or *q̇).

[4] The author expresses his deep gratitude to Prof. Herrmann Jungraithmayr and the Alexander von Humboldt-Stiftung (Bonn) for the support of his research at the Institut für Afrikanische Sprachwissenschaften (Frankfurt a/M, Germany) in 2002 when the present article has been prepared for publication.

Since we know little about the Proto-Afro-Asiatic vowel system, the list of the reconstructed Proto-Afro-Asiatic forms is arranged according to consonant roots (even nominal roots). Sometimes, nevertheless, it was possible to establish the root vowel, which is given in the paper additionally in brackets. In a number of cases, it is still difficult to exactly reconstruct even the root consonants on the basis of the available cognates (esp. when these are from the modern branches, e.g., Berber, Cushitic-Omotic, or Chadic).

**p-*

298. **AA *p-d** "to sprout": NBrb.: Iznasen ṯi-fifẹṭ, pl. ṯi-fifaḏ [-ṭ < *-d-t?] "inflorescence du palmier nain" [Rns. 1932, 297] || SBrb.: Hgr. ti-fadd-în (pl. tante) "bourgeons (d'arbres ou d'arbrisseaux qui perdent leurs feuilles en hiver)" [Fcd. 1951–2, 302] ||| WCh. *pūd- "to sprout" [GT]: Hausa hùùdá [hu- < *fu-] "to bud, blossom (locustbean, date-palm)" [Abr. 1962, 389] | Angas put [-t < *-d] "to sprout" [ALC 1978, 54].

299. **AA *p-d** "wooden plank (?)": Eg. pd (wood det.) "une partie du navire" (CT V 74u, *hapax*, AL 78.1543) = "*Deck (des Schiffes)" (GHWb 299) ||| NBrb.: Qabyle a-fud, pl. i-fud-en "bout de branche mal coupé, moignon de branche coupée qui reste sur un bâton, un manche" [Dlt. 1982, 191] ||| WCh.: Tangale pído "tree, log, plank, wood" [Jng. 1991, 131].
NB: Any connection to ECu. *bayt- "board" [GT]: Burji bóyt-ā "3. playing board (esp. for saddḗqa game)" [Sasse 1982, 41] | PDullay *payt-o "roasting plate (Röstplatte)" [GT]: Gorrose & Gollango & Gawwada payt-o [AMS 1980, 264]?

300. **AA *p-d ~ *p-ṭ** "wound, ulcer": SBrb.: Hgr. ti-fidi, pl. ti-fidi-w-in "plaie causée par le bât au garrot d'une bête de somme" [Fcd. 1951–2, 191], EWlm. & Ayr a-făḍay, pl. i-făḍay-ăn "plaie aux fesses", Ayr ə-fḍəy "avoir une plaie aux fesses (pour avoir monté un animal sans coussin)" [PAM 59] ||| WCh.: Tangale fədà "ulcer" [Krf. 1981, #256] = páḍi "boil, abscess" [Jng. 1991, 128], Pero pídà ~ píḍà "wound" [Frj. 1985, 45].
NB: A comparison to Eg. pdd.w (bodily efflux det.) "(Subst.)" (Med., Wb I 567, 7) = "?" (GHWb 300) is probably out of question, since—according to D. Meeks (p.c.)—it might in fact represent a miswritten form of Eg. rḏ.w "Flüßigkeit, Ausfluß" (PT, Wb II 469).

301. **AA *[p]-d-n ~ *[p]-n-d** "stone": Sem.: MSA *fVd(h)Vn "stone" [GT]: Jbl. fúdún "rock, stone", Sqt. fə́dhɔn [secondary *-h-?]

"mountain" (MSA: Jns. 1981, 51) ||| WCh.: BT *pand- [GT]: Tangale pandi̱ "stone, hill, mountain, rock" [Jng. 1991, 129], Dera póndó-póndí "rocks, boulders" [Nwm. 1974, 131].

NB1: Epenthetic -h- in Soqotri?

NB2: Perhaps here might belong WCh.: AS *ṗaŋ "stone" [Stl. & GT] (AS: Hfm. 1975, 17, #8; Stl. 1977, 156, #176), provided the AS *-ŋ was a resolution of the cluster *-nd or *-dn, i.e., AS *ṗaŋ < *pand- or *padn-.

NB2: Obscure is CCh.: Mofu-Gudur pərad̦ "rocher plat" [Brt. 1988, 219], in which -r- might be derived from *-n-, although -d̦ is unexpected.

302. **AA *p-t** "to look, watch": Sem.: MSA *ftš [GT: C_3 ext. *-š?]: Jbl. effúts̰ "to examine, look everywhere" [Jns. 1981, 65], Mhr. fatš "to examine, inspect" [Jns. 1987, 107] ||| CCh.: Gude fàtáfàtá "staring intently with head turned" [Hsk. 1983, 184] ||| ECh.: Bidiya ˀàpàt "1. voir, 2. contrôler" [AJ 1989, 53].

303. **AA *[p]-t** "to fall": perhaps ES: Gurage-Soddo fafat & Amh. fʷafʷate "waterfall" (ES: Lsl. 1979, 228 with dubious HECu. etymology) ||| SOm.: Dime fot- "to fall" [Bnd. 1994, 149] ||| WCh.: Hausa fáúčè [-če < *-te] "(bird) to swoop on to seize sg." [Abr. 1962, 261] || CCh.: Hurzo fat-day "to descend" [Rsg.], Moloko fàtáy "to descend" [Rsg.] (MM: Rsg. 1978, 236, #189) | Lame putu "tomber du haut de" [Scn. 1982, 272] || ECh.: Mubi fóót (pf.), ˀafad-é (inf.), ˀufát (impf.) "to fall" [Nwm. 1977, 183] (Ch.: JI 1994 II; Stl. 1996, 17).

NB: The uncertain reconstruction of PAA *[p]- is based on the supposed *p- in some eventual remote variant roots (cf. e.g. #307).

304. **AA *[p]-ṭ** (or *[f]-ṭ) "1. to fall, 2. (tr.) let fall": Sem.: Ar. faṭaˀa "(i.a.) jeter qqn. par la terre" [BK II 609] ||| NOm.: Shinasha-Bworo fèd̦d̦- "to fall" [Lmb. 1993, 301] | Sezo ṗɛṭɛš ṗɛ̃ṭɛ̃šá̱ "he falls down" [Sbr.-Wdk. 1994, 12] ||| Ch. *p-d̦ "to fall" [JS 1981, 98]: WCh.: perhaps Hausa fáád̦à "to fall into, on", fáád̦ád dà "to drop sg., cause sg. to fall", fáád̦ìì "to fall down, over, on to, into, off, out", fáád̦óó "to fall down, off" [Abr. 1962, 241–243].

NB: Cf. AA *[p]-t "to fall" [GT] (discussed above in #303).

305. **AA *p-ṭ-l** "fat": Sem. *pṭl [GT]: ES *fṭl [GT]: Amh. faṭula (adj.) "fat (man)", faṭṭälä "to become fat", Muher faṭula & Endegeny fāṭūlä "long and tall" (ES: Lsl. 1979, 250) ||| WCh.: Ron *fid̦ol "Fett, Mark" [GT]: Daffo fid̦ól, Sha fid̦ól, Kulere fid̦yól (Ron: Jng. 1968, 6; 1970, 284, 352, 389; JI 1994 II, 132) || CCh.: Gabin fid̦ète "oil", Hwona fɨd̦èrà "oil" (Tera gr.: Krf. 1981, #223).

NB: To be distinguished from AA *p-d-r ~ *p-r-d "fat" [GT].

306. **AA *p-t-Q** (perhaps ***-q**) "to pierce": Sem.: Akk. pataḫu (bab., nA) "durchstoßen, -bohren" [AHW 846] ||| CCh.: Mofu-Gudur

-pə́tkw- "percer (un bouton pour faire sortir le pus, un citron pour extraire le jus)" [Brt. 1988, 222].

NB: A PCh./PAA var. root *b-ṭ-K/Q (or sim.) [GT] has been preserved in CCh. *b-ḍ-kʷ [GT]: Mafa búḍúkw- "percer" [Brt.-Bléis 1990, 85] | Gude ɓə̀də́ku "poking through into hollow cavity" [Hsk. 1983, 165].

Lit.: the Akk.-Mofu etymology was published first by V.É. Orel & O.V. Stolbova (HSED #784). It was observed by me independently, being unaware of the suggestion in the relevant entry of HSED.

307. **AA *p-t-q̇ ~ *p-t-q** "to (let) fall": Eg. ptḫ "1. zu Boden werfen (PT), 2. sich niederwerfen (MK)" (PT, Wb I 565–566) ||| SBrb.: EWlm. & Ayr fətəqq-ət "tomber par terre (fruits, en abondance)", Ayr tə-ftəqq-et, pl. tyə-ftəqqa "chute par terre", cf. also EWlm. & Ayr fətəktək "tomber en grande quantité (pluie, fruits etc.)" [PAM 71] ||| HECu.: Sidamo fottoqa "to fall down" [Skn. 1996, 62, not found in Crl. 1938 II or Hds. 1989] ||| CCh.: Mofu-Gudur -pə́tk- "laisser tomber des déchets, vanner" [Brt. 1988, 222].

NB: Extension of AA *[p]-t "to fall" [GT] (discussed above).

308. **AA *p-t-r** "to untie, open, resolve": NWSem.: Hbr. ptr "auslegen, (Träume) deuten" [GB 669], NHbr. & JAram. ptr "deuten, auslegen" [GB] ||| CCh.: Daba pətar "déplier" [Mch. 1966, 146] || ECh.: Migama pòtôrtìrò "dérouler une bobine" [JA 1992, 117] | Birgit fičìrí [-či- reg. < *-ti-] "fendre" [Jng. 1973 MS].

NB: A var. (?) root (AA *p-s-r) might be preserved in Sem. *pšr [GT]: Akk. pašāru "lockern, (auf)lösen" [AHW 842] || Ar. fasara "1. découvrir ce qui était caché, 2. expliquer clairement, donner une interprétation de qqch." [BK II 593].

309. **AA *p-s** "1. to blow, 2. breathe → rest, 3. fart" [GT]: Sem. *pšw [GT]: Akk. pašû G "hauchen, leise furzen", Gtn "immer wieder rasselnd atmen" [AHW 846] || PB Hbr. pwš [met.?] "to breathe, rest one's self" [Jastrow] = NHbr. pwš "aufatmen" [WUS] || Ar. fsw: fasā "lâcher un vent (qu'on n'entend pas)", cf. also fissat- "pet" [BK II 595] || ES *fsw → *fʷs "to fart" [GT]: e.g. Geez fasawa "to break wind" [Lsl.] (ES: Lsl. 1956, 199; 1987, 168; Sem.: SED 1, 314–5, #56–57) ||| NOm.: Hozo pʊ́:šti, Sezo ṗű̃šɛ́ ~ fű̃šɛ́, Bambeshi pű̃šɛ́ "to blow" (Mao gr.: Sbr.-Wdk. 1993, 13; 1994, 10) ||| CCh.: Mbara pìsé "souffler" [TSL 1986, 275] || ECh.: WDangla píìsè "rester" [Fédry 1971, 64].

NB: The vocalism of the Chadic examples is obscure. A var. root can be found in Sem.: Ar. faššа "faire sortir l'air d'une outre en la comprimant" [BK II 595] ||| CCh.: Kotoko fàssə̀ "souffle" [Bouny 1978, 57]. Cf. also AA *b-s "1. to blow, 2. breathe, 3. rest" [GT] (discussed in "*Lexica Afroasiatica II*", #273).

310. **AA *p-s** (possibly ***pus-**) "1. to sting, 2. shoot an arrow": NOm.: Yemsa (Janjero) fus- "zwicken" [Lmb. 1993, 343] ||| WCh.: AS *pus "1. to shoot (arrow), 2. sting" [GT]: e.g. Angas pus, pl.

pwas "1. to shoot (as of an arrow), 2. shoot (of insects, of their stings), sting, 3. arrow" [Flk. 1915, 268–269] = puus "1. to shoot, 2. sting" [Grb.], Sura puus "1. to shoot, 2. sting" [Grb.] = pùs (sg.), pwas (pl.) "schießen" [Jng. 1963, 79], Kofyar fús [fu- < *pu- reg.] "to pierce" [Ntg. 1967, 13], Chip pùs "1. to shoot, 2. sting" [Grb.], Goemay puas (pl. of hes) "to pierce" [Srl. 1937, 184] (AS: Grb. 1958, 301, #2; Stl. 1977, 156, #170).

NB: J.H. Greenberg (1958, 301), V. M. Illič-Svityč (1966, 25, #3.9), followed by N. Skinner (1996, 66), identified AS *pus directly with OEg. pzḥ "to bite (PT), sting (Med.)" (FD 94), which was rejected by G. Takács (1999, 82; 1999, 368). The underlying PCh. root had a voiceless sibilant (cf. JI 1994 II, 2), although, in principle, the change Ch. *-Z > AS *-s seems plausible.

311. **AA *p-s** (perhaps ***pas- ~ *pis-**) "back": Eg. psḏ [reg. < *psg] "Rücken, Rückgrat" (OK, Wb I 556, 1–9) = "back, spine" (FD 95) ||| NOm.: Haruro pes-o ~ pis-o "deretano" [CR 1937, 657] ||| PCh. *pas- "back" [GT]: WCh.: presumably Hausa fáásà "to postpone (beginning sg.), be postponed indefinitely" [Abr. 1962, 257] || CCh.: Logone pásē "Gesäß, Hinterer" [Lks. 1936, 115] = mpa̱se̱ "cul" [Mch.] = páséé "podex" [IS].

Lit.: Mkr. 1981, 115, #24 (Gurage-Zayse); 1987, 360 (Logone-Burji-Zayse); Leslau 1979, 226; 1988, 188 (HECu.-Gurage).

NB1: The Egyptian counterpart has been extended by a third inetymological *-g (hence -ḏ), which occurs in a number of further Eg. body part names, cf. e.g. fnḏ "nose", mnḏ.t "cheek", nḥḏ.t "tooth", ẖnḏ "lower part, calf of leg" (meanings are quoted after FD). For the problem in detail cf. EDE II 577.

NB2: Not yet clear whether AA *p-s "back" [GT] is related to ES (borrowed from HECu.): Gurage: Selti fǟččo, Zway əfwaččo etc. "tail, hair of tail" (ES: Lsl. 1979, 226) ||| HECu.: Burji fǟ́č-o "bushy end of animal's tail" [Sasse 1982, 68: "ohne Etymologie"], cf. Darasa fǟč-ò ~ fǟčč-o "fly whisk" [Lsl.] ||| NOm.: Zayse fīc-o [-ts-] "tail" [Bnd.] = fīc-o [-ts-] "tail" [Mkr.] = fiš-o "tail" [Hyw. 1988, 285] = fic-o [-ts-] "tail" [Sbr. 1994, 20] ||| CCh.: Logone pisẖaa "tail" [Mkr.]. Should we assume AA *pis- "2. tail" [GT]?

312. **AA *p-ʒ** "to be agile, mobile": Sem. *pzz "to be agile" [GT]: Hbr. pzz qal "gelenk sein (von den Armen)" [GB] = qal "to be agile", piel "to leap" [Lsl.], MHbr. pzz "to be hasty" [Zbr. & Lsl.], NHbr. pzz "eilfertig sein" [GB], JAram. pəzīzā "übereilt" [GB], Syr. pzz "leicht beweglich sein" [GB] || Ar. fzz I "inquiéter qqn., le troubler dans qqch.", X "exciter, agacer, mettre dans un état d'excitation", fazz- "homme inquiet, toujours sujet à une agitation, 2 vif, alerte" [BK II 589–590] = fzz "to become excited with ardor" [Lsl.] || ES: Gurage: Chaha & Ennemor fuzz barä, Ezha fuzz männä "to walk quickly" (Grg.: Lsl. 1979, 253; Sem.: GB 838; Zbr. 1971, #177; Lsl. 1987, 167) ||| LECu. *fuzz- "agile, mobile" [GT]: Somali fúdud [d < *z reg.] (adj.) "1. leicht, beweglich,

flink, 2. leicht von Gewicht, 3. leicht, nicht schwierig, bequem zu machen" [Rn. 1902, 145] | Oromo fudud [d < *z regular] "sich schaukeln" [Rn.].

NB: Cf. also NEg. (loan from NWSem.?) pzz ~ pss (GW) "1. to exert oneself, strive, 2. undertaking" (NE, DLE I 182) = "1. sich (be) mühen, sich einsetzen, 2. Unternehmung, -en" (GHWb 294)?

313. **AA *p-Z** "vessel as measure (?)": Sem.: Akk. (Nuzi, nA) pūzu ~ būzu (f) "ein Meßgefäß" [AHW 145: "of unknown origin"] ||| NEg. pz "Art Krug oder Getränk" (NE, Wb I 553, 3) = "(vessel for beer)" (DLE I 182) = "ein Gefäß (für Bier, auch Maß für Bier)" (GHWb 293). Cultural loanword?

314. **AA *p-ʒ** "1. to puncture a suppurating wound (original sense), 2. sting (in general)": Sem.: Ar. fazza "saigner ou suppurer (une plaie)" [BK II 589] | MSA: Jbl. fzz: efzéz "1. to make a hole in, puncture (a tank, etc.), gore" [Jns. 1981, 68] ||| perhaps Eg. pzḥ [ext. -ḥ?] "beißen (Schlange, Löwe, Krokodil), stechen (Mücke, Fliege, Skorpion)" (PT, Med., Wb I 550) ||| WCh.: Tangale pide [-d- < *-z- possible] "to cut open, sting, puncture a boil, etc." [Jng. 1991, 131] || CCh.: Mafa fuza'a, fuz-fuzza'a, fuže'e, fuž-fužže'e "percé (pour une porte, un habit)" [Brt.-Bléis 1990, 139] || ECh.: Mokilko ˀáppìzá "1. faire les scarifications (tatouer), 2. percer (avec une lance)" [Jng. 1990, 59].

NB: Cf. AA *p-s "to sting, shoot" [GT] above.

315. **AA *[p]-s-q** "1. open, untie, 2. to spread out flat, 3. a wide flat surface (or sim.)": Sem.: Ar. fasaḫa "1. disjoindre, séparer, défaire, 4. résilier, dissoudre, 5. disperser" [BK II 592] ||| Eg.: perhaps psẖ (late var. pzẖ) "mat-like appendage on the prow of the solar bark" (CT, Faulkner 1973, 57, n. 9) = "platform on tip of solar bark's prow (from which the prow-mat [š3w] hangs)" (Ward 1981, 364, #15) = "Plattform (am Bug des Sonnenschiffes)" (GHWb 294) ||| SBrb.: EWlm. & Ayr ə-fsək "se désagreger" [PAM 69] ||| WCh.: Hausa fàskíí "1. breadth of sg., 2. being very broad" [Abr. 1962, 259] || CCh.: Mafa-Mada *p-s-k "to stretch open" (?) [GT]: Gisiga psak "entrollen (Matte)" [Lks. 1970, 134], Mofu pə̀skéy "to untie" [Rsg. 1978, 353, #773], Mofu-Gudur -pə̀sk- "détacher, défaire, découdre" [Brt. 1978, 140; 1988, 221].

NB: A var. root has been preserved in Sem. *pšḥ [GT]: OSA (Sab.) *fs₁ḥ: h-fs₁ḥ (caus.) "to enlarge (structure) (?)", m-fs₁ḥ-t "enlargement (?)" [SD 46], Ar. fasuḥa I "geräumig sein" [AHW 840] = I "to be wide, spacious", VII "to be dilated" [Lsl.] || Geez fḥs [met.] "to spread out, stretch out" [Lsl. 1987, 157: no etym.]. The NSem. correspondences are uncertain. L. Kopf (1976, 166) cited OHbr. pāsoᵃḥ "Raum machen" (contra KB 947) as cognate to Ar. fsḥ.

316. **AA *p-c-l** "to carve, hew": NWSem. *psl "to hew" [GT]: Ug. psl "ein Handwerker, der sich mit Behauen, Schnitzen beschäftigt", e.g. psl qšt "Bogenschnitzer" [WUS], Hbr. psl qal "behauen, zurecht hauen (e.g. steinerne Tafeln, ein Gottesbild)" [GB], Syr. psl peal "behauen" [WUS], NHbr. psl "behauen" [GB], Nabatean psl? "Steinmetz" [GB] (NWSem.: GB 561; WUS #2240) ||| ECh.: Lele pāsīlī "creuser dans un endroit dur" [WP 1982, 75].
NB: Cf. AA *b-s-l "long pointed tool" [GT] (debated in part 1, #32).

317. **AA *p-č** "1. to scatter (e.g. seed), 2. sow": presumably NEg. pjs (GW, corn det.) "*Saat (Korn)" (NE, GHWb 274) ||| NBrb. *a-yfs, pl. *i-yfs-an "seed" [GT]: NBrb.: Shilh i-fs-an "Saat, Samen" [Mkr.] | Tamazight (Beraber) i-fs-ān "semence" [Lst.], Ndir i-fs-an "sowing seeds" [Pnc. 1973, 105] | Mzab ə-fsa "répandre, verser" [Dlh. 1984, 54] | Nefusa a-ifs "semence" [Lst. 1931, 294] || SBrb. *ta-yfəs-t [GT]: Hgr. tê-fes-t [*ta-yfas-t], pl. tê-fs-în "semence (de végétal)" [Fcd. 1951–2, 362], Ghat či-fes-t "semence" [Nhl. 1909, 205] (Brb.: Mkr. 1969, 48, #40.1) ||| NAgaw *fäz- [*-z- < *-č- reg.?] "to sow" [Apl.]: Bilin fəd- ~ fäd-, Xamtanga fiz-u, Qemant fəz- ~ fäz- & NAgaw *fäz-än "seed" [Apl.]: Bilin fädän, Xamtanga fəza, Qemant fäzän (NAgaw: Apl. 1987, 505; 1989 MS, 9; 1991 MS, 11) || HECu.: Alaba fīšu "seed" [Bnd. 1971, 244, #70] || SCu.: Alg. pas-it- "to scatter (intr.)", pisari "seed", Brg. pisagariya "seed" (WRift: Ehret 1980, 161, #1) ||| WCh.: Hausa fáčá-fáčá "scattering" [Abr. 1962, 240] || ECh.: Toram fihaš- [-h- obscure] "to disperse, scatter" [Alio 1988 MS, 28].
Lit.: Mkr. 1981, 108, #5 (Brb.-Alaba-NAgaw).
NB1: Some authors (Dolgopolsky 1992 MS, 59–60, #63; Takács 1999, 17) linked the Brb. root to AA *p-Ŝ "to spread" [GT]), which is dubious due to Brb. *-s- ≠ AA *-Ŝ-.
NB2: AA *p-č has a var. root in AA *b-č "1. to scatter, 2. sow" [GT] (discussed in part 2 of "*Lexica Afroasiatica*", #276).

318. **AA *p-č̣** (or ***p-ṭ**?) "to sharpen": ES (from Cu.?): Amh. fäč̣č̣ä & Grg. *fč̣č̣ "to sharpen with a rasp, sharpen the edge" [GT] (ES: Lsl. 1979, 227 with dubious Sem. etym.) ||| ECh. *p-ḍ "to sharpen" [GT]: Kera féḍgé "an-, zuspitzen" [Ebert 1976, 45] | WDangla pááḍé "affûter une lame" [Fédry 1971, 53], EDangla pááḍé "schleifen" [Ebs. 1979, 133; 1987, 92], Migama páaḍó "aiguiser, affûter", páḍàwtà "tranchant" [JA 1992, 115], Bidiya paaḍ "affûter, aiguiser une lame" [AJ 1989, 105]?
NB: Cf. Ehret 1995, 101, #67 for further possible parallels.

319. **AA *p-ŝ** "to comb": Sem.: Ar. nafaša [prefix n-] "séparer la laine, le coton avec les doigts" [BK II 1311] = "to comb" [Brn.

1976, 820] ||| Eg. pšj (f) "Substantiv" (NE, Wb, I 560, 2) = "peigne" (AL 79.1049 after Zonhoven in JEA 65, 96, n. 65) = "divider, comb" (DLE I 184) = "Kamm (aus Elfenbein)" (GHWb 296) ||| WCh.: Hausa fííšíí "dressing woman's hair" [Abr. 1962, 269] | AS *pā₂s "to comb" [GT]: Angas pɛ̀ɛs (K) "rupfen (z.B. die Federn des Huhnes)" [Jng. 1962 MS, 32] = pes "to thin, comb" [ALC 1978, 51], Mupun pāas "to comb hair" [Frj. 1991, 47], Kofyar paas "to comb" [Ntg. 1967, 31], Goemay paas` "to clear, make a clearance through", paas dang goešing "to clear a horse's tail from entangled dirt by passing the hands through it" [Srl. 1937, 171].

Lit.: the Ar.-Mupun comparison was first suggested by O.V. Stolbova (in HSED #1918 & Stl. 1996, 121).

320. **AA *p-S** "to swell": Sem.: perhaps Ar. nfš [irreg. -š-]: muntafiš- & mutanaffiš- "gonflé et mou à l'intérieur" [BK II 1312] ||| NEg. pšj "a disease: pustule, swelling (?)" (NE, Edwards 1963, 11, fn. 30, not in Wb) = "pustule (?)" (AL 77.1503) = "*Eiterbläschen" (GHWb 296) → Cpt.: (S) paiše, paše, peše, piše, (S^A) pihe, (B) p^haiši, (O) *paeiše (f/m) "a disease producing pustules, swelling" (CD 278b) = "eine Hautkrankheit: Pustel, Blase" (KHW 145) = "ampoules, pustules" (DELC 159) ||| LECu.: Oromo fuš-ā, hence ES: Grg.-Ennemor fušä "boil at the joint of two parts of the body" [Lsl. 1979, 247] ||| WCh. *pačw- "to swell" [Stl.]: Daffo-Butura fos "geschwollen sein" [Jng. 1970, 214] | NBch. *p-č [GT]: Warji pəč- "to swell" [Skn.], Pa'a pɨčùù "to swell, puff up (as stomach after eating too many beans)" [MSkn. 1979, 200] = pu̱ču [Skn.], Diri fəču "to swell" [Skn.] (NBch.: Skn. 1977, 43; WCh.: Stl. 1987, 145, #9; 1996, 116) || CCh.: Balda mbèč [irreg. mb- < *p-] "enfler" [Trn. 1987, 55].

NB: It would be difficult to explain the Ar. and Eg. cognates from AA *p-č "to swell" [GT] as NBch. suggests. Note that AA *č → regularly Eg. s.

321. **AA *p-g** "far, long": EBrb.: Ghadames ṵ-fəġ "1. dépasser une limite, une mesure, 2. aller trop loin (ene verrou dans son logement)" [Lanfry 1973, 88, #382] ||| ECu. *fVg- "far" [Flm. 1969, 22, #11]: LECu.: PSom. *fog "far" [Ehret & Nuuh Ali 1984]: Somali fog ~ fug "1. Entfernung, 2. weit, fern" [Rn. 1902, 147] = fóg "far" [Abr. 1964, 80], Rendille fog-á "far" [Heine 1976, 215], Arbore feḳá ~ feḳ-í [irreg. -ḳ < *-g?] "far" [Hyw. 1984, 358], Dasenech (Geleba) fɨk "far, distant" [Flm./Dlg.] | Oromo fag-ō "far" [Gragg 1982, 139] = fag-oˀ "weit" [Sasse] | HECu.: Sidamo fag-o "far" [Hds. 1989, 362] = faf-ō [< *fag^w-] "lontano"

[Crl. 1938 II, 200] (ECu.: CR 1913, 421; Dlg. 1973, 320; Sasse 1975, 246) ||| SOm.: Ari feg-á "far" [Bnd. 1994, 149] ||| WCh.: Ngizim fák [irreg. -k < *-g?] "at a great distance (in time or space)" [Schuh 1981, 57].

322. **AA *p-g** "(to build a) wall": Eg. pḏ.wj (dual) [reg. < *pg] "Seitenwände (eines Gebäudes)" (XVIII. "old word", Wb I 569, 4) = "Seitenwände" (GHWb 300–301) ||| PCh. *pag- "to build wall" [GT]: WCh.: Angas pak "to put one thing on top of another", pak pang "to build up a stone wall" [Flk. 1915, 259] = pak (K) "to arrange stone (or other things) in form of a wall" [Jng. 1962 MS, 31] = pàk "to block, barricade" [ALC 1978, 50] || CCh.: Kotoko pfˀàgâ "encerclement" [Bouny 1978, 110].

NB: Cf. AA *p-Q̣ "to close" [GT] (below) and AA *b-K "wall" [GT] (presented in "*Lexica Afroasiatica* II", #278)?

323. **AA *p-g** "to sharpen": Eg. pḏj [reg. < *pgj] "wetzen (nur vom Scharfmachen des Feuersteinmessers)" (OK, Wb I 568, 14) = "to sharpen (a knife)" (FD 97) = "wetzen (das Feuersteinmesser" (GHWb 300) ||| NAgaw: Qwara fefagow "to polish" [Flad apud Rn. 1885, 57] || HECu.: Sidamo fāg- "to sharpen (wood, stake)" [Hds. 1989, 362: no etymology] ||| WCh.: Hausa fííḳè [irreg. -ḳ- < *-g-] "to sharpen sg. to a point", fììḳéé "filing one's teeth to a point" [Abr. 1962, 266].

NB: H.G. Mukarovsky (1982, 262) explained the Hausa word as a late loan from Lat. figere "etwas Spitzes einschlagen", which is clearly false.

324. **AA *p-k ~ *p-g** "1. to seize, take away, 2. plunder, rob": Akk. (aA-nA) puāgu G "gewaltsam wegnehmen" [AHW 874] ||| WBrb.: Zenaga f-k (impr. aᵘfuk) "faire une expédition de pillage, piller des biens", ĭufək "il a pillé, mis à sac" [Ncl. 1953, 197] || SBrb.: Hgr. feik "être dévalisé, dépouillé de" [Fcd. 1951–2, 311–2], EWlm. & Ayr fǎyku "être pillé, dévalisé" [PAM 73] ||| WCh.: Angas puk [-k reg. < *-g] "to take everything away, devastate, etc., in war (includes the burning and destruction of goods and houses)" [Flk. 1915, 267] = puk "to plunder" [ALC 1978, 53] || CCh.: Masa pēk-nà "saisir" [Ctc. 1978, 73] || ECh.: Tumak pə̀g "enlever, récolter" & pə̄g "1. enlever (plusieurs vêtements), 2. récolter (le coton, du miel . . .)" [Cpr. 1975, 91].

Lit.: the Akk.-Tumak etymology was first suggested in HSED #2021.

NB: Cf. AA *b-g ~ *b-ɡ "to rob" [GT] (discussed in part 1 of "*Lexica Afroasiatica*", #51).

325. **AA *p-k-r ~ *p-r-k** "tortoise": Common Brb. *i-fkər "tortoise" [GT]: hence Maltese fekruna "tortoise" & Ar. (Libya) fåkrū̀na,

fåkrôna "tartaruga" (Brb.: Aquilina 1975, 299, #13) ||| ECu.: (?) Yaaku parkílei, pl. parkileni (m) "turtle" [Heine 1975, 136].

326. **AA *[p]-K** "to fall": NOm.: Mao: Bambeshi φɛgá̲ ~ 'à̲ fɛká̲ "to fall" [Sbr.-Wdk. 1993, 15] ||| PCh. *p-k "to fall" [GT]: WCh.: Bade vg- "fallen" [Lks. 1974–75, 105], Ngizim vә̀gú "to fall down, descend down into, set (of sun)" [Schuh 1981, 165] = vә̀gә "to fall from high position" [JI] || CCh.: Bachama vùkɔ́, fùkɔ́ "to fall" [Skn.] = vúkó "to fall" [Crn. 1975, 463] || ECh.: Jegu pak- "herabfallen (Regen)" [Jng. 1961, 116] (Ch.: JI 1994 II, 130–131).

327. **AA *p-K** "to throw": NOm.: Janjero (Yemsa) foq- "scagliare (la lancia)" [Crl. 1938 III, 73] = fòkà "to throw spear" [Aklilu n.d.] | Mocha p̱òkkí-yé "to throw away" [Lsl. 1959, 45] = p·ok- "to throw away" [Flm.], Wombera hok-a [*pʰ-] "rubbish, garbage" [Flm.] (Kefoid: Flm. 1987, 157) ||| CCh. *p-k "to throw" [GT]: Gisiga mu-fko (nom. instr. prefix ma-) "Wurfmesser" [Lks. 1970, 131] | Lame pík "jeter (petites choses)" [Scn. 1982, 268], Zime-Dari pīk "jeter (petites choses)" [Cooper 1984, 21] || ECh.: Tumak pòg "abattre, faire tomber, terrasser (une personne . . .)" [Cpr. 1975, 91].

328. **AA *p-g** or ***p-ɡ** (perhaps ***pag-**?) "ring": SBrb.: Hgr. te-fagg-it, pl. ti-fugga "anneau de métal ou de cuir dur (servant à maintenir 2 choses l'une contre l'autre)" [Fcd. 1951–2, 309] || ECh.: Lele pàgà "anneaux de cheville (femme)" [WP 1982, 75].

329. **AA *p-Q** "to lead under control": perhaps Eg. pẖẖ "to control (?) (horses)" (XVIII., Urk. IV 1281, 13) = "dresser (des cheveux)" (AL 77.1481) = "Bändigung (Pferd), Schulung" (GHWb 292) ||| NBrb.: Iznasen e-tt-faq "convention, arrangement" [Rns. 1932, 284] ||| CCh.: Glavda poghw "to lead" [RB 1968] || ECh.: Somray pàgә̀ "élever (animaux)" [Jng. 1993 MS, 50].

330. **AA *p-Q** (either ***-q** or ***-ɡ**) "to close": Sem.: Akk. pḫʔ: (aAk) paḫāʔum, (spB) peḫû "verschließen, einschließen" [AHW 853] ||| CCh.: Daba pek "fermer" [Mch. 1966, 146] | Udlam (Uldeme) fәg "fermer" [Mch. 1953, 181].

331. **AA *p-q̇** (perhaps ***piq̣**) "to go round (or sim.)": NEg. pḫpḫ "Verbum: vom Gift, das in den Gliedern kreist" (NE, Wb I 544, 4) = "1. circuler (du venin dans le sang), 2. rôder (?)" (AL 77.1473 & 1481) = "kreisen (des Giftes im Körper)" (GHWb 291) ||| LECu.: OSomali *fīḳ- "kehren" [Lmb. 1986, 441] ||| WCh.: Ngizim vàikú "1. to encircle, surround (in the sense of actually forming a circle), 2. surround (be passively around), 3. go in circles", vàyák "detour, a wide circle made by a road or path" [Schuh 1981,

166–167] || ECh.: Kera ḅígí [< *piḳ-?] "umgeben (entourer)" [Ebert 1976, 34].

NB: Any connection to CCh.: Hitkala (Hide, Lamang) pγa "1. verser, renverser, 2. déshabiller" [Eguchi 1971, 224]?

332. **AA *p-ḫ-(ˁ)** "to put in": NEg. pḫʕ "to put in, place, install" (NE *hapax*, DLE I 180) ||| NAgaw *faγʷ- "to put in" [GT]: Falasha faw- [-w- reg. < *-γʷ-] "to bring in, put inside", Qemant faγ- "to marry" (NAgaw: Apl. 1996, 247) ||| WCh.: Bade fk- "eintreten" (intr. version of the same root?) [Lks. 1974–75, 101].

NB: The shift of meaning in Qemant is not unusual in Ethiopian language area, cf. e.g. ES: Amh. agäbba "1. to bring in, 2. marry" [Apl. 1977, .c.].

333. **AA *p-g-T** "trap (for catching bird or rat)": NBrb.: Qabyle f-ḫ-t: ti-feḫḫeṭ, pl. ti-feḫt-in "piège en fer (pour oiseau, souris)" [Dlt. 1982, 242] ||| ECh.: WDangla pùgùdùm "piège à trappe tombante, avec un van pour les oiseaux, avec une poterie pour les rats" [Fédry 1971, 69].

334. **AA *p-ḥ** (var. ***f-ḥ**) "1. breast, 2. milk": Sem.: ES: Amh. fäyä "to suck the breast, drink milk by suckling", Gafat fawatä "milk" [1945] = əfʷatä [1956], Gurage: Muher fʷat, Soddo äfat, Gogot äfʷat "milk" (ES: Lsl. 1945, 154; 1956, 172; 1979, 247: no Sem. etymology) ||| Eg. pḥ "Euter" (GR, Wb I 533, 9), cf. mnpḥ.t "Brust, Euter der Kuh" (NE, Wb II 79, 14–15) ||| SCu.: Ma'a ma-fwáha [irreg. f- < *p-] "fresh milk" [Ehret 1980, 151] ||| Ch. *p-y "1. breast, 2. milk" [GT]: WCh.: NBch. *-pi "milk, breast" [Skn.] = *(a)-pī [GT]: Warji pii-na, Kariya & Miya & Pa'a api, Diri yapu, Mburku pìì-hú, Tsagu ipən, Jimbin ifi [irreg. -f- < *-p-?] (NBch.: Skn. 1977, 14; Stl. 1987, 248, #2) || CCh.: Musgu fíau "milk" [Krs. in FMlr. 1886, 395] = fiáu "milk" [Rohlfs in Lks. 1941, 54] = fyaw ~ fya̱w "milk, breast" [Mch. 1950, 26, 38], Pus fiyaw "1. lait, 2. sein" [Trn. 1991, 88] | Lame pá "sein, mamelle" [Scn. 1976, 75; 1982, 267], Zime-Batna páʔ "breast" [Jng.] = pá "breast" [Scn.], Zime-Dari pāʔ "sein, mamelle" [Cooper 1984, 20], Masa pò "sein" [Ctc. 1983, 126] || ECh.: Sokoro paió "milk" [Lks. 1937, 37] (Ch.: IS 1966, 22, #2.14; JI 1994 II, 46–47).

NB: Areal parallels in further African language families: PCKhoisan *pī "breast", *pī "milk", *pī "to suck" [Baucom 1972, 19, 24, 27], Ubangi: PMundu-Ndogo *pī "to milk" [Saxon 1982, 77].

335. **AA *p-ḥ** "sheaf": Eg. pḥ.t "die Garbe des Korns" (OK, Wb I 533, 11) = "gerbe" (AL 78.1489) = "der Garbenhaufen (des Korns), Kornmiete" (GHWb 287) ||| NBrb.: Mgild a-ffa, pl. i-ff-an "stack of grain-sheaves" [Harries 1974, 222] | Iznasen & Rif & Senhazha ṯa-ffa, pl. ṯa-ffiw-in "meule de gerbes à dépiquer"

[Rns. 1932, 297] | Qabyle ta-ffa, pl. ta-ffw-in "tas de bois" [Dlt. 1982, 189] ||| WCh.: Tangale-Waja à bú̲w-à [irreg. b- < *p-] "to pile up, heap up (past)" [Kwh. 1990, 240] || CCh.: Margi pá "to pile up, fold" [Hfm. in RK 1973, 134, #123, #131, #135] | Bana pà "ramasser, rassembler" [Hfm. in Brt.-Jng. 1990, 86].

336. **AA *p-ḥ** "to strike, hit by shooting": SCu. *paḥ- [GT]: Dhl. paḥ- "to hit, strike" [Ehret 1980, 144] = paḥ- "to hit, shoot" [EEN 1989, 7] = paḥ- "to beat" [Tosco 1991, 145] ||| WCh.: Tangale pẹyị "to kick, shoot, sting" [Jng. 1991, 131] || CCh.: Bura pwa "to strike (in shooting)" [BED 1953, 177].

337. **AA *p-ḥ** "open(ing)": Eg. pḥ.w "ouvertures" (CT VI 94a, AL 78.1496) = "Öffnungen" (GHWb 289) ||| NBrb.: Iznasen t̲i-fi^{k}-t̲ [-^{k}- < *-y-] "entonnoir, orifice, trou" [Rns. 1932, 289] ||| CCh.: Margi pàhù̲ "open", pàpàhù̲ "open(ed)" [Hfm. in RK 1973, 135].

338. **AA *p-ḥ-s** (prob. ***piḥs-**) "hyena": NBrb. *i-f[ī]s "hyena" [GT]: Iznasen i-fis, pl. i-fis-a [Rns.], Tuzin i-fis, pl. i-fis-en [Rns.], Mzab i-fis, pl. i-fis-ən [Dlh. 1984, 54] (Zenet: Rns. 1932, 298) | Qabyle i-fis [Dlt. 1982, 233] | Nefusa fīs, pl. i-fīs-en [Bgn. 1942, 296] ||| SCu.: Ma'a mphiší "1. Hyäne, 2. Leopard", piši "Leopard" [Mnh. 1906, 314, 316].

339. **AA *p-ʕ ~ *b-ʕ** "man": Eg. pʕ.t "die Menschen" (OK, Wb I 503) = "patricians, mankind (the autochtonous inhabitants of Egypt from the earliest times)" (AEO I 98*, 110*; FD 88) = "mankind, men, people, citizens, human beings, patricians" (DLE I 171) ||| LECu.: Rendille ba (f) "Leute, Volk" [Schlee 1978, 110, #56] ||| WCh.: Kwami pée ~ fée "person" [Leger 1992, 25; 1993, 173], Kupto búu (m/f) "Mensch, Person, Mann" [Leger 1992, 18] || ECh.: Kabalay bă "man" [Cpr.], Lele bāy-ndí "man" [Garrigues] | Somray ʔàbé "man" [Jng.] (ECh.: JI 1994 II, 231).

340. **AA *p-[ʕ]** "to eat": SCu. *pa[H]- "to eat" [GT]: Qwd. p-is- (caus.) "to serve up portions of food" | Ma'a -pá "to eat (of people only)" (SCu.: Ehret 1980, 144) ||| WCh.: Pero púyù "to eat up" [Frj. 1985, 48], Kupto fòo "1. Nahrung, Essen, 2. Tuwo" [Leger 1992, 19] || CCh.: Mboku pa̲, Hurzo mpī "to eat" (CCh.: Mch. 1953, 177).

NB: For the *-[ʕ] in this PAA root cf. Eg. bʕ.t "aliments (?)" (CT, AL 78.1294) = "*Nahrung" (GHWb 248) < AA *b-ʕ "to eat" [GT] (derivatives presented in "*Lexica Afroasiatica I*", #93).

341. **AA *p-ʕ** "to suppurate": Eg. pʕpʕj.t "krankhafte Erscheinung an einer Geschwulst im Hals" (Med., Wb I 504, 9) ||| NBrb.: Qabyle fi "suppurer, jaillir" [Dlt. 1982, 188, 242] ||| WCh.: perhaps

Hausa fììyááyà ~ fííyààyéé "to be mildewed", fììyááyà (f) "mildew" [Abr. 1962, 272] | Waja puw- "to decay" [Kwh. 1990, 232] || CCh.: (?) Mada ífe "mûrir (abcès)" [Brt.-Brn. 2000, 104].

342. **AA *p-ʕ** ~ ***f-ʕ** "1. to swell, 2. grow, rise": SWSem. *ypʕ [prefix *y-?]: OSA (Sab.) yfʕ "to go up, approach (place/person), 2. rise up, oppose, 3. take a task in hand, 4. rise, spring (stream)" [SD 168] = "erhaben sein" [GB 310], Ar. yafaʕa "1. monter, 2. avoir grandi (jeune homme)" [BK II 1631] ||| NBrb.: Mzab ti-ffi-t, pl. ti-ffi-t-in "1. claque aux mains, ampoules, 2. excroissances de peau, filets de peau autour des ongles, envies" [Dlh. 1984, 46] || EBrb.: Ghadames i-ffu "il est enflé" [Lst. 1931, 232–233] ||| LECu.: Arbore foˀ- "to become full to overflowing (of a river)" [Hyw. 1984, 358] || SCu. *puʕ/ˀ- "to swell, rise" [Ehr.]: Qwd. puˀ-us- "to swell, rise", puˀ-us-iko "cow's hump" [Ehr. 1980 MS, 3] | Ma'a -puˀú "to rise (of sun)" [Ehr. 1980, 146] ||| WCh.: Goemay fuu "to be swollen" [Srl. 1937, 54] || CCh.: Margi fi "to swell" [Skn. 1977, 43] | Bana pə̀ "gonfler, enfler" [Brt.-Jng. 1990, 86].

NB1: Certain Chadic data speak for AA *f-ʕ (Goemay and Margi f- < AA *f-), while SCu. *p- speaks for PAA *p-.

NB2: F. Buhl (GB 310) combined SWSem. *ypʕ with Hbr. ypʕ hifil "Licht hervorbrechen lassen". Similarly, R.M. Voigt (1997, 174, fn. 18) took Ar.-OSA yfʕ from a basic meaning "sichtbar werden, leuchten". Unconvincing, since Hbr. ypʕ is cognate with Akk. wapû, which derives from a distinct AA root.

NB3: Ch. Ehret (1980, 339, #5) reconstructed PRift *piʕ- "to swell (of bud, fruit, flesh)" on the basis of SCu.: Irq. piʕ-amami "welt" | Qwd. piˀ-im- "to ripen", which is semantically unconvincing.

343. **AA *p-ʕ** (or ***p-ˀ**) "to defecate": SCu. *pU[ʕ]- "to defecate" [GT] = *pūˀ-/*pūˁ- "excrement" [Ehret]: Qwd. poˀo-tiko "mud" | Ma'a ki-pwúˀu "excrement", -pwúˀu "to defecate" (SCu.: Ehret 1980, 145) ||| SOm.: Hamer pio "feces, dung" [Bnd. 1994, 149] ||| CCh.: Nzangi poyəi "faeces" [Mch. in JI 1994 II, 129].

NB: Represents a var. of AA *b-ʕ "faeces, dirt" [GT]. For the AA etymology see also HSED #179 (CCh.-SCu.); Ehret 1995, 91, #39 (SCu.-Ngizim).

344. **AA *p-ʕ** (presumably ***puʕ-**) "to spit": Sem.: Ar. fwʕ, impf. yafūʕu "speien, vomieren" [Vcl.] ||| LEg. pʕ (or pʕj) "spucken" (GR, Edfu II 260, 12, Grdseloff, ArOr 20, 1952, 482–486) = "cracher" (Drioton, RdE 10, 1955, 91–92; AL 77.1381) = "speien" (Osing 1976, 195) ||| SCu. *paʕa- "spit, sputum" [Ehr.]: Ma'a ma-paˀé "spit, sputum" [Ehr. 1980, 143] ||| SOm.: Dime fuy- "1. to spit, 2. saliva" [Bnd. 1994, 159] ||| WCh.: Tangale puye "to expectorate, eject from mouth (anything unpleasant)" [Jng. 1991, 135]. Onom.

Lit.: Vcl. 1959, 73; 1959, 39; 1959, 29 (Eg.-Ar.); Takács 1998, 158, #4.3 (Eg.-Ar.-Ma'a); 2000, 75, #2.6 (Ma'a-Ch.-Ar.).

345. **AA *p-ʕ-m ~ *p-ʕ-n** (act. ***paʕam/n-**) "(sole of) foot, trace": Sem. *paʕam- "foot, leg" [GT] = *paʕm- "gamba" [Frz.] = *paʕm- ~ *paʕn- [SED]: Akk. (Bab.) pēmu ~ pēnu "Oberschenkel" [AHW 854] || Ug. pʕn "Fuß" [WUS #2243], Hbr. páʕam "2. Tritt, Schritt" [GB], Pun. pʕm pl. "Füße" [GB] || MSA *faʕm "foot, leg" [GT]: Hrs. fām, Jbl. faʕm, Mhr. fε̄m (MSA: Jns. 1977, 31; 1981, 51; 1987, 87; Sem.: GB 652; Frz. 1964, 49; SED 1, 183, #207) ||| SCu. *ṗaʕam- "sole of foot" [Ehr.] = *Pa[ʕ]am- (?) [GT]: Qwd. paˀam-uko "1. foot, 2. sole" [Ehr. 1980, 2] | Ma'a lu-bamé [Ehr.: b- < *ṗ-] "sole of foot" (SCu.: Ehr. 1980, 147).
Lit.: the Sem.-Qwadza etymology was first suggested by V.É. Orel & O.V. Stolbova (in HSED #828).

346. **AA *p-ʕ-l** "clever": presumably Eg. pʕn [provided < *pʕl] "klug" (PT, Wb I 504, 10–12) = "klug" (GHWb 274) ||| LECu.: Saho faʕal "(aus-, er)sinnen" [Rn. 1890, 128] ||| WCh.: Fyer ḅél [ḅ- from *p-H-] "klug werden" [Jng. 1970, 84] = ḅèl "cleverness" [Seibert 2000 MS, 2].

347. **AA *paˀr-** "locust" [GT]: SCu. *paˀar- [GT]: Qwd. paˀal-uko [-l- reg. < *-r-] "locust" [Ehret 1980, 143] ||| WCh.: Hausa fààráá, pl. fààríí "grasshopper, locust" [Abr. 1962, 251].

348. **AA *paˀl-** "wooden bed or stool": SCu. *paˀal- "wood" [GT]: Irq. páˀâlmo, pl. páˀâla "a wooden slat, placed across the bed as a mattress" [Wtl. 1953, 93] = paˀalmo "board, slat, lath" [Ehret] | Qwd. paˀal-uko "stool" [Ehr.] (SCu.: Ehret 1980, 143, #1) ||| WCh.: AS *p_2āl "bed made of palm or bamboo" [GT]: Angas pal "bed of strips of the tukurua palm, bore and threaded together (it serves as a solid mat to sleep on)" [Flk. 1915, 259], Sura pàal "Bett (aus Halmen)" [Jng. 1963, 78], Mupun pàal "bamboo bed" [Frj. 1991, 47], Kofyar pàal "wooden bed of palm ribs" [Ntg. 1967, 31], Goemay phaal "a bamboo stick" [Srl. 1937, 177] = pal "bamboo", pal-teŋ "flower (lit. 'bamboo-tree')" [Hlw. 2000 MS, 27] (AS: Stl. 1977, 156, #160).

349. **AA *p-H-n** (or ***p-y-n**?) "to disintegrate": Sem.: Akk. (jB, Nuzi) pênu "mahlen (?)" [AHW 854] (just a misreading of Akk. ṭênu?) ||| WCh.: AS *ṗīn ~ *ṗ^{y}e$_2$n, pl. *ṗ^{y}an "to break" [GT]: Angas piin "to break, divide", pyan "to split, tear apart", pyen "to break (of many things, as of eggs)", pyen "a crack (as in the drying of a mud house, etc.)" [Flk. 1915, 264, 270–271] = piin ~ pin (K), pl. pyan "to break (into pieces)" [Jng. 1962 MS, 33] = pin (sg.), pyan (pl.) "to smash" [ALC 1978, 52, 54] = pyin "to break in

pieces" [Krf.] = pīn, pl. pyān "to break (stone, dish, plate, not stick)" [Gochal 1994, 33, 62, 74], Sura piin (sg.), pyan (pl.) "schmelzen", piin gwak "spalten, aufteilen, zerreißen" [Jng. 1963, 79] = pìyìn "to break in pieces" [Krf.], Mupun pīin (sg.), pyān (pl.) "to shatter, break a round object" [Frj. 1991, 49, 51], Kofyar pin ~ piyán (sg.) "to break" [Ntg. 1967, 33], Chip piyən gwe "to break in pieces" [Krf.], Goemay p̣ian, pl. p̣iaram "1. to break, 2. pain" [Srl. 1937, 179] = piyan, pl. píyaram "brechen, zerbrechen" [Jng. 1962 MS, 9] = ni piyɛ̀n "to break in pieces" [Krf.] = pyan (sg.), pyaram (pl.) "to break e.g. a pot" [Hlw. 2000 MS, 28–29].

350. **AA *[p]-n** "to stretch out": Bed. fenin "(aus)strecken, dehnen" [Rn. 1895, 80, not in Rpr. 1928, 180 with this meaning] = f-n-n "sich ausstrecken", aor. afnā́n, pf. itfenin [Voigt 1987, 103] ||| CCh.: Mafa və́na [v- < *-VpV-] "2. (avec gé̩d 'tête') séparer, disperser, 5. (caus. vən-d-) disperser" [Brt.-Bléis 1990, 368] || ECh.: WDangla pààn̄yè, EDangla páanyé "s'étirer les bras" [Dbr.-Mnt. 1973, 237].

NB: Remotely related to AA *p-n "to scatter" [GT] (below)?

351. **AA *p-n** "1. to scatter, 2. sow": Eg. pnn "(ein Pulver) streuen" (Med., Wb I 510, 2) = "verser, saupoudrer, éparpiller" (NK, AL 77.1398, 78.1450) = "streuen (auf Augen)" (GHWb 277) ||| ECu. *finʕ/ḍ- [suffix *-ʕ/ḍ-?] "to scatter" [GT]: LECu. *finʕ- [GT]: Afar finʕa "scattering, wasting", finʕ-ite "to be sprinkled, scattered" [PH 1985, 103] | HECu. *finč̣- "to scatter (tr.)" [Hds.]: Hadiya fīnč̣-, Kambatta finč̣-, Sidamo finč̣- (HECu.: Hds. 1989, 129, 409) ||| WCh.: Tangale-Billiri pọọnẹ "to sow", pọọn "sowing" [Jng. 1991, 133], Kupto fóonì "Samenkorn" [Leger 1992, 19] || CCh.: Tera pòn "seed" [Nwm. 1964, 40, #168] | Bura piri [r reg. < *n] "pollen" [BED 1953, 173].

NB: A var. of AA *b-n "to scatter, sow" [GT] ("*Lexica Afroasiatica II*", #285).

352. **AA *p-n** "to roll": Eg. pn "zwirnen (o.ä.)" (CT III 133b, Osing 1976, 783–784, n. 980) = pnn (sic 2ae gem.) "retordre (le fil)" (AL 78.1451) = "drehen, zwirnen (Faden)" (GHWb 277–8) ||| WCh.: Hausa fúúnì "covering mouth and nose with ámááwàlíí of turban" [Abr. 1962, 273] = funi "wickeln" [Vcl.] || CCh.: Bura pira ~ pura [r reg. < *n] "to wrap around spirally", pirpirari "spiral, rolled up" [BED 1953, 172].

NB1: Nominal derivatives: Eg. pn "Name eines spindelartigen Gerätes" (OK, Wb I 508, 5) = "eine Art Spindel" (Vcl. 1934, 46) = "*Schiffchen (mit Schussfaden, spulenartig)" (GHWb 277), later attested as MEg. pnn "fuseau" (CT III 45a, AL

78.1452) = "Schiffchen" (GHWb 278) ||| ECh.: WDangla bɛ̀ɛ̀nɛ̀ [irreg. b- < *p-] "fuseau" [Fédry 1971, 83].
NB2: Remotely related with the underlying PAA root might be also:
1. AA *p-n-w "to turn (away from)" [GT]: Sem. *pnw "to turn" [GT]: Akk. panû (OAkk. panāʔum) "1. (aA) sich wenden an, 2. (bab.) voran-, vorausgehen" [AHW 822] || Ug. pn "1. sich wenden, 2. auf etwas merken" [WUS 256–7, #2230], Hbr. pny qal "wenden" [GB 645] ||| CCh.: Bura pura [r reg. < *n] "to stray, turn aside from the road" [BED 1953, 176] | (?) Mafa vəna "1. alterner, 2. faire à tour de rôle" [Brt.-Bléis 1990, 368]. Note that a direct equation of Sem. *pnw with Eg. pnʕ (which is so frequent in the literature) is mistaken. Cf. AA *p-n-ʕ [GT] below.
2. AA *p-n "twist with force" [GT]: Sem.: Hbr. *pnn "umbiegen, wenden", hence pinnā(h) "1. Mauerzacke, 2. Ecke (des Hauses)" [GB 650] ||| Bed. finin "to bend forcibly", finan "to bend oneself, carry oneself with chest thrust forward" [Rpr. 1928, 180] ||| ECh.: Mokilko (t)ìppìnyá "(com)presser, serrer, (se) traire, éssorer" [Jng. 1990, 113].

353. **AA *p-n-d** "to burn": NOm.: NMao pendí "pane, cotto sulla brace" [Grt. 1940, 358] = Hozo pēndi "ashes" [Flm. 1988, 38] ||| WCh.: Pero púndò "to cook" [Frj. 1985, 47] || ECh.: Gabri búndu "1. ashes, 2. coal" [Nct. in Lks. 1937, 87–88].

354. **AA *p-n-ṭ** "to fertilize by irrigiation": Sem.: Gurage *fnṭ "to spray water, sprinkle water, splash, bloom, blossom" [GT] (Grg.: Lsl. 1979, 237) ||| Eg. pnd "to make fruitful (?)" (Faulkner 1969, 142) = "benetzen, befruchten (o.ä.)" (Osing 1976, 303, note 1273 after Sethe) = "féconder, fertiliser" (AL 78.1457) = "befruchten, fruchtbar machen" (GHWb 278).

355. **AA *p-n-Z** "ashes": LECu.: PSomali *be(ze)mbez [irreg. *b-] "ashes" [Ehret & Nuuh Ali 1984, 218] ||| NOm.: (?) Sheko fɛmfus "burnt" [Flm. 1972 MS, 1] | PMao *pūz- [from *punz-?] "ashes": Bambeshi pù̱zè̱ [Sbr.-Wdk. 1993, 13], Diddesa pūse [Flm. 1990, 27] = EMao pūse ~ puse [Flm. 1988], Sezo pūsi ~ ṗūsi [Flm. 1988] (Mao gr.: Flm. 1988, 38) ||| CCh. *pinǯ- "ashes": Tera pəǯìt [Nwm. 1964, 40, #162], Pidlimdi pɨ̀zɨ̀di [Krf.], Ga'anda fiǯa [Krf.] | Bura pinǯu [BED 1953, 172] = pɪnǯu [Krf.], Ngwahyi pɪnǯu [Krf.], Margi pɪnsuḍu [Krf.] = ʔpǯínẑduuʔ [JI], Chibak pɪnzù [Krf.] = pinzu [Ibr.] = pənzu [IL] (CCh.: Krf. 1981, #128; Ibr. 1990, 88; JI 1994 II, 4).

356. **AA *p-n-g** "to kill": Eg. *png "to kill (?)" (GT) → Cpt.: (B) $p^{h}ōn^{e}ǯ$ "to overthrow, destroy" (CD 515a; CED 525) = "vernichten, zerstören" (KHW 149) ||| NOm.: Mao *pEng- [GT]: Hozo pēŋg- "to kill" [Flm.] = pɛŋgi [Bnd. 1994, 1158, #43], Sezo piyaŋ "to kill" [Flm.] (Mao: Flm. 1988, 38, #1) ||| CCh.: Mafa pə́ng- "égorger (plusieurs personnes, avec couteau)" [Brt.-Bléis 1990, 308].

357. **AA *p-n-ʕ** "to turn": Eg. pnʕ "umwenden, sich umwenden" (OK, Wb I 508–509) ||| PCh. *p-ŋ [reg. < *p-n-H] "to turn" [GT]: WCh.: Goemay phoeng "to turn, twist" [Srl. 1937, 178] = peŋ "to turn, spin, reel cotton into thread" [Hlw. 2000 MS, 28] || CCh.: PMasa *faŋ "1. to turn, 2. become" [GT]: Lame fáŋ "1. devenir, 2. grander, pousser, 3. transvaser" [Scn. 1982, 293], Zime-Dari fāŋ "1. devenir, 2. grandir, pousser, 3. transvaser, 4. revenir" [Cooper 1984, 6], Peve faŋ "to turn" [Venberg 1975, 37] = faŋ "to return" [Krf. 1981, #343].

NB: The Eg.-Ch. isogloss *p-n-ʕ [GT] is an extension of the biconsonantal PAA *p-n [GT] (above).

358. **AA *p-n-K** "to swim": NOm.: Oyda ṗīng- "to swim" [Bnd. 1971, 206] | Mao *pāŋg- "to swim" [GT]: Bambeshi pāŋg- [Flm.-Bnd.] = pāŋga [Mkr.], Diddesa pāŋg- [Flm.-Bnd.], Hozo pāŋg- [Bnd. 1990] = pāŋge [Bnd. 1971, 207] = pāŋgɛ [Bnd. 1994, 1159, #81], Sezo pāŋg- [Bnd.] = pʲá̲ŋá̲l pʲà̲ŋá̲ ~ φá̲ŋpȁŋá̲ [Sbr.-Wdk. 1994, 17] = payŋ- [Flm.] = paynɛ [Mkr.] (Mao: Mkr. 1981, 236; Flm. 1988, 38; Bnd. 1990, 603, #81) ||| WCh.: SBch. *pān(k)- "to swim" [GT]: Boghom pàanki, Jum pàanak, Mangas paan, Kir pane (SBch.: Csp. 1994, 71) || CCh.: Vulum fíní (adv. féng) [f < *b poss., vowel irreg.?] "flotter" [Trn. 1978, 293], Pus fini "flotter" [Trn. 1991, 88].

NB1: Weakening of PCh. *-nk > *ŋ in Musgu gr. as *-ny?

NB2: Cf. AA *b-n ~ *b-m "to swim" [GT] ("*Lexica Afroasiatica I*", #131).

359. **AA *p-r** "vessel": Sem.: Hbr. pārūr "Topf (irdener)" [GB 658] = "(≈ PAram. qidrā 'marmite')" [Rabin 1970, 295] ||| SBrb.: EWlm. ta-far-ē̄t "vieille vase de bois" [Ncl. 1957, 63] ||| SCu. *parer- [GT] = *pareh- "calabash sherd" [Ehr.]: Irq. parerehami (compound?) "calabash-sherd spoon" [Ehr.] | Ma'a mparé "half-calabash bowl" [Ehr.] (SCu.: Ehret 1980, 143) ||| WCh.: Tangale puuri "a large pot for keeping beer" [Jng. 1991, 135] | (?) Pa'a fə́rhà [f- irreg., -h- obscure] "small pot (for beer)" [MSkn. 1979, 176] || ECh.: Migama pòṛóòné "petite tasse en poterie pour servir la sauce" [JA 1992, 117] | Toram fooro (m) "small storage pot (for beer and in gen.)", fóoṛe (f) "water carrying pot" [Alio 1988 MS, 13, 24–25].

NB1: P. Haupt (1910, 714) combined Hbr. pārūr incorrectly with Akk. pūru ~ purru "(Stein)schale" [AHW 881] = "Vase, Urne, Büchse" [Haupt] || Hbr. pūrā "Kufe" [Haupt] (which are act. Sum. loans), suggesting a deverbal origin for these terms (Ar. fwr "sieden"). Cf. still Brockelmann 1932, 100, #1.

NB2: V.É. Orel & O.V. Stolbova (HSED #2010), in turn, mistakenly compared Hbr. pārūr & Tng. puuri to Akk. (a/jB) parūtu "eine Art von Köcher (?)" [AHW 837] and Eg. pr "box" (MK) (sic)!

360. **AA *p-r** "sort of bread": presumably Eg. p3.t (or p3w.t?) "Art Gebäck: Opferkuchen o.ä. als Speise der Götter und der seligen Toten" (OK, Wb I 495) = "cake or loaf (used in offerings)" (OK, FD 87) = "Opferkuchen, Opferbrot (viell. aus verschiedenen Sorten bestehend)" (GHWb 270) ||| SBrb.: Ayr u-f̱ər, EWlm. u-f̱f̱ər, pl. o-f̱r-an "pain en farine de jujubes" [PAM 64] ||| WCh.: Hausa fúr̃áá "balls of cooked flour for mixing up in milk" [Abr. 1962, 273].
NB1: E. Zyhlarz (1934–1935, 168) equated Eg. p3w.t with ONub. parou "bread".
NB2: C.T. Hodge (1966, 45, #28) erroneously combined Hausa fúr̃áá with Eg. p3q "a kind of cake".
NB3: For Eg. p3.t cf. alternatively LECu.: Saho fal-ṓ ~ fål-ṓ ~ fol-ṓ, pl. fṓlāl "1. Brot, 2. Nahrung, Speise" [Rn. 1890, 131], Saho-Assaorta fol-ȍ "pane" [CR 1913, 54], Afar fol-ṓ, pl. fṓlal (f) "1. Brot, 2. Speise" [Rn. 1886, 844].

361. **AA *p-r** "difficult": Eg. p3.wt [*pr.wt] "Last o.ä. (bildlich von einem Leiden)" (Med., Wb I 498, 4) = "burden (of illness)" (Pap. Ebers 19, 4, FD 87) = "Last (metaphorisch für Leiden)" (GHWb 271) ||| WCh.: Dera pə́rmá "difficult(y)" [Nwm. 1974, 132] || ECh.: EDangla péerì "lourd physiquement et moralement qui a du poids, pesant, dense, compact, épais, qui accable, érasant, pénible, désagréable" [Dbr.-Mnt. 1973, 242].
NB: Any connection to NBrb.: Mgild â-bṛ "to weigh" [Harries 1974, 227]?

362. **AA *p-r** "bad": Sem.: Gurage (from Oromo): Endegeny farä "sin" [Lsl. 1979, 240] ||| LEg. pr.t "Böses, Unreines (von dem man den Tempel säubert)" (LP-GR, Wb I 531, 7) ||| Bed. afrā̈y ~ afrä ~ áfre ~ áfri "schlecht, böse, häßlich, garstig" [Rn. 1895, 9] = afrɛi "bad", afrɛi "to be, go, turn bad" [Rpr. 1928, 144] || LECu.: Oromo farr-a "rancor", farr-ō "bad, mischivous" [Gragg 1982, 142] = far-a "sg. wrong" [Lsl.] | HECu.: Kambata farr- "to be bad", farr-a "bad" [Hds. 1989, 23, 315–316].
NB1: L. Reinisch (l.c.) connected the Bed. root to Ar. ʕafriyy- "vafer, malignus".
NB2: Ch. Ehret (1997 MS, 36, #1161) equated HECu. *far- "to be bad" (attested only in Kambata) with MEg. prj.t "crisis (?)" (FD) < AA *-far- "to be bad (off)", which is semantically less convincing.

363. **AA *[p]-r** "complete, full" [GT]: WBrb.: Zenaga tu-fuṛ-t "plein" [Ncl. 1953, 193] ||| WCh.: Hausa fúr "completely" [Abr. 1962, 273] || CCh. *p-r [GT]: Higi-Kamale pi̱rɛ "full" [Krf.] | Gude fyárə̀fyár "very full (of liquid)", fyárə́náʔ "full" [Hsk. 1983, 186] | Mada ppòr "complètement, définitivement" [Brt.-Brn. 2000, 228].
Lit.: the Zenaga-Higi parallel—to the best of my knowledge—was first suggested by the Russian linguists, e.g. A. Ju. Militarev (in Starostin etc. 1995 MS, 13). I only added the Chadic parallels.
NB: A. Ju. Militarev (1991, 261, #32.3) and V.É. Orel & O.V. Stolbova (1992, 200) supposed the Zenaga and the Higi root to be cognate with a certain Eg. ʕpr "full" (sic), which does not exist. False.

364. **AA *p-r** "1. to lie, 2. abuse": Sem.: Akk. (aA, jB) parû "etwa: Gemeines sagen" [AHW 837] || Ar. fry: farā I "6. inventer un conte, mensonge", IV "4. adresser à qqn. des reproches, blâmer qqn.", firy-at- "mensonge, imposture" [BK II 589] ||| Eg. p3.w [< *pr-w] "etwas das sich nicht zu sagen ziemt" (MK, Wb I 498, 3) = "falsehood (?), gossip (?)" (FD 87: stela of Usermontu, reign of Sesostris I, Sethe 1959, 79, l. 18) ||| NBrb.: Zayan s-fərr-ət "lügen" [Mlt. in SISAJa] ||| HECu.: Hadiya far- "to bewitch, deceive" [Sasse 1979, 18, 38] || SCu.: Qwd. pul-um- [l < *r] "to cheat" [Ehret 1980 MS, 3] ||| WCh.: Fyer fyéràt "Lüge" [Jng. 1970, 141] | Ngizim fə̀r̃fə̀r̃tú "to backbite, abuse someone when he is not present" [Schuh 1981, 56–57] || CCh.: Lame fár- "mentir (dans le sens de fabuler, raconter des bobards, enjoliver une histoire)" [Scn. 1982, 293] || ECh.: Lele pōryē ~ pōryī ~ pōyrē ~ pōyrī "1. mensonge, 2. se vanter" [WP 1982, 77].

Lit.: C.T. Hodge 1966, 26 (Eg.-Ar.); SISAJa I, #30 (Sem.-Brb.); Takács 2000, 76, #2.7 (Qwd.-WCh.-Lele-Eg.-Zayan-Ar.).

NB: Cf. also WCh.: Pero búrù "to deceive" [Frj. 1985, 23] || CCh.: Mwulyen mbwármà "Lüge" [Krf.], which seem to preserve a Ch. var. root *b-r.

NB2: Ch. Ehret (1980, 147) equated Qwd. pul-um- with Ma'a -bubúŝu "to startle, astonish" < SCu. *ṗuŝ-/*^{m}puŝ- "to fool (s'one)". False both phonologically and semantically.

NB3: The Russian linguists (SISAJa) equated the Sem.-Zayan isogloss with a number of semantically false parallels, too numerous to be listed here.

365. **AA *p-r** "worm": Sem.: Gurage: Chaha & Ezha & Endegeny & Gogot & Selti fərfər, Muher fərəffər "1. kind of worm, 2. eggs of the tick, disease that affects the food" (Grg.: Lsl.1979, 241: from Om.?) ||| Eg. p3wj.w [< *prwj.w] (worm det.) (pl.) "Bez. von Tieren die im Holz leben: Würmer (?), Ameisen (?)" (XVIII., Wb I 498, 5) = "Art Tiere (die im/am Holz leben): Würmer oder Ameisen" (GHWb 271) ||| NBrb.: Mzab ti-ffər-t ~ ti-frə-t "mites (insects)" [Dlh. 1984, 50] ||| NOm.: Mocha p̱irip̱iro "worm" [Lsl. 1959, 45], cf. Kafa hipper-ō [assim. < *p^{h}irper- < *p^{h}irp^{h}er-?] "verme" [Crl. 1951, 456] ||| WCh.: Hausa fùùráú (m) "larvae of digger-wasp" [Abr. 1962, 273] || ECh.: EDangla pír̃pìr̃ē (m) "le parasite du mil sorgho, 'coréides'" [Dbr.-Mnt. 1973, 245], Bidiya pirpìḍ "ver de terre" [AJ 1989, 108].

NB: C.T. Hodge (1961, 36) mistakenly identified the Mocha term with LEg. prpr "to jump about" (q.v.) and Hausa pílpílò "butterfly".

366. **AA *p-r ~ *p-ˀ-r** "to make a hole": Sem.: Ar. faˀara "creuser la terre" [BK II 529] = "to dig" [Lsl. 1987, 157] || ES: Gurage furä "hole in the wall or in the fence of the house, hole in a container", cf. Ennemor & Gyeto fəräfärä "to make a hole", Amh.

färäffärä "to make a hole", Tna. färfärä "to pierce, break" (ES: Lsl. 1979, 241) ||| Eg. pr.t "Öffnung des Höhle (?)" (NK, Wb I 532, 3) = "*Höhle (≈ qrr.t in anderen Versionen)" (GHWb 287) ||| NBrb.: Iznasen & Rif & Senhazha i-fri, pl. Iznasen & Tuzin & Uriaghel & Iboqqoyen i-fr-än, Ait Ammart i-farya-un, Senhazha i-frï-aw-en "caverne, terrier, trou" (NBrb.: Rns. 1932, 298) ||| SAgaw: Awngi fə́r "hole" [Apl. 1994 MS, 12.] || SCu.: perhaps Qwd. paˀal-uko [-l- reg. < *-r-] "hole, pit" [Ehret 1980 MS, 2] ||| NOm.: Kafa hir-o [h- reg. < *pʰ-] "Loch" [Lmb.], Shinasha-Bworo fur-à "Loch (zum Sehen)" [Lmb.] (NOm.: Lmb. 1993, 303) ||| WCh.: Kofyar pigar ~ piaŋar [< *piɣar] "to bore a hole" [Ntg. 1967, 32] | Ngizim pàarú "to make holes with planting hoe to drop seeds in" [Schuh 1981, 132] || CCh.: Gude fə́réeŋ "having one or more holes in it" [Hsk. 1983, 184].

NB1: Acc. to W. Leslau (1987, 157), the meaning of Ar. faˀara is secondary, being a denom. verbal root from Ar. faˀr- "rat, mouse", which would mean *"to dig as a rat does". Improbable. Leslau (1979, 241) explained ES *frfr "to make a hole" (or sim.) [GT] from Sem. *ḥpr (with met. in Ar.-ES *fḥr) "to dig", which is disproved by the clear distinction in Tigrinya between the reflexes with and without *-ḥ-, respectively, cf. Tna. färfärä "to pierce" vs. fäḥarä "to dig out".

NB2: Ch. Ehret (1995, 99, #61) equated the Ar.-Ngizim parallel with PCu. *paˀr-/ *baˀr- "field, cultivated ground" < AA *-pâˀr- "to dig up". False.

NB3: Awngi f- and Kefoid *pʰ- seem to point to AA *f- ≠ AA *p- (indicated by Eg. p- = Qwadza p-). Perhaps there were two distinct var. roots (AA *p-r vs. *f-r). Ehret (1987, #189) combined Awngi fər with ECu. *fur- "to open". An ultimate connection (at PAA level) to AA *p-r "to open" (or sim.) cannot be excluded.

NB4: Ehret (1980, 143, #7) derived Qwd. paˀal-uko from SCu. *paʕ- "to cut", which is certainly false. Qwadza paˀal- could be alternatively derived either from *paḳar-/*paḫar-/*paḥar-/*paʕar-.

367. **AA *p-r** "to rub" [GT]: SBrb. *f-r-(f-r) "to rub" [GT]: Hgr. fuffer-et [assim. < *furfər-ət] "frotter" [Fcd. 1951–2, 307], EWlm. f̱ur-ət "frotter avec qqch. de dur (une seule fois)", EWlm. & Ayr f̱ăr f̱ăr "1. se frotter les mains, 2. frotter le coude (chameau)" [PAM 64–65] ||| HECu.: Hadiya fur-š- (caus.) "to rub (off)" [Hds. 1989, 126, 278] ||| WCh. *pur- "to rub" [GT]: Goemay pûr "to rub" [Srl. 1937, 186] = phɪɪr [pʰʉ̄r] "to rub" [Hlw. 2000 MS, 29] | Tangale p̱uṟe̱ "to rub sg. in hands" [Jng. 1991, 135] | Ngizim fə̀rfə̀rú "to roll back and forth between hands" [Schuh 1981, 57] || CCh.: Mofu-Gudur -fáfər- "(se) gratter, frotter" [Brt. 1988, 113] || ECh.: Kera pápré "reiben (frotter), zerknittern (froisser)" [Ebert 1976, 87] (Ch.: Stl. 1996, 28 suggesting mistakenly Ch. *f- instead of *p-).

368. **AA *p-r** (var. ***p-ḥ-r**) "to run, flee": Eg. pḥrr [infix -ḥ-?] "laufen" (OK, Wb I 541, 2–13) = "to run" (XVIII., FD 92) = "to be swift, travel swiftly, run" (DLE I 180) ||| Bed. fōr "fliehen" [Rn. 1895, 81] = for "to flee" [Rpr. 1928, 181] ||| CCh.: Masa pīirà [-ii- < *-iH-?] "fuir (en courant)" [Ctc. 1978, 73] || ECh.: Mokilko pírpírá (f) "bon coureur" [Jng. 1990, 162].

369. **AA *p-r-s** "to penetrate": Sem.: (?) Ar. farasa V "1. plonger ses regards dans qqc., tenir ses yeux fixés sur qqc." [BK II 568] ||| NBrb.: Qabyle ffurres "présenter des perforations, des concavités sur sa surface" [Dlt. 1982, 228] ||| Bed. firis "to pierce, gap, break through" [Rpr. 1928, 181].

370. **AA *p-r-c** "vessel for water": Sem.: Akk. (aB) pirassum "ein Wassergefäß" [AHW 865] ||| Eg. p3z [-z < *-c reg.?] "Wassernapf, Wassernäpfchen des Schreibers" (MK, Wb I 499, 5) = "water-pot" (FD 88) = "le godet à eau du scribe" (CT, AL 77.1366) ||| ECh.: cf. WDangla pùrsìyè "calebasse grosse et épaisse utilisée pour la bière et pour l'eau" [Fédry 1971, 69].

371. **AA *p-r-ç ~ *p-r-ĉ̣** "to separate": Sem. *prṣ ~ *prḏ̣ "to break" [GT]: Akk. (bab., nA) parāṣu "durchbrechen" [AHW 832] || (?) Ug. prṣ "Öffnung (?)" [Ast. 1948, 216; WUS #2280], Hbr. prṣ qal "1. reißen, einen Riß hervorbringen, 2. (einen Schacht) brechen, 3. einreißen (Mauer), 4. in ein Haus einbrechen" [GB 661] || Ar. faraṣa "couper en deux" [BK II 572] = "to cut" [Lsl.] vs. faraḍa "tailler, faire des coches, des entailles dans un morceau de bois" [BK II 573] = "einschneiden, einen Einschnitt machen" [Barth apud GB] | MSA: Jbl. fɔ̃rɔ́ḏ̣ "to separate vertebrae from oa." [Jns. 1981, 59–60] || ES: Geez faraṣa "to break open, cut open, split" [Lsl. 1987, 167] ||| EBrb.: Ghadames e-frəḍ "ouvrir en deux (un fruit)" [Lanfry 1973, 96, #420] ||| WCh.: Hausa fàrḍáá "to hoe up (groundnuts)", fárḍà "to slit open front of animal", fárḍè "to slit up completely, hoe up all of" [Abr. 1962, 253] || CCh.: Mofu-Gudur pərḍaḍá ~ pərḍeḍé "(yeux) grand ouverts" [Brt. 1988, 219] || ECh.: Mokilko pôrḍyo "fissure, passage, espace étroit entre deux grosses pierres" [Jng. 1990, 161], Bidiya porḍòč "croquer (de la kola)", porḍòny "croquer" [AJ 1989, 108].

372. **AA *p-r-ḳ ~ *p-ḳ-r** "husk, shell": perhaps Eg. p3q.t [< *prḳ.t] "1. die Scherbe eines tönernen Topfes, 2. übertragen: als Bez. der Hirnschale des Menschen, 3. von der Schildkrötenschale" (Med., Westcar, Wb I 500, 1–3) = "1. shell (of turtle, skull) (Med.), 2. flake of stone (Westcar), 3. potsherd (Illahun, Ebers)" (FD 88) |||

SBrb.: EWlm. e-fărăγ, pl. a- & i-fărăγ-ăn "coquille" [PAM 66] ||| WCh.: Pero ṗékúrò "husk" [Frj. 1985, 44] || ECh.: Kera fékré "harte Schale (z.B. bei Nüssen)" [Ebert 1976, 45] | Sokoro fʋrkía "Rinde" [Lks. 1937, 33] | Mokilko pákìrtè "1. écorce, 2. ardoise (pour écrire), 3. morceau (poterie, calebasse)" [Jng. 1990, 160].

NB: Cp. also WCh.: Hausa ḅámḅáróókì "1. bark, 2. shell of egg, of groundnut, 3. scurf of scalp-disease, scab, bits of skin from desquamation" [Abr. 1962, 71] || CCh.: Mbara ḅólòkò "écorce" [TSL 1986, 257] < PCh. *ḅ-r-k from *b-r-ḳ (?).

373. **AA *p-r-K** "to squat": Eg. p3g "to squat (?)" (CT I 18a, FD 88) = "s'accroupir" (AL 78.1422) = "*knien" (GHWb 273) = "kauern" (Schenkel quoted by Hafemann, p.c. on 19 May 2000) ||| CCh.: Mafa fúrkw- "s'accroupir" [Brt.-Bléis 1990, 138], cf. perhaps also Gisiga hùrúk [hu- < *fu- not yet fully clear] "to squat" [Rsg. 1978, 334, #683].

374. **AA *p-r-ḳ ~ *p-r-Q** "to turn round": Sem.: Harari färäqa "to turn", Amh. färäqa "to turn" (ES: Lsl. 1963, 64) ||| Eg. pẖr [met. < *prẖ?] "umwenden, umdrehen" (PT, Wb I 544–7) ||| NBrb.: Mzab ə-frəγ "1. tourner, bifurquer, 2. être tordu, 3. (fig.) être mal venu, mal fait, défectueux" [Dlh. 1984, 52], Iznasen & Uriaghel & Senhazha e-fraγ "être courbe, tordu, sinueux" [Rns. 1932, 299] || EBrb.: Ghadames e-frəγ "être tordu" [Lanfry 1973, 98, #430] || SBrb.: Hgr. e-freγ "n'être pas droit (dévier de la ligne droite)" [Fcd. 1951–2, 355–6] ||| NOm.: Gimira pirik-o (?) "ritorna! (imprv.)" [CR 1925, 622] ||| CCh.: Mofu-Gudur -vərk- "(se) retourner, tourner" [Brt. 1988, 250], Mafa vərk- "retourner (un récipient)" [Brt.-Bléis 1990, 370] | Vulum f`r`k`: firkì "to turn upside down (renverser, retourner)" [Trn. 1978, 293; Brt. 1995, 213].

375. **AA *p-r-Q** "to scratch": Eg. p3ẖ [from *prẖ] "kratzen (in die Augen)" (PT 440, Wb I 498, 13) = "to scratch" (FD 87) ||| Ch. *p-r-Q "to scratch" [GT]: CCh.: Mada fròh fròh [-h < *-Q?] "se gratter" [Brt.-Brn. 2000, 105] || ECh. *p-r-k "to scratch" [GT]: Kera pírkí "kratzen" [Ebert 1976, 88] | Bidiya perékrèk "se gratter l'oreille (chien)" [AJ 1989, 107], WDangla pòrkè "égratigner" [Fédry 1971, 68].

NB1: An AA var. root *b-r-Q "to scratch" [GT] has been preserved in WCh.: Angas burk "to scratch, scratching" [ALC 1978, 5, not listed in Flk. 1915 & Jng. 1962 MS] | Tala birk "(finger)nail" [Csp. 1994, 27] || CCh.: Mbara mbròk "to scratch" [TSL 1986, 199, 256, 288], cf. perhaps also Vulum ŋùrkí [ŋ- < *mb-?] "égratigner" [TSL].

NB2: The third radical AA *p-r-q "to scratch" [GT] might be a root extension, cf. Ch. *p-r "to scratch" [GT]: CCh.: Mafa-Mada *fur "to scratch" [Rsg. 1978, 320, #610] || ECh.: Migama pòrrò "griffer", cf. pùrrùn "ongle, griffe" [JA 1992, 117].

Lit.: HSED #1988 (Eg.-Kera); Takács 1998, 159, #4.5 (Eg.-Kera); EEWC (Eg.-Ch.).

376. **AA *p-r-q** "to (split) open": MSA *frḫ: Jbl. férəḫ "(egg) to split open", fɔ́trəḫ "to open one's legs while lying down relaxing" [Jns. 1981, 62], Mhr. fərōḫ "(girl) to throw the legs wide apart in playing (which is punished by slap)" [Jns. 1987, 102] ||| perhaps Eg. pḫ3 [if met. < *p3ḫ = *prḫ] "spalten, öffnen" (MK, Wb I 542–3) ||| NBrb.: Shilh farkk "to separate" [Aplg. 1958, 52] | Qabyle fferk·ekk "1. se fendiller, 2. s'ouvrir, 3. se désagreger, tomber en miettes, 4. s'écailler (peinture)" [Dlt. 1982, 223] || EBrb.: Ghadames fərrək "séparer en deux" [Lanfry 1973] ||| WCh.: Ngizim pár̃ák "openness" [Schuh 1981, 132] || CCh.: Mofu-Gudur -vávə́rkw- "ouvrir (une fenêtre après la construction d'un mur)" [Brt. 1988, 251] | perhaps Logone paraka-ze "sich zerstreuen" [Lks. 1936, 115] || ECh.: Bidiya pírkàt "avoir les yeux écarquillés" [AJ 1989, 108].

377. **AA *p-r-[γ]** "to spit, vomit": Sem.: Akk. (jB) parû "(sich) erbrechen", (jB) parûtu ~ purâtu "Erbrochenes" [AHW 837, 880] ||| WCh.: Angas por "to spit, spit out" [Flk. 1915, 266] | Ngizim pùurú "to spray, spit out in spray" [Schuh 1981, 133] || CCh.: Mofu-Gudur -pápər- "projeter de l'eau avec la bouche (sur une plaie), vaporiser de l'eau (sur une natte)" [Brt. 1988, 218].

NB1: For the reconstruction of *-γ in this PAA root cf. the var. AA *b-r-γ "to spit" [GT] ("*Lexica Afroasiatica II*", #293).

NB2: The Sem. etymology of Akk. parû is obscure. F. Buhl (GB 660) suggests Sem. *prγ, cf. Ar. frγ "entleeren, (min) sich einer Sache entledigen, unbeschäftigt sein" [GB]. Cf. also MSA: Jbl. ṣə-fráγ "to be done, finished, empty" [Jns. 1981, 60], Mhr. fərōγ "to hatch (eggs, bird)", fátrəγ "to bloom", əftōrəγ "(gun) to fire, go off by itself" [Jns. 1987, 98] (doubtful). J. Huehnergard (1991, 694), in turn, compared it to ES *frh "to be afraid", which is semantically unconvincing.

NB3: O.V. Stolbova (1987, 146) mistakenly equated Angas par with Ngizim pàaḍú "to suck" [Schuh 1981, 131].

378. **AA *p-r-ʕ** "peak": SWSem.: OSA: Sab. frʕ "upper part, summit of building" [SD 46], Ar. farʕ- "sommet d'une branche d'arbre" [Lsl.] | MSA: Sqt. firfor "sommet" [Lsl. 1938, 342] ||| OEg. p3ʕr.t [< *prʕr.t] "subst. de sens inconnu, semble désigner 'une pointe (?)' (qui déchire le filet)" (*hapax*, CT VI 20k, AL 77.1415).

NB: The underlying Sem. verbal root is preserved in Ar. faraʕa "sorpassò, eccelse" [Frz.], SAr. frʕ "élevé, éminent" [Lsl.] | MSA: Mhr. frʕ: firā "(auf)steigen, hinaufklettern, aufgehen (Sonne)" [Jahn] = frā "to up up, ascent" [Jns. 1987, 97].

379. **AA *[p]-l** "full": Sem.: Gafat at-fälä "full" [Lsl. 1945, 154] ||| WCh.: Hausa fál "(chock-)full" [Abr. 1962, 246] || CCh.: Mafa pál "absolument (pas), (pas) de tout (placé devant une négation)" [Brt.-Bléis 1990, 306], Mada ppál "tout entier (mois, année, temps)" [Brt.-Brn. 2000, 226] | Musgu afalái "full" [Rohlfs in Lks. 1941,

cf. JI 1994 II, 157] || ECh.: Mokilko pèlèlé (adj.) "rempli, plein" [Jng. 1990, 161].

NB: W. Leslau (1945, 154) derived Gafat at-fälä from Sem. *mlʔ (phonologically improbable).

380. **AA *p-l** "1. up(per part), 2. sky" [GT]: NBrb.: Shilh flla- "over, in excess of" [Strm. 2000, 314] = a-fella "sur" [Jst. 1914, 117] | Mgild a-flla "1. place above, topside, 2. on top" [Harries 1974, 222] | Qabyle u-fella "au-dessus, en haut", fell- (prep.) "sur (etc.)" [Dlt. 1982, 217] || EBrb.: Siwa fəll "sur" [Lst. 1931, 298] || WBrb.: Zenaga a-fell "en haut" [Bst. 1909, 227] = a-fëlla "1. haut, 2. (le) dessus" [Ncl. 1953, 192] || SBrb.: Hgr. a-fella, pl. i-fellâ-t-en "haut (surface supérieure, dessus)", full (prep.) "(de) sur (etc.)" [Fcd. 1951–2, 318–9], EWlm.-Ayr a-fălla, pl. i-falla-t-ăn "haut(eur), surface ou partie supérieure", Ayr fel (prep.) "sur" [PAM 61] ||| NOm.: Gofa boll-a [irreg. b-] "1. cielo, 2. il di sopra, sopra" [Mrn. 1938, 139] || SOm.: Karo pol-a "sky" [Flm. apud Bnd. 1994, 158] ||| WCh.: Burma pɨlat "sky" [Krf. 1981, #116], Kir pɨlat "sky" [Csp. 1994, 65].

381. **AA *p-l** "sort of vessel": Sem.: Akk. (aB Susa) piltu "ein Gefäß (?)" [AHW 864] ||| NBrb.: perhaps Qabyle i-flu ~ i-flew, pl. i-felw-en "grande louche de bois", ti-flew-t, pl. ti-felw-in "louche" [Dlt. 1982, 208] ||| LECu.: Oromo fōll-ē "drinking cup" [Gragg 1982, 148] ||| WCh.: Bokkos pálán̰ "großer Bierbrautopf (mit Spitzboden)" [Jng. 1970, 145] || CCh.: Zime-Dari pēlé "marmite à terre cuite, sans colle" [Cooper 1984, 21] || ECh.: Sokoro fóliō "Kochtopf" [Lks.] = pólio "Trinkgefäß" [AF] (Ch.: Lks. 1937, 33, 38, 122).

NB: V.É. Orel & O.V. Stolbova (1989, 134) equated the Zime-Dari (quoted apud OS as Lame!) & Sokoro data with OEg. ʕpr.t "Art Krug" (OK, Wb I 181, 14), which is probably incorrect.

382. **AA *p-l** "lump, (small round) piece of sg.": perhaps Eg. pj.w (pl.) (grains det.), cf. pj.w nbs "Christusdornbeere" (GHWb 273) ||| NBrb.: Mzab a-fli, pl. i-fəly-an "1. miette, petit morceau, 2. grain concassé de blé, etc., brisure de grains" [Dlh. 1984, 49] || SBrb.: EWlm. te-fel, pl. ši-fel-en "1. pièce de métal, 2. pièce de monnaie" [PAM 60] ||| WCh.: Mupun píl "lump of food" [Frj. 1991, 49] || CCh.: Mofu-Gudur fafəla "1. boule (de mil, terre, tabac), 2. botte (de foin)" [Brt. 1988, 112] || ECh.: Somray pālā (m) "motte de terre", cf. pwʌ́lè ~ pólè (coll.) "tubercule (nom gén.)" [Jng. 1993 MS, 50, 52].

383. **AA *p-l** (act. ***pil-**) "to sweep": SCu.: Dhl. pēl-āð- "to sweep" [Ehr. 1980, 144, #12] ||| WCh.: Fyer fyâl ~ fyàl "1. reinigen, 2. reiben" [Jng. 1970, 141] = fyal "to sweep" [Magwa etc. 1985, 14].

384. **AA *p-l** "fresh, new" [GT]: Sem.: cf. perhaps Akk. papallu (j/spB) "Schößling, Zweig" [AHW 823] (unless it was a Sum. loan) (?) ||| Dem. ppj [reg. < *ppl] "kleiner, junger Vogel" (DG 131) → Cpt.: (S) papoi, (SA_2) papai (m) "junger Vogel, Küken, Huhn" (KHW 149) ||| NOm.: NMao pēll-i "vergine" [Grt. 1940, 358] ||| WCh.: AS *ṗal "fresh, unripe" [GT]: Angas pal "1. unripe, 2. fresh sprouts or buds" [Flk. 1915, 259], Kofyar pél "new, first" [Ntg. 1967, 32], Goemay ṗal "unripeness" [Srl. 1937, 172] | SBch. *p^y-l "new" [GT]: Guruntum pyàli [Csp.] = pyàalì [Jgr. 1989, 186], Tala pyaalii [Csp.] = pyaali [Smz.], Kir pyele [Csp.] = pyelè [Smz.], Laar pyella [Smz.], Mangas pyelà [Smz.] = pelàsà [Csp.], Soor (Zangwal) pyaalì [Smz.], Booluu pyaali [Smz.], Geji pyalì [Smz.], Zaranda pyààlè [Smz.], Zul pyel [Smz.], Barang & Dir pyèlì [Smz.], Buli pyel [Smz.], Zeem pyàlì [Smz.] (SBch.: Smz. 1978, 44, #96; Csp. 1994, 27, 60) || CCh.: Gude púl "very new" [Hsk. 1983, 260].

385. **AA *p-l** "to sprinkle": Sem.: Ug. pl "rieseln" [WUS #2219], Syr. pll "to sprinkle" [Lsl.] || Ar. fyl "vergießeln, rieseln" [WUS] || ES: Geez falfala "to gush out, spring forth, bubble up, break forth, burst out as a fountain, make gush, etc." [Lsl. 1987, 158] ||| SCu.: presumably Dhl. pill-ēð- "to shake water off the body (in manner of dog or duck)" [Ehret 1980, 144; EEN 1989, 7] ||| NOm.: Haruro (Kachama) pēl-uc [-ts] "to pour" [Sbr. 1994, 18] ||| ECh.: WDangla pâllè "asperger (équivalent profane de ḅâllè, réservé aux libations faites aux génies)" [Fédry 1971, 58].

386. **AA *p-l** "1. cloth, 2. loin-cloth": Sem.: (?) Akk. (Nuzi, Later Bab.) palīlu "ein Stoff (Nuzi: *palīlu* aus Leinen, Tücher *ana palīla*)" [AHW 816] ||| HECu.: Burji fel-o "loin-cloth" [Sasse 1982, 70] ||| (?) NOm. *afil-/*afill- "cloth" [GT]: Wolayta afil-ā "veste, toga" [Crl.], Gofa ˀapil-a "clothing" [Alm. 1993, 9] | Zayse afill-ā "veste, toga" [Crl.] | Chara afil-ā "veste, toga" [Crl.] = afl-a "clothes" [Bnd. 1974 MS, 9] (NOm.: Crl. 1938 III, 160, 198) ||| WCh.: Warji pààla "cloth (ткань)" [Stl., not found in Skn. 1977] | Guruntum pyelèe "loin-cloth" [Csp. 1994, 25].

387. **AA *p-l** "to open" [GT]: SBrb.: Hgr. felelli "être fixe et grand ouvert (un oeil)" [Fcd. 1951–2, 325] ||| HECu.: Qabenna fīll-oˀ

"to split, crack, tear" [Lsl. 1988, 188] ||| CCh. *p-l "to untie" [GT]: Higi pələntɛ̱ "to untie" [Hfm.] | Lamang (Htk.) pla "délier, dénouer" [Eguchi 1971, 224] | Glavda pəl "1. to untie, release, 2. change" [RB 1968] = "to untie" [Hfm.] | Mada pál "to loosen" [Rsg.], Gisiga pə̀lá "to loosen" [Rsg.], Zelgwa pla̩ "ouvrir" [Mch. 1953, 181] (MM: Rsg. 1978, 286, #439) | Kotoko fal "to untie" [Nwm.] | Musgu pela "to untie" [Hfm.], Pus pili "délier, détacher" [Trn. 1991, 111] (CCh.: Hfm. 1971, 11) || ECh.: WDangla pílè "ouvrir" [Fédry 1971, 64], EDangla pìlē "ouvrir, échancrer, entrouvrir, trouer, béer, bâiller" [Dbr.-Mnt. 1973, 244] = pìlē "aufmachen" [Ebs. 1979, 126; 1987, 75].

NB: Cf. AA *p-r ~ *p-ˀ-r "to open, untie" [GT].

388. **AA *p-l** "to plait, weave": NBrb. *f-l "to weave" [GT]: Mzab fəl "ourdir un tissage", ta-sə-flu-t, pl. ti-sə-fla "chaînette (en tissage), fil formant des boucles autours des fils de chaîne, tenants en boucles sur lesquels sont noués les bouts, extrémités des fils de chaîne" [Dlh. 1984, 48] | Senhazha fel "tisser" & Izn. a-s-fel "corde du turban", Iznasen & Senhazha i-filu, pl. i-fil-än "fil, fil de laine" (Zenet: Rns. 1932, 300) | Qabyle i-se-ffil, pl. i-se-ffil-en "fil de trame qui recouvre plusieurs fils de chaîne, soit exprès, pour un dessin ou une lisière, soit par erreur)" [Dlt. 1982, 203] ||| SCu.: Qwd. pal- [l < *r reg.] "to twist fibers into cord, rope" [Ehret 1980 MS, 2; 1980, 147] ||| WCh.: Tangale pe̩li̩ "to twist, plait (rope, of two threads), bind (hands), tie and take away, harden, stiffen" [Jng. 1991, 130].

389. **AA *p-l ~ *b-l** "sort of beer": Sem.: perhaps Akk. (jB) pillu ~ pilû "ein wilder Wein (?)" [AHW 863] (?) ||| Eg. pr.w "ein Getränk" (OK, V., Wb I 531, 9) = "une variété de bière" (AL 77.1451, 79.1014 after Roquet) = "*ein Bier" (GHWb 286) ||| WCh.: Kofyar pal "to wash brewing grain" [Ntg. 1967, 31], Goemay phal "beer on its second day of brewing" [Srl. 1937, 178] = n-tat pal "tuesday (lit. 'day of germinating')" [Hlw. 2000 MS, 34] || CCh.: Bura mbal [if l < *l] "beer" [BED 1953, 131] | Fali mbólo "beer" [Lks. 1937, 110] | Bata-Garwa bǎllé "beer" [Str. 1922–23, 127].

NB: W. von Soden (AHW l.c.) surmises in Akk. pillu a late Sum. loan (in LL, Akk. pillu = Sum. [giš]geštin-bíl). In the light of the AA data, an opposite way of borrowing (from the hypothetic OAkk. etymon of LBab. pillu) should not be excluded.

390. **AA *p-l ~ *p-H-l** "to knead": Eg. pjp ~ pjpj [reg. < *plp ~ *plpl] "(Lehm) kneten, (Ziegel) streichen" (NE, Wb I 502, 6–7) =

"mélanger, travailler (l'argile pour en faire des briques)" (AL 77.1378, 78.1430) ||| CCh.: Uldeme ḅāl-āy [ḅ- < *p-H-?] "pétrir, malaxer avec les pieds" [Clm. 1986, 131] | Lame púlú "malaxer la boule de mil avec de l'eau de façon à obtenir une bouillie qui tient lieu de sauce" [Scn. 1982, 273].

391. **AA *p-l-p** (or ***f-l-p**?) "to abuse, despise": Dem. prp [reg. < *plp] "verachten" (*hapax* in Pap. Rylands IX 20, 5, DG 136, 3) ||| WCh.: AS *fulup "to abuse" [GT]: Sura fulup "schmähen, fluchen", fúlúp "Fluch" [Jng. 1963, 65], Mupun fə̄lə̄p "to abuse" [Frj. 1991, 19], Goemay felep "to insult" [Srl. 1937, 48].

NB: Phonologically uncertain equation (AS *f- ≠ Eg. p-). The AS root seems to be a partial reduplication of *ful- (note that word-final *-f# becomes *-p in AS), which O.V. Stolbova (1987, 161) reconstructed as WCh. *ful- "ругать", quoting also Montol ful-ni [< *fulp-ni] "to curse", Gerka flup-ni "to curse", the source of which is Fitzpatrick. In any case, AA *p-l-p ~ *f-l-p might really be a partial reduplication of AA *f-l "to curse" [GT], cf. Sem.: ESA (Sab.) fˀl "to wish ill to so." [SD 43] | MSA: Jbl. fˀl: effél "to bring bad luck by cursing" [Jns. 1981, 50–51] ||| LECu. *fal- [GT]: PSam *fal "to curse" [Heine 1976, 214; 1978, 80/58]: Somali fal "to put a spell on" [Heine], Rendille fâl, pl. faló (m) "curse (n.)" [Heine 1976, 214] = fal- "to curse" [Sasse 1979, 18, 37–38] = a-fá̱la "ich verfluche", fá̱l-o "Fluch" [Schlee 1978, 120], Arbore fal- "to curse" [Hyw. 1984, 357] ||| WCh.: Bole full- "beschimpfen, verfluchen" [Lks. 1971, 135]. The Sem.-WCh. cognates was first proposed by the Russian linguists (HCVA 1, #67).

392. **AA *p-l-ˀ ~ *p-ˀ-l** "sort of rat, mouse": LECu.: Oromo fuliˀ-ō "rat" [Gragg 1982, 456] || SCu.: Qwd. pala-tiko [unless -l- < *-r-] "fat-mouse" [Ehret 1980 MS, 2] ||| ECh.: Bidiya paˀila "rat gris de dos et blanc de ventre, le plus petit de tous" [AJ 1989, 106].

NB: Cf. perhaps also ECh.: Mubi fólčók "rat géant (Xerus erythropus)" [Jng. 1990 MS, 15]. A compound?

393. **AA *p-l-ŝ** "to penetrate": Sem.: Akk. palāšu "durchbohren, einbrechen", cf. esp. pālišu "durchstoßend: (mA) ein Steinmeißel für den Wegebau" [AHW 815–816] || PBHbr. plš piel "to make a hole, pass through from end to end" [Lsl.], MHbr. plš piel "öffnen, durchbrechen" [Levy], Syr. plš "durchbohren" [GB] || (?) OSA flŝ-t-m "Ausgänge, Ausflüsse" [Müller] || ES: Amh. fälläsä "2. to dig the earth with the hands" [Lsl.] (Sem.: GB 644; Müller 1963, 313; Leslau 1969, 39; 1987, 160) ||| Eg. pjs [reg. < *pls] "(das Korn mit Eseln) einbringen" (MK, Wb I 502, 9, cf. already CT III 138b–139a in obscure context) = "to tread in (?) (seed)" (FD 88) = "faire pénétrer les semences" (Berlev 1978, 191, note 9) = "eintreten, eintrampeln (Saat in Boden), *einbringen" (GHWb 273) ||| NAgaw (from ES?): Qemant fäläs "creuser la terre de la corne" [CR 1912, 191], Xamir biles [irreg. b-] "ausbohren (mit dem

Bohrer)" [Rn. 1884, 348] || LECu.: Afar fuls-iyya "penetration" [PH 1985, 105].

394. **AA *p-l-k** "to turn around (?)": Sem. *plk "to be round (?)" [GT]: Akk. pilakku (a/jB, nA) "Stilett, Spindel", (a/jB, nA) pilku "Gebiet" [AHW 863] || Hbr. pélek "1. Kreis, Bezirk, 2. Spindel (urspr. wohl der Wirtel, Wertel)" [GB 643] || Ar. falak- "etwas rundes", falk-at- "Spindel" [GB] ||| perhaps Eg. p3ḏ [if < *plg with an irreg. *-g] (ball det.) "Kugel: 1. von der Kugel, zu der man Weihrauch formt, 2. ein Gebäck, runder Kuchen" (OK, Wb I 501, 9–13) ||| ECu.: Yaaku -pelk- (intr.), pelk-is- (tr.) "to shift" [Heine 1975, 133] (orig. *"to turn into" or sim.).

395. **AA *p-l-q̇** "1. to fear, 2. worship": Sem. *plḫ "to fear, respect" [GT]: Akk. palāḫu "1. sich fürchten, 2. verehren" [AHW 812] || BAram. plḥ peal "verehren, dienen (Gotte)", pālḥān- (st.cstr.) "Gottesdienst, Kultus" [GB 921] ||| SBrb.: Hgr. tă-felekḳ-at "lâcheté (manque complet de courage)", ă-felekḳa "homme/animal lâche" [Fcd. 1951, 327] ||| CCh.: Gude palhə "to worship aat pagan shrine or fetish" [Hsk. 1983, 257] || ECh.: Somray bə́lgə́ [irreg. b-] (f) "timidité" [Jng. 1993 MS, 5].

396. **AA *p-w-y** "to sit down": Sem.: Harari a-fōya "to be settled down" [Lsl. 1963, 66] ||| CCh.: Bura pwa "sich setzen, niederlassen" [Hfm. 1955, 134].

NB: Distantly related might be PCh. *p-y ~ *p-w "to lie down" [GT]: WCh.: NBch. *p̣iy- [*p̣- perhaps < *p^w-] "to lie down" [Skn.]: Warji p̣iy- ~ p̣iw-, Mburku & Tsagu p̣iy-, Kariya piy-, Miya piyo (NBch.: Skn. 1977, 29) || CCh.: Bura pi "liegen, die Nacht verbringen" [Hfm. in RK 1973, 95] = pi "1. to lie down, 2. recline", pupi "to lie down" [BED 1953, 171, 176], Chibak pí "sich hinlegen" [Hfm. 1955, 133] | Jimjimun pwáà-n "accoucher" [Hfm. apud Brt.-Jng. 1990, 88].

397. **AA *p-y ~ *p-w** "to go, pass": Eg. pj "sich begeben" (LP, Wb I 502, 3) ||| NBrb.: Shilh ffu "passer (le temps)" [Jst. 1914, 128] ||| Agaw *fi-t-/*fa-t- "to go" [GT] = *f-əT- "to go" [Apl.] = *f-ät- "to go" [Ehret 1987, #182]: e.g. Bilin. fə-r "to go" [Apl.], Xamir fi-t "fort-, weggehen" [Rn.] = fə-t [Apl.], Xamta fi-t "to go" [Apl.], Xamtanga fi-r "to go" [Apl.], Qwara fe ~ fē "(fort)gehen" [Rn.] = fe ~ fäy "to go" [Apl.], Falasha fia- "to go" [Apl.], Qemant fi "aller, sortir, partir, monter" [CR] = fäy ~ fəy "to go" [Apl.], Kailinya fäy "to go" [Apl.] | Awngi fa "andare, andarsene, passare" [CR] = fe-t- "to pass" [Apl.] (Agaw: CR 1905, 156–157; 1912, 190; Rn. 1884, 355; 1885, 55; 1887, 116; Dlg. 1966, 67; Apl. 1984, 39; 1986, 14; 1991 MS, 6; 1996, 15) ||| WCh. *pay-

[GT]: PRon *fay "to go" [GT]: Sha fay, Kulere fa (Ron: Jng. 1968, 8, #65; 1970, 284, 351) | Dera pú- "s'en aller" [Brt.-Jng.] (WCh.: Stl. 1987, 248) || CCh.: Masa pāì "se promener" [Ctc. 1978, 73] = pày [Ctc. 1983, 125], Lame pá "sortir" [Scn. 1982, 267].

NB1: A. B. Dolgopol'skij (1966, 67, fn. 8) considered the additional *-T- (hence -t-, -r-, -y-) in the Agaw reflexes as part of the root, which was later reinterpreted as the reflexive suffix. But the etymology proposed by Dolgopolsky is semantically unconvincing.

NB2: The same (?) Chadic root has been preserved in CCh. *v [< *-VpV- or *-VbV-?] "to go" [GT]: Gisiga vo, (Midjivin) vu [Lks. 1970, 137] | Musgoy va [Mch.], Daba va ~ vi [Pascal] = và [Lienhardt], Kola . . . va . . . [Schubert] | Vulum vì [Trn. 1978, 312; 1978, 91].

398. **AA *p-y** "log of wood": Eg. pjpj.t (wood det.) "der Kielbalken des Schiffes (?)" (NE, Wb I 502, 8) = "keel" (DLE I 170) = "la quille (?) d'un navire" (AL 79.0973) = "*Kiel" (GHWb 273) ||| Bed. fu (f) "die große Zeltstange in der Mitte des Zeltes" [Rn. 1895, 75] = fi (f), pl. fō-t "1. pole, prop, esp. of interior, 2. (*pars pro toto*) house, home" [Rpr. 1928, 177] ||| NOm.: Kafa pay-ō "canna con la quale si danno battiture" [Crl. 1951, 481] ||| CCh.: Hina pai "1. Baum, 2. Mattenstange" [Str.], cf. Daba paĭ ~ poĭ "Baum" [Str.] (CCh.: Str. 1922–1923, 129, 136).

Abbreviation of language names and related terms

(A): Ahmimic, AA: Afro-Asiatic (Afrasian, Semito-Hamitic), aAk: Old Akkadian, aAss.: Old Assyrian, aB: Old Babylonian, Akk.: Akkadian, Alg.: Alagwa, Amh.: Amhara, -ic, Ar.: Arabic, Aram.: Aramaic, AS: Angas-Sura, Ass.: Assyrian, (B) Bohairic, Bab.: Babylonian, BA(ram.): Biblical Aramaic, Bch.: Bauchi, Bed.: Bed'awye (Beja), BM: Bura-Margi, BN: Bade-Ngizim, Brb.: Berber (Libyo-Guanche), Brg.: Burunge, BT: Bole-Tangale, C: Central, Ch.: Chadic, Cpt.: Coptic, CT: Coffin Texts, Cu.: Cushitic, Dem.: Demotic, Dhl.: Dahalo, E: East, Ebl.: Eblaite, Eg.: Egyptian, ES: Ethio-Semitic, ESA: Epigraphic South Arabian, Eth.: Ethiopian, Eth.-Sem.: Ethio-Semitic, (F): Fayyumic, Gdm.: Ghadames, Gmy.: Goemay, GR: Ptolemaic and Roman period, Grg.: Gurage, Grw.: Gorowa, H: Highland (in Cushitic), Hbr.: Hebrew, Hgr.: Ahaggar, Hrs.: Harsusi (in MSA), IE: Indo-European, Irq.: Iraqw, irreg.: irregular, Izn.: Iznasen, JA(ram.): Jewish or Judeo-Aramaic, jB: jungbabylonisch, Jbl.: Jibbali, Kfy.: Kofyar, KK: Kera-Kwang group, L: Late, L: Low(land), lit.: literature, Lit.: literary texts, LL: lexical lists, LP: Late Period, M: Middle, Mag.: magical texts, mA: Middle Assyrian, mB: Middle Babylonian, Math.: mathematical papyri, Med.: medical texts, MK: Middle Kingdom, MM: Mafa-Mada group, Mnt.: Montol, Mpn.: Mupun, MSA: Modern South Arabian, Msr.: Mushere, Mzg.: Tamazight (Beraber), N: New, N: North, nA: New Assyrian, nB: New Babylonian, NC: Niger-Congo, NE(g.): New Egyptian, Nil.: Nilotic, NK: New Kingdom, NS: Nilo-Saharan, Nslm.: Taneslemt, O: Old, OInd.: Old Indic (Sanskrit), OK: Old Kingdom, Om.: Omotic, OSA: Old South Arabian, OT: Old Testament, P: Proto-, PB: Post-Biblical, PT: Pyramid Texts, Qwd.: Qwadza, reg.: regular, S: South, (S): Sahidic, Sab.: Sabaean, Sem.: Semitic, spB: Late Babylonian, Sqt.: Soqotri, Syr.: Syriac, TA(ram).: Aramaic of Talmud, Tna.: Tigrinya, Ug.: Ugaritic, W: West, Wlm.: Tawllemmed.

Abbreviations of author names

Abr.: Abraham, AF: Adolf Friedrich, AJ: Alio & Jungraithmayr, Alm.: Alema-yehu, AMS: Amborn & Minker & Sasse, Apl.: Appleyard, Aplg.: Applegate, Ast.: Aistleitner, Bgn.: Beguinot, BK: Bieberstein & Kazimirski, Bnd.: Bender, Brk.: Brockelmann, Brn.: Brunet, Brt.: Barreteau, Bst.: Basset, Clm.: Colombel, Cpr.: Caprile, CR: Conti Rossini, Crl.: Cerulli, Crn.: Carnochan, Csp.: Cosper, Ctc.: Caïtucoli, Dbr.: Djibrine, Dlg.: Dolgopolsky, Dlh.: Delheure, Dlt.: Dallet, Ebs.: Ebobisse, EEN: Ehret & Elderkin & Nurse, Ehr.: Ehret, Fcd.: Foucauld, Flk.: Foulkes, Flm.: Fleming, FMlr.: F. Müller, Frj.: Frajzyngier, Frz.: Fronzaroli, GB: Gesenius & Buhl, Grb.: Greenberg, Grt.: Grottanelli, GT: Takács, Hds.: Hudson, Hfm.: Hoffmann, Hlw.: Hellwig, Hnrg.: Huehnergard, Hsk.: Hoskison, Hyw.: Hayward, Ibr.: Ibriszimow, IL: Institute of Linguistics, IS: Illič-Svityč, JA: Jungraithmayr & Adams, Jgr.: Jaggar, JI: Jungraithmayr & Ibriszimow, Jng.: Jungraithmayr, Jns.: Johnstone, JS: Jungraithmayr & Shimizu, Jst.: Justinard, Krf.: Kraft, Kwh.: Kleinewillinghöfer, Lks.: Lukas, Lmb.: Lamberti, Lnf.: Lanfry, Lsl.: Leslau, Lst.: Laoust, Mch.: Mouchet, Mkr.: Mukarovsky, Mnh.: Meinhof, Mlt.: Militarev, Mnt.: Montgolfier, Mrn.: Moreno, MSkn.: M. Skinner, Ncl.: Nicolas, Nct.: Nachtigal, Nhl.: Nehlil, Ntg.: Netting, Nwm.: Newman, OS: Orel & Stolbova, PAM: Prasse & Alojaly & Mohamed, PH: Parker & Hayward, Pnc.: Penchoen, RB: Rapp & Benzig, RK: Reutt & Kogan, Rn.: Reinisch, Rns.: Renisio, Rpr.: Roper, Rsg.: Rossing, Sbr.: Siebert, Scn.: Sachnine, Skn.: N. Skinner,

Smz.: Shimizu, Srl.: Sirlinger, Ss.: Sasse, Stl.: Stolbova, Str.: Strümpell, Strm.: Stroomer, Sts.: Starostin, Trn.: Tourneux, TSL: Tourneux & Seignobos & Lafarge, Vcl.: Vycichl, Wdk.: Wedekind, WP: Weibegué & Palayer, Wtl.: Whiteley, Zbr.: Zaborski, Zhl.: Zyhlarz.

Bibliography

Abraham, R.C.: Dictionary of the Hausa Language.[2] London, 1962., University of London Press.

——: Somali-English Dictionary.[2] London, 1964., University of London Press Ltd.

AEO I–II = Gardiner, A.H.: Ancient Egyptian Onomastica. I–II. Oxford, 1947., Clarendon Press.

AHW = Soden, W. von: Akkadisches Handwörterbuch. I–III. Wiesbaden, 1965–1981., Otto Harrassowitz.

Aistleitner, J.: Untersuchungen zum Mitlautbestand des Ugaritisch-Semitischen.= Löwinger, S. & Somogyi, J. (eds.): Ignace Goldziher Memorial Volume. Part I. Budapest, 1948., Globus. Pp. 209–225.

AL I = Meeks, D.: Année lexicographique. Égypte ancienne. Tome 1 (1977). 2ème édition. Paris, 1998., Cybele.

AL II = Meeks, D.: Année lexicographique. Égypte ancienne. Tome 2 (1978). 2ème édition. Paris, 1998., Cybele.

AL III = Meeks, D.: Année lexicographique. Égypte ancienne. Tome 3 (1979). 2ème édition. Paris, 1998., Cybele.

ALC 1978 = Angas Language Committee (in Cooperation with Nigeria Bible Translation Trust): Shək nkarŋ kè shəktok mwa nḍən Ngas. Ngas-Hausa-English Dictionary with Appendix Showing Some Features of Ngas Grammar. Jos, Nigeria, 1978., Nigeria Bible Translation Trust.

Alio, Kh.: Allgemeine Kulturwortliste vom Toram. MS. Frankfurt a/M, 28 August 1988. 32 p.

Alio, Kh. & Jungraithmayr, H.: Lexique bidiya. Frankfurt am Main, 1989., Vittorio Klostermann.

Alemayehu, A.: Ometo Dialect Survey—A Pilot Survey Report.= Survey of Little-Known Languages of Ethiopia (S.L.L.E.) Reports 4 (1993), 1–10.

AMS = Amborn, H. & Minker, G. & Sasse, H.-J.: Das Dullay. Materialen zu einer ostkuschitischen Sprachgruppe. Berlin, 1980., Reimer Verlag.

Applegate, J.R.: An Outline of the Structure of Shilḥa. New York, 1958., American Council of Learned Societies.

Appleyard, D.: The Internal Classification of the Agaw Languages. A Comparative and Historical Phonology.= Bynon, J. (ed.): Current Progress in Afro-Asiatic Linguistics. Amsterdam, Philadelphia, 1984., John Benjamins. Pp. 33–67.

——: The Radical Extension System of the Verb in Agaw.= Goldenberg, G. (ed.): Ethiopian Studies. Proceedings of the Sixth International Conference, Tel-Aviv, 14–17 April 1980. Rotterdam, Boston, 1986., A.A. Balkema. Pp. 1–23.

——: A Grammatical Sketch of Khamtanga—I.= Bulletin of the School of Oriental and African Studies 50 (1987), 241–266.

——: A Grammatical Sketch of Khamtanga—II.= Bulletin of the School of Oriental and African Studies 50 (1987), 470–507.

——: Agaw and Omotic Links. The Evidence of the Lexicon. MS. Paper presented at the 2nd International Symposium on Cushitic and Omotic Languages, Torino, November 1989. Proceedings forthcoming.

——: Agaw Vocabulary Comparative Notes. MS. London, 1989. 24 p.
——: A Comparative Agaw Wordlist. MS. London, 1991. 13 p.
——: Preparing a Comparative Dictionary of Agaw. MS. Paper presented at the III. Kuschitisten- und Omotistenkongress, Berlin, March 1994. 4 p.
——: English-Awngi & Awngi-English Wordlists. Drawn from Hetzron, "The Verbal System of Southern Agaw", 1969, and Hetzron, "The Nominal System of Awngi (Southern Agaw)", BSOAS, 1978, together with additional material collected by D.A. in 1987–1991. MS. London, 1994. 16 p.
——: The Position of Agaw within Cushitic.= Zemánek, P. (ed.): Studies in Near Eastern Languages and Literatures. Memorial Volume for Karel Petráček. Praha, 1996., Academy of Sciences of the Czech Republic, Oriental Institute. Pp. 1–14.
——: Preparing a Comparative Agaw Dictionary.= Griefenow-Mewis, C. & Voigt, R. (eds.): Cushitic and Omotic Languages. Proceedings of the Third International Symposium. Berlin, March 1994. Köln, 1996., Rüdiger Köppe Verlag. Pp. 185–200.
Aquilina, J.: The Berber Element in Maltese.= Bynon, J. & Bynon, Th. (eds.): Hamito-Semitica. The Hague, 1975., Mouton. Pp. 297–313.
ArOr = Archív Orientální (Praha).
Baranov: Arabsko-russkij slovar'. Moskva, 1976., Nauka.
Barreteau, D.: Aspects de la morphologie nominale du mofu-gudur.= Caprile, J.-P. & Jungraithmayr, H. (eds.): Préalables à la reconstruction du proto-tchadique. Paris, 1978., SELAF. Pp. 95–113.
——: Structure du lexème verbal en mofu-gudur.= Caprile, J.-P. & Jungraithmayr, H. (eds.): Préalables à la reconstruction du proto-tchadique. Paris, 1978., SELAF. Pp. 115–142.
——: Description du mofu-gudur. Langue de la famille tchadique parlée au Cameroun. Livre II. Lexique. Paris, 1988., Éditions de l'ORSTOM.
——: Vowel and Tonal Variations within the Consonantal Framework of the Verbal System in Central Chadic Languages.= Ibriszimow, D. & Leger, R. (eds.): Studia Chadica et Hamitosemitica. Köln, 1995., Rüdiger Köppe Verlag. Pp. 197–228.
Barreteau, D. & Bléis, Y.: Lexique mafa. Langue de la famille tchadique parlée au Cameroun. Paris, 1990., ORSTOM, Librairie Orientaliste Paul Geuthner.
Barreteau, D. & Jungraithmayr, H.: Les verbes monoradicaux dans les langues tchadiques.= Jungraithmayr, H. & Tourneux, H. (eds.): Études tchadiques. Verbes monoradicaux suivis d'une note sur la negation en haoussa. Actes de la XIIème réunion de Groupe d'Études Tchadiques LACITO-CNRS-PARIS. Paris, 1990., Librairie Orientaliste Paul Geuthner. Pp. 37–214.
Barreteau, D. & Brunet, A.: Dictionnaire mada. Berlin, 2000., Dietrich Reimer Verlag.
Basset, R.: Mission au Sénégal. Tome I. Étude sur le dialecte zenaga. Paris, 1909., Ernest Leroux.
Baucom, K.L.: Proto-Central-Khoisan.= Third Annual Conference on African Linguistics, 7–8 April 1972. Bloomington, 1972., Indiana University. Pp. 3–37.
BED = Anonymous: Bura-English Dictionary. (Place unknown), 1953., (publisher unnamed). Master copy in the library of the Seminar für Afrikanische Sprachen und Kulturen der Universität Hamburg (inv. no.: 15 748 / JT 1526).
Beguinot, F.: Il berbero Nefûsi di Fassâṭo. Roma, 1942., Istituto per l'Oriente.
Bender, M.L.: The Languages of Ethiopia. A New Lexicostatistic Classification and Some Problems of Diffusion.= Anthropological Linguistics 13/5 (1971), 165–288.
——: Wordlist of Chara. MS. Carbondale, 1974.
——: The Limits of Omotic.= Hayward, R.J. (ed.): Omotic Language Studies. London, 1990., SOAS. Pp. 584–616.
——: Aroid (South Omotic) Lexicon.= Afrikanistische Arbeitspapiere 38 (1994), 133–162.
——: The Mystery Languages of Ethiopia.= Marcus, H. (ed.): New Trends in Ethiopian Studies. Vol. 1. Lawrenceville, 1994., Red Sea Press. Pp. 1153–1174.

Berlev, O.: Obščestvennye otnošenija v Egipte v épohu Srednego Carstva. Moskva, 1978.
Bieberstein Kazimirski, A. de: Dictionnaire arabe-français. I–II. Paris, 1860., Maisonneuve et Cie.
Bouny, P.: La formation du pluriel des nominaux en kotoko.= Caprile, J.-P. & Jungraithmayr, H. (eds.): Préalables à la reconstruction du proto-tchadique. Paris, 1978., SELAF. Pp. 51–65.
Brockelmann, C.: Ägyptisch-semitische Etymologien.= Zeitschrift für Semitistik 8 (1932), 97–117.
Caïtucoli, C.: Schèmes tonals et morphologie du verbe en masa.= Caprile, J.-P. & Jungraithmayr, H. (eds.): Préalables à la reconstruction du proto-tchadique. Paris, 1978., SELAF. Pp. 67–87.
——: Lexique masa. Paris, 1983., Agence de Coopération Culturelle et Technique.
Caprile, J.-P.: Lexique tumak-français (Tchad). Berlin, 1975., Verlag von Dietrich Reimer.
Carnochan, J.: Bachama and Chadic.= Bynon, J.; Bynon, Th. (eds.): Hamito-Semitica. The Hague, 1975., Mouton. Pp. 459–468.
CD = Crum, W.E.: A Coptic Dictionary. Oxford, 1939., Oxford, 1939., Oxford University Press.
CED = Černý, J.: Coptic Etymological Dictionary. London, Cambridge, 1976., Cambridge University Press.
Cerulli, E.: Studi etiopici. II. La lingua e la storia dei Sidamo. Roma, 1938., Istituto per l'Oriente.
——: Studi etiopici. III. Il linguaggio dei Giangerò ed alcune lingue Sidama dell'Omo (Basketo, Ciara, Zaissè). Roma, 1938., Istituto per l'Oriente.
——: Studi etiopici. IV. La lingua caffina. Roma, 1951., Istituto per l'Oriente.
Cohen, M.: Essai comparatif sur le vocabulaire et la phonétique du chamito-sémitique. Paris, 1947., Librairie Ancienne Honore Champion.
Colombel, V. de: Phonologie quantitative et synthématique. Propositions méthodologiques et théoriques avec application à l'ouldémé (langue tchadique du Nord-Cameroun). Paris, 1986., SELAF.
Conti Rossini, C.: Note sugli agau. 1. Appunti sulla lingua khamta dell'Averghellé.= Giornale della Società Asiatica Italiana 17/2a (1905), 183–242.
——: Note sugli agau. 2. Appunti sulla lingua Awiyā del Danghelà.= Giornale della Società Asiatica Italiana 18 (1905), 103–194.
——: La langue des Kemant en Abyssinie. Wien, 1912., Alfred Hölder.
——: Schizzo del dialetto saho dell'alta Assaorta in Eritrea. Roma, 1913., Tipografia della R. Accademia dei Lincei.
——: Studi su populazioni dell'Etiopia.= Rivista degli Studi Orientali 6 (1913), 365–426.
——: Sui linguaggi dei Naa e dei Ghimirra (Sce) nell'Etiopia Meridionale.= Rendiconti della Reale Accademia dei Lincei, Classe di Scienze morali, storiche e filologiche, ser. VI, vol. 1 (1925), 512–636.
——: Contributi per la conoscenza della lingua Haruro (Isole del Lago Margherita).= Rendiconti della Reale Accademia Nazionale dei Lincei, classe di scienze morali, storiche e filologiche, ser. VI, vol. XII, fasc. 7–10 (1937), 621–679.
Cooper, K.N.: Lexique zime-français. Vūn tàrí. Sarh (Tchad), 1984., Centre d'Études Linguistiques.
Cosper, R.: South Bauchi Lexicon. A Wordlist of Nine South Bauchi (Chadic) Languages and Dialects. Halifax, 1994., The Author (Saint Mary's University).
Dallet, J.-M.: Dictionnaire qabyle-français. Parler des At Mangellat (Algerie). Paris, 1982., SELAF (Société d'études linguistiques et anthropologiques de France).
Delheure, J.: Dictionnaire mozabite-français. Paris, 1984. Société d'Études Linguistiques et Anthropologique de France (SELAF).

DG = Erichsen, W.: Demotisches Glossar. Koppenhagen, 1954., Ejnar Munksgaard.
Djibrine, B.A.Z. & Montgolfier, P. de (etc.): Vocabulaire dangaléat. Kawo daŋla. (Place not indicated), around 1973., (publisher not indicated).
DLE = Lesko, L.H.: A Dictionary of Late Egyptian. Volume I, II, III, IV. Berkeley, 1982., 1984., 1987., 1989. B.C. Scribe Publications.
Dolgopol'skij, A. B.: Materialy po sravnitel'no-istoričeskoj fonetike kušitskih jazykov. Gubnye i dental'nye smyčnye v načal'nom položenii.= Uspenskij, B.A. (ed.): Jazyki Afriki. Voprosy struktury, istorii i tipologii. Moskva, 1966., Nauka. Pp. 35–88.
——: Sravnitel'no-istoričeskaja fonetika kušitskih jazykov. Moskva, 1973., Nauka.
——: From Proto-Semitic to Hebrew: Phonology. Etymological Approach in a Hamito-Semitic Perspective. MS. Haifa, 1992. 298 p. Forthcoming.
Ebert, K.H.: Sprache und Tradition der Kera (Tschad). Teil II. Berlin, 1976., Dietrich Reimer.
Ebobisse, C.: Die Morphologie des Verbs im Ost-Dangaleat (Guera, Tschad). Berlin, 1979., Dietrich Reimer Verlag.
——: Les verbaux du dangaléat de l'est (Guera, Tchad). Lexiques français-dangaléat et allemand-dangaléat. Berlin, 1987., Dietrich Reimer Verlag.
——: Die Morphologie des Verbs im Ost-Dangaleat (Guera, Tschad). Berlin, 1979., Dietrich Reimer Verlag.
——: Les verbaux du dangaléat de l'est (Guera, Tchad). Lexiques français-dangaléat et allemand-dangaléat. Berlin, 1987. Dietrich Reimer Verlag.
EDE I = Takács, G.: Etymological Dictionary of Egyptian. Volume One: A Phonological Introduction. Leiden, 1999., E.J. Brill.
EDE II = Takács, G.: Etymological Dictionary of Egyptian. Volume Two: b-, p-, f-. Leiden, 2001., E.J. Brill.
Edwards, I.E.S. (ed.): Hieratic Papyri in the British Museum. Fourth Series. Oracular Amuletic Decrees of the Late New Kingdom. I–II. London, 1963.
Eguchi, P.K.: Matériaux pour servir à l'étude de la langue hidé. Vocabulaire.= Kyoto University African Studies 6 (1971), 195–283.
Ehret, Ch.: The Historical Reconstruction of Southern Cushitic Phonology and Vocabulary. Berlin, 1980., Dietrich Reimer Verlag.
——: Kw'adza Vocabulary. MS. Los Angeles, California, 1980. IV + 17 p.
——: Proto-Cushitic Reconstruction.= Sprache und Geschichte in Afrika 8 (1987).
Ehret, Ch.: Reconstructing Proto-Afroasiatic (Proto-Afrasian). Vowels, Tone, Consonants, and Vocabulary. Berkeley, Los Angeles, California, 1995., University of California.
——: (Additions to the Afroasiatic reconstructions.) MS. Los Angeles, California, 1997. 522 p.
Ehret, Ch. & Ali, M.N.: Soomaali Classification.= Labahn, T. (ed.): Proceedings of the Second International Congress of Somali Studies. Vol. 1. Hamburg, 1984., Buske Verlag. Pp. 201–269.
Ehret, Ch. & Elderkin, E.D. & Nurse, D.: Dahalo Lexis and Its Sources.= Afrikanistische Arbeitspapiere 18 (1989), 5–49.
Faulkner, R.O.: The Ancient Egyptian Pyramid Texts. I. Oxford, 1969., Clarendon Press.
——: The Ancient Egyptian Coffin Texts. I. Warminster, 1973., Aris and Phillips.
FD = Faulkner, R.O.: A Concise Dictionary of Middle Egyptian. Oxford, 1962., Clarendon Press.
Fleming, H.C.: Asa and Aramanik: Cushitic Hunters in Masai-Land.= Ethnology 8/1 (1969), 1–36.
——: Sheko Word List. MS. Ca. 1972. 10 p.
——: Proto-Gongan Consonant Phonemes: Stage One.= Mukarovsky, H.G. (ed.): Leo Reinisch. Werk und Erbe. Wien, 1987., Verlag der Österreichischen Akademie der Wissenschaften. Pp. 141–159.

——: Mao's Ancestor. Consonant Phonemes of Proto-Mao. Stage One.= Gromyko, A.A. (ed.): Proceedings of the Ninth International Congress of Ethiopian Studies (Moscow, 26–29 August 1986). Vol. 5. Moscow, 1988., Nauka. Pp. 35–44.
——: Omotica, Afrasiana and More: Ethiopia as the Ever-Flowing Vase.= Mother Tongue 12 (1990), 22–30.
Foucauld, Ch. de: Dictionnaire touareg-français, dialecte de l'Ahaggar. Vol. I–IV. Paris, 1951–1952., Imprimerie Nationale de France.
Foulkes, H.D.: Angass Manual. Grammar, Vocabulary. London, 1915., Kegan Paul, Trench, Trübner and Co.
Frajzyngier, Z.: A Pero-English and English-Pero Vocabulary. Berlin, 1985., Dietrich Reimer Verlag.
——: A Dictionary of Mupun. Berlin, 1991., Dietrich Reimer Verlag.
Fronzaroli, P.: Studi sul lessico comune semitico. II. Anatomia e fisiologia.= Rendiconti delle Sedute dell'Accademia Nazionale dei Lincei. Classe di scienze morali, storiche e filologiche. Ser. VIII, vol. XIX, fasc. 7–12 (1964), 243–280.
GB = Gesenius, W. (bearbeitet von Buhl, F.): Hebräisches und aramäisches Handwörterbuch über das Alte Testment. Unveränderter Neudruck der 1915 erschienenen 17. Auflage. Berlin, Göttingen, Heidelberg, 1962., Springer-Verlag.
GHWb = Hannig, R.: Grosses Handwörterbuch Ägyptisch-Deutsch (2800–950 v. Chr.). Mainz, 1995., Verlag Philipp von Zabern.
Gochal, G.: A Look at Shik Ngas. Jos, 1994., Jos University Press.
Gragg, G.: Oromo Dictionary. East Lansing, Michigan, 1982., Michigan State University.
Greenberg, J.H.: The Labial Consonants of Proto-Afro-Asiatic.= Word 14 (1958), 295–302.
Grottanelli, V.L.: Missione etnografica nel Uollega Occidentale. Volume primo. I Mao. Roma, 1940., Reale Accademia d'Italia.
Harries, J.: Tamazight Basic Course. Ait Mgild Dialect. Final Report. Madison, Wisconsin, 1974., University of Wisconsin.
Haupt, P.: Elul und Adar.= Zeitschrift der Deutschen Morgenländischen Gesellschaft 64 (1910), 703–714.
Hayward, R.J.: The Arbore Language: A First Investigation Including a Vocabulary. Hamburg, 1984., Helmut Buske Verlag.
——: Remarks on Omotic Sibilants.= Becchaus-Gerst, M. & Serzisko, F. (eds.): Cushitic-Omotic. Papers from the International Symposium on Cushitic and Omotic Languages, Cologne, January 6–9, 1986. Hamburg, 1988., Helmut Buske Verlag. Pp. 263–299.
HCVA 1–5 = Diakonoff, I.M. & Belova, A.G. & Militarev, A.Ju.; Porhomovskij, V. Ja. & Stolbova, O.V.: Historical Comparative Vocabulary of Afrasian. Part 1–5.= St. Petersburg Journal of African Studies 2 (1993), 5–28 & 3 (1994), 5–26 & 4 (1994), 7–38 & 5 (1995), 4–32 & 6 (1997), 12–35.
Heine, B.: Notes on the Yaaku Language (Kenya).= Afrika und Übersee 58/2 (1975), 119–138.
——: Notes on the Rendille Language.= Afrika und Übersee 59 (1976), 176–223.
Heine, B.: The Sam Languages. A History of Rendille, Boni and Somali.= Afroasiatic Linguistics 6/2 (1978), 23–115.
Hellwig, B.: Goemai—English—Hausa Dictionary. MS. Draft. Printed out on 20 August 2000. 42 p.
Hodge, C.T.: Review of Leslau, W.: A Dictionary of Mocha (Southwestern Ethiopia).= African Studies 20 (1961), 113.
——: Hausa-Egyptian Establishment.= Anthropological Linguistics 8/1 (1966), 40–57.
Hoffmann, C.: Zur Sprache der Cibak.= Lukas, J. (ed.): Afrikanistische Studien. Berlin, 1955., Akademie-Verlag. Pp. 118–143.

Hoffmann, C.: Towards a Comparative Phonology of the Languages of the Angas-Goemai Group. MS. University of Ibadan, faculty seminar on 19 March 1975. 32 p.
Hoskison, J.T.: A Grammar and Dictionary of the Gude Language (Chadic). Ph.D. dissertation. 1983., The Ohio State University.
HSED = Orel, V.É.; Stolbova, O.V.: Hamito-Semitic Etymological Dictionary. Leiden, 1995., E.J. Brill.
Hudson, G.: Highland East Cushitic Dictionary. Hamburg, 1989., Buske.
Huehnergard, J.: Further South Semitic Cognates to the Akkadian Lexicon.= Kaye, A.S. (ed.): Semitic Studies in Honor of Wolf Leslau on the Occasion of His Eighty-Fifth Birthday, November 14th, 1991. Volume I. Wiesbaden, 1991., Otto Harrassowitz. Pp. 690–713.
Ibriszimow, D.: Towards a Common Chadic Lexicon.= Zeszyty Naukowe Universytetu Jagiellońskiego. Prace językoznawcze 102 (1990), 1–122.
Illič-Svityč, V.M.: Iz istorii čadskogo konsonantizma. Labial'nye smyčnye. = Uspenskij, B.A. (ed.): Jazyki Afriki. Voprosy struktury, istorii i tipologii. Moskva, 1966., Nauka. Pp. 9–34.
Jaggar, Ph.J.: Guruntum (gùrdùŋ) (West Chadic-B): Linguistic Notes and Wordlist.= African Languages and Cultures 2/2 (1989), 175–202.
JEA = Journal of Egyptian Archaeology (Birmingham).
Johnstone, T.M.: Ḥarsūsi Lexicon. London, 1977., Oxford University Press.
——: Jibbāli Lexicon. London, 1981., Oxford University Press.
——: Mehri Lexicon. London, 1987., University of London.
Jungraithmayr, H.: Beobachtungen zur tschadohamitischen Sprache der Jegu (und Jonkor) von Abu Telfan (Republique du Tchad).= Afrika und Übersee 45 (1961), 95–123.
——: Wörterbuch der Angas-Sprache. MS. 1962.
——: Wörterverzeichnis der Goemay-Sprache. MS. 1962.
——: Die Sprache des Sura (Maghavul) in Nordnigerien.= Afrika und Übersee 47 (1963), 8–89, 204–220.
——: A Comparative Word List of the Ron Languages (Southern Plateau, N. Nigeria).= Africana Marburgensia 1/2 (1968), 3–12.
——: Die Ron-Sprachen. Tschadohamitische Studien in Nordnigerien. Glückstadt, 1970., Verlag J.J. Augustin.
——: Dictionnaire birgit-français. MS. 1973.
——: Lexique mokilko. Berlin, 1990., Dietrich Reimer Verlag.
——: Lexique mubi-français (Tchad oriental). MS. Frankfurt a/M, 1990. 50 p.
—— (in collaboration with N.A. Galadima and U. Kleinewillinghöfer): A Dictionary of the Tangale Language (Kaltungo, Northern Nigeria) with a Grammatical Introduction. Berlin, 1991., Dietrich Reimer Verlag.
——: Lexique sibine (sumray)—français. MS. Frankfurt, 1993. 67 p.
—— & Adams, A.: Lexique migama. Berlin, 1992., Dietrich Reimer Verlag.
—— & Ibriszimow, D.: Chadic Lexical Roots. Volume II. Documentation. Berlin, 1994., Dietrich Reimer Verlag.
—— & Shimizu, K.: Chadic Lexical Roots. Vol. II. Tentative Re-construction, Grading and Distribution. Berlin, 1981., Verlag von Dietrich Reimer.
Justinard, (?): Manuel de berbère marocain (dialecte chleuh). Paris, 1914., Librairie Orientaliste Paul Geuthner.
KHW = Westendorf, W.: Koptisches Handwörterbuch. Heidelberg, 1977., Carl Winter Universitätsverlag.
Kleinewillinghöfer, U.: Monoradical Verbs in Waja.= Jungraithmayr, H. & Tourneux, H. (eds.): Études tchadiques. Verbes monoradicaux suivis d'une note sur la negation en haoussa. Actes de la XIIème réunion de Groupe d'Études Tchadiques

LACITO-CNRS-PARIS. Paris, 1990., Librairie Orientaliste Paul Geuthner. Pp. 229–241.
Kraft, Ch. H.: Chadic Wordlists. I–III. Berlin, 1981., Dietrich Reimer Verlag.
Lamberti, M.: Die Somali-Dialekte. Eine Vergleichende Untersuchung. Hamburg, 1986., Helmut Buske Verlag.
——: Die Shinassha-Sprache. Materialien zum Boro. Heidelberg, 1993., Carl Winter Universitätsverlag.
——: Materialien zum Yemsa. Heidelberg, 1993., Carl Winter Univer-sitätsverlag.
Lanfry, J.: Ghadames II. Glossarie. Alger, 1973., Le Fichier Périodique.
Laoust, E.: Siwa. I. Son parlier. Paris, 1931., Librairie Ernest Leroux.
Leger, R.: Sprachproblem aus dem Westtschadischen. Kupto- und Kwamitexte.= Afrikanistische Arbeitspapiere 28 (1992), 5–32.
——: Die Geschichte der Kwami nach einer Erzählung von Yerma Buba mit grammatischen Erläuterungen.= Mitteilungen des Sonderforschungs-bereichs 268 (1993), 143–177.
Leslau, W.: Lexique soqoṭri (sudarabique moderne), avec comparaisons et explications étymologiques. Paris, 1938., Librairie C. Klincksieck.
——: Gafat Documents. Records of a South-Ethiopic Language. Grammar, Text and Comparative Vocabulary. New Haven, Connecticut, 1945., American Oriental Society.
——: Étude descriptive et comparative du gafat (éthiopien méridional). Paris, 1956., Librairie C. Klincksieck.
——: A Dictionary of Moča (Southwestern Ethiopia). Berkeley, Los Angeles, 1959., University of California Press.
——: Etymological Dictionary of Harari. Berkeley, Los Angeles, 1963., University of California.
——: Southeast Semitic Cognates to the Akkadian Vocabulary. III.= Journal of the American Oriental Society 89 (1969), 18–22.
——: Etymological Dictionary of Gurage (Ethiopic). Vol. III. Etymological Section. Wiesbaden, 1979., Otto Harrassowitz.
——: Comparative Dictionary of Geʿez (Classical Ethiopic). Wiesbaden, 1987., Otto Harrassowitz.
——: Observations on Sasse's Vocabulary of Burji.= Afrika und Übersee 71 (1988), 177–203.
Lukas, J.: Die Logone-Sprache im Zentralen Sudan.= Abhandlungen für die Kunde des Morgenlandes 21/6 (1936).
——: Zentralsudanische Studien.= Abhandlungen aus dem Gebiet der Auslandskunde. Hansische Universität. Reihe B, Band 45, Band 24 (1937).
——: Zentralsudanische Studien.= Abhandlungen aus dem Gebiet der Auslandskunde. Hansische Universität. Reihe B, Band 45, Band 24 (1937).
——: Deutsche Quellen zur Sprache der Musgu in Kamerun. Berlin, 1941., Dietrich Reimer Verlag.
——: Studien zur Sprache der Gisiga (Nordkamerun). Hamburg, 1970., Verlag J.J. Augustin.
——: Die Personalia und das primäre Verb im Bolanci (Nord-nigerien). Mit Beiträge über das Karekare.= Afrika und Übersee 55 (1971), 114–139.
——: Studien zur Bade-Sprache (Nigeria).= Afrika und Übersee 58 /2 (1974–75), 82–105.
Magwa, J.G. etc. (20 members of the "Ron Language Committee"): A Ron Alphabet. Jos, Nigeria, 1985., Nigeria Bible Translation Trust.
Meinhof, C.: Linguistische Studien in Ostafrika. Fortsetzung.= Mitteilungen des Seminars für Orientalische Sprachen 9 (1906), 278–333.
Militarev, A. Ju.: Istoričeskaja fonetika i leksika livijsko-guančskih jazykov.= Solncev,

V.M. (ed.): Jazyki Azii i Afriki. IV, kniga 2. Moskva, 1991., Glavnaja Redakcija Vostočnoj Literatury. Pp. 238–267.
Moreno, M. M.: Introduzione alla lingua ometo. Milano, 1938., Mondadori.
Mouchet, J.: Vocabulaires comparatifs de quinze parlers du Nord-Cameroun.= Bulletin de la Société d'Études Camerounaises 29–30 (1950), 5–74.
——: Vocabulaires comparatifs de sept parlers du Nord-Cameroun.= Bulletin de la Société d'Études Camerounaises 41–42 (1953), 136–206.
——: Le parler daba: esquisse grammaticale précédée d'une note sur l'ethnie daba, suivie de lexiques daba-français et français-daba. Yaoundé, 1966., R.E.C.
Mukarovsky, H.G.: Baskisch-berberische Entsprechungen.= Wiener Zeitschrift für die Kunde des Morgenlandes 62 (1969), 32–51.
——: Einige hamitosemitische und baskische Wortstämme.= Jungraithmayr, H. & Miehe, G. (eds.): Berliner Afrikanistische Vorträge XXI. Deutscher Orientalistentag, Berlin 24.–29. März 1980. Berlin, 1981., Verlag von Dietrich Reimer. Pp. 105–118.
——: Wo steht das Saharische?= Afrika und Übersee 64 (1981), 187–226.
——: Lateinische Lehnwörter im Hausa.= Jungraithmayr, H. (ed.): The Cahd Languages in the Hamitosemitic-Nigritic Border Area. Berlin, 1982., Dietrich Reimer. Pp. 261–268.
——: Mande-Chadic Common Stock. A Study of Phonological and Lexical Evidence. Wien, 1987., Afro-Pub.
Müller, F.: Die Musuk-Sprache in Central-Afrika. Nach den Aufzeichnungen von Gottlob Adolf Krause herausgegeben.= Sitzungsberichte der Kaiserlichen Akademie der Wissenschaften. Phil.-hist. Klasse 112/1 (1886), 353–421.
Müller, W.W.: Altsüdarabische Beiträge zum hebräischen Lexikon.= Zeitschrift für die Alttestamentliche Wissenschaft 75/3 (1963), 304–316.
Nehlil: Étude sur le dialecte de Ghat. Paris, 1909., Éditions Ernest Leroux.
Netting, R.M.: Kofyar Vocabulary. MS. 1967.
Newman, P.: A Word List of Tera.= Journal of West African Languages 1/2 (1964), 33–50.
——: The Kanakuru Language. Leeds, 1974., The Institute of Modern English Language Studies, University of Leeds in association with The West African Linguistic Society.
——: The Formation of the Imperfective Verb Stem in Chadic.= Afrika und Übersee 60/3 (1977), 178–192.
Nicolas, F.: La langue berbère de Mauritanie. Dakar, 1953., Institut Français d'Afrique Noire.
——: Vocabulaires ethnographiques de la Tamâjeq des Iullemmeden de l'est (Touâreg de la Colonie du Niger, Afrique Occidentale Française).= Anthropos 52 (1957), 49–63, 564–580.
Orel, V.É. & Stolbova, O.V.: On Chadic-Egyptian Lexical Relations.= Shevoroshkin, V. (ed.): Nostratic, Dene-Caucasian, Austric and Amerind. Bochum, 1992., Brockmeyer. Pp. 181–203.
Osing, J.: Die Nominalbildung des Ägyptischen. I–II. Maiz/Rhein, 1976., Verlag Philipp von Zabern.
Parker, E.M. & Hayward, R.J.: An Afar-English-French Dictionary (with Grammatical Notes in English). London, 1985., School of Oriental and African Studies, University of London.
Penchoen, Th.G.: Tamazight of the Ait Ndhir (Afroasiatic Dialects, Volume 1). Los Angeles, 1973., Undena Publications.
Prasse, K.-G. & Alojaly, Gh. & Mohamed, Gh.: Lexique touareg-français. Copenhague, 1998., Museum Tusculanum Press, Université de Copenhague.
Rabin, Ch.: La correspondance d hébreu - ḏ arabe.= Cohen, D. (ed.): Mélanges Marcel Cohen. Paris, 1970., Mouton. Pp. 290–297.

Rapp, E.L. & Benzing, B.: Dictionary of the Glavdá Language. Frankfurt am Main, 1968., Bible Society Frankfurt am Main.
RdE = Revue d'Égyptologie (Paris).
Reinisch, L.: Die Chamirsprache in Abessinien. II. Chamir-deutsches Wörterbuch.= Sitzungsberichte der Kaiserlichen Akademie der Wissenschaften. Phil.-hist. Classe 106 (1884), 330–450.
——: Die Quarasprache in Abessinien. II. Quarisch-deutsches Wörterbuch.= Sitzungsberichte der Kaiserlichen Akademie der Wissenschaften. Phil.-hist. Classe 109/1 (1885), 3–152.
——: Die 'Afar-Sprache. II.= Sitzungsberichte der Kaiserlichen Akademie der Wissenschaften. Phil.-hist. Classe 113/2 (1886), 795–916.
——: Wörterbuch der Bilin-Sprache. Wien, 1887., Alfred Hoelder.
——: Die 'Afar-Sprache. III. Deutsch-'Afarsches Wörter-verzeichnis.= Sitzungsberichte der Kaiserlichen Akademie der Wissenschaften. Phil.-hist. Classe 114/1 (1887), 89–168.
——: Wörterbuch der Saho-Sprache. Wien, 1890., Alfred Hölder.
——: Wörterbuch der Bedawye-Sprache. Wien, 1895., Alfred Hölder Verlag.
——: Die Somali-Sprache. II. Wörterbuch. Wien, 1902., Alfred Hölder Verlag.
Renisio, A.: Étude sur les dialectes berbères des Beni Iznassen, du Rif et des Senhaja de Sraïr. Grammaire, textes et lexique. Paris, 1932., Éditions Ernest Leroux.
Reutt, T.E. & Kogan, E.Z.: Materialy po leksike jazykov margi i bura.= Bespis'mennye i mladopis'mennye jazyki Afriki. Moskva, 1973., Nauka. Pp. 83–147.
Roper, E.-M.: Tu Beḍawiɛ. An Elementary Handbook for the Use of Sudan Government Officials. Hertford, 1928., Stephen Austin & Sons.
Rossing, M.O.: Mafa-Mada: A Comparative Study of Chadic Languages in North Cameroun. Ph.D. dissertation. Wisconsin, 1978., University of Wisconsin-Madison.
Sachnine, M.: Notes sur le zime (lame) parlé au Cameroun.= Africana Marburgensia 9/1 (1976), 71–86.
——: Dictionnaire lamé-français. Lexique français-lamé. Paris, 1982., SELAF.
Sasse, H.-J.: Galla /š/, /s/ und /f/.= Afrika und Übersee 58 (1975), 244–263.
——: The Consonant Phonemes of Proto-East-Cushitic (PEC).= Afroasiatic Linguistics 7/1 (1979), 1–67.
——: An Etymological Dictionary of Burji. Hamburg, 1982., Helmut Buske Verlag.
Saxon, D.E.: Linguistic Evidence for the Eastward Spread of Ubangian Peoples.= Ehret, Ch. & Posnansky, M. (eds.): The Archaeological and Linguistic Reconstruction of African History. Berkeley, 1982., University of California Press. Pp. 66–77.
Schlee, G.: Sprachliche Studien zum Rendille: Grammatik, Texte, Glossar. Hamburg, 1978., Helmut Buske Verlag.
Schuh, R.G.: A Dictionary of Ngizim. Berkeley, California, 1981., University of California.
SD = Beeston, A.F.L. & Ghul, M.A. & Müller, W.W. & Ryckmans, J.: Sabaic Dictionary (English-French-Arabic). Dictionnaire sabéen (anglais-français-arabe). Louvain-la-Neuve, Beyrouth, 1982., Peeters, Librairie du Liban.
SED 1 = Militarev, A. & Kogan, L.: Semitic Etymological Dictionary. Volume One. Anatomy of Man and Animals. Münster, 2000., Ugarit-Verlag.
Seibert, U.: Comparative Ron Wordlist. MS. Frankfurt, 2000. 45 & 17 p.
Sethe, K.: Ägyptische Lesestücke zum Gebrauch im akademischen Unterricht. Texte des Mittleren Reiches.[3] Hildesheim, 1959., Georg Olms.
Shimizu, K.: The Southern Bauchi Group of Chadic Languages. A Survey Report.= Africana Marburgensia. Special Issue 2 (1978), 1–50.
Siebert, R.: Languages of the Abbaya/Chamo Area—Report Part I (with Notes on Koorete by L. Hoeft).= Survey of Little-Known Languages of Ethiopia (S.L.L.E.) Reports 21 (1994), 1–24.
Siebert, R. & Siebert, K. & Wedekind, K.: Survey on Languages of the Asosa—

Begi—Komosha Area.= Survey of Little-Known Languages of Ethiopia (S.L.L.E.) Reports 11 (1993), 1–22.
Siebert, R. & Wedekind, Ch.: Third S.L.L.E. Survey on Languages of the Begi/Asosa Area.= Survey of Little-Known Languages of Ethiopia (S.L.L.E.) Reports 15 (1994), 1–19.
Sirlinger, E.: Dictionary of the Goemay Language. Jos, Nigeria, 1937., Prefecture Apostolic of Jos.
SISAJa I = D'jakonov, I.M.; Belova, A.G.; Četveruhin, A.S.; Militarev, A.Ju.; Porhomovskij, V. Ja.; Stolbova, O. V.: Sravnitel'no-istoričeskij slovar' afrazijskih jazykov. Vypusk 1. p-p̣-b-f.= Pis'mennye pamjatniki i problemy istorii kul'tury narodov Vostoka. XV godičnaja naučnaja sessija Leningradskogo Otdelenija Instituta Vostokovedenija Akademii Nauk SSSR. Moskva, 1981., Nauka. Pp. 3–127.
SISAJa II = D'jakonov, I.M.; Belova, A.G.; Militarev, A. Ju.; Porhomovskij, V. Ja.; Stolbova, O.V.: Sravnitel'no-istoričeskij slovar' afrazijskih jazykov. Vypusk 2. t-ṭ-d.= Pis'mennye pamjatniki i problemy istorii kul'tury narodov Vostoka. XVI godičnaja naučnaja sessija Leningradskogo Otdelenija Instituta Vostokovedenija Akademii Nauk SSSR. Moskva, 1982., Nauka. Pp. 3–93.
SISAJa III = D'jakonov, I.M.; Belova, A.G.; Militarev, A.Ju.; Porhomovskij, V.Ja.; Stolbova, O. V.: Sravnitel'no-istoričeskij slovar' afrazijskih jazykov. Vypusk 3. s-c-ç-ʒ, č-ç̌-ǯ, ŝ-ĉ-ç̂ s labialami.= Pis'mennye pamjatniki i problemy istorii kul'tury narodov Vostoka. XVI godičnaja naučnaja sessija Leningradskogo Otdelenija Instituta Vostokovedenija Akademii Nauk SSSR. Moskva, 1986., Nauka. Pp. 3–46.
Skinner, M. G.: Aspects of Pa'anci Grammar. Ph.D. thesis. Madison, 1979., University of Wisconsin, Madison.
Skinner, N.: North Bauchi Chadic Languages: Common Roots.= Afroasiatic Linguistics 4/1 (1977), 1–49.
——: Hausa Comparative Dictionary. Köln, 1996., Rüdiger Köppe Verlag.
Starostin, S.A.; Dybo, V.A.; Dybo, A.V.; Helimsky, E.A.; Militarev, A. Ju.; Mudrak, O.A.; Starostin, G.S.: Basic Nostratic-Afrasian-Sino-Caucasian Lexical Correspondences. MS. Preliminary working version. Moscow, 1995.
Stroomer, H.: An Early European Source on Berber: Chamberlayne (1715).= Chaker, S. & Zaborski, A. (eds.): Études berbères et chamito-sémitiques. Mélanges offerts à Karl-G. Prasse pour son 70e anniversaire. Paris, Louvain, 2000., Éditions Peeters. Pp. 303–316.
Stolbova, O.V.: Opyt rekonstrukcii verhnezapadnočadskih kornej.= Jazyki zarubežnogo Vostoka. Sbornik statej. Moskva, 1977., Nauka. Pp. 152–160.
——: Sravnitel'no-istoričeskaja fonetika i slovar' zapadno-čadskih jazykov.= Porhomovskij, V. Ja. (ed.): Afrikanskoe istoričeskoe jazykoznanie. Problemy rekonstrukcii. Moskva, 1987., Nauka. Pp. 30–268.
——: Studies in Chadic Comparative Phonology. Moscow, 1996., "Diaphragma" Publishers.
Takács, G.: Refining Some Etymologies of the Root "Round" in Afrasian and Egyptian (A Return to the Discussion in GL 34/1, 1994).= General Linguistics 36/3 (1998), 153–166.
——: Afro-Asiatic (Semito-Hamitic) Substratum in the Proto-Indo-European Cultural Lexicon?= Lingua Posnaniensis 40 (1998), 141–172.
——: Development of Afro-Asiatic (Semito-Hamitic) Comparative-Historical Linguistics in Russia and the Former Soviet Union. München, Newcastle, 1999., Lincom Europa.
——: Contribution of V. M. Illič-Svityč to Chadic Comparative-Historical Linguistics.= Archív Orientální 67 (1999), 361–378.
——: South Cushitic Consonant System in Afro-Asiatic Context.= Afrikanistische Arbeitspapiere 61 (2000), 69–117.

Tourneux, H.: Le mulwi ou vulum de Mogroum (Tchad). Langue du groupe musgu—famille tchadique. Paris, 1978., Centre National de la Recherche Scientifique.
——: Racine verbale en mulwi.= Caprile, J.-P. & Jungraithmayr, H. (eds.): Préalables à la reconstruction du proto-tchadique. Paris, 1978., SELAF. Pp. 89–93.
——: Note complementaire sur les baldamu et leur langue.= Africana Marburgensia 20/1 (1987), 52–58.
——: Lexique pratique du munjuk des rizières. Dialecte de Pouss. Paris, 1991., Librairie Orientaliste Paul Geuthner.
—— & Seignobos, Ch. & Lafarge, F.: Les Mbara et leur langue (Tchad). Paris, 1986., Société d'Études Linguistiques et Anthropologiques de France.
Tosco, M.: A Grammatical Sketch of Dahalo. Hamburg, 1991., Helmut Buske Verlag.
Urk. IV = Sethe, K. & Helck, W.: Urkunden der 18. Dynastie. Heft 1–16 & 17–22. Berlin, 1927–1930. & 1955–1958., Akademie-Verlag.
Venberg, R.: Phonemic Statement of the Peve Language.= Africana Marburgensia 8/1 (1975), 26–43.
Voigt, R.M.: Derivatives und flektives ṯ im Semitohamitischen.= Jungraithmayr, H. & Müller, W. W. (eds.): Proceedings of the Fourth International Hamito-Semitic Congress, Marburg, 20–22 September 1983. Amsterdam, Philadelphia, 1987., John Benjamins. Pp. 85–107.
——: Die Wurzel i̯šʕ (*i̯θʕ) im Hebräischen sowie im Frühnord- und Altsüdarabischen.= Zeitschrift für Althebraistik 10/2 (1997), 169–176.
Vycichl, W.: Hausa und Ägyptisch. Ein Beitrag zur historischen Hamitistik.= Mitteilungen des Seminars für Orientalische Sprachen an der Friedrich-Wilhelms-Universität zu Berlin 37 (1934), 36–116.
——: Is Egyptian a Semitic Language?= Kush 7 (1959), 27–44.
——: Studien der ägyptisch-semitischen Wortvergleichung. Die Klassifikation der Etymologien. Zwölf neue Etymologien.= Zeitschrift für Ägyptische Sprache 84 (1959), 70–74.
Ward, W.A.: Lexicographical Miscellanies II.= Studien zur Altägyptischen Kultur 9 (1981), 359–373.
Wb = Erman, A. & Grapow, H.: Wörterbuch der ägyptischen Sprache. I–V.[2] Berlin, 1957–1971., Akademie-Verlag.
Weibegué, Ch. & Palayer, P.: Lexique lele-français. Sarh, Tchad, 1982., Centre d'Études Linguistiques.
Whiteley, W.H.: Studies in Iraqw. Kampala, 1953., East African Institute of Social Research.
WUS = Aistleitner, J.: Wörterbuch der ugaritischen Sprache.= Berichte über die Verhandlungen der Sächsischen Akademie der Wissenschaften zu Leipzig. Phil.-hist. Klasse 106/3 (1963).
Zaborski, A.: Biconsonantal Verbal Roots in Semitic.= Zeszyty Naukowe Universytetu Jagiellońskiego, prace językoznawcze 5 (1971), 51–98.
Zyhlarz, E.: Die Sprachreste der unteräthiopischen Nachbarn Altägyptens.= Zeitschrift für Eingeborenen-Sprachen 25 (1934–1935), 161–188, 241–261.

INDEX OF PERSONAL NAMES[1]

[1] Composed by G. Takács.

INDEX OF LANGUAGES[1]

[1] Composed by G. Takács.